These essays, as would be expected from their authors, manifest a high standard of scholarship and familiarity with current understandings. . . . The volume has a place on the desk of every reference librarian at the college and university level.

Bryn Mawr Classical Review

The arrangement of the contents and an index that provides coverage of all the essays, allows immediate targeting of specific topics and quick referencing, whilst in its entirety the book provides an excellent survey of tragedy as it is currently studied. Aimed primarily at undergraduates and useful to postgraduates needing to orientate themselves in the scholarship of this area, this title is a useful addition to the academic library.

Reference Reviews

D0860896

Blackwell Companions to Literature and Culture

This series offers comprehensive, newly written surveys of key periods and movements and certain major authors, in English literary culture and history. Extensive volumes provide new perspectives and positions on contexts and on canonical and post-canonical texts, orientating the beginning student in new fields of study and providing the experienced undergraduate and new graduate with current and new directions, as pioneered and developed by leading scholars in the field.

Published

A COMPANION TO
TRAGEDY

EDITED BY REBECCA BUSHNELL

WILEY-BLACKWELL

A John Wiley & Sons, Ltd., Publication

This paperback edition first published 2009
© 2009 Blackwell Publishing Ltd
except for editorial material and organization © 2005 by Rebecca Bushnell
Blackwell Publishing Ltd (hardback, 2005)

Blackwell Publishing was acquired by John Wiley & Sons in February 2007.
Blackwell's publishing program has been merged with Wiley's global Scientific,
Technical, and Medical business to form Wiley-Blackwell.

Registered Office
John Wiley & Sons Ltd, The Atrium, Southern Gate, Chichester,
West Sussex, PO19 8SQ, United Kingdom

Editorial Offices
350 Main Street, Malden, MA 02148-5020, USA
9600 Garsington Road, Oxford, OX4 2DQ, UK
The Atrium, Southern Gate, Chichester, West Sussex, PO19 8SQ, UK

For details of our global editorial offices, for customer services, and for information
about how to apply for permission to reuse the copyright material
in this book please see our website at www.wiley.com/wiley-blackwell.

The right of Simon Eliot and Jonathan Rose to be identified as the author of the editorial
material in this work has been asserted in accordance with the Copyright,
Designs and Patents Act 1988.

Library of Congress Cataloging-in-Publication Data

A companion to tragedy / edited by Rebecca Bushnell.
p. cm. —(Blackwell companions to literature and culture ; (32)
Includes bibliographical references and index
ISBN: 978-1-4051-9246-0 (pbk)
ISBN: 978-1-4051-0735-8 (hbk, alk. paper)
1. Tragedy—History and criticism I. Bushnell, Rebecca W., 1952–II. Series.

PNI892.C56 2004
809.2′512—dc22
2004018066

A catalogue record for this book is available from the British Library.

Set in 11/13pt Garamond
by SPi Publisher Services, Pondicherry, India
Printed in Singapore by C.O.S. Printers Pte Ltd

01   2009

For further information on
Blackwell Publishing, visit our website:
www.blackwellpublishing.com

Contents

Notes on Contributors

Rebecca Bushnell is a scholar of English Renaissance studies and comparative literature, and Professor of English and Dean of the School of Arts and Sciences at the University of Pennsylvania. In addition to her work on early modern English culture (including humanist pedagogy and early modern English gardens), her books on tragedy include *Prophesying Tragedy: Sign and Voice in Sophocles' Theban Plays* (1988), *Tragedies of Tyrants: Political Thought and Theater in the English Renaissance* (1990), and *Tragedy: A Short Introduction* (2008).

Deborah Boedeker is Professor of Classics at Brown University. Her research focuses on archaic and classical Greek religion, poetry, historiography, and especially the confluences among these areas. Recent publications include essays on Euripides, Herodotus, Simonides, and Sappho, as well as a number of edited volumes, including *Democracy, Empire, and the Arts in Fifth-Century Athens* (1998, with Kurt A. Raaflaub) and *The New Simonides: Contexts of Praise and Desire* (2001, with David Sider).

Claude Calame is Director of Studies at the École des Hautes Études en Sciences Sociales, Paris, and honorary professor of Greek at the University of Lausanne. His publications include *Le Récit en Grèce ancienne. Enonciations et représentations de poètes* (1986; translated as *The Craft of Poetic Speech in Ancient Greece*, 1995), *Mythe et histoire dans l'Antiquité grecque. La création symbolique d'une colonie* (1996; translated as *Myth and History in Ancient Greece. The Symbolic Creation of a Colony*, 2003), *L'Éros dans la Grèce antique* (1996; translated as *The Poetics of Eros in Ancient Greece*, 1999), and *Poétique des mythes dans la Grèce antique* (2000).

Barbara T. Cooper is Professor of French at the University of New Hampshire and a specialist in early nineteenth-century French theater. She has published extensively on topics including romantic drama, melodrama, vaudeville, neoclassical tragedy, theater censorship, and parody. She edited and contributed to the volume of the *Dictionary of Literary Biography* devoted to *French Dramatists, 1879–1914* and wrote the introduction and notes for a recent edition of Dumas's *The Three Musketeers* (2004).

Jeffrey N. Cox is Professor of English and of Comparative Literature and Humanities at the University of Colorado at Boulder, where he also directs the Center for Humanities and the Arts. His work on drama includes *In the Shadows of Romance: Romantic Tragic*

Drama in England, Germany, and France (1987) and the *Broadview Anthology of Romantic Drama* (2002, coedited with Michael Gamer).

Kathy Eden is Chavkin Family Professor of English and Professor of Classics at Columbia University. She is the author of *Poetic and Legal Fiction in the Aristotelian Tradition* (1986), *Hermeneutics and the Rhetorical Tradition: Chapters in the Ancient Legacy and Its Humanist Reception* (1997), and *Friends Hold All Things in Common: Tradition, Intellectual Property and the "Adages" of Erasmus* (2001).

Gail Finney is Professor of Comparative Literature and German at the University of California, Davis. Her publications include *The Counterfeit Idyll: The Garden Ideal and Social Reality in Nineteenth-Century Fiction* (1984), *Women in Modern Drama: Freud, Feminism, and European Theater at the Turn of the Century* (1989), *Look Who's Laughing: Gender and Comedy* (edited, 1994), and *Christa Wolf* (1999).

Richard E. Goodkin is Professor of French at the University of Wisconsin-Madison. His books include *The Tragic Middle: Racine, Aristotle, Euripides* and *Around Proust* (both 1991), and *Birth Marks: The Tragedy of Primogeniture in Pierre Corneille, Thomas Corneille, and Jean Racine* (2000). He also edited a volume of *Yale French Studies, Autour de Racine: Studies in Intertextuality* (1989).

Hugh Grady is Professor of English at Arcadia University in Glenside, Pennsylvania. He is the author of *The Modernist Shakespeare: Critical Texts in a Material World* (1991), *Shakespeare's Universal Wolf: Studies in Early Modern Reification* (1996), and *Shakespeare Machiavelli and Montaigne: Power and Subjectivity from "Richard II" to "Hamlet"* (2002). He is editor of *Shakespeare and Modernity: From Early Modern to Millennium* (2000) and co-editor (with Terence Hawkes) of *Presentist Shakespeares* (2007). His newest book is *Shakespeare and Impure Aesthetics* (2009).

Mitchell Greenberg is Professor and Chair of Romance Studies at Cornell University. He is the author of several books on seventeenth-century drama and culture: *Detours of Desire: Readings in the French Baroque* (1984), *Corneille, Classicism and the Ruses of Symmetry* (1986), *Subjectivity and Subjugation in 17th-Century Drama and Prose* (1992), *Canonical States, Canonical Stages* (1994; recipient of the MLA Scaglione Prize in Comparative Literature), and *Baroque Bodies: Psychoanalysis and the Culture of French Absolutism* (2001).

Margaret R. Greer is Professor of Spanish and Chair of the Department of Romance Studies at Duke University. Her publications include *The Play of Power: Mythological Court Dramas of Pedro Calderón de la Barca* (1991), *María de Zayas Tells Baroque Tales of Love and the Cruelty of Men* (2000), editions of Calderón de la Barca's plays *La estatua de Prometeo* (1986) and *Basta callar* (2000), and *Decolonizing the Middle Ages* (2000, edited with John Dagenais). Current book projects include *Approaches to Teaching Early Modern Spanish Drama* (forthcoming, with Laura Bass), a book on early modern Spanish tragedy, and a book on hunting.

Michael R. Halleran is Professor of Classics and Divisional Dean of Arts and Humanities in the College of Arts and Sciences, University of Washington. He is the author of *Stagecraft in Euripides* (1985), *Euripides:* Hippolytus, *with Translation and Commentary* (1995), and numerous articles and reviews on ancient Greek literature and culture.

Julia Reinhard Lupton is Professor of English and Comparative Literature at the University of California, Irvine, where she has taught since 1989. She is the co-author of *After Oedipus: Shakespeare in Psychoanalysis* (with Kenneth Reinhard, 1992) and the author of *Afterlives of the Saints: Hagiography, Typology, and Renaissance Literature* (1996) and *Citizen-Saints: Shakespeare and Political Theology* (2005). She is the founding director of Humanities Out There, a nationally recognized educational partnership between the University of California, Irvine and local schools.

Sheila Murnaghan is the Allen Memorial Professor of Greek at the University of Pennsylvania. She is the author of *Disguise and Recognition in the* Odyssey (1987) and the coeditor of *Women and Slaves in Greco-Roman Culture: Differential Equations* (1998, with Sandra R. Joshel).

Brenda Murphy is Professor of English at the University of Connecticut. Among her books are *American Realism and American Drama, 1880–1940* (1987), *Tennessee Williams and Elia Kazan: A Collaboration in the Theatre* (1992), *Miller:* Death of a Salesman (1995), *Congressional Theatre: Dramatizing McCarthyism on Stage, Film, and Television* (1999), *O'Neill:* Long Day's Journey Into Night (2001), and, as editor, *A Realist in the American Theatre: Drama Criticism by William Dean Howells* (1992) and the *Cambridge Companion to American Women Playwrights* (1999).

Michael Neill is Professor of English at the University of Auckland, New Zealand. He is the author of *Issues of Death Tragedy* (1997) and *Putting History to the Question* (2000), has edited *Anthony and Cleopatra* for the *Oxford Shakespeare* (1994), and recently finished *Othello* for the same series.

James I. Porter is Professor of Classics and Comparative Literature at the University of California, Irvine. His research areas are in literature, aesthetics, and intellectual history. He is the author of *Nietzsche and the Philology of the Future* (2000) and *The Invention of Dionysus: An Essay on The Birth of Tragedy* (2000), and editor of *Constructions of the Classical Body* (1999) and *Classical Pasts: The Classical Traditions of Greece and Rome* (2006). His book, *The Origins of Aesthetic Inquiry in Ancient Greece: Matter, Sensation and Experience*, is forthcoming from Cambridge University Press. His next projects include a study of the idea of Homer from antiquity to the present and another on ancient literary aesthetics after Aristotle.

Kurt Raaflaub is David Herlihy University Professor, Professor of Classics and History, and Director of the Program in Ancient Studies at Brown University, His main areas of interests are the social, political, and intellectual history of archaic and classical Greece and the Roman Republic. His most recent publications include *The Discovery of Freedom in Ancient Greece* (2004), an edited volume on *War and Peace in the Ancient World* (2007), and a co-authored volume on *Origins of Democracy in Ancient Greece* (2007), with Josiah Ober and Robert Wallace. He is currently working on a history of early Greek political thought in its Mediterranean context.

Timothy J. Reiss is Emeritus Professor of Comparative Literature and Distinguished Scholar in Residence at New York University. His recent books are *Against Autonomy: Global Dialectics of Cultural Exchange* (2002) and *Mirages of the Self: Patterns of Personhood in Ancient and Early Modern Europe* (2003), *Music, Writing, and Cultural Unity in the Caribbean* (2005) and the 2-volume co-edited *Topographies of Race and Gender: Mapping Cultural Representations* (2007–8). He is finishing a book on Descartes and the beginnings of the modern era and a collection on *Ngugi in the Americas*, working on rethinking the Renaissance as a process of cultural circulation between Africa, the Americas and Europe and preparing an anthology of tragedy of the African diaspora.

Simon Richter is Associate Professor of German and Comparative Literature at the University of Pennsylvania, editor of the *Goethe Yearbook*, and author of *Laocoon's Body and the Aesthetics of Pain* (1992).

Mark W. Roche is the Joyce Professor of German Language and Literature and Concurrent Professor of Philosophy at the University of Notre Dame, where he also served as Dean of the College of Arts and Letters from 1997 to 2008. He is the author of six books, including *Tragedy and Comedy: A Systematic Study and a Critique of Hegel* (1998) and *Why Literature Matters in the 21st Century* (2004).

Ralph Rosen is Associate Dean for Graduate Studies in the School of Arts and Sciences and the Rose Family Endowed Term Professor of Classical Studies at the University of Pennsylvania. He has published widely on archaic and classical Greek poetry, including *Old Comedy and Iconographic Tradition* (1988), *Andreia: Manliness and Courage in Classical Antiquity* (2002, with Ineke Sluiterr), and *Making Mockery: The Poetics of Ancient Satire* (2007).

Alessandro Schiesaro is Professor of Latin Language and Literature at King's College, University of London. His publications include *Simulacrum et imago: gli argomenti analogici nel De rerum natura* (1990) and *The Passions in Play: Thyestes and the Dynamics of Senecan Drama* (2003).

Ruth Scodel was educated at Berkeley and Harvard, and has been on the faculty at the University of Michigan since 1984. She is the author of *The Trojan Trilogy of Euripides* (1980), *Sophocles* (1984), *Credible Impossibilities: Conventions and Strategies of Verisimilitude in Homer and Greek Tragedy* (1999), *Listening to Homer* (2002), and articles on Greek literature.

Richard Seaford is Professor of Greek at the University of Nottingham. He is the author of numerous articles and reviews on Greek literature and religion from Homer to the New Testament, as well as *Pompeii* (1978), commentaries on Euripides' *Cyclops* (1984), and *Bacchae* (1996), *Reciprocity and Ritual: Homer and Tragedy in the Developing City-State* (1994), *Money and the Early Greek Mind: Homer, Philosophy and Tragedy* (2004), and *Dionysos* (Routledge 2006).

Alan H. Sommerstein is Professor of Greek at the University of Nottingham. His publications include *Aeschylean Tragedy* (1996), *Greek Drama and Dramatists* (2002), and editions of the plays and fragments of Aeschylus (2008) and of Aristophanes' eleven comedies (1980–2002). In a project funded by the Leverhulme Trust, he is preparing, with five collaborators, a two-volume study of *The Oath in Archaic and Classical Greece*.

Christiane Sourvinou-Inwood was born in Greece in 1945 and has taught Classics at the Universities of Liverpool, Reading, and Oxford. She has written many articles on the religion, mythology, women, tragedy, comedy, and art and archeology of Greece, and also the following books: *Theseus as Son and Stepson: A Tentative Illustration of the Greek Mythological Mentality* (1979), *Studies in Girls' Transitions: Aspects of the Arkteia and Age Representation in Attic Iconography* (1988), *"Reading" Greek Culture: Texts and Images, Rituals and Myths* (1991), *"Reading" Greek Death* (1995), and *Tragedy and Athenian Religion* (2003).

Matthew H. Wikander is Professor of English at the University of Toledo. His books include *The Play of Truth and State: Historical Drama from Shakespeare to Brecht* (1986) and *Fangs of Malice: Hypocrisy, Sincerity and Acting* (2002).

Victoria Wohl is Associate Professor of Classics at the University of Toronto. She is the author of *Intimate Commerce: Exchange, Gender, and Subjectivity in Greek Tragedy* (1998) and *Love Among the Ruins: The Erotics of Democracy in Classical Athens* (2003).

Acknowledgments

I would like to express my thanks to my colleagues Ralph Rosen, Sheila Murnaghan, and Phyllis Rackin, who offered invaluable advice at the beginning of this project when I was developing the proposal. Ralph Rosen, in particular, helped to shape the companion's dimensions and sustained me with his enthusiasm for the project. Thomas Lay provided excellent research assistance. Andrew McNeillie persuaded me to undertake the project, right after September 11, 2001, and Emma Bennett and Jennifer Hunt shepherded it to its conclusion.

R. B.

A Companion to Tragedy: Introduction

Rebecca Bushnell

In his searing comedy, *Frogs*, Aristophanes asked his audience which tragic playwright would be better suited to inspire Athens at a time of crisis: the heroic and stirring Aeschylus or the skeptical and emotional Euripides. Dionysus descends to Hades to satisfy his longing for Euripides, who has just died, but he stumbles into a competition between Aeschylus and Euripides for the name of the greatest tragic poet. The two tragedians battle it out over style, and both poets are mocked unmercifully, but finally Dionysus declares that what he really seeks is a poet who can serve the city. Once that end is declared, it is clear the deck is stacked: when it comes to saving cities, it appears, ironists need not apply. Aeschylus is chosen as the poet to cure the state and bring peace to Athens, and Euripides is abandoned in Hades.

The premise of *Frogs* – that the tragic playwright might indeed be able to rescue the state from disaster – is critical for understanding what tragedy might mean to us today. The increasing segregation of tragic theater from public life in our own time may have seriously diminished its claim to immediacy. But we still reach out to the idea of the tragic when confronted by horror or catastrophe. Tragedy can shape experience and history into meaning, and the shock of significance may have the power to transform us. The distinction between tragedy and the merely horrific accident or catastrophe lies in our expectation that knowledge might emerge out of the chaos of human suffering.

Of course, as Aristophanes' example of Euripides testifies, tragedy has also been thought to be able to undermine social and moral order. In *Frogs* Euripides is roundly criticized for slippery morality and dragging out the filth of real life on the stage. It was also Euripides who, through his own depictions of inexplicable human suffering, displayed the inadequacy of the consolations of divinity and justice, which were the foundations of the city-state. Tragedy can be dangerous, as much as redemptive, when it opens ups sores that cannot be healed.

In the West, in the centuries since Aristophanes, philosophers and poets have grappled with the question of how tragedy's formality, ethical example, and civic role intersect – for better or for worse. Plato believed that tragedy would undermine the city-state by inciting passion and disrespect for the gods. Aristotle responded by redeeming tragedy's emotional effect through catharsis, pulling tragedy back from the city into the mind and heart of the individual spectator. The English Renaissance poet Sir Philip Sidney reinserted tragedy into the political realm, when he asserted that the sweet violence of tragedy could make kings fear to be tyrants and tyrants abandon their cruelties; his contemporaries who opposed theater were convinced that tragedy would only drive spectators to imitate the violence they witnessed. The writers who fashioned neoclassical tragedy honed the aesthetics of tragic form, apparently severing tragedy from the welter of politics yet sending a more subtle message about social order. For Hegel and Nietzsche, in different ways, the conflicts of tragedy were to be played out in a world of spirit, more than on a civic scale, while to Freud, the tragic paradigm was the drama of the human psyche.

Tragedy can thus be construed in so many different ways – and those constructions themselves show what it means to us. It may be valued and defined in purely formal terms, or it may be understood as a spiritual or world view; it may be understood as an experience for the individual reader and thus a psychological phenomenon, or as a communal or political act, and thus an historical "event." The premise of this companion to tragedy is that in Western culture the meaning of tragedy is inseparable from history. The dramatic genre of tragedy has its roots in the religion and politics of the Greek city-state, and it lives still as a profoundly social art. Tragedy's subject is the relationship between the individual and the community in the face of a necessity that we may call the gods or history, and tragedy is performed to transform those who experience it. Tragedy's original form was shaped as much by Athenian democracy as it was by ancient religion, and its survival in European and American culture has been intertwined with the fate of dynasties, revolutions, and crises of social change. Yet, at the same time, this historical approach does not in any way devalue philosophical, religious, psychoanalytic, and anthropological readings of tragedy. While these forms of reading tragedy are themselves embedded in their own historical moments, they have powerfully affected how we have understood tragedy's cultural and ethical effects.

This companion presents tragedy as an artifact of Western culture and emphasizes its status as a dramatic genre. One could imagine composing a very different volume of chapters on the notion of the "tragic" more broadly construed, which would encompass global cultural manifestations of human suffering, especially in Asia, or one that would also extend beyond the narrower designation of tragic theater to include all performative expressions, including opera, music, film, and dance. But that is not the design of this book, which focuses on the complex *theatrical* inheritance from the Greeks to Rome and beyond, across Europe and North America, up through the twentieth century. The volume does end with an extended consideration of the appropriation and questioning of tragedy in African and Caribbean cultural traditions, where, as Timothy Reiss argues, we see how tragedy may be used against its makers.

The logic of the structure of this companion is thus twofold. The first set of chapters, on "Tragic Thought," unfolds a variety of modes of interpreting tragedy through different modes of thinking and experience, religious, philosophical, political, psychoanalytic, and historical. The chapters by Christiane Sourvinou-Inwood and Richard Seaford root our understanding of Greek tragedy in religion and in the practices of the worship of Dionysus, the god whose contradictions define the essence of tragic ambiguity. The contributions on tragedy, philosophy, and psychoanalysis by Kathy Eden, Mark Roche, James Porter, and Julia Reinhard Lupton take up the most important philosophical and theoretical framings of tragedy, beginning with Aristotle's extraordinarily influential *Poetics*. In different ways, Aristotle remains a point of reference for Hegel's refocusing on the tragic dialectic, Nietzsche's returning tragedy to Dionysus and redefining it as the essence of modernity, and Freud's and Lacan's reinterpretations of tragic paradigms in the psychic and symbolic orders.

The final part of this section on "Tragic Thought" takes up three ways of reading tragedy historically and politically, since recent scholarship on tragedy has turned strongly toward rooting tragic drama in the time that produced it. Deborah Boedeker and Kurt Raaflaub's chapter on tragedy and the Greek city-state complements the earlier chapters on tragedy and religion, in analyzing the function of Greek tragedy in the context of the Athenian politics. Hugh Grady looks at Marxist, cultural materialist, and new historicist interpretations of English Renaissance tragedy, while Victoria Wohl considers the evolution of feminist readings of Greek tragedy.

The second part of the companion, "Tragedy in History," follows the historical development of tragedy from classical Greece to modernity. Since the Greeks, the notion of tragedy has always been retrospective, looking backward with a sense of loss, and thus a great deal of attention is to be devoted to a fresh assessment of Greek tragedy. Rather than focusing on the individual Greek playwrights, the chapters consider issues that cross over the entire extant corpus of tragic theater. Alan Sommerstein's chapter on tragedy and myth and Ruth Scodel's on tragedy and epic explore the dimensions of Greek tragic plots and their relationship to the patterns defined by well-known stories of Greek culture. Michael Halleran discusses what we know of the performance of tragedy in ancient Greece. Claude Calame considers the unique role of the chorus, while Sheila Murnaghan uncovers the role of women in tragic drama (as an extension of the issues raised by Wohl's chapter). Ralph Rosen offers us the perspective that Old Comedy brings to fifth-century tragedy, and Alessandro Schiesaro concludes this section with a study of the Roman transformations of Greek tragedy.

The following three parts of this companion offer perspectives on critical moments in the afterlife of ancient tragic theater: the tragedies of Renaissance England and Spain; French, English, and German neoclassical and romantic tragedy; and the theatrical transformation of tragedy in the modern era. In each of these eras, we can see that writers and audiences struggled with the weight of the past. The models provided by Greek tragedy could be seen as the foundation on which a compelling new tragedy could be built, sweeping away the detritus of moribund, sentimental, or corrupt popular theatrical culture and restoring the mythic essentials of Western culture. However, classical tragedy could also be seen as the dead hand of the past, a frozen shell of a time long gone and of a world irrelevant to present values. The chapters on English and Spanish early modern tragedy by myself, Matthew Wikander, Michael Neill, and Margaret Greer open up a immensely vital moment in the history of tragedy, when playwrights were experimenting with new classical forms and played to kings and commoners alike, staging astonishing acts of violence and passion, regicide and rebellion. The following section on neoclassical and romantic tragedy shifts the focus to France and Germany (while Jeffrey Cox's chapter considers the extension of the conflicts of English Renaissance tragedy into the following two centuries). The three chapters on French tragedy by Richard Goodkin, Mitchell Greenberg, and Barbara Cooper follow the trajectory of French tragic drama from the overthrow of sixteenth-century Baroque theater through the extraordinary and rarefied phenomenon of neoclassical tragedy to its defeat, in turn, by melodrama and romantic theater in the nineteenth century. The final section, with chapters by Gail Finney, Brenda Murphy, and Timothy Reiss, offers an overview of the canonical modern reinterpretations of tragic theater in Europe, America, Africa, and the Caribbean. None of these chapters covering the history of tragic drama was intended to be comprehensive in covering all tragic authors or plays of a particular period. Rather, they are meant to suggest to the reader the critical questions of their time: how did tragedy, at that moment, *matter*, for writers and audiences alike.

Because of the companion's breadth, the contributors recognized that the chapters must be able to speak many different disciplinary languages but also be intelligible to nonspecialists. We wanted the chapters to enlighten readers across disciplinary divides, so that, for example, experts on Greek tragedy would communicate clearly to those in modern drama, or anthropologists and philosophers to literary scholars. It is an ambitious end, but all the more critical a task, given how the practice of reading tragedy has changed in the past two decades, especially in classical and Renaissance studies. At the same time, the chapters that follow here are not uniform, whether in style, method, or critical orientation, partly because they stem from many different disciplines and critical traditions. The reader will in fact find some disagreement among scholars on several contentious issues in the history of scholarship on tragedy, and quite appropriately so. This companion is not meant to provide a single point of view or narrative, but rather to give the reader a sense of the richness of the most current scholarship on the genre as reinvented across a great span of time and space.

What the contributors do clearly share is *their* conviction that tragedy matters: that is, that at critical points in the history of Greece, western Europe, and North America, tragic theater functioned as a vehicle for the expression of the deepest fears and most radical dreams of the society and culture that engendered it. The tragic scene may be played out in a stifling drawing room or on a battlefield, but wherever it happens, the experience has the power to evoke a culture's conceptions and questions about authority and the extent to which we determine the course of our own lives.

Part I
Tragedy and the Gods

1

Greek Tragedy and Ritual

Christiane Sourvinou-Inwood

Greek tragedies are not timeless. They are cultural artifacts embedded in the society that generated them, for they were produced and understood through the deployment of perceptual filters shaped by the cultural assumptions of fifth-century Athens, which the tragedians shared with their contemporary audiences. Moreover, they were performed in a ritual context, and this, as will become clear in this chapter, was not an incidental aspect that can be disregarded when we consider the meanings that these tragedies had for the ancient audiences, but a central element that shaped the tragedies and the ways in which those audiences made sense of them. Nevertheless, Greek tragedies can also be made sense of through filters shaped by cultural assumptions other than those that produced them, and they do have resonances for other societies, for they articulate rich, polysemic, and multivocal meanings, and explore problems that in some respects (albeit not in others) transcend the particular cultural forms that were specific to fifth-century Athens; this is partly because the tragedies were set in the audience's past, the heroic age, when men had walked with gods, and so even topical concerns were explored in a non-moment-specific version.[1] But modern readings can be very different from those that had been constructed by the fifth-century audiences.

For example, in Sophocles' *Antigone*, Antigone's disobedience of the edict of Creon, the King of Thebes, and her burial of her brother Polynices in defiance of that edict, have been seen by many modern readers as a noble act by a courageous individual rebelling against a tyrannical state, Antigone being perceived as a heroic figure who did her familial duty and obeyed the gods, privileging family and divine law over the law of an oppressive tyrant. This had great resonance for twentieth-century readers, in whose eyes the individual with a conscience who defies the state was of paramount importance, whether or not the individual readers had themselves lived under authoritarian regimes (see, e.g., Vidal-Naquet 2002: 47–9). But for the fifth-century audience the tragedy was much less predictable, much more complex and subtle, and so also richer.[2] For in the eyes of the ancient audience Antigone was, above all, a woman acting out of her proper place, in defiance of the decision of her community's leader, indeed, according to her sister Ismene, "against the will of the citizens" (v.79), at a moment when her community had just overcome a deadly danger, an attack from an invading foreign army brought against them by the traitor Polynices – and she was doing all that in the interests of that very traitor. There was no divine law that the audience knew to justify the fact that Antigone, a woman, acted out of her proper place, not only in defying her community, but also in performing a ritual act, the burial, which she was not, as a woman, supposed to perform (as opposed to lamenting, washing the corpse, and other rites which were a woman's proper role in the death ritual). Antigone, moreover, was the product of an incestuous union, the family she privileged was cursed, and her traitor brother Polynices, for whose sake she disobeyed the law, had killed their other brother, Eteocles, who had died a hero defending the city. Furthermore, in fifth-century Athenian terms Antigone's familial duty was to obey Creon, who was her uncle and became her legal guardian on the death of Eteocles.

Creon, on the other hand, was constructed, in the early parts of the tragedy, as the spokesman for the city, the polis, which itself, in ancient perceptions, was not a potentially threatening "state," but the community of citizens, the guardian and sole guarantee of civilized values, in which the religious sphere was an extremely important part. Creon begins by expressing sentiments that were the epitome of democratic patriotism and were indeed so understood by the fourth-century Athenian orator Demosthenes (19.247). It is only later in the tragedy that Creon makes tyrannical statements, thus sliding away from the concept "leader of the democratic polis," toward tyranny. Moreover, the ancient audiences would have perceived Creon as believing that in denying burial to Polynices he was only applying the principle (established in Athenian law and custom) that traitors were denied burial in their native land – a negative mirror image of the public burial and glorification of the war dead. It only eventually emerged that in denying Polynices any burial Creon had made a mistake, that he had extended that principle too far; that by keeping in the world of the upper gods a corpse, which belonged to the nether gods, Creon had upset the cosmic order and offended all the gods. This made for much more complex explorations, one of the main strands of which involved the exploration of the ultimate unknowability of the will of the gods, and correlatively of the fear that the religion of the polis, which articulated and guaranteed all religious activity, may sometimes get things wrong.

This was a very important problematization that modern readers would not register, unless familiar with Greek religion. Unlike Christianity, Greek religion did not have a canonical body of belief, no divine revelation nor scriptural texts – only some marginal sects had sacred books. It also did not have a "professional" divinely anointed clergy claiming special knowledge or authority; and there was no church. Crudely put, in Greek religion the polis (or, alternatively, ethnos, tribal state) played the role which in Christianity is played by the church: it was the polis who assumed the responsibility and authority to set a religious system into place,[3] structure the universe and the divine world in a religious system, articulate a pantheon with particular divine personalities; it established a system of cults, rituals, and sanctuaries, and a sacred calendar. The only guidance available was through prophecy; and, indeed, the various cities consulted the oracles on cultic matters. But while the god always spoke the truth, human fallibility could intervene and falsify the deity's words, and so the Greeks could never be certain that a particular prophecy was true.

This nature of Greek religion invited religious exploration, and so also the creation of a locus for this exploration of religious problems. I have argued that in fifth-century Athens this locus was, above all, tragedy (Sourvinou-Inwood 2003). We saw an illustration of such problematization in Sophocles' *Antigone*, where the exploration of the possibility that the polis' religious discourse may sometimes be mistaken was (as in other tragic explorations in other tragedies) distanced from the audience's realities; it was located at a safe symbolic distance through both its setting (Thebes, not Athens, the heroic age, not the present) and through Creon's tyrannical statements, which at a critical point distanced the world of the tragedy from the audience's democratic polis. When the tragedies are made sense of (as much as possible) through the (reconstructed) filters shaped by the cultural assumptions shared by the fifth-century tragedians and audiences, it becomes clear that the relationship between the world of the audience and that of the tragedy was not constant and inert, but shifting and dynamic, manipulated during the performance of each tragedy through devices that operated in interaction with those shared assumptions: "distancing devices," such as Creon's tyrannical statements, which distanced the action from the world of fifth-century Athens, sharply differentiating the two; and "zooming devices," which brought the tragic world nearer, pushed the audience into relating the play directly to their own experiences.[4]

The brief consideration of *Antigone* has illustrated how Greek tragedies can be read through filters other than those of the fifth-century Athenians and produce significant meanings, which, however, are radically different from those constructed by the ancient audiences; and also that the meanings created through the implicit deployment of modern assumptions have (naturally) more resonance for modern audiences than those reconstructed through the reconstruction of the ancient filters. Reading Greek tragedies through the (explicit or by default) deployment of modern assumptions is a legitimate part of modern theatrical discourses. But, in my view, modern readers should also take account of, and classical scholars must strongly privilege, the attempt to reconstruct as much as possible at least the parameters that had shaped the (varied) readings by the ancient audiences.

This discussion has also illustrated that an important element in the process of the construction of meanings by those audiences was the relationship between their ritual realities and the tragic rituals, for example whether the rituals enacted, or referred to in the tragedy (in *Antigone* burial by a woman, prohibition of the burial of traitors), were normative or transgressive. This element is marginalized in readings that deploy modern assumptions by default.

There is an intimate connection between fifth-century tragedy and ritual. Tragedies are articulated (some more densely than others) with the help of many rituals, such as sacrifices, prayers, and also divine epiphanies, which are not exactly rituals, but which, as we shall see, evoke rituals, and often explain and establish various cults and rites. This is one facet of that intimate connection. Another is the context of the performances: tragedies and comedies were performed during a festival of Dionysus, above all the City Dionysia, in a sanctuary, the theater in the sanctuary of Dionysus Eleuthereus underneath the Acropolis in Athens, in the presence of the statue of Dionysus.[5]

If Greek tragedy had been the cultural artifact of a newly encountered society it would have been classified, I suggest, as a type of performance which was, at the very least partly, ritual. However, historically the dominant perception of Greek tragedy has been as the literary genre which gave birth to Western theatrical tradition – which, of course it is, but this knowledge should be blocked, to avoid reading a cultural artifact through filters derived from its distant descendants, a methodologic-ally flawed procedure when the aim is to understand how that "ancestor" artifact functioned in the society that produced it. The perception of the relationship between Greek tragedy and religion in classical scholarship has changed over the years. When the ancient Greeks were perceived to be "like us," and the reading of texts a matter of common sense, with little or limited reflection of the ways in which meanings were inscribed and read through perceptual filters shaped by cultural assumptions, the religious dimension of Greek tragedy was generally underplayed, and the resulting readings reflected the rationality-privileging perceptions of (especially twentieth-century) Western intellectuals. In recent years there has been a much greater accept-ance of the religious dimension of Greek tragedy, with the emphasis on the articu-lations and manipulations of rituals in the creation of tragic meanings. (Zeitlin 1965: 463–508; Vidal-Naquet 1972: 133–58; Vernant 1972: 99–131; Easterling [1988] 1991: 87–109; cf. Friedrich 1996: 269–70), and the character of the dramatic performances as part of a festival has been stressed (see Goldhill 1990: 97–129). But not everyone accepts that the ritual context of the performance and the import-ance of religious elements in the tragedies are connected, let alone that they may indicate something about the ways in which the ancient audiences perceived the tragic performances. (see, e.g., Heath 1987: 48).

I have recently set out (Sourvinou-Inwood 2003) a detailed case for the view that tragedies were perceived by the ancient audiences as ritual performances, not as a purely "theatrical" experience simply framed by ritual and articulated through ritual, and that the rites, gods, and other religious elements in the tragedies were perceived to be representations of parts of the audiences' religious realities; and also that Greek tragedy was, among other things, but very importantly, also a discourse of religious exploration, one important locus where the religious discourse of the Athenian polis was explored and elaborated in the fifth century; and finally, that this religious exploration was intimately connected with the ritual context in which tragedies were performed, and within which tragedy had been generated. I am not, of course, suggesting that tragedies were simply discourses of religious exploration, or doubting that many other important problems are also explored, or that tragedies involve emotional experiences. What I am suggesting is that the reasons why the exploration of so many human problems is closely intertwined with religion are, first, the Greek perceptions of the world, in which the mortals' interactions with the divine was of crucial importance for, and affected the course of, human lives, behavior, and relationships; and second, tragedy's nature as a ritual performance which developed out of a ritual matrix conducive to religious problematizations and exploration. I also argued that, though in the fifth century tragedy changed significantly, and came to encompass a wide variety of problematizations, it did not lose its role as a locus of religious exploration, and did not cease to be perceived as a ritual performance. Let us briefly consider some of the arguments.

I will first illustrate how densely ritual elements are deployed in, and help articulate, Greek tragedies with two examples: Aeschylus' *The Libation Bearers*, the middle play of the *Oresteia* trilogy, and Euripides' *Electra*, a later tragedy focused on the same myth, a matricide, the killing of Clytemnestra and her lover Aegisthus by Clytemnestra's son Orestes, with the help of her daughter Electra, in revenge for Clytemnestra's murder of their father Agamemnon, on the oracular advice of the god Apollo.

The first part of *The Libation Bearers* is focused on the offering of chthonic libations. The original purpose of this rite, as intended by Clytemnestra, was to placate the angry shade of Agamemnon on her behalf, but this purpose was perverted and the rite turned against her: it became the starting point for Clytemnestra's murder, and Agamemnon's shade was asked to help his children avenge him by killing their mother.

The Libation Bearers begins with a prayer, then the chorus of female slaves bearing chthonic libations enters, together with Electra; the libations are poured, and Electra invokes Hermes Chthonios (the god responsible for the passage between the world of the living and the land of the dead) and asks him to summon the infernal gods, while she pours libations as she invokes, and addresses a prayer to, her dead father and asks his help for herself and her brother and against his killers, their mother and her lover Aigisthos. This is followed by lamentations by the chorus, and then the discovery of Orestes' offering of hair to their father's tomb. Then there is another prayer, and then Orestes reports a ritual, his consultation of the Delphic oracle, and Apollo's response: the god had urged him to avenge his father by killing his murderers and had enumerated the punishments inflicted by the infernal gods to those who do not avenge their kin. This report is followed by a lament, itself followed by a segment which includes further addresses to the dead Agamemnon, and requests for his help, invocations of, and prayers to, chthonic deities, and also the recounting of Clytemnestra's prophetic dream which had motivated her to send the chthonic libations in an attempt to placate her dead husband.

Most of the choral ode which begins at v. 783 consists of a prayer, and there is another prayer by the chorus at 855–68; at 900–2 there is a significant religious reference that affects the course of action, a reminder to Orestes of Apollo's oracular command. The choral ode at 935–71 is a song of victory and thanksgiving sung to celebrate that Dike, the goddess who personifies justice, has come. What follows after 973 can be considered to be enacting a rite of supplication, since Orestes is holding the suppliant's bough. At 1029–39 Orestes, having mentioned that it was Apollo's inducements that led him to kill his mother, announces that, on Apollo's instructions (part of the original oracular response), he is now going to Delphi as a suppliant to be purified. At 1048 he begins to describe his vision of the Erinyes, the Furies, whom no one else sees. At 1057 he invokes Apollo, and the chorus urge him to go to the Delphic sanctuary of Apollo. He then exits, fleeing, to go to Delphi, pursued, the audience will understand, by the Erinyes.

Thus, a very considerable part of this tragedy is articulated by ritual, there are religious references everywhere, and the Delphic Apollo has a central role.

The main ritual skeleton articulating Euripides' *Electra* is focused on a ritual that is reported in detail by a messenger (vv. 783–851), the sacrifice performed by Aegisthus, in the course of which he was murdered by Orestes. This sacrifice was referred to before its description, and then again afterwards. In the description we are told (vv. 825–9) that Aegisthus had taken the omens and that the organs of the sacrificial victim were abnormal and diseased, that is, the omens were bad. The predicted misfortune came to pass when Orestes, almost immediately afterwards, killed Aegisthus. This is a sacrifice corrupted by murder.[6] This corrupted sacrifice is part of a wider web which also includes other, associated, rites, some reported, others enacted. Thus, the messenger reports that when Orestes revealed his identity the palace servants raised the ritual cry of triumph and crowned him with a wreath. When the messenger departs the chorus performs a victory dance and invites Electra to join in the dancing and singing. Electra will fetch a wreath to crown her brother, but it is the chorus who do the singing and dancing. At vv. 874–9 the chorus – in this tragedy a chorus of young women in the heroic age – refers to its singing and dancing in a way that will have zoomed the audience's perception to their identity as a chorus of Athenian men in the present, singing in honor of Dionysus at the Dionysia in the theatre in the sanctuary of Dionysus (see Henrichs 1994/5: 87–8). I shall return to this.

The next enacted ritual, Electra's crowning of Orestes at 880–9, is a disturbing victory celebration, for the killing of Aegisthus, which could have been presented as a legitimate act of punishment, is made problematic in this tragedy through the outrage of the ritual order during the sacrifice (Easterling [1988] 1991: 101); also potentially disturbing is the fact that the corpse of Aegisthus is brought on to the stage and treated with disrespect (Easterling [1988] 1991: 107).

The murder of Clytemnestra involves a deception also centered on a ritual. At 1124–38 Electra tricks her mother by pretending to have given birth and asking her to perform the sacrifice offered on the tenth night after childbirth. Clytemnestra goes into the house believing she will perform the role of sacrificer, while in fact she will be the sacrificial victim. When, after the murder, Orestes and Electra come out of the house, appalled at their actions, they continue with religious language. At 1198–9

Electra mentions choral performances and weddings as rites from which she will be excluded. This would have evoked for the audience her earlier statement (in 309–13) that she was isolated because she was excluded from ritual, deprived of participation in festivals and dances because she avoided the group of which she was supposed to be a member, that of married women, since in reality she was a virgin. (Aegisthus had given her in marriage to a peasant, to ensure that her husband could not become a threat to him, but this peasant respected Electra and did not consummate the marriage). At 1177–93 Orestes invokes three deities to look upon his deeds, Gaia, Zeus, and Apollo. Finally, the brothers of Clytemnestra, Castor and Polydeuces, who had become gods, appear in epiphany. The epiphany of deities to mortals in the world of the tragedies corresponded to a real-life religious experience in the world of the audience; for deities, it was believed, occasionally manifested themselves to mortals and gave them instructions, as a result of which very often a cult was instituted (Versnel 1990: 190–3; Burkert 1985: 186–8; Henrichs 1996: 546). The representation of a deity by an actor evoked, for the ancient audience, the ritual impersonation of divinities by priestly personnel during certain religious ceremonies (Burkert 1985: 186, 1997: 27–8).

The following rites also helped create the ritual web that articulated the tragedy but are not part of the central segment of its main ritual skeleton. Electra's informal lament (vv. 112–66); the reference (167–97) to the forthcoming festival of Hera, aspects of which are evoked by both chorus and Electra; a double report of a ritual in the Old Man's account to Electra of his visit to the tomb of Agamemnon: he mentions his own lament and the fact that he offered a libation and deposited myrtle branches, and also reports that he saw evidence of a previous sacrifice of sheep and offering of hair; the prayer by Electra, Orestes, and the Old Man (671–82). There is also a prolonged reference to a human sacrifice, the sacrifice of Iphigenia (1011–50). The choral odes contain ritual and other religious references. At 737 ff. the chorus express their disbelief of the story that (after Atreus' faithless wife had given a golden lamb to her lover) the sun had changed its course, to the misfortune of mankind, for the sake of mortal justice, adding that frightening stories are profitable to men in furthering the service of the gods and that Clytemnestra, not remembering such stories, killed her husband. This passage affirms the gods' intervention in human affairs on the side of justice; it is this that Clytemnestra should have remembered (Stinton 1976: 79–82; cf. also Cropp 1988: 152, 743–4.) The comment concerning Clytemnestra shows that the notion of "frightening stories conducive to piety" is not presented by the chorus with a rationalist's sneer, but as something good, since they remind people of the existence of divine justice.

The corruption of two rites, Aegisthus' sacrifice and the enticing of Clytemnestra inside the house on the pretext of her participation in a ritual, helps color the two murders negatively. The corruption is less serious in the case of Clytemnestra, correlatively with the fact that matricide was in any case negatively colored. The central strand of religious problematization in this tragedy is focused on the role of Apollo in instigating murder, especially matricide. As well as deploying complex explorations of human relationships, passions, behavior patterns, and characteristics,

Electra problematizes not simply the killing of the mother to avenge the father (which involved both human relationships issues and issues involving the gods, pollution, and divine punishment), but also the notion of revenge in general, suggesting the possibility that it is in itself a corrupting act. Most importantly, this exploration problematized the role of Apollo and the Delphic oracle. However, the ancient audience would not have perceived this as a "criticism" of Apollo and his oracle, but as an illustration of the dark side of life; once one is caught up in a cycle of destruction there will be a lot of suffering. But ultimately Orestes will be saved. So, if one acts on divine instructions, even if they make no sense, or seem wrong, there may be intense suffering, but there will be an end to the suffering and an end to the self-perpetuating cycle of destruction.

Euripides' *Electra*, then, is articulated by a dense web of ritual elements, which is intertwined with rich religious problematization; thus, for example, the corruption of a rite colors an action negatively; the oracular consultation makes clear what it is that the god advises in a particular situation.

To move on. In terms of form, Greek tragedies are structured through songs sung by the chorus. The first song, called parodos, is sung as the chorus enters; the others, sung while they were in the orchestra, are called stasima. The role of the chorus in the tragedies diminished in the course of the fifth century, as individual characters acquired greater importance. However, the terminology used by the Athenians to speak of tragedy places the chorus at the center, defines tragedy through the chorus, and the chorus remained central in the organization of the production.[7] *Tragodoi*, "tragic singers," continues to be used to denote tragic performances in, for example, Aristophanes, Lysias, and Plato. Clearly, this does not mean that the chorus was perceived to be dramatically more important, especially given its decreasing role within the tragedies, so this centrality may be reflecting the importance of the tragic chorus in the wider context of the festival. An explanation in terms of the ritual importance of the chorus would coincide with the ritual importance of choruses in Greek festivals in general.

The festival of the City Dionysia included sacrifices, a very elaborate procession, and competitions, elements that formed the basic template for major Greek festivals, occurring in particular variants in particular festivals, depending on the specificities of each cult. In the Dionysia the competitions were connected with Dionysiac cult in that they were dramatic and dithyrambic competitions – dithyrambs being hymns, usually to Dionysus, sung by choruses who danced in a circular formation. Another element specific to the City Dionysia was a preliminary rite: just before the festival proper started, the statue of Dionysus was removed from the sanctuary of Dionysus Eleuthereus and taken to a shrine a little outside the center of Athens, in the Academy; eventually it was ceremonially escorted back to the theatre in the sanctuary, where the performances took place in its presence.

According to the myth associated with the festival,[8] a man from Eleutherai called Pegasos brought Dionysus' statue to Athens, but the Athenians did not receive the god with honor. Dionysus, enraged, struck the male sexual organs with an incurable disease. Instructed by the oracle to bring in the god with honor, the Athenians manufactured phalluses, penises made of wood and leather, and with these they honored the god, commemorating their misfortune. The City Dionysia, then, celebrated the introduction of the cult of Dionysus in Athens, and reenacted that introduction, and this is why the statue of Dionysus was removed from its sanctuary, taken to the Academy and then ceremonially escorted back, reenacting the introduction and giving the god an honored reception, both in the present, and as an reenactment of the hospitality offered him at the introduction of the cult. The festival was focused on a rite of receiving and entertaining a deity, a rite of xenismos, common in the Greek world, which involved the offering of a meal to a god or hero.[9]

The word *tragodos*, which denoted above all a member of the tragic chorus (though it was also used for the tragic poet and actor), means, according to its most widely accepted and best interpretation, either "singer at the sacrifice of a billy goat (*tragos*)," or "singer for the prize of a billy goat" – or both together, since the prize animal would have been sacrificed to Dionysus (Burkert 1990: 16–18). A singer at the sacrifice of a billy goat makes perfect sense, since in Greek ritual practice songs, hymns, were indeed sung at sacrifices.[10] In at least some sacrifices in which several hymns were sung, there was a basic bipartite articulation: a processional hymn, sung as the sacrificial procession moved toward the altar, and one or more songs sung by the altar. There are good reasons for thinking that the nexus of choral songs sung at the sacrifice of a billy goat in the rite of xenismos at the early City Dionysia was articulated in this way. This reconstructed nexus of songs sung at the sacrifice of a tragos in that xenismos bears a striking resemblance to the articulation of choral songs in tragedy, the basic skeleton of parodos and stasima. This suggests that this schema articulating the tragic choral odes may be reflecting the ritual schema of songs that had been part of the sacrificial ritual during the xenismos of Dionysus; that those songs sung at that sacrifice had produced the template of the basic schema structuring tragedy, the parodos and stasima.

The centrality of the chorus in Athenian perceptions of tragedy, the fact that the terminology used by the Athenians to speak of tragedy defines tragedy through the chorus, and the fact that the chorus remained central in the organization of the production, are important not simply because they show that tragedy was perceived in ways that placed it close to its ritual roots, but also, and especially, because, I will now try to show, in the eyes of the fifth-century audiences the tragic chorus was not only perceived as a group of people in the world of the play, in the audience's past, but also as a chorus, a group of male citizens acting as ritual performers, in the here and now, a chorus to Dionysus in the world of the present.

An element that indicates that tragic choruses were also perceived as ritual choruses in the present is the fact that the members of tragic – as well as dithyrambic – choruses had to be citizens (see, e.g., Plutarch *Phokion* 30; MacDowell 1989: 69–77; Csapo and Slater 1995: 351), and thus that they were, like other choruses, singing as representatives of the polis – while actors and poets could be foreigners. Also, as Easterling has stressed ([1988] 1991: 88–9), in tragedy the chorus is never simply a

group of bystanders or witnesses reacting and commenting; they are also a chorus
ready to perform lyrics patterned on ritual song and dance and accompanied by
appropriate music, for example, a paean giving thanks for victory, as in the parodos
of *Antigone*.[11] I would take this further and suggest that, for example in the particular
case of the parodos of *Antigone*, as the chorus processed in, singing a cult song the
usual mode of performance of which was processional, it would have been difficult for
the audience not to perceive this hymn as being sung also in the real world of here and
now. Then, there are choral passages in which references to choruses amount to choral
self-referentiality (Henrichs 1994/5: 56–111; Wilson and Taplin 1993: 170–4), in
which choruses "draw attention to their ritual role as collective performers of the
choral dance-song in the orchestra" (Henrichs 1994/5: 58). We saw an example of that
in Euripides' *Electra*.

Let us see how this self-referentiality works by considering another, striking,
example (see Henrichs 1994/5: 65–73) from an ode in Sophocles' *Oedipus Tyrannus*:
in vv. 883–910 the chorus of Theban elders ask, if people act without fear of Dike,
Justice, and without reverence for the gods and get away with it, "why should I
dance?," that is, why should I worship the gods through being a member of a chorus?
Then they sing that they will not visit the oracles any more if oracles do not come
true. Finally, they pray to Zeus not to allow this present situation to escape his power
– a situation which involves Oedipus' patricide and incest, though at this point in the
tragedy neither is clear to the tragic characters, who only know of the possibility that
Oedipus had killed Laios, his wife's first husband; the fact that Laios was his father is
not yet known. The verses activate the audience's knowledge that nothing will go
unpunished and that the oracles will come true in this case. Of course, the religious
problematization in this ode is located above all in the world of the tragedy, but when
the chorus sing "why should I sing and dance as a member of a chorus?," in a context
in which the meaning "worship the gods through being a member of a chorus" was
also constructed, at the very moment when they are singing and dancing as members
of a chorus, their song inevitably activated the audience's awareness that they were at
this very moment singing and dancing as members of a chorus in honor of Dionysus
in the present. This activated the perception of tragedy as a ritual performance. At the
same time, the complex and ambiguous relationship between the chorus's two
personae allowed the religious problematization they set out to take place at a
distance, and in a context in which the audience's knowledge about the play would
lead them to give reassuring answers. The questions were articulated simultaneously
in both worlds, but the audience's knowledge allowed them to place the questions the
chorus asks in the world of the play in their proper perspective, and give reassuring
answers, for they know that nothing will go unpunished and that the oracles will
come true. Clearly, the activation of the perception of the tragedy as a ritual
performance is intertwined with religious problematization, the basic question, "if
evil goes unpunished, why should we worship the gods?"

Choral self-referentiality, then, activated for the audience the chorus's identity as
chorus in the present performing in honor of Dionysus. The mask, while locating the

chorus in the other world of the heroic past, at the same time draws attention to the fact that the members of the chorus are not in fact "other," that their otherness is constructed, and located above all in the mask, while they are also, underneath the masks, a chorus of male Athenians in the present.

Another argument for the view that the identity of the chorus as a chorus in the present was not wholly neutralized is provided by Plato (*Laws* 800C–801A). Plato expresses his disapproval of the fact that, as he puts it, after a public sacrifice many choruses, standing not far from the altars, pour blasphemies over the sacrifices by singing mournful songs and racking the souls of the listeners and making them cry. The fact that this idiosyncratic polarization about tragic choruses was possible indicates that in the Athenian assumptions, the shared assumptions that have to be taken for granted for Plato's articulation to work, the tragic chorus was also perceived as a chorus in the present; for unless that was the case such a polarization would not make sense. The Platonic image entails that it could be presented as being the case that the world of the present could be penetrated by the world of the tragedy, that the mourning songs could be presented as constituting blasphemy within the ritual performed in the here and now.

Another argument in favor of the view that the chorus was also perceived as a chorus in the present may be provided by the tailpieces addressing Nike, the goddess of Victory, and requesting a prize in Euripides' *Orestes*, *Iphigenia in Tauris*, and *Phoenician Women*.[12]

If tragic choruses were indeed also perceived (albeit not dominantly) as choruses for Dionysus in the present, it follows that in the fifth century tragic performances were perceived as ritual performances also in the sense that they were shot through by rituals performed as rituals in the present, since the choral songs which structured the tragedies were not only perceived as sung in the world of the tragedy but also in the here and now, by a chorus of Athenian men in honor of Dionysus at his festival in his sanctuary. This perception would inevitably have affected the perception of the tragic performances as a whole. These performances, taking place in a sanctuary, during a ritual, in the presence of a god, and involving the representation of rituals and often also of gods, and named after, and also otherwise focused upon, the one element which was also perceived to be a ritual element in the present, could not have been perceived as other than ritual performances, in the presence of the statue of Dionysus, part of the ritual entertaining Dionysus at his festival.

But, it may be asked, if the case is so clear, why did previous generations of classical scholars not perceive tragedy in this way? There are several interacting reasons why the ritual, and generally religious, dimension of tragedy was underplayed. To begin with, the implicit perception of Greek tragic performances through the filter of modern theatrical experiences led to the implicit underprivileging of their ritual context and the concentration on their content, taken in isolation, wrenched from that context. Then, the absence of awareness of the role of assumptions in the construction of meaning led to the tragedies being made sense of through the (by default) deployment of modern assumptions, especially the rationalizing filters of modern scholars, which in turn led to the underprivileging of the importance of the religious dimension and the correlative reinterpretation of tragic religious discourses as ironic and/or critical of traditional religion – readings which could only be sustained by virtually eliding the importance of the ritual context of the tragic performances by marginalizing it as "simple" "framing."

This process was facilitated by the influence of Aristotle's *Poetics*, a treatise which radically underplays religion, and generally presents a perception of tragedy shaped by rigidly rationalizing filters and structured through the conceptual schemata Aristotle set out to construct, which reflected his own preoccupations and assumptions – the preoccupations and assumptions of a philosopher who was not even a participant in the culture, since he did not live in the fifth century and he was not Athenian. The distorting selectivity of Aristotle's presentation of tragedy has been stressed in recent years (Taplin 1995: 94–6; Gould 1996: 217; Goldhill 1996: 244; Hall 1996: 295–309, esp. 296); but its influence has not entirely disappeared, or at least a conceptual bias ultimately based on that perception of tragedy has not.

The belief that some tragedies, above all by Euripides, were challenging established religion was an important element in this nexus of interacting factors that shaped earlier perceptions of tragedy in which its religious dimension was underplayed. The notion that Euripides was an atheist has been shown to be wrong;[13] it is a modern construct produced through the deployment of modern filters and the taking at face value of what ancient audiences would have understood to be the comic distortions in Aristophanes' comedies (Sourvinou-Inwood 2003: 294–7). One of the main modalities of misreading that generated such interpretations is that which mistakes the dark problematizations in Euripidean tragedies (such as that in *Electra*) for criticisms of traditional religion. Such misreadings are produced when the tragic explorations are made sense of through modern filters shaped by assumptions which are not sympathetic to those of the Greek religious universe. I will now illustrate this, by briefly considering another instance of religious exploration and its articulation through ritual, an exploration which involves very dark problematization in Euripides' *Orestes*, where Apollo is repeatedly criticized by the dramatic characters, blamed for Orestes' matricide, and the notion that gods cause troubles and woes to humans is repeatedly expressed.

Euripides' *Orestes* deals with events that took place after the events represented in Aeschylus' *The Libation Bearers* and Euripides' *Electra*. In *Orestes* Orestes is pursued by the Erinyes after the matricide and he has also been condemned to death by the Argives. Because his uncle Menelaus had not come to his assistance, Orestes intends to punish him by killing his wife Helen and daughter Hermione. However, the gods snatch Helen away, so Orestes threatens to kill Hermione and burn down the palace, unless Menelaus convinces the Argives to spare his life. Catastrophe is averted by Apollo, who appears in epiphany, accompanied by Helen. He announces that Helen is now deified and tells Orestes that he is to undergo purification and then rule Argos – and also that he must marry Hermione and that Orestes' friend Pylades must marry Electra.

Many modern scholars have interpreted this ending of Orestes as an ironic construct, for they perceive an incongruity between this unexpected happy ending and
the earlier bleakness. However, as I will now try to show, an ironic reading (besides
being both a priori and culturally determined) cannot function when we deploy the
(reconstructed) filters shaped by the ancient assumptions through which the tragedy
was made sense of by the ancient audiences,[14] in that a series of interacting factors
make such an interpretation impossible. First, throughout the tragedy Apollo had
been zoomed to the audience's religious realities, through references that would have
evoked the audience's own consultation of the Delphic oracle, so that they would have
identified the Apollo of the tragedy with their own god, not perceived him as a
literary construct. Second, the epiphany of deities in the tragedies activated, and so
was perceived with the help of, two religious schemata, real-life epiphany (corresponding to the perspective of the dramatic characters) and (from the perspective of
the audience) "ritual impersonation of deities by priestly personnel." This also would
have led the audience to perceive the god on stage as a representation of the god they
worshiped, a perception further reinforced by the fact that this was a performance at a
festival of Dionysus in the sanctuary of Dionysus in the presence of the statue of
Dionysus, in which, moreover, the chorus was also as a chorus for Dionysus in the
present – (a persona confirmed and stressed by its concluding words in which it is
asking Nike for victory in the competition). All these interacting factors would have
inescapably have led the audience to perceive Apollo on stage as a representation of
their own god, not as a theatrical device of closure constructing an ironic ending.

After telling Orestes that he must go to Athens to stand trial for the matricide and that
he will be victorious at this trial Apollo promises that he will reconcile him to the city of
Argos, because, he says, "I forced" Orestes to kill his mother. Throughout the tragedy,
Apollo was repeatedly blamed for the matricide, which was characterized as unholy, and
for its consequences, and here he accepts that responsibility. But things are not that
simple. The audience would have perceived the notion that Apollo was alone responsible
for the matricide as one possible way of presenting a complex situation, but not as the
whole picture. For the Greek – and tragic – perception of double motivation, divine and
human, in which the gods will something but mortals' actions bring it about, would have
deconstructed the notion that the god alone was responsible. More importantly, there is
another recurrent theme in Orestes, which also deconstructs the notion of Apollo's sole
responsibility: the notion that these disasters were the result of an ancestral curse, and the
consequent operation of an avenging demon. This affects the way in which the audience
would have made sense of the notion that Apollo had forced Orestes to kill his mother.
Since, in the eyes of the audience, an avenging demon triggered off by the curse was
operating, it was inevitable that Orestes should have suffered, so Apollo's command was
good advice on how to deal with a dreadful situation. Apollo stresses his own responsibility, focuses on his own role, because he is stressing that Orestes obeyed him, a god, and
he wants to marginalize Orestes' choice in this context, in which he is speaking of
reconciling him to the people of Argos; it is as though he is presenting the case for
Orestes that he will make to the Argives.

Consequently, the superficial impression that Apollo is to blame for Orestes' matricide was modified, for the audience, through their perception that Orestes had ultimately made his own choices, and also, very importantly, through the perception of the workings of the avenging demon. Nevertheless, Apollo was responsible; he had ordered Orestes to kill his mother. Does this entail that the audience would have perceived Apollo to have been wrong, and worthy of criticism? Surely, gods should not instigate matricide. These, I suggest, are culturally determined questions. For the ancient audience Apollo was right, in that the fact that Orestes followed his advice has led, after suffering, to the present situation, in which it is clear that order will eventually be restored, and Orestes' sufferings will come to an end. This does not alter the fact that his guidance involved the commission of an unholy deed. The themes of "vengeance" and "reaction to injustice and wrongdoing with further wrongdoing" are explored in many tragedies. The answer is not simple. The ideology of the society in which tragedy was generated led to an hierarchy of wrongness. In Greek discourse the father, and the father–son relationship, were privileged, and a woman who betrayed and killed her husband was perceived, as Clytemnestra is described in this tragedy, as a threatening figure, representing the dangers of complete disorder. But the matricide is also presented in very negative colors, and also threatens disorder. Because of this hierarchy of wrongness, order will be eventually restored after a matricide, but the other side is also strongly articulated, and the prospective happy ending does not obliterate Orestes' suffering which the audience has witnessed.

Would the audience have perceived that there were alternatives to what Apollo had advised Orestes to do? From the human perspective one character, Tyndareus, believes that there were. But in the Greek representations the human perspective is limited. So, the audience's perception, I suggest, would have been that in those circumstances, only part of which are intelligible to mortals, Apollo's command revealed what was the best way to deal with an extremely bad situation – however dreadful that remedy. So, one of the perceptions articulated in this tragedy was that the ways of the gods are unfathomable, but this is intertwined with the perception that even when people think that the gods have abandoned them, it is not true – if they have followed the gods' will; ultimately the gods help those who obey them, whatever it may look like; there is suffering, and this suffering is not annihilated by what will happen in the future, but eventually the suffering will come to an end, and things will work out. This is a reassuring message. However, this reassurance is partly deconstructed, as far as the world of the audience is concerned, by Orestes' reply. Orestes acknowledges that Apollo is a true prophet. His fear had been that it might have been a false oracle, not Apollo's voice, but an avenging demon attempting to deceive him. This would have evoked the fact that in the audience's reality people did not know if the prophecy they received was right, for there was always the danger, in their perceptions of prophecy, that human fallibility might interfere to distort the god's message. But again, the very fact that there is an order and a divine plan in the cosmos is itself reassuring. *Orestes*, then, does not criticize the gods or challenge established religion; it sets out a complex religious exploration.

Euripidean tragedies often explored problematic areas in the Greek religious system and the human relationships that were grounded in that system. They explored, among other things, the empirically observable fact that the world is cruel, and people suffer, by articulating the darkness and bleakness and offering "answers," which were ultimately, in complex ways, reassuring.

The perception that Apollo was a representation of the audience's god was, we saw, an important element in their reception of the religious exploration in *Orestes*. Since this perception was to a large extent constructed through the activation of ritual schemata from the audience's lived religion, it is clear that here also the discourse of religious exploration is constructed through (among other things, but especially) the deployment of ritual. This is another illustration of the articulation of religious explorations (and the explorations of associated issues pertaining to human inter-actions) through the ritual web that structures the tragedies. Indeed, on my view, which I will now summarize, tragedy was generated through the interaction between ritual performance and religious exploration. The festival myth of the City Dionysia is not the only myth of resistance to the introduction of Dionysus' cult. The best known among such myths is that of Pentheus, King of Thebes, as told in Euripides' *Bacchae*. In this tragedy Dionysus, the divine son of Zeus and the mortal Semele, arrived at Thebes, bringing his cult; his mother's sisters challenged his divinity and he punished them by sending them madness which drove them to the mountain where they were raving, joined by the other Theban women, to whom Dionysus had also sent frenzy. Dionysus' cousin, Pentheus, resisted the introduction of Dionysus' rites and impri-soned Dionysus and his followers – though they all escaped from prison miraculously. Pentheus was punished by being torn apart by his mother and the other raving women who mistook him for a mountain lion. Pentheus, and all the others who, like the Athenians, resisted the cult of Dionysus, had followed surface logic, not realizing that this stranger who brought disordered behavior was a god. On the surface the behavior of Dionysus and his retinue was wrong, mad; but in the deeper reality that was inaccessible to human logic that disorder was good. What seemed madness was right; and what had seemed right – the exclusion of disorder – turned out to be madness. For this disorder was inspired by Dionysus and opposition to it was an offense against the gods. This is a paradox, and paradox characterizes religion and the world of the gods which is unknowable to men. One of the perceptions expressed in such myths is that ultimate religious reality lies beyond the limits of human rationality. This Dionysiac challenge of human rationality invites exploration, both in itself and also insofar as it presents a polarized version of the unknowability of the divine will and so appropriate human behavior – at least in cases in which the latter is not based on customs hallowed by tradition, practices that, as the Greeks saw it, had proved their efficacy through the longevity and prosperity of the communities that practiced them.

I have argued (Sourvinou-Inwood 2003: 67–200) that it was through the inter-action between the myth of Athenian resistance to Dionysus, which raised complex religious problems and invited exploration, and choral performances at the sacrifice of a goat during the rite of xenismos of Dionysus, the focus of the City Dionysia, that tragedy was generated in the particular historical circumstances of sixth-century Athens and thanks to the contribution of particular poets. For the focus of the xenismos, and so also of the hymns accompanying its sacrifice, was the festival myth, the rejection of Dionysus' cult and the realization that this was a terrible mistake, and so also the problematization of the paradox that these myths of resistance to Dionysus set out. In other words, the hymns would have implicated a subject highly conducive to religious exploration, of a type that also raised wider questions pertaining to religion in general, and this was one of the factors that led to the generation of new forms that eventually led to the emergence of tragedy. On my argument, the ritual performance and the exploration had began by focusing on the festival myth, which involved a world that was both other, part of the heroic past, and part of the world of the present, in that it involved the introduction of the cult of Dionysus which was part of the Athenian present, as were the relationships between the god and the Athenians set up in that heroic age. Subsequently, these explorations encompassed other Dionysiac myths, comparable to the festival myth, that also invited the generation of comparable explorations. Eventually, these explorations widened their scope to take in non-Dionysiac religious matters; new forms developed, and tragedy was born.

On my thesis, tragedy in the fifth century was still a ritual performance which explored – among other things – the religious discourse of the polis. When the plague, which began at 430 BCE, brought about moral and religious "turbulence," insecurity, anxiety, and questioning (Thucydides 2.47.4, 2. 53.4; see Parker 1996: 200) that religious exploration (in the extant Euripidean tragedies) acquired greater urgency and intensity, and set out a darker problematization, but it still offered "answers," which were ultimately, in very complex ways, reassuring.

NOTES

1   I discuss the preferred setting of Greek tragedy in the heroic age and its implications in Sourvinou-Inwood (2003: 15–66).

2   For the detailed arguments on which what follows is based see Sourvinou-Inwood (1989: 134–48, 1990b: 11–38).

3   Sourvinou-Inwood (1990a: 295–322 [2000: 13–37], 1988: 259–74 [2000: 38–55]).

4   Sourvinou-Inwood (1989: 134–48, 2003: *passim*, esp. 15–66); cf. Pelling (1997: 217–18, 228–9, 233–4).

5   See Pickard-Cambridge (1968); Csapo and Slater (1995); Goldhill (1990: 97–129); Sourvinou-Inwood (2003: 67–200, cf. 40–5). They were also performed at the Lenaia, in some

local communities at the Rural Dionysia, and from the late fourth century BCE at the Anthesteria. But the City Dionysia was their primary and most important context.

6   See Easterling ([1988] 1991: 101–8); Henrichs (1994/5: 86); cf. Cropp (1988: 153–7, 747–858).

7   See, e.g., Winkler (1990: 42); Wilson and Taplin (1993: 170); Wilson (2000: 54–5, 61–7).

8   Scholia Aristophanes *Acharnians* 243a; Pickard-Cambridge (1968: 57–8); Garland (1992: 159); Cole (1993: 26).

9   On this rite see Jameson (1994: 35–57); Burkert (1985: 107).

10 The detailed argument on which what follows is based is set out in Sourvinou-Inwood (2003: 141–200).

11 See Rutherford (1994/5: 127): "the parodos of the Antigone can itself be thought of as a paean, although this would be a celebratory victory paean, contrasting with the fearful and apotropaic song of Pindar."

12 Especially if they were Euripidean. But even if they were actors' interpolations they would still testify to perceptions in which the chorus was also perceived as a chorus in the present. The notion that they are post-classical is based on the circular argument that "the break of illusion is foreign to tragedy" (Mastronarde 1994: 645, 1764–6); but the notion "break of illusion" is too crude a concept for the complex situation that tragic performances involved; the argument is circular because it becomes invalid if it is right that the tragic chorus was also perceived as a chorus in the present – with this part of the chorus's persona being zoomed at the end of some tragedies (see also Sourvinou-Inwood 2003: 66 n.135, and esp. 415–17).

13 See esp. Lefkowitz (1987: 149–66, 1989: 70–82). I added some further arguments to this discussion in Sourvinou-Inwood (2003: 291–458, 489–500).

14 A detailed discussion with bibliography is in Sourvinou-Inwood (2003: 386–402, 410–14).

References and Further Reading

Burkert, W. (1985). *Greek Religion. Archaic and Classical*, vol. 2. Oxford: Basil Blackwell.

Burkert, W. (1990). *Wilder Ursprung. Opferritual und Mythos bei den Griechen* [Savage origin. Greek victim ritual and myth]. Berlin: Wagenbach.

Burkert, W. (1997). "From Epiphany to Cult Statue: Early Greek Theos." In *What Is a God? Studies in the Nature of Greek Divinity*, ed. A. B. Lloyd. London: Duckworth, 15–34.

Cole, S. G. (1993). "Procession and Celebration at the Dionysia." In *Theater and Society in the Classical World*, ed. R. Scodel. Ann Arbor: University of Michigan Press, 25–38.

Cropp, M. J. (1988). *Euripides: Electra*. Warminster: Aris & Phillips.

Csapo, E. and Slater, W. J. (1995). *The Context of Ancient Drama*. Ann Arbor: University of Michigan Press.

Easterling, P. E. (1988) [1991]. "Tragedy and Ritual. 'Cry "Woe, Woe", but May the God Prevail."' *Metis* 3, 87–109.

Friedrich, R. (1996). "Everything to Do with Dionysos? Ritualism, the Dionysiac and the Tragic." In *Tragedy and the Tragic. Greek Theatre and Beyond*, ed. M. S. Silk. Oxford: Clarendon Press, 257–83.

Garland, R. (1992). *Introducing New Gods. The Politics of Athenian Religion*. London: Duckworth.

Goldhill, S. (1990). "The Great Dionysia and Civic Ideology." In *Nothing to Do with Dionysos?: Athenian Drama in Social Context*, ed. J. J. Winkler and F. Zeitlin. Princeton, NJ: Princeton University Press, 97–129.

Goldhill, S. (1996). "Collectivity and Otherness – The Authority of the Tragic Chorus: Response to Gould." In *Tragedy and the Tragic. Greek Theatre and Beyond*, ed. M. S. Silk. Oxford: Clarendon Press, 244–56.

Gould, J. (1996). "Tragedy and Collective Experience." In *Tragedy and the Tragic. Greek Theatre and Beyond*, ed. M. S. Silk. Oxford: Clarendon Press, 217–43.

Hall, E. (1996). "Is There a Polis in Aristotle's Poetics?" In *Tragedy and the Tragic. Greek Theatre and Beyond*, ed. M. S. Silk. Oxford: Clarendon Press, 295–309.

Heath, M. (1987). *The Poetics of Greek Tragedy*. London: Duckworth.

Henrichs, A. (1994/5). "Why Should I Dance?": Choral Self-Referentiality in Greek Tragedy. In *The Chorus in Greek Tragedy and Culture, One*, ed. H. Golder and S. Scully, *Arion* 3.1, 56–111.

Henrichs, A. (1996). "Epiphany." In *The Oxford Classical Dictionary*, ed. S. Hornblower and A. Spawforth, 3rd edn. Oxford and New York: Oxford University Press, 546.

Jameson, M. H. (1994). "Theoxenia." In *Ancient Greek Cult Practice from the Epigraphical Evidence*, ed. R. Hägg. Stockholm: Svenska Institut i Athen, 35–57.

Lefkowitz, M. R. (1987). "Was Euripides an Atheist?" *Studi italiani di filologia classica* 5, 149–66.

Lefkowitz, M. R. (1989). " 'Impiety' and 'Atheism' in Euripides' Dramas." *Classical Quarterly* 39, 70–82.

MacDowell, D. M. (1989). "Athenian Laws about Choruses." In *Symposion 1982. Vorträge zur griechischen und hellenistischen Rechtsgeschichte* [1982 symposium. Lectures on Greek and Hellenistic historical jurisprudence], ed. F. J. Fernandez Nieto. Cologne: Pöhlau, 65–77.

Mastronarde, D. J. (ed.) 1994. *Euripides, Phoenissai*. Cambridge: Cambridge University Press.

Parker, R. (1996). *Athenian Religion. A History*. Oxford: Clarendon Press.

Pelling, C. (1997). "Conclusion." In *Tragedy and the Historian*, ed. C. Pelling. Oxford: Clarendon Press, 213–35.

Pickard-Cambridge, A. (1968). *The Dramatic Festivals of Athens*, 2nd edn, revised by J. Gould and D. M. Lewis. Oxford: Clarendon Press.

Rutherford, I. (1994/5). "Apollo in Ivy: The Tragic Paean." In *The Chorus in Greek Tragedy and Culture, One*, ed. H. Golder and S. Scully, *Arion* 3.1, 112–35.

Sourvinou-Inwood, C. (1988). "Further Aspects of Polis Religion." *Annali Istituto Universitario Orientale di Napoli: Archeologia e storia antica* 10. Naples, Dipartmento del mondo classico e del mediterraneo antico, 259–74. Also in *Oxford Readings in Greek Religion*, ed. R. Buxton, Oxford: Oxford University Press, 2000, 38–55.

Sourvinou-Inwood, C. (1989). "Assumptions and the Creation of Meaning: Reading Sophocles' *Antigone*." *Journal of Hellenic Studies* 109, 134–48.

Sourvinou-Inwood, C. (1990a). "What is Polis Religion?" In *The Greek City from Homer to Alexander*, ed. O. Murray and S. Price. Oxford: Oxford University Press, 295–322. Also in *Oxford Readings in Greek Religion*, ed. R. Buxton. Oxford: Oxford University Press, 2000, 13–37.

Sourvinou-Inwood, C. (1990b). "Sophocles' Antigone as a 'Bad Woman'." In *Writing Women into History*, ed. F. Dieteren and E. Kloek. Amsterdam: Historisch Seminarium van de Universiteit van Amsterdam, 11–38.

Sourvinou-Inwood, C. (2003). *Tragedy and Athenian Religion*. Lanham, MD: Lexington Books.

Stinton, T. C. W. (1976). " 'Si credere dignum est': Some Expressions of Disbelief in Euripides and Others." *Proceedings of the Cambridge Philological Society* 22, 60–89.

Taplin, O. (1995). "Opening Performance: Closing Texts?" *Essays in Criticism* 45, 93–120.

Vernant, J.-P. (1972). "Ambiguité et renversement. Sur la structure énigmatique de l'"Oedipe roi' " [Ambiguity, and inversion. On the enigmatic structure of *Oedipus the King*]. In *Mythe et tragédie en Grèce ancienne* [Myth and tragedy in ancient Greece], ed. J.-P. Vernant and P. Vidal-Naquet. Paris: Maspéro, 99–131.

Versnel, H. S. (1990). *Ter Unus. Isis, Dionysos, Hermes. Three Studies in Henotheism*. Leiden: Brill.

Vidal-Naquet, P. (1972). "Chasse et sacrifice dans l'*Orestie* d'Eschyle"[Hunting and sacrifice in Aeschylus' *Oresteia*]. In *Mythe et tragédie en Grèce ancienne*, ed. J.-P. Vernant and P. Vidal-Naquet. Paris: Belles lettres, 133–58.

Vidal-Naquet, P. (2002). *Le miroir brisé. Tragédie athénienne et politique* [The broken mirror. Athenian and political tragedy]. Paris: Maspéro.

Wilson, P. (2000). *The Athenian Institution of the Khoregia. The Chorus, the City and the Stage*. Cambridge: Cambridge University Press.

Wilson, P. and Taplin, O. (1993). "The 'Aetiology' of Tragedy in the *Oresteia*." *Proceedings of the Cambridge Philological Society* 39, 169–80.

Winkler, J. J. (1990). "The Ephebes' Song: Tragoidia and Polis." In *Nothing to Do with Dionysos?*, ed. J. J. Winkler and F. Zeitlin. Princeton, NJ: Princeton University Press, 20–62.

Zeitlin, F. I. (1965). "The Motif of the Corrupted Sacrifice in Aeschylus' *Oresteia*." *Transactions of the American Philological Association* 96, 463–508.

2
Tragedy and Dionysus

Richard Seaford

In Athens of the classical period tragedy (as well as comedy and satyric drama) was performed at the theater of the god Dionysus, in his cult. A strong association of Greek drama with Dionysus persisted throughout antiquity, and it is virtually certain that drama also *originated* in Dionysiac cult. Myths were told about Dionysus, notably about his arrival in a new place where he was resisted by the local ruler, for example by Pentheus of Thebes. And yet, because most surviving tragedies and comedies dramatize stories that are not about Dionysus, it is legitimate to ask whether the cultic connection of Dionysus has any relevance to our understanding of the surviving plays. My answer – though not everybody will agree – is that it does.

The Genesis of Tragedy in Dionysiac Cult

Our most reliable source by far for the genesis of tragedy is the fourth chapter of Aristotle's *Poetics*. Though his testimony has been doubted, he could draw on research (now lost) into the early theater, and does indeed state (1449b37) that the process by which tragedy came into being is known. He makes three remarks of particular interest, that tragedy had an improvisatory beginning, that it came into being "from the leaders of the dithyramb," and that it developed *ek tou satyrikou* – that is, from something like the satyric drama. We should add the ancient tradition that, when the themes of tragedy ceased to be about Dionysus, it was decided that a satyr play was to be performed after each set ("trilogy") of three tragedies, i.e., to be a reminder of tragedy's humble origins. A satyr play was a boisterous drama, written by the author of the preceding tragedies, but with a chorus of satyrs – naked, hedonistic followers of Dionysus, with some equine characteristics. Only one satyr play survives complete, Euripides' *Cyclops*. The dithyramb was a hymn to Dionysus, probably once consisting of solo improvisation and choral refrain – sometimes sung by men dressed as satyrs – in a procession escorting Dionysus into the city.

To answer the question why it was the cult of Dionysus that produced tragedy, we must look not just at the main context for the performance of tragedy, the City Dionysia, but also at the other main polis festival of Dionysus at Athens, the "older Dionysia" (Thucydides 2.15.4), called Anthesteria. The City Dionysia (or "Great Dionysia") was – unlike the traditional Anthesteria – created or amplified as late as the sixth century BCE. The Anthesteria, a spring festival of Dionysus, seems to have derived its name from the Greek word for flower (*anthos*). It was a festival of the whole community of Athens, lasted three days, and included the opening and drinking of the new wine, as well as various other components. I will focus on five of these components.

The first component is that during this spring festival men and boys dressed up as (and wore the masks of) *satyrs*. This belonged to the hedonistic, wine-drinking aspect of the festival.

Second, it is likely that at some point in this festival Dionysus was escorted into the city, in a cart shaped like a ship, by satyrs playing pipes.

Third, Dionysus (whether impersonated, or in the form of an image) was united with the wife of the "king" archon (magistrate), in a "sacred marriage," as one element of female ceremonies that were celebrated in what was imagined to be the old royal dwelling, and that included mystic ritual, perhaps at the conclusion of the processional escort of Dionysus.

Fourth, these and other elements of the festival were associated with *myths*. For instance, the escort of Dionysus into the city was no doubt envisaged as a celebration or reenactment of his original arrival. The "sacred marriage" was seen as the union of Dionysus and Ariadne. The practice of drinking the new wine in silence and at separated tables was explained as a result of the hospitality once given at Athens to the polluted matricide Orestes. The story was told of Ikarios, who was given wine by Dionysus, gave it to his neighbors, and was killed by them because they became drunk and imagined that Ikarios had poisoned them. His daughter Erigone eventually found his body in a well, and hanged herself: the ritual of swinging at the Anthesteria was explained as propitiating her. And so on.

Fifth, the ritual was one in which, in a sense, the whole city took part (including children and slaves). This *inclusiveness* probably involved a sense of communality: collective wine-drinking may promote dissolution of distinctions, and in Euripides' *Bacchae* it is explicitly stated that Dionysus wants everybody to join in his worship, and "to be magnified while distinguishing nobody" (209).

Each of these five elements of the ancient Anthesteria contributed to the genesis of drama at another Dionysiac festival at Athens, the newly founded (or reorganized) City Dionysia, in the latter half of the sixth century BCE.

First, a precondition for drama is the *transformation of identity*, such as we find in the transformation of men and boys into satyrs at the Anthesteria, as well as predramatic (sixth-century) representations of *masks* of Dionysus. That boisterous performance by satyrs played an important role in genesis of tragedy is suggested, as we have seen, by Aristotle in the *Poetics*.

Second, with Aristotle's remark that tragedy arose from "the leaders of the dithyramb" (an originally processional hymn accompanying Dionysus), we should compare not only the *parodos* (entry-song) of Euripides' *Bacchae*, but also the processional entry of Dionysus at the Anthesteria, which was certainly musical (in the vase-paintings of the festival the satyrs are shown playing pipes) and, indeed, precisely the kind of ritual that the dithyramb originally accompanied. A fourth-century BCE Athenian (Phanodemos *FGrH* 325 F 12) tells us that in their songs and dances at the Anthesteria the Athenians addressed Dionysus as (among other titles) "Dithyrambos."

Third, the procession seems to have been associated with a myth, and with female *mystic ritual*. That female mystic ritual, which certainly involved transformation of identity, was an important factor in the genesis of satyric drama and of tragedy, I have argued elsewhere (Seaford 1994).

Fourth, the various rituals performed seem each of them to have been imagined as reenacting a mythical event. Moreover, the myths are *etiological* in that they explain why the ritual began to be performed. Similarly, tragedy reenacts myth, in particular, *etiological* myth of cult.

Fifth, tragedy, like the Anthesteria, is an institution of the polis and is addressed to the whole polis; and many tragedies seem to take the polis as a central theme.

Of course the combination of these five elements in the ancient Anthesteria was not sufficient to create drama. Something extra is required, which was supplied in the creation (or reorganization) – probably by the tyrants – of another Dionysiac festival (the City Dionysia) in the latter half of the sixth century BCE. It is beyond the scope of this chapter to investigate what this something extra was. Suffice it here to say that whereas the ancient festival of the Anthesteria had long centered around a key moment in the agricultural year, the opening of the new wine, the new Dionysia was largely designed to serve a *political* end: the *display* of the strength and magnificence of Athens – to itself and to others. We should also note that the organization and coordination of the new urban festival was greatly facilitated at this time by the introduction into Attica of (recently invented) coined *money*: the universal power of money, deployed at a single center or even by a single individual, is especially good at coordinating a complex new initiative, and tends in our period to replace the less flexible power of barter and traditional observance.

It is implied by what I have said so far that the myths dramatized in the earliest tragedies were likely to have been about Dionysus, as indeed an ancient tradition states. There are two reasons why the cult of Dionysus could contain, as it did throughout the classical period, dramatic enactments of myths that had nothing to do with the god. The first is that the number of myths about Dionysus is relatively small, so that the demands of originality resulted – in dithyramb, in tragedy, and even in satyric drama – in the adoption of non-Dionysiac myth. The other is that Dionysiac cult seems early on to have had elements in common with another kind of cult, that held in honor of heroes, usually at their tombs and often involving lamentation. The similarity and potential for synthesis between the Dionysiac cult and hero-cult is exemplified by an instance which has, again, a political aim: in early sixth-century

Sikyon the cult of the Argive hero Adrastus contained "tragic choruses" about his sufferings, which the tyrant Kleisthenes transferred to Dionysus while transferring the rest of the cult to the hero Melanippus (Herodotus 5.67).

Of the very earliest tragedies – those attributed to the four tragedians older (it seems) than Aeschylus – we possess 18 titles, of which only two indicate myths about Dionysus. These are *Pentheus*, attributed to Thespis, and *Dymainai*, or *Karyatides*, attributed to Pratinas. *Dymainai* are said by the fifth-century AD lexicographer Hesychius to be choral *bacchae* (maenads, women performing cult for Dionysus) at Sparta. Heracleides of Pontus, who lived in the fourth century BCE, was accused by his contemporary Aristoxenos of forging plays by Thespis, but may have followed Thespis' titles. Two fragments (2, 4) with Dionysiac content, attributed to Thespis, may well be forgeries.

Tragedies about Dionysus

The first dramatist of whom we possess complete plays is Aeschylus (ca.525–456 BCE). The surviving titles of tragedies attributed to him number about sixty, of which two may well have been about myths involving Dionysus (*Athamas* and *Toxotides*), and seven certainly were: *Edonians*, *Bassarids*, *Neaniskoi*, *Bacchae*, *Pentheus*, *Semele*, and *Xantriai* ("Wool-carding Women").

The only certainly attested Aeschylean trilogy on a Dionysiac theme, consisting of *Edonians*, *Bassarids*, and *Neaniskoi*, dramatized the story of the arrival of Dionysus from the east to establish his cult in Thrace, where the local ruler Lycurgus resisted it. In the drama the maenads were imprisoned and miraculously liberated, and it seems that Lycurgus was maddened by Dionysus, killed his own son Dryas, mistaking him for a vine (a subject represented in several vase-paintings), and was punished by Dionysus, probably by being taken off to imprisonment in Mount Pangaion so as to cure the land of sterility.

It is possible that only the resistance to Dionysus occurred in *Edonians* and that his punishment was dramatized in *Bassarids*, but it is more likely that resistance and punishment both occurred in *Edonians*, like the resistance of Pentheus and his punishment by Dionysus in Euripides' *Bacchae*. Indeed, *Edonians* resembles Euripides' *Bacchae* (the only surviving tragedy about Dionysus) not only in its plot but also – to judge from its few surviving fragments – in detail, notably in the king's taunting interrogation of the captive Dionysus as effeminate (fr. 61) and in the Dionysiac shaking of the king's house (fr. 58).

If both resistance and punishment were dramatized in *Edonians*, what was the theme of *Bassarids*? The title refers to Thracian maenads, who were sent by Dionysus to dismember Orpheus. This was almost certainly the theme of the play. And of all the various reasons given for this punishment of Orpheus, the most likely to have occurred in this drama is the one contained in the reconstructed Chapter 24 of Eratosthenes' *Katasterisms*:

Having gone down to Hades for his wife, and seen what things were like there, Orpheus no longer honoured Dionysus, by whom he had been made famous, but regarded the sun as the greatest of the gods, and called him Apollo. And so Dionysus was angry and sent the Bassarids against him, as Aeschylus the tragic poet relates, . . .

This has been argued in detail by M. L. West (1983). I add only that it is worth asking why experience of the underworld turned Orpheus into a devotee of the sun. The answer is, I think, provided by the amazing light that frequently marks the unforgettable transition from anxiety to joy for the mystic initiand, as it does also in the modern near-death experience. This light was, in mystery-cult, sometimes envisaged as the sun (cf., e.g., Aristophanes *Frogs* 155, 454–5). Mystery-cult was a rite of passage that had to be kept secret from the world at large: it often involved the imagined death of the initiate as a rehearsal for real death, as well as transition from ignorance to knowledge and from anxiety to joy. At *Bacchae* 629–30, in a passage full of correspondences with mystic initiation, Dionysus makes a "light" (this is the word in the manuscript, which scholars have mistakenly altered) which Pentheus *attacks* – an extreme expression of the individualistic obstinacy of his resistance to mystery-cult. And Sophocles, perhaps influenced by Aeschylus, made Lycurgus "put out . . . the fire" (*Antigone* 964). Orpheus is in myth associated with both Dionysus and Apollo. His choice of the sun (Apollo) implies its superiority to the mystic light of Dionysus.

The theme of the third drama in the trilogy (*Neaniskoi*, "Young men") is unknown. M. L. West argues that, given that Dionysus has destroyed his enemies, balance has finally to be restored by honoring Orpheus and Apollo. Perhaps cult was founded in their honor.

Of the four remaining titles of Aeschylean tragedies about Dionysus (see above), at least one may have been an alternative title (e.g., *Bacchae* may have been the same play as *Pentheus* or *Bassarids*). If so, then Aeschylus may have written only one other trilogy on Dionysiac myth, for instance, in the order *Semele, Xantriai, Pentheus*. Such a trilogy would, it seems, have told of the pregnancy and death of Semele (along with the birth of Dionysus), disbelief of Semele's story of union with Zeus, Dionysus' sending of Theban women in a frenzy to Mount Kithairon, and the resistance and punishment of Pentheus, i.e., the events leading up to and including the theme of Euripides' *Bacchae*. Although almost nothing survives from these plays, we do know that it contained the appearance of Hera (fr. 168) – as enemy of Semele and of Dionysus – and of Lyssa (Frenzy) inspiring maenads (fr. 169); and it is likely that those who touched the belly of the pregnant Semele were thereby possessed by the god (Schol. Ap. Rhod. 1. 636).

The birth of Dionysus, accompanied by thunder and lightning, must have been a remarkable event, even if in Aeschylus' drama only narrated. It was a myth closely associated with (and indeed probably experienced in) a ritual – initiation into the Dionysiac mysteries – and hence was a common theme of the dithyramb. It plays a prominent part in Euripides' *Bacchae*: it is mentioned by Dionysus in line 3, and in 6–12 he mentions Semele's tomb converted into a shrine, together with the royal house destroyed (along with Semele) by the "still-living flame" of Zeus; the same myth is then narrated in the dithyrambic entry-song of the maenads (88–95); and when Dionysus later makes his epiphany with the destruction of the royal house by earthquake, thunder, and lightning, in a passage full of evocations of mystic initiation, Semele's tomb flares up again with "the flame that once Zeus's hurled thunder left" (598–9, 623–4). We are reminded of the most substantial fragment surviving from Aeschylus' *Edonians* (57), apparently from the (again, dithyrambic) entry-song of the Dionysiac chorus, in which there is mention of voices resembling roaring bulls from some invisible place, and the frightening sound of drums as of thunder under the earth (Seaford 1996: 155, 195–8).

Other Aeschylean titles of plays in which Dionysus may have been involved (if only by narration) are *Toxotides* ("Archeresses") and *Athamas*. *Toxotides* was about Actaeon, torn to pieces by his own hounds on Mount Kithairon. Actaeon is the cousin of Pentheus, who was torn apart by "hounds of Frenzy" (Euripides *Bacchae* 977; Seaford 1996: 230) in exactly the same place as Actaeon (Euripides *Bacchae* 1291). Actaeon's crime is, in the oldest attested version, not that he saw Artemis bathing (later frequently attested), but that he desired to take his aunt, Semele, as a wife. Several later texts associate him with Pentheus, in one case as an enemy of Dionysus. All this, together with various other considerations (Kossatz-Deissman 1978: 142–65), suggests that Dionysus may have had a role in the dramatized myth. Intriguingly, the drama is mentioned as one of those in which Aeschylus is said to have profaned the mysteries (Radt 1985: 63). These may well have been the Eleusinian mysteries of Demeter, but may conceivably have been those of Dionysus. Given the use of the mirror in the mysteries of Dionysus, which is probably alluded to in Euripides' *Bacchae* (Seaford 1996: 223), it is of interest that Actaeon was said to have seen his horned head reflected in water shortly before his death.

The plot of Aeschylus' *Athamas* is unknown. In one of the myths in which Athamas is involved, he, together with his wife Ino, brings up the infant Dionysus, with the result that Hera drives them both mad and they destroy their own children. It is not impossible that this was the theme of Aeschylus' *Athamas*.

Sophocles wrote a *Hydrophoroi* ("Water-carriers"; no doubt describing the chorus), which – given that an alternative title of Aeschylus' *Semele* was *Hydrophoroi* – may have been about Semele giving birth to Dionysus. And he may have written a *Bacchae* (Radt 1977: 170), of which nothing survives.

Of Euripides the only known play on a Dionysiac theme is his *Bacchae*, which survives almost entirely complete. This text, which has been hugely influential both in antiquity and since the Renaissance, is by far our fullest source for Dionysiac cult in the classical period. It dramatizes the resistance of Pentheus to the new cult of Dionysus, his imprisonment of the god, the miraculous escape of the god with his destruction of Pentheus' house, Pentheus' sudden agreement to dress as a maenad in order to spy on the Theban maenads on Mount Kithairon, and his savage dismemberment by those maenads led by his own mother Agave. The drama contains throughout – in the experience of Pentheus – evocations of Dionysiac initiation, many of them probably already there in the myth, albeit without revealing the mystic secrets that might have incited the kind of legal prosecution suffered by Aeschylus.

Other tragedies called *Bacchae* were produced by Xenokles (415 BCE), Sophocles' son Iophon, and (probably in the fourth century BCE) Cleophon. There had been a tragic trilogy on the story of Lycurgus (*Lykourgeia*) by Polyphrasmon (467 BCE). And there was a "Semele Thunderbolted" (*Semele Keraunoumene*) by Spintharos, a *Semele* by Carcinus, a *Semele* by Diogenes, and a *Dionysus* by Chaeremon, all probably of the fourth century BCE. We know almost nothing about any of these Dionysiac plays by minor tragedians. But from the titles, taken together with what does survive, it seems that in its frequent and powerful evocation of the birth of the god, combined with the dramatization of his defeat of resistance, *Bacchae* was typical of tragedy on a Dionysiac theme.

We should also note the existence of lost plays in which, whether or not Dionysus himself appeared, there may have been much mention of him or of his maenads, for instance, plays entitled *Actaeon*, Sophocles' *Tereus*, and Euripides' *Ino* and *Antiope*.

Tragedy and the Dionysiac

Certain features of extant tragedy may be said to derive from its origin in Dionysiac ritual: the centrality of the chorus, the tendency of the chorus to associate its own dancing with Dionysus (Henrichs 1995), the use of masks (used in the predramatic cult of Dionysus), the ubiquity (in contrast to Homer, for example) of the evocation of ritual, perhaps the thematic importance of a suffering individual. We have also traced the presence of Dionysus himself in what we know of Athenian tragedy. But clearly most of what survives is not about Dionysus. Can it make sense to call a narrative or drama Dionysiac if Dionysus himself plays no part in it?

The obvious answer is no. But the question raises a broad issue. The Greek deities, we need to remind ourselves, are no more than human constructions. About each of them we need to ask: in what social circumstances did human beings need to imagine her or him? The question may be, in certain divine manifestations, unanswerable. And even when it is answerable, the answer may consist of various social circumstances which have nothing to do with each other; or the same social circumstances may inspire the imagining of different deities (or no deity at all) in different places and times. Nevertheless, the question is worth asking, and we should ask it about Dionysus.

In Homeric epic Andromache is twice compared to a maenad (see below), and Dionysus has only four mentions. Three of these are brief: he is twice associated with death (*Odyssey* 11.325, 24.74), and once called the son of Semele and "a joy for mortals" (*Iliad* 14.325, i.e., as associated with wine). In the fourth he escapes from King Lycurgus into the sea, and Lycurgus is consequently blinded by Zeus (*Iliad* 6. 130–40).

All three of these Homeric associations – with death, with wine, and with autocratic resistance – persist throughout pre-Christian antiquity. Is it possible to find any connection between them, any formula which subsumes them all? One possibility is the idea that has its most influential form in Friedrich Nietzsche's *The Birth of Tragedy* (1872; see chapter 5 in this volume), namely that Dionysus embodies the confusion of boundaries, which may result in the unity of opposites. He writes, for instance, that "the primary effect of Dionysiac tragedy is that ... the divisions between man and man yield to an overwhelming feeling of unity, which goes back to the heart of nature": this is because "the man of culture (*Kulturmensch*) felt himself nullified in the presence of the chorus of satyrs" who embody nature (§7).

We can use this notion to subsume our three Homeric associations. First, Dionysus presided, throughout pre-Christian antiquity, over mystery-cult, which provided happiness in the next world by rehearsing the transition to it, and so was imagined as uniting the opposites of life with death. Second, wine, by collapsing the conventional boundaries of perception, tends to unite individuals, especially at a wine festival of the whole community such as the Anthesteria. Third, it is clear from Euripides' *Bacchae* that such indiscriminate communitarianism (208–9) threatens autocratic control. And we can extend the idea to cover other fundamental forms of the unity of opposites, notably human–animal, man–god, and male–female, each of which was associated with Dionysus (notably in *Bacchae*) and occurred in the ritual of mystic initiation.

Extant tragedy can be called Dionysiac not just as originating and performed in the cult of Dionysus, but also in the tenuous sense that – in sharp contrast to, say, Homeric epic – it tends to embody all the aforementioned unities of opposites even when Dionysus himself is not involved. But there is a further confusion of boundaries that is, I suggest, fundamental to tragedy. This is a consequence of what I have called Dionysiac communitarianism (or unity). I mean the dissolution of the boundary between the community as a whole and autocratic rule. This remains, even in our "Western democracies," an idea whose appeal should not be difficult to understand. It is most visible perhaps in the two most accessible tragic treatments of Dionysus, Aeschylus' trilogy about Lycurgus and Euripides' *Bacchae*. Nietzsche's distaste for the politics of his own time made him imagine Dionysus as a metaphysical principle with nothing to do with "the state and society." In this he was profoundly mistaken.

In the Homeric version Lycurgus is punished by being blinded by Zeus. But in Aeschylus it is Dionysus who does the punishing, by inciting Lycurgus to a frenzy in which he kills his own son. In Euripides, too, the resistant autocrat is punished by the Dionysiac frenzy that inspires the maenads, led by his own mother, to tear him apart. Homeric epic, by contrast, tends to avoid mention of frenzy (apart from the frenzy of battle) and of kin-killing. In Aeschylus the trilogy may have ended with the founding of cult, for Apollo or Dionysus. And in Euripides' *Bacchae* it is virtually certain that Dionysus, in the lost part of his final speech, founded Dionysiac cult for the polis of Thebes (Seaford 2000: 83–91). What we have is the disruption inherent in kin-killing followed by the foundation of cult for the whole polis. This is a surprisingly common pattern (though not universal) in extant tragedy, and so does not require the agency of Dionysus, although it does, as we shall see, frequently attract Dionysiac metaphor. I have elsewhere suggested that the pattern derives from the Dionysiac origins and early themes of tragedy (Seaford 1994). Athenian tragedy was (in contrast again to Homer) a product of the polis, and in tragic myths the polis tends to benefit from the foundation of polis cult, which should not – tragedy insists – be resisted or neglected, and from the tendency of the ruling family to *destroy itself*, sometimes under the influence of deity (notably Dionysus), and never producing the collective guilt that would result from its destruction by the polis. Dionysus is god of the whole community: for instance, we have seen this in Euripides' *Bacchae*, and an oracle cited by Demosthenes (*Against Meidias* 52) insists that Dionysus be worshiped by the Athenians "all mixed up together." A fundamental boundary that Dionysus dissolves is between community and ruling family. In Euripides' *Bacchae* this also takes the subjective form of opposition between the almost impenetrable individualism of the autocrat Pentheus on the one hand and the chorus that aspires to "merging the soul in the thiasos" on the other (75). The dissolution of this opposition is initiated by Dionysus persuading Pentheus – suddenly and somewhat improbably – to dress as a maenad (a change that can also be seen as belonging to the experience of mystic initiation projected onto Pentheus).

But is the presence of our pattern enough to allow us to call a tragedy Dionysiac, even where Dionysus himself does not occur in it? The answer is a matter of choice. What is important is the social process, sometimes but not always associated with Dionysus himself. In some tragedies the family destroys itself under the influence of another deity, such as Aphrodite in Euripides' *Hippolytus*. In Euripides' *Medea*, where we might have expected that for a mother to kill her children was possible only in the frenzy inspired by Dionysus (as in *Bacchae*), the autonomous sanity of Medea adds pathos.

Whatever terminology we decide to use, I maintain that the pattern I have identified, which is alien to, for example, Homeric epic, derives from the genesis of tragedy in Dionysiac cult. And the same may be said perhaps of other features of extant tragedy, for instance, the fundamental opposition between the powerful (and sometimes impenetrable) individual and the anonymous communality of the chorus, and perhaps even the social marginality of the chorus, who are only very occasionally able-bodied males. Then there are the frequent evocations of Dionysiac cult, not necessarily in dramas involving Dionysus himself. I conclude by looking at these.

The first category consists of various mentions or brief descriptions, by several tragedians, of Dionysus or of Dionysiac cult. In the case of fragments quoted without specification of the play (e.g., Aeschylus frr. 341, 382, 355), it may be that they are from plays involving Dionysus himself (e.g., the Lycurgean trilogy). Where we know the context (i.e., normally of passages from extant plays) it is sometimes difficult to evaluate the tone of the reference to Dionysus. When, for instance, in Sophocles' *Oedipus at Colonus* there is mention of the presence of Dionysus and his nurses at Colonus in Attica, this seems entirely positive, cohering completely with the praise of Colonus and of Athens that is at the heart of the play. But when, on the other hand, in the same author's *Women of Trachis*, Heracles is said to be "from Bacchic Thebes"

(510–11), our knowledge of the ambivalent role of Dionysus at Thebes, well known from Euripides' *Bacchae* (e.g., 860–1), may suggest that the phrase may perhaps hint at the terrible death that we are about to see inflicted (inadvertently) on Heracles by his own wife, especially as the tuft of wool with which she had smeared Heracles' garment with the dead centaur's blood caused to "erupt from the earth on which it lay clotted foam, as of the rich liquid...from the bacchic vine poured on the ground" (703–4). Even the other Dionysiac reference in the play (219), to the ecstatic dancing of the female chorus on the news of Heracles' return, may seem ominous (Schlesier 1993).

There is something similar in the same author's *Antigone*. Thebes has been delivered from the onslaught of Polynices and his allies, and the chorus evokes celebrations in which Dionysus will rule and shake Thebes (i.e., with dancing, but with the inevitable suggestion of his power to create the kind of earthquake that in *Bacchae* destroyed Pentheus' palace). Moreover, a mere 18 lines earlier, the ecstatic aggression of Capaneus, one of Thebes' attackers, is described with the image of bacchic revelry (as is another of Thebes' attackers, Hippomedon, by Aeschylus *Septem* 498). The other references in the play to Dionysus are to Liturgies' suppression of bacchic cult (956–64, see above), and then the vain choral invocation of the god to come to purify Thebes (1115–52): he is invoked, I believe, not only as god of the whole community (and so naturally opposed to the introverted, incestuous Theban ruling family), but also as *Iakchos* (1152), the form he takes in the Eleusinian mysteries (1120), in which the emergence of a young girl (*Kore*) from the earth brings salvation, in contrast to the failure to rescue Antigone from below the earth (Seaford 1990).

The second category of evocations of Dionysiac cult consists of what seem to be metaphors, drawn from the ("bacchic") frenzy that was, in life as in drama, imagined as inflicted by Dionysus, notably on his female followers, known as "maenads." Here too there is frequently the possibility of a negative association. And there is a further complication. Although "bacchic frenzy" (e.g., Cassandra *bakcheuousa* – "in a bacchic frenzy" – at Euripides *Trojan Women* 342) was in tragedy a way of describing frenzy in which Dionysus himself is not necessarily in the mind of the author, such expressions evoke the possibility – hard to exclude, given the impossibility of knowing which deity is responsible for any particular case of frenzy – that Dionysus himself is involved. Moreover, it seems that the metaphor (or idea) of "bacchic frenzy" tended to describe the kind of frenzy (imposed by Dionysus on Lycurgus in Aeschylus or on Agave in Euripides, and in various other myths) that produces killing within the family and so the self-destruction of the household: i.e., frenzy is the means by which Dionysus creates the "Dionysiac" tragic pattern described above.

A prime exhibit is Euripides' *Heracles*. Heracles has returned home, rescued his family from the tyrannical usurper Lykos, and slaughtered his enemies. Iris and Frenzy (Lyssa) then arrive, sent by Hera, to inspire Heracles with a frenzy in which he will kill his children, and to make a physical assault on Heracles' house. This process is embellished with comparisons with the Dionysiac, even if sometimes only to be *contrasted* with the Dionysiac, so that, for instance, one of the first reactions of the chorus is to say that "dancings are beginning without the drum and not embellished with the thyrsos of Dionysus" (892–3). Heracles is repeatedly said to be in a bacchic frenzy (896–7, 966, 1086, 1119, 1122, 1142). The combination of kin-killing frenzy and physical destruction of the house (864–5, 905, 1007) is the same as that imposed by Dionysus in Euripides' *Bacchae. Bacchae* undoubtedly was influenced, even in detail, by Aeschylus' *Edonians* (see above); and it has been argued on the basis of various vase-paintings that this scene of Euripides' *Heracles* was influenced, even in respect of the appearance of Lyssa, by Aeschylus' *Edonians* (Sutton 1975). A fragment of *Edonians* – (58: "the house has the god in it, the roof is in a bacchic frenzy") suggests the destruction by Dionysus of the house of Lycurgus comparable to those by Dionysus in *Bacchae* (cf. esp. 587–93, 726) and by Lyssa in *Heracles.* And so we have three instances of a typical scene of divine destruction of a royal house (together with frenzied intrafamilial killing), two involving Dionysus himself; the other without him (but with Dionysiac imagery). A pattern of activity that is strongly associated with Dionysus (but without requiring the involvement of Dionysus himself) attracts sustained Dionysiac imagery. This exemplifies a key transition in the history of tragedy, from myths involving Dionysus to those that do not.

Another instance of sustained Dionysiac metaphor in Euripides is from his *Trojan Women*. In Aeschylus' *Agamemnon* Cassandra is an inspired prophetess. In Euripides she has just been allocated as concubine to Agamemnon after the fall of Troy, and appears not only as an inspired prophetess but as a bride and as a maenad. There is frequent reference to her maenadism and bacchic revelry (169, 171, 307, 341, 367, 408, 415, 500). To be sure, her frenzy is caused not by Dionysus but by Apollo (408). But when she says that she will kill Agamemnon and destroy (in return) his house (359, 461), and that her union with Agamemnon will cause matricide and the upturning of the house of Atreus (363–4), the Dionysiac imagery seems especially apt.

Cassandra in *Trojan Women* appears *running* (307, 349). Emphasized in *Bacchae* is the ability of the maenads to *run* (731, 748, 1091–2). In Euripides' *Suppliants* Evadne comes "running from my house in a bacchic frenzy" (1000–1) to jump onto the funeral pyre of her husband. Whereas Cassandra sees herself as about to destroy her consort and his household, and so appears as a ghastly bride, Evadne appears as a (suicidal) bride because she is reacting to the destruction of her household by wanting to share the death of her husband.

Another running maenadic bride is Iole, who is represented in a choral strophe of Euripides' *Hippolytus* as responsible for the destruction of her husband (550–4); interestingly, in the antistrophe another instance of the association of sex with death is the birth of Dionysus at Thebes, which involved the killing of his mother Semele by the thunderbolt of her lover Zeus (554–62). This was (we have seen) a central theme of the song that developed into tragedy, the dithyramb; and it suggests the association of the unity of opposites (here sex, new life, and violent death) with the cult of Dionysus. The main theme of *Hippolytus* is the illicit passion – that will destroy the household – of Phaedra for her stepson Hippolytus. In the pain of her suppressed passion she expresses the desire to be hunting hinds on the mountainside, i.e., to be a maenad (Schlesier 1993: 109–10).

Another tragic "maenad" who, it seems, rushes out of the house and imagines herself as a bride is Antigone in Euripides' *Phoenician Women*. There is evocation of the bridal ceremony of unveiling (*anakalypteria*). The same rare word for veil (*krēdemnon*) is used in the Homeric description of Andromache, on the death of her husband Hector, rushing out of her house "like a maenad" to the city walls and throwing off the veil given to her on her wedding day (Seaford 1993: 115–21). But what interests us in the Euripidean passage is the self-description of Antigone as "maenad of the dead" (1489). The dead are her brothers Eteocles and Polynices, whose mutual slaughter has destroyed their own household. The idea "maenad of the dead" occurs also, in a slightly different form, as "maenads of Hades" in Euripides' *Hecuba* (1076), of the "mothers" (1157) who killed Polymnestor's children, and should, in Aeschylus' *Agamemnon* (1235), be restored, as "maenad of Hades," of Clytemnestra.

Some tragic "maenads" are (at least indirectly) agents of the destruction of the household (e.g., Cassandra and Iole). To these we should add the real maenad Agave as well as the male Heracles (and probably Lycurgus). The "maenadism" of another male kin-killer, Orestes in Euripides' *Orestes*, is the frenzy of remorse. The blood of his mother is said to put him in a bacchic frenzy (339; cf. 411, 835). The consequent association of maenadism with the Furies maddening him (e.g., 319) had already appeared in Aeschylus' version of the story (*Eumenides* 500). The maenadism of Euripides' Heracles is (at least as believed by Amphitryon) a *result* of killing (his enemies; 966–7), as well as its cause.

Other "tragic maenads," by contrast, merely react to killing performed by others. There may be influence here from a general tendency, derived perhaps from cult, to associate maenadic ecstasy with the ecstasy of lamentation (Seaford 1994: 322–3). The female chorus of Aeschylus' *Septem* applies a word for maenad (*thuias*) to themselves as lamenting (835–6), and Hecuba calls her lament for her dismembered (716) son a bacchic tune (Euripides *Hecuba* 685–6).

We have seen that the maenadic metaphor may be attracted by a female character exhibiting one or more of the characteristics of maenadism (as we find them, above all, in *Bacchae*). These characteristics are frenzy (Heracles, Cassandra, Evadne, Iole, Phaedra, Antigone, Orestes, the Furies, Clytemnestra, etc.), running (Cassandra, Evadne, Iole, Phaedra (?), Antigone), intrafamilial killing and destruction of the household (Heracles, Cassandra, Iole, Orestes, Clytemnestra), and lamentation for family members (Antigone, Hecuba). The captive mothers of *Hecuba*, "maenads of Hades" according to Polymnestor, dismember children in the wild (1075–8) – another imagined characteristic of maenads. All these characteristics embody the reversal of norms expected of the female (especially as wife and mother) – even the *running*, which expresses potential uncontrollability, as, for instance, in a Dionysiac ritual described by Plutarch (*Moralia* 299e), in which the female followers of Diony- sus are chased by a male priest.

Several such maenadic characteristics are combined in the figure of Clytemnestra as described by Aeschylus at *Agamemnon* 1235, where the case for reading "maenad of Hades" is reinforced by the immediate context, in which she is described as raving and breathing unlimited aggression against her own (family) and as having uttered a cry (*ololyge*) of triumph, as in the turning point in battle (1235–7). All this is typically maenadic. Maenads, like Clytemnestra, kill their own family members, utter the *ololyge* (e.g., *Bacchae* 689), and behave like males – even to the point of engaging males in battle (e.g., *Bacchae* 731–5). There are even fourth-century vase-paintings from southern Italy, inspired, it seems, by a reperformance of Aeschylus, in which Clytemnestra, wielding her axe, is dressed as a maenad.[1] Clytemnestra's anomalous rule over the household seized from the husband she has killed is called an "evil bacchic revel" (Aeschylus *The Libation Bearers* 690).[2]

To conclude, we have discussed some but not all of the references in tragedy to Dionysus or his cult. Among those which we have discussed, a distinct group is formed by those in which behavior not apparently influenced by Dionysus is nevertheless described in Dionysiac terms, for instance, as "bacchic frenzy." Even in such cases it seems rash to exclude entirely the possibility that Dionysus himself is imagined as somehow involved, especially given that tragedy originated – and continued to be performed – in the cult of Dionysus. Further, such Dionysiac "metaphors" tend to be applied to people who destroy (or are faced with the destruction of) their own household, notably by killing (as maenads do in myth) their own kin. And this self-destruction, followed by the institution of cult for the whole polis, is a typical pattern of tragedy.

NOTES

1 Leningrad Hermitage 812; Bari 1014 (Trendall and Cambitoglou 1988: 933 n.126); Kossatz-Deissman (1978: 91, 99–100).

2 With Portus' κακ*J*φ for καλ*J*φ; for the case for retaining καλ*J*φ see Schlesier (1993: 113).

REFERENCES AND FURTHER READING

Bierl, A. F. (1991). *Dionysos und die griechische Tragödie* [Dionysus and Greek tragedy]. Tübingen: Classica Monacensia 1. A detailed analysis of the appearances and mentions of Dionysus in Greek tragedy.

Carpenter, T. H. and Faraone, C. A. (1993). *Masks of Dionysus*. Ithaca, NY and London: Cornell University Press. Essays by various scholars on aspects of Dionysus (archaeological, literary, inscriptional, etc.).

Dodds, E. R. (1960). *Euripides* Bacchae, 2nd edn. Oxford: Oxford University Press. Once the definitive commentary on *Bacchae*, now somewhat outdated by archaeological discoveries and by much scholarly work on Dionysus.

Henrichs, A. (1978). "Greek Maenadism from Olympia to Messalina." *Harvard Studies in Classical Philology* 82, 121–60. An excellent and lucid history of maenadism (ecstatic women in the cult of Dionysus).

Henrichs, A. (1995). " 'Why Should I Dance?': Choral Self-referentiality in Greek Tragedy." *Arion* 3:1, 56–111. On the association of Dionysus with tragic choruses referring to themselves.

Kossatz-Deissman, A. (1978). *Dramen des Aischylos auf Westgriechischen Vasen* [Aeschylean drama on western Greek vases]. Mainz: Phillip von Zabern. A detailed account of the reflection of Aeschylus' dramas in fourth-century-BCE vase-painting of southern Italy and Sicily.

Nietzsche, F. [1872] (1993). *Die Geburt der Tragödie aus dem Geist der Musik* [The birth of tragedy from the spirit of music]. Stuttgart: Reclam. Nietzsche's influential text, influenced by Wagner, on Greek tragedy as a synthesis of the Apolline and the Dionysiac.

Otto, W. F. (1965). *Dionysus. Myth and Cult*, trans. R. B. Palmer. Bloomington: Indiana University Press (originally published in German, 1933). An idiosyncratic but influential account of Dionysus as a god of the irreducible experience of epiphany.

Radt, S. (1985). *Tragicorum Graecorum Fragmenta*, vol. 3 (vol. 4, 1977). Göttingen: Vandenhoeck & Ruprecht. Indispensable collections of the fragments (in Greek) of lost tragedies.

Schlesier, R. (1993). "Maenads as Tragic Models." In *Masks of Dionysus*, ed. T. H. Carpenter and C. A. Faraone. Ithaca, NY and London: Cornell University Press, 89–114. On the descriptions (in tragedy) of women as maenads more than just metaphors.

Seaford, R. (1990). "The Imprisonment of Women in Greek Tragedy." *Journal of Hellenic Studies* 110, 76–90. On the theme (in tragedy) of the imprisonment of women as associated with endogamy and structurally antithetical to Dionysus.

Seaford, R. (1993). "Dionysos as Destroyer of the Household." In *Masks of Dionysus*, ed. T. H. Carpenter and C. A. Faraone. Ithaca, NY and London: Cornell University Press, 115–46. On destruction of the household as characteristic of Dionysus, especially in tragedy.

Seaford, R. (1994). *Reciprocity and Ritual. Homer and Tragedy in the Developing City-State*. Oxford: Oxford University Press. On the difference in the shaping of myth between Homer and tragedy and its relation to the development of the city-state.

Seaford, R. (1996). *Euripides:* Bacchae. Warminster: Aris & Phillips. A commentary on *Bacchae* with an introduction and translation.

Seaford, R. (2000). "The Dionysiac Don responds to Don Quixote: Rainer Friedrich on the New Ritualism." *Arion* 8:2, 74–98. A defense of the importance of evocations of ritual in tragedy.

Segal, C. (1997). *Dionysiac Poetics and Euripides' Bacchae*, 2nd edn. Princeton, NJ: Princeton University Press. A very detailed analysis of *Bacchae* that combines New Critical, structuralist, psychoanalytic, and postmodern perspectives.

Sutton, D. F. (1975). "A Series of Vases Illustrating the Madness of Lycurgus." *Rivista di Studi Classici* 23, 356–60. Describes vase-paintings that suggest that the madness of Heracles in Euripides was influenced by the madness of Lycurgus in Aeschylus.

Trendall, A. D. and Cambitoglou, A. (1988). *The Red-Figure Vases of Apulia*, vol. II. Oxford: Oxford University Press. The standard and detailed collection of these fourth-century-BCE vases.

West, M. L. (1983). "The Lycurgus Trilogy." *Bulletin of the Institute of Classical Studies* 30, 63–71, 81–2 (a revised and expanded edition can be found in *Studies in Aeschylus*, ed. Teubner, Stuttgart, 1990, 26–50). A detailed reconstruction of the lost trilogy by Aeschylus.

Zeitlin, F. (1993). "Staging Dionysus between Thebes and Athens." In *Masks of Dionysus*, ed. T. H. Carpenter and C. A. Faraone. Ithaca, NY and London: Cornell University Press, 147–82. Thebes represented in tragedy as embodying inversion of Athenian values.

Part II
Tragedy, Philosophy, and Psychoanalysis

3

Aristotle's *Poetics*: A Defense of Tragic Fiction

Kathy Eden

Aristotle's *Poetics* is arguably the first and also the most influential work ever to address the subject of tragedy. Written sometime between the 360s and 320s BCE, it looks back somewhere between fifty and a hundred years to the heyday of Greek drama, with the philosophical agenda of distilling from tragic practice a theory that explains the genre from its early development to its full maturity.[1] Probably the remains of lecture notes, this abridged and often puzzling explanation is organized into 26 chapters. Nearly all of them have at some time or other occasioned controversy, even while setting the conditions for centuries of literary theory and practice – not only for tragedians but for fiction-writers more generally. Throughout the *Poetics*, in fact, Aristotle characterizes tragedy in terms of what it does and does not share with other literary genres.

In the last chapter of the *Poetics* (ch. 26), Aristotle finally resolves one of these comparisons – the one between tragedy and epic – by finding in favor of tragedy on the grounds of both form and function. More unified than epic, tragedy is also more vivid (*enargēs*). Consequently, Aristotle argues, it packs more pleasure. If this closing judgment highlights the differences between the two genres, however, much of the argument of the *Poetics* up to this point foregrounds their similarities.[2] Indeed, tragedy and epic together constitute a kind of literary making or fiction – *poiēsis* – that differs not only from other kinds of fiction, such as comedy, but also from nonfictional discourse such as philosophy and history. Although Homer and Empedocles compose in the same meter, as we learn in the opening of the *Poetics*, one is a poet (that is, a maker of fictions); the other a philosopher (ch. 1, 1447b17–20). On the same principle, Herodotus, even if he wrote in verse, would still be an historian (ch. 9, 1451a38–1451b4). In his effort to play advocate for tragic fiction, in other words, Aristotle first settles the claim of fiction before he clinches the case for tragedy.

The aim of this chapter is to outline some of the main arguments that support Aristotle's case for the value of the genre he so vigorously defends. Before doing so, however, I want briefly to remind the reader that many aspects of his treatise, including the competition between the discourses, figure in the dialogues of his teacher, Plato, who is, not incidentally, the unacknowledged antagonist in the debate about tragedy's value. In the *Republic*, to take only the most obvious example, Socrates, citing the long-standing *agōn* or contest between philosophers and poets (607B), levels very damaging charges against the mimetic arts, including poetry or fiction. Some of these charges he aims at *what* the poets imitate: heroes who behave irrationally and gods who behave like their irrational human counterparts. Others he aims at *how* the poets imitate, namely by copying the distortions of the sensible world. Ignorant of the realities his imitations only inadequately represent, Plato's poet can provide his audience with pleasure but no real knowledge or understanding. Despite his traditional authority, such a poet is no true "teacher of men." For, Socrates insists, the poet cannot teach what he himself does not understand.

Aristotle agrees with his own teacher not only about the relation between teaching and understanding (*Metaphysics* 981b7–10), but also about what it means to understand. In contrast to the casual or accidental knowing of the sophist, philosophical knowledge (which *is* knowledge properly speaking) is a knowledge of causes: *why* something is *what* it is (*Posterior Analytics* 71b10–13; cf. *Metaphysics* 981a24–30). With this assumption about knowledge and causality in mind, Aristotle counters Plato's objection, noted above, that the poets please with their imitations but cannot teach. Quite on the contrary, Aristotle argues, imitation or *mimēsis* causes human beings generally to understand through a learning process that begins in childhood. Understanding, in turn, causes pleasure (ch. 4; cf. *Rhetoric* 1.11.23). As a particular kind of imitation, Aristotle will undertake to demonstrate, tragedy provides a special kind of understanding that leads to its own peculiar pleasure.

If in Chapter 4 of the *Poetics* Aristotle makes the case for imitations in general, in Chapter 6 he narrows the focus to tragic imitation, defining it as follows: *an imitation of human action that is serious, complete, and of a certain magnitude; that is enacted dramatically rather than narrated, in language appropriately ornamented; and that arouses pity and fear* (ch. 6, 1449b24–8; emphasis added). In good philosophical fashion, this definition addresses the *what*, *how*, and *why* of tragedy, in that order. Elsewhere in the argument Aristotle answers the first two questions – what and how – in the shorthand of two separate lists. First is the tripartite division into *object* (what), and *mode* and *media* (how) (ch. 1, 1447a16–18), followed by the division into six constituent parts: plot, character, thought (objects/what), style, melody (media/how), and spectacle (mode/how) (ch. 6, 1450a7–12). (Like most shorthands, Aristotle's are nearly incomprehensible to the uninitiated.) By far the most important of these six parts is the plot, which Aristotle calls the starting point, the endpoint and the soul of tragedy (ch. 6, 1450a38–9, 1450a22–3, 1450a38–9). And *what* tragedy imitates with its plots is unambiguously a certain kind of action.[3]

By characterizing this action as serious, *spoudaia*, Aristotle contradicts Plato, who dismisses all imitation as "child's play" or *paidia*, the antithesis of whatever is worthwhile (*Republic* 602B). With this characterization, Aristotle also distinguishes tragedy from another kind of enacted as opposed to narrated fictional imitation, namely comedy. Whereas these two genres share a single mode – dramatic as opposed to narrative – and some overlap on media in their use of language and meter, their objects differ significantly. Both represent actions, but comedy treats actions performed by agents who are lesser human beings, while the agents of tragic action belong to the better sort (ch. 2, 1448a16–18; ch. 4, 1448b24–7; ch. 5, 1449a32–4) (see chapter 15 in this volume). And if tragedy is more serious or worthwhile – *spoudaia* – than comedy, fiction (*poiēsis*), and especially tragic fiction, is more serious than history. Whereas history deals only with the actions of particular people, fiction shares with philosophy its access to universality. "It is for this reason," Aristotle argues (ch. 9, 1451b5–11),

> that poetry is both more philosophical (*philosophōteron*) and more serious (*spoudaioteron*) than history, since poetry speaks more of universals, history of particulars. A "universal" comprises the *kind* of speech or action which belongs by probability or necessity to a certain *kind* of character – something which poetry aims at *despite* its addition of particular names. A "particular," by contrast, is (for example) what Alcibiades did or experienced.

Fiction's claim to universality – kinds or types rather than individuals – is crucial to Aristotle's argument because it is in universals that the philosopher or anyone else looking for knowledge most readily discovers cause (*Posterior Analytics* 86a4–10; *Metaphysics* 981a15–981b6). And knowing an object, as we have seen, requires knowing its causes. Aristotle's poet, in sharp contrast to his historian, imitates not just *what* happened but *why*. Whereas the historian represents events that happen one after another, in temporal sequence (*pros allēla*) (ch. 23, 1459a24), the poet or fiction-writer imitates events which occur because of one another (*di'allēla*) (ch. 9, 1452a4).

These causal connections between the events of the fictional plot also account for the unity or wholeness of the tragic action; and unity, alongside seriousness, figures prominently in the definition of tragedy in Chapter 6 noted above. In Chapter 7, Aristotle gives a fuller account of this wholeness by differentiating the beginning, middle, and end of the tragic action in terms of causality: the beginning is not caused by anything that comes before; the middle is caused by the beginning and causes the end; the end is caused by beginning and middle but causes nothing further. To this wholeness and seriousness, as we have seen, Aristotle adds "magnitude," which he goes on to define as "the scope required for a probable or necessary succession of events which produce a transformation either from affliction to prosperity, or the reverse" (ch. 7, 1451a12–15).

The magnitude of a tragic action, in other words, is indefinable in terms of length or, following later dramatic theory and practice, a specified number of acts.[4] Rather, it must be long enough to allow for a probable or necessary change. Here, as throughout the *Poetics*, Aristotle's brevity obscures several important points. One is the emphasis on change or *metabolē*, which, considered indispensable by Aristotle, is flatly condemned by Plato. In the *Republic* (604E), Socrates singles out the changeability of the tragic agent in the face of misfortune as *the* characteristic that disqualifies him as an object suitable for representation. And representing the gods as changeable is no less objectionable (380D–381D). Just as Aristotle disagrees with Plato on this issue, later dramatic theorists will disagree with Aristotle, not because they will reject change, however, but because they will accept for tragedy a change only from good fortune to bad.[5]

Another important point involves the role of probability, which raises from Socrates objections as fierce as those he levels against change. Condemned most roundly in the *Phaedrus* (272D–273D), probability, according to Plato, sidesteps the truth in favor of credibility – what most people believe. Vestiges of this Platonic position are recognizable in the *Poetics*, especially its final chapters, where Aristotle recommends both that the poet avoid at all costs whatever is implausible (ch. 24) and that he counter critics' charges of the impossibility of fiction with its believability (ch. 25). "Poetic requirements," he cautions, "make a plausible impossibility preferable to an implausible possibility" (ch. 25, 1461b11–12). For most of the argument, however, Aristotle propounds a very different notion of probability – one responsive to fiction's intense focus on human action.

In discussions elsewhere of such varied topics as metaphysics and ethics, Aristotle first divides human endeavor into three categories – doing, making, and thinking – and then identifies the ways that doing is like and unlike the other two (*Nicomachean Ethics* 6.3.1–6.6.2; cf. *Metaphysics* 981b25–982a1). Both doing and making are matters of practice; they lead to some activity. Thinking, in contrast, is theoretical. It does not culminate in any action. On the other hand, thinking and doing (well) are alike in that both are ends in themselves, whereas making (*poiēsis*) – even making tragedies – is not. In starkest contrast to a more modern aesthetic that embraces art for its own sake, Aristotelian *poiēsis* is always the means to some further end. For this reason, Aristotle finds it necessary in his definition cited above to address the *why* as well as the *what* and *how* of tragedy.

Despite this crucial distinction between what we do and what we make, however, our actions are like our products but unlike our contemplation in another regard. Belonging to the natural world or physics, the supernatural world or metaphysics, and the formal world of mathematics, the objects of thinking are invariable. They cannot be otherwise. Being so, they operate according to fixed, unchanging laws that can in turn predict their operations with great precision. Once the scientific thinker understands the laws governing the sun, for instance, she can predict with great accuracy its rising and setting tomorrow and the next day.

Though similarly true for the equilateral triangle, this degree of predictability is not true for human action – even for the actions of those who are more than usually consistent or very familiar to us. Like human production, human behavior is variable. It can be otherwise; and so its operations and outcomes are not knowable with anything like the same precision as the sun or the triangle. Indeed, the laws governing what we do, like those governing what we make, are only very infrequently necessary; for the most part they are probable. And so Aristotle warns that (*Nicomachean Ethics* 1.3.1.) "the same exactness must not be expected in all departments of philosophy alike, any more than in all the products of the arts and crafts...It is equally unreasonable to accept merely probable conclusions from a mathematician and to demand strict demonstration [necessary conclusions] from an orator."[6]

Aristotelian probability, in other words, is not, as it was for Plato, a mere strategy or trick for exploiting popular opinion. On the contrary, it characterizes the kind of knowing commensurate with its object, human action, as the focus of tragedy. When Aristotle repeats throughout the *Poetics* that the elements of the plot, like those of character, must obey either necessity or probability (chs. 7, 8, 9, 10, 15), he is safeguarding tragic imitation from the Platonic charge that all imitations are the products of ignorance. Insofar as the tragic poet constructs his fiction according to the laws governing human action, that fiction will disclose the causal connection between events and so deepen our understanding of those events – *why* they happened as they did.

For the causes of human action, in turn, the fiction-writer must look to the moral and intellectual qualities – character (*ēthos*) and thought (*dianoia*) – of the agents. In the *Nicomachean Ethics*, especially book 6, Aristotle develops this complex causality in some detail. In the *Poetics,* he states it more baldly (ch. 6, 1449b36–1450a3): "tragedy is a representation of an action, and is enacted by agents, who must be characterized in both their character (*to ēthos*) and their thought (*tēn dianoian*) (for it is through these that we can also judge the qualities of their actions, and it is in their actions that all men either succeed or fail)." Aristotle's previously enumerated list of the six constituent parts of tragedy, in other words, fails through its abbreviation to disclose the causal relation among the first three: plot (*mythos*), character (*ēthos*), and thought (*dianoia*). The actions of the plot are what they are in no small part *because* of the ethical and intellectual qualities of their agents. If tragic and comic plots differ, as we have also seen, that is precisely because of such qualitative differences.

In the *Nicomachean Ethics*, moreover, Aristotle's analysis of action includes a crucial element not on the list of the *Poetics*. "Now the origin of the action," Aristotle explains in the *Ethics* (6.2, 1139a31–35),

> the source of the movement, not the action's goal – is decision (*prohairēsis*), and the origin of decision is desire together with reason that aims at some goal. Hence decision requires understanding and thought (*dianoia*), and also a state of character (*ēthike*), since doing well or badly in action requires both thought (*dianoia*) and character (*ēthos*).

Our decisions, as we learn from this explanation, are what they are *because* of our characters and thoughts; and our actions are what they are *because* of our decisions.

Despite its shorthand for treating the causes of action, the *Poetics* nevertheless acknowledges this same indispensable intermediate step in the psychological process that culminates in action. Both chapter 6 and chapter 15 underscore the causal relation between the character of the agent and his decisions or choices, insisting that "the character will be good when the choice (*prohairēsis*) is good" (ch. 15, 1454a18–19). But choice plays an even more prominent role in Aristotle's literary theory than the brief treatment of *prohairēsis* in the *Poetics* suggests.

Like the *Nicomachean Ethics,* the *Poetics* assumes that actions in general are some-where between the extremes of wholly voluntary (*hekōn*) – the immediate consequence of our decisions or choices – and wholly involuntary (*akōn*), the consequence of causes completely out of our control. When in chapter 13 (1453a10) Aristotle characterizes the tragic act as a *hamartia*, he is specifying the extent to which the agent can be said to have caused the act through his choices. On this point, the difficult shorthand of the *Poetics* gains clarity from the *Rhetoric*, where Aristotle divides acts into three kinds: mistakes (*atuchēmata*), personal failings (*hamartēmata*), and unjust acts (*adikēmata*) (*Rhetoric* 1.13.15–16; cf. *Nicomachean Ethics* 5.8.6–11): "Mistakes are unexpected actions and do not result from wickedness; personal failings are not unexpected and do not result from wickedness; [and] unjust actions are not unexpected and do result from wickedness." As we learn in chapter 13 of the *Poetics*, unjust actions are inappropriate for tragedy. For the agent of an unjust act, whether he experiences a change from prosperity to affliction or the reverse, will not provoke the spectators' fear and pity. Those who are the victims of chance misfortunes – mistakes – are also disqualified since it is "neither fearful nor pitiful but repulsive" when preeminently good men "[pass] from prosperity to affliction" (ch. 13, 1452b34-36). Furthermore, because a mishap is by definition without cause – a product of chance – this kind of action cannot be qualified by the intellectual and ethical qualities of the agent.

The *hamartia* or *hamartēma*, on the other hand, is precisely suited to tragic fiction: while it is not, strictly speaking, voluntary, in that the agent does not freely choose the act with full knowledge of its particulars, neither is it, strictly speaking, invol-untary, in that it is not wholly unforeseen. Aristotle's tragic *hamartia*, then, falls somewhere between an act that is fully intended and one that is completely unex-pected. Or as Aristotle puts it in chapter 9 (1452a4), tragic events happen "contrary to expectation yet still on account of one another."

That Aristotelian tragic action occupies this middle condition between the fully intended and completely unexpected is confirmed by the discussion that follows. Chapter 14 of the *Poetics* lays out the possibilities for tragic action as (1) intended and committed, (2) intended but not committed, (3) not intended but committed, and (4) neither intended nor committed. Medea illustrates the first, Haemon in *Antigone* the second, Oedipus in *Oedipus the King* the third, and Iphigenia in *Iphigenia in Tauris* the last. The third and fourth combinations make for the best tragedies, according to Aristotle, because their tragic agents do not fully intend the acts they commit or almost commit. If the common factor in the two approved tragedies, *Oedipus the King* and *Iphigenia in Tauris*, is the lack of intention, moreover, the difference between them turns on whether the unintended act is discovered before or after it is committed. And this conjunction of intentionality with the timing of discovery also accounts for a structural feature of the best tragedies: what Aristotle calls the *anagnōrisis* or recog-nition, one of the two features of the complex plot.

Like all tragic plots, even the simplest ones, scenes of recognition require change – in this case, a change from ignorance to knowledge (ch. 11, 1452a30–1). Like only the very best tragic actions, however, the best recognitions occur contrary to the intentions of the agents. Accordingly, Homer shows himself a more skillful poet in crafting Eurycleia's discovery of her master Odysseus in book 19 than he does in Eumaios' in book 14. In the one, Odysseus intends to keep his identity a secret from his nurse, who recognizes him against his will, whereas in the other he intentionally identifies himself to the swineherd. And the same criterion serves to distinguish the two recognitions in *Iphigenia in Tauris*. While Iphigenia identifies herself unintentionally through a letter, thereby earning for Euripides Aristotle's approval, her brother Orestes in the same play fully intends to make his identity known, thereby effecting a recognition less deserving of praise.

The other feature of the complex plot is *peripeteia*, or reversal, which shares certain characteristics with recognition. Both involve change. And both occur in the best cases not only according to probability or necessity (chs. 10, 11), but also contrary to the intentions and expectations of the agents. So Aristotle illustrates *peripeteia* with an episode from *Oedipus the King* (ch. 11, 1452a25–6), "where the person comes to bring Oedipus happiness and intends to free him from his fear about his mother; but he produces the opposite effect, by revealing Oedipus' identity." In addition to these similarities, recognition and reversal also share their singular impact on the emotions (ch. 6, 1450a33–5).

Like his teacher, Aristotle takes into account the power of fiction through these and other features to provoke strong emotion in the audience. Plato would just as soon eradicate fiction's so-called *psychagogic* power – that is, its power, literally, to lead the minds of those in the audience.[7] Aristotle, in contrast, prefers to harness this power for some socially useful end. Like any other made thing, we recall, a tragic poem is never an end in itself but a means to some further end. As we have already seen, Aristotle acknowledges this end in chapter 6, where, defining the kind of fiction or *poiēsis* under consideration, he introduces not only the *what* and *how* of tragedy, but also the *why*. And the *why* he identifies unambiguously with the provocation of strong emotion – an identification he later confirms (ch. 25, 1460b24–6) when advising other defenders of fiction to justify apparent errors in poetry on the very grounds that these errors serve to heighten poetry's emotional impact.

But why the emotions, and why fear and pity in particular? Aristotle answers the first question, directed somewhat predictably at Plato's objections to fiction's *psychagogic* power, in the *Rhetoric* (2.1.8): "The emotions are those things through which, by undergoing change, people come to differ in their judgments and which are accompanied by pain and pleasure, for example, anger, pity, fear, and other such things and their opposites." Over and against Plato's call for eradication, Aristotle affirms the role of human emotion (as well as change) in the activity of judging human action, whether we encounter these actions in the law courts, the assembly, or the theater.[8] An action arousing our fear, he argues by way of example (*Rhetoric* 1.14.5), deserves a harsher judgment than one arousing our pity.

In his handbook for the fiction-writer as well as the orator, Aristotle describes the two emotions of fear and pity as both especially instrumental in judging action and inextricably related to one another. In the *Poetics* (ch. 13) we pity those agents who suffer unfairly, while we fear for those who are like us (*homoios*). This latter quality of likeness is, moreover, essential to the best tragic characters (ch. 15, 1454a24). In the *Rhetoric*, we similarly pity those who have not deserved their suffering (2.8.1), but we also pity those who are like us (2.8.13) – provided they are not so like us as to be us or those closest to us. In such cases, Aristotle reasons, we feel fear rather than pity. Accordingly, Amasis, King of Egypt, was seen to weep at the sight of a friend reduced to poverty but not to have wept at his son's execution, the sight of which terrified him (2.8.12). In general, however, "people pity things happening to others in so far as they fear for themselves" (2.8.13; cf. 2.5.12).

As characterized in the *Rhetoric*, then, pity is the more sympathetic counterpart to fear, although both are engaged by another's suffering. Fear is intensified, moreover, by those events that occur contrary to our expectation. If you want to terrify your audience, Aristotle informs the student of rhetoric (2.5.13), "make them realize that . . . there are others like them suffering [now] (or who have suffered) and at the hands of those from whom they did not expect it and suffering things [they did not expect] and at a time when they were not thinking of [the possibility]." With this advice in the *Rhetoric* Aristotle inadvertently fills out the truncated argument of the *Poetics*.

In some of the best tragic fiction, as we have seen, a basically good character suffers because he takes responsibility for an action with unforeseen consequences. He commits (and regrets) a *hamartia* (cf. *Nicomachean Ethics* 3.1.13). Many of these same tragedies turn on tragic recognitions and reversals that terrify us precisely *because* their changes are sudden and contrary to expectation. Such rapid, unexpected change also causes wonder (ch. 9, 1452a4–7; cf. *Rhetoric* 1.11.24 and *Poetics* 24, 1460a17). Wonder, in turn, provokes the desire to understand (*Metaphysics* 1.1, 980a21–7; *Rhetoric* 1.11.24), and both wondering and understanding cause pleasure (*Rhetoric* 1.11.23, *Poetics* 4, 1448b4–19).

Aristotle's defense of tragic fiction, then, addresses both of Plato's charges against it: that it is the product of ignorance and that it inflames the emotions. In response to the first charge, Aristotle requires from the tragic plot a carefully constructed sequence of events causally rather than just temporally related. In order to fulfill this requirement, the tragic poet himself must understand the causes of human action in the ethical and intellectual qualities of the agents. Furthermore, he must know how to build these qualities of character and mind into the structure of events. Thus carefully crafted, Aristotelian tragedy challenges and even sharpens its audience's ability to judge human action. In doing so, it performs no small psychological and social function.

But making judgments engages our emotional as well as our rational powers; and so this same tragedy, if its aim is really to deepen our understanding of human action, must also provoke our fears about and our compassion for the human suffering that those who act very often bring on themselves and those closest to them. Rather than answering Plato's second charge, in other words, Aristotle refutes its most basic assumption. The intense pleasure that comes from our emotional engagement with the tragic action and its agents is inseparable, he argues, from the pleasure associated with our instinct to admire them and our efforts to understand them.

But the emotions do more than account for the effectiveness of tragic fiction. As mentioned in my introduction, they also help to explain tragedy's superiority to epic. Sharing many features of this older and longer form of fiction, tragedy surpasses epic in Aristotle's estimation for two related reasons: one is its greater unity; the other, the greater compression and therefore, we can assume, emotional impact that such structural tightness affords (ch. 26, 1462a12–13). These generic advantages, Aristotle insists, belong as much to reading tragedy as to seeing it performed (ch. 26, 1462a17–18). If reading fiction serves better than reading history because fictional structure in general foregrounds the causal relations between the qualities of human agency and human action, then reading tragic fiction is best of all. Its peculiar structure intensifies our emotional engagement, thereby deepening our understanding and increasing our pleasure.

NOTES

1   On the dating of the *Poetics* see Halliwell (1986: 324–30).

2   For a couple of exceptions, anticipating the final chapter, see ch. 4, 1449a5–6 and ch. 5, 1449b18–20.

3   With the exception of a few remarks on spectacle (ch. 6, 1450b16–20; ch. 14, 1453b1–10; ch. 26, 1462a16), indicating its secondary role in tragic fiction, the *Poetics* more or less confines its discussion of *how* tragedy imitates to its treatment of style in chs. 19–22. See Halliwell (1986: 337–49).

4   See Halliwell (1986: 286–323; Herrick (1950: 32–3); Weinberg (1961: 402).

5   See Halliwell (1986: 228) and Weinberg (1961: 416).

6   Although Aristotle routinely couples probability and necessity together in the shorthand of the *Poetics*, he does sometimes refer to probability alone (ch. 16, 1455a16–19; ch. 18, 1456a23–5). See Eden (1986: 69–70) and Halliwell (1986: 99–102).

7   For Aristotle's use of this term in the *Poetics* see ch. 6, 1450a33; 1450b16–17 and Halliwell (1986: 64).

8   For Plato and Aristotle on the commonalities between legal and dramatic theory see Eden (1986: 3–61).

REFERENCES AND FURTHER READING

Aristotle. (1985). *Nicomachean Ethics*, trans. T. Irwin. Indianapolis: Hackett (fourth century BCE).

Aristotle. (1987). *Poetics*, trans. S. Halliwell. Chapel Hill: University of North Carolina Press (fourth century BCE).

Aristotle. (1991). *On Rhetoric*, trans. G. A. Kennedy. Oxford: Oxford University Press (fourth century BCE).

Dale, A. M. (1969). "Ethos and Dianoia: 'Character' and 'Thought' in Aristotle's *Poetics*." In *Collected Papers*. Cambridge: Cambridge University Press, 139–55.

Eden, K. (1986). *Poetic and Legal Fiction in the Aristotelian Tradition*. Princeton, NJ: Princeton University Press.

Else, G. F. (1957). *Aristotle's Poetics: The Argument*. Cambridge, MA: Cambridge University Press.

Frede, D. (1992). "Necessity, Chance, and 'What Happens for the Most Part' in Aristotle's *Poetics*." In *Essays on Aristotle's Poetics*, ed. A. O. Rorty. Princeton, NJ: Princeton University Press, 197–219.

Halliwell, S. (1986). *Aristotle's Poetics*. Chapel Hill: University of North Carolina Press.

Halliwell, S. (1992). "Pleasure, Understanding, and Emotion in Aristotle's *Poetics*." In *Essays on Aristotle's Poetics*, ed. A. O. Rorty. Princeton, NJ: Princeton University Press, 241–60.

Herrick, M. T. (1950). *Comic Theory in the Sixteenth Century*. Urbana: University of Illinois Press.

Janko, R. (1984). *Aristotle on Comedy*. Berkeley: University of California Press.

McKeon, R. (1952). "Literary Criticism and the Concept of Imitation in Antiquity." In *Critics and Criticism: Ancient and Modern*, ed. R. S. Crane. Chicago: University of Chicago Press, 147–75.

Nehamas, A. (1992). "Pity and Fear in the *Rhetoric* and the *Poetics*." In *Essays on Aristotle's Poetics*, ed. A. O. Rorty. Princeton, NJ: Princeton University Press, 291–314.

Plato (1992). *Republic*, trans. G. M. A. Grube. Indianapolis: Hackett (ca. 380 BCE).

Stinton, T. C. W. (1975). "*Hamartia* in Aristotle and Greek Tragedy." *Classical Quarterly* 25, 221–54.

Trimpi, W. (1982). *Muses of One Mind: The Literary Analysis of Experience and Its Continuity*. Princeton, NJ: Princeton University Press.

Weinberg, B. (1961). *A History of Literary Criticism in the Italian Renaissance*. Chicago: University of Chicago Press.

4

The Greatness and Limits of Hegel's Theory of Tragedy

Mark W. Roche

Hegel's Theory of Tragedy

Next to Aristotle's account of tragedy, the theory of tragedy developed by the German philosopher G. W. F. Hegel (1770–1831) has become the most studied and quoted in the West. Even scholars who openly criticize Hegel sometimes unwittingly reproduce aspects of his theory (Moss 1969–70). Tragedy arises, according to Hegel, when a hero courageously asserts a substantial and just position, but in doing so simultaneously violates a contrary and likewise just position and so falls prey to a one-sidedness that is defined at one and the same time by greatness and by guilt.

Born the same year as the composer Ludwig van Beethoven (1770–1827) and the poets Friedrich Hölderlin (1770–1843) and William Wordsworth (1770–1850), Hegel lived in an era of transition. Raised in the provincial Duchy of Württemberg in southern Germany, Hegel celebrated the advent of the French revolution while he was still a teenager, only to be sobered by the subsequent movement to terror. By the time of his death in 1831, the Industrial Revolution was well underway in Europe, though still barely on the horizon in the German-speaking principalities. Hegel lived in an age of the flowering of German letters. The philosophers Immanuel Kant (1724–1804), Johann Gottlieb Fichte (1762–1814), and Friedrich Schelling (1775–1854) and the writers Johann Wolfgang Goethe (1749–1832), Friedrich Schiller (1759–1805), and Friedrich Schlegel (1772–1829) were all contemporaries. After a slow start as a professional philosopher, Hegel became the leading philosophical figure of his day, gaining chairs in philosophy, first in Heidelberg and then in Berlin. He was the first great philosopher to have detailed knowledge of non-European cultures and to integrate them into his thinking.

Hegel was one of the broadest minds in the history of philosophy. His writings, which are all interconnected, range widely and address, for example, logic, the philosophy of nature, the philosophy of history, political philosophy, aesthetics, the philosophy of religion, and the history of philosophy. Hegel sought to develop a complex logic of categories that illuminated the absolute and its appearance in the world. In the Hegelian dialectic, which encompasses both thought and history, each category or thesis reveals its one-sidedness and passes over into its antithesis, which is likewise recognized as one-sided, eventually giving way to a synthesis, which both negates and preserves the earlier terms; the synthesis itself becomes absorbed in a larger process in which it, too, is recognized as partial, though at a higher and more complex level. This continual progression, whereby partial categories give way to their own internal contradictions, leads to an ever greater realization of reason, self-consciousness, and freedom. Hegel's influence on Western thought is immeasurable to this day. Even many thinkers who are skeptical of the Hegelian system recognize Hegel's extraordinary powers of integration and his profound insights into wide-ranging areas of human inquiry.

Tragedy plays a role in both Hegel's *Phenomenology of Mind* and his *Lectures on the Philosophy of History*, arguably his two best-known works in the Anglo-American world. In chapter 5 of the *Phenomenology* Hegel discusses character, ethical action, and guilt partly by way of an analysis of Sophocles' tragedy *Antigone*. In his introduction to the *Lectures on the Philosophy of History* Hegel analyzes the world-historical individual who shapes history often beyond her conscious intentions; such figures emerge ahead of their time, come into conflict with their ages, and prepare a new world. In his *Lectures on the History of Philosophy* Hegel offers a fascinating portrait of Socrates in the light of this tragic dialectic. Also in his *Lectures on the Philosophy of Religion* Hegel touches on tragedy, especially in the Greek world and in relation to reconciliation. Tragedy is most prominent in Hegel's *Lectures on Aesthetics*, which is one of his most accessible texts. The *Aesthetics*, which was compiled and edited by Hegel's student Heinrich Gustav Hotho, is based on Hegel's lecture notes and on student transcriptions of the lectures. Hegel lectured on aesthetics in Heidelberg in 1818 and in Berlin in 1820/1, 1823, 1826, and 1828/9. Toward the end of his lectures Hegel discusses drama and devotes most of his attention to tragedy. These reflections represent Hegel's most mature and most extended discussion of tragedy, and they relate to his entire corpus insofar as the structure of tragedy parallels the dialectic and insofar as the content of tragedy involves the most essential dimensions of human action and divine providence (15:502; A1179).[1]

For Hegel tragedy is the conflict of two substantive positions, each of which is justified, yet each of which is wrong to the extent that it fails either to recognize the validity of the other position or to grant it its moment of truth; the conflict can be resolved only with the fall of the hero, such that unity is restored and the whole of ethical life is purged of its one-sidedness.

> The original essence of tragedy consists then in the fact that within such a conflict each of the opposed sides, if taken by itself, has *justification*, while on the other hand each can establish the true and positive content of its own aim and character only by negating and *damaging* the equally justified power of the other. Consequently, in its moral life,

and because of it, each is just as much involved in *guilt*. (15:523; A 1196, translation modified)

Hegelian tragedy is the conflict of two goods. What should be a single unity has been split into two. For Hegel, this is an inevitable consequence of the absolute realizing itself in individuals. In order to become manifest, the absolute must pass over into the particular; this generates conflict within the absolute, to be resolved only with the transcendence (or death) of the particular (15:523–4; A 1196–7). In the course of history one-sided positions emerge that transcend previous errors but which still contain within themselves their own limitations (15:486; A 1167); these, too, eventually give rise to conflict and transcendence, such that history progresses dialectically, through contradiction and negativity, toward an ever more comprehensive and rational goal.

Not only does the tragic hero refuse to acknowledge the validity of the other position; the other position – or at least the sphere it represents – is also an aspect within the hero even as she denies it. This is especially clear in Sophocles' *Antigone*, which Hegel describes as the most beautiful of all tragedies (15:550; A 1218; see also 17:133). In this play Creon, King of Thebes, decrees that because of treason the body of Polynices may not be buried. Antigone, Polynices' sister, recognizes a higher, divine law and tries to cover his body. Though Antigone is affianced to Creon's son, Haemon, Creon sentences Antigone to death. Before the sentence is carried out, Antigone and Haemon commit suicide, as does Creon's wife, leaving Creon devastated and alone. Not only is Creon stubborn and steadfast in Sophocles' play; Antigone, too, fails to recognize a legitimate conflict of goods and is in this sense as single-minded as her nemesis, if nonetheless more valid in her stance. According to Hegel, the action of each hero is both destructive of the other and self-destructive: Antigone is not only a family member but a member of the state, Creon not only a ruler but a father and husband; the tragic heroes transgress

> what, if they were true to their own nature, they should be honouring. For example, Antigone lives under the political authority of Creon [the present King]; she is herself the daughter of a King [Oedipus] and the fiancée of Haemon [Creon's son], so that she ought to pay obedience to the royal command. But Creon too, as father and husband, should have respected the sacred tie of blood and not ordered anything against its pious observance. So there is immanent in both Antigone and Creon something that in their own way they attack, so that they are gripped and shattered by something intrinsic to their own actual being. (15:549; A 1217–18)

According to Hegel, the tragic hero adheres to a one-sided position, denies the validity of its complementary and contrasting other, and eventually succumbs to the greater process in which it is submerged. The tragic adherence to a partial position is stripped away and yields to the larger rational process of historical development. Tragedy thus contains within itself a hidden moment of resolution and reconciliation (15:524; A 1197; 15:526; A 1198; 15:547; A 1215).

The Greatness of Hegel's Theory of Tragedy

Most interpreters of tragedy, beginning already with Aristotle, focus their accounts of tragedy on the effect of tragedy, on its reception. Hegel, along with Hölderlin, Schelling, and Peter Szondi (1929–79), is one of the few figures in the tradition to take a different path. Here is the first appealing feature of Hegel's theory. The history of the philosophy of tragedy is marred by an overemphasis on reception, an undue focus on the (emotive) effect of tragedy at the expense of tragic structure. Hegel, in contrast, focuses on the core structure of tragedy. Hegel does share with Aristotle an interest in organic plots, with an appropriate reversal and an ensuing recognition, but Hegel's aspirations for organic structure may be said to exceed Aristotle's: Hegel places far more emphasis on the way in which the hero's flaw must be intertwined with, and in a sense result from, her greatness.

Paradoxically, Hegel's focus on the structure of tragic collision gives him a new angle on the traditional motifs of fear and pity. For Hegel the audience is to fear not external fate, as with Aristotle, but the ethical substance which, if violated, will turn against the hero (15:525; A 1197–8). Insofar as suffering flows inevitably from the tragic hero's profound identification with a just and substantial position, suffering for Hegel is not quite the undeserved suffering that for Aristotle elicits pity. Hegel reinterprets pity as sympathy not merely with the suffering hero as sufferer but with the hero as one who, despite her fall, is nonetheless in a sense justified. According to Hegel we fear the power of an ethical substance that has been violated as a result of collision, and we sympathize with the tragic hero who, despite having transgressed the absolute, also in a sense upholds the absolute. Thus, Hegelian tragedy has an emotional element: we are torn between the values and destiny of each position; we identify with the character's action but sense the inevitable revenge of the absolute, which destroys the hero's one-sidedness.

Second, collision draws out the ambivalence central to the tragic intertwining of greatness and limits, divinity and nothingness. Because the tragic hero acts both for and against the good, her nature is as paradoxical as the situation in which she finds herself: she is both great and flawed; indeed, her very greatness is her flaw, since greatness comes at the price of excluding what the situation also demands. The hero is both innocent and guilty: innocent insofar as she adheres to the good by acting on behalf of a just principle; guilty insofar as she violates a good and wills to identify with that violation. Guilt presupposes action for which the hero is responsible; as a result, the hero seeks not sympathy or pity but recognition of the substance of her action, including its consequences. In this spirit Hegel offers the paradoxical formulation: "It is the honour of these great characters to be culpable" (15:546; A 1215). The traditional notion of *hamartia*, often misunderstood simply as a tragic flaw, can be grasped with the help of Hegel as an error or disaster that is nonetheless related to a greatness. Kurt von Fritz argues that *hamartia* is best understood as action according to an immanent necessity that nonetheless leads to catastrophe (1962: 3–14). In other words, the hero suffers from her greatness (which necessarily also violates a good) rather than simply from a weakness (or a flaw). Hegel's theory is more complex than either the traditional notion of tragic flaw or the counterstrand that elevates greatness: for Hegel the hero's greatness and flaw are one and the same; in fulfilling the good, the hero violates the good. Not surprisingly, the audience likewise experiences both admiration and despair, pleasure and pain, renewed reconciliation and irretrievable loss.

Third, we might note the dramatic intensity generated by Hegelian tragedy. The collision of two goods is *in principle* the dramatically richest structure of tragedy. Even Arthur Schopenhauer, who develops a concept of tragedy in *The World as Will and Representation* (1819) that is far removed from Hegel's reconciliatory focus, privileges that form of tragedy defined by a collision of goods; it is the most dramatic and most powerful. Our understanding of a work that seemingly lacks a collision may be enriched by a reading that recognizes submerged moments of collision. An interpretation of Goethe's *Faust*, for example, that stresses moments of collision between Faust and Mephistopheles, might shed a different and fuller light on the play than a reading that argues merely for the conflict of good and evil. So, too, might one emphasize the structure of tragic collision in works such as Euripides' *Bacchae*, Schiller's *Wallenstein*, Ibsen's *Ghosts*, and Brecht's *The Good Person of Sezuan*.

As if to underline the hidden identity of the two forces, the competing heroes in a Hegelian tragedy are often presented, despite their obvious differences, as mirror images of one another. Antigone and Creon, for example, are specular figures: each pursues justice in a narrow way, each is isolated, stubborn, imperious toward others, and the cause of doom for self and others. A mirroring structure is also evident in Shakespeare's *Julius Caesar*, where the similarities of Caesar and Brutus are presented in parallel and adjoining scenes (2.1 and 2.2), and in Büchner's *Danton's Death*, where both Robespierre and Danton compare themselves with Christ and near one another, intellectually, in their soliloquies.

Fourth, great psychological depth is found within the complex reactions of a hero who is aware of competing and equally justifiable demands. I would make a distinction within tragic collision which Hegel does not make. In some tragedies the conflict of goods is represented by more than one person or institution, what one could call external collision, for which Sophocles' *Antigone* would be an example. In other tragedies a single hero is aware of competing obligations, what one might call internal collision; an example would be Shakespeare's *Hamlet*. In external collision the hero sees only her own perspective and fails to recognize, as the audience does, that her position is as invalid as it is valid. Some tragic heroes, however, see both sides of the conflict. In not differentiating the two types of collision, Hegel appears to be overestimating the role of reception. For Hegel the two goods are united in the consciousness of the audience as it sees the fall of the hero and her one-sided principle. It makes a great difference, however, whether the hero is aware of the collision; this affects not only the dramatic and psychological complexities of the work but also the movement toward reconciliation on the stage itself.

External collision offers us the most dramatic form of tragedy. An internal collision may become less dramatic because of the unity of two positions within a single self; on the other hand, internal collision tends to be intellectually and psychologically more differentiated. It allows for richer characterization, a trait Hegel admired in modern drama, and conduces to a more explicit thematization of tragic essence, that is, the connection between greatness and suffering. Internal collision is also formally rich, giving rise to some of the greatest rhetoric of world drama, monologues and dialogues that presuppose awareness of an ineradicable conflict of goods. That the hero must sacrifice her naive belief in a just world – by violating one good in order to preserve another – has extraordinary intellectual and emotional consequences.

The danger may, of course, arise that the hero will simply waver back and forth between one pole and the other, thus destroying the hero's resolve and any unity of character, and that this indecisiveness, not the substance of the poles, will be heralded as the essence of art (13:312; A 241; 15:562–3; A 1228–9). In this context Hegel distinguishes characters who hesitate because they are confused and weak from those who see a genuine and irresolvable conflict of goods.

> It is already different if two opposed spheres of life, duties, and so forth, seem equally sacrosanct to a self-assured character, and yet he sees himself compelled to align himself with *one* to the exclusion of the other. In that case the vacillation is only a transitional phase and does not constitute the nerve of the person's character. (15:563; A 1228–9, translation modified)

A central insight in Hegel's analysis of tragedy in the *Phenomenology* is that, even when the tragic hero becomes conscious of the justice of a competing position, character demands consistency, and with this not vacillation, but action, acknowledgment, and guilt (3:348). According to Hegel, Shakespeare's characters are defined by their passions and their compelling action, not their vacillation or hesitation. Hegel describes Macbeth:

> In the beginning he hesitates, but then he stretches out his hand to the crown, commits murder to get it, and, in order to maintain it, storms away through every atrocity. This reckless firmness, this identity of the man with himself and the end arising from his own decision, gives him an essential interest for us. Not respect for the majesty of the monarch, not the frenzy of his wife, not the defection of his vassals, not his impending destruction, nothing, neither divine nor human law, makes him falter or draw back; instead he persists in his course. (14:200–1; A 578, translation modified)

Writing later not only of Macbeth, Othello, or Richard III, Hegel comments:

> It is precisely Shakespeare who gives us, in contrast to that portrayal of vacillating and inwardly divided characters, the finest examples of firm and consistent figures who come to ruin simply because of this decisive adherence to themselves and their aims. Without ethical justification, but upheld solely by the formal inevitability of their

individuality, they allow themselves to be lured to their deed by external circumstances, or they plunge blindly on and persevere by the strength of their will, even if now what they do, they accomplish only from the necessity of maintaining themselves against others or simply because they have reached the point that they have reached. (15:564; A 1229–30, translation modified)

To elevate to tragic status Hamlet's lack of will as a simple inability to act, the common view among Hegel's contemporaries, is to transform tragedy into mere suffering (13:316; A 244). For Hegel the apparent weakness of Hamlet derives, rather, from the energy of his thought, which recognizes a conflict between the emotional need to act in the face of corruption and indecency and insight into the immoral nature of the contemplated action. Because Hamlet is idealistic, conscientious, and sensitive, he hesitates to add to the pollution and sickness of the age; he must first weigh the merits of restoring justice and order through treachery and murder. Thus, he hesitates, disgusted with the world, but tormented in his conscience, weary within himself (14:207–8; A 583–4; 15:559; A 1225–6; 15:566–7; A 1231–2).

Fifth, we see with the help of the Hegelian model how tragedy, like much of art, also has a proleptic function: presenting the boundary cases of ethics, it not only exhibits the good; it portrays conflicts that can in turn give rise to philosophical reflection on the good. Any Hegelian tragedy implies alternatives; the hero of internal collision knows of these alternatives. Her choice is conscious, and her act of deliberation brings forth the fullest range of consciousness, the weighing of ends and means, of duties and obligations, the totality of conflicting claims. Traditional definitions of tragedy often stress knowledge and self-recognition; these aspects receive their fullest development in the tragedy of internal collision. Hegel argues in the *Phenomenology* that even when two individuals collide and recognize only their own ethical values, in violating the other and destroying self and other, they gain a late recognition of the validity of the contrasting ethical power (3:348).

For Hegel tragic fate is rational: reason does not allow the individuals to hold onto their positions in their one-sidedness. Because each stance is constituted through its relation to the other, the elimination of one stance leads to the destruction of the other. The human result is death, but the absolute end is the reestablishment of ethical substance. This unity is, for Hegel, the catharsis of tragedy, which takes place in the consciousness of the audience, as it recognizes the supremacy of the whole of ethical life and sees it purged of one-sidedness. Catharsis, then, is for Hegel an act of recognition; tragedy gives us ethical insight into the untenability of one-sided positions.

Sixth, we recognize the utility of Hegel's theory for a philosophy of history that stresses the importance of paradigm shifts. Hegel's theory of tragedy deals not just with conflict but with the dynamics of historical change. Tragedy rarely occurs in an eminently ordered universe, such as the Christian Middle Ages, where suffering is fully rationalized, or in a chaotic age such as our own that is less attuned to the idea of binding ethical norms and views suffering as either arbitrary or external to greatness. Tragedy is more likely to arise when there is partial order and partial disorder, a transition between paradigms, and thus often a collision.

Precisely because tragedies of collision frequently arise during paradigm shifts, Hegelian tragedy has particular relevance for historical drama. Hegel is attuned to historical conflicts, crises, and transitions; periods of tranquility and happiness, according to Hegel, are "empty leaves" in the annals of world history (12.42). Hegel invites audiences to ask: Which values have come into conflict? Which positions are rooted in the past and which are harbingers of the future? In what ways do individual characters embody the conflicting strands of history? To what extent are forces beyond the hero's intentions and passions shaping the events as they unfold? The importance of historical drama has been developed partly under Hegelian influence by the nineteenth-century German dramatist Friedrich Hebbel (1813–63), who tries to show the clash of values as one norm is pushed aside and another comes into being. Often a self-sacrificing hero arrives before a new paradigm is set and collides with tradition, or a stubborn hero holds onto her position long after a new norm has taken shape. Both moments are present in Schiller's *Don Carlos*. It is important to note that for Hegel the individual can be morally right, the state retrograde, such that the individual person is more aligned with the universal, the state more with the false particularity that must ultimately give way (or adjust to the ideas represented by the moral individual). In this sense we should be careful not to see in Hegel's view of tragedy simply a deflation of the value of the person in the march of history. After all, for Hegel the telos of history is freedom and self-consciousness.

According to Hegel tragedy presupposes profound identification with normative values, to which a hero is attached and for which the hero is willing to sacrifice herself. Hegel recognizes a shift from tragedy to comedy when what is substantial gives way to what is subjective, and the particular becomes more important than the universal (15:527–31; A1199–1202; 15:552–5; A 1220–2; 15.572–3; A 1236). For Hegel, like Nietzsche, tragedy vanishes in an age of self-consciousness and enlightenment. For Nietzsche, however, the obstacle to tragedy is the abandonment of irrationality; for Hegel the problem is the dissolution of objective values.

Finally, whereas Aristotle, along with certain formal theorists in the mid twentieth century, developed ahistorical theories of tragedy, and contemporary critics tend to dispute any transhistorical concept of genre, Hegel was aware of both, offering a universal definition, but suggesting at least one significant shift in its articulation, the difference between ancient and modern tragedy. In ancient tragedy the characters completely identify with the substantive powers and ideas that rule human life; characters act "for the sake of the substantial nature of their end" (15:558; A 1225). In modern tragedy, in contrast, we see greater internal development of character as well as the elevation of more particular concerns: "what presses for satisfaction is the *subjectivity* of their heart and mind and the privacy of their own character" (15:558; A 1225). Also the complexity of modern causality diminishes the extent to which one single person can affect the world around her; complexity and the contingency of circumstances play a greater role in modern tragedy (15:537; A 1207;15:558; A 1224;15:560; A 1226).

The Limits of Hegel's Theory of Tragedy

Several criticisms of Hegel's theory of tragedy have been advanced, some legitimate, others less so. I have already made one modest criticism: that Hegel fails to distinguish collisions between individuals and collisions within individuals. In truth, this is less a criticism than an attempt to build on what Hegel has already sketched, for the distinction between external and internal collision parallels in some respects Hegel's account of the difference between ancient and modern tragedy. More formidable criticism has been launched at Hegel's claim that the tragic heroes embrace conflicting positions that are "equally justified" (15:523; A 1196; cf. 3:349). I concede that this criticism is valid; Hegel cannot be right when he says that all tragic collisions contain poles of *equal* value; this is already clear in the problems classical philologists have found in Hegel's otherwise magisterial reading of *Antigone*. Even Hegel, in fact, despite his overarching interpretation, is in his language slightly more sympathetic to Antigone. Nonetheless, Hegel is right if we understand him to mean that in the *best* tragedies the conflict is equal. In works where the conflict is unequal, tragic intensity diminishes.

In response to this criticism, one might propose two forms of collision where the poles are not equally weighted, the tragedy of self-sacrifice and the tragedy of stubbornness. These would represent modified versions of Hegelian collision. The tragedy of self-sacrifice would be a collision not of two goods but of good and evil, whereby the hero does the good knowing that she will suffer for it. To preserve a value, its bearer must sometimes perish. One thinks of Gryphius' *Catharina von Georgien*, Eliot's *Murder in the Cathedral*, or Miller's *The Crucible*. The tragedy of self-sacrifice is the noblest and most didactic of tragic subforms, though it is dramatically – owing to the simplicity and nonambiguity of the conflict – the weakest. Heroes of self-sacrifice ideally trigger transitions in history even as they give their lives for these transitions. The other, often the state, adheres to a principle of the past, yet it still holds power; the tragic hero of self-sacrifice represents the future. Self-sacrificing heroes stand for truths that are too new to have a majority behind them; after the hero's sacrifice the situation will change. We can cite Hegel on this issue:

> That is the position of heroes in world history generally; through them a new world dawns. This new principle is in contradiction with the previous one, appears as dissolving; the heroes appear, therefore, as violent, destructive of laws. Individually, they are vanquished; but this principle persists, if in a different form, and buries the present. (18:515)

The unambiguous contrast between good and evil evident in self-sacrifice often weakens the potential richness of the work, reducing complex art and intricate questions to an almost black-and-white formula. The audience has unadulterated compassion for the tragic hero of self-sacrifice (there is no awareness of the complexity of action or of moral choice) and clear disdain for the enemy (there is no awareness of the good that sometimes lies hidden behind the façade of evil). Hochhuth's *The Deputy*, considered by many the one tragedy in twentieth-century German literature, is weakened by the clearly evil nature of the other, in this case the pope. An admirable and a good work, it is nonetheless not great. Modern Britain's most significant contribution to tragedy, Robert Bolt's *A Man for All Seasons*, a play about Sir Thomas More, is likewise a noble but undramatic tragedy of self-sacrifice.

The tragedy of stubbornness is morally less admirable than the tragedy of self-sacrifice but formally and, in most cases, dramatically richer. Here the hero adopts an untenable position but nonetheless displays formal virtues: courage, loyalty, or ambition, for example. Stubbornness – or for the general case let us say steadfastness – belongs as a moment to all tragedy. The greatness of the tragic hero of stubbornness lies in the consistency with which she adheres to a position, false and one-sided though it may be. The hero will not yield; she has no capacity for, or interest in, moderation or compromise, and there is something impressive, even inspiring, about this intensity and perseverance. Ajax wants the world on his own terms and is willing to destroy himself and others to get it. Medea would have profited empirically from stilling her anger, but she remains steadfast in her hate, consistent in her desire for vengeance. Coriolanus could have won the favor of all Romans by being flexible, perhaps simply by being mild, but he will not stray from his principles and resoluteness. His honor and pride will not bear it. Though Hegel does not introduce the idea of tragic stubbornness, he is, as we have seen, not blind to the "greatness of spirit" in a character such as Macbeth (13:538; A 420), and he presents an insightful description of what is necessary for any successful aesthetic portrayal of evil: "Here above all, therefore, we must at least demand formal greatness of character and a subjectivity powerful enough to withstand everything negative and, without denying its deeds or being inwardly shattered, to accept its fate" (15:537; A 1207, translation modified).

One form of tragic stubbornness comes especially close to a concept of collision. I'm thinking of a particular manifestation of what is traditionally called tragedy of character. The collision is not of two justified goods, but instead of two formal virtues. An asymmetry arises, with one virtue being cultivated, the other neglected. The hero has a particular greatness (one formal virtue in excess), coupled with a weakness (another virtue neglected). Coriolanus, for example, is a great warrior but incapable of peaceful compromise. Goethe's Egmont exhibits honesty, openness, and trust but is unaware of the need for caution and calculation. Dr. Stockmann in Ibsen's *An Enemy of the People* exhibits the virtues of truth, honesty, and fearlessness at the expense of pragmatism, restraint, and considered action, and so he, too, represents this type of tragic hero. When Gregers Werle in Ibsen's *The Wild Duck* elevates honesty over sensitivity, he also becomes a tragic hero of stubbornness who exalts one formal virtue at the expense of another. Precisely in these cases greatness stands in a dialectical relationship to the traditional concept of tragic flaw. The hero becomes great by neglecting a contrasting virtue, which is thus the hero's flaw.

Let us return briefly to *Antigone*. Hegel views this play as the paradigmatic tragedy of collision. His view has been frequently contested, but if we see in the play a conflict not between Antigone and Creon but between Antigone and the institution of the state, then we could view the work in modified Hegelian terms (Hösle 1984: 97). Antigone's resistance to the state is based on her adherence to the law of the family, but in following this law, she violates the law of the state. Creon's particular law may be unjust (it is not an established law but a subjective decree); nonetheless, it belongs to the idea of the state that its laws be just and that they be obeyed. Hegel writes: "For the first principle of a state is that there is no reason, conscience, righteousness, or anything else higher than what the state recognizes as such" (18:510). Creon's decrees are wrong, such that law and justice do not coincide. Thus, the state here is only formally right; in terms of content it is wrong. Antigone's act of resistance is just (and so it belongs to self-sacrifice), yet she collides with the state (and so it is collision), even as the state is weakened by a ruler whose position is untenable (Creon represents stubbornness).

Self-sacrifice and stubbornness, along with the drama of suffering, a genre in which we see suffering independently of greatness, might be viewed as deficient forms of the Hegelian model. In a tragedy of collision one hero will likely exhibit the supremacy of a position by pledging her life for it; another is stubbornly unwilling to compromise, even when the limits of her position are evident; and in the wake of such a collision innocent persons suffer. In their autonomy the forms are deficient. They render individual moments absolute: content at the expense of complexity, form at the expense of content, and suffering at the expense of conflict and greatness. What they gain in terms of focus, they lose in terms of wholeness. The greatest tragedy has all moments: moral goodness, formal strength, complexity, and suffering.

Self-sacrifice reaches a peak when it borders on collision, when it is presented as a conflict of goods (the hero's life or well-being versus action on behalf of the good). Likewise, stubbornness fulfills its highest potential when it points toward a collision, the conflict of goodness versus formal virtues or, in a particular variant, the elevation of one virtue at the expense of another. Even as self-sacrifice and stubbornness differ from collision, they find therein their greatest fulfillment. In addition, both self-sacrifice and stubbornness surface more frequently and are more dramatic in periods of conflict, that is, during paradigm shifts, which are in part pushed forward or held back by the tragic heroes. Heroes who are in advance of their time, as are many heroes of self-sacrifice, invite a conflict of values. At times the herald of the new pursues her course in such a way as to ignore the value of the present or to undermine her own position, thus embodying stubbornness. More commonly, however, the stubborn hero holds onto the stability or formal greatness of the past and is destroyed by historical developments that transcend her. From a reverse angle, we can say that certain instances of collision contain within them subordinate moments of self-sacrifice and stubbornness. The claim of equal justification, then, is best dealt with by recognizing also unequal collisions (self-sacrifice and stubbornness) and by acknowledging the virtues of any tragedy that equalizes the conflict.

A third criticism of Hegel's theory is that Hegel insists on an element of harmony in tragedy, which is anathema to the modern insistence on ineradicable and unrelieved suffering. Hegel argues that despite negativity and destruction, despite the hero's suffering and death, tragedy also offers us a window onto reconciliation and harmony. This point has been criticized most especially in modernity (for references, see Roche 1998: 355). Goethe, writing in Hegel's day, argues, with Hegel, that "a reconciliation, a solution is indispensable as a conclusion if the tragedy is to be a perfect work of art" (1986: 198). Rare, however, is the modern reading of tragedy that sees in tragedy even a glimmer of reconciliation or rational order. Almost accentuating his critique of Hegel's thesis that tragedy contains a moment of reconciliation, Ludwig Marcuse elevates the modern drama of suffering, which he calls "the tragic tragedy," insofar as suffering is given no meaning, no context, no reason: "The absolute tragic essence of the tragic tragedy is suffering without meaning" (Marcuse 1923: 17–18). Marcuse continues his definition: "Modern tragedy is now only a cry of existence; not overcoming, not mitigation of suffering: only a compression and formulation as last and only reaction still possible" (Marcuse 1923: 20). In this account tragedy becomes simple suffering – removed from greatness, from causality, from its position within any overarching narrative. Recognizing neither an overarching order nor any absolutes that might give meaning to suffering, many contemporary theories of tragedy, like Marcuse's, along with an abundance of contemporary "tragedies," elevate suffering and the irrational, chaotic, and often arbitrary forces that elicit suffering. Suffering in this context becomes the whole of tragedy.

In analyzing tragedy, Hegel stresses not the hero's suffering, nor even her endurance in suffering, but her relation to the absolute. For Hegel, as we have seen, the essence of tragedy is structural conflict, not the effect of suffering. Critics of Hegel are sometimes led to equate tragedy with suffering and so divorce tragedy from greatness. I side with Hegel on this issue. Obviously not all suffering need derive from greatness and not all great heroes need suffer. The richer argument is that some suffering is linked to greatness and some forms of greatness cannot avoid suffering; this specifically organic sphere defines the tragic.

Nonetheless, and here I come to a fourth criticism, Hegel might have more clearly differentiated tragedy from the drama of reconciliation, a genre that greatly interested such early Hegelians as Carl Ludwig Michelet (1801–93) and Moritz Carriere (1817–95). Some of the contradictions in Hegel's discussion of drama derive from the failure to differentiate these two genres adequately. Though there is a connection between catharsis and reconciliation, a significant difference exists between tragedy and the drama of reconciliation, namely, whether reconciliation takes place in reception, that is, in the consciousness of the audience, or in the story line itself, that is, in the action on stage. Hegel mentions in this context Aeschylus' *Eumenides* and Sophocles' *Philoctetes* as well as Goethe's *Iphigenia*, which he elevates even higher than the Greek plays insofar as its harmonious resolution is unambiguously organic, deriving as it does from the action itself (15:532–3; A 1203–4). In his *Lectures on the Philosophy of Religion* Hegel returns to this elevation of resolution, arguing again for a transcendence of tragedy: "The higher reconciliation would be that the attitude of one-sidedness would be overcome *in the subject* . . . and that it renounce injustice in its mind" (17:134). In Hegelian terms, tragedy portrays the transcendence of one-sided positions through death, thus offering an objective reconciliation. The drama of reconciliation, in contrast, exhibits a shift of consciousness on stage; the warring forces give way, thus creating a subjective or "inner reconciliation" (15:550–1; A 1219).

That a nondualistic philosopher like Hegel should articulate a harmonic form of drama, is natural, especially when we consider that Hegel consistently views art in connection with what he calls the speculative, or the higher unity of two conflicting forces (8:176–9). Hegel claims, for example, that the either-or mentality of understanding cannot grasp the unity of art (13:152; A 111), and that poetic, as opposed to prosaic, consciousness represents the literary equivalent of the speculative (15:240–5; A 973–7). Unfortunately, Hegel never fully develops his brief discussion of the drama of reconciliation, and when he does return to it, his comments are as frequently derogatory as they are laudatory. The form is "of less striking importance" (15:531; A 1202). It runs the danger of not fully developing a conflict (15:533; A 1204). The hero who alters his position may appear to lack character (15:550; A 1218). Such changes may diminish the determination and pathos of the hero's position (15:568; A 1233). Finally, harmonic resolutions are frequently unearned (15:569; A 1233). Most of these points can weaken a drama of reconciliation, but they do not belong to it in principle. Hegel himself seems unsure whether these characteristics are contingent or necessary.

If Hegel were to have analyzed the drama of reconciliation more fully and stressed more clearly the difference between it and tragedy, he may not have been led to overstress the reconciliatory moment within tragedy itself. To a degree the critics who assert that Hegel over-idealizes tragedy and gives insufficient attention to the moment of ineradicable suffering are right: the genre is not exhausted by its harmonic resolution; tragedy also suggests the inevitable calamities and inconsolable suffering that result when greatness surfaces in a complex world. On the other hand, it is equally one-sided to assert, as many contemporary critics do, that tragedy offers us only destruction, uncertainty, and gloom, and that any hidden visions of greatness, harmony, or hope are anathema to the tragic spirit. Tragedy is too multifaceted and complex for an either-or reception.

A fifth and related criticism involves the claim that the Hegelian universe in which all conflict is in principle solvable is incompatible with tragedy. Why doesn't the possibility of the drama of reconciliation eliminate the reality of tragedy? Aren't, as Otto Pöggeler (1964) suggests, Hegel's dialectical–teleological reflections and his optimistic worldview in the long run incompatible with the gravity of tragedy? One might answer in the following way. First, according to Hegel, already in tragedy a moment of reconciliation surfaces – though this reconciliation comes at a price (the hero's destruction) and may be visible only to the audience. Second, tragedy can in many cases be overcome. Either under alternative conditions or from the perspective of the universal many conflicts are in principle solvable. Even the collision of two goods can often be resolved by the argument that in such a conflict, one good can and *should* be violated on the basis of another good whose value is greater and in the interest of whose preservation the violation of the lesser good is demanded. From this perspective tragedy can be partially overcome, but this is not the entire picture.

In some instances tragedy is not only possible, it is unavoidable. That is, even if it is possible to justify the morality of violating one good in favor of a higher good, we still transgress a good. Such a violation is tragic, even when it is justified, even when it is inevitable, even when it alone leads to the preservation of the higher good. One must recognize the importance of contingency for Hegel. If from the perspective of the universal, tragic failure is frequently overcome, from the perspective of the concrete such transcendence is rare. Moreover, only in the particular, in history is the universal realized; tragedy is indispensable for the realization of spirit in history. Here Hegel would agree with Hölderlin's stimulating reflection in his drama and essays on Empedocles that in tragedy the universal comes to itself through the particular, as sacrifice. When faced with a collision of goods, the great and tragic hero does not simply choose the higher good and feel she has made the correct choice, she senses also the loss of the lesser good, which is indeed still a good. She chooses with regret and remorse, if also with necessity. Duke Ernst in Hebbel's *Agnes Bernauer* knows how he must act, but this does not erase his guilt. Moreover, even if we recognize history as generally progressive, at any given time there are both individual conflicts engendering tragedy and broader conflicts, shifts between paradigms, that create inevitable collisions. In addition, conflicts exist where there is no Hegelian resolution or synthesis whatsoever. No hierarchy of values can solve the hero's dilemma. Which is higher in a conflict between freedom and life, for example? The answer is not so simple, for, whereas freedom is the ideal meaning of life, life is the necessary condition of freedom; conflicts between the two are in many cases irresolvable. The drama of reconciliation thus supplements, rather than replaces, tragedy.

A sixth criticism of Hegel's theory is the claim, advanced, for example, by Johannes Volkelt (1897: 28–32, 300), that tragedy portrays particular individuals, not metaphysical ideas. We can defend Hegel by saying that the two are not mutually exclusive. It is, of course, possible to stress the metaphysical at the expense of the psychological, but that is in no way the necessary result of a Hegelian approach. Indeed, in his account of Hegel's aesthetics, Peter Szondi speaks with admiration of "the extraordinary capacity of his thinking, in the abstract dialectic of thought not, let's say, to dissolve the concrete but rather first and foremost to make it transparent" (1974: 445). Hegel himself insists that dramatic works should not offer "abstract presentations of specific passions and aims" (15:499; A 11777). Instead, they should contain the subtlety and vitality of life, truly living individuals, "the all-pervasive individuality which collects everything together into the unity which is itself and which displays itself in speech as the one and the same source from which every particular word, every single trait of disposition, deed, and behaviour springs" (15:500; A 1177–8). Tragic collision can in principle run the danger of being overly schematic and allegorical – an abstract weighing of position *x* versus position *y*, but that is the opposite of Hegel's explicit preference. If art is defined by its empirical concreteness and sensuous externality, with which it distinguishes itself from philosophy, and its wholeness and harmony, which it shares with philosophy, the artist should present full and whole and concrete characters, and the artist who presents abstractions – be it Corneille, Racine, or Ernst – falls short of the aesthetic ideal. The best tragedies avoid this danger by focusing on character as well as conflict, by presenting strong if complex individuals, and by rendering the conflict not only complex and multifaceted in its ramifications and consequences but also immediate and existential. Indeed, authors who reach this level of tragedy tend to satisfy audiences in this regard. No one would argue that Sophocles' *Oedipus the King*, Shakespeare's *Hamlet*, or Kleist's *Penthesilea* lack the fullness of character, the subtlety and complexity, the irresolvable questions and inevitability of suffering, in short, the mystery and awe we associate with tragedy. Allegory is a potential danger but in no way a necessary consequence of Hegelian tragedy.

Finally, the claim has been made that Hegel's theory applies to only a handful of plays. Hegel's typology of tragedy, brilliant though it is, appears to exclude all but a dozen or so world tragedies. The true Hegelian may want to assert "so much the worse for the plays," and indeed she would be right in arguing that Hegel's typology, normative as it is, cannot be refuted by individual dramatic texts. Just because a work is called a tragedy does not mean that it is a tragedy or deserves to be called one. Consensus and usage are for Hegel no grounds for legitimation. Nonetheless, self-sacrifice and stubbornness, modified versions of Hegelian collision if you will, suggest that other types of tragedy exist, even if they fail to reach the heights of the Hegelian model.

Note

All references to Hegel are to his collected works (indicated by volume number and page number). Most of the passages stem from the *Aesthetics*. In those instances I have also given page numbers to the Knox translation, prefaced by the letter A.

References and Further Reading

Bradley, A. C. (1903–4). "Hegel's Theory of Tragedy." *Hibbert Journal* 2, 662–80. Reprinted in *Oxford Lectures on Poetry*. London: Macmillan, 1909, 69–95. Presents an original theory of tragedy and remains one of the best introductions to Hegel's theory.

Bremer, Dieter. (1986). "Hegel und Aischylos" [Hegel and Aeschylus]. In *Welt und Wirkung von Hegels Ästhetik*, ed. Annemarie Gethmann-Siefert and Otto Pöggeler. Bonn: Bouvier, 225–44. Argues that Hegel's theory is most strongly influenced by Aeschylus' *Oresteia*, the model of Greek tragedy as reconciliation: it alone survives as the complete articulation of what all Greek tragedy ultimately included, a final or reconciliatory moment.

Bungay, Stephen. (1984). *Beauty and Truth: A Study of Hegel's Aesthetics*. Oxford: Oxford University Press. A comprehensive evaluation and critique of Hegel's aesthetics, which includes a discussion of Hegel's theory of tragedy (165–78).

Donougho, Martin. (1989). "The Woman in White: On the Reception of Hegel's *Antigone*." *The Owl of Minerva* 21, 65–89. An account of the reception of Hegel's reading of *Antigone*, which forms the core of Hegel's view of tragedy.

Finlayson, J. G. (1999). "Conflict and Reconciliation in Hegel's Theory of the Tragic." *Journal of the History of Philosophy* 37, 493–520. Notes similarities between Aristotle and Hegel on tragic action and seeks to distinguish two forms of reconciliation, only one of which is tragic.

Fritz, Kurt von. (1962). "Tragische Schuld und poetische Gerechtigkeit in der griechischen Tragödie" [Tragic guilt and poetic justice in Greek tragedy]. In *Antike und moderne Tragödie*. Berlin: Walter de Gruyter, 1–112. A discussion of tragic guilt, which includes an insightful commentary on *hamartia* (3–14) and an analysis of Hegel (81–100).

Goethe, Johann Wolfgang. (1986). "On Interpreting Aristotle's *Poetics*." In *Essays on Art and Literature*, trans. Ellen and Ernest H. von Nardroff, ed. John Gearey. Vol. 3 of *Goethe's Collected Works*, ed. Victor Lange, Eric Blackall, and Cyrus Hamlin. 12 vols. New York: Suhrkamp, 197–9. Elevates, with Hegel, the moment of reconciliation in tragedy.

Hegel, G. W. F. (1975). *Aesthetics: Lectures on Fine Arts*, trans. T. M. Knox, 2 vols. Oxford: Clarendon Press. The standard English translation of Hegel's *Aesthetics*, which is based on the Hotho edition.

Hegel, G. W. F. (1978). *Werke in zwanzig Bänden* [Works in twenty volumes], ed. Eva Moldenhauer and Karl Markus Michel. Frankfurt: Suhrkamp. The most accessible edition of Hegel's collected works, containing in volumes 13, 14, and 15 the Hotho edition of the *Aesthetics*. Although other editions of the *Aesthetics* are available in German, they are restricted to the student transcriptions of single lectures. The Hotho edition, though filtered through Hotho's own thinking, is the most comprehensive edition.

Hösle, Vittorio. (1984). *Die Vollendung der Tragödie im Spätwerk des Sophokles: Asthetisch-historische Bemerkungen zur Struktur der attischen Tragödie*. [The culmination of tragedy in the late work of Sophocles: aesthetic-historical comments on the structure of Attic tragedy]. Stuttgart–Bad Cannstatt: Frommann-Holzboog. A fascinating account of Greek literature and drama, partly influenced by Hegel.

Houlgate, Stephen. (1986). *Hegel, Nietzsche, and the Criticism of Metaphysics*. Cambridge: Cambridge University Press. Culminates in a comparison and evaluation of Hegel and Nietzsche on tragedy (182–220).

Jaspers, Karl. (1952). *Tragedy is Not Enough*, trans. Harald A. T. Reiche, Harry T. Moore, and Karl W. Deutsch. Boston: Beacon. Justly argues that Hegel renders tragedy overly harmonic (79), yet recognizes the validity of the Hegelian definition of tragedy as collision (57, 95), and skillfully deflates the anti-Hegelian view that there is nothing but tragedy and within tragedy nothing but ambiguity and despair (80–7, 97–101).

Kaufmann, Walter. (1971). "Hegel's Ideas about Tragedy." In *New Studies in Hegel's Philosophy*, ed. Warren E. Steinkraus. New York: Holt, 201–20. A useful introduction to Hegel's theory, with a positive assessment of its applicability to dramatic works.

Marcuse, Ludwig. (1923). *Die Welt der Tragödie* [The world of tragedy]. Berlin: Schneider. A classic modern account of tragedy as commensurate with unsublated suffering.

Moss, Leonard. (1969–70). "The unrecognized influence of Hegel's theory of tragedy." *Journal of Aesthetics and Art Criticism* 28, 91–7. A fascinating study of Hegel's influence, even on those who are critical of Hegel.

Paolucci, Anne and Paolucci, Henry, eds. (1962). *Hegel on Tragedy*. New York: Doubleday. Gathers into one volume Hegel's various comments on tragedy.

Pöggeler, Otto. (1964). "Hegel und die griechische Tragödie" [Hegel and Greek tragedy]. In *Heidelberger Hegel-Tage 1962*, ed. Hans-Georg Gadamer. Bonn: Bouvier, 285–305. Raises the question whether Hegel's optimistic worldview is ultimately compatible with tragedy.

Roche, Mark William. (1998). *Tragedy and Comedy: A Systematic Study and a Critique of Hegel*. Albany: State University of New York Press, 1998. A comprehensive analysis, evaluation, and development of Hegel's theories of tragedy and comedy, with illustrations also from modern drama.

Szondi, Peter. (1974). "Hegels Lehre von der Dichtung" [Hegel's teachings on poetry]. In *Poetik und Geschichtsphilosophie* [Poetry and historical philosophy], ed. Senta Metz and Hans-Hagen Hildebrandt. Frankfurt: Suhrkamp, 267–511. Very brief on tragedy, but otherwise a superb introduction to Hegel's *Aesthetics*.

Volkelt, Johannes Immanuel. (1897). *Ästhetik des Tragischen* [Aesthetics of the tragic]. Munich: Beck. Criticizes Hegel with the argument that tragedy portrays particular individuals, not metaphysical ideas.

5

Nietzsche and Tragedy

James I. Porter

Friedrich Nietzsche (1844–1900) gave new life to the modern reception of tragedy, especially in its ancient Greek form. Thanks to Nietzsche, tragedy not only rose to prominence as a supreme literary and cultural achievement. At the same time tragedy also became a clarion call for modernism and a benchmark by which to measure the claims and aspirations of the modern world against the classical past. Indeed, henceforth world history and worldviews could be conceived in terms of literary genres, with tragedy occupying pride of place.

Nietzsche coined the term *tragic age*, and he left behind innumerable suggestions, which are really just provocations, about extending the moniker from ancient Greece to modern Europe. In a word, with Nietzsche *tragedy* became a powerful label, one that could be applied to cultures, mentalities, historical moments, and sweeping historical patterns. Tragedy likewise came to be applied to aspects of Nietzsche's own intellectual achievements, and at times to the coherence and tenor of his thinking as a whole. But by the same token, because Nietzsche's thought was as suggestive and provocative as it was, in his wake the very idea of tragedy became something of a challenge and a puzzle. Nietzsche bequeathed to posterity not a clear view of tragedy but a series of urgent problems and questions: Did the Greeks experience a tragic age? Can modernity experience tragedy again and attain the vanished heights of the classical period? Is there such a thing as a tragic view of the world, and is that view valid today? Is Nietzsche himself possibly a tragic thinker? If it is difficult to separate out the fascinations with tragedy from the uncertain boundaries of the concept, Nietzsche is not entirely to blame, but neither can he be lightly exempted from the charge.

Nietzsche's influence was both vast and lasting. It is doubtful that thinkers as diverse as Miguel de Unamuno, Karl Jaspers, and Raymond Williams would have given tragedy the central importance they did were it not for Nietzsche and his clamoring reception. This is not to say that Nietzsche directly influenced how all who came after him chose to read the idea and phenomenon of tragedy, but rather that he made it difficult for anyone not to think of these things whenever the topic of modern life was on the table. Hegel may have located tragedy within the evolution of the human spirit as one of its key transitory stages. But it was Nietzsche who made tragedy into a touchstone of the future, and consequently of paramount importance for the present, a thing not only born once and then rendered *passé* and of antiquarian interest, but a form, less of art than of *experience*, that had once struggled to come to life and that was now on the verge of being born again – not least due to the promising successes of the new total art form, or *Gesamtkunstwerk*, of Wagnerian opera. Tragedy was no longer a dry article of history but a sign of possibilities hitherto untapped. It was a sign and symbol of life.

While it was a significant element of historical consciousness, tragedy for Nietzsche thus had the potential to transcend history, and so, too (as the example of Wagner suggested), the generic boundaries of the art form. With Nietzsche tragedy suddenly became existentially relevant, a kind of primordial experience that brought one back not only to the depths of the human heart but to the roots of human history and human existence. The challenge of this conception was that to be incapable of tragedy was to be incapable of being fully human. Tragedy was not simply permitted again: it was imperative, to be ignored at one's peril.

It is no small paradox that tragedy, that harbinger of disaster and grim fatality, should be associated with human flourishing and abundance and with hopes for cultural renewal. But this, too, is part of the Nietzschean inheritance, and, indeed, its most distinctive feature. Likewise, if tragedy points to the future, it is nonetheless in the classical roots of the Western tradition that one must go to seek tragedy in its purest and most natural form. It is there one can trace the sources of the tragic essence, of both tragic writing and tragic performances on the one hand and of the very idea of tragedy on the other – what is frequently referred to, in an alluring if vague way, as *the tragic* and sometimes as *the tragic vision*. In one respect, at least, Nietzsche's thinking about tragedy is entirely conventional: it merely rephrases a long standing tradition that looked to an archetypal Greece whenever tragedy came to mind. What is novel about Nietzsche's thinking on the subject is his reversal of this commonplace gesture. Tragedy for Nietzsche is the single pivot around which antiquity, indeed world history, turns: everything leads up to its development, gradually and over millennia, from Asia to Europe, and then just as slowly and inexorably culture falls off from this unparalleled height of achievement. And because tragedy occupies so central a place in Nietzsche's view of the classical world, it is also the case that in Nietzsche's eyes the modern world must define itself in relation to tragedy.

To be sure, Nietzsche's reading of tragedy would not have resonated the way it did had he not been capitalizing on a peculiarly modern set of desires and fears, although specifying what these were would be a study unto itself (the acceleration of modern life, feelings of cultural crisis or cultural exhaustion, a reaction to materialism, a foundering spirituality, and the need to lay claim to a legitimating and authoritative past are all contributing factors). Classics had long been a conduit and a symptom of these worries, at least in Europe. Nietzsche's peculiar contribution lay in his revealing a dimension of classical culture, especially in one of its most revered relics, that was literally hidden by its obviousness: namely, its turbulent, ritualized violence. In this way Nietzsche opened the floodgates of Greek tragedy, and so too of classical antiquity, unleashing an energy that has yet to have completely dissipated. In his wake, tragedy and the tragic became points of ferment across an array of inquiries – in philosophy, aesthetics, and literary criticism generally, and in the study of classical antiquity in several domains, but above all in myth, ritual, and anthropology. Hellenism and primitivism were among the primary beneficiaries of this trend: the cult of the early Greek past and the cult of the cultic itself (most notably J. G. Frazer's *The Golden Bough* of 1890 and the work of the so-called Cambridge Ritualists, who sought to trace the origins of tragedy in myth and ritual). And Nietzsche was himself a beneficiary of this trend, as his name became attached to a long line of developments that he could now be held responsible for having spawned. Whether he would have approved of these developments is an open question. Indeed, whether Nietzsche's view of human life or his philosophy are fundamentally tragic, like that of the Greek Presocratics whom he frequently adored, is likewise open to question. As with other aspects of his philosophy, it is probably safe to say that Nietzsche stimulated more opinions than he ever would have shared. His writing was suggestive, if nothing else.

The Birth of Tragedy and Nietzsche's *Curriculum Vitae*

The writing that contains Nietzsche's most concentrated reflections on tragedy is *The Birth of Tragedy*. First published in 1872 as *The Birth of Tragedy out of the Spirit of Music* when he was 27, the book was republished in 1886 as *The Birth of Tragedy, or, Hellenism and Pessimism*, with a new preface that revived the earlier controversy and in ways sought to palliate it as well. It is a labyrinthine and mystifying work, and impossible to classify. Only a classical scholar could have written it, but no scholar of the classics would have dared to sign his name to such a book. Presented as an inspired essay, lacking notes and apparatuses of any kind, and overtly hostile to scientific method and to classical philology in particular, *The Birth of Tragedy* was bound to cause a sensation. Speculative in the extreme, the work contained a good deal of modern mythmaking – a fact that ought to be a clue to some of its larger purposes. Nor was Nietzsche unaware of this problem. When one classical scholar later asked him for a bit of "proof, just a single piece of evidence, that in reality the strange images on the *skênê* [stage] were mirrored back from the magical dream of the ecstatic Dionysian chorus," Nietzsche soberly replied, as he only could, "Just how, then, should the evidence approximately read? . . . Now the honorable reader demands that the whole problem should be disposed of with an attestation, probably out of the mouth of Apollo himself: or would a passage from Athenaeus do just as well?" (letter to Rohde, 4 August 1871). Whatever else Nietzsche may have been trying to do with *The Birth of Tragedy*, he was surely guided by a certain perversity of mind. "Oh, it is wicked and offensive! Read it furtively in your closet," he confided to his friend Gustav Krug in December of 1871 while the book was at the publisher's waiting to be printed. But neither was this the first sign of Nietzsche's desire to shock his readers, or of his willingness to put his career, or at least his professional image, on the line in the process.

So eventful was *The Birth of Tragedy* to Nietzsche's life that his profile and identity as a thinker and a cultural force could not help but be bound up with his views on tragedy, and consequently with the way he would be remembered, whether in terms of his career (which at least outwardly plots a course from old-fashioned philology to radical philosophy) or in terms of his thinking, given the place – though not quite centrality – of tragedy in his thought. Conventionally, *The Birth of Tragedy* is seen as occupying an uncomfortable and transitional middle ground in Nietzsche's development: for all its rebelliousness, the work is too metaphysical, too earnest, and too beholden to modern German myths of cultural renewal to typify the later free-spirited thinker. But there is something wrong with this way of characterizing the *curriculum vitae* of Nietzsche's thought.

For one thing, Nietzsche's writing during his academic period is every bit as radical – as daring, unsettling, subversive, and self-subverting – as it is at any other time in his productive life. Like the later productions, his writings up to and including *The Birth of Tragedy* engage a reader in the perils of establishing safe and final meanings, and they render Nietzsche less the producer than the *occasion* of those meanings. At the same time, Nietzsche is unafraid to be contaminated by the objects of his critique. As a result, Nietzsche is a most unreliable witness to his own purported meanings. His interest is first and foremost in the *staging* of meaning and its perplexities. As a rule, his writings provide a sampling, and a hyperbolizing, of culturally available assumptions and counter-assumptions, at times extrapolated into mind-spinning hypotheticals intended to make vivid the psychology, and above all the frequent illogic, of everyday belief ("What would follow if reality really looked like this or that?"). The ultimate object of Nietzsche's writings, both early and late, is thus not abstract philosophical truths, but the all-too-human nature of humanity and its endlessly marvelous and criticizable dissonances. "If we could imagine dissonance become man – and what else is man?," Nietzsche asks (*The Birth of Tragedy* §25; trans. Kaufmann), posing a hypothetical that is perhaps the hardest of all to conceive and imagine. *The Birth of Tragedy* typifies Nietzsche's presentational styles, both early and late, not least because it is more a processual object than a stable text: its controversial qualities originate from within itself. At the limit, it is literally an incredible work, one that sets up a long list of improbabilities and then dares us to believe in them.

Without going into all of the work's dimensions, we can trace some of the essentials of Nietzsche's views of tragedy in one of the central motifs of *The Birth of Tragedy*, which doubles as its main methodological problem, namely the way it accounts for the mere apprehension of the various truths it names. The concepts in question here are three: intuition, appearances, and imagination. But before that, it will be useful to sketch out the general outlines of Nietzsche's first book, and in particular its surface plot.

At the heart of *The Birth of Tragedy* lies the opposition between the two Greek gods, Apollo and Dionysus, who in turn stand for two antagonistic aesthetic principles that are nonetheless complementary and equally vital to the production of the highest art. Apollo and his abstraction the Apollonian represent the realm of clear and luminous appearances, plastic images, dreams, harmless deception, and traits that are typically Hellenic and classical, at least to the modern imagination (simplicity, harmony, cheerfulness, tranquility, and so on), while Dionysus and the Dionysian represent hidden metaphysical depths, disturbing realities, intoxication, music, and traits that are typically exotic and therefore unclassical (ecstasy, disorderliness, dance, orgy). The history of Greek art is the history of the relation between these two principles. At its origins Greek art is naïve and Apollonian, as in the epic world of Homer. All surface, Apollonian art is blissfully ignorant of any dimensions of reality beyond the immediately visible. Instead, it is rapt by objective images (appearances) that are as vivid and certain as marble. Lyric poetry in Homer's wake marks a heightening of the powers of music and a loss of individuality: it is the heartfelt cry of Dionysian passions that echo the depths of the world's soul.

At its peak, the Dionysian nearly gains the upper hand and obliges the Apollonian to speak its own truths. As from behind a screen, another reality is revealed to the aesthetic spectator, who is henceforth the privileged focus of artistic effect, but no longer its perceived cause. The culmination of this process is the rapid flowering of Greek tragedy, first with Aeschylus and then Sophocles, in which music and dance, song and speech, and spectacle are magnificently coordinated in a first anticipation of the Wagnerian total work of art. But just as rapidly a decline sets in during the last third of the fifth century BCE, with the rise of dialectic (Socratic–Platonic philosophy) and its tragic equivalent in Euripidean theater. Tragedy is debased, brought down to the level of the banal and the everyday, and no longer spiritually significant. Music and spectacle give way to the calculations of garrulous speech, while the balance between quiet and ecstasy gives way to a violent oscillation between the twin excesses of rationality and momentary passion. As Apollonianism is replaced by Socratism (science), Dionysianism retreats into the mystery cults. Both gods await a rebirth in a world that is now rendered thoroughly Alexandrian and unclassical, which is to say degenerate, epigonal, and modern.

So much for the overall plot of Nietzsche's first book. If this was all *The Birth of Tragedy* contained, it would have been an interesting work but not an original or remarkable one. The modern German tradition of Hellenism alone supplied all the materials one needed to develop this nostalgic reading of Greek tragedy and classical culture (Baeumer 1976; Silk and Stern 1981; Behler 1986; Henrichs 1986; Courtine 1993; Porter 2000b, chs. 4 and 5). However, on this rather conventional story about Greece Nietzsche overlays an unconventional metaphysical scheme and a daring epistemology. These new elements raise the stakes of his project considerably, but they also put a heavy strain on its coherence.

Aesthetic Intuitions

The Birth of Tragedy opens with a remarkable assertion: "We shall have gained much for the science of aesthetics, once we perceive not merely by logical inference, but with the immediate certainty of vision [*zur unmittelbaren Sicherheit der Anschauung*], that the continuous development of art is bound up with the *Apollonian* and *Dionysian* duality." One of the problems with this claim is that the immediacy it awards to the modern mind is in turn "borrowed" from the Greeks: "The terms Dionysian and Apollonian we borrow from the Greeks, who disclose to the discerning mind the profound mysteries of their view of art, not, to be sure, in concepts, but in the intensely clear figures of their gods," which is to say, once again, through direct intuition, and not logic. Through a borrowed distinction, borrowed names, and a borrowed perception we are to attain a vision of the Greek world that is evidently illusion-free and unmediated.

This dilemma, or rather glaring improbability, is directly paralleled by the way Nietzsche frames the metaphysics of *The Birth of Tragedy*, which both puts on offer and withdraws the possibility of an immediate intuition of reality. And this in turn sets up the conditions for tragedy, because tragedy embodies this kind of direct and shocking encounter with the real, the meaning of which forever eludes one's grasp. The problem can be simply stated. Being (reality, truth, "the ground of our being," "the eternally suffering and contradictory primal unity," *das Ur-Eine*, or the One Will) is seemingly accessible in brief, unmediated glimpses (tragic knowledge is predicated on this possibility), but in point of fact no glimpse of reality can be had except through the filtering and distortive agency of appearances. Not even the so-called "primal unity," that curious entity postulated by Nietzsche and seemingly invented *ad hoc* as a grotesque calque on the (already bizarre) Schopenhauerian Will, can have an immediate intuition of itself. Indeed, appearances just are the illusions by means of which the primal unity finds a numbing joy and pleasure and so heals its pains, although what the exact nature of these pains or their redemption is Nietzsche nowhere clarifies.

The duality is in ways Kantian, with Apollo representing the warm and familiar realm of phenomenal appearances and Dionysus representing the chilly and inaccessible reality of things in themselves. But it is also Schopenhauerian, with Apollo standing for the principle of individuation, the instrument by which the metaphysical Will (represented by Dionysus) that lies at the bottom of all things acts out its contradictory urges to enter the world of appearances even as it struggles agonizingly, but not inexplicably, to return to its original primordial state of unity and quiescence. Apollo placates the self-tormenting Will, but the Will needs Apollo to act out its urges. This is their basic collaborative pact, which gives rise not only to sweet dreams but to art and culture, and above all to tragedy, the culminating form of both.

Lodging contradiction in reality in this way has the advantage at least of making reality in a sense tragic. Meanwhile, tragedy is the most intense experience of metaphysics one can have, inasmuch as the conditions for simultaneous pain and pleasure are in tragedy intensified to the greatest bearable limit. Approximating to a metaphysical experience, tragedy is painful and pleasurable at once – painful because it hurts simply to touch ground, as it were, without the protections of appearance, pleasurable because it puts us into communication with our original reality. And yet, while tragedy "forces" a recognition of the reality that Being dwells in (§7), there is nothing tragic about the final result, because pain, whether tragic or primordial, is converted into pleasure ("aesthetically justified"), seemingly in its very apprehension. Tragic pleasure is for this reason comparable to the "primordial joy experienced even in pain," which in turn resembles "the joyous sensation of dissonance in music" (§24). As a consequence, experiencing metaphysical reality through tragedy is in the last analysis profoundly life-affirming.

Thus, so far from being tragic, Nietzsche's view of life is, on the contrary, one of tragedy averted. Reality's ongoing redemption in appearances saves the metaphysics of *The Birth of Tragedy* from collapsing into unbridled pessimism. In this way tragedy no longer has to be the sign of nihilism and of oppressive fatalism (as it was, for instance, in Schopenhauer). Rather, it is the promise of aesthetic fullness and of a complex joy – even ecstasy – that is tinged (and so, too, heightened) with pain and loss. Pain and suffering are never a reason for despair: instead they are a motive for their own conversion into pleasure. But Nietzsche can arrive at this cheery conclusion only by ensuring that his account is at bottom a perceptual one and grounded in lies and illusions: metaphysical pain, to be felt, has to appear. In this way, pain is not only "obliterated by lies [*hinweggelogen*] from the features of nature" (§16), it can never quite get off the ground. The significance of this perceptual bias emerges in Nietzsche's portrayal of the way tragedy evolved, with its emphasis on the spectator (see below).

To this metaphysical scheme Nietzsche adds a psychological scheme to help map out the metaphysical undertow of tragedy and to render it anthropologically plausible – a much needed step, given the blatant anthropomorphism of *The Birth of Tragedy*'s metaphysics, with its thrashing and restless Will yearning for aesthetic redemption. Dreams and music, the provinces of Apollo and Dionysus respectively (so Nietzsche, but with little ancient warrant), short-circuit ordinary consciousness and put the mind "directly" (intuitively) in touch with reality, at once revealing reality's hurtful pains and protecting us from them. And yet, as we saw, the immediate intuition into metaphysical truth seems a priori excluded on this picture. Indeed, all that seems immediate is the spontaneous urgency of the process being described, which conflates art and nature at every turn. The Primordial One suffers in us and through us, while what we suffer is its pain, not our own. Not even the nihilistic core of tragic knowledge – knowledge that "what is best of all is utterly beyond your reach: not to be born, not to *be*, to be *nothing*. But the second best for you is – to die soon" (§3) – can be immediately apprehended: it must pass through an aestheticizing filter. (Here, truth is put into the mouth of a mythical being, a "fictitious natural being" [§7], Silenus.) It is for this reason that the aesthetics of *The Birth of Tragedy* can be aptly called an "artists' metaphysics" (as in the preface from 1886), which is also why tragedy is at bottom a metaphysical experience – or, rather, an experience of metaphysics. Tragedy shows us the illusion that we are.

Is our experience of reality direct and unmediated, or is it not rather our access to *illusion* that is direct and immediate? Nietzsche's language in places strongly suggests the latter. Not even the Primordial Being seems to have direct access to itself, as we saw. It is a fair question whether metaphysical pain is ever experienced in itself, or whether all that is ever experienced of metaphysical pain is its appearance as such. By the same token, it is unclear whether reality consists in the experience of pain or in its evasion, and finally whether this latter isn't better called a "deception" (§21; see "obliterated by lies" in §16, quoted earlier). Metaphysics, after all, confronts us in the end not with metaphysical pain but with "the metaphysical comfort . . . that life is at the bottom of things, despite all the changes of appearances, indestructibly powerful and pleasurable" (§7; cf. §8). This comfort is interestingly propositional.

Immediacy of perception, straining credulity by itself, is, moreover, something that Nietzsche's earlier and contemporary writings explicitly reject on epistemological and psychological grounds, putting in its place *the illusion of immediacy* and of a totalizing perception (see his inaugural university lecture, "Homer and Classical Philology," 1869 = *KGW* 2.1: 247–69, with Porter 2000b, 62-81). Is Nietzsche now, or rather again, commending an illusion? If he is, then his stance is suspect, and the surface meaning of *The Birth of Tragedy* has to be seen in an entirely different light. The chief difficulty with the scheme of this book is that the whole of it seems to be the product either of an illusion or a dream, or both. The metaphysical principles involved are as mythical as the gods that represent them – a point made abundantly clear by Nietzsche in his essay "On Schopenhauer" (1867/8 = *BAW* 3: 352–61, with Porter 2000a, 57–73). And where does our knowledge of these latter gods come from? It is plainly mediated, "borrowed from the Greeks," as we've seen. But then where did the Greeks come across this knowledge? Nietzsche's answer, which appears on the first page, is unequivocal: "It was in dreams, says Lucretius, that the glorious divine figures [of Apollo and Dionysus] first appeared to the souls of men; in dreams the great shaper beheld the splendid bodies of superhuman [*übermenschlichen*] beings" – whence "the intensely clear figures of their gods" (§1).

Is Nietzsche's work possibly *Lucretian*? If so, the Schopenhauerianism of that work stands in need of recasting (Schopenhauer was an uncompromising critic of atomism.) However we decide the issue, we are still left with the puzzling suggestion that the Greeks *dreamt up* their gods, and that consequently we – Nietzsche's generation and our own – are the inheritors of those dreams. It may be that "in our dreams we delight in the immediate understanding of figures; all forms speak to us; there is nothing unimportant or superfluous" (§1). But this is the immediacy experienced by the mad and the deluded. How illusory is our grasp of the antique past if it comes to us channeled through dreams? The risk here is not only that dreams distort some original reality, but that they invent it to begin with.

That they do is a possibility contemplated in a draft of a text that never found its way into the final draft of *The Birth of Tragedy*, in which Nietzsche confesses that delusions are a necessary condition of life, and

> that this whole process [namely, of the Will and its miseries and actions] is only our necessary form of appearance and thus utterly lacking in any metaphysical reality... If above I dared to speak of Genius and appearance, as if I had access to a knowledge surpassing those limits, and as if I were able to look out from the pure, great eye of the world [*Weltauge*], let me explain after the fact that I don't believe that I have stepped beyond the anthropomorphic circle with that figurative language. *But who could endure existence without such mystical possibilities?* (14:541 = *KGW* 3.5.2:1060–1; emphasis added)

A parallel insight leads to Nietzsche's exposure of Greek religion, where he holds that the appearance of each of the gods, be they Olympian or pre-Olympian, is the work of Apollo, who "rules over the beautiful illusion of the inner world of fantasy" (*The Birth of Tragedy* §1), which is to say the work of Greek fantasy itself. Nor is Dionysus with his metaphysical underworld exempt from this retroactive invention:

> The divine world of beauty [namely, of Apollo] produces the chthonic divinities [viz., the "horrible" pre-Olympian dark underworld gods and "then Dionysus"] as its own supplement. These latter, more formless in themselves [*an sich*] and closer to the Concept, increasingly gain the upper hand and [then] cause the whole Olympian world to vanish together with the heroes, as symbols of their [sc., the chthonic gods' own] secrets. (*Encyclopedia of Classical Philology*, *KGW* 2.3:415 n. 37; cf. 413)

In this light, the Dionysian may turn out to be not the index of some vaguely horrific realm of metaphysical truth lying beyond our ken but just a bad dream – the dream-work of Apollo ("the *dream-world* of a Dionysian intoxication," §14), or, what is worse, an idealization of the "horrible oppressiveness" of waking reality itself, that truest of all horrors, made metaphysically attractive. More horrible than any metaphysical horrors, in other words, is the *horror vacui*, the prospect of a world shorn of any metaphysical supplement and lacking any metaphysical justification. Beauty in that case would be how we confront or rather evade this void, by filling the void of metaphysics *with (the mere prospect of) metaphysics itself,* and then by converting that image into a reason for pleasure. "Metaphysical comfort" is on this approach simply the comfort of having a metaphysics: it is the ultimate aesthetic redemption of reality and daily life. *The Birth of Tragedy* is in this sense a story about the aestheticization of reality. It describes the historical process by which art felt its way into metaphysics, and it outlines the conditions of the possible reemergence of this high point in the history of appearances, in the hope that all human endeavor will acknowledge itself as the art, and the art of metaphysics, that it is.

The Dionysian, in other words, risks being part of a fantasy-construct, much like the veil (of *mâyâ?*) painted by Parrhasius so convincingly that it seemed to cover a "real" painting, when all it concealed was the fact that there was nothing to conceal. Such is "the mysterious background" of tragedy (§24, a passage that directly echoes this anecdote from Pliny). Just when this elaborate construct first originated is a distinctly harder question to answer. One clue, which we've come across already, attributes this construction to the Greeks, and the point is reinforced a bit later on: "It was in order to be able to live that the Greeks had to create these gods [sc., the Olympians, but also, *a fortiori*, their Titanic and Chthonic counterparts] from a most profound need" (§3). The Greeks here retain their exemplary function familiar from Winckelmann and company. Only the state they model is not one of naïve moral perfection but of profound and all-too-human self-deception and disavowal (see also *On the Genealogy of Morals*, Second Essay, §§19–20, 23). Another possibility, which is not ruled out by the first, is that some or much of this construction is of modern origin, a modern myth about ancient myths. Either way, the argument of *The Birth of Tragedy* can no longer be taken at face value. The implications of this turn can be further traced in the finer details of Nietzsche's conception of the tragic phenomenon in its Greek form.

Tragedy, the Tragic, and the Dionysian

One of Nietzsche's signal innovations in his construction of the tragic is that he views tragedy above all from the perspective of its beholder, a fact that is entirely in keeping with the artists' metaphysics of that work. Tragedy is first and foremost an aesthetic phenomenon, which means that it is grounded in perceptual experience, but also at a remove from its objects. Nietzsche's model is constructed not from the viewpoint of the tragic hero but rather from that of the observer: what matters is not the experience of Oedipus, say, but that of the audience coming close to, but never really touching, his experience. It is thus a model not of any immediacy of experience, but of mediating distance and of that distance's sublimation in the very experience of immediacy.

For these reasons, Nietzsche's theory stands in contrast to its nineteenth-century predecessors in the German idealist tradition, such as those of Schelling, Hegel, Vischer, and Schopenhauer. These latter theories one could call essentializing, inasmuch as they reify the tragic in an objective event, or rather archi-Event, that takes place with all the immediacy of a schoolbook lesson. Thus for the early Hegel

> tragedy consists in the fact that the moral nature separates from itself its inorganic nature and opposes this to itself in the form of Fate, lest it get entangled with this latter; and it achieves a reconciliation with Fate through the recognition of the same in the struggle [*Kampf*] with divine nature, which is the unity of both moral and inorganic nature. (Hegel, *Über die wissenschaftlichen Behandlungsarten des Naturrechts*, 1802–3, cited in Szondi 1964: 20)

Schelling's definition from the same year breathes in the same atmosphere of romantic idealism, although the modern notion of the tragic owes its existence to still earlier writings by Schiller and Schelling: "The essence of tragedy is an actual conflict between the freedom of the subject and objective necessity, which ends...in a complete [and mutual] indifference" (cited in Szondi 1964, 15; cf. ibid., 13; Schiller [1791–2] 1993; Schiller [1790–2] 2003; Courtine 1993).

The focus in these philosophies is the tragic action unfolding on the stage, emblematic of a world stage upon which larger-than-life metaphysical forces play themselves out, recklessly, and seemingly indifferent to the world. These forces impress themselves on the tragic form, but they do so from without, not from within: tragedy models itself on an action that can in principle take place without the benefit of an audience. The ultimate referent of tragedy, the Tragic or the Tragic Idea, shines translucently through the aesthetic performance, effacing it. Thus, a tragic figure like Oedipus is not interesting as an actor on the stage repeating a drama for a public: he is an idealist Subject moving and acting in the abstract landscape of a timeless metaphysical reality. Worse still, the peculiars of the tragic action in which Oedipus is enmeshed are not even interesting in their own right. Tragic actions are effectively interchangeable, and so too dispensable. As a result, we can say that in German idealism there are no tragedies, but only a singular Tragedy of which individual plays (optimally, Greek) are the pale reflection and a mere mnemonic, lacking any sense of history or phenomenology, and ultimately uninteresting as aesthetic phenomena.

Not so in Nietzsche, for whom the structure, circumstances, and the psychology of the tragic performance are everything. Nietzsche's theory of tragedy is, to be sure, permeated by metaphysics. But it is also historically located in a then and now, and it is a fundamentally theatrical theory, in the sense that it is about the staging, at specific historical conjunctures, of metaphysical appearances, or rather of the appearance of metaphysics itself through ritual, art, and drama. Nietzsche's *Birth of Tragedy* thus offers something like an *affective* history of metaphysical consciousness, one of its aims being to demonstrate how metaphysics just is a psychological phenomenon, linked as it is to pleasure, pain, and disavowed self-consciousness, as we saw. But in one significant respect, Nietzsche's theory does resemble that of his landsmen. For it too claims to work out an allegory of reconciliation according to which

> not only is the union between man and man reaffirmed, but nature which has become alienated, hostile, or subjugated, celebrates once more her reconciliation with her lost son, man...Now, with the gospel of universal harmony, each one feels himself not only united, reconciled, and fused with his neighbor, but as one with him, as if the veil of *mâyâ* had been torn aside and were now merely fluttering in tatters before the mysterious primordial unity. (§1)

But two characteristics set Nietzsche's theory apart from its predecessors. The tragic reconciliation may be of the highest metaphysical order, in theory transcending the individual who has become the "work of art" of the Will and so a "Dionysian world-artist." Nevertheless, this reconciliation is phenomenologically available to the individual and meaningless without him. Second, the metaphysical event remains *staged* even in its culmination, as an object for viewing and consumption. The veil of *mâyâ*, of Illusion and Appearances, may be torn aside, but it remains firmly in place, "fluttering in tatters before the mysterious primordial unity," like a curtain in a theater.

These two characteristics are actually one and the same: tragic artistry is located in the experience of the individual, but that experience is of a phenomenon in which the categories of artist, subject, and spectator coalesce. There is an immediacy to the experience, which is rooted in the body and physiology of a subject. But the experience is, structurally speaking, that of a visual perception, not of a physical sensation, which gives the lie to the object of the experience, which is supposed to entail the dissolution of subject and object in a blinding immediacy, a moment of ecstatic union, and a loss of individuation. That is, the tragic experience must necessarily be that of an *individual*, even if it involves the momentary hallucination of her no longer being one.

Spectatorship is for this reason of the essence for Nietzsche. It is the point of departure in *The Birth of Tragedy* and the way it ends. Qualifying the effacement through rapt absorption of the self in the visionary world that it beholds is the fact that the spectacle of the tragic always comes framed, whether by the horizon of a dream, the circle of a chorus, the context of a ritual, or the *skênê* of the stage (these are formally indistinguishable Nietzsche, and they interpenetrate as well): "The form of the Greek theater recalls a lonely valley in the mountains: the architecture of the scene appears like a luminous cloud formation that the Bacchants swarming over the mountains behold from a height – *like the splendid frame in which the image of Dionysus is revealed to them*" (§8; emphasis added). *The Birth of Tragedy* traces the evolution of this revelation, which is to say the gradual manifestation (appearance) of the godhead (Dionysus, the One, representing – but not identical to – the Will, *das Ur-Eine*, the Primordial Unity of Being), effectuated through the ministrations of Apollo over time, from the visions of the lyric poet in the archaic age of Greece to the rise of the satyr chorus, to its transformation into the tragic chorus, and then to the demise of tragedy at the hands of Platonic philosophy. Tragedy thus has the structure of a revelation. But *is* it a revelation?

In point of fact, the revelation is described by Nietzsche as a projection. Consider how membership in the satyr chorus of Dionysian revelers, the original form of tragedy and "the dramatic proto-phenomenon," involves a complex chain of assignments: "the Dionysian reveler sees himself as a satyr, *and as a satyr, in turn, he sees the god*" (§8; emphasis in original). Further, "this process of the tragic chorus [namely, its projective mechanisms] is the *dramatic* proto-phenomenon: to see oneself transformed before one's own eyes and to begin to act as if one had actually entered into another body, another character. This process stands at the beginning of the origin of drama" (§8).[1] At every point along tragedy's evolution this doubling of consciousness is at work. But there is more, for as the revelations of the god intensify, which is to say as the god becomes increasingly present and concrete, so does the degree of consciousness of the tragic viewer, as he stands increasingly removed from the scene of action, observing and delighting in appearances as such, but also watching the surrogates of his now increasingly vicarious experience (the actors and the chorus), which, as we saw, are in fact projections of himself. Ironically, the culmination of these two progressions results in the death of tragedy. This progression can be briefly sketched.

At the beginning of things stand the satyr chorus, who simultaneously comprise the spectators, dancing, as it were, round an empty stage, ecstatically, and projecting a vision of the god: "*Dionysus*, the real stage hero and center of the vision, *was . . . not actually present at first*, in the very oldest period of tragedy; *he was merely imagined as present*" (first emphasis added; last two in original). This is the strictly choral origin of tragedy, which involved dancing and music but no dramatic representation: the god was not permitted to appear except to the mind's eye. "Later the attempt was made to show the god as real to represent the visionary figure together with its transfiguring frame as something visible for every eye – and thus 'drama' in the narrower sense [sc., of "action" and "enactment"] began" (§8). So it happened, on Nietzsche's scheme of things (which in its rudiments may be historically accurate, if we take Aristotle as a witness), that tragedy evolved into a chorus with actors: first there was one, then two, and finally three actors, while the role and power of the chorus, and thus of the tragic form itself, correspondingly dwindled.[2]

The final blow to tragedy comes when Dionysus, "initially absent," finally takes the stage in Euripides' last and posthumously performed play, *Bacchae*, in 406 BCE – indeed, precisely in a play that turns on the contested appearance and the final, vengeful epiphany of the god ("I *am* a god. I was blasphemed by you," *Bacchae* v. 1347; cf. vv. 41–2). It is striking that tragedy should dissolve at the moment when Dionysus, "initially absent," finally claims his rightful due on the tragic stage.

Nietzsche is not falsifying history, but he is being quietly and creatively selective, and so too highly distortive, for the sake of his own plot line. Though you would never know it from *The Birth of Tragedy*, Dionysus did *not* make his first and only appearance on the Greek stage in 406 BCE. Aeschylus is responsible for two (now lost) Dionysiac tetralogies, and at least five other tragedians had composed plays with titles such as *Bacchae*, *Pentheus,* and *Semele*, while the comic stage had itself experienced as many or more sightings of Dionysus since the time of Aeschylus.[3] Euripides was closely following tradition in his own *Bacchae*, and many of the features of his passion play about Dionysus seem to be borrowed from Aeschylus.[4] Why is Nietzsche silent about these known facts? Evidently, Euripides must be shown to have innovated by rationalizing the imaginary devices of tragedy – whence his innovations in the tell-all prologues, his introduction of the *deus ex machina*, his realism, his debasement of tragic speech at the expense of music and in favor of the chatty and pattering language of the everyday. But most of all, Nietzsche says, Euripides flattens out the metaphysical dimensions of tragedy. Unable to make sense of what is no more than a blur to his keen eye, that "enigmatic depth, indeed infinitude" that lurks in the background of prior tragedy, which is to say its intimation of a deeper metaphysics, Euripides puts everything into the foreground and the broad daylight for inspection (§11).[5] Along with the spectator he brings Dionysus onto the stage as well: it is not enough that the god should shine through the masks of tragic heroes (§10): he must literally *appear* and in human form at that ("disguised as a man," *Bacchae* v. 54). Whence his culminating epiphany as a literal *deus ex machina*, which has tragic consequences to those who deny him and to the form of tragedy itself.

Is Euripides' final "glorification of the god" a last-minute confession by the former unbeliever (§12), or is it not rather a sign of the god's declining grip on the Greek imagination that Dionysus must completely submit to appearances in order to be? It is as if the Greeks for Nietzsche no longer could sustain an imaginary connection to the Dionysian: they were obliged to bring Dionysus before their very eyes (and indeed, as a human masked as a god), their powers of projection having been fatally weakened by the diseases of their culture. But if so, then this decline in imagination had to have begun early on. The gradual concretizing of the god's presence defines the earliest evolution of tragedy, as we saw, and there is in fact nothing exceptional about Euripides' dramatic staging of the god. The development is in every way comparable to the puzzle of the metaphysical Will that *needs* appearances, which is to say the realm of degeneracy and derogation vis-à-vis Being, in order to be at all. What is more, far from being a progression that was willfully imposed on Dionysus by Nietzsche, the evolution of the god perfectly matches his original cultic functions. As a god of masks and appearances, of vision and theater (Otto 1960; Henrichs 1993, esp. 17), Dionysus was from the very beginning a perfect avatar of Apollo, indeed, his "supplement" (see p. 73 above).[6]

No sooner does Dionysus erupt into palpable reality, and in fully human form, than he is just as quickly banished again, forced to seek "refuge in the depths of the sea, namely the mystical flood of a secret cult which gradually covered the earth" (§12). Nietzsche has more to say about the postclassical cult of the Dionysian in his various notes and in later writings (some of them published). That cult, drawing as it does on the earlier forms of Dionysianism, with their eschatological fixation on rebirth and salvation in the afterlife and on revealed truth, is none other, it turns out, than *Christianity*. And if Greek tragedy's proximate, but not necessarily final, goal is buried in the latency of the Christian faith – that is, if Greek culture is indeed a preliminary stage of Christian culture – it ought to come as no surprise when Dionysus emerges on the other end as a seeming transfiguration of Christ (a connection already foreshadowed in §4 of *The Birth of Tragedy*, in the analysis of Raphael's devotional painting, *The Transfiguration*). This story about the rise of Christianity out of the spirit of Dionysus may seem something of a stretch at first, but it, too, is a conventional topos in prior German thought. It is one of the ways by which modernity made legible to itself a distant pagan reality (and justified the need to do so).[7] Likewise, the symbolic link between Dionysus, violence, and the exotic, but above all the violence of alienated and vicariated identity, is another characteristic feature of modern German classicism, and yet one more form of "metaphysical comfort." Closely connected to both of these aspects of the Dionysian is the nineteenth-century brand of antisemitic Aryanism that is retrojected onto Greece and organized around Dionysus, and not only in §9 of *The Birth of Tragedy* (Porter 2000b, 274–86). Is Dionysus Greek or

Christian – or is he simply *German?* Whatever else he may be, Nietzsche's Dionysus is symbolic of this perplexity.

Is Nietzsche's Philosophy "Tragic"?

Nietzsche's first and best known book, *The Birth of Tragedy*, was an instant sensation and scandal. How much of an impact its initial reception had on Nietzsche can never be known, but emotional scarring aside (the book nearly cost him his career), it is conceivable that he would have enjoyed none of his later notoriety if he had not made such a spectacular début in 1872. It was perhaps inevitable that Nietzsche should have revisited the idea of tragedy in his subsequent writings, given the radically innovative nature of his views at the time. But opportunism cannot be ruled out as a motivating factor either. The reissue of the book in 1886, with its brash new preface, did as much to stir the ashes of the old controversy as it sought to realign Nietzsche's early and later styles of thought. And although tragedy nowhere receives the same intensity of focus in any of his subsequent writings, it does survive in them as a powerful and colorful leitmotif, not least because of the frequently retrospective nature of his own writing. Nietzsche is fond of playing the literary narcissist who cultivates his *curriculum vitae*, revising it as he revisits it. Tragedy was first and foremost a theme to be *cultivated* in Nietzsche's self-presentation, and not merely an abiding concern.

Tragedy, with its darkness and death-dealing attributes and its portentous thunder, held an immediate and irresistible appeal for Nietzsche. And having set himself up as a prophet of culture and announcing the arrival of a second tragic age that in effect never arrived, Nietzsche had something like a public relations crisis on his hands. A decade and a half on still finds him beating the same drum: "I promise a *tragic age*: the supreme art in the affirmation of life, tragedy, will be reborn when mankind has behind it the consciousness of the harshest but most necessary wars *without suffering from it*" (*Ecce Homo*, "The Birth of Tragedy," 4, emphasis in original). But to palliate the still unfulfilled promises of his youth, a few revisions are first in order. Wagner has to be dismissed as a typographical error, a slip for "Zarathustra," at least in *The Birth of Tragedy* (ibid.), while Dionysus and the Dionysian must be conjured forth again with a new and brutal energy, bidding adieu, or nearly so, to the all-too-classicizing attributes of the Apollonian, as Nietzsche claims in notes from 1875:

> The psychology of the orgy as an overflowing feeling of life and energy within which even pain acts as a stimulus provided me with the key to the concept of the *tragic* feeling, which was misunderstood as much by Aristotle as it was by our pessimists . . . Affirmation of life even in its strangest and sternest problems, the will to life rejoicing in its own inexhaustibility through the *sacrifice* of its highest types – *that* is what I called Dionysian, *that* is what I recognized as the bridge to the psychology of the *tragic* poet . . . And with that I again return to the place from which I set out – the *Birth of Tragedy* was my first revaluation of all values: with that I again plant myself in the soil

out of which I draw all that I will and *can* – I, the last disciple of the philosopher Dionysus – I, the teacher of the eternal recurrence. (*Twilight of the Idols*, "What I Owe to the Ancients," 5; trans. Hollingdale)

"*Incipit tragoedia*" (*The Gay Science*, 342), indeed.

Yet even with these cosmetic changes there is something unsatisfying about Nietzsche's revised pronouncements. The tragic age remains as vague as ever, conceptually and temporally, banished as it is to the realm of the possible and the future, one that perhaps might be glorified as an Eternal Recurrence, though that is itself an eternal refrain in the later Nietzsche.[8] Just when *were* the Greeks properly *tragic*? The "tragic age of the Greeks" Nietzsche dates not to the fifth century but to the time of the Presocratics, assigning its acme to the sixth century during the *floruit* of Heraclitus, Empedocles, and Pythagoras, well before Aeschylus could arrive on the scene. What is more, the Tragic Age is populated not by artists or satyr choruses but by philosophers who are out of touch with their times and who inaugurate a revolution in thought that, Nietzsche claims, utterly failed: "they had a gap in their nature" (*KGW* 4.1:180). Consequently, decline in Greek culture sets in already with the Presocratics, which leaves that *other* tragic age, the age of Aeschylus to Euripides, and, indeed, the very meaning of "tragic knowledge," in a precarious state indeed. One has to suspect that the Presocratics inaugurated a tragic age because of what they tragically failed to achieve. "Tragic knowledge" can hardly be anything other than this intuited and repressed self-knowledge (Porter 2000b: 236–8).

All of this notwithstanding, Nietzsche would come to be identified as a latter-day Presocratic ushering in a second tragic age (an identification he also encouraged). The apparent goal of his later philosophy is to breed just such a type through a kind of Schillerian ascesis of the self (Schiller [1791–2] 1993: 4) – one strong enough to withstand the shocks of a fluxing world driven no longer by the Primal One agonizing in its reflection in appearances, but by the Will to Power coursing through all things in an endless and restless becoming, violently tossing up entities and engorging them again. The Dionysian man is someone capable of staring this meaningless surge in the face and deriving solace, indeed, a kind of "metaphysical comfort," from its very ceaseless quality: he dances on the edge of an abyss.[9]

All this is well and good, but wherein lies the tragic here?, we might well ask. One possibility is that tragic knowledge consists in the devastating realization that all meaning is in vain. Another is that it consists in the cathartic lessons learned from this agonizing revelation: tragedy encompasses an affirmation of life wrested from the moment of its regenerative extinction, the way this is embodied in the death (say) of a tragic hero, who is a stand-in for life's ultimate value and meaning. But the Dionysian man isn't pained by the destruction of meaning; he exults in it. Indeed, his exultation is the sign of life's inextinguishable powers working through him. But if so, then tragedy no longer seems the appropriate term. Or is it? Drawn to a point where it could encompass both total expenditure and total recuperation, the meaning of tragedy and the tragic seems stretched to an improbable limit. Perhaps Nietzsche is

not redirecting the meaning of tragedy and the tragic but is instead merely redescrib-
ing these things, demonstrating with chilling accuracy what they ever only were.
Tragedy was always invested in the extraction of pleasure from pain, an eerie paradox
that prior theory, from Aristotle to Schiller, could only domesticate but could never
fully comprehend. Nietzsche may well be setting his face against the moralizers of
tragic effect, but whether he has earned the label of tragic philosopher remains open to
question. Is Nietzsche celebrating tragic violence or critiquing the established order's
secret fascinations and hypocrisies in the realm of tragedy?

As it happens, much of the time Nietzsche's position stands a good deal nearer to
comedy than to tragedy. The Free Spirit, delighting in his Gay Science – literally,
cheerful knowledge, the direct opposite of tragic knowledge – is a light-stepping
dancer "pregnant with lightning bolts that say Yes and laugh Yes, soothsaying
lightning bolts – blessed is he who is thus pregnant!" (*Zarathustra*, Third Part,
"The Seven Seals (Or: the Yes and Amen Song)," 1; trans. Kaufmann). Laughter,
after all, is the other face of Dionysianism, represented perhaps less by the god than by
his votaries and companions, the Sileni, the satyrs, the fools, and the buffoons – and
now, Zarathustra. "*Learn* – to laugh!," the preface to the 1886 edition of *The Birth of
Tragedy* urges at its close, quoting from *Thus Spoke Zarathustra*. Perhaps comedy,
hinging upon tragedy in the form of the burlesque satyr play in Greek practice
(tragedy's supposed *Ur*-form), is tragedy in its most affirmative aspect, but then it is
this minus any sense of the tragic, blissfully unaware of darkness and danger (and
perhaps all the more dark and dangerous to an onlooker for that reason), blithely
disengaged in its oneiric joyfulness and its redemptive, healing indifference. On this
view of things, tragedy is forever "short," "vanquished by laughter," and "returned to
the eternal comedy of existence," for " 'the waves of uncountable laughter' – to cite
Aeschylus [!] – must in the end overwhelm even the greatest of th[e] tragedians" (*The
Gay Science*, 1; trans. Kaufmann). In this mood, Nietzsche is no longer keen to
proclaim the coming of a new tragic age. Quite the contrary, he is doing all he can
to subvert the tragic spirit and to *exit* the tragic age of his own day: "For the present,
the comedy of existence has not yet 'become conscious' of itself. For the present, *we
still live in the age of tragedy*, the age of moralities and religions" (ibid.; emphasis
added). To the previous tragic age (or is it two tragic ages?) we must now add a third:
our own, teeming as it is with moral maladies and degenerate instincts.

To call Nietzsche either a tragic or a comic philosopher obviously won't do. His
positions can hardly be confined to a genre, and the effect they leave us with is not one
of tragic insight or giddy amusement but only a feeling of puzzlement and uncertainty and a need to ponder all the harder and more critically what we are about, and
so too to examine the very terms by which we apprehend ourselves and our world.
Laughter and gaiety shade off into various tonalities. At times they pass into intense
superficiality and serenity – not Dionysianism now, but (of all things) Apollonian
classicism, as Nietzsche in places allows: "Oh, those Greeks! They knew how to live.
What is required for that is to stop courageously at the surface, the fold, the skin, to
adore appearance, to believe in forms, tones, words, in the whole Olympus of

appearance" (*The Gay Science*, Preface for the Second Edition, 3; cf. *Twilight of the Idols,* "Expeditions of an Untimely Man," 10; *The Will to Power,* §§798–9). At other times, Nietzsche has to describe himself all over again lest his readers take him too literally and too seriously: " '*Incipit tragoedia*' we read at the end of this awesomely aweless book," he writes in his preface to the reedition of *The Gay Science*, which evidently stands in need of a corrective emphasis: "Beware! Something downright wicked and malicious is announced here: *incipit parodia*, no doubt" (ibid., 1).

The sudden and shifting positionalities that Nietzsche assumes and then drops like so many masks bespeaks a kind of perversity in itself. In a word, there is nothing self-evidently tragical about either tragedy or the tragic in the later writings, as indeed there never was even in *The Birth of Tragedy*. Greek cheerfulness was always tied to the subtle undertone of Nietzsche's first book, which was that of a disdainful comic artist gazing haughtily upon "the whole divine comedy of life" and upon "this comedy of art" by which the Primordial One "prepares a perpetual entertainment" for itself, by staring deeply into, and then somehow beyond, "the eternal joy of existence," healing life of its ills through the only "notions with which one can live:...the *sublime...* and the *comic*" (*The Birth of Tragedy* §§1, 5, 7, 17). There *is* something sublime and comical about mankind's persistent inability to live in the absence of metaphysical illusions. And that is the nub of the problem of tragedy in Nietzsche, who in the end stands mesmerized, as he did at the beginning, by the richest and yet most problematical of all phenomena, the dissonance that is "man."

NOTES

1 Similarly, the musical effusions of the lyric poet, that Dionysian artist *par excellence*, are "only different projections of himself" (§5).

2 It is a sign of Nietzsche's powerful influence that Raymond Williams takes over this conceit from him and its implications for cultural decline without compunction (1966: 18).

3 For the tragedians, see Euripides (1960: xxviii–xxxiii). Most of these titles are known to have antedated Euripides' play. For the comic playwrights, see Aristophanes (1996: 11). This omission by Nietzsche is rarely noted, although see Henrichs (1986: 393–6), who, however, does not mention the comic tradition and arrives at a different conclusion from the one presented here.

4 Euripides (1960).

5 It is worth toying with the thought that Euripides' reading is fatal to tragedy, not because he gets tragedy wrong, but because he has *correctly* analyzed its contrived and shadowy suggestiveness: "How questionable the treatment of the myths!" (§11), etc.

6 Dionysus was also, exceptionally, a frontally facing god: his images show him full-face and frequently surrounded by winged eyes – another index of his intimate connection to the visible realm.

7 Cf. Nietzsche's notebook entries such as the following from 1870/1: "The Hellenic world of Apollo is gradually overcome from within by the Dionysian powers. Christianity was already in place"; also: "With the rise of the Oriental–Christian movement the old Dionysianism inundated the world, and the work of Greek antiquity seemed all in vain." See Porter (2000a: 154 – to which one could add *Ecce Homo*, "The Birth of Tragedy," 1: "In one place

the Christian priests are alluded to as ... 'sub-
terraneans,' " a seeming reference to the last
sentence of *The Birth of Tragedy* §12, "the
mystical flood of secret cults which gradually
covered the earth, " 2000b: 220–1 with
377n.161–381 n.179; Baeumer (1976) on
the Romantic identification of Christ with
Dionysus, which Nietzsche is playing off of –
without, one should add, merely restating
Heine's subversion of that identification; Henrichs (1982: 159–60), on the modern sequel,
in the wake of W. Robertson Smith and Frazer.

8　A note from the spring of 1887, contemplat-
ing a future title, reads: "The Tragic Age: The
Doctrine of the Eternal Recurrence."

9　The will to power is every bit as much a
metaphysical postulate (*Annahme*) as the primordial One Will that antedates it in *The Birth
of Tragedy*, offering perhaps not quite "a metaphysical comfort in the old style" (as a note
from 1887/8 puts it), but at least one such
comfort in a new style. The reasons why this is
so cannot be argued for here. For the direct
Kantian echoes, see *The Critique of Judgment*
A33/B33, likewise postulating ("*wir. . . anneh-
men*") the existence of a "will."

References and Further Reading

Aristophanes. (1996). *Frogs*, ed. A. H. Sommerstein. Warminster: Aris & Phillips.

Baeumer, M. (1976). "Nietzsche and the Tradition of the Dionysian." In *Studies in Nietzsche and the Classical Tradition*, ed. James C. O'Flaherty, Timothy F. Sellner, and Robert Meredith Helm. Chapel Hill: University of North Carolina Press, 165–89.

Behler, E. (1986). "A. W. Schlegel and the Nineteenth-century *Damnatio* of Euripides." *Greek, Roman and Byzantine Studies* 27, 335–67.

Bishop, P., ed. (2004). *Nietzsche and Antiquity: His Reaction and Response to the Classical Tradition*. Rochester, NY: Camden House.

Cancik, H. [1995] (2000). *Nietzsches Antike: Vorlesung* [Nietzsche's antiquity: lectures], 2nd edn. Stuttgart: Metzler.

Courtine, J.-F. (1993). "Tragedy and Sublimity: The Speculative Interpretation of *Oedipus Rex* on the Threshold of German Idealism." In *Of the Sublime: Presence in Question. Essays by Jean-François Courtine, et al.*, trans. Jeffrey S. Librett. Albany: State University of New York Press, 157–74.

Euripides. (1960). *Bacchae*, ed. E. R. Dodds, 2nd edn. Oxford: Clarendon Press.

Frazer, James George. (1890). *The Golden Bough: A Study in Comparative Religion*, 2 vols. London: Macmillan.

Henrichs, A. (1982). "Changing Dionysiac Identities." In *Jewish and Christian Self-Definition. Volume Three: Self-Definition in the Greco-Roman World*, ed. Ben F. Meyer and E. P. Sanders. Philadelphia, PA: Fortress Press, 137–60.

Henrichs, A. (1986). "The Last of the Detractors: Friedrich Nietzsche's Condemnation of Euripides." *Greek, Roman and Byzantine Studies* 27, 369–97.

Henrichs, A. (1993). " 'He Has a God in Him': Human and Divine in the Modern Perception of Dionysus." In *Masks of Dionysus*, ed. Thomas H. Carpenter and Christopher A. Faraone. Ithaca, NY: Cornell University Press, 13–43.

Friedrich Nietzsche. Kritische Gesamtausgabe, Werke [Nietzsche's critical works], ed. G. Colli and M. Montinari (1967–) Berlin: Walter de Gruyter. (= *KGW*).

Otto, W. F. [1933] (1960). *Dionysos: Mythos und Kultus* [Dionysus: myth and cult], 3rd edn. Frankfurt/ Main: Vittorio Klostermann.

Porter, J. I. (2000a). *The Invention of Dionysus: An Essay on "The Birth of Tragedy"*. Stanford, CA: Stanford University Press.

Porter, J. I. (2000b). *Nietzsche and the Philology of the Future*. Stanford, CA: Stanford University Press.

Rampley, M. (2000). *Nietzsche, Aesthetics, and Modernity*. Cambridge and New York: Cambridge University Press.

Schiller, F. [1790–2] (2003) "On the Reason Why We Take Pleasure in Tragic Subjects." In *Friedrich Schiller: Poet of Freedom*, trans. G. W. Gregory. Washington, DC: Schiller Institute, 4: 267–83.

Schiller, F. [1791–2] (1993). "On the Art of Tragedy." In *Friedrich Schiller: Essays*, ed. Walter Hinderer and Daniel O. Dahlstrom. New York: Continuum, 1–21.

Silk, M. S. and J. P. Stern. (1981). *Nietzsche on Tragedy*. Cambridge and New York: Cambridge University Press.

Sloterdijk, P. (1989). *Thinker on Stage: Nietzsche's Materialism*, trans. Jamie Owen Daniel. Minneapolis: University of Minnesota Press.

Szondi, P. [1961] (1964). *Versuch über das Tragische*, 2nd edn. Frankfurt/Main: Insel-Verlag. (Available in English as *An Essay on the Tragic*, trans. Paul Fleming. Stanford, CA: Stanford University Press, 2000.)

Williams, R. (1966). *Modern Tragedy*. Stanford, CA: Stanford University Press.

6
Tragedy and Psychoanalysis: Freud and Lacan

Julia Reinhard Lupton

In 1900, Sigmund Freud published *The Interpretation of Dreams*, altering the course of medicine, art, and literature in their relation to the conditions and possibilities of socio-sexual life. *The Interpretation of Dreams* is above all a science of hermeneutics or interpretation, but it also a prose epic and autobiography, in which the hero-author descends into the undiscovered country of the unconscious, using his own memories and dreams to scan the shaping force of repression in the chains of association that measure out human thought. *The Interpretation of Dreams* also institutes psychoanalysis's ongoing reflections on tragedy, for it is here that Freud first published the twinned readings of *Oedipus the King* and *Hamlet* that would become emblematic of the psychoanalytic enterprise more generally. Freud's brief but powerful interpretations of these two plays, taken together and separately, lay out the four fundamental directions that psychoanalytic criticism would take in the next century: character analysis, hermeneutics, genre and narrative structure, and the dynamics of the psychoanalytic situation. In order to indicate the deep affinity and fundamentally literary rationality that links Freudian thought to the history and theory of tragic form, I have mapped these four areas onto categories provided by Aristotle's foundational anatomy of tragedy in the *Poetics*. The psychoanalysis of literary persons takes its bearings from the Aristotelian category of *ethos* or character; psychoanalytic hermeneutics develops the interplay of *lexis* and *dianoia*, or diction and thought, in the *Poetics*; narratology emphasizes the centrality of *mythos* – both plot and myth – in psychoanalysis and tragedy; and the dynamics of the psychoanalytic situation returns both implicitly and explicitly to the function of catharsis as a dramatic therapeutics for Aristotle.[1] Freud's engagement with tragedy is one moment in the constitutive dialogue between tragedy and theory that first assumed a systematic form in Aristotle, a repeated set of encounters that weaves the forms, moods, and shapes of tragedy into the scenes and dreams of Western thought in antiquity and modernity.

These four fundamental concepts represent both the main moments in the history of psychoanalytic criticism since 1900, and a set of continually operative critical possibilities. *Character criticism* unfolds between the poles of brute personification or impersonation ("putting the character on the couch") and more subtle forms of analysis that respect the fictional being of literary characters. *Hermeneutics* takes the simple form of searching for hidden meanings; in its more elaborate variations, psychoanalytic interpretation follows the operations by which meanings are transformed and redistributed in their passage between conscious and unconscious planes, replacing the search for latent contents with the dynamism of rhetorical transformation. *Narratology* focuses on the structure of dramatic narratives, the storytelling styles of Freud's own writing, and the transformations undergone by tragedy as a genre over time. Finally, approaches that take the *psychoanalytic situation* as their point of orientation try to map key features of the psychoanalytic session and the transferential dynamics of the analyst–analysand relationship onto the text–reader relation, an approach anticipated by Freud's engagement with *Oedipus* and *Hamlet* in his own self-analysis. In the following pages I recover the outlines and interplay of these four directions of psychoanalytic criticism in Freud's inaugural readings of Oedipus and Hamlet, not in order to imply a progressive history of increasingly nuanced psychoanalytic approaches to tragedy, but rather to insist on the ongoing urgency of these fundamentally linked vectors of thought, in both their genesis in Freud's early writing and their unfolding in later schools and moments of literary criticism and psychoanalytic theory. I end by suggesting the convergence of both Lacanian psychoanalysis and classical studies of tragedy around the question of citizenship. Not quite a history (of critical approaches), not quite a reading (of *Hamlet* and *Oedipus*), and not quite a theory (of psychoanalytic criticism), this chapter convenes key moments in the psychoanalytic conversation with tragedy in order to invite us to think broadly and generously about both their past and future conjunctions.

Origins

Hamlet and Oedipus first appear in Freud's writings in a letter written to his friend Wilhelm Fliess on October 15, 1897. The first half of the letter in question recollects a scene from Freud's childhood: "I was crying my heart out, because my mother was nowhere to be found. My brother Philipp (who is twenty years older than I) opened a cupboard [*Kasten*] for me, and when I found that mother was not there either I cried still more, until she came through the door, looking slim and beautiful" (Freud 1954: 222). Freud links this poignant but elliptical memory to the fate of an old nurse who had been arrested or "boxed up" (*eingekastelt*) for theft; he was fearful that his mother, too, might disappear forever. (He will later link his mother's reappearance, "slim and beautiful," to her recent pregnancy and confinement [*SE* VI: 51].) Unable to proceed further with the interpretation, Freud then confesses to Fliess that "Only one idea of general value has occurred to me. I have found love of the mother and jealousy of the father in my own case too, and now believe it to be a general phenomenon of early childhood" (223).[2]

As if to bridge the abyss between the intimate enigma of the mother in the cupboard on the one hand and the speculative generalization of its possible meaning on the other, Freud turns fatefully to the example of *Oedipus the King*:

> If that is the case, the gripping power of *Oedipus Rex*, in spite of all the rational objections to the inexorable fate that the story presupposes, becomes intelligible... The Greek myth seizes on a compulsion which everyone recognizes because he has felt traces of it in himself. Every member of the audience was once a budding Oedipus in phantasy, and this dream-fulfillment played out in reality causes everyone to recoil in horror.

Caught up in this productive train of associations, Freud is next struck by the proximity of *Hamlet* to this scenario: "The idea has passed through my head that the same thing may lie at the root of *Hamlet*." He goes on to roll out a cascade of details in Shakespeare's play that make a new kind of sense when read as expressions of a repressed Oedipal scenario, culminating in the spectacular puppet show of engineered death that ends the drama: "And does not [Hamlet] finally succeed, in just the same remarkable way as my hysterics, in bringing down his punishment on himself and suffering the same fate as his father, being poisoned by the same rival?" (1954: 224).

In the letter to Fliess, Freud takes *Oedipus* and *Hamlet*, in their associative conjunction, as diagnostic mirrors of his own subjective formation, articulating their power at a turning point in his self-analysis. It is no accident that Freud conducts the self-analysis that led him to many of the key formulations published in *The Interpretation of Dreams* in the form of an epistolary exchange: these letters, collected in a volume appropriately entitled *The Origins of Psychoanalysis,* are addressed to a friend and interlocutor who clearly focalizes (often precisely in his noncommittal or unresponsive stance) the powerful structural and affective relationship that Freud would later call "transference." The screen memory in its inchoate particularity only becomes susceptible to analysis via the act of address to another person (Fliess) and the mediation of tragedy (Oedipus/Hamlet), itself a genre organized around the turning point of recognition and reversal.

In *The Interpretation of Dreams,* Freud for the first time links the two heroes in print, disclosing their affinity beyond the intimate circle of friendship and the terrifying semi-privacy of self-analysis:

> Another of the great creations of tragic poetry, Shakespeare's *Hamlet* has its roots in the same soil as *Oedipus Rex*. But the changed treatment of the same material reveals the whole difference in the mental life of these two widely separated epochs of civilization: the secular advance of repression in the emotional life of mankind. In the *Oedipus* the child's wishful phantasy that underlies it is brought into the open and realized as it would be in a dream. In *Hamlet* it remains repressed; and – just as in the case of a neurosis – we only learn of its existence from its inhibiting consequences. (*SE* 4: 264)

Here, as in the letter to Fliess, Oedipus enters the scene of Freudian thought just a few steps ahead of Hamlet. Oedipus functions in this couple as the clearer, more primal, more realized version of the son's infantile wish to marry one's mother and kill's one's father; Hamlet, on the other hand, figures for Freud the repressed and distorted replay of the same scenario, whose motivating function in the drama is evident only negatively, in its "inhibiting consequences." Even before he learns of his father's death from the Ghost, for example, Hamlet is "sullied" by a sense of guiltiness and despair, his outlook colored by a disgusted fascination with his mother's sexuality and a crippling identification not with his idealized father but with the grotesque figure of his uncle, the satyr-king.[3] Freud attributes Hamlet's inability to murder the man who has killed the King and married the Queen not to hypertrophied intellectualism, but rather to the debilitating burden of his own desire to have achieved what Claudius has pulled off: "Hamlet is able to do anything – except take vengeance on the man who did away with his father and took that father's place with his mother, the man who shows him the repressed wishes of his own childhood realized" (*SE* IV: 265).

Freud's initial foray into literary criticism responds to and reflects on the agony and ecstasy of literary characters. It is the horrifying sight of Oedipus's recognition, and the equally horrifying specter of Hamlet's delay, that rivets the audience, fastening us in the grips of identification. Character criticism was, and, indeed, remains, a necessary first stop in psychoanalytic criticism – a starting point determined not only by Freud's driving concern with the fate of the individual subject, but also by the primacy of *ethos* or character in modern tragedy, an orientation toward individual subjectivity and consistency itself emblematized by the figure of Hamlet. Greek tragedy, as theorized by Aristotle, is a genre governed by the organic machinery of *mythos* or "plot," designating the clean economy of a dramatic action in which the moment of tragic recognition cascades into a series of ironic reversals (Aristotle 1449b–1450b). For Aristotle, who, not like Freud, took *Oedipus the King* as an exemplar of classical tragedy, *ethos* or character was always subordinate to *mythos* or plot. Modern tragedy would, however, give center stage to increasingly complex and compelling characters, a transformation exemplified for many later theorists, critics, and writers by Shakespeare's Hamlet, whose ruminative magnificence is matched only by his chronic disability in the area of dramatic action. In the modern theatre of the ego, Hamlet's fascination with his own subjective extravagance replaces the clarity and objectivity of classical *mythos* (plot) with the libidinal and linguistic interest of *ethos* (character). Since tragedy itself had devolved into a drama of character in the productions of Shakespeare and his Romantic heirs, applying the paradigms of psychoanalysis to characters on stage or page was, as it were, pre-scripted both by the psychoanalytic enterprise itself and by the changes undergone by tragedy as a genre.

Ethos

In the decades following the publication of *The Interpretation of Dreams*, Freud's initial analyses of Oedipus and Hamlet would be extensively excavated, remapped, and extended by both psychoanalysts and literary critics working in a Freudian vein. In 1949, Ernst Jones devoted an entire book, succinctly entitled *Hamlet and Oedipus,* to the comparative analysis of Freud's odd couple. Critics and analysts also drew other tragic dramas into the circuit of psychic life, especially the *Oresteia,* whose father-loving Electra and mother-hating Orestes offered important variations on the Oedipal theme (e.g., Jung 1915). Hamlet, a young man sent away to school during the period when his mother remarries the man who has killed his father, is certainly closer to Orestes than to Oedipus in his immediate situation. Hamlet's revulsion before the sexuality of his mother, flowering into a death wish against Gertrude that demands constant self-policing by both himself and the Ghost, competes with and overshadows Hamlet's resolve to avenge his father. Moreover, the politics and ethics of revenge are clearly at stake in both the *Oresteia* and in *Hamlet,* but not in *Oedipus the King.*[4] Such comparisons fill out the central Freudian insight, engaging the fuller resources of the classical canon of tragedy in order to fathom the dramatic shape of human motivation and desire. Does this mean that Hamlet has an "Orestes complex," and that Greek tragedy provides an infinite set of templates for mapping human desire? Far from it. In respect to Freud's foundational reading and dialectical mind, Hamlet's mother-hate and father-love is best described as the "negative Oedipus complex," retaining the essential referent to the enunciation of Oedipus in the formative scene of Freud's self-analysis, rather than dissolving the singularity of that initial insight into the sea of vague analogies (with women from Venus and men from Mars) that has become pop-psychoanalysis.

Within the domain of character criticism, the Orestes reference brings forward the importance of the mother in the scene of Hamlet's desire. We might recall here the *Kasten* memory that introduces Freud's initial double reading of *Hamlet* and *Oedipus* under the sign of a deeply unreliable and divided maternity (Lupton and Reinhard 1993: 17–19). The enigmatic box formed by the *Kasten* (box, wardrobe, casket) functions like an illuminated rubric in a medieval manuscript, a concentrated cipher of the discursive text that follows. Although the father in *Hamlet* is most clearly split between obscene and normative figures, the mother, too, is subject to division: is Gertrude the lustful bearer of excessive desire, or is she the pragmatic widow who has taken the best road available to her in a state of emergency? T. S. Eliot formulated the "objective correlative," the equivalence between an object and its affect that, in Eliot's judgment, makes a work of art convincing, in relation to the felt disparity between these two versions of Gertrude: "Hamlet is up against the difficulty that his disgust is occasioned by his mother, but his mother is not an adequate equivalent for it; his disgust envelops and exceeds her" (25). Jacques Lacan, in his seminar of 1958–9, on "Desire and Its Interpretation," also emphasized the importance of Gertrude in Hamlet's psychic state. According to Lacan, Hamlet is stalled because he is always at "the hour of the Other," playing out even in his final moment of achieved revenge the scripts imposed by Claudius and the Ghost. The true Other of the play in Lacan's reading, however, is not the father in either his ghostly or his obscene instantiations, but rather the mother, who, as the first bearer of nourishment, the agent and object of primal loss, and the original source of language, occupies the field in which the child's desire is first "alienated" – takes shape, comes into being, but never as its own desire, never as an expression of its own subjective autonomy. Lacan characterizes the dominant linguistic relation between mother and child as one of "demand," the fundamental stance and tone taken by the small child and his caretaker. For Lacan, the incessant demands placed by each on each are always demands for the same thing: not for the toy, or the juice, or the bowel movement, elicited in the painful decibel of the infantile whine or the maternal nag, but rather, in and beyond these objects, the demand for love, for a recognition of absolute value that would magically reinstall the infantile subject in a scene unmarked by the threat of castration or the scandal of the mother's desire (her libidinal distraction by other persons, objects, and activities).

For Lacan, demand stands as an intermediary term between (quasi-biological) need and (thoroughly dialecticized and linguistic) desire. Demand, surging beyond the ache of need into the register of language, borrows its irritating, even exasperating, insistence from the frustration of need, but without symbolizing lack into new forms of mediation and substitution. Gertrude poses a problem to Hamlet because she embodies the purity of demand in its contiguity with need: "His mother does not choose because of something present inside her, like an instinctive voracity. The sacrosanct genital object . . . appears to her as an object to be enjoyed in what is truly the direct satisfaction of a need, and nothing else" (Lacan 1958–9: 12–13). This is, I would insist, the Gertrude of Hamlet's imaginings and not the Gertrude of the play, who, in T. S. Eliot's astute phrase, remains "negative and insignificant"; no Clytemnestra, Gertrude does not provide an adequate referent or "objective correlative" for the intensity of Hamlet's misogynistic revulsion.

Hamlet has been unable to wrest from this imaginary mother the subjective mobility provided by the empty space of desire; "confronted on the one hand with an eminent, idealized, exalted object – his father – and on the other with the degraded, despicable object Claudius, the criminal and adulterous brother, Hamlet does not choose" (1958–9: 12–13). In *Hamlet,* the Oedipal situation, Lacan writes, "appears in the particularly striking form in the real" (51). The subjectivization that Hamlet achieves in the final "interim" of the play, after his abrupt return from his English misadventure, comes about, Lacan suggests, because he has managed to grasp the phallus in its symbolic function: "It is a question of the phallus, and that's why he will never be able to strike it, until the moment when he has made the complete sacrifice – without wanting to, moreover – of all narcissistic attachments, i.e., when he is mortally wounded and knows it" (51). The phallus in its symbolic function is not the obscene, over-present object of Gertrude's imagined desire, but rather, Lacan says, an ordering function of signification: "one cannot strike the phallus, because the phallus, even the real phallus, is a *ghost*" (50). By recognizing the phallus as a symbolic function behind or beyond rather than in or on the king – a feature of his office rather than his physical body – Hamlet is able to achieve a degree of subjective autonomy relative to Gertrude, to Claudius, and to the Ghost. In the final scene of the play, in the interim opened up by his rapidly approaching mortality, Hamlet at the very least intuits a larger design in his own passivity, wresting some kind of *subjectivity* from the very fact of his *subjection* to the games and commandments of ghosts and counselors, kings and queens. If he is an instrument of Claudius – reduced to a poisoned rapier and a player-recorder in a game of blindman's bluff scripted by the Other – he now conceives of this instrumentalization in terms of a larger symbolic design at work beyond the usurping policies of the satyr-king. And if Hamlet has been trapped in the claustrophobic field of Gertrude's imagined demands, he is able in his final speech to say farewell to her, to separate without further incrimination: "I am dead, Horatio. Wretched Queen, adieu!" (5.2.275). No longer trapped in the specter of her sexual demands, Hamlet may in this final parting accept Gertrude's desire as an indeterminate quantity (does she or doesn't she love Claudius?) rather than a fantasy of realized enjoyment ("honeying and making love / Over the nasty sty," 3.4.92–4). I will return in the final pages of this chapter to the question of the precise nature of the margin of freedom won by Hamlet with respect to the phallus: does the prince of Denmark access the phallus in its relation to the sovereign singularity that marks primal repression and the absolutist state, or does he rather intuit its role in establishing a signifying chain ruled by political and ethical equivalence among members of an emergent body politic?

Hermeneutics

Although Lacan's reading of Hamlet is undeniably an attempt to account for the subjective predicament of the title character, Lacan's emphasis on demand as a certain mode of language identifies a feature of subjectivity that pulses within and beyond the pull of characters and character in the play. Lacan's impact on psychoanalytic criticism would fall much less in the area of character analysis, and much more powerfully in the regions of hermeneutics, narratology, and the dynamics of the psychoanalytic situation. It is significant, for example, that the selection from Lacan's seminar on Hamlet available in English first appeared in a double issue of *Yale French Studies* in 1977, later published as a separate volume entitled *Literature and Psychoanalysis: The Question of Reading: Otherwise* (Felman 1982). For many critics like myself who came of age by coming to terms with the essays collected in this volume, "reading otherwise" meant above all reading for something *other than character*, venturing into fields of literary signification beyond the lure of identification. Indeed, in the original scenes of Freud's conjunction of psychoanalysis and tragedy, we see that Freud is at least as concerned with the techniques of hermeneutics or interpretation as he is with analyzing the characters of Hamlet and Oedipus. In Freud's method of interpretation, manifest contents (what we see, say, or hear in our dreams; the recorded elements of the dream-text itself) carry latent or unconscious meanings, archaic sexual wishes that have been "repressed," rendered unthinkable, by the civilizing processes that forcibly channel the polymorphous perversity of children into the regulated heterosexuality of adulthood. In Freud's scheme, *Oedipus the King*, a play in which the horror of father-death and mother-love is actually achieved, represents the latent content or repressed meaning that both backlights and inhibits the thoughts and actions of *Hamlet*. This scheme authorized a whole strain of psychoanalytic hermeneutics committed to unlocking the sexual significance of literary images and symbols. At the local level of poetic analysis, this remains a powerful interpretive and pedagogical tool today, not the least because it can be conducted on textual instances – jokes, figures of speech, slips of the tongue; advertisements, images, and product designs – that are easily disengaged from the imaginary coherence of a literary or dramatic character. In Aristotelian terms, psychoanalytic hermeneutics invites the critic to attend to the local play of *lexis* (diction) in its relation to *dianoia* (thought) apart from the march of characters across the stage. A rich bouquet of sexual significations, for instance, animates the fantastic garlands of Ophelia, woven from "crow-flowers, nettles, daisies, and long purples, / That liberal shepherds give a grosser name" (5.1.140–1). Although scholars did not need Freud to discover country matters within Ophelia's pretty posies (what are flowers, after all, than the sexual organs of plants?), the psychoanalytic perspective allowed these local instances of sexual punning to inseminate whole networks of image patterns with scenes of seduction, desire, and loss.[5]

The surface-depth model of hermeneutics, already pushed beyond its limits in stress points of Freud's own writing and thinking, underwent extensive revision under the impact of semiotics, structuralism, and poststructuralism – furthered, for example, in the publication of the *Yale French Studies* volume that introduced Lacan's Hamlet to America. These discourses of the sign, which placed a new, counter-hermeneutic emphasis on the rule of the signifier over the signified, of the letter over the spirit, encouraged critics to invert the logical relationship between Oedipus and Hamlet in Freud's original scene of reading tragedy. If interpretation must always begin with surface, is not *Hamlet* rather than *Oedipus* the logically "prior" play, its palimpsest of historical, dramatic, biographical, and editorial versions and variants initiating Freud into the seductive dynamics of repression? In this vein, critics emphasized the importance of the "dreamwork" [*Trauerarbeit*] itself – the forms and mechanisms of substitution and displacement – over the meanings secreted on the far side of the dream (e.g., Weber 1982). A tour de force in this area is Joel Fineman's "The Sound of O in *Othello*"; arguing ingeniously that "Othello," a name apparently of Shakespeare's invention, derives from the Greek *ethelō*, " 'wish,' 'want,' 'will,' 'desire,' " Fineman traces the catastrophic reduction of Othello through the course of the play into a headless subject "inflated with his loss of self" (1991: 148). "The sound of O in *Othello*," Fineman argued, serves "both to occasion and to objectify in language Othello's hollow self" (151), culminating in his keening cry, "O, Desdemona dead, Desdemona dead, O, O" (5.2.288). Fineman's fearless pursuit of the Greek letter in Shakespeare's text echoes Lacan's aside in the *Hamlet* seminar, "I'm just surprised that no one has pointed out that Ophelia is *O phallus*" (20). Indeed, Fineman's essay was first presented at a 1987 conference devoted to Lacan's *Television*, sponsored by the journals *October* and *Ornicar?*. "The Sound of O" represents a sustained attempt to remain at the level of the letter without relinquishing interest in the drama's production of what Fineman calls "the subjectivity effect," a formulation that at once recognizes the pull of *ethos* and insists on its life and death in *lexis*.

Mythos

For Aristotle, however, *mythos* was the prime mover of tragedy. *Mythos* can be translated as "plot," but also as "myth"; it designates the structural and temporal element in drama, the architecture of its action. For Freud, *Oedipus the King* staged a fundamental plot of human desire and development, the crystalline clarity of its dramatic action bearing the structural stamp not only of literary art, but also of ritual and archetype. Moreover, Freud compares the diagetic or narrative sequence of *Oedipus the King* to the temporality of a psychoanalysis: "The action of the play is nothing other than the process of revealing, with cunning delays and ever-mounting excite-ment – a process that can be likened to the work of a psychoanalysis – that Oedipus himself is the murderer of Laïus, but further that he is the son of the murdered man and of Jocasta" (*SE* IV: 261–2). Freud initiates here a comparative analysis of his own narrative techniques that would be picked up in later literary theory and criticism by Peter Brooks, Charles Bernheimer, and others interested in the narrative features shared by psychoanalysis and literature. Claude Lévi-Strauss, following Freud's in-sight into the formative character of myth, would develop the structuralist approach to narrative, organizing mythic action into symbolic formulae (e.g, the raw and the cooked) that could account for huge areas of cultural life.

The work of Jacques Lacan is once again a major factor in the rise of structuralist approaches to psychoanalysis and tragedy. Like Lévi-Strauss, Lacan is interested in the basic schemata that underlie various subjective configurations and confrontations. Lacan, writes Alenka Zupančič, "treats myth and tragedy themselves as instantiations of formal structures" (171). When Lacan turns to a reading of *Antigone* in his seminar on the ethics of psychoanalysis, conducted a year after his sessions on *Hamlet*, he refers to conversations with Lévi-Strauss on the play. He tells us, "To put it in the terms of Lévi-Strauss – and I am certain that I am not mistaken in evoking him here, since I was instrumental in having had him reread *Antigone* and he expressed himself to me in such terms – Antigone with relation to Creon finds herself in the position of synchrony in opposition to diachrony" (1959–60: 285). In structuralism, synchrony refers to language as system or code, and diachrony to its historical development.[6] Antigone's uncanny location between real and symbolic death, according to Lacan, "suspends everything that has to do with transformation, with the cycle of generation and decay or with history itself, and it places us on a level that is more extreme than any other insofar as it is directly attached to language as such" (285). Antigone suspends diachrony, argues Lacan, by enshrining the irreparable loss of her brother in the barest outlines of a tomb (the pouring of dust on his corpse), a symbolic act that serves to dislodge human being from the temporal flux of both natural and historical change.

Lacan's remarks on *Antigone* center on the moment when Antigone, having sung her own dirge on her road to death, makes the following troubling declaration about the singularity of her brother's case:

> Had I had children or their father dead,
> I'd let them moulder. I should not have chosen
> In such a case to cross the state's decree.
> What is the law that lies behind these words?
> One husband gone, I might have found another,
> Or a child from a new man in first child's place,
> But with my parents hid away in death,
> No brother, ever, could spring up for me.
>
> (905–12)

The Romantic author Goethe, in his conversation with Eckerman in 1827, was appalled: how could Antigone, the paragon of filial piety, imagine leaving the bodies of her children and husband to rot unburied in the fields (Lacan 1959/60: 255)? Analyzing the intensity of Goethe's reaction, Lacan takes Antigone's declaration as a model of the relation between a chain of signifiers (what he will call S_2, defined by their replaceability in a line of associations and substitutions) and the singular signifier, or S_1, that anchors the shifting meanings of the signifying chain by being itself irreplaceable, not subject to any substitution. Installed by and as trauma, this singular signifier refuses to budge, forming the immovable cornerstone of the fantasmatic architecture of the unconscious. Lacan says of Antigone's declaration that she invokes

> a right that emerges in the language of the ineffaceable character of what is –
> ineffaceable, that is, from the moment when the emergent signifier freezes it like a
> fixed object in spite of the flood of possible transformations. What is, is, and it is to
> this, to this surface, that the unshakeable, unyielding position of Antigone is fixed.
> (279)

Antigone fastens on her brother as the one immovable element in the world of *philôtes*, the pre-political rituals of reciprocity that encompass the bonds of kinship, friendship, and hospitality. She has defended these bonds in a more global manner up until this point; now she singles the brother out as the one person who cannot be exchanged for another, and in doing so she singles herself out, becoming in Lacan's description similarly "unshakeable" and "unyielding." She speaks for the irreplaceability of her brother, a stance that irrevocably isolates her from the polis, but she does so while also allowing – and here lies the scandal for Goethe – the total exchangeability of other elements in the world of intimate bonds, namely husbands and children. If one point is unmovable, then it is precisely this anchoring point that allows her to release other forms of relation to the regime of equivalence in the polis (cf. Tyrrell and Bennett 1998: 115–17).

When Antigone hangs suspended within the tomb of her live burial, she becomes, as Lacan's structuralist reading suggests, an image of synchrony as such, the structure and field of language that wrestles objects from the flux of temporal transformation by granting them both their fixed and their moveable places in a signifying system. Passing through Freud and Lacan, the synchrony of *mythos* is projected onto the very body and being of Antigone, in three senses. First, she is a figure of suspension and arrest, from her fixation on the singularity of her brother to the hanging of her body in the cave of live burial. Second, Antigone materializes the incestuous union between Oedipus and Jocasta, hence concretizing and concentrating the consequences of the Oedipal plot within the very genealogy and substance of her being. Finally, her refusal of a sexual relation (her choice of the dead Polynices over the living Haemon) links the hollow space of the cave to the uncanny *Kasten* or cupboard of the maternal body as well as to the disquieting question mark of feminine desire (Copjec 2002: 22).

Transference

Lacan associates Antigone with the specter of beauty, which forms a blinding spot within the clarity of the structure of *mythos* in its signifying function:

> The violent illumination, the glow of beauty, coincides with the moment of transgression or of realization of Antigone's *Até* [infatuation, impulse, drive]... it is in that direction that a certain relationship to a beyond of the central field is established for us, but it is also that which prevents us from seeing its true nature, that which dazzles us and separates us from its true function. The moving side of beauty causes all critical judgment to vacillate, stops analysis, and plunges the different forms involved into a certain confusion or, rather, an essential blindness. (1959/60: 281)

Beauty materializes a moment of intense and overwhelming affect, bearing the sublime charge of the real, that accrues at and as the limits of the symbolic structure called myth. Lacan associates the power of Antigone's terrible beauty with the Aristotelian function of catharsis (245–6), which in turn leads us from the formal structure of tragedy to its social and psychological function, and hence from the critical perspectives of character, hermeneutics, and narrative to that of the psychoanalytic situation itself: how, namely, does the staging of tragedy itself institute a kind of psychoanalytic process, resulting in something like a cure? And to what extent does the audience submit to this experience (as patient or analysand) rather than dictate the terms and rhythm of its interpretation (as analyst)? This is not a late question on the scene of criticism, but rather an originary one, insofar as Freud's analysis *of* tragedy was also at the same time his (self)analysis *by* tragedy, conducted in the absent presence of the friend, Wilhelm Fliess.

Hamlet's play-within-a-play stages the transferential effects and potentialities of literature, forming a central cog in what Richard Halpern has provocatively termed the "Hamletmachine" (1977: 227–88), the mechanical reproduction of *Hamlet* in modernity. Hamlet writes the play for diagnostic purposes, in order to test the veracity of the Ghost by measuring the impact of the re-narrated crime on the purported villain, Claudius. The layering of dramatic versions within the play (dumb show nested in Mousetrap, which is in turn framed by *Hamlet*) figures the layering of analogues, sources, and replays in *Hamlet* and its reception (good and bad quartos, Greek and Senecan reminiscences, Ur-Hamlets and their modern ghosts). These multiple screens trigger not only the drive to interpretation (the hermeneutic impulse) but also the shock of encountering oneself within the scene (the transferential act), a movement, translation, or transfer into the drama that can both hit upon and obscure truths concerning one's subjective position. Claudius is appalled to see his own act in the mirror presented "by one Lucianus, nephew to the King" (III.ii.223). Hamlet, in recognizing Claudius' recognition, is lured into mis-recognizing, or failing to recognize, his own complicity with Claudius' desire. Hamlet, too, is "nephew to the King" and hence bound up in Claudius' guilt. As Jean-François Lyotard has argued, "What this scene offers Hamlet is an alibi: I am Laertes (= I am not Claudius), I must still fulfill the paternal word (= I haven't already fulfilled it by killing Polonius)" (1977: 409). Transference in its imaginary function encourages us to identify with characters at the level of *ethos* or character – the function of pity as com-passion or sym-pathy that forms one strand of catharsis in Aristotle's famous formula. Transference in its symbolic and real dimensions, however, locates us in contradictory places within the *mythos* of the drama, and the *mythos* of our lives, corresponding to the fear or terror that wrenches us out of imaginary identification with a character and forces us into contact with the unconscious plot and repressed words that shape our desire.

Lacan writes of the terrifying image of Antigone: "through the intervention of pity and fear...we are purged of everything of that order. And that order, we can now immediately recognize, is properly speaking the order of the imaginary. And we are purged of it through the intervention of one image among others" (1959–60: 247–8). The fascinating image of Antigone, like the specter of Lucianus that takes shape in the hall of mirrors constituted by Hamlet's play-within-a-play, leads us both in and through the drama, transferring our subjective interest across competing positions and levels of meaning in the play, in order to rearrange or shake up our unconscious knowledge. As such, catharsis and/as transference involves a certain bringing-into-action or subjective effectuation of the formal dimensions of character, plot, and language.

Psychoanalysis and Citizenship

Where do psychoanalytic studies of tragedy stand today? Although Lacan's approach to psychoanalysis builds in part on structuralist conceptions of language, kinship, and social order, in French classical studies, the structuralist approach to myth and tragedy would develop largely apart from psychoanalysis, culminating in the work of Marcel

Detienne, Pierre Vidal-Naquet, and Jean-Pierre Vernant, their student Nicole Loraux, and English and American scholars such as Charles Seaford, Froma Zeitlin, Charles Segal, William Tyrell, and Larry Bennett. The political anthropology of Greek tragedy has used the resources of myth criticism to uncover the tension in Greek tragedy between the myths of the great aristocratic houses, marked by self-destructive crises of incest and familiacide, and the new institutions of citizenship on the other, which smashed the charisma of authority based on kinship in order to reorganize political life in terms of the equivalences of citizenship. My final question is the following: can the *political anthropology of citizenship* and the *psychoanalysis of kinship* be brought together productively in new readings of tragedy?

At first glance, citizenship and psychoanalysis would appear to have little to say to each other. Psychoanalysis, with its emphasis on the singularity of subjectivity, the force of fantasy, and the unsettling effects of desire and enjoyment, presents itself as the inverse and underside of citizenship, with its normative presentation of the public life and juridical definition of persons. The word "citizen" does not appear in the General Index to the *Standard Edition* of Freud, nor does it figure in any substantial way in the teaching of Lacan. Yet the two discourses can be joined around the dialectic between subjective alienation in the symbolic order (the institution of norms) and subjectivizing separation from symbolic systems (the taking exception to norms that forms the action of many tragedies, notably *Antigone*). Moreover, psychoanalysis and citizenship are drawn together *by, in and as the field of drama itself*, in its dialectic between the family and the polis and between ancient and modern forms of tragic narrative. New work by Lacanian theorists, especially those in the "Slovenian School" associated with Slavoj Žižek as well as critics affiliated with the journal *October* (e.g., Joan Copjec) have developed the political implications of psychoanalysis for this new century. Much of this work has been conducted via structuring references to *Antigone*, *Hamlet*, and other works of tragedy from the canon of psychoanalysis, often juxtaposed with examples from film and new media in order to focalize the ongoing cogency of tragic scenes and dreams whose formative function cannot be dissolved into the multiplicity and relentless particularism of "culture."

In Ernesto Laclau's account of hegemony (1996), the war of individual interests coalesces around points of social identification – whether sent from above, in the fictions of unity authored by the state, or emanating from below, in the struggles of individual groups (the poor, religious minorities, immigrant groups, and so on). In the very intensity of their particularism, such struggles have the capacity to galvanize the disparate interests of others, achieving a provisional universality around a broadened roster of citizenship. Yet such moments of signification remain contradictory and inadequate, rendering the social forever unstable, always an incomplete mapping of the field it attempts to master. Posing the question of psychoanalysis and citizenship does not mean applying a universal form of explanation (Lacan) to a local instance (be it to Athenian, Elizabethan, or Stalinist political culture), but rather mobilizing within citizenship itself the dialectic of the particular and the universal, the specific case of citizenship and the impulses toward both normative expression and internal critique immanent within citizenship as a discourse. The difference made by psycho-analysis is to insist on the singular place of sexuality, desire, and enjoyment in shaping both the exploitative and the utopian dimension of every social arrangement, includ-ing democratic ones; again and again, citizenship comes up against the differences made by gender, kinship, and cultic forms of group identity in attempting to fashion a world that founds itself on their neutralization, equalization, or disremption.

With these possibilities in mind, let us revisit our earlier comparison of *Hamlet* and the *Oresteia*. Both the *Agamemnon* and *Hamlet* begin with scenes of a night watch, commanded by a royal household in a state of sovereign transition. In both cases, the night watch is dramatized as a sequence or rotation that evokes the signifying chain as such. In the opening scene of Aeschylus' trilogy, a relay of lights, what we might call a pure sequence of signifiers, transmits the message of Agamemnon's imminent return from the ruins of Troy all the way to Argos. In the opening of *Hamlet*, the changing of guards on the ramparts of Elsinore establishes equivalence among the young men who take turns guarding the castle; they too form a kind of signifying chain or relay race of transferred duties. We might say that both plays are divided between hierarchical structures based on the family triangle, with the child placed beneath and outside a parental couple in a state of emergency; and horizontal structures based on social equivalence (the band of brothers, the circle of friends, the chain of signifiers). The family triangle is anchored by the sublime singularity of the Father, identified with the symbolic function of the phallus; in relation to this evacuated slot, Orestes and Hamlet must figure out how, if at all, to assume a relation to the phallus. Over against the despotic singularity of sovereignty, and set into motion by the very fragility and crisis suffered by the paternal function, flows the sequence of equivalence, laying out a horizontal plane of action and interaction, and of possible subjectivization.

Orestes will go on to avenge his father by killing his mother and her lover. Although he achieves this deed at the end of the second play, the result is subjective catastrophe: the son is driven mad and into exile by a swarm of Furies, archaic goddesses of blood-right and the aristocratic rule of kinship, who revisit the rage of the dead mother on her son. As spirits of vengeance, the Furies represent the threat of an ongoing legacy of perpetual guilt and reciprocal violence. Resolution is found in Athens, on the Areopagus, site of the future high court of Athens, where Athena oversees a trial of Orestes. Ten jurors are assembled to deliver their judgments, recalling in their formal parity the relay of lights that opens the trilogy. Athena breaks the tie among the ten, inserting the continuing necessity of a singular moment of sovereignty within the new constitutional order. Although Orestes has been exonerated, the trial transfers adjudication of murder from the family to the court. At the end of the trilogy, a certain passage has been effected from aristocratic kinship to constitutional citizenship, but not without retaining in reserve a founding moment of sovereign violence, preserved in the tragic mythoi of the House of Atreus and visualized in the domesticated but still vital presence of the Furies, now transformed into the "Eumenides" or "Kindly One" of the third play's title and given cultic place next the court.

The Denmark of Shakespeare's Hamlet is, of course, no Athens, and constitutional conditions and outcomes hang very far on the horizon indeed. Nonetheless, the comparison with the *Oresteia* allows us to bring forward several features that bear on citizenship, from the night watch that opens the play to the circle of friendship that ends it. Hamlet's Denmark is an elective monarchy, representing a certain hybrid between absolutist and constitutional frameworks. In his last moments, Hamlet gives his "dying voice" to Fortinbras and "prophesies his election." He turns, that is, to the phalanx of doubles and foils – Horatio, Laertes, Rosencrantz, Guildenstern, Fortinbras – that have assembled around him in the course of the drama. If Hamlet has, in Lacan's reading from 1958–9, claimed a new freedom with respect to the phallus at the end of the play, the phallic function, I would argue, orients him more toward the horizontal scene of friendship (and hence of proto-citizenship) than toward the singularity of the sovereign position held by the dead father. We might note here that "prince" comes from the Latin "princeps," meaning "first"; in Roman law, *princeps* meant "first citizen," and it came to designate the emperor's nominal relation to the constitutional order of the Republic that remained officially in effect long after its actual eclipse. Hamlet is, from the beginning to the end of the play, the "Prince" of Denmark: does this mean he is always a little less than a sovereign, enunciating a principle of One, but in miniature and in minority, or is he rather the "first Citizen," the first in a row of equals in a civic order, who nonetheless lays claim to a quotient of exceptional sovereignty, in the form of achieved subjectivity?

In electing Fortinbras, Hamlet, I would argue, does not choose his own successor (one sovereign choosing another in a conservative enunciation of elective monarchy; Schmitt 1956), but rather speaks for the body politic, called to give its minimal consent to the person of the new king. At the end of *Hamlet*, the monarchy remains a monarchy, and a brutalized and debased one at that, in the hands of a new prince who is more thug than scholar, more dictator seizing the occasion of emergency than anointed king in an orderly succession. Yet, as Christopher Pye has argued, the "interim" claimed by Hamlet as his own ("It will be short; the interim's mine," 5.2.73) becomes an opening for subjectivity. In and through this interim, Hamlet transforms the passivity of delay within the endless cycle of revenge into the activity of an anticipatory deadline, a call to action that allows the prince to become a subject: "The 'interim' that Hamlet speaks of is the split and pause that haunt the male revenger's act, now miraculously transformed into the enabling measure of his life" (Pye 1999: 112). Hamlet, not unlike Orestes, passes through but also out of the modality of revenge, discovering something like citizenship on the other side of reciprocal violence. The subjectivizing "interim" marked by the act and fact of election orients Hamlet in a sequence of equivalent figures, his foils and doubles, his friends and his successors. Hamlet's final words announce not his accession to some form of kingship in the moment of death, but rather his passage into the chain of friendship that will survive Hamlet and take up his story: "Horatio, I am dead. / Thou liv'st. Report me and my cause aright / To the unsatisfied" (5.2.280–2).

The Hamlet–Horatio couple is minimally anticipated in the friendship between Orestes and Pylades, which we might in turn transfer, with some caution, to the friendship between Freud and Fliess. If Hamlet is the object and mirror of our imaginary fascination, Horatio directs the symbolic dimension of our subjective capture within the scenes before us. Moreover, a remnant of the classical chorus, Horatio performs this work in the mode of public opinion formation, testing, evaluating, and summarizing the state of the union throughout the drama, but always against the backdrop of unconscious knowledge (including the textual variants, generic transformations, and classical recollections gathered up by *Hamlet* as an instance of modern tragedy). As such, Horatio is another figure for us, the audience, not a *princeps* or First Citizen like Hamlet, functioning at the head of the signifying chain, but rather situated discreetly within the devolution of both public reason (*orratio*) and unconscious knowledge, a figure of normative consciousness within the play, between the play and its audience, and in the constitution of tragedy as a genre with a history, that is, a shifting set of aesthetic norms.

Recall Hamlet's cosmic musings: "this brave o'erhanging firmament, this majestical roof fretted with golden fire, why, it appeareth nothing to me but a foul and pestilent congregation of vapours" (2.2.300–4). To the excellent canopy of the Globe Hamlet opposes a fundamentally social term: the foul *congregation* of vapors. "Congregation" – social yet not national, a body without a politic – evokes here the new forms of association emerging in Shakespeare's plays and in Shakespeare's time. If Hamlet's margin of subjectivity is "sovereign," this hard-won sovereignty is not based on kingship and kinship, but rather, I would argue, on friendship in both its sociosexual ambiguity and its emancipatory promise (as *philadelphia*, brotherly love). In this analysis, Hamlet's final moments on stage cast the drama not simply as a mourning play, but also as a modern play. This modernity, however, is native to tragedy itself. For does not every tragedy (if not every work of art) instantiate the passage from a collective to an individual moment, from pre-Oedipal to Oedipal formations, from an archaic economy to a system of exchange, from the anonymity of religious ritual to some new form of expression, founding in each case the possibility of modernism even in the depths of antiquity? We might point here to the Homeric exodus from the domestic economy of the aristocratic household to the possibility of the political at the very end of the *Odyssey*, the same passage re-marked and formalized in the *Oresteia*, which definitively positions Athenian tragedy between ritual and democracy, and between kinship and citizenship. Such forms are radically new because radically contingent, yet, like any authentic beginning (including the beginning made by Freud in his letter to Fliess on October 15, 1897), they instantiate the eternal recurrence of the same: moments of genuine creation that build synapses between epochal moments and hence ground the narratives of history that close around them.

NOTES

1   Missing from this scheme is the authorial approach; because it is not a significant feature of the Aristotelian graphing of tragedy, I have omitted it from this account of tragedy and psychoanalysis.

2   This letter has received extensive analyses; see, for example, Swan (1974) and Bröser (1982).

3   See Hamlet's first soliloquy, 1.2.129–59; for an analysis of the soliloquy in terms of Oedipal guilt, see Lupton (2001: 146).

4   On Shakespeare's possible access to Aeschylus, see Schleiner (1990).

5   On the sexuality of Shakespeare's language outside a psychoanalytic perspective, see Partridge (1948) On Freud and the language of flowers, see Lupton (1996).

6   See Ducrow and Todorov (1979: 137): "A linguistic phenomenon is said to be *synchronic* when all the elements and factors that it brings into play belong to one and the same moment of one and the same language. It is *diachronic* when it brings into play elements and factors belonging to different states of development of a single language."

REFERENCES AND FURTHER READING

Aristotle. (1984). *The Complete Works of Aristotle*, 2 vols., ed. Jonathan Barnes. Princeton, NJ: Princeton University Press.

Bernheimer, Charles and Claire Kahane, eds. (1990). *In Dora's Case: Freud/Hysteria/Feminism*. New York: Columbia University Press.

Brooks, Peter. (1985). *Reading for the Plot: Design and Intention in Narrative*. New York: Vintage.

Bröser, Stephen (1982). "Kästchen, Kasten, Kastration." *Cahiers Confrontation* 8 (Autumn), 87–114.

Copjec, Joan. (2002). *Imagine There's No Woman: Ethics and Sublimation*. Cambridge, MA: MIT Press.

Ducrow, Oswald and Todorov, Tzvetan. (1979). *Encyclopedic Dictionary of the Sciences of Language*, trans. Catherine Porter. Baltimore, MD: Johns Hopkins University Press.

Eliot, T. S. (1920). *The Sacred Wood*. New York: Methuen.

Felman, Shoshana, ed. (1982). *Literature and Psychoanalysis: The Question of Reading (Otherwise)*. Baltimore, MD: Johns Hopkins University Press.

Fineman, Joel. (1991). *The Subjectivity Effect in Western Literary Tradition: Essays Towards the Release of Shakespeare's Will*. Cambridge, MA: MIT Press.

Freud, Sigmund. [1952] (1974).*The Standard Edition of the Complete Psychological Works*, trans. and ed. James Strachey, 24 vols. London: Hogarth Press. [= *SE*]

Freud, Sigmund. (1954). *The Origins of Psychoanalysis: Letters to Wilhelm Fliess, Drafts and Notes: 1887–1902*, trans. Eric Mosbacher and James Strachey, ed.. Marie Bonaparte, Anna Freud, and Ernst Kris. New York: Basic Books.

Green, André. (1979). *The Tragic Affect: The Oedipus Complex in Tragedy*, trans. Alan Sheridan. Cambridge: Cambridge University Press.

Halpern, Richard. (1997). *Shakespeare Among the Moderns*. Ithaca, NY: Cornell University Press.

Jones, Ernest. [1949] (1976). *Hamlet and Oedipus*. New York: W. W. Norton.

Jung, Carl. [1915] (1970). *The Theory of Psycho-Analysis*. New York: Johnson.

Lacan, Jacques. (1958–9). "Le Séminaire, Livre VI: Le désir et son interprétation." Unpublished. Sections translated as "Desire and the Interpretation of Desire in *Hamlet*" in *Literature and Psychoanalysis: The Question of Reading (Otherwise)*, ed. Shoshana Felman, Baltimore, MD: Johns Hopkins University Press, 11–52.

Lacan, Jacques. (1959–60) (1992). *Seminar VII: The Ethics of Psychoanalysis, 1959-60*. Text established by Jacques-Alain Miller, 1982, trans. Dennis Porter. New York: Norton.

Laclau, Ernesto. (1996). *Emancipations*. London: Verso.

Loraux, Nicole. (1986). *The Invention of Athens: The Funeral Oration in the Classical City*, trans. Alan Sheridan. Cambridge, MA: Harvard University Press.

Lupton, Julia Reinhard. (1996). "Sphinx with Bouquet." In *Excavations and Their Objects: Freud's Collection of Antiquity*, ed. Stephen Barker. Albany: State University of New York Press, 107–26.

Lupton, Julia Reinhard. (2001). "The Gertrude Barometer: Teaching Shakespeare with Freud, Eliot, and Lacan." In *Approaches to Teaching Shakespeare's* Hamlet, ed. Bernice W. Kliman. New York: Modern Language Association, 146–52.

Lupton, Julia Reinhard and Reinhard, Kenneth. (1993). *After Oedipus: Shakespeare in Psychoanalysis*. Ithaca, NY: Cornell University Press.

Lyotard, Jean-François. (1977). "Jewish Oedipus," trans. Susan Hanson. *Genre* X:3 (Fall), 395–412.

Partridge, Eric. [1948] (1960). *Shakespeare's Bawdy*. New York: Dutton.

Pye, Christopher. (1999). *The Vanishing: Shakespeare, the Subject, and Early Modern Culture*. Durham, NC: Duke University Press.

Schleiner, Louise. (1990). "Latinized Greek Drama in Shakespeare's Writing of *Hamlet*." *Shakespeare Quarterly* 41:1 (Spring), 29–48.

Schmitt, Carl. (1956). *Hamlet oder Hekuba; der Einbruch der Zeit in das Spiel* [Hamlet or Hecuba: the breakdown of time in the play]. Düsseldorf: E. Diederichs.

Shakespeare,William. (1997). *The Norton Shakespeare*, ed. Stephen Greenblatt et al. New York: Norton.

Sophocles. (1954). *Sophocles I: Oedipus the King, Oedipus at Colonus, Antigone*, trans. David Grene, Robert Fitzgerald, and Elizabeth Wyckoff. Chicago: University of Chicago Press.

Swan, Jim. (1974). "*Mater* and Nannie: Freud's Two Mothers and the Discovery of the Oedipus Complex." *American Imago* 31:1, 1–64.

Tyrrell, William Blake and Larry J. Bennett (1998). *Recapturing Sophocles'* Antigone. Lanham, MD: Rowman & Littlefield.

Weber, Samuel. (1982). *The Legend of Freud*. Minneapolis: University of Minnesota Press.

Zeitlin, Froma. (1986). "Thebes: Theatre of Self and Society in Athenian Drama." In *Greek Tragedy and Political Theory*, ed. J. Peter Euben. Berkeley: University of California Press, 101–41.

Žižek, Slavoj. (1989). *The Sublime Object of Ideology*. London: Verso.

Zupančič, Alenka. (2000). *Ethics of the Real: Kant, Lacan*. London: Verso.

Part III

Tragedy and History

7

Tragedy and City

Deborah Boedeker and Kurt Raaflaub

Tragedy and Civic Education

In the year 405, shortly before the disastrous end of the Peloponnesian War and soon after the deaths of both Sophocles and Euripides, Aristophanes produced his brilliant comedy *Frogs.* Disgusted with the poor quality of the surviving poets, the god Dionysus descends into the underworld to bring Euripides back. He arrives just in time to judge a contest between Aeschylus and Euripides for the chair of tragic poet (757ff.). The two dead poets, having outrageously criticized one another's diction and plots, soon focus on the tragedian's central function. To Aeschylus' question, "For what should a poet be admired?," Euripides responds, "For skill and good advice, and because we make men better in their cities" (1008–10). In the ensuing debate, Euripides is accused of making tragedy democratic: he has given everyone a voice, and has portrayed even the vices and weaknesses of ordinary characters. We will return to this charge, which we think points to one of tragedy's vital political functions. In the comic Aeschylus' view, however, this democratization is reprehensible; the poet's duty is not to describe normal life, let alone its scandalous aspects, but to portray noble ideals and behavior, to instill virtue into the body politic. Unlike Euripides, Aeschylus claims, he has presented models of patriotic and martial conduct in plays like *Seven against Thebes* and *Persians*; his drama was intended to bring out the audience's bravery.

In highlighting the playwright's obligation not just to entertain but also to improve and inspire, Aristophanes caricatures both Euripides and Aeschylus beyond recognition. Yet we should not doubt that his Athenian audience accepted the tragic poet's didactic function – indeed, in *Frogs* even the comic playwright prays to "speak much in fun [*geloia*] and much in earnest [*spoudaia*]" (389–90). Not surprisingly then, as the debate concludes, the emphasis switches even more directly to communal concerns. Dionysus explains: "I came down here for a poet . . . so that the city may survive and keep presenting its choral festivals. So whichever of you is going to give the city some good advice, that's the one I think I will bring back" (1418–21). In the end, more fully understanding his initial purpose of saving the *theater*, Dionysus decides to bring Aeschylus back to the upper world to bring blessings to his fellow-citizens and save the *city* (1487). Hades bids farewell to the poet: "Save our city with your good counsels, and teach the fools – of which there are many!" (1500–3).

Behind its witty excesses, Aristophanes' comic contest reflects the venerable Greek tradition that the poet is a teacher of the people. Aristophanes' Aeschylus cites the famous poets of old, Orpheus, Musaeus, Hesiod, and Homer, as models of the poet-educator (1030–6). Of these, Homer and Hesiod were credited with creating the Greeks' religious framework (Herodotus 2.53), and already in the sixth century they were criticized for the way they did this (Xenophanes fr. 11 Diels-Kranz). More generally, recent scholarship has recognized the Homeric poet's role as political thinker and educator (Raaflaub 2000: 23–34; Hammer 2002). Beyond these epic "teachers," the fragments of archaic lyric and elegiac poetry include many passages that reflect the polity's ethos and transmit its ideology. The martial elegies of Spartan Tyrtaeus and Callinus of Ephesus, for example, clearly enunciate civic and military ideals; even such works as Alcman's *parthenia*, "maiden songs," induct the young female chorus members into the lore and values of Spartan society. Alcaeus' political and social advice to his comrades in Mytilene is part of a long tradition of advice poetry, with parallels in Hesiod, Archilochus, Theognis, and from Athens itself, in Solon. Later in the sixth century, Xenophanes of Colophon addresses his audience on matters of public interest.

Athens' tragedians were not excluded from the assumption that poets are teachers. As we saw, Aristophanes' parody of advice given by Aeschylus and Euripides indicates that this didactic role would seem "normal" to the comedian's audience (which was also the audience of tragedy).

The orator Demosthenes (19.246–8), attacking a political opponent who was also a tragic actor, makes much of the "fine and useful" speech that "the wise Sophocles" wrote for Creon in his *Antigone* (ll. 175–90), declaring that love for one's country far outweighs other sentiments and bonds. A Hellenistic summary of *Antigone* even states that Sophocles was elected a general in the war against Samos because the Athenians were so impressed by this play.

Aristotle, too, seems to have accepted the role of poet-teacher, believing that tragedy could improve citizens by persuading them to live seriously, virtuously, and thoughtfully (see Salkever 1986), but in this view he differed conspicuously from his teacher Plato. In *Republic*, Plato's Socrates objects to tragedy on two grounds, both of them derived from its being a mimetic genre, in which actors imitate behavior of various kinds. (This criticism applies even to Homeric epic, whose speeches are mimetic, but Plato is concerned most of all with tragic drama.) First, Socrates argues that it would be deleterious for the Guardians of his ideal city to be influenced by tragedy's imitations of inferior kinds of people, or even of superior men behaving in accord with emotions rather than reason and law (394c). Second, the Guardians should be educated only with the truth, not an imitation, but dramatic mimesis is far removed from reality, being the mere imitation (in performance) of a fiction (602b–d). In *Republic* 3, Socrates argues that tragedy should be restricted to imitations of good and noble actions (401b–c); by Book 10 (607a), he is in favor of banning it altogether. In *Gorgias* (502b–c), Plato's Socrates makes a further charge. Tragic poets, he argues, cannot really educate their large and heterogeneous audience; to compete successfully, like flute-players or orators, they must flatter their hearers rather than teach them. For Plato, then, tragedy is a powerful, influential medium, but rather than being truly educative, it is harmful and meretricious.

The question of the tragedian's role within the city lies at the center of a current, as well as an ancient, controversy. Political interpretations of tragedy have proliferated in recent years (e.g., Meier 1993; Seaford 1994). That the community or specifically the democracy forms the crucial, even indispensable, background for understanding tragedy has almost become an orthodoxy (e.g., Winkler and Zeitlin 1990; Sommerstein et al. 1993; Pelling 1997; see Saïd 1998 for an excellent summary and discussion). Such views, sometimes exaggerated or presented without sufficient support from ancient evidence, have prompted protest and refutation, challenging scholars to step back, reconsider, and seek a more balanced and comprehensive assessment (e.g., Griffin 1998, 1999; Kurke 1998; Rhodes 2003). It is not our purpose to take sides in this debate. Rather, we wish here to illuminate three issues: the civic context of tragic performances in fifth-century Athens; the politics of tragedy in selected plays whose content is clearly political; and the complexity of content, meaning, and function against which such political interpretations need to be assessed. We shall return briefly to the current controversy at the end of this chapter. Despite the primacy given to it in *Frogs* and *Republic*, we are far from claiming that the role of educator of the polis was a tragedian's only or even most important function – though we do think it was important. As will become clear, however, we would not limit the poet's educative role to advocating specific policies or behaviors.

Tragedy in a Civic Context

We discussed briefly the long-standing tradition that saw the poet (whether epic, lyric, or tragic) as an educator or teacher. Yet certainly in fifth-century Athens there was no lack of those who, officially or unofficially, for pay or without, were happy to offer their advice and wisdom: philosophers, sophists, other intellectuals such as historians or physicians (Thomas 2000), and of course the politicians. Moreover, Athens was politicized to an extraordinary degree; every year thousands of citizens participated in multiple assembly meetings or sat on large judicial panels, hundreds were allotted to offices small and large. Of those over forty, probably two-thirds of the citizens, had even been members of the central administrative Council of Five Hundred for at least one year (Hansen 1999: 249). In all these capacities, Athenian men constantly received advice from fellow-citizens and various "experts" (Plato

Gorgias 455b–d; *Protagoras* 319b–d). Why, then, would they consider, or even need, a tragic poet as political advisor?

We can approach an answer by exploring more broadly the political nature of Athenian theater. Unlike most modern Western theatrical performances, ancient Athenian dramas were public events in public space at the heart of civic festivals, imbued with overtly political overtones. Let us survey this aspect of tragedy in more detail (see also chapter 12 in this volume; Pickard-Cambridge 1968; Csapo and Slater 1995).

Dramatic performances were initially limited to the Great (or City) Dionysia, the main festival of Dionysus (on which we will focus here), and later spread to lesser festivals of the same god (Lenaea, perhaps also Anthesteria). In addition, several of the rural districts (demes) of Attica featured dramas at their own Dionysiac festivals. Performances at the Great Dionysia originally took place in a temporary wooden structure erected each year at the orchestra in the Agora, the most important public square in the city (Travlos 1971: 1–3). By the mid-fifth century at the latest, performances were moved to a permanent outdoor site connected with the sanctuary of Dionysus on the south slope of the Acropolis. By the fourth century, this theater accommodated 15,000–20,000 spectators, a substantial percentage of the city's population – indeed, far more than the political assembly place on the Pnyx, which held about 6,000. Even before the Peloponnesian War, when the population of Athens was much greater (and, since the theater fund had not yet been established, tickets were still expensive, costing two obols or half a day's wage: Sommerstein 1997: 66–7), the theater would have held five to seven percent of the whole population of Attica. The audience consisted mostly of male citizens but included also resident aliens (metics), foreign visitors, and probably some women and slaves (Csapo and Slater 1995: 286–7; Goldhill 1995; Sommerstein 1997). Both in quantity and distribution, it was thus in some ways representative of the entire polis. The chorus members were amateur citizens; although usually they played the role not of Athenian citizens but of foreigners, women, slaves, or even divine beings, they nevertheless often functioned as an internal audience for the actions on stage, voicing reactions and sentiments that would be shared by many in the external audience. Polis, theater community, and stage were deeply interconnected.

The Great Dionysia included four or five days of dramatic performances every spring. Three tragic poets produced "tetralogies," consisting of three tragedies (sometimes thematically connected) followed by a satyr play, which was a kind of burlesque on a mythical subject; five comic poets produced one comedy each. The performances were financed by a special tax levied on the wealthiest citizens, one of several such obligations ("liturgies"). The sponsor (*chorêgos*) paid for the equipment, costumes, and maintenance of chorus, actors, and director (often the poet himself) during rehearsals and performance. One of the highest officials (archons) selected the *chorêgos* who then assembled the chorus, hired or was assigned the actors, and was assigned a poet (probably by lot). No explicit evidence survives about how the poets who were going to perform their plays were selected. Statements made in passing, especially in comedies, suggest that the poets applied, presumably with the text or a sketch of the play, and the archon in charge made the decision, perhaps together with his two assistants (*paredroi*). Two aspects are extraordinary here. One is the procedure itself: decision by a single office holder, in a democracy that otherwise operated through committees. The other is that this issue apparently was uncontroversial and taken for granted in antiquity. It is perhaps best explained by the fact that it was embedded in tradition and cult – two reasons that helped defy adaptation to democratic practices in other religious respects as well (Csapo and Slater 1995: 139–57; Schuller and Dreher 2000: 523–6, 533–4).

A few days before the festival, the poets introduced their plays at an event in the Odeon next to the theater. In a solemn procession, recalling the introduction of Dionysus from the Boiotian village Eleutherai to Athens in the sixth century, the wooden image of Dionysus was carried out to the grove of the hero Academus (later the site of Plato's Academy) on the way to Eleutherai, and later brought back to his sanctuary in a torchlight parade before the festival began. At the end of the performances, a board of judges, selected by a complicated procedure designed to avoid partisanship and bribery, determined the ranking among poets, actors, and *chorêgoi*, who all received prizes (Csapo and Slater 1995:158–65; Schuller and Dreher 2000: 526–36). An assembly held in the theater reviewed the entire event. In addition to all these official public procedures, the first day of the festival opened with a series of explicitly civic and political ceremonies in the theater. The ten elected generals (not the priests) poured libations for the gods. The war orphans, who had been raised by the city and reached adulthood, were introduced with their own and their fathers' names, equipped with a panoply, and discharged to their families. Meritorious citizens were honored with a crown and public acclamation. And the tribute of the empire was displayed in the orchestra (Goldhill 1990). All these ceremonies reminded the audience not least of their city's imperial might, and all were set in an overtly civic, political, and imperial context (ibid., 39–40; Smarczyk 1990: 155–67).

We might explore a little further the possible range of political components at the Dionysia. How exactly the dramatic performances were distributed over four or five days is much debated: one opinion places all five comedies on the first day, followed by a tragic tetralogy on each of the next three, another has the comedies spread over five days, joined on the first two by dithyrambic contests, on the last three by tragedies (Csapo and Slater 1995: 107). Whatever the exact program, it seems that comedies preceded tragedies. Now, as Aristophanes' extant plays and numerous fragments of his competitors attest impressively, comedies in the fifth century tended to be intensely and directly political. The comic poets routinely poked fun at their fellow citizens both collectively and individually, criticizing and satirizing the demos, the jurors, politicians, generals, poets, sophists, and other eminent personalities. With very few exceptions, freedom of speech was virtually unlimited, and, as the case of Aristophanes' feud with Cleon shows, a sore victim's angry and inappropriate reaction could easily backfire (Henderson 1998).

Comic characters sometimes addressed the audience directly, and the poet, speaking through the chorus in the *parabasis*, might even do so in his own persona, explaining, defending, or advertising himself, or offering his advice to the community. Even if the political immediacy of the *parabasis* in *Frogs* (686ff.) is an exception, justified by the emergency of the final phase of the Peloponnesian War, the comic poet apparently saw it as one of his primary functions to comment on the civic life of the community and the tensions caused by it. Through the experiences and figures it satirized, comedy placed the community itself on stage. Whether ridiculing it relentlessly (as in *Knights* or *Wasps*) or drawing on deeper registers beneath hilarious fantasy (as in *Birds* or *Lysistrata*), comic satire often targeted problems and behaviors that were directly connected with the community's way of life and politics and, since Athens at the time was a democracy, especially with democratic ways of doing things.

Most of this decidedly does not apply to tragedy, but it prompts the question whether the audience, "primed" by the politics of comedy, did not attend tragic performances with certain expectations that carried over from previous days and plays. Other considerations also suggest that the audience would be prepared to find contemporary, communal relevance in tragedies. As mentioned earlier, with rare exceptions tragedy's subject matter was taken from myth, and mythical poetry had always had the potential of dramatizing communal concerns. Moreover, a particular group of these mythical themes – focusing on Athenians' selfless dedication to helping the oppressed and saving their fellow Hellenes from barbarian onslaught or tyrannical injustice (such as their protection of the children of Heracles, or intervention to secure the burial of the seven heroes who had fallen in attacking Thebes) – formed an essential component of Athens' self-presentation and imperial ideology, as pronounced annually in the Funeral Oration (Lysias 2.1–16). Such myths were occasionally put on stage, especially in the "suppliant plays" (e.g., Euripides' *Heraclidae* and *Suppliants*). Further, these same themes, as Herodotus (9.27) and Thucydides (1.73; 5.89; 6.83) emphasize, also served as serious arguments in foreign policy debates and diplomatic exchanges. Finally, at least one of these myths, the defeat of the Amazons, along with other deeds of Athens' "national hero" Theseus (Castriota 1992), was prominently represented in public art, such as the "Painted Stoa" in the Agora, friezes and metopes of sanctuaries (e.g. the Parthenon, temple of Hephaestus, and Nike temple), and in independent sculptures (the base of the statue of Athena Parthenos). Such representations contributed to forming an ideological panorama that decisively shaped the self-perception and identity of the Athenians (Hölscher 1998) and conditioned them to consider emulation of their ancestors' great deeds as a primary civic virtue (Raaflaub 2001). Myth thus was a common object of civic and political interpretation and instruction. It is reasonable to assume that it could play that same role in tragic adaptations of mythical stories and that the theater audience, used to multiple aspects of this function, was prepared to recognize it on the tragic stage as well.

It is time, then, to examine in some detail the civic or political content of a few tragedies.

The Politics of Aeschylus' *Suppliants* and *Eumenides*

Aeschylus' *Suppliants*, usually dated to 463, was performed in a time of great political turmoil. After repelling Persian invasions in 490 and 480–79, the Athenians had continued the war against Persia, set their military organization, based on naval power, on a permanent foundation, organized their own alliance (the "Delian League"), and transformed it into a naval empire. The fleet maintaining this empire was rowed largely by lower-class citizens. In contrast to earlier periods, when they had counted for little, these citizens now assumed a military role that was crucial to their city's safety and power, and that raised the possibility (and probably their demand) that they were entitled to a more significant political role as well. In 462 the Athenians enacted reforms that shifted important political powers from the traditional Areopagus Council to the Council of 500, the assembly, and the law courts, that is, to bodies that represented the demos as a whole. Subsequent reforms further facilitated popular participation in politics, and simultaneously made citizenship more exclusive.

The reforms of 462, fully establishing democracy, coincided with a drastic realignment of foreign policy (from collaboration to open rivalry with Sparta) and with the ousting of the long-popular leader Cimon. They were apparently experienced as the victory of one part of the citizen body over the other, bitterly contested and resented by the defeated, and resulted in acute civil strife. This outcome was, of course, not yet known at the time of the performance of *Suppliants*. Still, we may safely assume that an emotional debate about the planned changes was raging for sometime before 462.

In this situation Aeschylus chose to dramatize a myth that played not in Athens but in Argos (a polis traditionally hostile to Sparta, with which the Athenians at the time were seeking closer relations). The chorus consists of the Danaids, daughters of Danaus, descendants of the Argive princess Io who, for reasons familiar to the audience, had ended up in Egypt. Escaping from an unwelcome marriage, pursued by their bridegrooms (with an army), the Danaids seek refuge in their ancestress's home town. After much worry and debate, the Argive leader brings the issue to the assembly, which decides to offer the women shelter and to defy the Egyptians' demand for their extradition. The Argives defeat the Egyptians in battle and integrate the Danaids into their polis. The play's theme thus focused on the protection of suppliants and as such connected it, despite geographical displacement, with a major component of Athenian ideology (mentioned above). Moreover, in their new polis the Danaids became metics (resident aliens). Unusual emphasis is placed in this play on this civic status – an issue of great significance in Athens around that time (Bakewell 1997). All this is likely to have signaled to members of the audience that other issues in the play, too, could be seen as relevant to their community.

The Danaids, with their Egyptian background, hold views about political power and decision-making that contrast starkly with those of the Argives, a typical Greek polis. The former expect the King to decide autocratically, as any eastern monarch would, but the Argive king himself is unwilling to decide in such an important matter without consulting his people (365–75). His dilemma is simple but extreme (as is typical of tragedy). He is confronted by the clash of two almost irreconcilable claims: the demand of the suppliants for protection (backed by Zeus, the divine protector of suppliants, who threatens violators with divine wrath and punishment) and the responsible leader's concern for the safety of his community (which forces him, if at all possible, to avoid war with its inevitable risks and losses). This conflict increases in intensity (341–489) and climaxes in the Danaids' suicide threat (which would add religious pollution to the city's plight). To the Argive leader, the resolution of this dilemma is a matter of communal urgency: if the entire community will be affected by a decision, all citizens have to participate in it.

Hence the leader cannot but let the community decide. The poet stresses often that *all* citizens (the *entire* polis) need to be involved (366–67, 398–9, 483–5, 517–18, 942–3), and he draws attention to the importance of persuasion (523, 623–4). This strand of development in the play culminates in the description of the crucial assembly and its unanimous decision in favor of the suppliants (605–24, 942–9). Accordingly, the choral ode thanking Argos (625ff.) combines traditional physical blessings with explicitly political aspects (the avoidance of civil war, and close collaboration and balance between council and people).

All this helps us recognize the gist of the poet's political concern. In a time of rapid and fundamental social and economic change (Boedeker and Raaflaub 1998: Ch.2), when distinctions between citizens and non-citizens became blurred in many spheres, it seemed all the more important to emphasize the citizens' share in political power, government, and responsibility. This need was even more urgent when the polis was faced with extraordinary outside challenges – as Athens was in the decades following the Persian Wars. When the wellbeing of the entire community was at stake, all the citizens who would have to bear the consequences of political decisions needed to participate in those decisions. It is difficult not to think that this argument was intended to help the theater audience understand one of the most effective justifications of the planned democratic reform. The poet, however, did not formulate a direct political recommendation. Rather, by dramatizing in a mythical story some crucial aspects of the current debate, he drew the citizens' attention to these aspects, raised their critical awareness, and made them conscious of their civic responsibility. By interpreting myth from the perspective of his own time, he made it immediately relevant to his community – especially when the mythical king acted like a model democratic leader, the assembly operated like an exemplary democratic assembly, and the protagonists came to grips with dilemmas that were all too familiar to the audience.

We should not conclude too quickly, though, that Aeschylus the poet here played the role of a thinly disguised pro-democratic activist. Five years later, when the reforms' impact on the community and the negative reaction of the losers had become fully visible, he highlighted the other side of the coin. In the last play of the *Oresteia*,

Orestes, killer of his mother and her lover, avenger of his father's murder, tyrannicide and liberator of Argos, and restorer of legitimate rule, is being hounded by the Furies, avenging spirits of murdered relatives. He has acted upon the orders of Apollo, and Apollo cleanses him of his bloodguilt. A new court, founded by Athena herself on the Areopagus hill in Athens, acquits him. But this does not eliminate all threats: old family claims and the traditional demand for revenge (represented by the Furies) have not been satisfied. This problem is resolved by appeasing the Furies, integrating them into the community, and turning them from hostile outcasts to "well-meaning" powers (*Eumenides*). Conflicts that emerged on three levels in the preceding plays of the trilogy (*Agamemnon* and *The Libation Bearers*) are resolved in this final play. On the level of the family, the action moves from killing and counter-killing (vendetta in an unintegrated community) to court action in the integrated polis; on the divine level, the Furies with their ancient rights yield to the new justice of Zeus which is represented by Apollo and Athena; and on the political level, violent coup and counter-coup, threatening to tear the community apart, are replaced by broad-based communal action, compromise, and vote.

Ingeniously, the poet merges all these strands into one major conflict and its resolution. The Furies are represented as primeval deities (as also in Hesiod's divine genealogy: *Theogony* 185), ordained by fate with a specific function (*timē*) that they have fulfilled from time immemorial and which is thus not subject to any time's judgment. By contrast, Apollo, Athena, and the other gods descended from and ruled by Zeus are young gods. The Furies describe them as violent usurpers, tyrants, who destroy old rights and claims and have no understanding and respect for the old gods. Apollo indeed seeks victory in confrontation, but Athena, sponsor of the new court and protectress of Athens, uses a more diplomatic, conciliatory approach. In this confrontation, an old system of justice, based on fixed claims (oaths), in which every case is the same and neither logic nor mitigating circumstances count, clashes with a new system of justice which is differentiated, takes arguments into account, and is based on persuasion and vote.

Athena justifies her decision to install a new court by pointing out that both claims are powerful, constituting a "crisis either way" (similar to the leader's dilemma in *Suppliants*), a confrontation that cannot be resolved by any one person, even one god (particularly since she is one of the new gods). As in *Suppliants*, therefore, the decision must be made by the community, here represented by the judges. Again ingeniously, the poet lets their votes to acquit or condemn Orestes turn out even. This suffices to release Orestes (with Athena's vote clinching the decision), but an even vote knows no loser, and this opens the way for a compromise solution on other levels.

For it is not enough to reach and announce a verdict in court. If the losing side does not accept this verdict, the conflict will continue. The play thus demonstrates how such a crisis can be resolved – here concerning a murder case, but the implications reach much farther. For the Furies initially are not willing to accept anything but victory; they consider defeat a sign of tyranny and anarchy, an irreparable loss of honor and elimination of their age-old rights, and in revenge they threaten the community with destruction. Athena skillfully overcomes this danger by using rational argument against irrational anger, patient persuasion against desperate threats, and generosity toward the losing side against self-asserting stubbornness: the Furies are offered a position of great importance in the heart of Athena's city, they will become the guardians of domestic prosperity and peace, and they will receive special honors forever. This approach works: the Furies are eventually appeased and allow themselves to be integrated into the community and to contribute their efforts for the good of the community. (For a darker reading of this resolution, focusing on what the Furies have lost and how, see chapter 9 in this volume.)

This play also contains unmistakable references to contemporary conditions or events, such as the alliance with Argos promised by Orestes (significant in Athens' recent turn against Sparta) or the appropriation of Troy in Asia Minor by Athena herself (alluding to the crucial importance of that area for Athenian imperial policies). Even more importantly, this drama plays out in Athens, and its focus on the Areopagus, the very institution that was deprived of its ancient powers by the new democracy just four years earlier, makes it clear that the tragedy's tensions and resolutions relate in very tangible ways to Athenian ones. Hence Athena's warning against tyranny, anarchy, and the pollution of law by inconsiderate innovation must be taken seriously. Other pointers are provided by the poet's urgent call for domestic peace, condemnation of civil strife, and appeal to engage in war, if at all, united against foreign enemies. Finally, we should pay attention to Aeschylus' emphasis on vote, persuasion, and conflict resolution by compromise and integration.

All this appears directly significant in the situation of 458, still full of tensions and potential civil strife. What happened in Argos and the house of Atreus did and might happen in Athens: violent coup and counter-coup, dividing the community and prompting more violence. The old powers (the Furies, in some ways analogous to Athens' traditional aristocratic government) have been ousted by new powers (the young gods, perhaps corresponding to the new democracy). Despite their defeat, they do not accept the verdict and threaten the community with further violence. In order to bring out these claims more sharply, the poet grants the defeated side a higher legitimacy, and compares the victorious side with tyranny. In this constellation, to hold power does not suffice to guarantee peace and durable government; victory by vote is not sufficient to overcome partisanship and hatred. What is needed is patient persuasion and compromise, integration (with high honors) of the old system into the new, and collaboration for the common good (Meier 1990: Ch.5; 1993: 102–37).

In sum, then, *Eumenides* complements *Suppliants*. Under the specific conditions prevailing in Athens, broad-based rule by the entire community makes sense. But democracy as partisan rule without respect for older claims and traditions will be self-destructive and cannot last: it needs to rule by persuasion and compromise, and it must find a way to integrate opposing elements. Seen in this light, *Eumenides* is a powerful example of political thought and an impressive testimony of the tragic poet's independent position and sociopolitical responsibility.

The Politics of *Antigone*

In the 450s and early 440s, large-scale military ventures forced the Athenians to close ranks and focus on foreign policy. War with the Persians ended by ca.450, with Sparta in 446. In the late 440s, the large island of Samos revolted from the Delian League and was subdued in a long and costly war, in which Sophocles himself served as a general. On the domestic scene, in the 440s Pericles proposed a grandiose program of construction on the Acropolis (where the sanctuaries, destroyed by the Persians in 480, had been left in ruins as memorials). This proposal and its funding (in part by the allies' tribute) became the focus of a long power struggle between two factions that ended in 443 with the ostracism of Thucydides (son of Melesias, not the historian) and initiated Pericles' 15-year domination of Athenian politics. (Thucydides 2.65.9 describes this as democracy in name but in reality rule by the first man.) Already in the 440s comedy mocked Pericles as "Olympian" and "tyrant." By the time of *Antigone*'s performance (probably in the late 440s), the impact of democracy on Athenian society and politics had become fully visible. Presumably the civic ideology summarized in Pericles' Funeral Oration (Thucydides 2.36–46) was in place by that time as well: it emphasizes service to and sacrifice for the community and the primacy of the citizens' political over their social identity (Meier 1990: Ch.6); the citizen's relationship to the polis is compared to that of a lover (*erastês*) to his beloved, subordinating his own interests to the community's well-being.

The subject matter of *Antigone* is part of the Theban cycle of myths. Oedipus' children have grown up. His sons, Eteocles and Polynices, have agreed to take turns in ruling Thebes, but Eteocles has refused to relinquish power. Polynices and six other heroes have led an army against Thebes; the assault has failed, and the two brothers have killed each other in a duel. Creon, heir to the Theban throne, prohibits by decree the burial of Polynices, the traitor and enemy of his fatherland. Antigone, Polynices' sister, defies this order, sprinkles dust on the corpse, and is captured by guards. Since she refuses to yield to the king's decree and threats, Creon condemns her to be buried alive. Haemon, Creon's son and Antigone's fiancé, fails to change his father's mind. Confronted by the seer Tiresias, Creon first threatens even the god's prophet but then, urged by the chorus, understands that the gods themselves oppose his view and disapprove of his treatment of Polynices and Antigone, which, reversing divine order, keeps the dead above and entombs the living in the earth. He hurries to free Antigone and bury Polynices but comes too late: Antigone has hanged herself in her tomb, Haemon kills himself over her body, and the queen, hearing the disastrous news, ends her life as well, leaving Creon standing alone in despair over the ruins of his house.

In this play, Antigone and Creon can be identified with contrasting principles that clash violently because of the protagonists' intransigence. Antigone defends family interests and obligations, divine laws that demand the burial of the dead, the autonomy of the individual and the private sphere, and the women's world (*oikos*, home, inside, and love), while Creon insists on obedience to the laws of the city and decrees of the ruler, on the primacy of the state and the public sphere over the private, of the common good over individual interests; he represents the men's world (community, outside, strictness and toughness).

Creon's leadership reveals crucial flaws. Although initially evoking principles (the primacy of the common good and of allegiance to the community) that seem right and are accepted by the chorus of Theban Elders, he demonstrates a level of strictness and harshness that does not bode well; nor does his paranoia about conspiracies and opposition based on corruption – a paranoia that will emerge ever more clearly. News about an attempt to bury Polynices' corpse prompts him to suspect bribery and treason. As he meets resistance, first on the part of Antigone, then of Haemon, he insists ever more rigidly on his principles (including absolute control over family members), fears to lose face, considers it unthinkable to yield to a woman or a younger man, and eventually proclaims his absolute right to make decisions by himself. Power and rule, he declares, are his property, he possesses the city. His understanding of leadership is thus unmasked as tyranny in the harshest sense – not just a self-proclaimed monarch, but an unjust and peremptory one as well. In the course of his confrontation with Tiresias, whom he groundlessly accuses of being bribed as well, he even refuses to yield to the gods and Zeus himself. Creon's personal catastrophe can thus be seen as divine punishment for tyrannical arrogance and *hubris*.

Various people interact with Creon in characteristically different ways. Antigone, fiercely independent (described in her last scene as autonomous, living according to her own laws), bases her defiance on principles; she is the first to accuse Creon openly of tyranny. Confrontational and uncompromising, she consciously risks meeting a violent end. Ismene, Antigone's sister, dares not to stand up against law and authority. The Elders in the chorus, initially deferential and supportive, grow increasingly more doubtful but avoid open resistance. Haemon is at first polite, loyal, and deferential to his father and ruler; when his attempts at persuasion fail, however, he opposes Creon vigorously. Discovering Antigone dead in her underground chamber, he turns violently against Creon and when this attack fails, Haemon kills himself instead, joining Antigone in death. The average citizens, we hear from Creon's opponents, are oppressed by fear but agree with Antigone and hate Creon; they form a silent opposition.

As often, the choral odes offer important insights. Zeus' power is the only stable element in the world; he hates and punishes human self-aggrandizement. Mythical examples illustrate the fate of such overbearing personalities. Wisdom is what we learn from such examples and experiences. The famous "Ode to Man" (332–83) is crucial: humans have mastered the earth and the animals, taught themselves all the skills, speech and quick thought and laws to rule cities, even the healing of illness; but death they have not mastered.

> Humankind – clever , with ingenuity
> in skill unimagined–

moves ahead, sometimes to ill,
at other times to good ends. Who interweaves
the laws of the land and the gods' sworn justice
is elevated in his city [*hupsipolis*]—
but he is cityless [*apolis*]
who associates with baseness
because of daring.
(365–1, trans. Robert Fagles, slightly modified)

All these highly political issues encourage us to find in this play also, among many other perspectives, a pointedly political emphasis. The conflict between Antigone and Creon has often been understood as a contest pitting superior divine, unwritten laws against inferior human laws decreed by polis or tyrant; in this view, Antigone, though dying, would be the moral winner. Many scholars, however, see the conflict as raging between two important prerogatives taken equally to extremes. In this view, both protagonists insist intransigently on their position and on confrontation, and suffer irreversible harm. The solution, conspicuously not achieved in this tragedy, must lie in a compromise. As suggested by the Ode to Man, peace, stability, and the city's prosperity can be achieved only by respecting, reconciling, weaving together the two sets of values. (In the Funeral Oration, Pericles too emphasizes this principle: Thucydides 2.37.3.) What may have prompted the poet's focus on this problem is democracy itself: democracy's process of decision-making allowed for only one winner and one solution; in extreme cases, the loser was ostracized, removed from the polis, and the winner took all, dominating the polis. Laws and decrees passed by the demos allowed no appeal. Against the backdrop of the conflict between Pericles and Thucydides, and of decisions about policies connected with this conflict, we understand why such issues would have troubled many citizens.

Another question is why Sophocles characterizes Creon as a tyrant. This makes it difficult to empathize with him but brings out starkly the conflict between the primacy of the polis and that of the family – a conflict heightened by the fact that Creon's main opponent is a woman and one of his own family. Especially in democracy, the question of the state's interference in areas that traditionally were the family's prerogative must have become a major issue and caused manifold tensions. (The conflict over Polynices' burial reminds us of the Athenian burial of the war dead in a public cemetery, a custom introduced soon after the Persian Wars, in which the state clearly arrogated a family function: Thucydides 2.34.) Creon's decree is called a pronouncement (*kêrugma*); he himself speaks of a law (*nomos*). In fifth-century democracy, decrees on specific issues and the enactment of new laws were not clearly distinguished; some of these "laws" must have appeared to many as arbitrary decisions, dictated by interest groups rather than serving the common good. Questions raised by this experience, then, were likely to concern relations between majority decisions, based on specific constellations, and traditional social norms, and the limits of public authority and legislation.

Furthermore, given the potentially enormous influence of a popular leader in a democracy, it was necessary to ask how such a leader could be prevented from becoming so self-possessed that no sane advice could reach him, so obsessed with power that he considered it his right and possession. This explains the emphasis the poet places on the importance of flexibility, listening, and learning – crucial steps for the success of the democratic process. Finally, Antigone is no revolutionary. She opposes not Creon's rule but one particular decree. She thinks as an independent individual and has the courage to differ. This attitude – made more conspicuous and problematic because attributed to a woman – is crucial in a democracy, but it can be destructive if confrontation and independence become an end in themselves. From this perspective, too, the variety of reactions to Creon's decree and behavior are surely intended to stimulate the audience's thinking.

Antigone is typical of Athenian tragedy in being a complex creation, weaving together multiple strands of characters, actions, ideas, and conflicts. Various versions of the political interpretation presented here have been proposed by many scholars, and other perspectives have been argued as well (see Saïd 1998). In general, we believe, this tragedy, like most, did not take sides in political conflicts, and it is therefore better to avoid one-on-one identifications. Polemics against individuals and specific policies were comedy's domain. Although many Athenians probably thought of Pericles when they watched Creon, this is not to say that Sophocles intended to identify the two. Nor does it seem likely that the play was meant to confirm the Athenians in their devotion to democracy by assuring them that the conflict dramatized here could happen only in a tyranny, not at home. On the contrary, the play questions, probes, exposes weaknesses and potential dangers; it places on stage important tensions that accompanied, though they were not limited to, the rise of democracy. After all, not only a powerful individual, but the demos, too, was capable of tyrannically abusing the power of decrees, causing clashes between public and private, state and family, that resulted in conflict and alienation and that needed to be overcome by mutual respect and understanding.

Tragedy and the Polis

Admittedly and intentionally, the plays we selected here for closer analysis are among the most explicitly political in the preserved corpus. But political or civic issues play crucial roles in many other tragedies as well. Aeschylus' *Persians*, to which we return below, and *Seven against Thebes* (467) are obvious examples. Political interpretations of Sophocles' *Ajax, Oedipus the King, Philoctetes,* and *Oedipus at Colonus* are common, if more controversial. They impose themselves for Euripides' Trojan War plays (*Hecuba, Trojan Women, Andromache, Helen*) and *Phoenician Women*, all performed during the Peloponnesian War (Gregory 1991; Croally 1994). Political themes are also prominent, though less predominant, in *Medea, Ion, Orestes,* and other plays.

Scholars have often tried to identify some of the tragic heroes with specific Athenian politicians: Sophocles' Creon or Oedipus with Pericles, Polynices in *Phoenician Women* with Alcibiades. While it is likely that such correlations may have occurred to audience members, especially since comedy frequently and overtly engaged in them (Philocleon and Bdelycleon, "Lovecleon" and "Hatecleon" in Aristophanes' *Wasps* could not possibly be misunderstood), we do not think that sustained direct correspondence with current events or prominent individuals is typical of tragedy. With rare exceptions, tragedians formed their plots from traditional, broadly familiar mythical tales rather than using historical themes or inventing their own stories. Of course the poets did not hesitate to adapt the plots freely and sometimes radically to serve their purposes – and some of those purposes relate to political discourse. Euripides' Jocasta in *Phoenician Women*, for example, survives the revelation of her incestuous marriage with Oedipus so that she can mediate between her sons in a great debate about power and equity; in *Suppliants*, the same poet has Adrastus describe the "Seven against Thebes," traditionally exemplars of hubris, as ideals of civic virtue. Moreover, tragedians freely interpreted persons, institutions, and events "anachronistically" from a contemporaneous perspective – thus, for example, transforming mythical kings such as Theseus into democratic leaders. Yet the stories and their protagonists remained set apart in the heroic age, the realm of myth.

Like the geographic separation afforded by using myths set in alien places such as Thebes (see Zeitlin 1990), Argos, or Troy, mythic distancing offered the poets great advantages. They could present tragic events as taking place far from the here-and-now, while retaining the freedom to dramatize problems and concerns that were in some ways relevant. The distancing could even allow some viewers to discern important issues (including but not limited to political matters) that were obscured by prevailing ideologies, or that tended to be overlooked in the heat of current controversies.

Keeping in mind this temporal and geographical distance, as well as our conviction that tragedy avoided sustained correspondence with specific political figures and situations, we return to our suggestion that the Athenian audience may have been conditioned to look for contemporary relevance in tragic performances. For their part, the poets occasionally provide clues that they intended a dramatic situation to be politically relevant, by using buzzwords, phrases, or concepts that would bring to mind contemporaneous events or concerns. In this effort they would have been aided by the fact (commented upon by Aristophanes' Praxagora in *Ecclesiazusae* 241–4 and by Thucydides' Cleon in the Mytilenian Debate, 2.38) that their (ideal) audience regularly attended both theater performances and political debates, and thus was skilled in the nuances of political discourse. Obvious examples of a tragic reference intended to be relevant would be the promise of a treaty with Argos, or the foundation of the Areopagus Court, both in Aeschylus' *Eumenides* (discussed above).

Such clues encouraged the public to make the intended connections, but even so, we maintain, the plays generally were not created to support or oppose a specific person, policy, or decision. Whatever he may have thought personally about such issues, in our judgment Aeschylus' purpose in *Eumenides* was not primarily to recommend the treaty with Argos or the restoration of the Areopagus Council's powers. Rather, tragedies illuminated broader attitudes and problems, including critical aspects of Athenian polity. It might be useful to illustrate this assertion with a further example. Aeschylus' *Persians*, performed in 472, only eight years after the event, is a highly political play. Focusing on the magnificent description of the Battle of Salamis, we can read it as patriotic, celebrating the Greek triumph over the Persians. The setting in Susa and the Persian protagonists (including Xerxes himself) clearly provide a Persian perspective, and we can understand the drama's emphasis on divine punishment for human *hubris* and aggrandizement. Yet we should not overlook two striking innovations. Darius who, according to history, almost perished in an ill-conceived and badly executed campaign to conquer the Scythians (Herodotus 4.1–144) is idealized as a king who never jeopardized the safety of his people by aiming at large-scale foreign conquests. Darius' moderation contrasts pointedly with his son Xerxes' *hubris* in having ignored and willfully disrespected a divinely ordained separation between the Asian lands (the Persians' domain) and Europe and the sea (the Greeks' prerogative). In bridging the Hellespont and aiming at conquering Europe, Xerxes trespassed into forbidden realms. Many spectators may have been perfectly happy to revel in patriotic pride and the arrogant king's demise. More critical viewers, however, might have thought of their city's ongoing efforts to establish its control over vast areas along the Anatolian coast that had been "the king's land," and wondered about how the gods might react to trespasses in the other direction.

At the beginning of this chapter, we mentioned the current controversy about the predominant scholarly tendency to consider political meanings pervasive throughout the corpus of extant tragedies. Without denying the political nature of a small number of plays, critics have rightly pointed out that such interpretations often seem arbitrary, fanciful, and ill-founded. Different political interpretations of the same play frequently contradict each other. The role of the community and especially of democracy in shaping tragic concerns has been exaggerated; standard civic, ethical, and religious concerns, shared among democratic and oligarchic poleis, are much more prevalent. Focus on political aspects may ignore or obscure other aspects that are much more widely shared among the extant plays, that indeed were noticed by ancient observers, and that have secured the continuing attractiveness of many plays. "Tragedy is, rather, to be seen as providing a uniquely vivid and piercingly pleasurable enactment of human suffering, magnified in scale and dignity by the fact that the agents were the famous people of myth, and winged with every refinement of poetry and music" (Griffin 1998: 60).

Much of this criticism seems justified. The pendulum has swung too far in one direction. Yet, as so often, the truth may lie in the middle. At the high point of tragedy, nine plays were produced every year for the Dionysia alone (more than a thousand plays overall in the fifth century), each intended to be performed only once for the sponsoring community (before it might be taken "on the road" and later reperformed in other poleis and at kings' courts). For most of that time, Athens, after all, was a democracy – and ruler over an empire. It is easy to underestimate the profound impact, on this community as a whole and on the intellectuals of the time, of the two major transformative experiences of the time: democracy and imperialism. Tragedy shares with other genres of literature (not least historiography) an abiding interest in and concern about these phenomena. The greatest challenge we face is how to develop reliable and verifiable interpretive methodologies that help us avoid guesswork, unfounded assumptions, even mere fantasy, and enable us to base our interpretations on sound foundations. Future discussions should focus more explicitly on this problem. One approach seems most promising: to pay close attention to the clues the poets themselves provide, not least in word choice and terminology; this requires close reading and attention to details (see, e.g., Knox 1979: chs. 9, 11, 21).

All this raises a further (and final) question. Even by a cautious assessment, we hope to have shown, many tragedies were markedly political. Often, it seems, the poets did not hesitate to raise unsettling questions about various aspects of their community's policies and official ideologies. If so, did they have any impact on the citizens' attitudes and decisions? Did what these citizens experienced in the theater influence their vote in the Pnyx? In one area, that of Athens' attitudes toward war, the answer seems to be negative, and reasons can be adduced to explain this (Raaflaub 2001). Yet the evidence available to us is far too limited and unspecific to permit a more general assessment.

One conclusion can be drawn with confidence, however, about tragedy's relation to the polis that produced it. In Aristophanes' *Frogs*, as we have seen, Aeschylus criticizes Euripides for allowing *everyone* to talk in his plays – men of all classes, women, slaves, foreigners. Plato's Socrates warned that tragedy's imitation of all kinds of human behavior would provide the Guardians of his ideal state with too many models, not all of them meritorious. In just that noisy dialogism, in its disagreements, verbal contests, dismayed reactions, doubts, and second thoughts, Athenian tragedy largely reflects the discursive civic context in which it flourished. The dramas provided provocative models both negative and positive for ways that opposing positions could share the public stage and lead to unexpected but, in retrospect, not unintelligible results. In this sense at least, the tragic poet served as a teacher of his audience: not so much by providing specific advice, but by illuminating aspects of the process in a political culture where dialogue really did have immediate and immense consequences.

REFERENCES AND FURTHER READING

Bakewell, Geoffrey W. (1997). "*Metoikia* in the *Supplices* of Aeschylus." *Classical Antiquity* 16: 209–28.

Boedeker, Deborah and Raaflaub, Kurt A. (eds.) (1998). *Democracy, Empire, and the Arts in Fifth-Century Athens*. Cambridge MA: Harvard University Press.

Castriota, David. (1992). *Myth, Ethos, and Actuality: Official Art in Fifth-Century B.C. Athens*. Madison: University of Wisconsin Press.

Croally, N. T. (1994). *Euripidean Polemic: The Trojan Women and the Function of Tragedy*. Cambridge: Cambridge University Press.

Csapo, Eric, and Slater, William J. (1995). *The Context of Ancient Drama*. Ann Arbor: University of Michigan Press.

Goldhill, Simon. (1990). "The Great Dionysia and Civic Ideology." In *Nothing to Do with Dionysos? Athenian Drama in Its Social Context*, ed. John J. Winkler and Froma I. Zeitlin. Princeton, NJ: Princeton University Press, 97–129.

Goldhill, Simon. (1995). "Representing Democracy: Women and the Great Dionysia." In *Ritual, Finance, Politics: Essays Presented to David Lewis*, ed. Robin Osborne and Simon Hornblower. Oxford: Clarendon Press, 347–69.

Gregory, Justina. (1991). *Euripides and the Instruction of the Athenians*. Ann Arbor: University of Michigan Press.

Griffin, Jasper. (1998). "The Social Function of Attic Tragedy." *Classical Quarterly* 48: 39–61.

Griffin, Jasper. (1999). "Sophocles and the Democratic City." In *Sophocles Revisited: Essays Presented to Sir Hugh Lloyd-Jones*, ed. Jasper Griffin. Oxford: Oxford University Press, 73–94.

Hammer, Dean. (2002). *The Iliad as Politics: The Performance of Political Thought*. Norman: University of Oklahoma Press.

Hansen, Mogens H. (1999). *The Athenian Democracy in the Age of Demosthenes: Structures, Principles, and Ideology*. Norman: University of Oklahoma Press.

Henderson, Jeffrey. (1998). "Attic Old Comedy, Frank Speech, and Democracy." In *Democracy, Empire, and the Arts in Fifth-Century Athens*, ed. Deborah Boedeker and Kurt A. Raaflaub. Cambridge, MA: Harvard University Press, 255–73, 405–10.

Hölscher, Tonio. (1998). "Images and Political Identity: The Case of Athens." In *Democracy, Empire, and the Arts in Fifth-Century Athens*, ed. Deborah Boedeker and Kurt A. Raaflaub. Cambridge, MA: Harvard University Press, 153–83, 384–7.

Knox, B. M. W. (1979). *Word and Action. Essays on the Ancient Theater*. Baltimore, MD: Johns Hopkins University Press.

Kurke, Leslie. (1998). "The Cultural Impact of (on) Democracy: Decentering Tragedy." In *Democracy 2500? Questions and Challenges*, ed. Ian Morris and Kurt Raaflaub. Archaeological Institute of America: Colloquia and Conference Papers 2. Dubuque, IA: Kendall/Hunt, 155–69.

Meier, Christian. (1990). *The Greek Discovery of Politics*. Tr. David McLintock. Cambridge, MA: Harvard University Press.

Meier, Christian. (1993). *The Political Art of Greek Tragedy*. Tr. Andrew Webber. Baltimore, MD: Johns Hopkins University Press.

Morris, Ian, and Raaflaub, Kurt, eds. (1998). *Democracy 2500? Questions and Challenges*. Archaeological Institute of America: Colloquia and Conference Papers 2. Dubuque, IA: Kendall/Hunt.

Pelling, Christopher, ed. (1997). *Greek Tragedy and the Historian*. Oxford: Clarendon Press.

Pickard-Cambridge, A. [1968] (1988). *The Dramatic Festivals of Athens*, revised by John Gould and David Lewis. Oxford: Clarendon Press.

Raaflaub, Kurt A. (2000). "Poets, Lawgivers, and the Beginnings of Political Reflection in Archaic Greece." In *The Cambridge History of Greek and Roman Political Thought*, ed. Christopher Rowe and Malcolm Schofield. Cambridge: Cambridge University Press, 23–59.

Raaflaub, Kurt A. (2001). "Father of All – Destroyer of All: War in Late Fifth-Century Athenian Discourse and Ideology." In *War and Democracy: A Comparative Study of the Korean War and the Peloponnesian War*, ed. Barry S. Strauss and David McCann. Armonk, NY: M. E. Sharpe, 307–56.

Rhodes, P. J. (2003). "Nothing to Do with Democracy: Athenian Drama and the *Polis*." *Journal of Hellenic Studies* 123: 104–19.

Saïd, Suzanne. (1998). "Tragedy and Politics." In *Democracy, Empire, and the Arts in Fifth-Century Athens*, ed. Deborah Boedeker and Kurt A. Raaflaub. Cambridge, MA: Harvard University Press, 175–95, 410–15.

Salkever, Stephen. (1986). "Tragedy and the Education of the *Demos*: Aristotle's Response to Plato." In *Greek Tragedy and Political Theory*, ed. Peter Euben. Berkeley: University of California Press, 274–303.

Schuller, Wolfgang, and Martin Dreher. (2000). "Auswahl und Bewertung von dramatischen Aufführungen in der athenischen Demokratie." In *Polis & Politics: Studies in Ancient Greek History Presented to Mogens Herman Hansen on his Sixtieth Birthday*, ed. Pernille Flensted-Jensen, Thomas Heine-Nielsen, and Lene Rubinstein. Copenhagen: Museum Tusculanum Press, 523–39.

Seaford, Richard. (1994). *Reciprocity and Ritual: Homer and Tragedy in the Developing City-State*. Oxford: Clarendon Press.

Smarczyk, Bernhard. (1990). *Untersuchungen zur Religionspolitik und politischen Propaganda Athens im Delisch-Attischen Seebund* [Investigations into the religion, politics, and political propaganda of Athens in the Delian-Attic sea-federation]. Munich: Tuduv-Verlagsgesellschaft.

Sommerstein, Alan H. (1997). "The Theatre Audience, the *Demos*, and the *Suppliants* of Aeschylus. In *Greek Tragedy and the Historian*, ed. Christopher Pelling. Oxford: Clarendon Press, 63–79.

Sommerstein, Alan H., Halliwell, Stephen, Henderson, Jeffrey, and Zimmermann, Bernhard, eds. (1993). *Tragedy, Comedy and the Polis*. Bari: Levante Editori.

Thomas, Rosalind. (2000). *Herodotus in Context. Ethnography, Science and the Art of Persuasion*. Cambridge: Cambridge University Press.

Travlos, John. (1971). *Pictorial Dictionary of Ancient Athens*. New York: Praeger.

Winkler, John J. and Zeitlin, Froma I., eds. (1990). *Nothing to Do with Dionysos? Athenian Drama in Its Social Context*. Princeton, NJ: Princeton University Press.

Zeitlin, Froma I. (1990). "Thebes: Theater of Self and Society in Athenian Drama." In *Nothing to Do with Dionysos? Athenian Drama in Its Social Context*, ed. John J. Winkler and Froma I. Zeitlin. Princeton, NJ: Princeton University Press, 130–67.

8
Tragedy and Materialist Thought

Hugh Grady

I should begin with an explanation of this chapter's title, which uses a term developed over the last two to three decades in English studies, particularly in the field of Shakespeare and the early modern, the academic area I know best. Since sometime between 1980 and 1985[1] the leading critical methods in the field have involved varying combinations of structuralist and poststructuralist ideas of language and textuality, Marx-, Foucault-, and feminist-inspired contextualizing strategies of interpretation, and a concurrent openness to the political dimensions of literary works in both their original contexts and those of the present. To oversimplify a complex array of contemporary practices, we could speak of three major divisions among critics influenced by the currents indicated above: American new historicism, exemplified by Greenblatt; British cultural materialism, represented by Dollimore, Sinfield, and Drakakis; and international feminism, an approach that is both part of but also autonomous from the others. There was no universally accepted umbrella term to designate all three of these clearly interrelated critical methods, but sometime in the 1990s the term "materialism" began to perform this office, at least among some critics.

The term has proven useful, not least in helping to indicate the ambiguous relationship of these new methods to the convoluted and controversial legacy of Marxism as a method of critical analysis. On the one hand, "materialism" correctly suggested some level of affinity to a series of Marxist texts which designated themselves as versions of a broader philosophical materialism: "materialism" and "materialist" were favorite terms of Marx and Engels for designating their methods of analysis, and they were associated with various interpretations of Marxism in the twentieth century through terms like "historical materialism" or Stalin's "dialectical materialism." On the other hand, without any such qualifying adjectives, the term "materialism" *tout court* suggested not so much a specific version of Marxism but a general approach to theory free to choose and select from the large array of Marxisms and, in addition, from other critical social theories like those of feminism or Michel

Foucault's singular materialist theoretical construct. To be sure, British critics like Dollimore and Sinfield aligned themselves with one strand of the complex array of Marxisms by adopting the coinage "cultural materialism" from Raymond Williams, a prominent independent leftist critic from the previous generation who had long dialogued with and dissented from what he thought of as "Marxism" – until Marxism itself was transformed in the 1960s and 1970s by the New Left, after which Williams declared himself a Marxist (Williams 1977: 1–7). Trying to avoid misunderstandings of his position, however, he created a special term to refer to his own and allied theoretical systems, overlapping with, but distinct from, the larger, variegated Marxist theoretical archive: "cultural materialism" (1977: 5). As will become clear below, I think Williams's work, among that of several others, is still highly relevant to contemporary critical theory – especially in discussions of tragedy. But Williams had developed his theory independently of the poststructuralist revolution that soon overtook his successors in the 1980s, whereas the materialism of the last two decades has been deeply shaped by structuralist and poststructuralist concepts and practices, giving it a quite different texture from Williams's writings. In any case the trend in recent years has been to drop Williams' "cultural" qualifier in favor of the unmodified term "materialism," creating a loosely defined but not completely indeterminate theoretical field, including borrowings from any number of other unorthodox *Marxisant* critics such as those of the Frankfurt School. More recently still, the term "materialism" has been appropriated by critics either indifferent or hostile to the Marxist tradition who favor what has been called a "new materialism" of localizing, nontheoretical investigations of material artifacts and practices as a favored method of critical analysis.[2] "Materialism," cultural or otherwise, is now a contested term, and I will necessarily be developing a specific interpretation of it in what follows. As a critic of "the new materialism" (Grady 1996: 4–6, 23–5), I will be focusing on materialist approaches to tragedy closer to but not identical with the cultural materialism which began to be defined in the 1980s and continues to the present.

But one of the unfortunate outcomes of 1980s and 1990s materialism – one greatly exacerbated by the development of a radically localizing "new materialism" – has been suspicion of terms like "tragedy," often thought to be complicit with discredited ideas of transcendent literary significance. The major trend of the last two decades of Shakespearean criticism has been to ignore the category of the tragic altogether, unless to show how an earlier nineteenth- and twentieth-century discourse of the tragic embodied numerous illusions about transcendent value and served conservative political and cultural ends. "Tragedy is an unfashionable subject these days," says Terry Eagleton, but he added, "which is one good reason for writing about it" (2003: ix). And there are important additional reasons. Eagleton, in his new book *Sweet Violence* (2003), describes how the Left has in effect given over discourse on the tragic to the Right, by dismissing or ignoring the term. Eagleton's book is an impressive, almost encyclopedic approach to the long history of discourse about tragedy from the Greeks to the present. But the book strives not only to critique and synthesize the discourse but also to demonstrate that the idea of the tragic is indispensable for grasping the sweep of history, the situation of humanity in the present, and the possibility of moving from this point. Like Raymond Williams, Eagleton shows that the twentieth century, while through many of its leading theorists and artists proclaiming the impossibility of tragedy within advanced capitalism, was itself the most tragic of centuries and capitalism the most tragic of social arrangements. Rather than resist the idea of tragedy, we need to embrace it in its complexity and contradictoriness. Eagleton's ambitious aim is ultimately to define the tragic dimension of history and human life in a very broad-ranging materialist synthesis. I recommend it strongly to all those who wish to pursue the subject more deeply.

My aim here is much more modest: to discuss the tragic in the context of the many important insights of materialist literary and cultural theory since the 1970s, with a view to defining what the (literary and aesthetic) idea of tragedy can mean to us now, in the postmodernist present in relation to materialist thought broadly construed. There is always an important "presentist" dimension involved when we reread the works of the past,[3] and in any case the works of Aeschylus, Sophocles, Euripides, Marlowe, and Shakespeare – not to mention a host of others discussed elsewhere in this anthology – have never been mere exemplars of a later discourse on the tragic. Tragic discourse necessarily failed to encompass their richness and openness to interpretation. "In every era the attempt must be made anew to wrest tradition away from a conformism that is about to overpower it," Walter Benjamin wrote (1968: 255), and this includes the well-intentioned conformism induced by a generation of often polemical and therefore one-sided battles in academia over critical methods. Materialist thought, I believe, if it is redirected, is a major, probably the major vehicle through which to rethink tragedy for the twenty-first century. The following paragraphs should be considered notes toward that project.

Tragedy, Human Nature, and Historical Difference

Tragedy is a concept that has been falsely universalized over and over in its long critical history, both in its guise of designating a particular set of perceptions and feelings and in naming a literary genre of differing times and places. Raymond Williams eloquently wrote on this issue, "Tragedy is . . . not a single and permanent kind of fact, but a series of experiences and conventions and institutions" (1966: 45–6). In one of the finest chapters of his *Modern Tragedy* (1966), "Tragedy and Contemporary Ideas," Williams goes right to the question of how various twentieth-century ideologies have shaped thinking on the issue. His first move is to focus in on "the assumption of a permanent, universal and essentially unchanging human nature (an assumption taken over from one kind to Christianity to 'ritual' anthropology and the general theory of psychologists" (45).

In this critique Williams was undoubtedly influenced by Bertolt Brecht's anti-essentialist theatrical practice and theoretical writings from the 1930s on.[4] Even though some aspects of Brecht's classical criticism now seem dated, Brecht should still be considered one of the sources of both American new historicism and British cultural materialism in passages like the following, from his *A Short Organum for the Theatre* (1949):

> In other words we must drop our habit of taking the different social structures of past periods, then stripping them of everything that makes them different, so that they all look more or less like our own, which then acquires from this process a certain air of having been there all along, in other words of permanence pure and simple. Instead we must leave them their distinguishing marks and keep their impermanence always before our eyes, so that our own period can be seen to be impermanent too. (Brecht 1964: 190)

The widespread idea of a permanent, fixed human nature which Brecht alludes to in the above passage has been, in fact, perhaps the chief target of the materialist criticism since the 1980s. Under the influence of Foucault and Lacan especially, and of a certain "antihumanist" interpretation of Marxism in addition, numerous British and American critics have attacked the "essentialism" of the idea of a general human nature, charted its uses in support of discrimination against women and stigmatized races and ethnic groups, probed its intellectual inconsistencies and evidentiary distortions, and championed notions of decentered selves designed to avoid essentialist ideas of humanity. The idea of "Man," Foucault wrote in his most famous pronouncement on the subject, was invented in the Enlightenment, perfected in the nineteenth century, and had been largely demolished at the end of the twentieth. Man will be replaced by the Being of Language, he concluded – and good riddance (Foucault 1973: 373–87). Jonathan Dollimore, in his seminal *Radical Tragedy* (1989), besides invoking Williams and Foucault, emphasized in this connection as well Marx's famous dictum that "It is not the consciousness of men that determines their being, but, on the contrary, their social being that determines their consciousness" (Marx [1859] 1970: 21; quoted in Dollimore 1989: 153), and he found in Brecht's writings on the theater further development of what he called "this materialist, anti-essentialist conception of subjectivity" (Dollimore 1989: 153). The alternative to an essentialist idea of "man" with a fixed, static nature was the idea of the "decentered self" – that is, a recognition that human consciousness is contradictory and filled with ideology, the commonplace beliefs of one's culture which justify the culture's (unequal) distribution of wealth and power. The term "decentered," originally coined by Lacan, also implied a division between conscious and unconscious thinking which Dollimore did not emphasize, but which a number of other materialist critics – especially feminists – attempted to develop through Lacanian and other forms of psychoanalytic theory.[5]

These basic insights into the socially regressive, ideological effects of prevailing ideas and attitudes about a fixed human nature seem to me, as they do to many others, among the most valuable contributions of the materialist thought of the last two decades, and they need to be incorporated into any materialist theory of tragedy – but not as one-sidedly as they have been to this point. Tragedy, we might say, is universal in its exploration of human suffering, but human suffering itself takes different forms and meanings from era to era, culture to culture. The identity crises suffered by Oedipus, Hamlet, and Nora Helmer, for example, are all wrenching and painful, but the ideas of identity, the moment of disentanglement from a previously taken-for-granted identity, are profoundly different – and revelatory of the societies which created these plays. All three of these plays have plenty to say, directly and indirectly, about "human nature" – but the Greek dynastic curse, the Renaissance humanist alienation from Machiavellian politics, and the emergent nineteenth-century feminist consciousness achieved by Nora at the very end of *A Doll's House* all imply different ideas about what matters most in human life, what can be changed and cannot be changed.

This is not to say, however, as Terry Eagleton has recently argued, that we cannot find limits to human malleability. Many materialists, in their zeal to expose the ideological content of the various appeals to human nature continuing to proliferate in our time,[6] have been reluctant to cede any ground whatsoever to "nature" instead of "nurture," to biology instead of culture. But this ultimately leads to a wholly untenable materialism which denies the influence of biology on human life – leading to a very strange materialism and to bad tragic theory.

Shakespeare's *King Lear* is a play that has inspired volumes of criticism, most of it since the beginning of the twentieth century recognizing at one level or another that much of this great play's thematics center around Lear's probing for the degree-zero of human nature, for "the thing itself" as he calls "unaccommodated man," man outside of culture and its systems of signification, the man he sees figured in the unclothed person of Tom o'Bedlam – who is, of course, the disguised, much wronged Edgar. There is no single answer to Lear's questions in the play. Instead, we witness the wildly contrasting cases of benevolent, generous characters in battle with the malevolent and the cruel ones. The answer to the question seems to be: "man" is both these things, neither necessarily cruel nor necessarily kind. But in the central figure of Lear himself we witness a transformation – wrenching, even cruel in the suffering which the change demands – from one state to the other. Do we want to say, with the Dollimore of *Radical Tragedy*, that the valorization of this change is an instance of essentialist humanism and that the materialist critic's task in addressing this play is "to make visible social process and its forms of ideological misrecognition" (1989: 189–203)? As I argued elsewhere, such procedures leave the critic largely silent before the grand themes and issues of this great tragedy, valuing it exclusively for its exposure of early modern ideologies rather than for any positive insights of its own into suffering, death, identity, and redemption (Grady 2002: 103–4).

Instead of fearing the consequences of positing some basic human genotype – what the young Marx called our species-being – materialism, I believe, needs to acknowledge the existence of and the limits to human nature, underlining the unknown dimensions of the boundaries formed by these limits. Several centuries of tragic investigations into these boundaries constitute an enormous resource for human self-understanding. Shakespeare alone provides a considerable library of possibilities. Indeed, social theorist Agnes Heller, in a new book which brings the insights of a lifetime of work and writing in social philosophy to bear on Shakespeare's plays, suggests that virtually all models of human nature ever produced are represented somewhere in Shakespeare (Heller 2002: 149–60 *et passim*). Similarly, the extant plays of Greek tragedy hardly fit into any single mold either, with Euripides especially diverse in his representations. Terry Eagleton is cogent on this point:

> Historicism is mistaken to believe that what belongs to our species-being must invariably be politically retrograde or irrelevant. It can indeed be this; but one would expect such devotees of cultural relativity to be a little less inflexibly universalist in their opinions. It is true that there is much about our species-being which is passive, constrained, and inert. But this may be a source of radical politics, not an obstacle to it. Our passivity, for example, is closely bound up with our frailty and vulnerability, in which any authentic politics must be anchored. Tragedy can be among other things a symbolic coming to terms with our finitude and fragility, without which any political project is likely to founder. But this weakness is also a source of power, since it is where some of our needs take root. (2003: xv)

Putting it simply, a basic datum of human nature is mortality, and tragedy is centrally about some of the consequences of our mortality, or it is about nothing. The responses to the universal fact of death made by humans in our long history and prehistory are staggeringly different, but common emotions of fear, grief, and mourning are not hard to perceive in all of them. Along with Eagleton, I believe this is one of several starting points for a materialist view of tragedy.

Order and Tragedy

In his highly useful and insightful anatomy of significant theories of the tragic for contemporary thinking, British cultural materialist John Drakakis drew attention to the priority accorded by several of them to the idea that tragedy always represents a violation of the natural order which it is the hero's task to restore through suffering and death. Twentieth-century Anglo-American Shakespearean criticism, from A. C. Bradley through E. M. W. Tillyard and into the mainstream of modernist Shakespeare criticism, repeatedly invoked the idea of tragedy as a loss of natural order which the suffering of the tragic hero somehow restores. This was especially true of one of the most influential of all works about Shakespearean tragedy, A. C. Bradley's 1904 Romantic-realist synthesis, *Shakespearean Tragedy*, continually in print from its date of publication to the present. Bradley wrote, for example, "The ultimate power in the tragic world is a moral order," an order which "does not show itself indifferent to good and evil, or equally favourable or unfavourable to both, but shows itself akin to good and alien from evil" (Bradley 1904: 23; quoted in Drakakis 1992: 11). Drakakis goes on to show how Bradley's interpretation of tragedy as asserting a moral order violated by a substantial, metaphysical evil plays through the modernist Shakespeare criticism of such figures as L. C. Knights, Irving Ribner, Clifford Leech, and Northrop Frye (1992: 12–15). The list could of course be extended, and it certainly should include the vastly influential figure of E. M. W. Tillyard, who seldom if ever wrote directly on tragedies, but whose argument for an underlying sense of order in all of Shakespeare's plays, indeed in all the other literary works of the early modern, was transmitted as a received truth by many, probably the majority of critics and teachers throughout the 1950s and 1960s. As is shown by any number of American textbooks for Introduction to Literature college courses, the idea could be and was extended to Greek tragedy as well – despite the resistances to such an interpretation in texts like *Antigone*, *Medea*, or *Bacchae*, for which a moral interpretation of the outcome seems rather hard to hold to. The power of the idea, I would argue, rests on two different but related qualities. First, it assumes an ultimately benevolent universe of order and justice and is therefore compatible with the Western religious beliefs which permeate our culture. It is thus a comforting doctrine. Second, now as in the Elizabethan age, it legitimates the existing order and authority of state and status quo, stabilizing the current distribution of wealth and power, disallowing challenges to what is seen as a natural order in harmony with an inherent human nature.

Recognition of the ideological dimension of the idea of order in many theories of tragedy is a strength of recent materialist criticism which should be continued in any emerging materialist theory of tragedy. In this connection, Drakakis points out quite cogently that the classic writings on tragedy of both Nietzsche and Freud make exactly the opposite assumptions. For both of these theorists, tragedy reveals the disorder inherent in human nature underneath the ego's Apollonian appearances. This is particularly true of Nietzsche's *The Birth of Tragedy*, with its critique of Apollonian rationality and its assertion of the reality of power and desire – all central issues for Foucault, and therefore for contemporary materialist theory. Given this centrality, in fact, it is somewhat puzzling that instead of recognizing the relevance of materialist theory to tragedy, most materialist critics have in fact ignored them. Even Drakakis, despite his interest in aspects of the previous philosophical discourse on the tragic, moves in the direction of dismantling rather than reconfiguring this discourse (1992: 37).

Drakakis's critique, particularly of the dominant twentieth-century discourse on tragedy in English studies, rightly targets a recurring conservativism, a dubious assumption of unchanging, universal human nature, and a recurrent emphasis on a substantive, metaphysical concept of evil in most of these works, and I am in complete agreement that a materialist contribution to a theory of tragedy would attempt to reverse all three of these assumptions. It is rather the trend in much contemporary materialist criticism to abandon the enterprise of defining a workable category of the tragic, which I think is shortsighted.[7]

If, as I think, tragedy in several major instances from different eras, has been concerned with questioning human nature and probing its limits, it is therefore also necessarily concerned with the contours of the myriad of social orders in which humanity has lived over thousands of years. And therefore it is necessarily concerned with issues of order.

But does tragedy always assume an underlying natural order, as so many critics have asserted? The cosmologies of most human societies seem to have done so. One of the lasting achievements of the work of French anthropologist Claude Lévi-Strauss, whose name was once on everyone's lips, was to show how mythologies create mental orders which get embodied in concrete human societies and the structures, physical and social, which they build – and in the stories they compose or write. Traditional societies create cosmologies which justify the social order, as the grand correspondences of the European idea of the Great Chain of Being show us. Tillyard assumed that the same was true of Shakespeare's plays and the works of all his companions.

The problem with this idea, however, as a generation of scholars has subsequently demonstrated, is that early modern culture, precisely because it was in the midst of a profound cultural paradigm shift, did not work that way, and neither did those of other transitional societies which produced tragedy. We can identify moments – fifth-century-BCE Greece, sixteenth- and seventeenth-century Europe – in which traditional cosmologies were challenged by new forms of rationality (as I will discuss below, critical and instrumental reason) which called them in doubt. These are of course precisely the points of the most creative upsurge in the writing of tragedy. "And new Philosophy calls all in doubt," wrote John Donne in his 1611 poem "The First Anniversarie" (Donne 1967: 207, l. 205), and his contemporaries Christopher Marlowe, William Shakespeare, and John Webster, among others, showed us numerous examples of this phenomenon on the stage, just as Sophocles and Euripides had done in their day in their own terms. Traditional theories of tragedy have understood that tragedy continually disrupts order and calls it in doubt, but they assume that at the end of the play, traditional order is reestablished and the good prevails. Knowing what we know about the cultural histories of Athens and Renaissance London, however, it is hard to see what justification there is for this assumption. When Medea rides away from her pursuers in the chariot of the sun at the end of her tragedy, what moral order has been reestablished? When Tamburlaine continues his unbroken chain of triumphs and demonstrates the military efficacy of killing civilians, what moral order is restored? The same might be and has been asked of the deaths of Hamlet, Cordelia, and Lear. An equally plausible interpretation of all of these representative plays would be to say that the universe appears indifferent to moral orders, and what order is reestablished – or fails to be reestablished – is a (merely) human and historical matter which perhaps helps chart for us, provisionally, the limits of the human under great duress. And as Bertolt Brecht, Jonathan Dollimore, and a long line of more traditional Marxist critics have demonstrated, tragedy can be a marvelous vehicle for the exposure of and protest against injustice and repression. There is nothing at all inherently conservative about it.

Historicize, Always Historicize! But How?

I mentioned earlier in this chapter that the localistic and particularist tendency in 1980s new historicism has developed in the last decade into a "new materialism" which appears indifferent to the large-scale historical issues (on the nature of modernity, the historicity of selfhood, for example) which were central in founding new historicist (and cultural materialist) works. This development retrospectively demands questioning the particular elements of the new historicism which created the potential for this development. I believe the anthropological moment of the method was always to some extent in conflict with its historicizing impulses. The founding notion of "culture" within anthropology was inherently spatial, not temporal, synchronic, not diachronic. Anthropologists use thick description to anatomize currently existing societies and to discover their social arrangements and the belief systems which inform them. To this extent, cultures – as they exist in anthropology – have no histories. In the works of the new materialism, this anthropological tendency has triumphed, into a historicism so finely textured and detailed that its development over long-range time is occluded. We see trees, but no forests.

The idea of tragedy, with its transhistorical dimension, resists such localization. I would say that there is no reason in principle why the fine details could not finally be woven into a larger historical perspective. Walter Benjamin's *Arcades Project* (1999) – more properly the notes to the project which constitute the work published and translated decades after Benjamin's death – is nothing if not a mind-boggling demonstration of a critic intent on just such a minute labor, and he achieved some dazzling successes within his uneven, voluminous material. But few, if any, will be able to follow his audacious lead. In practice, localism has meant a radical shrinkage of the levels and the durations of history taken into account.

On the other hand, one of the great strengths of almost all the Marxisms has been their historical sweep, the grand narrative which encompasses all of human history and leads triumphantly into an emancipatory future. Of course, few of us participate in this grand proletarian myth these days; our fear of *les grands récits* is based on very good reasons. However, versions of postmodernist Marxism have arisen,[8] and they retain analytic narrative as a chief method of thought, even though these narratives are no longer considered teleological. And I believe these narrativizing methods of the variegated Marxist tradition constitute important resources for an adequate material-ist theory of tragedy. For me the most interesting of these, and the one with the most relevance for almost all the texts we call tragic, is the inverted Hegelian history of rationality outlined by Horkheimer and Adorno in their 1944 *Dialectic of Enlighten-ment*, which I will discuss below.

Reason and Unreason in Tragedy

Oedipus in *Oedipus the King*, Creon in *Antigone*, Pentheus in *Bacchae*, and perhaps even Apollo and Orestes in *The Oresteia* all enunciate forms of rationality which are tested and found wanting in the tragedies in which they appear. Scholars connect this new rationality with the rise of rhetoric as a technology of persuasion in the new democracy of fifth-century-BCE Athens and with new notions of what would later be called *raisons d'état* to defend the new collectivist institution of the state against older traditions. As Nietzsche famously asserted, we can watch a slow trajectory from Aeschylus to Sophocles to Euripides which culminates in the birth of Socratic philosophy in the next generation, a trajectory of a growing, illusion-filled Apollonian rationality, obscuring the Dionysian will-to-power which tragedies manifested underneath their apparent rationality ([1872, 1887] 1956).

Shakespearean tragedy similarly stages contests of forms of rationality, as has long, if sporadically, been noted.[9] In *Othello*, for instance, Iago consistently enunciates a narrow, highly efficacious form of complex rationality which combines a series of calculated rhetorical arguments continually shifting in assumptions, evidence, and logic, but consistent in intent: they are designed to persuade their targets of falsehoods by mobilizing unconscious assumptions and desires within their hearers, Roderigo and Othello. Iago in this sense is like a contemporary copywriter for an advertising agency, pursuing an instrumental rhetoric indifferent to any other values than its own efficacy. Ultimately, as I have argued elsewhere, close textual analysis will show that despite the apparent value-free, instrumental quality of the rationality, it consistently advances an agenda of erotically charged aggression motivated by a generalized, largely irrational sense of both envy and jealousy (Grady 1996: 95–109). It is, finally, a deeply irrational rationality.

In *King Lear* a similar rationality is at work in the actions and speech of the so-called "evil" camp, enunciated most explicitly by Edmund in his "Thou, Nature, art my goddess" speech, but implicitly in the deceptive words and actions of Cornwall, Goneril, and Regan. The memorable, searing scene of the blinding of old Gloucester, which occurs just after the great heath scenes with their praise of unreason and madness as truer vehicles to truth than rationality, is the play's epiphanic judgment on instrumental reason, demonstrating its potential cruelty, its undermining of tradition, its "unnaturalness." Lear himself had participated in such instrumental rationality in his foolish attempt to quantify his daughters' love in the opening scene, and the play is focused around his and Gloucester's recovery and repentance from succumbing to the deceptive rhetoric and manipulation of "unnatural" children. Famously, the play pits alternative uses of the words "nature" and "natural" against each other, highlighting its representation of competing rationalities. The traditionalists like Gloucester and Albany – Lear himself at first seems to be a traditionalist with modernizing tendencies – affirm the view of an inherent natural order governing cosmos, state, family, and individual; the others, Edmund especially, evoke a "nature" that is a Dionysian repository of power, desire, and aggression.

For a long time, under the influence of critics like Bradley and Tillyard, it was assumed that Shakespeare, because in the Jacobean tragedies especially he painted instrumental reason with such dark colors, was a conservative traditionalist. What this traditional view ignored or underemphasized, however, were the foolish colors in which Shakespeare arrayed the supposed "traditionalists" like Othello, Lear, or Gloucester. Rather, the plays seem to follow a more Hegelian pattern, posing two problematic forms of rationality against each other, enacting the defeat of tradition by modernizing instrumental reason, only to show the subsequent collapse of instrumental reason. At the end of *King Lear*, especially, the audience is teased, made to imagine hope and despair, as Cordelia and Lear appear now to have lived, now to have died. The space is created for a new form of rationality, which would be neither of the other two. But the space is, as it were, blank, not filled in, symbolized but not enunciated in discourse. In short, the dialectic is a negative one, never arriving at a final synthesis, but certainly going beyond its two previous stages.[10]

This clash of rationalities is a central one for Shakespearean tragedy, history, and some of the comedies, but it is, I think, an essentially tragic idea which tends to add a tragic dimension to the histories (it is present in virtually all of them) and the comedies (for example, in *As You Like It*, *The Winter's Tale*, and *The Tempest*) in which it is developed.[11]

As mentioned above, the materialist work which most illuminates Shakespeare's probing of rationality is *Dialectic of Enlightenment*. Writing during the tragic events of World War II, with its culminating revelation of the Holocaust and its development of nuclear weapons, drawing on a broad counter-Enlightenment tradition, including German Romanticism, and radicalizing and deepening Max Weber's studies of administrative reason and its paradoxes, Horkheimer and Adorno identified instrumental reason as one of the chief harbingers and products of capitalist modernity, and one which was a crucial component of the major catastrophes of twentieth-century history – Nazism, Stalinism, and totalistic war. Less starkly but crucially, instrumental reason also underlay the development of the mass consumer society they witnessed in New York and California in the 1940s, and their pioneering, prescient work on what they termed "the culture industry" has remained crucial. But Max Horkheimer had had an earlier interest in the Renaissance, and in an essay from the 1930s he identified the Renaissance as the moment when modern, instrumental reason came into existence, in the works of Machiavelli, the early Renaissance scientists, and Francis Bacon (Horkheimer [1930] 1993). Modernity proper, it might be said, begins its self-perpetuating dynamic of modernization when instrumental reason marries capitalist economics, and the two autotelic systems reinforce each other in a fatal feedback loop. Shakespeare comes back over and over in his works to the dynamics of the dialectic of enlightenment theorized by Horkheimer and Adorno three and a half centuries after his death.

The connection of this dynamic with ancient Greek society in the clash of rationalities in Greek tragedy and philosophy, which I briefly discussed above, might at first seem remote from all this, but appearances can be deceiving. Fredric Jameson very usefully underlined in his recapitulation of the theory of instrumental reason (Jameson 1990) that the dialectic of enlightenment is a relative process with major eruptions but continuing throughout human history. "No universal history leads from savagery to humanitarianism," wrote Theodor Adorno, "but there is one leading from the slingshot to the megaton bomb" (Adorno 1973: 320). In military science, rhetoric, and political-administrative technology, the ancient world developed forms of instrumental reason potent enough to culminate in the vast Roman Empire. These impulses were contained and even reversed in the Christianization and infrastructure-dismantling of the so-called transition to feudalism in a complex process, but one whose outlines (in this regard at any rate) seem clear and set the stage for the European Renaissance – a process, therefore, with a dark side as well as its much celebrated bright one. In the two high points of Western tragedy, the Greek and the Shakespearean, we are situated at transitional points, when instrumental reason is challenging tradition, when mythos is giving way to logos.[12] And this transitional zone, as others have suggested before me, seems to be the privileged ground for the development of tragedy, which in this light appears to be a potent combination of traditional, poetic modes of rationality fused with newer, more unilinear, "modern" ones.

Is this a "materialist" theory? I would argue that it is, since materialism in such major figures as Marx and Foucault has been centrally concerned with the history of *mentalités*, ideologies, and worldviews, developing in innumerable complex relations to more obviously "material" factors like city-building, changing agricultural and productive technologies, warfare, conquests, and, of course, economic modes of production – but with a logic of their own which gives mental structures a relative autonomy long recognized in the Marxist tradition in numerous classic passages from Marx and Engels onward – and repeatedly underlined in recent materialist theorizing. In short, structures of thought are crucial elements of major versions of materialism.

Tragedy, Modernity, and Value

It is a commonplace of literary history that the medieval period could make little sense of the tragic tradition of antiquity. Chaucer's woeful series of one-paragraph "tragedies" in "The Monk's Tale" is an oft-cited example, one which seems to show that in the fourteenth century, tragedy was seen as a certain type of narrative with the repetitive moral mission of underlining the fickleness of fortune in the world. Traditionally, it has been said, this reduction of tragedy was a result of the incompatibility of classical ideas of tragic suffering with the received truths of Christianity, especially their built-in happy ending. Raymond Williams cast some doubt on this traditional view. Why is the still very Christianized early modern period suddenly receptive to the idea of tragedy, he asked (1966: 19) – but then he goes on to answer his own question, and I think his answer makes for a good starting point of a longer one. The dissolution of the feudal world, Williams says, allows tragedy to reunite what the medieval era had separated, common human experience and the misfortune of the great. In the less rigidly divided society that evolved in the England (especially the London) of the sixteenth century, tragedy became more resonant with a larger part of the population (1966: 23–5). But there is much more to the difference between the high Middle Ages of Chaucer's time and the early modernity of Shakespeare's than that. Even Williams in 1966 seems to have been swayed by the reign of Tillyard into believing that the Elizabethan and Jacobean tragedians were order-affirming traditionalists who managed to create tragedy despite their orthodox Christian beliefs. Forty years later, as I have emphasized, this assumption is no longer convincing. As numerous contemporary critics have noted in passing, and as Agnes Heller ([1967] 1981) and I (1996) have each shown at greater length, Shakespearean drama is more compatible with the skeptical–pragmatic philosophies of Machiavelli and Montaigne than with received Christianity, especially so in the great tragedies *Hamlet*, *Troilus and Cressida*, *Othello*, and *King Lear*, each of which in its own way posits a universe indifferent to moral outcomes and a human world of autotelic power politics and free-flowing, identity-shifting subjectivity. In the late tragedy *Timon of Athens* and in the tragic comedy *The Merchant of Venice*, in substantial portions of *Troilus and Cressida* and in passages in *Othello*, power and subjectivity are in turn linked with commodity trade and commodity fetishism. In short, Shakespeare's tragic world is a world of modernity, replete with three of the defining characteristics of modernity as it has been theorized by numerous historians and social philosophers: a secular, post-religious mentality; instrumental, value-free rationality; and a developing (preindustrial) capitalist economy. Except for Shakespeare's Roman and Greek plays, the histories and tragedies are also fully involved in a fourth central category of the modern, a nation-state system operating according to Machiavellian politics. But if the Roman and Greek history-tragedies necessarily avoid the idea of the nation, they are still among the most Machiavellian (and in that sense "modern") of all Shakespeare's plays: *Timon of Athens*, *Troilus and Cressida*, *Titus Andronicus*, *Julius Caesar*, and *Antony and Cleopatra* especially read like thought-experiments for imagining post-religious societies in which mercantile capitalism, power politics, and unrepressed sexual desire are allowed to operate without any of the restraints of traditional society. The same could be said of the major works of both Corneille and Racine a half-century later in a France still transitional between feudalism and modernity. Few would contest this claim for the works of "modern tragedy" which Williams identified in the nineteenth and twentieth centuries (1966). Tragedy, for us, at this time (and at least since the advent of literary Modernism around 1910) is implicated in the values and characteristics of modernity.

There is obviously a paradox involved in claiming for the discourses of modernity artworks of the ancient world like the surviving Greek tragedies from fifth-century-BCE Athens. But this a point where a recognition of an inevitable and enabling presentism is crucial in understanding the ways in which even Greek and Roman tragedies manifest (for us) characteristics of modernity. As in the Renaissance, classical societies represent for us non-Judeo-Christian (and to that extent non-traditional) societies, ones in which ambition, jealousy, and revenge can manifest themselves in the same primal zone theorized by Lear in his speculations on "unaccommodated man." As we have seen, we can recognize in major Greek tragedies versions of instrumental rationality crucial to modernity and the operations of aggression and sexual desire we have learned to see in ourselves in a post-Freudian world. That is why classical Greek settings or repeated allusions have been important for twentieth-century tragic writers like O'Neill, Sartre, and Beckett. I have before me a paperback edition of translations of three plays by Euripides (1988) whose cover illustration is Picasso's Cubist *Women Crying*, and it is far from a unique example of a cultural impulse to link Greek tragedy with modernist art. Twentieth-century stage history is full of attempts to adopt elements of ancient Greek dramaturgy — masks, choruses, stylized movements — to modernist aesthetic (and at times political) ends.

This oxymoronic marriage of classical and modernist aesthetics is centrally concerned, I believe, with issues of value, of our ability to assess and understand good and evil in a post-traditional world. In ancient Greece, the source of value was largely unquestioned, seen as residing in a natural material world of inherent goodness (or at least one without the slightest taint of Manichaean inherent evil) in porous interactions with humanistic gods, goddesses, and spirits. Homeric society, Lukács famously asserted, had answered mankind's questions (of meaning, relation of humanity to nature, and of purpose in life) before the developing history of mankind enabled us to pose them (Lukács [1920] 1971: 29–30). For this reason, I believe, the Homeric poems have not been associated with modernist art in the way Greek tragedy has been. In the much later Athenian tragedies, human alienation from the social and the natural is clearly in evidence, in fact, center-stage. And while the different tragedians take characteristically different attitudes toward the gods (Aeschylus, we might say, a proto-monotheist, Euripides a proto-atheist, Sophocles somewhere between), for us in late modernity the skies in the works of all three surviving playwrights are empty, the gods metaphors for an array of natural and human powers. In short, Greek tragedy is always materialist-for-us, more starkly even than is Shakespeare. The difficulty of founding a stable sense of good and evil, of right and wrong, is as problematic for Orestes, Oedipus, Antigone, Creon, Pentheus, and Phaedra as it is for Faustus, Hamlet, Lear, Macbeth, Timon, and the others — and as it is for us in the early twenty-first century. "Tragedy," Terry Eagleton wrote, "is an imaginary solution to a real contradiction plaguing modernity" (2003: 119). And a sufficiently self-conscious materialist criticism would be presentist enough (in the good sense of the word) to recognize and develop this reconfiguration of the ancient and the (post-) modern.

Materialist thought as it was reformulated in late twentieth-century literary studies has had, until very recently, a one-sided relation to ideas of the tragic, more suspicious and skeptical than sympathetic and accepting. But in two new works, Terry Eagleton's *Sweet Violence* (2003) and Agnes Heller's *The Time is Out of Joint* (2002), the tide seems to be shifting into a more appreciatory relationship with the tragic, like a rebellious daughter rediscovering her mother. It is a shift that promises a new generation of critical creativity.

Notes

1   Two of the major paradigm-changing books appeared in 1980: Greenblatt (1980) and the feminist critical anthology Lenz, Greene, and Neely (1980). In 1985 three seminal critical anthologies appeared – Dollimore and Sinfield (1985), Drakakis (1985), and Parker and Hartmann (1985).

2   This evolution of the term was documented and analyzed incisively by American critics (Harris 2001 and Bruster 2003).

3   I argued various aspects of this position in Grady (1991, 1996, 2002); see also Hawkes (2002).

4   Williams (1966) discusses Brecht in a chapter, finding several of his plays among the most significant twentieth-century examples of what he calls "modern tragedy," but he complains that Brecht's critical terminology of "epic" vs. "Aristotelian" theater is misleading and inconsistent.

5   The turn to psychoanalytic theory by feminists in the 1980s and 1990s might be surprising to those who remember classic feminist denunciations of Freud by pioneering 1970s feminist critics, but it became widespread because Freudian theory – if not every jot and tittle of Freud's specific analyses – was deemed to offer the best prospects for an "anti-essentialist" theory of gender and sex, and this trend has continued into the new millennium, particularly in the innovative work of Judith Butler.

6   The widely popularized theories of the so-called evolutionary psychologists, with their "just-so story" approach to evidence, are the latest in a long line of sexist and racist theories of human nature in the last two centuries.

7   See Grady (1999) for an earlier statement of this position, along with some of the other themes of this chapter.

8   Eagleton (2003) would be an excellent example of such a phenomenon, despite his earlier critique of many aspects of the theoretical confluence he calls postmodernism, as would the theory developed across a myriad of works by either Fredric Jameson or Gayatri Spivak. In my view both Adorno and Benjamin were theoretical postmodernists, and I have applied the same label to the theory I developed in Grady (1996). For further discussion and examples see Callari, Cullenberg, and Biewener (1995).

9   For example, Coleridge (1930: 2: 210, 286–7); Lewis (1927), and Heilman ([1956] 1977: 222).

10 If all this sounds too formulaic, let me plead that I tried to work out the fine details of this dynamic of rationality (and related forms of what I term "reification") at length in my 1996 book *Shakespeare's Universal Wolf*, with chapters on *Troilus and Cressida*, *Othello*, *King Lear*, and *As You Like It*, and I continued the study of Shakespeare's (sometimes sympathetic) critique of instrumental reason, this time identifying it with Machiavelli's *The Prince* and showing a different set of dynamics in the earlier plays *Richard II*, *1 and 2 Henry IV*, *Henry V*, and *Hamlet* in my 2002 *Shakespeare, Machiavelli, and Montaigne*.

11 Heller (2002: 15–31) makes a similar argument in somewhat different but related terms.

12 Eagleton (2003: 144) adds that political transition may be important in this connection as well, with the transition to a democratic polis in fifth-century-BCE Athens and to the modern nation-state in sixteenth-century Europe.

REFERENCES AND FURTHER READING

Adorno, T. (1973). *Negative Dialectics*, trans. E. B. Ashton. New York: Continuum. Adorno's major epistemological statement, highly relevant to issues of rationality within materialist theory.

Benjamin, W. (1968). *Illuminations*, ed. H. Arendt, trans. H. Zohn. New York: Schocken.

Benjamin, W. [1982] (1999). *The Arcades Project*, trans. H. Wiland and K. McLaughlin. Cambridge, MA: Belknap.

Bradley, A. C. (1904). *Shakespearean Tragedy: Lectures on "Hamlet," "Othello," "King Lear," "Macbeth."* London: Macmillan. A vastly influential synthesis of romantic characterology, realist notions of a stable reality underlying the texts, and Aristotelian and Hegelian ideas of tragic meaning and structure, all presented through an unstable aporia gliding between moralism and aestheticism.

Brecht, B. (1964). *Brecht on Theatre: The Development of an Aesthetic*, ed. and trans. J. Willett. New York: Hill & Wang.

Bruster, D. (2003). *Shakespeare and the Question of Culture: Early Modern Literature and the Cultural Turn*. New York: Palgrave. Presents a critique of new historicism and "new materialism" and advocates alternative models for materialist criticism.

Callari, A., Cullenberg, S., and Biewener, C., eds. (1995). *Marxism in the Postmodern Age: Confronting the New World Order*. New York: Guilford. A varied anthology of contemporary writings in what can be called "postmodernist Marxism."

Coleridge, S. T. (1930). *Shakespearean Criticism*, ed. T. M. Rayser, 2 vols. Cambridge, MA: Harvard University Press.

Dollimore, J. (1989). *Radical Tragedy: Religion, Ideology, and Power in the Drama of Shakespeare and his Contemporaries*, 2nd edn. London: Harvester. A seminal work for British cultural materialism and its approach to tragedy.

Dollimore, J. and Sinfield, A. (1985). *Political Shakespeare*. London: Cornell University Press, 1985.

Donne, J. (1967). *John Donne: Poetry and Prose*, ed. F. J. Warnke. New York: Modern Library

Drakakis, J., ed. (1985). *Alternative Shakespeares*. London: Methuen. An influential set of essays that helped define British cultural materialism in the 1980s.

Drakakis, J. (1992). Introduction. In *Shakespearean Tragedy*, ed. J. Drakakis. London: Longman, 1–44. A highly useful survey of major thinkers on tragic theory critiqued from a cultural materialist perspective.

Eagleton, T. (2003). *Sweet Violence: The Idea of the Tragic*. Oxford: Blackwell. An original, provocative rethinking of the idea and practice of tragedy from a leading British materialist, arguing that the Left has abandoned the idea of tragedy to the Right and should instead engage in rethinking the necessity of the idea of the tragic for our age.

Euripides. (1988). *Plays: One*. London: Methuen.

Foucault, M. [1966] (1973). *The Order of Things: An Archaeology of the Human Sciences*. New York: Vintage.

Grady, H. (1991). *The Modernist Shakespeare: Critical Texts in a Material World*. Oxford: Clarendon Press. Argues a "presentist" and materialist thesis that twentieth-century Shakespearean criticism until about 1980 was unconsciously shaped by modernist aesthetic notions, the ideology of professionalism, and various political currents.

Grady, H. (1996). *Shakespeare's Universal Wolf: Studies in Early Modern Reification*. Oxford: Clarendon Press. A consciously "presentist" and materialist study of *Troilus and Cressida*, *Othello*, *King Lear*, and *As You Like It*, showing how Shakespearean themes in the plays parallel many of the insights of Marx, Lukács, Horkheimer and Adorno, Foucault, and Habermas on issues of political power, sexual desire, commodification, and reification.

Grady, H. (1999). "Thinking Shakespearean Tragedy in the Late Twentieth Century." *In-between: Essays and Studies in Literary Criticism* 8, 1: 11–25. Argues that the nonspecialist literary world still follows the lead of A. C. Bradley's views on Shakespearean tragedy, that the possibility for a late twentieth-century theory of tragedy exists in the works of central materialist thinkers, and sketches some elements of such a theory.

Grady, H. (2002). *Shakespeare, Machiavelli, and Montaigne: Power and Subjectivity from "Richard II" to "Hamlet."* Oxford: Oxford University Press. A "historicist" complement to earlier "presentist" works which argues that Shakespeare's parallels to nineteenth- and twentieth-century materialist thought can be explained by his borrowings from or parallels with concepts of Machiavelli and Montaigne, exemplified here most prominently in the second historical tetralogy.

Greenblatt, S. (1980). *Renaissance Self-Fashioning: From More to Shakespeare.* Chicago: University of Chicago Press. The seminal work of American new historicism.

Greenblatt, S. (1990). *Learning to Curse: Essays in Early Modern Culture.* New York: Routledge.

Harris, M. (2001). *Cultural Materialism: The Struggle for a Science of Culture.* Walnut Creek: AltaMira Press.

Hawkes, T. (2002). *Shakespeare in the Present.* London: Routledge. A "presentist" manifesto which makes the case for the necessary influence of contemporary culture on how readers and viewers construe Shakespeare's plays in particular.

Heilman, R. [1956] (1977). *Magic in the Web: Action and Language in "Othello."* Westport, CT: Greenwood Press.

Heller, A. [1967] (1981). *Renaissance Man*, trans. R. E. Allen. New York: Schocken.

Heller, A. (2002). *The Time Is Out of Joint: Shakespeare as Philosopher of History.* Lanham, MD: Rowman & Littlefield. A Hungarian post-Marxist social philosopher defines the philosophy of history implicit in Shakespeare's plays, primarily the English histories and Roman tragedies.

Horkheimer, M. [1930] (1993). "Beginnings of the Bourgeois Philosophy of History." In *Between Philosophy and Social Science: Selected Early Writings*, ed. M. S. Kramer and J. Torpey, trans. G. F. Hunter. Cambridge, MA: MIT Press, 313–88.

Horkheimer, M. and Adorno, T. W. [1944] (1972). *Dialectic of Enlightenment*, trans. John Cumming. Boston: Seabury. Seminal work connecting shifting modes of rationality to the dynamics of modernization and the problems of capitalist societies.

Jameson, F. (1990). *Late Marxism; or, Adorno and the Persistence of the Dialectic.* London: Verso.

Lenz, C., Greene, G., and Neely, C., eds. (1980). *The Woman's Part: Feminist Criticism of Shakespeare.* Urbana: University of Illinois Press.

Lewis, W. (1927). *The Lion and the Fox: The Role of the Hero in the Plays of Shakespeare.* London: G. Richards.

Lukács, G. [1920] (1971). *The Theory of the Novel*, trans. A. Bostock. Cambridge, MA: MIT Press.

Marx, K. [1859] (1970). Preface. In *A Contribution to the Critique of Political Economy*, ed. Maurice Dobbs, trans. S. W. Ryazanskaya. New York: International.

Marx, K. (1964). *The Economic and Philosophic Manuscripts of 1844*, ed. D. Struik, trans. M. Milligan. New York: International.

Nietzsche, F. [1872, 1887] (1956). *The Birth of Tragedy and The Genealogy of Morals*, trans. F. Golffing. New York: Doubleday.

Parker, P. and Hartmann, G., eds. (1985). *Shakespeare and the Question of Theory.* New York: Methuen.

Shuger, D. (1999). "The 'I' of the Beholder: Renaissance Mirrors and the Reflexive Mind." In *Renaissance Culture and the Everyday*, ed. P. Fumerton and S. Hunt. Philadelphia. University of Pennsylvania Press, 21–41.

Veeser, H. A., ed. (1989). *The New Historicism.* New York: Routledge. An early and still useful anthology of essays defining and critiquing American new historicism.

Williams, R. [1958] (1966). *Culture and Society, 1780–1950.* New York: Harper. Williams's major work on the development of the complex word "culture" in British letters from Wordsworth to Orwell.

Williams, R. (1966). *Modern Tragedy.* Stanford, CA: Stanford University Press. A seminal work for subsequent materialist discussions of tragedy.

Williams, R. (1977). *Marxism and Literature.* Oxford: Oxford University Press.

Williams, R. (1980). *Problems in Materialism and Culture.* London: Verso.

Wilson, S. (1995). *Cultural Materialism: Theory and Practice.* Oxford: Blackwell. A very useful sympathetic overview of major themes and sources of British cultural materialism, its relations to American new historicism, and its strengths and weaknesses.

9

Tragedy and Feminism

Victoria Wohl

The tide of rumor will turn and bring our lives renown: glory will come to the female race. No longer will a discordant reputation oppress women; the Muses will leave off their ancient songs of our faithlessness. Not to us did Phoebus, lord of songs, grant the inspired strain of the lyre, or else we would have sung a hymn in answer to the race of men. The long ages have much to tell of women's fate and men's.

Euripides *Medea* 418–30

Within the Western humanist tradition that traces its origins to classical antiquity, tragedy holds pride of place. It is the humanist genre par excellence, treating the questions that seem most profoundly to define mankind. Within this tradition, Oedipus is a tragic "everyman," illustrating man's tragic blindness and the cosmic limitations upon his knowledge and free will. The moral of Oedipus' story applies to all men: "count no man happy until he is dead." For many scholars and lay readers alike, its universal humanist message makes tragedy the most classic of the classics, and its dark conclusions about the mortal condition virtually define the genre from its ancient origins to its contemporary incarnations.

Feminist scholars of tragedy, both classical and post-classical, have questioned the universality of tragedy's humanism, asking what bearings its insights into the nature of "man" have upon "woman." They have resisted the adequation of humanity and masculinity upon which this humanism rests. This is an ancient catachresis: Greek tragedy often expresses its universal message in explicitly gendered terms, as when the chorus of Sophocles' *Oedipus the King* responds to Oedipus' fatal discovery by lamenting the generations of mortals (*brotoi*) and the shadowy existence of man (*anêr*, 1186–96). Aristotle likewise describes the ideal tragic plot in terms that make it clear that the tragic everyman is, literally, a man (e.g., *Poetics* 13). The Greeks' own equation of the masculine and the human is perpetuated in modern scholarship by the slippage in English between "man" in a universal and a specific sense: even where Athenian tragedy did distinguish between man (*anêr*) and human (*anthrôpos*), modern translations tend to blur that distinction, for instance rendering *Antigone's* famous ode to human ingenuity (*anthrôpou*, *Antigone* 332) as "The Ode to Man." Feminist scholars seek to pry apart man and human, *anêr* and *anthrôpos*, and to show that the two are not, in fact, coterminous. They highlight the exclusions that have historically secured claims of universality, the politics behind seemingly neutral truths, and the power relations that have sustained Western humanism from the Greeks on.

It is little surprise, then, that feminists have maintained a love-hate relationship with tragedy. Tragic theater ancient and modern abounds in memorable female characters. In the case of ancient tragedy, female characters play substantial parts in virtually all of the 32 surviving plays, and only one extant tragedy (Sophocles' *Philoctetes*) contains no female character at all. This prominence is all the more remarkable for being out of all proportion to women's status in contemporary Athenian society. Women were almost completely excluded from public life in ancient Athens; considered lifelong minors, they were unable to vote, own substantial property, or represent themselves in court. While men competed for glory in the public arena, respectable women were largely restricted to the household, where their greatest glory was chastity and silence. On the tragic stage, by contrast, we find an array of strong and active women, women who deliver persuasive public addresses, enter into debates with men, sacrifice themselves for their families or their countries, even exercise political rule (cf. chapter 14, this volume). For many feminist readers, tragedy's dominant women have offered a counterweight of optimism against the pervasive misogyny of Athenian culture, suggesting that either women were not, in fact, as thoroughly marginalized as they appear from other sources or, if they were, at least the culture was capable of thinking critically about its own oppressions and exclusions.

While the prominence and ubiquity of female characters makes tragedy a natural object of feminist interest, its representation of women is far from unequivocal. To turn again to the ancient example, we often find attractive female characters sharing the stage with virulent expressions of misogyny. Euripides, for instance, offers us both Medea's self-conscious critique of the iniquities facing women in a male-centered world ("I would rather stand in the battle-line three times than give birth once," *Medea* 250–1) and Jason's misogynist opinion that "it would be better if men found another way to bear children and there were no race of women" (573–5). With its horrific description of Medea's vengeance and matricide, the play hardly offers the revisionary history the women of the chorus anticipate in the epigraph to this chapter, yet many readers find its depiction of Medea's plight insightful and sympathetic. Already in antiquity, these contradictory representations generated debate over Euripides' attitude toward women. In Aristophanes' *Thesmophoriazusae*, the women of Athens attack Euripides for exposing their adulterous stratagems to their husbands (383–458); in *Frogs*, by contrast, Euripides claims that he wrote "democratically" by giving women a voice in his plays (948–52). It is impossible, then, to view Euripides – or tragedy in general – as either "misogynist," blithely reproducing the gender stereotypes and inequalities of a sexist society, or "feminist," radically challenging those same stereotypes and inequalities. If tragedy as a genre has often seemed to sing a hymn of the female race (as the chorus of *Medea* puts it), that hymn has remained difficult to interpret and its ambivalent message has been the object of much productive debate among feminist scholars.

This chapter surveys that debate, focusing on the tragedies produced in Athens in the fifth century BCE and the scholarship on those plays. One persistent theme throughout this scholarship has been the attempt to understand the connection between tragedy's representation of the feminine and the institutional, experiential, or ideological status of women beyond the tragic stage. This question has real stakes for feminist classicists, trying to reconcile their love of ancient literature with their commitment to fight the social inequalities it so often enshrines. But it is also vitally relevant for feminist work on post-classical drama. In Shakespearean tragedy too, for example, a contradictory representation of women reflects their ambiguous position in a largely androcentric culture (see, e.g., Callaghan 2000). Virtually all historical texts encode elements of their cultural milieu that a modern reader might wish to oppose – sexism, racism, imperialism, class bias, etc. – while not tossing away the literary baby with the cultural bathwater (as happened, for instance, with the banning of *Huckleberry Finn* from school curricula). Thus the debate among feminist classicists on tragedy's relation to Athens' oppressive gender norms resonates across disciplinary boundaries, and its conclusions are potentially valuable for any scholar seeking a way of reading the text that recognizes its more oppressive aspects without condoning them, or that locates resistance within the text without retrojecting an anachronistic political sensibility.

Before delving into that debate, however, it may be helpful first to define what constitutes a feminist interpretation. This is, of course, a fraught question. At a moment when many Women's Studies departments are changing their name to Gender and/or Sexuality Studies and the very category of "woman" has come under question from postmodern theory, the object of feminist interpretation is no longer simply the lives and writings of women. In the case of Greek tragedy, "woman" is mediated by a text written and produced exclusively by men – with all-male actors and probably an all-male audience – and thus the study of women has always been a study of gender, the cultural construct of femininity in its differential relation to masculinity. In Greece, that construct was also tied up with notions of the body and sexuality, and so feminism has from the start necessarily and productively intersected with sexuality studies.

Methodologically feminist scholars have employed a variety of approaches to tragedy, including anthropology, film theory, deconstruction, and psychoanalysis, but have tended to share certain basic assumptions and concerns. Feminists assume that gender – generally an asymmetrical arrangement of gender – fundamentally structures society and discourse; their aim is to excavate that structure. Their guiding questions when they approach a text concern its latent power relations: Who is speaking? To whose advantage or disadvantage? What sort of gender (and other) hierarchies does the text inscribe or prescribe? What interests lie beneath statements that claim to be interest free, and what exclusions lie behind statements that claim to be all-inclusive? Feminism tends to operate through a hermeneutics of suspicion, skeptical of claims to neutrality on the part of the text or its reader. This has also made feminist scholarship self-reflective about its own practice: Who is reading? What desires animate that reading? What power dynamics are reproduced by it? Thus, for example, Karen Bassi (1998) identifies the nostalgia at work in our contemporary readings of Athenian tragedy, a desire to preserve the idealized masculine subject of antiquity and be at one with him.

While feminists argue that all readers bring their own desires and concerns to the text, they are particularly open about their own. And this is perhaps what most distinguishes feminism from other methodologies: its commitment to reading as a vehicle for social change. Feminists are often accused of having a "political agenda," and in a sense it is true. Implicitly or explicitly, feminists bring to the texts they study a desire to transform the way gender is understood and lived, to resist sexism, rethink confining notions of femininity and masculinity, and challenge the inevitability or necessity of gender arrangements they find oppressive in their own lives. This scholarly activism, the belief that critical reading can have real-world results, means that for feminist historians the study of the past is immediately relevant to the project of understanding the present. Some explain that relevance in terms of a continuous history of misogyny (e.g., Peradotto and Sullivan 1984: 1–4); others find the value of the past in its difference from modernity and the opportunity that affords for rethinking our own assumptions about gender (e.g., duBois 1988). But all believe that the study of the past is and should be useful to the present, that we turn to the past hoping to find something, and that this desire is not only inevitable in scholarship, but in fact beneficial. Thus feminist classicists argue simultaneously against those feminists who reject ancient Greece as the progenitor of a misogynist legacy best ignored, and those classicists who argue that to expose the violent substrate of classical literature denudes it of the grandeur and beauty that constitute its timeless relevance. The feminist scholar of ancient tragedy – like feminists working on any historical literature – tries to mediate between these two positions, finding the relevance and timeless appeal of the plays precisely in the complex way they challenge, as well as reflect and affirm, the androcentric tradition they are too often assumed to simply embody. Feminist scholars of non-contemporary tragedy, then, be it Sophocles or Shakespeare, bring to their work a desire not only to show the relevance of the literature of the past to the politics of the present, but also to redefine the very criteria of relevance, to posit a different sort of universalism and resituate tragedy within a more inclusive tradition of humanism.

The first major feminist discussion of Athenian tragedy came in Sarah Pomeroy's groundbreaking book *Goddesses, Whores, Wives, and Slaves* (1975), which aimed to bring to light the life of average women in classical antiquity, and thus redress the balance of a historical tradition that had mostly ignored them. Pomeroy approached tragedy as a potential source for the lives of contemporary women and judged it by its verisimilitude: Aeschylus' and Sophocles' heroines reveal little about women in contemporary Athens, while Euripides' are truer to life (1975: 92–112). This empiricist approach may seem rather naive now, when many feminists would critique the very notion of "the lives of real women" as a unitary, knowable (much less empirically describable) object, and would find fault with the presumption that texts mirror an autonomous reality that exists outside of them. Yet the assumptions and questions that ground Pomeroy's work have persisted throughout feminist scholarship. Tragedy is rarely still mined for nuggets of reality, but it is broadly assumed to bear *some* relation – whether active or passive, direct or inverted – to the world outside it. And although many feminists would now be wary of reifying "the life of real women" as if it were an ontological given, not a discursive construct, nonetheless "real women" – women outside the theater of Dionysus – have remained an implicit reference point for most subsequent feminist work on tragedy.

Pomeroy pointed the way for future scholars when she suggested that the women who were excluded from male life "returned to haunt men's imaginations, dreams, and nightmares" (1975: 229). The second generation of feminists shifted the emphasis from "women" and their lived experience to "woman" as a cultural concept. A notable representative of this trend was Helene Foley's important article, "The Conception of Women in Athenian Drama" (1981). Foley begins by contrasting the images of women in drama to the view of their legal and institutional position gleaned from nonfiction prose. But rather than put the former at the service of the latter – drama as a reflection of the reality embodied in prose – she posits a symbiotic relation between the two:

> [W]e must begin by accepting all of the complex distortions of life which belong to the genre [of tragedy]. Then we must go on to categorize the precise nature and range of these distortions in the context of the symbolic systems presented in Athenian literature, systems in which sex roles obviously play a central part. In short, we must investigate how the concept of woman operates in the symbolic systems of drama as a whole. At the same time we should not despair of uncovering comprehensible – if oblique – relations between life and literature ... [T]he Athenian audience must have brought to their experience of the remarkable women of drama a way of understanding these characters which grew out of their psychological, religious, political, and social lives and problems. (1981: 35–6)

Tragedy and life are semiautonomous but mutually informing symbolic systems; tragedy incorporates and speaks to the lived experience of its (male) audience without simply mirroring it. In the discussion of structural anthropology that follows, Foley refines this symbiosis by suggesting that the same polarities (nature vs. culture, public vs. private) informed conceptions of gender in both the tragic text and the democratic city, with woman functioning as a shifting sign within these fundamental cultural oppositions.

Foley closes her article with the famous remark of Lévi-Strauss that women are not only signs but also generators of signs. One criticism leveled by feminists against this type of work is that in emphasizing the former it overlooks the latter. It reduces woman to an object within a male text, a sign manipulated by men for male aesthetic pleasure or moral edification, and thus loses sight of women as subjects who themselves manipulate tragedy's symbolic systems, including its gender system. Tragedy does, indeed, stage women as "generators of signs," as subjects of language, desire, and action. At the same time, these characters are constrained by the symbolic systems within which they are constructed: as characters within male-authored texts, they are signs even when they are subjects. This paradox generates much tension, as heroines try to assert themselves as subjects in a poetic and social universe that treats them as symbols of male heroism, virility, or honor. Thus, for example, when Clytemnestra deploys the traditional tropes of femininity and domesticity to lure her husband to his death in Aeschylus' *Agamemnon* (offering him a warm bath then killing him in it), her action shows her as a skillful manipulator of signs, and simultaneously fixes her as herself a sign of monstrous inversion within the play's hierarchies of gender and power. This tension between woman as sign and woman as (the sign of) a producer of signs may help explain the jarring juxtapositions of misogynist and "feminist" statements within a single play. Medea may be the product of a discourse that dreams of a world without women (in a passage I cited earlier), but as soon as she is imagined as a speaker and (in accordance with tragedy's practice of *ethopoieia*) is given lines appropriate to her character, she can deliver speeches that go against (while still being contained within) that discourse.

Treating tragedy's female characters not as reflections (accurate or inaccurate) of "real women" but as symbols operating complexly within textual and cultural symbolic systems opened two interrelated avenues of inquiry, one literary and one socio-historical. The first – the function of the female within the thematic, metaphoric, visual, and spatial codes of a literary text – is pursued with particular sophistication by Froma Zeitlin. If Pomeroy asks what tragedy can teach us about Athenian women, Zeitlin asks what attention to women can teach us about tragedy. In her early article, "The Dynamics of Misogyny: Myth and Mythmaking in the *Oresteia*" (1978, reprinted in her 1996 collection, *Playing the Other: Gender and Society in Classical Greek Literature*), she examines how tragedy constructs the female and uses her to construct its own imagined world. She shows how Aeschylus' trilogy posits female power as dangerous, a rule of women that threatens to overthrow the rule of men, and by turning Clytemnestra into a monster justifies her murder and the eventual exclusion of women from the civic sphere. The trilogy achieves this progress from "rule of women" to "rule of men" in part by linking the opposition between male and female to other cultural polarities: culture over nature, god over mortal, life over death. The structural oppositions so prevalent in tragic thought are neither natural nor neutral, as Zeitlin shows, but instead are generated and consolidated through violent textual manipulation. The homologies she draws between different hierarchies explain both the depth of misogyny in Athens and the stakes involved: once the binarism of male and female is yoked to that of order and chaos, for example, control of women becomes "the social and cultural prerequisite for the construction of civilization" (1996: 88).

Given the importance of the feminine to tragedy's project of "world-building," Zeitlin emphasizes inclusion and negotiation over oppression and exclusion (1996: 8). Through transaction with the idea of the feminine, tragedy addresses its most fundamental concerns: the nature of the male self and society, the mysteries of desire and reproduction, man's relation to the cosmos and the gods. Women are so prominent in tragedy, then, not for their own sake (not because the tragedian or the tragedy is either "misogynist" or "feminist"), but because their presence as "other" illuminates the male world and self:

> From the outset, it is essential to understand that in the Greek theater, as in Shakespearean theater, the self that is really at stake is to be identified with the male, while the woman is assigned the role of the radical other... Even when female characters struggle with the conflicts generated by the particularities of their subordinate social position, their demands for identity and self-esteem are still designed primarily for exploring the male project of selfhood in the larger world. These demands impinge upon men's claims to knowledge, power, freedom, and self-sufficiency – not, as some have thought, for woman's gaining some greater entitlement or privilege for herself and not even for revising notions of what femininity might be or mean... [F]unctionally women are never an end in themselves, and nothing changes for them once they have lived out their drama on stage. Rather, they play the roles of catalysts, agents, instruments, blockers, spoilers, destroyers, and sometimes helpers or saviors for the male characters. (1996: 346–7)

Women are instrumental in tragedy, but in no way incidental: they are not mere intruders within male social or psychic space, but instead are woven into the metaphoric and thematic weave of the play, integral to its language, its philosophical concerns, even its generic form and dramatic enactment. In "Playing the Other: Theater, Theatricality, and the Feminine in Greek Drama" ([1985] 1996: 341–74), Zeitlin argues that tragedy as a genre shares an intrinsic affinity with the feminine. She identifies four defining elements of the tragic experience – the representation of the body, the arrangement of space, the strategies of plot, and dramatic mimesis – all of which, she argues, were coded as feminine in Athenian thought. So, for example, when male characters appear on stage weakened and in physical pain, like Heracles in Sophocles' *Trachiniae*, poisoned (accidentally) by his wife, they experience a corporeality associated primarily with women. By "playing the other" – both literally, as male actors playing female characters, and imaginatively, as a male audience entering into feminine experience – Athenian men achieved a broadened understanding of what it meant to be a man.

Zeitlin's analysis, then, looks inward and finds the answer to questions about tragic women not in the external world but on the tragic stage, in the theatrical resources, generic structure, and thematic preoccupations of tragedy (1996: 347). She does at times gesture beyond the stage. The *Oresteia*, she says at the end of "The Dynamics of Misogyny," not only reflects Athenian thought about women, but also contributes to it: through "a continuing reciprocity between external and internal, between individual psyche and collective ideology," it "organizes and manipulates reality" (1996: 119). That tragedy may shape – not merely reflect – the extra-theatrical world is an important insight. But that world is glimpsed only occasionally in Zeitlin's work and appears almost as an epiphenomenal effect of the text. And that world, too, is textual, as much a matter of mythical patterns and literary paradigms as social institutions and legal rights: the extra-textual woman she refers to most is not "the real Athenian" but Hesiod's Pandora, the first lady of Greek myth. This opens Zeitlin's work (and other work in this literary vein, like Loraux [1985] 1987 or Goff 1990) to accusations of apoliticism, a failure to contextualize tragedy within the specific ideological struggles of fifth-century Athens. These works exemplify feminist philology at its most insightful; by focusing on the textual role of the feminine they illuminate the metaphorical density and structural nuance of tragedy, but also risk fetishizing both tragedy and its women by deracinating them from the society that produced them and from the political and ideological conflicts that shaped their textual ambiguities.

But as Peter Rose notes, there is a potentially political reading implicit within this literary approach (Rose 1993: 221–3). Because tragedy was a site of active ideological struggle, he argues, it contains contradictory impulses toward affirming the status quo (a negative hermeneutic) and challenging it (a positive hermeneutic). Reworking this double hermeneutic slightly, we can see how the literary and theatrical richness that readings like Zeitlin's uncover itself dismantles any simple ideological claims that tragedy may ultimately make. Zeitlin comments that in many tragedies "the project is to lay the female to rest, at least temporarily, and to define the parameters of male hegemony. But in the course of its enactment, the dynamic impulse belongs to the female" (1996: 171). Thus the *Oresteia* moves from a chaotic rule of women through matricide and demonization of the woman to the ultimate establishment of the rule of law in a world of male citizens. Yet we reach this final scene of world-building by way of both a plot driven by women and imagery and language saturated with gender. So when the virgin Eumenides are set at the end to preside over holy sacrifices for the city (*sphagiôn … semnôn*, *Eumenides* 1007), the celebratory language cannot help but evoke what it most wishes to obscure: not only Clytemnestra's murder of Agamemnon (*sphagên*, *Agamemnon* 1389), but also the sacrifice of the virgin Iphigenia (*parthenosphagoisin*, *Agamemnon* 207), whose pathetic murder symptomatized the violence of the old order even as her enforced silence presaged the violent exclusion of the female from the new order. The dramatic structure and metaphoric texture of the trilogy thus work simultaneously toward and against its final resolution. By highlighting the ways in which the theatrical and textual means (which often operate through the female) destabilize the ideological end (which generally reaffirms male hegemony on the stage and beyond it), we can politicize textual analysis, situating it critically within its historical context while sacrificing none of its literary sophistication.

This project of situating tragedy historically once again takes center stage with the "return to history" that characterizes most recent feminist work on tragedy in general (and indeed, much recent work across the humanities). This approach has sought to elucidate tragedy's representation of women not in terms of the texts' metaphorical systems but in relation to contemporary social institutions or broader ideological structures (see Goff 1995, Winkler and Zeitlin 1990 for this trend in classical tragedy scholarship; many of the essays in Callaghan 2000 exemplify the same trend in Shakespeare scholarship). Often anthropological or sociological in orientation and intersecting productively with cultural and postcolonial studies, it has sought to theorize the relation between tragedy and its sociocultural environment, asking how tragedy not only reflects but also supports, shapes, and sometimes subverts cultural norms. If Pomeroy asks what tragedy can tell us about women, and Zeitlin asks what women can tell us about tragedy, these studies ask what tragic women can tell us about the society that gave them dramatic existence.

Within classics, much of this work has focused on marriage, kinship and social exchange (Loraux [1984] 1993, Rabinowitz 1993, Wohl 1998, Ormand 1999, Foley 2001). Because so many Greek tragedies treat myths of domestic disharmony and highlight tensions between the public sphere and the private, marriage is a ubiquitous concern. Marriage is staged in tragedy as the keystone of human society — defining male and female identities, creating kinship bonds within and between cities, securing social continuity through the production of legitimate heirs — but also as a site of potential social crisis. This crisis is often precipitated by the woman, whose sexual jealousy or infidelity, loyalty to her natal household and status as outsider in her husband's household, insufficient or excessive devotion to her children, refusal to subordinate her own desires to her husband's (or unhappiness in doing so) all enact various structural tensions within the Athenian marriage system. And because marriage functioned as "a metaphor for civic life" (Foley 2001: 103), marital crisis is often the occasion for exploring further social questions, including the definition of citizen status, the struggle between egalitarianism and elitism, and the obligations of reciprocity and economic exchange. This metaphorical mode of reading has been extremely productive for feminist scholars, as it places gender at the very heart of the city's most vital concerns and shows how "the feminine... haunts the Athenian civic imagination," shaping even realms from which women were excluded in practice (Loraux [1984] 1993: 11). In the process, however, sometimes the female herself is lost, becoming a pure and vacant vehicle for other, more important, male social relations or civic issues. Modern scholarship thus risks reproducing the dynamic of the ancient texts, instrumentalizing the woman as a symbolic means to the larger goal of (re)constructing the male world.

One way scholars have tried to avoid this pitfall is by focusing on female agency and analyzing the ways in which the dramatization of a woman's subjective experience can complicate her structural position within the institutions and relations of tragedy's masculine world. Thus in Ormand's view, the woman's experience of marriage as unfulfilling and alienating is one source of instability in tragic marriage (1999: 25–35), while for Foley, the contradictory cultural demands upon women insistently raise the problem of an autonomous female ethical agent (2001: 109–23). Likewise, in *Intimate Commerce: Exchange, Gender, and Subjectivity in Greek Tragedy* (1998) I examined the subjectivities, male and female, generated by the tragic exchange of women between men (in marriage, gift-exchange, war, or sacrifice). These exchanges require a female object in order to consolidate male identities and relations, but tragic heroines often refuse that role. Even when they fail to position themselves successfully as active partners in exchanges with men (as they invariably do), their very attempt shows tragic subjectivity under construction and illuminates both the nature and limitations of the self, female or male. Whereas I see tragedy's frequent dramatization of the female psyche as part of its attempt to develop a language and theory of the self, Nancy Rabinowitz (1993) argues that the plays grant their heroines an illusory subjectivity the better to control them, representing them as either uncannily powerful or sacrificial victims in order to justify their containment. For both of us, tragedy ultimately forecloses the possibility of a viable female subject; but while Rabinowitz emphasizes the inevitability of that foreclosure, I find it remarkable that tragedy keeps open the space of the female psyche for as long as it does. After we have heard Medea lament the plight of women, seen her agonize over the decision to kill her children, and gained such intimate insight into her desires and motivations, can we easily condemn her as a monster at the end?

Rabinowitz and I both argue for the importance of the psychological in understanding the role of women in tragedy. But while this approach has proved extremely fruitful in feminist readings of post-classical tragedy, the psychological – and particularly psychoanalysis – is by and large an underutilized resource in feminist work within classics. Whether this is due to a wariness of psychoanalysis' supposed phallocentrism or its ostensible ahistoricism, it is a regrettable absence. As critics of Renaissance drama have shown (e.g., Kahn 1981, Belsey 1985), the nature of the self is a central problem in tragedy: complexly enmeshed in relations to the family and state, shaped not only by gender but by class and other ideologies, limited in freedom but not responsibility, the individual is often staged as a psychologization of the social. This is especially true for female characters, who are less secure as social agents and therefore offer a test case in tragedy's epistemology of the self. If gender is a point of convergence between the psyche and the social, as the individual internalizes the norms of society, then psychoanalysis offers indispensable tools for feminist critique, diagnosing the ways in which characters inhabit gender norms or (more often and more interestingly) fail to inhabit them fully. Moreover, these same dynamics operate at the level of the text as a whole. If, as Judith Butler suggests (1997: 86), those social injunctions which we cannot fully incorporate become the loam of the unconscious, then we might understand the plays' profound ambivalence toward the female – the simultaneous aggression and dependence, desire and fear, that permeate the language and shape the structure of these texts – as the unconscious trace of their uneven internalization of the gender imperatives of their society. Approached in this way, a psychoanalysis of the text is neither necessarily phallocentric nor necessarily ahistorical, and could be a valuable instrument for feminist classicists (as it has been for scholars of post-classical tragedy) as they try to theorize the gendered construction of the self on stage and off.

In this way psychoanalysis might add to the project that more than anything else characterizes recent work on Greek tragedy, the intensive investigation of tragedy's relation to Athenian ideology. This investigation has been central to feminists' concerns since the 1970s, as I have suggested, although it has taken different forms and emphases over time. In its current instantiation, it assumes that tragedy bears an active relation to Athenian social and sexual norms, not only reflecting but contributing to them; the guiding question then becomes the nature of that contribution. Does tragedy reaffirm Athens' oppressive gender hierarchy or does it resist, even subvert it? If it does both simultaneously (as many conclude), how can we theorize the relation between the two? On the one hand, tragedy was a civic institution, part of a civic festival sponsored by and held in honor of the city (a fact discussed most famously by Goldhill in Winkler and Zeitlin 1990). Bearing that in mind, several scholars have viewed tragedy as an "ideological state apparatus," and have argued that tragedy as a civic practice functioned to naturalize and reproduce existing social relations, consolidate existing ideologies (including gender ideologies), and hail both its characters and its audience into specific (gendered) subject-positions (Rabinowitz 1993, Wohl 1998, Ormand 1999; cf. Rose 1993). On the other hand, since Vernant's famous 1969 essay "Tensions and Ambiguities in Greek Tragedy" ([1972] 1988: 29–48) it has been common to view tragedy as a staging of questions rather than answers. Exposing the rifts and fissures within Athens' dominant ideology, tragedy (by this view) poses a challenge to Athenian gender relations, questioning their necessity and naturalness, revealing their structural or systemic incoherences. The former approach situates tragedy firmly within its historical context, tying it directly to other ideological and discursive formations, but it runs the risk of turning the plays into monovocal ideological documents – propaganda for the patriarchy. The latter captures well the dense texture of tragedy, in which virtually every word bristles with double meaning, but risks naive apoliticism or even aporia – ambiguity for its own sake.

For feminism the debate between these two views of tragedy is not merely academic. Instead, it is a question of how to read both as a classicist and as a feminist (Rabinowitz and Richlin 1993), affirming the value of Athenian literature while acknowledging the oppressions and exclusions of Athenian society. In this sense, it is a question of saving tragedy from the worst aspects of Athens – and Athens from the worst aspects of itself – and in this way redeeming both for feminist study. Thus the theoretical debate over tragedy's relation to Athenian gender ideology is replicated on the hermeneutic level in a division between "optimists" and "pessimists." Rabinowitz argues the pessimist's position: viewing tragedy as a "technology of gender" that hails its audience (male and, she believes, female) as gendered subjects in accordance with the unequal gender norms of Athenian society, she proposes that the plays' primary function was to reinforce male control over women and in this way "to keep the system going" (1993: 21). This conception of tragedy raises obvious problems for the feminist critic, as Rabinowitz acknowledges: in her quest for a "third position," she looks to those moments when the plays fail in their relentless ideological intent and takes hope in the idea of a "resisting [female] reader" who saw through tragedy's violent containment of women to "the female power that may well have inspired this male reaction" (1993: 23).

Even if we accept the premise that women were in the audience and viewed the plays resistantly, this is a shaky ground for optimism, as it situates any progressive impulse outside the texts themselves. Others have accordingly sought signs of subversion or resistance within the plays and have based a cautious optimism on the notion that tragedy questions the status quo (as well as representing it) and that "by giving a public voice to those who were normally silent in the political arena . . . it can open fresh perspectives on and restore some balance to a civic life and dialogue otherwise dominated by citizen males" (Foley 2001: 18). But this optimism is tempered by the acknowledgment that tragedy's questions often serve ultimately to reinforce the system they seem to challenge:

> tragedy can invert and destabilize norms in a fashion that questions the cultural status quo . . . Yet such temporary inversions and queries can also serve in the end to reinforce cultural ideologies, and we should not be fooled into thinking that the prominent, articulate, active, or resistant women of tragedy represent a genuine impulse for social change. (Foley 2001: 333)

Asking about the real-world effects of tragedy's "tensions and ambiguities" drives even the optimistic feminist to pessimism.

How, then, can we reconcile these two positions and theorize the relation between tragedy's function as an ideological apparatus reproducing and reinforcing Athens' oppressive gender norms, and tragedy as a site of institutionalized questioning of or even resistance to those norms? Tragedy was a site of ideological contest, a struggle over the terms in which the world will be conceptualized and organized. This struggle is always ongoing and its conclusions always provisional; it is not the victory of one position over the other that constitutes ideology, but the struggle itself. This means that ideology always contains both hegemonic and subordinate positions, and the relation between them is not fixed or inevitable, but contingent and variable. As an ideological apparatus, tragedy reflects and reproduces ideology *as conflict*: tragedy's "tensions and ambiguities" are thus in fact an essential aspect of its ideological role, and tragedy mirrors reality precisely in its contradictions (Rose 1993; Wohl 1998: xviii–xxiv). And if tragedy's ideology is not monolithic, neither is its ambiguity neutral: tragedy's allusive language and indeterminate images condense different and competing ideological positions, positions that could potentially be actualized in the real world.

The woman, I believe, is the locus, as well as object, of tragedy's most intense ideological negotiations. She is simultaneously the cornerstone in tragedy's project of world-building and a point of instability within the world that results. Sophocles' *Trachiniae* provides a good example. The play closes with a scene of patrilineal succession, as the dying Heracles, poisoned unintentionally by his wife Deianira, hands to his son Hyllus a bequest of legitimacy, royalty, and heroic identity – as well as his concubine Iole, who drove Deianira to murder and then suicide. Such scenes of male bonding close several tragedies and seem to strongly reaffirm an androcentric ideology in which relations between men constitute the social order and the patriline guarantees its perpetuation in future generations. This productive, patriarchal world order – sanctified on the highest level by Zeus himself (*Trachiniae* 1278) – is secured at the expense of the woman, who is either driven to death (Deianira) or reduced to a silent, passive object of male exchange (Iole). But this new social order falters precisely where it should be most secure, the exchange of the woman: Hyllus is reluctant to accept Iole as his bride. This reluctance is not merely the scruple of a son against marrying his father's concubine and the woman he blames for both his parents' deaths. It is the textual trace, in the midst of this inaugural moment, of the tragedy of Deianira, which occupied the first two-thirds of the play. Through Deianira's eyes we see the cost for women of the social transactions that are so productive for men. We are told how she watched the terrifying marriage-contest between Heracles and the river-god Achelous, waiting to see which would be her husband; how she was ripped from her mother ("like a calf abandoned," *Trachiniae* 530) and carried far from her family to become the wife of a hero who seldom comes home and, when he does, brings with him Iole, a captive from his latest expedition and his "hidden bedmate" (*Trachiniae* 360). Deianira speaks of her jealousy of, but also sympathy for, the silent girl, whose experience she compares to her own. Her unhappiness, presented in painful detail, constitutes a critique of a heroic – and tragic – order that trades in women and predicates male subjectivity and social relations on the reduction of women to objects.

Deianira attempts actively to save her marriage by sending Heracles a "gift in exchange for the gift" of Iole (*Trachiniae* 494), but her gift, a robe smeared with what she thinks is a love-potion but is actually poison, is fatal, and when she discovers this Deianira kills herself. Her death and subsequent vilification pave the way for the play's final scene of patrilineal bonding and masculine world-building, but do not erase the pathos of her story, which lives on after her, embodied in the silent Iole. The final scene, then, reproduces a heroic male order along with its oppression of women; but at the same time it also reproduces Deianira's unhappy perspective on that world, which lingers on in Hyllus' reluctance to accept Heracles' gift of Iole, and in a pall of unease and coercion that clouds this ostensibly celebratory moment. In this way the play subtly incorporates alternatives it manifestly rejects, installing them as a point of silent but persistent critique within the world it creates.

It is in the woman as an institutionalized point of resistance to the oppressive systems she is used to consolidate that I find some basis for optimism. Tragedy does actively reproduce the unequal gender relations of Athenian society; it does reinforce the ideological status quo. But if we view ideology as contested and provisional instead of fixed and invariable, then there is some hope for change, a hope that tragedy encrypts within its contradictory representations of the female. Though we should not ignore the forces within society that make some ideological positions more viable in practice than others, we also need not, I think, dismiss the radical potential of tragedy's critique, its implication that liberatory alternatives subsist within the very structures of the hegemonic. Thus for me the solution to the *hermeneutic* problem – how to read tragedy as a feminist – is reached only by working toward a solution to the *theoretical* problem of tragedy's relation to Athenian gender ideology. In tragedy's interweaving of reaffirmation and resistance lies the answer both to feminists who revile Athens as the origin of misogyny – it is, but it is also the origin of a critique of misogyny – and to those humanist philologists who decry feminism for sullying the beauty of the classics – for if the beauty of timeless and apolitical truths is lost, another sort of beauty is found precisely in tragedy's complex ideological negotiations.

Feminism brings to the study of tragedy in general less a new object of inquiry (for scholars had always noticed the genre's foregrounding of the female, even if they had not fully appreciated its extent and depth) than a new awareness of the ways in which gender (and other power) relations structure drama in its language, theatrical performance, and ideological effect. I hope that my survey of the scholarship on classical tragedy has illustrated this point, but to underline it we need think only of how feminism has changed the way scholars view Greek tragedy's pervasive structural oppositions. Although the genre's ubiquitous play of dark and light, nature and culture, house and city – to say nothing of female and male – is hard not to notice, feminist critics revealed the hidden connections among these various oppositions and the ways in which, within an ostensibly balanced dialectic, one side was implicitly valorized and the other subordinated; they made visible a politics of structure. Furthermore, by focusing on the minor term in the dyad – the woman and all she is aligned with – they uncovered buried alternatives within hegemonic hierarchies. An excellent example of this is Helene Foley's reading of *Antigone*. Many readers have echoed Hegel's interpretation of the play as a transcending of the family (and the feminine) by the masculine state; they assume that in the gendered oppositions that structure this play Creon's position – representing masculinity, authority, civic order – must be the stronger. But Foley restores equal weight to the "slave" position in this dialectic, arguing that Antigone offers an alternate mode of ethical reasoning to Creon. Instead of a zero-sum game of opposites, the polarities in this play exist in a complementary relation; their synthesis is achieved not through the victory of one over the other (in the Hegelian tradition) but through the expanded morality that their juxtaposition affords: "the gendering of ethical positions," Foley concludes, "permits the public exploration of moral complexities that would not otherwise have been possible" (2001: 172). If structural polarities are themselves objects of ideological contest (not essential and universal modes of human thought), then not only are their hierarchies always in theory reversible, but their synthesis is greater than the sum of its parts.

Finally, feminism has challenged the political neutrality not only of tragedy's structuring metaphors but also of the ways in which it has been read. It has argued for the need to critique our own investment in the texts we study and to expose the desires behind our continuous return to tragedy. If feminism debunks the timeless truths and claims to universality of the Western humanist tradition fathered by tragic

Oedipus, it suggests that there might be a different humanist tradition – perhaps one mothered by Antigone who, with her oppositional ethics, exposes the limits and limitations of the masculine universal and reminds us that critique, too, is a legacy we inherit from Greek tragedy.

ACKNOWLEDGMENTS

My thanks to Rebecca Bushnell, Kate Gilhuly, Melissa Mueller, and Sheila Murnaghan for helpful comments.

REFERENCES AND FURTHER READING

Bassi, K. (1998). *Acting Like Men: Gender, Drama, and Nostalgia in Ancient Greece*. Ann Arbor: University of Michigan Press. A fascinating study of the performance of masculinity and the gendered dynamics of spectatorship in classical Athens on and off the stage.

Belsey, C. (1985). *The Subject of Tragedy: Identity and Difference in Renaissance Drama*. London: Methuen. A history of the subject, male and female, in Renaissance tragedy and other contemporaneous literature.

Butler, J. (1997). *The Psychic Life of Power: Theories in Subjection*. Stanford, CA: Stanford University Press. Essays on power and subjectivity from the premier theorist of gender.

Callaghan, D., ed. (2000). *A Feminist Companion to Shakespeare*. Oxford: Blackwell. A wide-ranging collection of feminist approaches to Shakespearean drama and Elizabethan England.

duBois, P. (1988). *Sowing the Body: Psychoanalysis and Ancient Representations of Women*. Chicago: University of Chicago Press. An insightful historicizing critique of psychoanalytic representations of the feminine.

Foley, H. P. (1981). "The Conception of Women in Athenian Drama." In *Reflections of Women in Antiquity*, ed. H. P. Foley. New York: Gordon & Breach, 127–68. A seminal article in a seminal early collection.

Foley, H. P. (2001). *Female Acts in Greek Tragedy*. Princeton, NJ: Princeton University Press. Brings together and expands essays written over the previous decade by one of the foremost feminist tragedy scholars.

Goff, B. (1990). *The Noose of Words: Readings of Desire, Violence, and Language in Euripides' Hippolytus*. Cambridge: Cambridge University Press. A beautifully nuanced deconstructive reading of Euripides' play.

Goff, B., ed. (1995). *History, Tragedy, Theory: Dialogues on Athenian Drama*. Austin: University of Texas Press. Contains a number of superb essays reading tragedy from a historicizing perspective; the introduction offers an excellent discussion of this theoretical approach.

Kahn, C. (1981). *Man's Estate: Masculine Identity in Shakespeare*. Berkeley: University of California Press. An important study of masculinity in Shakespeare from a psychoanalytic perspective.

Loraux, N. [1984] (1993). *The Children of Athena: Athenian Ideas About Citizenship and the Division Between the Sexes*, trans. C. Levine. Princeton, NJ: Princeton University Press. Focusing more on myth than tragedy, this book illuminates the place of the feminine in the Athenian democratic imagination.

Loraux, N. [1985] (1987). *Tragic Ways of Killing a Woman*, trans. A. Forster. Cambridge, MA: Harvard University Press. A subtle and provocative analysis of the semiotics of women's deaths in Greek tragedy.

Ormand, K. (1999). *Exchange and the Maiden: Marriage in Sophoclean Drama*. Austin: University of Texas Press. A detailed study of marriage in five plays of Sophocles.

Peradotto, J. and Sullivan, J. P., eds. (1984). *Women in the Ancient World: The Arethusa Papers*. Albany: State University of New York Press. An early collection of important feminist articles on a number of different topics within classical studies.

Pomeroy, S. B. (1975). *Goddesses, Whores, Wives, and Slaves*. New York: Schocken Books. One of the first and most influential studies of the life and status of women in the ancient world.

Rabinowitz, N. S. (1993) *Anxiety Veiled: Euripides and the Traffic in Women*. Ithaca, NY: Cornell University Press. Analyzes Euripides' treatment of women's role within male society from a theoretical (largely psychoanalytic) perspective, offering interesting in-depth readings of numerous plays.

Rabinowitz, N. S. and Richlin, A., eds. (1993). *Feminist Theory and the Classics*. New York: Routledge. Collects original feminist readings on a variety of classical topics and from a variety of theoretical perspectives; more overtly political than most collections on the subject.

Rose, P. (1993). "The Case for Not Ignoring Marx in the Study of Women in Antiquity." In *Feminist Theory and the Classics*, ed. N. S. Rabinowitz and A. Richlin. New York: Routledge, 211–37. A strong argument for the relevance of Marxism to feminism, including a smart theorization of tragedy's political and gender ideologies.

Vernant, J.-P. [1972] (1988). "Tensions and Ambiguities in Greek Tragedy." In *Myth and Tragedy in Ancient Greece*, ed. J.-P. Vernant and P. Vidal-Naquet, trans. J. Lloyd. New York: Zone Books, 29–48. A highly influential theorization of the nature of tragedy and its relation to its historical moment.

Winkler, J. J. and Zeitlin, F. I., eds. (1990). *Nothing to Do with Dionysos? Athenian Drama in Its Social Context*. Princeton, NJ: Princeton University Press. Still the most important collection of contemporary tragedy scholarship; contains many influential and important pieces, most with a historicizing slant.

Wohl, V. (1998). *Intimate Commerce: Exchange, Gender, and Subjectivity in Greek Tragedy*. Austin: University of Texas Press. Studies exchanges of women in three Greek tragedies, drawing upon psychoanalytic and post-Marxist theory.

Zeitlin, F. I. (1996). *Playing the Other*. Chicago: University of Chicago Press. A seminal collection of essays written over the previous decade by one of the foremost feminist tragedy scholars; every essay is worth careful reading.

Part IV
Tragedy in Antiquity

10

Tragedy and Myth

Alan H. Sommerstein

Virtually all ancient Greek tragedy was based on myths about the doings of gods and heroes in ages long past. We know of three tragedies in the fifth century BCE (Phrynichus' *Capture of Miletus* and *Phoenician Women*, and Aeschylus' surviving *Persians*) that dealt with contemporary events, and of a few in Hellenistic times that drew their plots from Herodotus; we also know of one play (*Antheus*, by Agathon) whose plot and characters were freely invented (Aristotle *Poetics* 1451b21–2). But myth was the basis of well over 99 percent of all the tragedies that were written – and often the same stories were returned to, over and over again: for example, our meagre sources mention eleven tragedies entitled *Thyestes* (three of them by Sophocles alone).

Myth, History, and Poetry

In discussing what we call "Greek myth" or "Greek mythology" it is important to remember two things in particular. One is that the distinction between "myth" and "history" was, for an ancient Greek, far from clear-cut. Learned commentators of the Hellenistic period and later can complain that a poet's version of a story is "contrary to history," or report that "X says [so-and-so], but the true history is [something different]"; the often skeptical historian Thucydides (1.4–12), while making much allowance for "poetic exaggeration" and discounting the supernatural element, takes it for granted that the major events of the heroic age (such as the reign of Minos, the Trojan War, and the return of the descendants of Heracles to the Peloponnese) had actually happened, and uses them as evidence for his reconstruction of the social, economic, and political structure of early Greece; and Aristotle's explanation of tragedy's preference for mythical over fictional stories is that tragedy must deal with "the sort of thing that could happen," and mythical events, unlike fictional ones, are *known* to be the sort of thing that could happen because they *did* happen (*Poetics* 1451b15–19). The ordinary fifth-century Athenian did not have the perception that we have, or that Hellenistic scholars had, of a continuous, measurable time-line connecting past, present, and future. He had a rich collection of tales, with an elaborate genealogical organization, about a distant past. He also had a much less well-organized collection of memories – his own, his parents', his friends' – of outstanding persons and events of the last seventy years or so. In between, there was hardly anything, except for two names, Draco and Solon, which were remembered because they were attached to codes of law that were still in operation, and the Peisistratid tyranny, which was remembered because it was the "other" against which democracy defined itself. Cleisthenes, now regarded (and already regarded by Herodotus 5.66–78 and 6.131.1) as the creator of Athenian democracy, is only once mentioned in any text composed for performance or delivery in the theaters, law courts, or assemblies of classical Athens – and that one instance (Isocrates 16.26) is an exception that proves the rule, for the speaker (the younger Alcibiades) is Cleisthenes' great-great-great-nephew and would know about him from family tradition. The heroic age was in a way more real to the average Athenian than the Athens of four or five generations back: he had, or thought he had, a clear idea of the main personalities and their relationships, of the main events in each saga cycle and their sequence and causal linkages (cf. Antiphanes fr. 189).

A clear idea, but an ever-shifting one. For the other point that it is vital to understand about Greek myth is that, in one sense, there was no such thing; or, to put it in a less startlingly paradoxical way, there was never any single, authoritative, canonical version of the traditional stories. The only exceptions, and then only partial ones, because of their unique cultural and educational status, were the two great Homeric poems, the *Iliad* and the *Odyssey*; and even they had no absolutely binding force on later poets (in whatever genre) or visual artists.[1]

Classical Greeks themselves sometimes said – and tragedians sometimes made their characters say – that the myths were the creations of poets.[2] Many of them, to be sure, will have been learned by children literally at their mother's knee (Plato *Republic* 377b–c), but from school age onwards it will have been mainly poetry that developed and consolidated their mythical knowledge. The children of the well-to-do learned large amounts of epic, didactic, and lyric poetry by heart at school. All alike heard Homer recited at the Panathenaea, and could form part of the vast audiences for the performances of tragedy, satyr drama, comedy, and dithyramb at the Dionysia and other festivals, both in the city and in local communities (demes). The only other media whose influence could be remotely comparable were certain types of public oratory (notably funeral speeches for those killed in war) – which by their nature concentrated almost entirely on stories about Athens or about Athenian heroes like Theseus – and public art in the form of sculptures and mural paintings (no text of the classical period makes any mention of vase-painting, which has so greatly enriched our own detailed knowledge of many myths).

How to Make a New Myth

Did the poets, in truth, create the myths? It depends what one means by "create." Even the most innovative of them were working within an existing framework and largely with existing personages. The action of a tragic drama, in particular, could cover only a short period of time, and the characters had to be left at the end in a position consistent with their future fate as known to the audience from other sources. Occasionally this limitation could be avoided or evaded. A good way to do this was to create a story that reached an existing destination by an entirely novel route. This, in effect, is what Sophocles did in *Antigone*.

For the familiar story of how Antigone defied her uncle Creon's edict forbidding the burial of her brother Polynices, of how Creon's son Haemon, to whom she was betrothed, pleaded in vain for her life to be spared, of how Creon relented too late, and of how first Antigone, then Haemon, then his mother committed suicide leaving Creon desolate, is virtually all, so far as we can tell, brand-new myth: there is no evidence whatever, in literature or art, that any such story existed before Sophocles (for the last scene of Aeschylus' *Seven against Thebes* is a later addition based on Sophocles' play). There were the names of Antigone and Ismene, as daughters of Oedipus. There were stories about how they met their deaths; we know only of one about Ismene – that she had an illicit affair with the Theban warrior Periclymenus, and that the Argive warrior Tydeus surprised them together and killed Ismene[3] – but the tradition must also have found a way to dispose of Antigone. There was a Haemon, son of Creon, but he was killed by the Sphinx long before Antigone was born (*Oedipodeia* fr. 3 Davies). And, perhaps most importantly, there was an Athenian tradition according to which the victors did deny burial, not just to Polynices but to all the Seven, until Theseus on the appeal of their kinsfolk made the Thebans surrender the bodies for burial at Eleusis, either by persuasion or by military force. This story had been dramatized in Aeschylus' lost *Eleusinians*, and would be again in Euripides' surviving *Suppliants*; certainly in the latter, probably in both, Creon was the ruler of Thebes. But the concentration on Polynices, the lone opposition of Antigone (with Ismene as a foil to her), the devastating effects of the collision between Creon's statecraft, Antigone's love of the dead, and Haemon's love of Antigone – these all seem to be Sophocles' invention. And yet the conclusion of his story allows the saga to continue almost exactly as it traditionally did, with Antigone and Haemon dead, Creon still in power (he is not expendable, since he will later become the father-in-law of Heracles), and the bodies of six of the Seven still unburied (cf. *Antigone* 1080–3) until Theseus comes to rescue them. The popularity and fame of Sophocles' play made his innovations almost immediately the constitutive elements of a new Antigone myth, which soon spawned further variants (often greatly developing the Antigone–Haemon "love-interest") (Zimmermann 1993) and which has remained fresh, powerful, and productive to this day (Steiner 1984).

Similar in principle is the sequel that Euripides, in *Iphigenia in Tauris*, creates to the long-familiar tale of the sacrifice of Iphigenia. The story that Iphigenia was snatched away by Artemis from the altar at Aulis, and taken to the land of the Taurians (the Crimea), was already told in the cyclic epic, the *Cypria*; Iphigenia was there said to have become immortal, and the story is doubtless connected with the existence in that region of a cult of a virgin goddess involving human sacrifices (Herodotus 4.103). But Euripides' tale of Iphigenia living among the Taurians, not as a goddess but as the priestess of this cult, of Orestes being sent there by Apollo in quest of an image of Artemis, of his reunion with his sister, and of their escape and return to Greece, as far as we can tell is entirely novel. It is pasted to the end of Orestes' story as known from Aeschylus by the transparently artificial device of assuming that after his trial and acquittal at Athens, some of the Furies continued to pursue him (*IT* 968–75) until he appealed to Apollo, who told him he could save himself by bringing the image of Artemis to Attica. At the end of the play nothing at all is said about Orestes' future, except that his "present troubles" will be over (1441b): Iphigenia will become priestess of Artemis at Brauron in Attica, where she will die and be buried (1462–4).

The establishment of the *deus ex machina* convention provided another method whereby a dramatist could create a new story within an existing mythical framework. It enabled him, in fact, to let his plot go in any direction he chose, and leave it for the *deus* to put it back on its traditional track. The most spectacular surviving example of this is Euripides' *Orestes*. In this play Orestes is (in effect) tried for the murder of his mother, not by the gods or the Areopagus council at Athens but by the people of Argos, and he, his accomplice Pylades, and his sister Electra are sentenced to death but allowed to commit suicide rather than suffer the disgrace of execution. They use their brief respite to hatch a daring plot. They seize Hermione, daughter of Menelaus, as a hostage; they murder her mother Helen – or at least they believe they have done so; they take control of the palace, and when Menelaus attacks it they threaten to burn it down and destroy Hermione together with themselves. At this point Apollo appears as *deus ex machina* – accompanied by Helen, who is not dead after all but has become a goddess – and proceeds, in effect, to cancel everything that has happened in the play. Orestes, after a year's exile in Arcadia, is to go to Athens and be tried and acquitted there; he is then to marry Hermione (at whose neck his sword is still poised!) and settle down as King of the Argives (who an hour or so before had condemned him to death) while Menelaus rules Sparta (Apollo considerately encourages him to take a new wife!). And thus, as in *Antigone*, the play can end with everyone in more or less the situation where their traditional future requires them to be.

Innovation within Existing Myths

But more usually what poets, tragic and other, do with myth is to take an existing story and *modify* it in one or several respects so that, to a greater or lesser extent, it becomes a somewhat different story with somewhat different implications. Some modifications were undoubtedly easier than others. It was one thing, as Sophocles does, to substitute Neoptolemus for Diomedes as Odysseus' companion on the mission to bring Philoctetes to Troy; it would have been quite another for Neoptolemus, won over by pity and affection for Philoctetes, to take him home instead – and in fact, when Neoptolemus is about to do this, Heracles appears as *deus ex machina* and orders the two men to go to Troy where both will win glory. Were there any modifications that were *completely* impossible? Is it ever true to say that a dramatist made his plot develop in this or that way because "the myth" left him no alternative?

Our evidence suggests that the answer is: yes, but only to a very limited extent. It was not normally possible to make alterations that would disrupt the basic genealogical framework of the mythical corpus. The story of the Danaids, for example (presented in the tetralogy from which Aeschylus' *Suppliants* survives, and in several lost plays by other authors), must always end with the confirmation of the marriage of Hypermestra, daughter of Danaus, to Lynceus, the only surviving son of his brother Aegyptus, because this couple become the founders of a long, much-branching tree of descendants including Perseus, Heracles, and other major heroes. Crucial and focal events, too, which involve many characters from a range of families – events like the voyage of the Argonauts, the attacks on Thebes by Adrastus and the Seven (unsuccessfully) and by the Epigoni (successfully), or the Trojan War – cannot be abolished. But beyond this, scarcely anything is sacrosanct: one can broadly say that *in a telling of any given story, any element may be altered, so long as the alteration does not impact severely on other stories which are not, on that occasion, being told*. This applies both to stories forming the main plot of a play (or other poetic text) and to those which are introduced by way of illustration (e.g., in a tragic choral ode).

Let us consider a few pieces of data, from myths used in tragedy, which might have seemed (and some of which have actually been alleged, by ancient or modern writers) to be unalterable.

Oedipus blinded himself on discovering that he had killed his father and married his mother. So he does in Sophocles' *Oedipus the King*, and so he is reported as having done in Aeschylus' *Seven against Thebes* (778–84), Sophocles' *Antigone* (49–52) – both produced earlier than *Oedipus the King* – and in Euripides' *Phoenician Maidens* (59–62) which was produced later; but from one ancient commentator on the last-mentioned play we learn that in Euripides' lost *Oedipus*, Oedipus was overpowered and *forcibly* blinded by "the servants of Laius" (presumably immediately after he had killed their master), and from another that a version of the story existed in which Oedipus was blinded by his adoptive father, Polybus, before he ever left Corinth, when Polybus learned of the prophecy that Oedipus would kill his father.

Orestes killed his mother. So he does in every account, dramatic or other, that we know of – with one important exception. The *Odyssey*, while never explicitly denying the matricide, never explicitly affirms it either, and its statement that after killing Aegisthus Orestes held a funeral feast for him and Clytemnestra (3.309–10) strongly implies, without actually stating, that Clytemnestra is to be assumed to have committed suicide. Having the authority of Homer, this version was always available to later poets; we know of none who actually used it, but I have argued elsewhere (Sommerstein 1997) that Sophocles in *Electra* encourages us for some time to believe that he is going to[4] (just as later in the play, when Electra believes Orestes to be dead, we are encouraged to expect that he will innovate in a quite different way and have her, not Orestes, kill Clytemnestra[5]). Even Aristotle, however, could write (*Poetics* 1453b22–4) that no poet could abolish the death of Clytemnestra at the hand of her son – forgetting that the greatest poet of all had in effect done just that.

Medea murdered her children. This crime, which has more and more come to seem constitutive of the mythical persona of Medea, was in all probability invented by Euripides. In accounts which are, or may be, of earlier date, we find her causing their death unintentionally by laying them in the sanctuary of Hera Akraia in the belief that the goddess would make them immortal (Eumelus, *FGrH* 451 F 2a); we also find them being killed at Hera's altar by the Corinthians (Parmeniscus, cited by an ancient commentator on *Medea* 264), or by friends of Creon (Creophylus, *FGrH* 417 F 3), and it was asserted (Parmeniscus, cited by an ancient commentator on *Medea* 9) that the Corinthians had paid Euripides five talents to transfer the blame for the children's deaths from themselves to Medea (obviously a fabrication, but further evidence that Euripides' account was an unusual one). Having made this drastic innovation (though one, be it noted, thoroughly consistent with Medea's traditional persona – consider how she murdered and dismembered her brother, duped the daughters of Pelias into killing their father, and later plotted to destroy the young Theseus), Euripides had to find some way to link it with the Hera Akraia cult with which all previous versions of the story had been closely connected. He does so, quite artificially, at the end of the play (1378–83) by having Medea interrupt her miraculous flight to safety at Athens to bury the two boys in Hera's sacred precinct (so that the hostile Corinthians will not be able to destroy their tombs), and establish a cult there which these same Corinthians will maintain for ever – and he evidently expects us not to notice the inconsistency.

Paris took Helen to Troy. One might suppose that if this elopement (or abduction) was abolished, it would destroy with itself the whole saga of the Trojan War. In the sixth century, however, the lyric poet Stesichorus[6] created a version of the story in which it was not Helen that went to Troy but a phantom in her shape, and Euripides uses this version in *Helen*.

Tragedians never felt in the least inhibited about presenting or presupposing different and incompatible versions of a story in different works. It is true that a poet was equally entitled to presuppose, as background to his new work, a particular account of earlier events by himself or another, as Oedipus' claims of moral and legal innocence in *Oedipus at Colonus* (265–72, 988–96) presuppose, and are not convincing without, the precise account of Laius' death which he gave in *Oedipus Tyrannus* (800–13); but we cannot *in general* read material from one play into another without specific authority, unless the plays are part of a connected sequence produced together as a unit. Euripides dramatized the story of Phaedra and Hippolytus twice, with drastically different presentations of Phaedra and probably of Hippolytus too. In

Sophocles' *Antigone* Creon is a vigorous ruler and is never called an old man (except possibly in the very last line of the play, when his misfortunes have broken him); in *Oedipus at Colonus*, whose action is to be imagined as taking place perhaps a month or two earlier, he is explicitly presented as elderly – because the play's central figure is the aged Oedipus, so that his uncle Creon must be aged too. In Sophocles' *Philoctetes* Odysseus is an unscrupulous villain; in *Ajax* his sympathetic understanding of Ajax, and awareness of his own human frailty, put Athena herself to shame. In Euripides' *Helen*, Helen is a virtuous woman who for seventeen years has been slandered worldwide without justification; three years earlier, in *The Trojan Women*, she had been portrayed as a spoilt playgirl, unscrupulously using her erotic magnetism to escape well-merited death at her wronged husband's hands; four years later, in *Orestes*, she has to sneak into Argos at night, loathed by its people and well aware that she deserves to be (*Orestes* 56–9, 98–104), and Orestes and his fellow-conspirators know that they have only to kill her to wipe out, in the mind of the Argive public, the stain of Orestes' matricide (*Orestes* 1134–42).

Mythical Innovation and Audience Expectation

The flexibility of myth was an invaluable resource to the tragedian, not only in constructing his plot and molding his characters but in playing on the expectations and emotions of his audience. Since no dramatist ever presented a story in precisely the same way as any of his poetic predecessors, the audience could be certain that the play they were going to see would contain some completely novel features or combinations of features. However, they would have no idea just *what* innovations it was going to contain, and this had two effects. In the first place, paradoxically, while they knew that the play *as a whole* would contain some innovations, with respect to any *particular* story element the likeliest outcome was that it would remain unchanged – so although innovation in the abstract was expected, any particular innovation would be a surprise. In the second place, it was possible for the author to bluff the audience by seeming to foreshadow an innovation and then presenting a different innovation or none at all (Sommerstein 1997). But we will never perceive such effects unless we think away our knowledge of how a play actually ends and put ourselves in the position of an audience seeing it for the first time, knowing one or (usually) several past versions of the story, able to infer with moderate confidence which elements of it would be effectively unalterable, but not knowing (though eager to guess) which elements would in fact be altered.

Euripides' *Hippolytus*,[7] for example, shows that an audience can be bluffed even if they are explicitly and authoritatively told in advance how the action is going to go. Our evidence suggests that, in most earlier versions of the Phaedra–Hippolytus story, Phaedra had killed herself after Hippolytus' death, when in some manner it had become known to Theseus and the world that she had not only fallen in love with Hippolytus but had made or authorized an adulterous proposition to him. The order of events was approximately: (*a*) Phaedra, rebuffed by Hippolytus, accuses him to Theseus of actual or attempted rape; (*b*) Theseus curses Hippolytus and he is killed; (*c*) the truth about Phaedra's passion is revealed to Theseus; (*d*) Phaedra commits suicide. This appears to have been the pattern of the plot both in Euripides' first *Hippolytus* play and in Sophocles' *Phaedra* (from both of which we possess only fragments). At the beginning of the surviving *Hippolytus*, Euripides' second treatment of the story, Aphrodite tells the audience what will happen: Phaedra, though smitten with love for Hippolytus, is keeping silent and confiding in no one; however: "that is not the destined outcome of this passion; I will reveal the matter to Theseus, and it will be brought into the open. And the young man who is my enemy will be slain by his father with the curses which the sea-lord Poseidon granted him . . . ; and Phaedra will perish with a good name, but will nevertheless perish" (*Hippolytus* 41–8).

In terms of the older tale, Aphrodite mentions coming events in the order (*c–b–d*), indicating one other modification (that Phaedra will die "with a good name"), and omits (*a*) altogether. This may well bewilder the spectator. If Theseus knows about "this passion" before he has cursed his son, how comes it that he utters the curse at all, and how can Phaedra possibly die with a good name? Again, Aphrodite says nothing of the rape allegation, and Theseus' early knowledge of Phaedra's passion would seem to leave no place for it: what entirely new twist, then, is Euripides meaning to substitute for it? Only as the action develops will the audience realize how Euripides has played fast and loose with them. Aphrodite has not told any lies, but neither has she told the whole truth, and what she has told she has put in a misleading order. The actual order of events turns out to be close to (*d–a–b–c*). The rape allegation is there after all, though it is made posthumously and Phaedra's motives for it are in part different from those portrayed in earlier treatments. The curse and Hippolytus' fatal injury occur, as tradition and logic require, *before* Theseus knows the truth, though he – and Hippolytus himself – are undeceived before Hippolytus dies. Aphrodite has led the spectator to expect far-reaching plot innovations; only one such innovation actually occurs (the retiming of Phaedra's suicide), and it occurs *contrary* to what Aphrodite's words seemed clearly to imply.

Let us now put ourselves in the position of the spectators watching another play of Euripides, *Medea*, and assume (as we have seen to be likely[8]) that in no previous version of the story has Medea been imagined as having deliberately killed her children – though in all of them, one way or another, the children have perished at Corinth. As we see the play in real time, what will our expectations be, and how will they develop, regarding Medea's intentions and the children's likely fate? At the outset we are quickly told the current situation: after living in Corinth for some time with Medea and their children, Jason, despite his sworn pledges of fidelity to her, has decided to marry the daughter of King Creon,[9] leaving Medea in desolate misery. We can guess that a person with her past record and her magical abilities will probably be determined, and able, to seek revenge; and her nurse indeed fears an act of violence against one or more of her declared enemies (37–45).[10] She also reports that Medea "hates the children and takes no joy in looking at them" (36); this will seem sinister only because we are sure that the children will die *somehow* before the play is over.

The early indications thus point to a murder-plot against Jason,[11] or his new bride, or Creon, or all three; in that case the children will probably be killed by the Corinthians in revenge. Consistent with this is the news that Creon is intending to send Medea and her children into exile (70–2), evidently fearing just such a move by her. The boys' tutor has learnt this with distress, but *we* may wonder if it offers a loophole whereby (contrary to all precedent) his charges can perhaps be saved. It is, to be sure, unlikely that Medea will simply depart without more ado (because then there can be no tragedy), but she might quite plausibly depart with the children leaving behind a deadly "present" for the new bride. A moment later the nurse (assumed to have gained through long intimacy a unique understanding of her mistress's mind) warns both the children and their tutor to beware of Medea, whose powerful emotions may drive her to some act of violence (89–104). This raises a fresh possibility – that Medea may kill her own children in a fit of anger – and this fear will be strengthened in a moment when Medea's voice is heard from within, cursing her children as well as Jason, and expressing loathing of herself as well (112–14, cf. 144–7); soon she is also cursing the new bride and her family (163–4). Almost all possibilities now seem open, except what actually happens: the deliberate, calculated killing of the children for the purpose of causing the maximum harm and pain to Jason. A complicating factor is that whereas *we* know that Medea is to be banished, she herself does not, and the knowledge, when it comes, may change her feelings and preferences.

Presently Medea comes on stage and makes a long and very rational speech (214–66), ending by asking the chorus to keep silent about any means she may discover to punish Jason for what he has done to her. In this speech she does not mention her children, and it must now seem unlikely that she will kill them in anger; we will probably go back to our former assumption that she is planning to strike down the wedding party. The chorus promise to keep her secret – but at this moment Creon arrives. He orders her immediate departure into exile, because she is making threats against him, his daughter, and his future son-in-law (287–9). She supplicates him for one day's respite, mainly for her children's sake (340–5), and he is not brutal enough to refuse. When he has gone, Medea firmly declares that she is going to "make corpses of three of my enemies, the father, the girl, and my husband" (374–5). She is aware that she will then find it hard to escape or find refuge (386–8), so she decides to wait a little to see if some hope of safety appears; if not, she will go ahead anyway even at the cost of her life (392–4). Knowing that Medea has to survive,[12] we will doubtless guess that a refuge will present itself.

Certain now, as we think, that Jason is doomed, we listen to Medea wiping the floor with him in a set-piece debate scene (446–626). We may briefly wonder if she will be tempted to accept (treacherously, of course) his offer of money, and introductions to his friends, to ease her and her children's path in exile (610–15), but we are not surprised when she refuses to accept anything at all from him. And then, after Jason's departure and a choral song, a saviour enters in the bumbling shape of

Aegeus of Athens; Medea secures asylum with him by making another supplication, promising to use her magic to enable him to beget children, and making him swear that he will neither banish her nor surrender her to her enemies. The oath she administers (735–55) is the most solemn and precise in all surviving tragedy, and we soon discover why. No longer is Medea thinking of killing Creon, his daughter and Jason. Now, as she reveals at 792–3, she means to kill Creon, his daughter – and Jason's children: Jason himself is now envisaged as surviving to suffer their loss (803–4, 817), which Medea perceives to be a worse punishment than mere death. That she is also inflicting the same punishment on *herself* is pointed out by the chorus (818), but brushed aside, though it will influence her, momentarily, later on (1044–8).

Now at last we *do* know how things will end, and the only uncertainties that seem to remain are how Medea will escape from Corinth and how she will ensure, as her new plan demands, that her device to kill Creon and his daughter does *not* also kill Jason.[13] But we may be surprised when, sending the children with Jason to take the "present" to his bride, she asks him to ask Creon to spare them from exile (939–45); surely, if the petition is granted, they will stay with the wedding party (cf. 939), and probably be killed when they are discovered to have been the bearers of death to the king and princess? Is this perhaps a devilish device of Medea's to cause the death of the children without getting their blood on her own hands? But no: immediately after the following choral ode, the children return with their tutor (1002ff). If they are to be killed, it must be their mother that kills them – though even now Euripides continues to play with alternative denouements, as Medea thinks momentarily of taking the children to Athens (1044–8).[14]

Presently we, and Medea, learn of the horrible death of Jason's bride and her father. If she is going to complete her revenge, Medea must now kill her children at once (1236–7); she steels herself to do it with the thought that otherwise they will die by "another, more hostile hand" (1239) – which had been their fate in most earlier accounts. She goes inside, and presently the children's final cries are heard.

Shortly afterwards Jason arrives, desperate to save his children – from the Corinthians (1303–5); when told that things are far worse than he imagines, he asks whether Medea is planning to kill him too (1308). He is, one might say, in the wrong script, and presently Medea is seen aloft in her winged chariot, her grief almost, but not quite, lost in her triumph over him – while he is the same Jason as ever, still quite unaware that he has ever done her any wrong. The inauguration of the cult of Hera Akraia (discussed above) provides a link back to more familiar versions of the story, as probably does the reference to Jason's unusual death.[15] But Euripides has innovated here too. So far as we know from other sources, nothing significant happens to Jason between his children's death and his own – indeed, as we have seen, in at least one account he dies shortly *before* them – unless his assistance to Peleus in capturing Iolcos (Pherecydes *FGrH* 3 F 62) is to be taken as a later event. It would seem to follow that he was normally thought not to have lived long after his parting from Medea. In Euripides' version he certainly will, as witness her gleeful response when he laments his bereavement: "You've not started grieving yet: just wait till you're old!" (1395). *That* is to be Jason's greatest punishment: the curse of long life!

Thus, while in one sense we have known from the moment *Medea* began how it would end – with Jason's children and his new bride dead, and Medea on her way to Athens – in another and perhaps a more important sense we have often had very little idea what was going to happen until shortly before it did happen, and have sometimes been carefully led astray by the planting of false expectations. Not every tragedy plays these games with the audience quite as intensively as *Medea* does, but it happens far more frequently than has traditionally been allowed.

Etiology

Medea's foundation of a cult in honor of her children at the sanctuary of Hera Akraia exemplifies a very common feature in tragic poets' treatment of myth: the creation of links, or the highlighting of existing links, between the mythical past and the world of the poet's own time. Almost every surviving play of Euripides ends with a statement (by a *deus ex machina*, if there is one) of some kind of etiological connection to the contemporary world. Sometimes the etiological connection may have been obvious to the audience from an early stage. In *Medea* it seems to have already been part of the story before Euripides, and the only uncertainty will have been how it could be combined with a deliberate murder of the children by Medea, once it had become clear that such was her intention. In *Iphigenia in Tauris*, we learn very early on (85–92) that Orestes is on a mission to steal an image of Artemis from the Taurians and take it to Attica; there was probably already a well-established association between Iphigenia and the cult of Artemis at Brauron in eastern Attica (cf. *IT* 1462–7), although the link between the Taurian image and the cult of Artemis *Tauro*-polos at nearby Halae Araphenides, which is given greater prominence by the *dea ex machina* (1449–61), may well be a Euripidean invention (Scullion 2000).

Other Euripidean etiologies are of a political nature. In *Andromache* (1247–9) the connection is the foundation, by Andromache's son, of the still reigning royal house of Molossia; in *Suppliants* (1191–1209) it is an eternal treaty of nonaggression between Athens and Argos; in *Ion* it is the nomenclature of the four traditional Athenian tribes, descended from Ion, and the division of the Hellenic people into Ionians, Dorians, and Achaeans (*Ion* 1575–94) – and a traditional genealogy is modified so as to give the Dorians of the Peloponnese an Athenian ancestry (1589–91), with obvious contemporary political implications. In one or two plays the concluding etiology is rather trivial – notably in *Helen* (1670–5), where a tiny island off the Attic coast is named after Helen – but there is only one Euripidean tragedy that we know to lack one altogether, *The Trojan Women*, whose relevance to the contemporary world was only too plain anyway.

Perhaps the most celebrated of all tragic etiologies are those in Aeschylus' *Eumenides* for the homicide jurisdiction of the Areopagus council (681–710), for the rule in

Athenian trials that equal votes mean acquittal (735–41), and for the Athenian alliance with Argos (289–91, 667–73, 762–77) – all three probably, and the last certainly, invented by Aeschylus. Generally, though, both in Aeschylus and in Sophocles, links between the drama and the contemporary world are made by implication rather than explicitly; the late *Oedipus at Colonus*, with its prophecy (409–11, 621–3) of an Athenian victory over Athens' current enemy Thebes at the site of Oedipus' tomb, is an exception.

It is striking that it is hardly ever possible to determine, on the basis of internal evidence alone, whether a tragic etiology (or similar linkage between the world of the play and the world of the audience) was taken from existing tradition (with or without modification) or was wholly invented by the dramatist. What matters, apparently, especially in Euripides, is that the connection should be made, and the question of its mythical or cultic "authenticity" does not arise. Once again we must bear in mind that there was no fixed entity called "Greek myth."

Secondary Mythical Allusions

Let us turn now to a quite different kind of linkage: the many cases in which characters or choruses in a drama try to illuminate the story being enacted by referring or alluding to a different story that can be seen as in some way related to it – as when, just after the killing of Medea's children, Euripides' chorus sing of Ino (*Medea* 1282–92), calling her the only other mother to have killed her own offspring. For us today, such references may also, contrariwise, throw new light on the story being referred to – and sometimes on other stories not even mentioned. That is the case with this Ino passage. As has recently been pointed out (March 2003), if it can be said by a chorus in 431 BCE that Ino is the *only* woman before Medea to have killed her children, that proves not only that Sophocles' *Tereus* (in which Procne takes revenge on her husband Tereus for his rape and mutilation of her sister Philomela by killing her son Itys) is later than 431, but that in earlier versions of the story Procne (or whatever she was then called) had not killed her own child, or at least had not done so deliberately. Another possible parallel known to all students of tragedy, the killing of Pentheus by his mother Agave in Euripides' posthumously produced *Bacchae*, was probably like-wise unknown in 431 (March 1989: 50–2): on fifth-century and earlier vase-paintings showing the killing of Pentheus by Dionysiac maenads, their leader is never named Agave, and on one she is named as Galene.

If a myth is alluded to only very briefly, especially if the allusion is indirect, it will usually not be possible to alter it in the process; at the most, the poet may be able to indicate which of various existing versions of the story is being referred to. But even brief references can be used in surprising ways. In Aeschylus' *Eumenides* there are two references to the story of Ixion. When Athena comes to her temple on the Acropolis, finds Orestes embracing her image there and the Furies surrounding him, and is told by the latter that they are pursuing him because he has killed his mother but are willing to submit the case to her judgment, she turns to Orestes and asks him what he has to say for himself "if it is with trust in justice that you sit guarding this image near my hearth, a suppliant deserving respect in the manner of Ixion" (*Eumenides* 439–41). Later, while the votes are being cast at the end of Orestes' trial, there is an altercation between the Furies and Apollo (who has been acting as Orestes' advocate): the Furies charge Apollo with having allowed his sanctuary at Delphi to be polluted by the blood on Orestes' hands, and Apollo retorts with a rhetorical question: "did my Father [Zeus] also make a wrong decision on the occasion when Ixion, the first murderer, was a suppliant for purification?" (*Eumenides* 717–18) – which the Furies evade answering.

If this was all we knew about Ixion, we would gather that he killed someone, supplicated Zeus for purification, and was granted it; moreover, both Athena and Apollo – and even, to judge by their failure to challenge Apollo, the Furies – seem to regard it as obviously true that Ixion justly deserved this favor from Zeus, and from this one would naturally presume that, as in Orestes' case, there were strong and well-known reasons for holding that the killing was to some degree excusable.

Yet when we turn to Pindar's *Second Pythian* (21–48), to our fragments of Aeschylus' own *Ixion* and *Women of Perrhaebia*, and to a variety of later sources, we find they tell a coherent tale which is very hard to reconcile with the assumptions that seemingly underlie the *Eumenides* references. The following account is based on the ancient commentary to the Pindar ode, with additional material from Pindar's text (in angled brackets) and from Diodorus Siculus 4.69.3 5 (in square brackets).

> Ixion married Dia, the daughter of Deioneus.... After the marriage Deioneus, according to custom, demanded that Ixion hand over the bride-gifts [and, when he refused to do so, seized his horses in pledge]. So Ixion dug a pit, filled it with fire, and invited his father-in-law as if to a feast, [promising full compliance,] and the latter, unaware of the contrivance, came in, fell into the fire-pit, and perished in the flames. <Ixion thus became the first man to shed kindred blood in a treacherous murder.> No one was willing to purify him, and his pleas were rejected also by most of the gods, but Zeus took pity on him, purified him of the murder, took him up to heaven, and let him share his home. But they say that he attempted a second crime, falling in love with Hera [and having the audacity to proposition her sexually], and that Zeus, learning of this, fashioned a cloud in the shape of Hera: Ixion, seeing it, approached it and lay with it, and from this union was born a savage and monstrous man to whom they gave the name Centaurus, <who in turn lay with some Magnesian mares on the slopes of Mount Pelion and begot the hybrid Centaurs>. Afterwards Ixion's hands and feet were bound to a <winged> wheel <on which he rolls around everywhere, proclaiming to mortals that they must repay their benefactors with kind deeds in return>.

No source gives the slightest indication of anything that might excuse Ixion – and the second half of the story shows, moreover, that Zeus' merciful behavior toward him was about as misguided as could possibly be imagined. At least from the beginning of the fifth century BCE (when the wheel first appears in art) Ixion was one of the archetypal great sinners of myth. The two allusions in *Eumenides* are thus likely initially to bemuse the audience, and on reflection to raise serious questions about the attitude of the Olympians to homicide and in particular to Orestes. Ixion had used deception to kill his father-in-law (who must also have been a blood-kinsman, perhaps an uncle); Orestes had used deception to kill his mother, which must be even worse – with the approval of Apollo and therefore (*Eumenides* 19, 616–18) of Zeus. Do Apollo, Athena, and Zeus not care about such things? Do the Furies not know what is known to everyone to whom Ixion's name means anything at all? These questions arise from the very fact that the allusions are too brief to include any data that might change our view of the story. They are never directly answered. But they may serve, like the equally divided vote of the jury, to counteract any temptation we may be under to see the case of Orestes in simplistic, black-and-white terms; to emphasize that his action, like Ixion's, was an enormous evil – even if, unlike Ixion's, it was an absolute necessity in the given situation – and that it is essential to ensure that such a situation never arises again; and perhaps also to suggest that the automatic forgiveness, regardless of the circumstances, which Zeus extended to Ixion, is as unacceptable a policy as the automatic retribution, regardless of the circumstances, on which the Furies insisted so passionately for so long.

When we are told a little more than this, it does become possible to alter a myth in the process of alluding to it. Midway in Aeschylus' *Choephoroi* the chorus, reflecting on Clytemnestra's crime which is soon to be avenged, recall various other atrocious crimes committed by women, such as the killing of Meleager by the action of his mother Althaea, or of all but one of the men of Lemnos by their wives, or:

> . . . another hateful woman in story,
> the bloody maiden
> who caused the death of one close to her
> at the hands of enemies,
> persuaded by a gold-crafted
> Cretan necklace, the gift of Minos,
> she, with the mind of a bitch, robbed Nisus
> of his lock of immortality
> as he snored in unwary sleep;
> and Hermes touched him.
>
> (*Choephoroi* 613–22)

The maiden is easily identifiable as Scylla, who betrayed her father Nisus, and her city of Megara, to the army of Minos of Crete. Nisus could not die so long as a particular lock of hair was on his head; Scylla cut it. We have no other references to the story before Roman times, but it is striking that this passage implicitly denies an element present in all later accounts:[16] they all, whether in Greek or in Latin, say that Scylla was *in love* with Minos. If she was in love with him, and if he and her father were implacable enemies (so that a normal marriage to Minos was an impossibility), she would need no gift of jewelry to persuade her to kill Nisus, particularly (one might think) in a choral ode whose declared subject is the disastrous effects of *desire (eros)* in women (*Choephoroi* 596–601). It appears, therefore, that in Aeschylus we are to suppose that she commits the crime purely for a bribe. It is possible, of course, that the love element is a later invention and that the bribery story was the normal one in Aeschylus' time, but the love element is attested by eight different authors who are certainly not all dependent on each other, and none of them mentions a gift by Minos to Scylla. The story would be well known at Athens, Nisus being the brother of the Athenian king, Aegeus; so if Aeschylus was here modifying it, the modification would be noticed, and spectators would ask themselves why it had been made. Their likeliest answer would perhaps be, especially after hearing some more of the ode, that the feminine "desires" which are its subject are turning out not to be exclusively or even mainly sexual. By the time they reach the end of the ode, they will have encountered four instances of women murdering those close to them, motivated by four different kinds of desire: Althaea (602–12) by vengeance, Scylla by material gain, the Lemnian women (631–8) by sexual jealousy, and Clytemnestra, to judge by what is said of her in 623–30, mainly by power. On still further reflection they may conclude that these four motives were all in fact present in the Clytemnestra they saw in *Agamemnon*: vengeance for Iphigenia, sexual jealousy of Cassandra, and the chance to gain control of Agamemnon's great wealth (cf. *Choephoroi* 135–7, 275, 301) and effective rulership of Argos (cf. *Choephoroi* 302–5). The ode may on the surface be telling four different stories; but at a deeper level it is telling just one – the story of the woman who in a few moments will appear yet again at the door of the house whose headship she has usurped.

Conclusion

Thus, whether on a small or large scale, we can see tragedy exploiting, renewing, and sometimes creating myth, holding its audience in a varying combination of knowledge and ignorance, creating and frustrating their expectations. Whether in the construction of his plots and the events surrounding them, or in the illustrative exploitation of stories other than the one being enacted, or in building connections between the heroic age and the present day, the tragic poet was the master of myth, not its servant. Perhaps this was even more powerfully true of him than it was of his epic or lyric brethren. They could *tell* a story, fully or briefly, explicitly or allusively; the dramatist, at least so far as concerned the actual plot of his play, was committed to having it *enacted* in a manner that could persuade an audience that it was seeing "the sort of thing that could happen"; committed, that is, to imagining and credibly re-creating at least some episodes at a level of detail that other genres could always avoid if they wished, and forming them into a structure that would make, as a whole, an effective and appealing theatrical experience. The stories that had been handed down by tradition provided admirable raw material for this purpose; but ancient artists, unlike some modern ones, gained no prizes by presenting their material raw. Myth was tragedy's framework, but never its straitjacket.

Notes

1 See chapter 11 in this volume.

2 See, for example, Herodotus 2.53 ("Hesiod and Homer ... are the ones who created the genealogy of the Greeks' gods"); Plato *Republic* 377d ("Hesiod and Homer ... and the other poets ... told and still tell men false stories of their own composition"); Euripides *Heracles* 1346 (Heracles rejecting myths of divine immoralities and conflicts: "these are the wretched tales of poets").

3 Mimnermus fr. 21 West (where the name is Theoclymenus); Pherecydes *FGrH* 3 F 95; and at least two archaic vase-paintings (see *LIMC* Ismene I 3–6). Tydeus acts at the behest of Athena, and it has been suggested that in this story Ismene was a cult-servant of Athena bound to virginity.

4 The key false clue is planted in lines 121–8, when the chorus address Electra as "child of a most wretched mother," recall the death of Agamemnon "most impiously caught by the deception of your guileful mother" – and then end by praying "May *he* that brought these things about perish!" In speaking of the murder they mention only Clytemnestra, and yet it is Aegisthus whom they curse: if they, who are not Clytemnestra's children, cannot bring themselves even to pray for her death, how much less will those who *are* her children be willing actually to kill her! As late as lines 453–71, when Electra asks the cautious, timid Chrysothemis to pray that Orestes should "live, get the upper hand, and plant his foot upon his enemies," and she agrees to do so, we can hardly be meant to suppose that Chrysothemis is agreeing to pray that Orestes should kill his mother.

5 We know, of course, that Orestes is close at hand, but we cannot be sure that he will carry out his plans before she has had time to act on her declared intention (1019–20, 1045) of avenging her father's murder herself (Chrysothemis having refused to assist her).

6 *PMG* 192, 193; cf. Plato *Republic* 586c.

7 This paragraph is taken, with minor modifications, from Sommerstein (1997:195–6).

8 See p. 168 above.

9 No connection with the Creon of the *Antigone* story.

10 This fear may have been expressed vaguely or precisely, depending on whether the disputed lines 38–42 are genuine.

11 In most other accounts Jason survives (to perish later by accident or suicide), but in one (Hyginus *Fabulae* 25) he dies, together with his bride and Creon, in a conflagration caused by Medea.

12 For she has an important role to play later in Athens as a wicked stepmother to Theseus.

13 The dramatist eventually solves this problem for her by having Jason leave the palace, with the children, as soon as their petition has been accepted by his bride (1158); he does not trouble to explain how in that case it comes about that when the children are returned to their mother (1002), Jason is not with them.

14 A second reference to this possibility at 1058 is probably, with its context, a spurious addition (the passage makes Medea not merely inconsistent but incoherent: 1058 takes it for granted that she will be able to take the children with her to Athens, the next sentence without argument takes it for granted that she will not).

15 He will die after being hit on the head by "a relic of the *Argo*" (1387), explained by an ancient commentator as referring to the ship's stern-post falling off the wall of the temple where it had been dedicated.

16 *In Greek:* Pseudo-Apollodorus 3.15.8; Pausanias 2.34.7; scholia to Euripides *Hippolytus* 1200 and to Lycophron *Alexandra* 650. *In Latin:* [Virgil] *Ciris*; Propertius 3.19.21–8; Ovid *Metamorphoses* 8.6–151; Hyginus *Fabulae* 198.

References and Further Reading

Burian, P. (1997). "Myth into *Muthos*: The Shaping of Tragic Plot." In *The Cambridge Companion to Greek Tragedy*, ed. P. E. Easterling. Cambridge: Cambridge University Press, 178–208. A sensitive study of how myth and tragedy helped to fashion each other.

Buxton, R.G.A. (1994). *Imaginary Greece: The Contexts of Mythology*. Cambridge: Cambridge University Press. On the contexts in which myths were told and portrayed, their presentation of key aspects of the world, and their functions as perceived in ancient and modern times.

Clauss, J. J. and Johnston, S. I., eds. *Medea: Essays on Medea in Myth, Literature, Philosophy and Art*. Princeton, NJ: Princeton University Press. A collection of studies on a wide range of aspects of the figure and myth of Medea from our earliest evidence to the present day, with Euripides' play as a constant point of reference.

Dowden, K. (1992). *The Uses of Greek Mythology*. London: Routledge. Discusses the uses to which myths were put in Greek society, and ancient and modern theories about them.

Gantz, T. R. (1993). *Early Greek Myth: A Guide to Literary and Artistic Sources*. Baltimore, MD: Johns Hopkins University Press. The only handbook of Greek mythology that treats it as a dynamic, developing entity, presenting an exhaustive, source-based analysis of the known myths, covering all versions that originated, or may have originated, before about 450 BCE.

Graf, F. [1987] (1993). *Greek Mythology: An Introduction*, trans. T. Marier. Baltimore, MD: Johns Hopkins University Press. Probably the best introductory text on Greek mythology; see especially Chapter 7 on lyric and tragedy.

Hard, R. (1997). *Apollodorus: The Library of Greek Mythology*. Oxford: Oxford University Press. A translation of the most complete ancient mythological compendium that survives, with valuable endnotes discussing alternative versions and their history.

Kirk, G. S. (1974). *The Nature of Greek Myths*. Harmondsworth: Penguin. A classic and still valuable study, notable for its wide range, its interest in comparison of Greek myth with the mythologies of other cultures, and its sceptical attitude to all comprehensive theories.

March, J. R. (1987). *The Creative Poet. Bulletin of the Institute of Classical Studies* Supplement 49. London: Institute of Classical Studies. Traces the development of selected myths in the archaic and classical periods, stressing the poets' role as (sometimes drastic) innovators.

March, J. R. (1989). "Euripides' *Bakchai*: A Reconsideration in the Light of Vase-paintings." *Bulletin of the Institute of Classical Studies* 36, 33–65. Argues that two key features of Euripides' *Bacchae* (Pentheus being dressed as a woman, and being killed by his mother) are Euripides' own inventions.

March, J. R. (1998). *Cassell Dictionary of Classical Mythology*. London: Cassell. A handy guide, alphabetically arranged (by character or event), with sources given *en bloc* at the end of each major entry.

March, J. R. (2003). Sophocles' *Tereus* and Euripides' *Medea*. In *Shards from Kolonos: Studies in Sophoclean Fragments*, ed. A. H. Sommerstein. Bari: Levante, 139–61. Argues that Sophocles in his lost *Tereus* invented Procne's deliberate killing of her son Itys on the model of Euripides' novel version of the Medea story.

Prag, A. J. N. W. (1985). *The Oresteia: Iconographic and Narrative Traditions*. Warminster: Aris & Phillips. A detailed study of versions of the Agamemnon–Orestes myth in art and poetry down to and including Aeschylus.

Scullion, S. (2000). "Tradition and Invention in Euripidean Aetiology." In *Euripides and Tragic Theatre in the Late Fifth Century*, ed. M. Cropp et al. *Illinois Classical Studies* 24–5, 217–33. Argues that the tragedians, especially Euripides, not only often invent etiologies but sometimes for this purpose invent nonexistent cults or add invented details to actual cults.

Shapiro, H. A. (1994). *Myth into Art: Poet and Painter in Classical Greece*. London: Routledge. Studies the relationships between the treatment of myth in art and in poetry (Chapter 4 is on tragedy).

Sommerstein, A. H. (1997). "Alternative Scenarios in Sophocles' *Electra.*" *Prometheus* 23, 193–214. On how Sophocles, by misleading his audience (twice) into expecting *Electra* to end in untraditional ways, increases the tragic power of its (traditional) ending.

Steiner, G. (1984). *Antigones.* An immensely stimulating study of the impact of the Antigone myth, and its many realizations, in the twenty-four centuries since Sophocles.

Stinton, T. C. W. (1985). "The Scope and Limits of Allusion in Greek Tragedy." In *Greek Tragedy and its Legacy: Essays Presented to D. J. Conacher*, ed. M. Cropp et al. Calgary: University of Calgary Press, 67–102. Reprinted in T. C. W. Stinton, *Collected Papers in Greek Tragedy*, Oxford: Oxford University Press, 1990, 454–92. On "how far … the tragic dramatists [could] count on their audience taking the allusions in their plays and filling in for themselves what was not actually stated; and … how far … their audiences [could] be counted on to recognize a departure from traditional legend, that is, *not* to fill in for themselves what was not intended to be filled in."

Zimmermann, C. (1993). *Der Antigone-Mythos in der antiken Literatur und Kunst* [The Antigone myth in ancient literature and art]. Tübingen: Narr. Presents and analyses all available evidence for the story, its variations, its main themes and its development, seeing it as essentially Sophocles' creation.

In addition, almost every modern edition of a Greek tragedy contains in its introduction a section headed "The myth," "The history of the legend," or the like, which discusses the evidence for the development of the relevant myth(s) before the date of the drama in question and the significance of the choices and innovations made by the dramatist.

11

Tragedy and Epic

Ruth Scodel

Epic Stories and Allusions

When tragedy began in Attica in the sixth century BCE, epic was the most important source for the new genre. Tragedy's great innovation was to combine the existing genres of epic recitation and choral song in dramatic form. Although it replaced the epic narrator with actors and a chorus, it was in many ways a continuation of the epic tradition.

The epic foundation was very rich. By the latter part of the sixth century BCE the Homeric epics were regularly performed in Athens by professional reciters (*rhapsodes*) in a four-yearly contest at the Great Panathenaea. This contest gave Homer a special status, but other epics, of which only fragments remain, were familiar to the tragedians and many members of their audiences: poems about Theban legend, the *Oedipodeia* and *Thebais*, and the poems now called the "Epic Cycle," which collectively told the entire history of the Trojan War (Homer's authorship of all these was disputed); Hesiod's *Theogony*. There was an old Heracles-epic, the *Capture of Oechalia* (attributed to Homer or Creophylus); Panyassis, a contemporary of Aeschylus, composed a long epic on Heracles' life. An epic about the most important figure of Athenian legend, Theseus, was probably composed in the sixth century BCE. The epic on Corinthian history by Eumelus included at least some material about the Argonauts. The genealogical poem attributed to Hesiod, the *Catalogue of Women*, was almost an encyclopedia of Greek legend, providing family trees with brief narratives.

The Homeric poems were unlike these other epics. They had more dialogue, less narration; more focus on fewer characters and events, and more connection among episodes (plots rather than a succession of actions); less magic (Griffin 1977). Homeric epic was already, as the ancient critics realized, highly dramatic: most of the first book of the *Iliad*, for example, consists of a series of dialogue scenes with narrative bridges between them. Drama was a development from an already dramatic epic. Tragedy could not do everything epic could. The narrator could not comment directly on the action, for example, and the dramatic form imposed severe limits on the length of individual tragedies. Yet tragedy also could adapt the most powerful elements of epic and intensify their effects through its special resources of spectacle and song.

Tragedy had considerable freedom in using epic tales and characters (see chapter 10, this volume). No single narrative ever told the whole story of a traditional character, and no single version, even the Homeric epics, had absolute authority. So lyric, and then tragedy, could endlessly fill in and readapt the old material. Poets frequently created new stories by interpreting familiar ones. For example, both Sophocles and Euripides composed tragedies about the youth of Paris/Alexander. His parents, frightened by omens that he would cause the destruction of Troy, exposed him at birth. After growing up as a herdsman, he competed in his own funeral games and was recognized by his father. This does not seem to have been an epic story, but it has obvious parallels with such familiar myths as those of Oedipus and Perseus, and it resembles Herodotus' account of the childhood of Cyrus the Great. In Homer, the Trojans loathe Paris, yet seem unable to resist him, as if they believe that the evil he would bring is inevitable. In the logic of Greek story, it would be surprising if there had been no omens to warn Paris' parents of how dangerous he was. The invented story is thus a "reading-out" of the existing epic, an interpretation.

The stories could be changed, as long as the overall outcomes remained. Aeschylus, in a tragedy called *Myrmidons*, made Achilles older than Patroclus, though the *Iliad* explicitly says that Patroclus was older. Aeschylus made the two men lovers, and so imagined Achilles, the more powerful hero, as the lover, the dominant partner in a homoerotic relationship. Phoenix, Achilles' tutor, describes in the *Iliad* how he fled home after he seduced his father's concubine and his father cursed him; in Euripides' *Phoenix* this episode became a Potiphar's-wife story with an innocent hero (who was blinded instead of cursed). Euripides was fascinated by Potiphar's-wife stories. When the tragic poets rethought an epic story, they changed not just details but the motivations of characters. They reconsidered how events could have happened, what kind of people could have performed the actions attributed to the epic characters, and where an audience's sympathies should be directed. Homer avoids ever mentioning Agamemnon's sacrifice of his daughter, while Hesiod's *Catalogue* mentioned her miraculous rescue by Artemis. Even Aeschylus is interested in Agamemnon's feelings more than hers: she is pathetic, but is seen only as the chorus remembers seeing her. Euripides, in two tragedies about her, makes her two, very different, fully imagined people: the desperate and resourceful woman whom Artemis rescued but made her priestess in a remote country in *Iphigenia in Tauris*, and the naïve, frightened, and finally resolute victim in *Iphigenia at Aulis*.

The qualities of the Homeric poems themselves prepared for tragedy's adaptations. Both epics, but especially the *Iliad*, are profoundly generous in their treatment of their characters. The poet seems continually aware that while he cares most about Achilles and Odysseus, other characters, even minor ones, have their own stories. Homer does not give much attention to Nausicaa once she serves her function of bringing Odysseus to her parents, but it is enough to make an audience wonder how the rest of her life was affected by her meeting with the hero. Sophocles composed a *Nausicaa* from Homer's episode. Furthermore, the *Iliad*-poet is a Greek, but his Trojans are sympathetic and richly imagined characters. Even though the *Iliad* does not tell the fall of Troy, Homer's Andromache and Hecuba invited Euripides to imagine the fates given them in the Cycle as their stories, not those of the conquerors.

In general, tragedy took much of its technique and its sense of narrative possibility from Homer, but many of its stories and atmosphere from the rest of the epic inheritance (Herington 1985: 133–6). The claim that tragedy is so profoundly dependent on epic may seem surprising, since tragedy arose in a very different social and political context from archaic epic. Many critics see tragedy as intimately connected with Athenian democracy. Indeed, some important features of Attic tragedy belong exclusively to this "tragic moment" (see chapter 7, this volume). Certainly tragedy shows a distinct tendency to give stories an Attic connection, even when they derive from old, non-Athenian myths. Aeschylus' *Eumenides* is an outstanding example: the traditional story of the royal house of Argos ends with the foundation of an Athenian institution. Not infrequently, too, tragedies confront contemporary issues – the function of the Areopagus council and the Argive alliance in *Eumenides*; the scope and limits of mathematical and rational investigation in Sophocles' *Oedipus Rex*; political faction and rhetorical maneuvering in Euripides' *Orestes*.

Despite these real differences from epic, tragedy throughout its history depends on epic for actual stories, for a ready made fictional world, for resonant language, for narrative devices, for allusive depth. Differences between Homeric and fifth-century values that seem obvious now were not salient for the fifth-century audience, who did not read Homer exactly as we do. In modernizing epic material, tragedy helped make epic modern (Plato's Socrates effortlessly compares himself to Achilles at *Apology* 28c–d). Tragedy mined the epic tradition for pathetic and sensational material, stories of violence, cruelty, intrigue, and sexual transgression. It presented these in an exalted, solemn register, with a rich admixture of theological and moral speculations, meditations, and platitudes. In characterization, in plot construction, and in emphasizing the detailed representation of crucial moments, tragedy imitates Homer; but it is more like the Cycle in its interest in the erotic and cruel. Homer mutes the nastier familial violence of his stories (the *Odyssey* manages to avoid mentioning Orestes' killing of his mother), while tragedy seems to revel in it (Seaford 1994: 11–13).

Often, non-Homeric epics, especially the Epic Cycle, were a direct source for the stories of tragedies. Relatively few plays were based directly on the two Homeric poems. Aeschylus had an *Iliad* and an *Odyssey* trilogy. Sophocles composed two plays possibly based on the *Odyssey*, *Nausicaa* and *Niptra*, but many on other Trojan War subjects. Euripides seems never to have challenged Homer directly in a tragedy, although his surviving satyr-play, *Cyclops*, deals with Odysseus' most famous adventure, and the fourth-century tragedy in his style that survives with his plays, *Rhesus*, is based on the tenth book of the *Iliad*. Euripides expanded the brief narrative of how Phoenix, Achilles' old teacher and friend, left his home into a tragedy – changing the hero's seduction of his father's concubine into a false accusation. Similarly, the *Odyssey* briefly describes the family of Aeolus, who married his sons to his daughters. In Euripides' tragedy, one of the sons had a sexual relationship with his sister, and persuaded his father to marry his children incestuously. The father, however, assigned the daughters by lot, and the son was unlucky. Euripides, however, was especially fond of stories from the *Cypria* (Jouan 1966).

Sophocles' surviving Trojan dramas illustrate the complexity of the literary sources of tragedies. The fate of Telemonian Ajax was told in the *Aethiopis* and Little *Iliad*, but before Sophocles it had been dramatized by Aeschylus, while Pindar offers several, slightly different, short versions. Sophocles' *Philoctetes* treats a tale told in the *Aethiopis*, but already put on the stage by Aeschylus and Euripides. Similarly, Aeschylus' *Seven against Thebes*, Sophocles' *Oedipus the King*, and Euripides' *Phoenician Women* may all reflect the poets' familiarity with the Theban epics, but Sophocles and Euripides both surely knew Aeschylus' trilogy, of which only *Seven against Thebes* survives, and a papyrus first published in 1977 has fragments of a previously unknown poem of Stesichorus that clearly influenced Euripides. The *Nostoi* told the story of Agamemnon's murder and his son's vengeance (also the subject of extended digressions in the *Odyssey*), but Stesichorus' long lyric *Oresteia* was probably the single most important literary version for Aeschylus' *Oresteia*.

When poets renew familiar stories, they invite their audiences to compare their new versions with old ones, or tease them with expectations derived from familiar, epic versions. In *Agamemnon*, the opening song ignores the story, familiar from the epic *Cypria*, that Agamemnon at Aulis, after a deer hunt, boasted that he had excelled Artemis. She then made it impossible for the army to sail until Agamemnon sacrificed his daughter Iphigenia to her. Artemis, however, actually rescued Iphigenia and made her immortal, although the mortals present probably did not realize what had happened. In Aeschylus, the chorus describes an omen in which two eagles devour a pregnant hare, foreshadowing the destruction of Troy; Artemis' anger seems to be caused by the omen itself (*Agamemnon* 104–59). The singers describe the preparations for the sacrifice in detail, but insist that they did not see what finally happened (248). The effect is profoundly disconcerting, for Artemis either confuses the omen with the reality, or punishes an action before it takes place. The audience does not know whether Iphigenia was saved or died. Such an effect is possible only in drama, for an omniscient epic narrator who failed to explain such important events would be intolerable. In Sophocles' *Electra*, Clytemnestra justifies her murder of Agamemnon as vengeance for the killing of Iphigenia, complaining that if a war needed to be fought for Menelaus, a child of Menelaus should have been sacrificed. Electra replies by referring to the story of the deer hunt (516–609). Versions from different texts have become competing accounts of the past.

Tragedy also invents new sequences that invite comparison to familiar epic material. The plot of Euripides' *Iphigenia in Tauris* is loosely based on the epic story of Jason and the Argonauts (Lange 2002: 107). Here the epic source provides a general plausibility for the invented plot – this kind of quest is typical of the heroic world.

Sometimes borrowings are far more specific, as when the hero of Sophocles' *Ajax* says farewell to his son (545–51). When he holds the boy, insisting that he will not be frightened by his blood-soaked father, and prays that his son may be like his father, but luckier, he strongly recalls the episode in the *Iliad* (6.466–82) when Hector's son cries in fear at his father's helmet, and Hector prays that he may be "much better" than his father. The boy's mother, the concubine Tecmessa, echoes the Homeric Andromache when she pleads with Ajax not to kill himself, but to protect her. The resonances complicate the moment in various ways. That *Ajax* echoes his greatest enemy shows an underlying similarity among all the heroes. Ajax's prayer shows a pride that is especially striking in contrast to Hector's modesty. Yet Hector's prayer works against the hearer's knowledge that the boy will not survive the fall of Troy, while the prayer of Ajax reminds the Athenian audience that Eurysaces, like his father, was among their heroes – Sophocles composed a tragedy about him. So the prayer of Ajax, unlike that of Hector, will be fulfilled. The echo of the famous Hector–Andromache scene is especially striking because Eurysaces is not a legitimate son, Tecmessa a concubine, not a wife, but Ajax behaves as though they were (Easterling 1984 gives a discussion of this scene).

The connections between tragedy and epic are various and complex. Non-Homeric epic provides the stories, but the resulting dramas are frequently profoundly engaged with the *Iliad* or *Odyssey*.

Epic Thematics

In the *Odyssey*, Penelope decides to challenge her suitors to match Odysseus' skill with the bow just when he has returned in disguise. Many critics have thought that Penelope must know that the beggar is Odysseus, although the text tells us clearly that she does not. Others have guessed that our *Odyssey* has borrowed its plot from a version of the story in which she had recognized her husband. As it stands, however, the *Odyssey*'s climax takes place at a murky boundary between coincidence and divine management, between a theological level at which the gods bring about their chosen outcomes, and a narratological one at which the will of Zeus is that part of the story that cannot be changed. The gods promise that Odysseus will avenge himself on the suitors, but only Penelope's decision, which no god directs, makes the actual outcome possible. Again, the *Iliad* is deeply ambiguous at the divine level. Initially, Zeus is unwilling to agree with Thetis to help Achilles, but once his Plan is in motion, it leads to the fated destruction of Troy, through consequences Achilles did not intend, Hector's killing of Patroclus and Achilles' consequent killing of Hector. The deaths of Sarpedon and of Hector both belong to this sequence and are said to be fated: how would they have happened without Achilles' anger?

Tragedy delights in such situations, variously mixing human causality, chance, and divine meddling. The Homeric epics do not overtly draw the audience's attention to the difficulty of understanding how divine plans and human choices work together, or to the apparent contradictions in Zeus' direction of events, but tragedy often develops this aspect of the epics. Homeric epic is full of prophecies, but these are rarely primary motivators of the action. Tragedy uses communication from the gods to make the ambiguities of the gods' plans a central feature of its plotting. In Aeschylus' *Agamemnon*, the omen of the eagles and the hare reveals at once the support of Zeus for the Trojan War and the anger of Artemis. In *Oedipus the King*, the divine warning itself inspires the human reactions that fulfill the prophecy. In *Philoctetes*, mortal attempts to fulfill a prophecy lead to complete frustration, until Heracles comes from heaven. Euripides often builds a complex web of divine and human motivation, only to end with a direct divine intervention. Euripides' *Iphigenia in Tauris* has the heroes' intrigue almost fail at the last moment, as it appears that Poseidon will not allow their ship to escape. Then Athena, as *deus ex machina*, intervenes, and announces that Poseidon, for her sake, is calming the sea (1444).

Tragedy derives its most characteristic event, the recognition, from Homer. The *Odyssey* provides the models for the many episodes of long-separated relatives who learn each others' identity. Yet the Odyssean recognitions are tame compared to many in tragedy, which often makes its recognitions as sensational or pathetic as possible. Aeschylus' Clytemnestra recognizes her son when the slave says that the dead are killing the living (886); Euripides' Ion is given his recognition tokens as he is about to murder his mother; Sophocles' Orestes reveals himself to Electra only after she has mourned over the urn that she believes holds his ashes.

The *Iliad* is the main source for tragic recognition in the broader sense – those moments when the characters realize that the stories of their lives have not been the stories they thought they were. Achilles in the *Iliad* thinks that he is in control of the narrative. When his best friend Patroclus is killed, he realizes that he was wrong. Just before he receives the news of Patroclus' death, he remembers a prophecy that the best of the Myrmidons would die before him, and suddenly realizes that it could apply to Patroclus (18.9–14). The misunderstood oracle, of course, is a typically tragic device for signaling such disjunctures between human plans and understandings and the divine plans in which human beings are entangled (see Rutherford 1982). But Hector also has a moment of such recognition. First he realizes his own folly in not listening to the wise advice of Polydamas and keeping the Trojans outside the walls after Patroclus' death; then, when he realizes that he has been tricked by a god into believing he had Deiphobus beside him, he sees that the gods have determined his death (22.296–305; Redfield 1975: 128–59).

Tragedy offers a rich repertory of variants on these themes. Sophocles' Oedipus is the most famous, but we should not make it a universal model. Eteocles in Aeschylus' *Seven against Thebes*, when the messenger announces that his brother Polynices is the attacker at the seventh and last gate, sees that his father's curse is being fulfilled (655). He insists on going to fight his brother, even though the chorus tries to convince him to avoid such pollution. Eteocles is surely right in seeing supernatural forces in his placement against his brother, but his acceptance of the curse is horrifying. Sophocles' *Women of Trachis*, when Hyllus tells Heracles how Deianira was tricked into poisoning him, recalls two oracles (1159–71). One, a version of the oracle that has been quoted many times in slightly different forms, said that at this time Heracles would be freed of labors. The other said that he would be killed by someone who was dead. Combining the two, he sees that release from labors means his death. Instead of exploring his new understanding of his own fate and Deianira's, however, he immediately turns to managing what will happen next. His own share in the responsibility for what has happened was to take Iole as a concubine (sacking her city for this purpose), and now he insists that Hyllus marry her. He also forces his son to prepare a pyre for him. The Spartan kings claimed descent from Hyllus and Iole, and the story that Heracles ascended to Olympus from the pyre was probably already familiar to the original audience; but Heracles gives no explanation for his demands. So as soon as one gap between human knowledge and fate is closed, Heracles opens another. The spectator cannot tell whether he actually has access to divine knowledge or is simply acting in accordance with it when he insists on these perverse actions. In Euripides' *Hippolytus*, the goddess Artemis coolly explains what has happened; she is critical of Theseus, but acknowledges that the goddess Aphrodite caused the events (1325–8). Theseus learns of both his own, human errors, and of the divine plan behind them. Hippolytus, like Hector, has a double recognition. Defending himself to his father, he shows some understanding of Phaedra and so of his own role in his calamity (1034–5); only in the final scene does he learn, just before his death, that Aphrodite was actually responsible at the divine level. Here, though, the emphasis seems to lie less on the human experience of recognition than on the contrast between the mortals' response to it (Hippolytus forgives his father) and the gods' remoteness.

Such recognition is "tragic" even when the reinterpretation is benign rather than disastrous. Euripides' "romances" all have plots that center on recognitions in the literal sense, but that also demand that the characters profoundly reinterpret the past. The *Helen* is the richest of these, for the play provides both a happy outcome for the main characters, Menelaus and Helen, and a version of the Trojan War that deprives it utterly of meaning; the Helen for whom Greeks and Trojans died was an illusion. The *Ion* makes the theme most salient; Creusa at 1501–9 sings of how "we are whirled around from there to here by misfortune and again by good fortune" and at 1609 says, "I praise Phoebus, though I did not praise him before."

Even when the characters do not come to understand what has happened, Homer already combines characters' inability to do what they know is best with the gods' broader plans. The *Iliad*'s Priam surely realizes that Paris is bringing ruin to Troy, but cannot bring himself to oppose him. When he refuses to blame Helen, because the war is the gods' fault (3.164–5), he is simultaneously correct and foolish. The gods are at work, but his and Helen's weaknesses are essential to their plan. Even in the *Odyssey*, where the suitors are for the most part entirely unsympathetic, there are two "good" suitors. Odysseus warns Amphinomos that he should leave, but the narrator tells us, in an unusually strong example of divine causation, that Athena has willed that all the suitors must die (18.124–57). Such instances of weakness helped Aeschylus create his Agamemnon, who agrees to walk on the tapestries against his better judgment, just as he sacrificed his daughter. The example of Amphinomos (as well as Polydamas' advice to Hector in the *Iliad*, 18.249–309) shows the Homeric antecedents of the characteristically tragic "warning" sequence. A servant advises Euripides' Hippolytus to revere Aphrodite (88–107 – the audience knows that the goddess' vengeance is already planned); Tiresias and Cadmus warn Pentheus to honor Dionysus in *Bacchae* (266–342).

Closely related to tragedy's theme of recognition and disaster half-foreseen is the characteristic tragic theme of the suddenness of changes of fortune. This, too, has epic antecedents, of course – one might consider the astonishing changes of fortune in the tale the disguised Odysseus tells Eumaeus (14.192–359). The *Odyssey* is very concerned with a special, significant time. At its opening it emphasizes that its narrative begins at a particular point in the story, the time that the gods had fated for Odysseus' return (1.16–18), and the predictions of his homecoming in Ithaca refer to a mysterious unit of time, the *lycabas*. The formulaic system of epic insists on the importance of the day with expressions like "day of return," "day of freedom," and "day of slavery." Greek lyric, in its recurring concern with human vulnerability, frequently uses the epithet *ephemeroi*, "beings of a day." Tragedy, however, is profoundly aware not only of its epic origins, but also of its differences from epic, particularly its concentration and brevity. Although Greek tragedy does not strictly observe the unity of time, since the passage of time during a choral song is undefined, most tragedies seem to take place in a time only a few hours longer than their actual duration. Tragedy thus thematizes "the day" in which lives can be rescued or ruined (or both, as in Euripides' *Heracles*, where the hero returns just in time to save his family from the tyrant Lycus, and then goes mad and kills them himself). Tiresias warns Creon in *Antigone* that he will pay for his confusion of dead and living within a few days (1064–5). Haemon in fact dies on this same day. The possibility of radical change on the day is at once a moralizing platitude and a generic marker of tragedy.

Tragedy takes from Homer the ambition to depict certain kinds of experience with emotional depth. *Women of Trachis* and Sophocles' *Electra* both present a central character whose suffering is modeled on that of the waiting Penelope. *Women of Trachis* alludes to the *Odyssey*: when Deianira sends her son to find her husband, the ideal spectator surely compares Deianira to Penelope directly. Yet what really matters is less that we think about Penelope than that Sophocles recognized in Homer's attention to Penelope a subject worthy of attention. Because the poet is so familiar with Penelope, he thinks about the story of Deianira and Heracles as the story of a woman left alone, not knowing what has happened to her husband. (He then, with the arrival of the husband's concubine, can turn Deianira/Penelope into a potential Deianira/Clytemnestra). In Sophocles' *Electra*, the main character is a sister, not a wife, and the echo of the *Odyssey* is less vivid. Yet when Orestes hears Electra lament, but does not stay to listen and perhaps reveal himself, the audience is invited to remember Odysseus' choice to test his wife rather than trust her in his intrigue. Because the themes of waiting and trust are so familiar from Homer, the tragedian can make them effective quickly.

From the *Iliad* come tragedy's great explorations of the experience of betrayal. Achilles, when Agamemnon takes away his prize of honor, becomes profoundly disillusioned with the heroic system, in which the hero risks his life in battle and is rewarded with honor. The intensity of his anger estranges him from the rest of the Greek army and leads to the death of Patroclus. Euripides' *Medea* and Sophocles' *Philoctetes* are the two surviving masterpieces in which the protagonist most develops the themes of the angry Achilles. Medea, abandoned by Jason, for whom she has betrayed her own family and committed murder, is willing to cause herself the worst imaginable pain in order to make him suffer, by killing their children. The play gives an Achillean need for vindication to a foreign woman who uses cunning and deceit. Philoctetes, left on an uninhabited island by the Greeks, would rather die in misery than return to Troy and achieve heroic glory. Early in the play, Neoptolemus, Achilles' son, wins Philoctetes' sympathy by telling a false story of how the Greeks refused to give him his father's armor. He claims to be sailing home in anger, though he is serving as an agent of the Greek army, under Odysseus' command. Sophocles' audience is supposed to realize that Neoptolemus is using the story of the *Iliad* as well as the Cycle to fabricate this tale. Only Philoctetes, in his isolation, does not know the most familiar of all stories, even though he is truly Achilles-like, while Neoptolemus is betraying his father's memory by evoking it to deceive a friend.

Epic Style and Decorum

Even when a particular play tells a story that has no epic antecedent, however, epic is essential for understanding tragedy's generic aspirations, freedoms, and boundaries. Epic is the basic source of the tragic world. Epic contributes one strain to the tragic language. Much early tragic lyric was probably in the dactylic rhythms that evoked epic, and tragic speech admits distinctly epic words and forms that were foreign to contemporary Attic speech. Even more, epic gives tragedy the rules of what human experiences may be represented. Familiarity and the canonical status of the epic and tragic traditions lead us to take their decorum and the rules of their imagined world for granted, but these deserve a little attention. The epic presents a world in which gods frequently intervene in the lives of individuals; so does tragedy. Ghosts appear but not Lamias; monsters, following Homer, tend to be kept at the periphery. Even more than epic, tragedy prefers horses to donkeys. The chorus of *Antigone* sings of how men exhaust the untiring Earth by turning the soil "with the race from horses" – in the *Iliad*, Hermes himself drives Priam's horses, but though he breathes energy into his mules, the god does not handle them (24.440–2). Like epic characters, tragic characters often weep and bleed, and sometimes belch or vomit (blood or human flesh), but never fart. Narrative triviality is excluded, so that a hero may forget to sacrifice to the right god, but he never forgets his helmet. The economy is strict.

Both genres, though, sometimes flirt with the limits of their own high decorum. An important character in the *Odyssey* is a swineherd. His pigs do not seem to stink, although the seals of Proteus do (4.441–2). Aeschylus in *Agamemnon* allows the Greek army to suffer, euphemistically but clearly, from mildew and bugs in their clothes (560–2; neoclassicism would surely forbid both the seals and the lice). Homer admits humor (especially when gods are involved); tragedy does too (Seidensticker 1982). Drunkenness and invective appear now and then. Tragedy can achieve special effects by playing its own testing against that of epic. Euripides' *Electra* evokes the *Odyssey*, and its setting in a humble farmer's house in the countryside recalls Eumaeus. Yet precisely because the *Odyssey* keeps epic grandeur amid rusticity, the play is striking when it makes the characters no grander than their surroundings. When Electra scolds her husband for inviting noble guests despite his poverty, and sends him to invite the old family slave and ask him to bring dinner (404–5, 408–14), we are a distinct step below the small pig Eumaeus sacrifices for his guest. When Orestes is recognized by a scar, it is not the mark of a brave hunter, but the remains of a childhood accident with a pet. Orestes is not the hero Odysseus was (Goff 1991).

Greek epic achieves its grandeur through meter, through being composed in an artificial dialect, and through rich ornamentation. Tragic speech is mostly in the Attic dialect of its primary audience, but it borrows many of epic's tools (and takes its songs from the tradition of choral lyric). Although there is occasional colloquialism in tragic speech, tragedy does not often test the limits of language and of subject matter at the same time. The speech of slaves can be less elevated than that of the noble characters, but the language tends to be euphemistic when the topic is vulgar or dangerous. Tragedy can be sexually explicit, but tends to use grand language (*Women of Trachis* 539–40). Clytemnestra calls Cassandra a "pole-rubber," *histotribes* – the reference is utterly vulgar, but the word is a unique compound. Euripides, whose language is the plainest, shows Phaedra's desire for Hippolytus through her fantasies of wandering in the woods as he does. The Nurse tells Phaedra, "what you need is not specious [i.e. moral] talk, but the man" (490–1). Such bluntness, which almost demands that Phaedra stop being a tragic character, can appear in an argument but not as an expression of feeling, where it would be too transgressive. Tragedy's decorum is in some ways stricter than epic's. The word *kopros*, "manure," appears several times in Homer, but is banned from tragedy – perhaps because tragedy, performed at the same festival as comedy, had a greater need to define itself by contrast.

Tragedies were normally set in the remote past familiar from epic poetry. The epic heroes were stronger and braver than contemporary mortals, and they require elevated language and respectful attention. The epic world is both an ordinary past, historically linked to the present, and a different reality from the everyday world, where gods intervene, words have special power, and the rules of plausibility are slightly different.

Epic customs were different from those of the fifth century, but not too different, especially because fifth-century readers looked for similarity rather than difference. Some differences were useful. The Iphigenia of *Agamemnon* has sung at her father's banquets (242–5), which would be unimaginable in contemporary Athens, but Medea can complain to the Corinthian women about how women "buy" their husbands (232–4), although Homer's culture practices bride-price. Sophocles' Orestes can compete in the Pythian Games, although they had not yet been founded. In his *Ajax*, the debate between Teucer and the Atridae evokes at least three different contexts at once. Is Ajax a Homeric hero, who, like Achilles, is entitled to demand the honor he deserves, even if he injures the common cause? Is he a contemporary Athenian military leader and aristocrat, whose loyalty the city expects even when it has treated him unfairly – although, in fact, such men sometimes conspired with foreign enemies to recover the status that they believed they deserved? Is he a representative of the Athenians' allies?

Tragedy loved to mix distance and difference with contemporary norms and problems. When Aeschylus ends the *Oresteia* with the establishment of the Areopagus court, he retroactively implies that the struggles over justice enacted in the horrifying murders of the last two plays belonged to the past. Yet the killing of Agamemnon is also a coup d'état, and civic institutions cannot operate against a dictatorship. The fear of tyranny was real in Athens, so that the trilogy can address old history and present concerns simultaneously.

In the epic world, gods frequently have sexual relations with women. In epic, gods' children are usually reared by a grandfather and the women make appropriate marriages (so, for example, Polymele at *Iliad* 16.179–92). Nor do the illegitimate children of the great heroes seem to be an embarrassment. In tragedy, however, these stories are seen through contemporary eyes. So the mothers typically hide their pregnancies and expose their children, and tragedy then generates a variety of stories of the woman's suffering and eventual reunion with her son(s). The *Ion* is the only one of these to survive in full, but there are extensive papyrus fragments of Euripides' *Hypsipyle* and *Antiope*. Tyro, according to the *Odyssey*, fell in love with the river-god Enipeus and would walk by the river's banks, where she was raped by Poseidon. Her sons were the heroes Pelias and Neleus. She married Cretheus, and although Poseidon warns her not to announce her sexual encounter with him, there is no hint that she suffered (*Odyssey* 11.235–59). Sophocles composed two plays called *Tyro*. In one, Tyro was persecuted by a stepmother named "Iron" (and proud of it; fr. 658). In another fragment she laments that her hair has been cut off (659). Such plots about the reunions of separated parents and children then proliferated in New Comedy. As so often, tragedy expanded an epic narrative element so that its possibilities were visible for later authors and genres.

Epic Narrative

Epic forms the basic model for tragic plots. Many Greek tragedies have happy endings: so does the *Odyssey*. The *Odyssey* brings the human actors to a situation of near-disaster, as Odysseus and his supporters begin a battle with the families of the suitors, but Athena suddenly appears to bring about peace. This is the origin of the tragic *deus ex machina*. Many other tragedies end with a lament, like the *Iliad*. It is probably from the *Iliad* that the tragedians acquired their interest in narratives of two opposed focal characters. Hector and Achilles are the main characters of the poem, each extensively developed in his own social world, though Achilles is clearly more important. They meet only once, when they finally fight in Book 22, but everything else leads toward and away from that encounter. Hector kills Achilles' surrogate, Patroclus, and Achilles then kills Hector. When Achilles finally ransoms Hector's body, he also releases the Trojan half of the story, so that it can come to an end. Sophocles' *Antigone*, like the *Iliad*, brings two opponents together and then separates them. In Euripides' *Hippolytus*, the two never actually meet directly at all, but the scene where they are on stage together and Phaedra's intermediary, the Nurse, approaches Hippolytus, is the moment at which the disaster takes place. In Sophocles' *Women of Trachis*, Deianira and Heracles never meet at all (they were played by the same actor). Critics have traditionally argued about who is the "hero" in these plays, but mutual destruction is what these plots are about.

From the Cycle, on the other hand, Euripides took his plots whose focus shifts drastically with a dizzying succession of incident. In *Andromache*, the initial dramatic problem is Hermione's threat to kill Andromache, the concubine of her husband Neoptolemus, and Andromache's child. Andromache is rescued by Peleus, then Hermione is terrified but is rescued by Orestes. Then the messenger reports Neoptolemus' murder by Orestes at Delphi. *Phoenician Women* begins with Jocasta, then moves its attention from Antigone to Eteocles and Polynices, to Menoeceus the son of Creon, back to the warring brothers and the death of Jocasta, and to Oedipus.

Tragedy depends profoundly on epic narrative technique. Of course, drama is in some respects inherently different from epic. One is obvious: Homer can tell, while tragedy must show (though it can show a character who narrates). Homer, however, does not provide a single, authoritative voice. He is often secretive or ambiguous, so that the contrast between telling and showing is not always as great as one might imagine. The other difference, though it sounds banal, is not. Tragedies are short, and the choral songs make the action-time shorter. All the spoken episodes of tragedy tend to resemble the most intense passages of Homer. Homer is full of formulaic narrations of journeys, feasts and sacrifices. In tragedy, if the journey can be taken for granted, it is skipped. Messengers begin their stories when they arrive at the setting of the event. Tragedy narrates only astonishing journeys, like the path of Agamemnon's beacons, or Io's fated wandering through the exotic edges of the world. Homer has long similes, but tragedy is typically metaphorical. Homer is expansive. Although Homeric digressions serve to mark the significance of the episodes they amplify, they nonetheless give the impression that the poet is interested in them for their own sake. Tragedy tends to be tightly constructed.

Still, Homeric epic was the tragedians' abiding model for what made a good story and how to tell it. Their dramatic form often made their needs different from Homer's, but even when they are different it is often revealing to see them in relation to Homer. For example, Sophocles often uses what Barbara Goward has called a "narrative loop" (Goward 1999: 87–118). A false or ambiguous narrative within the tragedy threatens to send the plot in the wrong direction, but in the end the "true" plot is restored. Euripides does something similar, though in his own manner, in *Orestes*. The *Iliad* is actually a model for the loop, when Zeus is first distracted and then deceived by Hera, so that Poseidon can intervene to make the Achaeans win.

Homer observes a careful distinction between his own omniscient narrative, which often explains events as the work of particular gods, and his characters, who do not know about divine interventions unless they are given supernatural access to this information through prophets or by the gods themselves. Hence mortals speak of "some god" or "Zeus," even though the narrator tells the external audience that an individual god has acted. The tragedians play endless variations on mortals' inability to know the gods' plans and actions. In Aeschylus' *Agamemnon* and *Choephori*, the characters talk about what various gods demand, but in the final play the gods themselves appear. In Euripides' Hippolytus, the Nurse argues with Phaedra that her passion for her stepson has been caused by Aphrodite, and that she is therefore wrong in trying to resist it (443–76). Phaedra wins sympathy by rejecting this attitude. Yet the audience knows from Aphrodite herself that Phaedra is, indeed, the victim of direct divine intervention. In *Antigone*, the poet has the guard describe the burial of Polynices as astonishing: first somebody manages to slip by the guards and cover the body; then, during the day, a dust-storm forces the guards to close their eyes, and when they can see again, Antigone is beside the body, lamenting. It looks as if the gods might be involved, just as in epic they rescue their favorites in battle or help them reach their goals without being seen. Here, however, the external audience can only share in the wonder of those who see a stranger suddenly before them. No omniscient narrator clarifies the event. If the gods have helped Antigone in reaching the body of Polynices, their failure to help her later is even more striking.

Homer provided the basic canon of verisimilitude and the rules of what makes narrative sense. Homer and tragedy share a rule, for example, that prophecies and predictions by gods are always true, but may be imprecise. In Homer, characters' versions of the narrator's story, whether anticipatory or retrospective, are never too accurate, because the character's point of view infiltrates them. Prophecies are a special case, and serve simultaneously to inform the audience of what will come without abandoning the possibility of surprise. Inaccurate details by Zeus or a prophet, however, do not limit the speaker's overall authority. The prologue of Euripides' Hippolytus implies that Theseus will curse Hippolytus after learning of his wife's love. The events that actually transpire clearly fit what Aphrodite intended, but not what she says. On the other hand, in Euripides' *Ion*, Athena explains at the end that Hermes' prediction in the prologue that Creusa would recognize her son after they had returned to Athens was not just a misleading detail. Apollo was wrong about what was going to happen.

In the *Odyssey*, the same prophet, Theoclymenus, interprets the same omen slightly differently in different passages: first he tells Telemachus it means no family will be more "kingly" than his (15.531–4), but later he tells Penelope it means that Odysseus is nearby, preparing death for the suitors (151–61). These interpretations are different aspects of the same essential message. Similarly, in Sophocles the same prophecies are quoted in different forms in different circumstances – most strikingly in *Women of Trachis*, since Deianira emphasizes that the oracle is written down.

Tragedies approach epic most directly in messenger-speeches. The convention of the tragic messenger is not primarily a way to avoid representing violence before the audience. Messenger speeches allow epic scale and actions impossible within the narrow dramatic space. Narrative allows for movement, summary, the description of silent actions and of masses of people. The messenger in Agamemnon describes a storm at sea, the messenger in *Persians* an entire battle. The old man in Sophocles' *Electra* delivers a false, but splendidly detailed account of Orestes' death in a chariot-race at the Pythian Games. Narrative has further positive advantages: above all, because the messengers of tragedy are ordinary mortals, it allows for ambiguity and mystery about divine intervention.

The tragic messenger speech develops the first-person narrative of epic – not the reports of messengers, but autobiographical narratives. Here, as in other ways, epic's conventional allowances are very useful for the tragedian. Homer's first-person narrators stay generally within the limits of what they know, but not entirely. Although they typically use mostly "experiencing" focalization, they are prone to add not only hindsight, but knowledge they could not have at all. They are held strictly only to the restrictions limiting human awareness of divine interventions. Eumaeus, for example, tells the story of how his nurse abducted him from home when he was a child (*Odyssey* 15.403–84). He includes events at which he was not present, and throughout he remembers far more accurately than a small child could have. Epic characters tell their own versions of stories, and these are always self-interested – but sometimes they seem to have borrowed some of the epic narrator's basic fairness, his sense that everybody has a point of view. Eumaeus is the victim of the story, but his narrative seems to sympathize with the nurse in her longing to return to her home. Similarly, tragic messengers are simultaneously eyewitnesses, whose knowledge is confined to what they personally saw, and quasi-epic narrators, whose sight is greater than any individual's could naturalistically be. The messenger in Aeschylus' *Persians* sees the entire battle-field and hears what the Greeks call to each other. Unlike Homeric narrators, tragic messengers are not significant participants in the events they describe. They always have a particular, clearly defined sympathy and their reports are emotionally colored, yet their facts are always correct.

Only rarely does a messenger express hesitation in his reporting or differentiate his observations from his inferences. Usually messengers avoid transgressing human knowledge of the divine. So the messenger in *Oedipus at Colonus* conveys the boundary precisely in his inability to say what happened to Oedipus (1656–6). At the end of Euripides' *Iphigenia in Tauris*, however, the messenger seems to know not only that Poseidon has caused a powerful current to force the Greeks' ship back against the shore, but that he is acting from hatred of the Pelopidae (1414–19) – although he cautiously adds "so it seems" to his statement that Poseidon will give Orestes and his sister to the Taurians. He also refers to Iphigenia as "forgetful" of the help Artemis gave her at Aulis. A moment later, Athena appears to explain the future of Artemis' image and of Iphigenia as Artemis' priestess. The messenger is not wrong, exactly, but his knowledge about the gods is incomplete. Euripides loves to play messenger-narrative, action, audience knowledge and inference, and omniscient narrative against each other: in *Ion* we hear how the hero is saved from being poisoned when doves drink the wine he has poured in libation (1196–208; did Apollo send them? Probably). We suspect Apollo's intervention when the Pythia enters to stop Ion from killing Creusa (1320–3); then Athena says that Apollo feared Creusa would kill Ion and Ion Creusa, and saved them "by contrivances" (1565).

Tragedy constantly adapts and transforms epic methods. On the large scale, epic provides not just stories, but models of plot. The tragedians use it as a repertory of the possible. Frequently, tragedy seems haunted by the epic poet's omniscience. Homer already plays with the distance between what he can tell the external audience and what his characters can know. Dramatic form, with its fewer opportunities for presenting divine knowledge, invited the poets to play with the audience's uneasy position between the characters' limited knowledge and the full information only epic promises.

Tragedy into Epic

The passage of story, technique, and sensibility from epic into tragedy did not go all one way. In Homer, characters faced with difficult decisions sometimes speak to their own hearts. These are practical decisions: they set out the reasons for each side and make up their minds. Tragedy did not at first adapt this epic convention, but it fully developed speeches by perplexed characters who reason acutely even while expressing intense emotion. Sophocles' disgraced Ajax considers his alternatives, while Euripides' Admetus realizes how lost he is without the wife who died for him. Euripides finally used the Homeric form for Medea's great speech in which she hesitates between murdering her children and giving up her revenge (1021–80). This speech became a model for later epic. The monologue became a powerful vehicle for Apollonius of Rhodes' Medea. Her descendents, in turn, are Virgil's Dido and the tragic women of Ovid's *Metamorphoses* – Iphis, Byblis, Myrrha, Procne. Epic, having created tragedy, re-created itself on the model of its creation.

If tragedy became an important source for epic, it has been just as important in directing readers of Homer. Even without Aristotle's influence, we would see Achilles and Hector as tragic figures. Thanks to the *Poetics*, it is often impossible to distinguish what tragedy took from Homer from what we see in epic because tragedy, and the history of the criticism of tragedy, has directed our vision. Epic and tragedy are inextricably entangled.

REFERENCES AND FURTHER READING

Barrett, J. (2002). *Staged Narrative: Poetics and the Messenger in Greek Tragedy*. Berkeley, Los Angeles, and London: University of California Press. A study of authority, knowledge, and fictionality in messenger-speeches.

Easterling, P. E. (1984). "The Tragic Homer." *Bulletin of the Institute of Classical Studies* 31: 1–8. A sensitive study of the complexities of Sophocles' use of Hector and Andromache in *Ajax*.

Easterling, P. E. (1985). "Anachronism in Greek Tragedy." *Journal of Hellenic Studies* 105: 1–10. A survey of tragedy's mixture of contemporary and epic elements.

Goff, B. (1991). "The Sign of the Fall: The Scars of Orestes and Odysseus." *Classical Antiquity* 10: 259–67. Shows how Euripides' Homeric echoes mark the un-Homeric qualities of his characters.

Goldhill. S. (1986). *Reading Greek Tragedy*. Cambridge: Cambridge University Press. Chapter 6, "Text and Tradition" (138–67), is an important discussion of how tragedy modifies epic sources.

Gould, J. (1983). "Homeric Epic and the Tragic Moment." In *Aspects of the Epic*, ed. T. Winnifrith, P. Murray, and K. W. Gransden. London: Macmillan, 32–45. A discussion of the continuing relevance of Homer for the Athenian democracy and his importance for tragedy.

Goward, B. (1999). *Telling Tragedy: Narrative Technique in Aeschylus, Sophocles, and Euripides*. London: Duckworth. A narratological study of tragedy whose approaches to tragic structure suggest links to Homer that have not been explored.

Griffin, J. (1977). "The Epic Cycle and the Uniqueness of Homer." *Journal of Hellenic Studies* 97: 39–53. A classic demonstration of how different the *Iliad* and *Odyssey* were from other early epics.

Herington, J. (1985). *Poetry into Drama. Early Tragedy and the Greek Poetic Tradition*. Berkeley, Los Angeles, and London: University of California Press. A study of the origins and development of tragedy in the context of Greek "song-culture."

Jouan, F. (1966). *Euripide et les légendes des chants cypriens* [Euripides and the legends of the Cyprian songs]. Paris: Les Belles Lettres. A careful and insightful examination of Euripides' use of the epic *Cypria*, which narrated the origins and early part of the Trojan War.

de Jong, I. F. (1991). *Narrative in Drama: The Art of the Euripidean Messenger-Speech*. Mnemosyne Supplement 116. Leiden: Brill. Analyzes Euripidean messenger-speeches narratologically.

Lange, K. (2002). *Euripides und Homer. Untersuchungen sur Homernachwirkung in Elektra, Iphigenie im Taurerland, Helena, Orestes und Kyklops* [Euripides and Homer. Investigations into the influence of Homer in *Electra*, *Iphigenia in Tauris*, *Helen*, *Orestes*, and *Cyclops*]. Hermes Einzelschriften 86. Stuttgart: Seiner. A careful study of the importance of the *Odyssey* for late Euripides.

Lowe, C. (2000). *The Classical Plot and the Invention of Western Narrative*. Cambridge: Cambridge University Press. The "classical plot" is that of Homeric epic, tragedy, New Comedy, and the Greek novel.

Pratt, L. (1993). *Lying and Poetry from Homer to Pindar*. Ann Arbor: University of Michigan Press. Argues that truth-claims in archaic poetry need to be understood within their poetic contexts rather than literally.

Redfield, J. (1975). *Nature and Culture in the Iliad. The Tragedy of Hector*. Chicago and London: University of Chicago Press. Includes an extended discussion of tragic elements in the *Iliad*.

Rutherford, J. B. (1982). "Tragic Form and Feeling in the *Iliad*." *Journal of Hellenic Studies* 102: 145–60. A brief and clear demonstration of the *Iliad*'s use of such tragic themes as misunderstood oracles, late learning, stubbornness, and the value of pity.

Schadewaldt, W. (1926). *Monolog und Selbstgespräch. Untersuchungen zur formgeschichte der griechischen tragödie*. [Monologue and discussion. Investigations into the historical form of Greek tragedy]. Neue philologische Untersuchungen Heft 2. Berlin: Weidmann. A study of how tragedy handles "talking-to-one's-self" where tragedy does not use a Homeric model until Euripides.

Seaford, R. (1994). *Reciprocity and Ritual. Homer and Tragedy in the Developing City-State*. Oxford: Oxford University Press. Argues for profound differences between Homer and tragedy, with tragedy seeking to create a social cohesion Homer lacks.

Scodel, R. (1999). *Credible Impossibilities: Conventions and Strategies of Verisimilitude in Homer and Greek Tragedy*. Stuttgart and Leipzig: Teubner. Looks at how tragedy uses Homer as a guide for how consistent and rationally motivated narrative should be.

Seidensticker, B. (1982). *Palintonos Harmonia. Studien zu komischen Elementen in der griechischen Tragödie* [Palintonos Harmonia. Studies in the comic elements of Greek tragedy]. Hypomnemata. Heft 72. Göttingen: Vandenhoeck & Ruprecht. A study of humor in tragedy, with attention to Homer's comic elements.

12

Tragedy in Performance

Michael R. Halleran

In Aristophanes' comedy *Frogs*, Dionysus journeys to Hades in search of a talented poet. With the recent deaths of Sophocles and Euripides, the god of the theater seeks to restore to Athens one of her great poets from among the shades. This search leads to a raucous contest between two of Athens' greatest playwrights, Aeschylus and Euripides, representing respectively, in rough terms, traditional and newfangled tastes, poetics, and values. Underlying the comic treatment of Athenian drama, mores, and politics (and the three are closely linked) is a core assumption that tragedy is central to Athenian life and prosperity. To understand this centrality of tragedy to Athenian life, we need to situate it in the context of performance.

We are accustomed to reading plays as verbal texts accompanied by stage directions and notes that *suggest* a performance. For the fifth-century Athenians, however, tragedy was performed. Etymologically, *drama* is a Greek word meaning "something done." Tragedies were performed during an important religious/civic holiday in a large open-air theater. Written texts were still rare in this period, and the experience of drama was primarily, if not exclusively, in performance. We should consider the performative aspect of Greek drama as part of the fabric of a predominantly oral culture, which Athens continued to be during this period.

On many points our information about Greek theatrical productions of this period is sketchy. What knowledge we do have comes from the archaeological remains of the theaters, the iconography on vase-paintings, comments from ancient authors, and the plays themselves. Almost every statement needs to be qualified by "as far as the evidence suggests," or the like. In the sketch that follows I will not try to qualify every statement but rather to present a consensus overview of the circumstances of ancient production.

Contemporary stadia for American football stand idle most of the time. Often seating over 70,000 people, costing huge amounts of public funds to build, and located commonly on prime real estate, they reflect the cultural capital devoted to the contests played therein. These athletic events constitute a gathering of a large portion of the local population, isolated from mundane concerns, and enjoying a contest in a special space. Without carrying any further this analogy between modern sporting events and ancient theater, this modern counterpart may help us to understand the cultural significance of the ancient experience.

The tragedies were performed at a festival known as the Dionysia (or City Dionysia, to distinguish it from celebrations of the Rural Dionysia). To call this early spring festival religious is anachronistic, for the festival was both civic and religious at once. The city-state of Athens had a full calendar of state-sponsored celebrations of local and Panhellenic deities. These festivals marked the progress of the year, recognized the important gods, and brought the community together in religious/civic celebration. For the Greeks, an agonistic people, these were also occasions for competition. Three playwrights were chosen to produce plays at the festival, and first, second, and third prizes were awarded; in 449 BCE a token prize was introduced for the best actor.

That the great dramatic festival was connected to the god Dionysus is no surprise, reflecting, it seems, both historical accident and broad cultural beliefs. The origins of Greek tragedy remain obscure. *Tragoidia*, the Greek word, etymologically means "goat song," and it has been forcefully argued that a song sung at a ritual of Dionysus involving the sacrifice of a goat (or with the prize of a goat) is the earliest form of what became Greek tragedy (Burkert 1966).[1] Obviously, there would be many stages in development, from song at a goat sacrifice to a song at a ritual, to a song responded to by an actor, to the full-blown dynamic of choral song and actors' dialogue creating a story drawn from traditional Greek mythology. Whatever the particulars of its origins, Greek tragedy had a natural affinity with the god Dionysus. Dionysus was not simply a god of wine; he represented the sap of life and ecstatic experience. Tragedy, with its intense explorations of the essence of human life and death and its structural otherness (masked actors claiming to be characters in a long-ago story), had an appropriate patron in Dionysus (see chapter 2 in this volume).

It is important to stress that Greek tragedy, although originating in ritual and performed during a religious festival, was not religious in any common sense of the term. Greek tragedies did not deal with dogma, or seek to justify the ways of the gods. Their plots came from the rich trove of traditional tales and were not chiefly about the gods at all – except in an important sense that gods were a routine feature of Greek myth. By their artistic excellence, these plays honored the god at whose festival they were performed, but were not religious beyond that.

A question of considerable and recently rekindled interest is whether women were allowed among the spectators. Many bits of evidence suggest that they were. For example, a remarkable, if fanciful, anecdote[2] relates that the horrifying appearance of the Furies in Aeschylus' *Eumenides* caused women to miscarry. Even if this account is not literally true, it assumes the presence of women in the theater. But, in general, women were not part of the public and civic life of fifth-century Athens, and many doubt that they were in attendance at these plays. On balance, it seems most likely that women were allowed to attend the theatrical productions, but in fact did so only in small numbers (see chapter 9 in this volume).

At the City Dionysia, each of three dramatists who had been selected for this honor produced four plays – three tragedies and one satyr play. The three tragedies might be connected by a mythological thread or have little or nothing in common with each other. With the exception of the three plays of Aeschylus' *Oresteia*, all of the plays that survive come down to us without their trilogic partners. The original theatrical experience, however, entailed viewing all three tragedies and the following satyr play consecutively, and the ways in which these dramas might echo or engage the others is something that is lost to us. Satyr play, an example of which survives in Euripides' *Cyclops*, was a boisterous genre, with a chorus of satyrs ("good-for-nothings" is Hesiod's description of them) and a plot often involving sex, assault, and rescue. Aeschylus' *Oresteia* did not end with the triumphant pageant of Athenians and a newfound system of justice, but with the *Proteus*, a send-up, it seems, of Menelaus' homecoming, one which spoofed his brother Agamemnon's tragic return.

Theatrical Space

The ancient Theater of Dionysus, built into the southeast slope of the Acropolis, was a prominent public space set aside for a variety of functions, including the theatrical productions of the city's religious festivals. For the fifth-century dramas (all surviving tragedies, with the possible exception of the *Rhesus*, implausibly ascribed to Euripides, were performed between 472 and 401 BCE), our information is fractured.[3] The Theater of Dionysus that survives reflects multiple later alterations and additions, including ones from the Roman period. We know that the material conditions of performance in the fifth century were, by later standards, stark. Most of the audience sat on the hillside into which the theater was built. Estimates of the seating capacity run between 15,000 and 20,000. The stage building (*skene*) was made of wood and built and razed annually. Stage design and scenery were minimal. But within these stark conditions lay the potential for striking theatrical performances.

One arresting convention of the Attic theater, from our perspective, was that all the action took place outdoors. The "missing" fourth wall of the modern theater that allows the audience to see within the interior of a house, cottage, or building of any sort was not a convention of the fifth-century stage. The intimacy and domesticity of so much modern European drama was foreign to the Greek theater. While much is made of Euripides' "domesticating" tragedy by bringing on stage servants and beggars, even his drama did not focus on the interior spaces of home and hearth, but on the public sphere and how "private" matters were played out in the public arena. It is also worth remembering that much of Athenian life took place outdoors – the market, the assembly, the law courts, and much of religious ritual were outdoor activities – and so the outdoor settings of the plays conformed with the basic facts of Athenian life.

The dramatic space consisted of two chief components – the *orchestra* and the *skene*. The *orchestra* was a large circular space largely encompassed by the semicircular

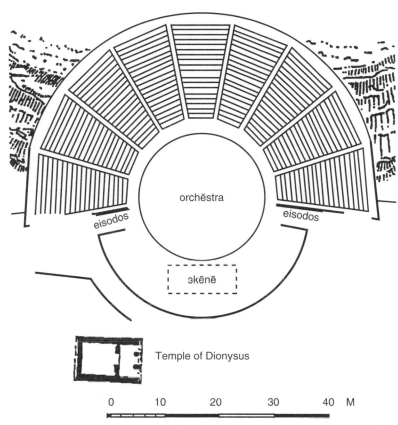

Figure 1 A reconstruction of the theater of Dionysus in Athens during the second half of the fifth century BCE. Based on J. Travlos, *Pictorial Dictionary of Ancient Athens* London: 1971, p. 540.

viewing area (*theatron*; originally, this space may have been rectangular). It measured perhaps 70 feet in diameter, offering an impressive area for the singing and dancing of the chorus. (The Greek word *choros* meant song and dance, and the two were closely interwoven in Greek culture and performance: See chapter 13 in this volume.) Whereas the *orchestra* was the chorus's space, the *skene* was more closely associated with the actors. The *skene* was located at the edge of the *orchestra* across from the center of the *theatron*. It stood about 12 feet high and ran about 35 feet in length. First and foremost, the *skene* represented part of the world of the play, most commonly palaces, since Greek tragedy focused on regal families. But it could also represent a cave (Sophocles' *Philoctetes*), tents (Euripides' *Trojan Women*), or a hut (Euripides' *Electra*). Secondarily, the *skene* served also as a changing room for actors and as a backdrop to aid voice projection in this large open-air theater.

Actors would also enter into and exit from this building. The other chief avenues for entrances and exits were the two long ramps that came at angles into the *orchestra*, the *eisodoi* (often called, less correctly, *parodoi*). These long and visually prominent ramps allowed for impressive and significant comings and goings. Aeschylus' *Agamemnon* is based on the theme of *nostos* (homecoming), with the entire first half of the play preparing in disturbing ways for the return of the Greek king and warrior after ten years at Troy. When Agamemnon takes the stage, he enters on a chariot and with a retinue. During this visually arresting entrance along one of the *eisodoi*, the chorus addresses him with a long, honorific, and troubling greeting (782–809), in which it refers to his errors as well as successes in the broader context of human failing and punishment. Another effective use of a slow entrance along an *eisodos* is in Sophocles' *Oedipus the King*. When Tiresias, twice sent for and eagerly awaited, finally appears, he is addressed at length by Oedipus (300–15), who hopes that this prophet can solve the mystery of the plague devastating Thebes. This prophet brings to Oedipus not his hoped-for solution but news that he, Oedipus, is responsible for the land's pollution. The fulsome greeting, delivered while Tiresias walks along the *eisodos*, creates a sharp contrast with Oedipus' vicious attack on the blind prophet in the following scene.

In a later period of the theater, a convention developed that "stage left" led out to the town and "stage right" led to the country. There is no evidence for this convention in the fifth century. The world of the play indicated (often only in broad strokes) what the offstage areas represented, with a consistency only for that particular play.

I have already used the word "stage," but was there a raised platform for the actors in the fifth-century theater? Remarkably, this question does not have a definite answer. Most likely (and this is the working assumption of the majority of scholars) there was a slightly raised (by three feet?) platform in front of the *skene* building that served as a stage. This was the world of the actors – from here they delivered their speeches and engaged in dialogue. The chorus's area was the *orchestra*. There it sang and danced, and there it remained in between its songs while the actors delivered their lines. It is important to observe that although the actors remained on stage and the chorus remained in the *orchestra*, the two worlds were not fully separated. Actors spoke to, argued with, and even threatened the members of the chorus. The chorus, for its part, engaged with the actors in conversation, often announced their arrivals, and at times considered entering the *skene*, although it did so only very rarely.

Attending a play by Shakespeare, one will at times see six, seven, or more actors on stage at a time. This was decidedly not the case in fifth-century tragedy. By convention, only three actors with speaking parts were permitted for any production. Ancient sources relate the "history" of the actor: Thespis, a shadowy figure, "answered" the chorus and became the first actor; Aeschylus added a second actor, and Sophocles a third, where the number stopped, giving rise to the so-called "three-actor rule," by which the tragedians could employ only three actors with speaking parts in any play. (There are a handful of exceptions to this "rule.") Silent "extras" were also employed. Whatever the reasons for the limited number of actors with speaking parts (fairness in the competition no doubt was a key issue), it is important to note that the ancient stage was not nearly as "busy" as many later ones. In fact, even with the "three-actor rule," having three actors on stage concurrently was unusual and three-way conversation among them rare; most scenes involved one or two actors (and the chorus). The chorus leader, the *coryphaeus*, in addition to serving as a member of the collective chorus, could also play the part of a single individual and engage in dialogue with the actors. It is remarkable to turn from Aeschylus' *Persians*, produced in 472 BCE, to his *Oresteia*, produced 14 years later, and note the much more flexible use of multiple actors in the latter plays.

Fifth-century theater, at least in the latter part of the century, had two stage devices for expanding the performative scope of the dramas – the *ekkyklema* and the *mechane*. The *ekkyklema* was a wheeled platform that could be brought forth from the opened doors of the *skene* to reveal an interior scene. Since Greek theater had no "missing" fourth wall, this was a way of bringing interior space before the eyes of the audience. Corpses were often revealed in this way, and a frequent pattern was for the visual display to come after the events had been reported or heard (from the *skene*), with the display on the *ekkyklema* marking visual confirmation of what had transpired. The *mechane* was a crane-like device to carry characters aloft. In Greek thought, gods occupied the upper air and the *mechane* was most frequently used for divine characters (hence the phrase, as it developed in Latin, *deus ex machina*), who became more common in Euripidean drama. This space could also be appropriated by mortals, with arresting effect. At the end of *Medea*, after Medea has murdered her children and is being pursued by Jason, who threatens to knock down the door to Medea's house, she appears aloft, totally in command, thwarting Jason's feeble attempts to rescue his children and punish her. Like gods at the end of several other Euripidean plays, she predicts a future cult in honor of the children and Jason's death, before departing unscathed from Corinth to a welcoming Athens.

Actors and Chorus

Actors spoke their parts; the chorus sang and danced its part. That, in a nutshell, is the dynamic from which the rich and supple tapestry of Greek drama emerges in performance. We have already noted the origin of Greek tragedy in ritual song, but by the fifth century (and earlier) it was very well developed, with the alternation of speech and song. In broad terms, the spoken verse of the actors was the language of declamation, explanation, debate, and argument, while the sung verse of the chorus was the language of evocation, imagination, fractured narrative, and highly charged images. Spoken and sung verse differed in other, fundamental ways, as well. Not only were the rhythms completely different, but spoken verse was composed in the Attic dialect, the language of the Athenians, while the lyrics were in a pseudo-Doric, an artificial literary version of the Doric dialect.

The above description does not adequately convey the nuances and variations of Greek drama. Actors spoke their lines – primarily. But they also could deliver sung monodies (comparable to operatic arias) and participate in duets with fellow actors and the chorus. In Euripides' later plays such monodies sung by the actors became increasingly frequent, and his *Orestes* (408 BCE) contains a monody that must have been an amazing tour de force for the actor who played the Phrygian slave (1369–1502). Earlier plays also had impressive songs sung by actors – the intricately structured *kommos* (lament) in Aeschylus' *The Libation Bearers* is shared by the chorus and the actors playing Orestes and Electra (306–478). And "spoken" lines had a range of delivery. The standard iambic trimeter (the verse form for over 90 percent of the spoken lines in Greek tragedy, which Aristotle said was the genre's "appropriate meter," *Poetics* 1449a 24) was spoken, while other meters, such as anapests, for example, were more likely recited, accompanied by a reed instrument called the *aulos*. As already noted, the chorus leader (*coryphaeus*) not only performed as part of the collective chorus, singing and dancing lyric song, but also could engage in spoken dialogue with the actors. In short, the richness of Greek tragedy's language and dramatic structure came from both the alternation of spoken and sung verse *and* variations on this underlying dynamic.

A refinement of the structural pattern of alternating speech and song has been observed more recently, namely that the alternation of song and speech is punctuated by exits and entrances (Taplin 1977: 49–60). An episode typically concludes with an exit of one or more characters, leading into a choral song, while the conclusion of a song is commonly followed by a character's arrival, giving shape to the ensuing episode. This pattern is reinforced by another of Greek tragedy's "rules": a character arriving on stage immediately after a choral song receives no entrance announcement, while a character arriving later in the episode generally does (Hamilton 1978; Halleran 1985: 11–20). On a mechanical level, this pattern of exit/song/entrance reflects the small number of actors with speaking roles and the necessity of allowing them to exit in order to return as another character. These junctures of exit and song and song and entrance form the very joints of an ancient dramatic production and should be considered carefully in any interpretation of the drama.

While actors and chorus were in various ways separated – by mode of speech and space especially – they shared several characteristics, including costume. All wore a full-length robe (*chiton*) with an outer garment (*himation*) over it. Theatrical footwear in this period was flat-soled shoes or boots. Different characters within productions and different productions would show variation in wardrobe, reflecting nationality, gender, status, and so on.

Most striking to a modern audience would be the full-face mask, likely made from reinforced linen, worn by actors and chorus alike. Perhaps stemming from the ritual origins of the genre, the mask allowed for the easy distinction between characters needed in the large Theater of Dionysus. It would mark a character as the old man, the young woman, the Greek, or the barbarian. Since Greek tragedy employed only three actors with speaking parts, there was a frequent doubling of roles (and occasionally even a splitting of one role between two different actors), and so the mask played a key role in defining the character. The same actor, wearing a different mask and costume, playing two or more roles, raises some intriguing questions. What, for example, would the audience watching Sophocles' *Women of Trachis* make of the same male actor (all actors were men) appearing first as Deianira, Heracles' wife, who unintentionally poisons her husband, and then the hero himself, wracked with pain and complaining that in his current state he has been feminized (1075)? Or how would they respond to seeing the same actor who had played Pentheus in *Bacchae* return as Agave, his mother, who has just dismembered her son in a fit of bacchic frenzy?

The wearing of a mask, along with other features of the Theater of Dionysus, had further implications. The outdoor setting of the plays, the large theater, and the wearing of full-face masks all combine to turn our attention, in the words of one scholar, "not to the unexpressed thought inside, but to the distant, heroic figures, whose constant ethos it portrays" (Taplin 1978: 14). The mask "presents, it does not re-present" (Jones 1962: 59) the character. We are very accustomed to dramas, films, and novels that explore in depth the interior states of characters; we expect, more than anything else, psychological drama. But for the fifth-century Greeks, the focus was elsewhere. Conceptions of the self were differently constructed compared to the modern period, and the focus in dramatic (and nondramatic) literature was not on personality. In a famous definition, Aristotle declares that tragedy is an imitation of an *action*, and polemically claims that drama is about action, not about human beings (*Poetics* 1450a 15–16). Of course, tragedy involved human beings. But the exploration of what motivates, say, Agamemnon or Oedipus is not foregrounded, and even Euripides' characters – Medea or Phaedra, for example – are not developed in any degree comparable to what one would find in characters in Shakespeare, Ibsen, or O'Neill.

The presence of a chorus challenges a modern audience.[4] We are unaccustomed to such a collective (originally 12 in number, later in the fifth century 15), singing and dancing as integral parts of a drama. Modern musicals offer something of a parallel with its "spontaneous" outbursts of song and dance, but in musicals the singing and dancing are distributed among the characters in the story, while in Greek drama, these activities belong (with some exceptions, of course) to the chorus alone, which remains a constant presence in the orchestra during the drama's episodes. Some have imagined that the chorus represented a super-dramatic perspective, aloof from the stresses and biases of the characters in the action. This is not true. In some cases, the characters in the chorus are integral to the action (suppliants in several plays, a band of bacchants in Euripides' *Bacchae*, for example). Even in other cases, where the characters are less essential to the story at hand, the chorus is first and foremost a dramatic character (or, rather, group of characters) with an ethos and viewpoint. It offers in its songs another and different kind of voice to the drama, but not the "right" one. Agathon, a younger contemporary of Euripides and Sophocles, was said to have composed *embolima* (intermezzos) for the chorus of his plays (*Poetics* 1456a 29). In this he prefigured a later development of Greek drama but did not reflect standard fifth-century practice. Not only were the members of the chorus characters in the drama, but their songs were integral to the action, background, themes, tone, and movement of the plays.

Over the course of the fifth century, the choral role diminished in quantity, but not in importance.

Conventions

All genres have conventions, principles that the audience accepts as true in order for the world of the genre to make sense, many of which have already been surveyed in this chapter. What allows these conventions to work is the "willing suspension of disbelief," to use Coleridge's term. Sitting in the Theater of Dionysus and seeing a man dressed as a woman, claiming to be Oedipus' daughter, as she explains (in beautifully turned iambic trimeters) why she buried her brother in defiance of the king's edict, one accepts *by convention* that he is Bronze Age Antigone offering her valiant defense in a painful struggle with Creon. Without acceptance of such conventions, dramatic art (and much other art) does not work. But these conventions could be overturned and exposed in episodes of metatheatricality.

Comedy, tragedy's close generic cousin, routinely violated the dramatic illusion. In fact, one standard feature of fifth-century comedy was the *parabasis*, the moment in the play when the chorus, at times claiming to speak directly as the playwright, openly and directly addressed the audience. In Aristophanes' *Clouds*, for example, the playwright complains about the audience's negative judgment of an earlier version of the play (519ff.). In addition, comedy frequently broke the dramatic illusion with jokes scattered throughout the play. Tragic examples, however, are rare and mild.

In contrasting tragedy with comedy, I have exaggerated the differences. The dramatic illusion is not binary: even while accepting the terms and premises of the genre and a particular tragedy, a member of the audience can still be aware that s/he is watching a dramatic production. For the audience in the Theater of Dionysus, Athens is visible beyond the orchestra; fellow-citizens are seated all around; references to the contemporary world draw attention away from the world of the play; and perhaps simply the discomfort of one's seat reminds one of the fact that one is viewing a play. But comedy is upfront, blunt, and frequent in its violations of the dramatic illusion, while tragedy is oblique, subtle, and uncommon in its breaking of it.

A look at some of the rare cases of tragedy's metatheatricality gives a sense of its function in this genre. Halfway through *Oedipus the King*, the chorus of Theban citizens is at a loss. The play opens with a vivid description of the plague that torments their city; they have heard Oedipus boldly accused by the prophet Tiresias of being the murderer of King Laius and the cause of the land's pollution; they have seen Oedipus quarrel fiercely with his brother-in-law (and uncle) Creon; and they have heard Jocasta, fearing that her husband may in fact be Laius' murderer, dismiss divine prophecy altogether. Under this stress, the Theban elders sing a song in which they express their desire to believe in a theodicy, but when such deeds as they have seen and imagine take place unchecked, they ask, "Why should I sing and dance?" (896). This powerful rhetorical question resonates at two levels. As characters in a play, the

Theban elders wonder why they should sing and dance (in the rituals common in Greek life). Sung by members of a chorus as they dance in a publicly sponsored religious festival, these words also extend beyond the world of the play, remind the audience of the conditions of performance, and raise questions about divine justice in the contemporary world.

No play among the surviving tragedies revels in brutal reversals more than Euripides' *Heracles*. The hero's family has been threatened with death by the new ruler in Thebes, Lycus. Having taken refuge at the altar of Zeus Soter (Zeus the Savior), they yield to the tyrant's threat to burn them at this shrine if they do not yield, and prepare for death. As they await their doom, Heracles, long absent in Hades and presumed dead, returns to rescue his family and leads them indoors with the comment, "So your exits into it are fairer / than your exits from it, right?" (623–4). The oblique reference to the actual stage actions underscores the seemingly incomprehensible change of fortune they underlie.

On a much larger scale, metatheatrical elements abound in *Bacchae*. From the opening prologue in which the god of the theater, Dionysus, explains (four times) that he is in disguise, to the "collapse" of the palace, to the scene of Pentheus adjusting his bacchant garb, the tragedy plays repeatedly with and against the conventions on which it is based.

Stage Properties

If tragedy ends in funerals, it is no surprise that corpses serve as important visual elements – both at the end and also during tragic productions. It is well known that tragedy did not generally depict murder or violence on stage. (Ajax's onstage suicide was highly unusual.) But tragedy did show the results of violence, displaying both corpses and the wracked pain of those near death. The howls of pain from the dying Heracles in Sophocles' *Women of Trachis* and the moribund Hippolytus in Euripides' drama are impressive instances of the genre's frequent displays of raw emotion. The lyric grief of Xerxes in Aeschylus' *Persians*, Hecuba in *Hecuba*, Evadne in Euripides' *Suppliants*, and many others all indicate the high emotion of performed lamentation.

Sophocles' *Ajax* stands out for its innovative use of a corpse. The Greek hero, distraught that his attempted revenge against the Greeks for denying him the dead Achilles' armor has met with failure and disgrace, decides to take his own life. Deceiving his wife and comrades about his intentions, he departs to the shore, where he falls on his own sword. At this point, the play is barely half completed. For the rest of the drama, the corpse of Ajax is the focus of the action. The corpse becomes the object of fierce debate – does it deserve burial? It also serves as a shrine, protecting Tecmessa and Eurysaces from the blustering threats of Agamemnon, and near the end of the play it is predicted that the corpse will become an object of worship in hero cult, a role it has in a sense already begun to take on (Burian 1972: 151–6).

The tone of *Alcestis* is odd. It was presented fourth among Euripides' plays in 438 BCE, but it is not a satyr play. Yet it is not like other tragedies either. It is built on several folktale motifs (dying in someone's stead, wrestling with Death) and in many ways doesn't have a consistent tone – tragic or satyric. One of many such ambiguous scenes is the heroine's funeral procession. A moment of expected somber emotion goes astray when Admetus' father, Pheres, who, having refused to die on his son's behalf, has come to share his grief, meets the grieving husband and the funeral procession. Admetus angrily dismisses his father's concern and the two argue over their decisions – Pheres' not to die for his son and Admetus' acceptance of his wife's death on his behalf. The entire argument takes place before Alcestis' corpse, undercutting the arguments of both men and underscoring her heroism.

Euripides' *Hippolytus* shows a more pointed and tonally simpler use of a corpse. When she fails to control her passion for her stepson, Phaedra decides to take her life; then, when she believes that Hippolytus is going to reveal her passion, she determines to forestall that and punish his arrogance by leaving a note falsely accusing him of rape. When her husband Theseus comes on the scene, he is confronted with her death, her corpse (wheeled out on the *ekkyklema*, on which see above, p. 203) and the lying note. The argument that he then engages in with his son is played out with the corpse before them. Each of them appeals to the corpse, with Theseus calling it "the surest witness" (972). The constant presence of the dead Phaedra makes a mockery of their arguments, since prima facie it both wrongly condemns Hippolytus and falsely justifies Theseus in his destruction of his son.

No scene involving a corpse is more piteous than the return of Pentheus' corpse in *Bacchae*. The young ruler of Thebes has foolishly opposed the new god Dionysus and his worship by Theban women acting as maenads, and in his ardor to thwart this worship, he has yielded to a desire to see the god's devotees in the mountains. There the god turns on him and Pentheus is killed, torn apart by the frenzied maenads, among whom is his mother Agave. The return of Pentheus' corpse comes in two stages. First, a jubilant and ecstatic Agave comes to the palace with Pentheus' head, represented by the actor's mask, on her bacchic wand. In her altered state of consciousness, she believes that she holds the head of the savage beast that she killed in joyous celebration of Dionysus, and she proudly displays her prize before the chorus of bacchants. But her gruesome exultation changes when Cadmus, her father and former King of Thebes, enters, followed by attendants carrying the remains of Pentheus' ripped-apart corpse. In a painful scene (1244 ff.), Cadmus slowly gets Agave to recognize that what she holds in her hands is not the head of a fierce beast but that of her son, savagely murdered by her and her fellow-bacchants in their rage.

Significant use of stage properties other than corpses was uncommon in this period (see below, however, on a striking example from Aeschylus' *Agamemnon*). In his *Electra*, Sophocles makes ironic use of an urn which is said (falsely) to contain the ashes of the dead Orestes. Having lamented her brother's "death," and holding this urn, Electra finally meets her not-yet-recognized brother and, in stichomythia (one-line exchanges), comes to learn that her brother lives and their vengeance against Clytemnestra and Aegisthus can go forward (1098ff.).

More sustained is the use of the bow in Sophocles' *Philoctetes*, throughout which play both the question of possession of the bow and its symbolic value ("traditional" heroism) are underscored by the physical bow and its transfer – first from Philoctetes to Neoptolemus, and then back again to the wounded hero. As these two men, secure in their friendship, prepare to leave for Philoctetes' home – and the play seems likely to end contrary to the mythological "requirement" that Philoctetes sack Troy – Heracles, the bow's original owner, appears on high to persuade them to seek their glory in capturing Troy.

Although the Theater of Dionysus had few stage properties, it did make frequent use of an altar as the focus of attention. Many plays follow the pattern of "suppliant drama," in which someone takes refuge at an altar, giving rise to a contest for the suppliants' safety. Aeschylus' *Suppliants* and *Eumenides*, Sophocles' *Ajax* and *Oedipus the King*, and Euripides' *Suppliants*, *Children of Heracles*, *Heracles*, and *Helen* are among those that follow this pattern to some degree. An altar was believed to offer protection, provided that the suppliants retained physical contact with it, and thus the physicality of supplication is fundamental to its success and reinforced in performance.

The *skene* itself could have an impact on the audience viewing a tragic production, as the ways in which and the degrees to which it took on significance varied from play to play. Aeschylus' *Oresteia* has a lengthy and thematically well-developed function for the house. In the trilogy's first two plays, the setting is the same – the palace at Argos. The dramas' emphasis on internecine bloodshed and the self-destructive history of the house of Atreus is played out against the backdrop of the palace. This focus is announced and highlighted by the remarkable opening scene of *Agamemnon*, where a watchman delivers the prologue from the palace's rooftop and emphasizes in this speech the house of Atreus. In both *Agamemnon* and the following *The Libation Bearers*, we see an ongoing struggle for control of the house (Taplin 1977: 276–361, esp. 299–300, 306–8, 310–16, 342–4). It is no coincidence that the stalemate over vengeance, sanctioned by the *lex talionis*, reached at the end of the second play leads to a change of scene: the third play opens not with the house of Atreus but the temple of Apollo at Delphi, and then shifts again to the Areopagus in Athens.

Whereas the *Oresteia* used the palace as a site (and sight) of marital and familial discord and death, Euripides' *Alcestis* establishes the house as a symbol of marital harmony and rebirth. Alcestis was the only one willing to die on her husband Admetus' behalf, and halfway through the play, a dead Alcestis is carried out from her house on a bier, toward her burial. But her death, which keeps Admetus from death, makes his own life not worth living. His excessive hospitality – hosting a visiting Heracles despite his promise to his dying wife that their house would hold no feasts – both shows his house's predisposition to *xenia* (guest–host friendship: "My house does not know how to turn away or dishonor friends," 566–7), and wins for him a new life with Alcestis. Inspired by what Admetus has done for him, Heracles wrestles with Death and returns at the play's end with a veiled and mute woman (Alcestis), whom Admetus receives as a groom would receive a bride and leads into the house (Halleran 1988: 123–9).

Gestures and Silence

Even in a genre that was fairly stylized in its performance, human contact can shift the direction, tone, or meaning of a Greek tragedy. A few examples, including two of the supplication of a person, show how powerful such seemingly simple acts could be. Supplication of a person was a socio-religious custom in ancient Greece involving the touching of another's knees, hands, and/or chin while making a request of him or her. Behind this custom stood the authority of Zeus, who protected suppliants. While one was not religiously or legally obliged to respond positively to supplication, the presumption was that the act of supplication, since it debased the individual making the request, would be rare and extended a kind of moral suasion on the one supplicated. In *Medea*, the Corinthian King Creon has ordered immediate exile for Medea out of fear of her harming his daughter, Jason's new bride, and his family. A foreigner and a woman, Medea has no rights in Corinth, but she thwarts Creon's demand for immediate exile by grabbing his knees and hand with the act of supplication. Against his express better judgment (350–1), Creon yields to Medea's supplication, made in part (iron-ically) to him as a fellow-parent, and allows her to stay in Corinth for one more day. With immediate exile, Medea's plans for vengeance – and the plot itself – would be thwarted. The tragedy of revenge becomes possible only through this simple act.

Supplication in *Hippolytus* plays an equally pivotal role. Phaedra's Nurse, eager to save her life at whatever cost, cannot learn from her mistress what is driving her to suicide, and Phaedra is determined not to reveal her passion for Hippolytus. The Nurse takes the unusual and drastic measure of making a formal supplication of Phaedra, who reluctantly yields and only gradually reveals her illicit passion. Phaedra is shown to reveal what she wanted to keep secret only through the compulsion of supplication, while the Nurse, despite assurances to the contrary, reveals this passion to Hippolytus, which moves the play in another direction and allows the tragedy to unfold.

The end of *Hippolytus* shows another scene highlighted by physical contact. Hip-polytus, mangled by his horses in their frantic response to the bull sent from the sea by Theseus' curse, returns to the palace wracked with pain. Artemis, his patron deity, has already appeared on high to reveal the truth of Hippolytus' virtue. Theseus, who had so misconstrued his son's character in their previous encounter and who had cursed him with death and proclaimed his exile, now realizes that he was terribly wrong. As his son is about to die, he seeks forgiveness. While we may think of forgiveness as routine in such a situation, for the Greeks this concept was much less fully ingrained. For Hippolytus, with Artemis' urging, to forgive his father is thus striking. And the play concludes, after Artemis' departure, with father embracing son.

Something often lost in reading dramatic texts is silence. Characters on stage but not speaking can be lost on the page but not in the theater. Silence – and the breaking of it – can be as powerful as speech. Aeschylus was noted – and spoofed by Aristophanes – for his "silent" characters (Taplin 1972: 57–97). According to the lively parody in *Frogs*, Aeschylus would bring a character on stage at the start of a play, and have him or her stay silent beyond any reasonable time and then burst forth in speech. In the extant plays of Aeschylus, we have no such examples from the beginning of a play, but all three surviving tragedians successfully exploit dramatic silences.

Riding in a chariot and with attendants, victorious after ten years of battle at Troy, Agamemnon is met by his wife, Clytemnestra, when he enters in Aeschylus' play. The preceding part of the drama has been filled with descriptions of domestic and political turmoil, with hints – and more than hints – of conflict between husband and wife. Now that Agamemnon has returned and is eager to dismount and enter his palace, Clytemnestra engages him in a battle of words and wills (905ff.). She wants him to come into the house, but only by treading on valuable and fragile tapestries, which she has had laid out for him. Agamemnon is reluctant: this is a needless wasting of the house's prosperity, an act that symbolically will recall to the audience his sacrifice of Iphigenia to ensure the success of the Greek expedition against Troy. But Clytemnestra is persuasive and, with misgiving, Agamemnon enters the house, walking on and thereby destroying these household tapestries.

Throughout this entire scene, silent but visible, a young captive from Troy is present. The audience would surely have inferred that this is Cassandra, one of the princesses from the fallen city, whom Agamemnon was rumored to have taken as his concubine. While Clytemnestra and Agamemnon argue about how he will enter the house, an argument that is ultimately about which of them is in control, the audience sees this final Trojan victim. Later in the play (1412–18, 1438–9), Clytemnestra will explain that she killed her husband in revenge for his callous sacrifice of their daughter and for his many infidelities. Here, the silent Cassandra – another young female victim and the latest instance of Agamemnon's sexual indiscretions – visually underscores the queen's complex motivations and the play's multiple layers of causation, both domestic and political. And Cassandra's role is not over. Following a brief choral song, after which there is every reason to believe we will learn of Agamemnon's murder, Clytemnestra returns to the stage to bring Cassandra into the house as well. In response to the queen's curt commands that she leave the chariot and come inside, Cassandra remains silent, and the audience probably continued to think of her as a "mute" character. It is only after the queen, frustrated by Cassandra's refusal to accompany her, departs, that she breaks out into initially incoherent cries, which lead, ultimately, to a brilliant visionary description of the past and future ills of this house. The silent Cassandra, at first a mute icon of the troubles in the house of Atreus, becomes a powerful prophetic voice of familial bloodshed, past, passing, and to come.

Perhaps the most effectively painful silent character in all of extant tragedy is Jocasta in a scene from Sophocles' *Oedipus the King*. Impressively tight in its dramatic structure, this play pivots around the twin and related mysteries of Laius' murder and the prophecy that Laius' son, Oedipus, would kill his father and marry his mother. When a messenger from Corinth comes with news that seems to join and solve these two mysteries, Jocasta is silent for some 70 lines (989–1055). Oedipus, her husband and son, has questioned the Corinthian messenger in rapid stichomythia leading to the key question of the identity of the shepherd who took the infant Oedipus from Laius' house. During this fast-paced dialogue, Jocasta, who in the previous scene was concerned to establish that Oedipus could not have murdered Laius, now concludes that he is both a regicide and a parricide and that she is his mother, as well as his wife. When finally made to speak, she tries to dissuade Oedipus from pursuing these leads. Unsuccessful, she enigmatically rushes from the stage. During the taut dialogue of discovery, Jocasta's silence clues the audience in to the truth and serves as a painful symbol of the twisted tale Oedipus is seeking to unravel.

Hippolytus and Phaedra never speak to each other in Euripides' *Hippolytus*. A previous dramatic treatment of this myth by Euripides contained, it seems, a scene in which Phaedra, filled with passion for her stepson, confronts him directly and is rebuffed by the shocked young man. In the version that survives, Euripides takes great pains to portray a virtuous Phaedra, one who will do anything, even take her own life, to keep from acting on her passion. But Phaedra's Nurse is eager to save her mistress and hopes that her approach to Hippolytus will find a way to end her passion. Hippolytus is outraged and rails against the Nurse, Phaedra, and all woman-kind. While he rejects the Nurse's pleas and declaims on women's evils, Phaedra is on stage throughout, silent and not participating (601–68) (Halleran 1995: 200–1). Miscommunication, a theme that lies at the heart of this drama, shows itself vividly as these two characters fail to communicate at all and, through the well-intentioned machinations of the Nurse, misunderstand each other profoundly.

Just as verbal images may be repeated and echo throughout any literary work, visual images can be repeated and resonate in the performance of Greek tragedy. *Oedipus the King* ends contrary to expectation in at least one respect. We fully anticipate that the king will learn the harsh truth of his origins and his ghastly situation – mythological and dramatic pressure both require it. But throughout the play we have heard that the murderer of Laius must go into exile and Oedipus himself, after learning who he is and what he has done, blinds himself and demands to be exiled. And yet the play concludes with his return into the palace. At the start of the drama, Oedipus emerged from the palace seeking to help the suppliants before him, eager to end the plague's ravages of his land and people. Now, at the play's end, he returns to the palace, denied exile, denied the release that exile might bring, forced to confront the site of his incest and Jocasta's suicide, the site of his birth, his discovery, and ongoing pollution. The house, as Oedipus reenters it, has been, in a sense, as transformed as he has been. In this "mirror scene" lies the tale of Oedipus' reversal (Taplin 1978: 46, citing Colin McLeod).

Perhaps the most elaborate set of repeated visual images, in connection with verbal links, comes in Euripides' *Heracles*, part of which was described above (p. 207). The entrance from the house seemed to portend the family's death, but death is overturned with their triumphant exit into the house and Heracles' soon-to-be-accomplished defeat of Lycus. But this safety proves illusory: Heracles, having dispatched Lycus, is maddened by Hera into murdering his own family. Heracles goes from family rescuer to murderer, a transformation marked by the self-conscious echo between the two stage actions. Heracles himself is rescued at the end of the drama. Ashamed of his unspeakable deeds, he is determined to take his own life. But Theseus, arriving in the nick of time, persuades his friend to continue with his life and live with him in Athens. As they depart, Heracles leans on Theseus for support and describes himself as a "little boat in tow" (1424), the very same (and rare) image that he had used of his children (631) when they clung to him as they entered the house to apparent safety earlier in the play. The sequence of these three prominent stage actions outlines the play's progress – from apparent death to illusory rescue to true rescue – and Heracles' transformation from rescuer to rescued (Halleran 1985: 84–5, 91–2).

Dionysus in *Bacchae* develops from hunted to hunter. In his first encounter with Pentheus, he arrives as a prisoner, captured in the hills of Cithaeron. The young king mocks his prey, making fun of his effeminate bacchant garb, and has him thrown into prison. But in the second of three encounters with Pentheus, Dionysus seems slowly to be taking over, offering the young king the opportunity to see the bacchants in the mountains. In the third scene, Pentheus, who had mocked his captive's dress, is now wearing a bacchant outfit, while his captive leads him on to the mountains, to his death at the hands of the women whose god he ridiculed. The lacunose ending of this play's text precludes full appreciation of the final turnaround. Dionysus had emphasized his mortal appearance in the play's prologue. Near the end of the drama (of which we are missing a key portion), he appears in his full glory – aloft, powerful, and unforgiving in his theater.

Notes

1 This argument cannot be *proven*, but it is a powerful explanation of the evidence.
2 Vita. Aesch. 9; Pollux iv.110.
3 On the key issues of the physical theater, see Pickard-Cambridge (1946).
4 Among several recent excellent treatments of the tragic chorus, see Henrichs (1994–5), Gould (1996), and chapter 13 in this volume.

References and Further Reading

Burian, P. (1972). "Supplication and Hero Cult in Sophocles' *Ajax*." *Greek, Roman and Byzantine Studies* 13, 151–6. An exploration of the echoes of Greek rituals and hero cult in Sophocles' play.

Burkert, W. B. (1966). "Greek Tragedy and Sacrificial Ritual." *Greek, Roman and Byzantine Studies* 7 (1966) 87–121. A strong case for a (particular) ritual origin of Greek tragedy and echoes thereof in some plays.

Gould, J. (1996). "Tragedy and Collective Experience." In *Tragedy and the Tragic*, ed. M. S. Silk. Oxford: Oxford University Press, 217–43. A discussion of choral role as "collective" and "other."

Halleran, M. R. (1985). *Stagecraft in Euripides*. London and Totowa, NJ: Croom Helm. A focus on entrances, exits, and choral songs, with special attention to Heracles, Trojan Women, and Ion.

Halleran, M. R. (1988). "Text and Ceremony at the Close of Euripides' *Alkestis*." *Eranos* 86, 123–9. A discussion of the echoes of Greek betrothal and wedding rituals at this play's ending.

Halleran, M. R., ed. (1995). *Euripides:* Hippolytus, *with an Introduction, Translation, and Commentary*. Warminster: Aris & Phillips. A commentary on the play with particular attention to literary, thematic, and cultural issues.

Hamilton, R. (1978). "Announced Entrances in Greek Tragedy." *Harvard Studies in Classical Philology* 82, 63–82. A definition of the "rules" for entrance announcements in Greek tragedy.

Henrichs, A. (1994–5). " 'Why Should I Dance?': Choral Self-referentiality in Greek Tragedy." *Arion* 3, 56–111. A study of self-referentiality in the Greek tragic chorus.

Jones, J. (1962). *On Aristotle and Greek Tragedy*. Oxford: Oxford University Press. A bracing reading of Aristotle's focus on action, not individual character.

Pickard-Cambridge, A. W. (1946). *The Theatre of Dionysus in Athens*. Oxford: Oxford University Press. A comprehensive, if dated, overview of the physical Theater of Dionysus.

Rehm, R. (2002). *The Play of Space: Spatial Transformation in Greek Tragedy*. Princeton, NJ and Oxford: Princeton University Press. A discussion of plays using a taxonomy of different theatrical spaces in the Theater of Dionysus.

Taplin, O. (1972). "Aeschylean Silences and Silences in Aeschylus." *Harvard Studies in Classical Philology* 76, 57–97. A discussion of Aeschylus' use of silent characters.

Taplin, O. (1977). *Stagecraft in Aeschylus: The Dramatic Use of Exits and Entrances in Greek Tragedy*. Oxford: Oxford University Press. A fundamental scholarly study of stagecraft in Greek tragedy.

Taplin, O. (1978). *Greek Tragedy in Action*. Berkeley and Los Angeles: University of California Press. An exploration of several dramaturgical perspectives on nine plays (three each from Aeschylus, Sophocles, and Euripides).

Wiles, D. (1997). *Tragedy in Athens: Performance Space and Theatrical Meaning*. Cambridge: Cambridge University Press. A semiotic analysis of the Theater of Dionysus.

13
The Tragic Choral Group: Dramatic Roles and Social Functions

Claude Calame

Translated by Dan Edelstein

"We can stitch back together and rearrange, or rip apart a second time the fraying shreds of the ancient tradition: this tradition tells us with utmost certainty that *tragedy was born from the tragic chorus*, that it was originally the chorus and nothing but the chorus." With this categorical assertion, Friedrich Nietzsche begins the paragraph in *The Birth of Tragedy* dedicated to determining the origin of the genre (1872: §7, 1.9). According to Nietzsche's claims regarding the "Dionysio-Apollonian genius" that produced classical tragedy (1872: §5, 1.2), Greek tragedy is thus anchored in the collectivity of the "fictional natural beings" that constitutes the satyrs' chorus. In this manner, Nietzsche privileges the satyric collectivity over the two other representatives in the romantic triad: on the one hand, epic poetic images, and on the other, lyrical individual being. While referring back to the Dionysian ecstasy supposed to free the self from civilized reality, this definition of the tragic chorus is in fact polemically opposed to August Wilhelm Schlegel's famous theory, as well as to Friedrich Schiller's practical application, visible in his own drama.

Like his successors, Nietzsche only retains from Schlegel's definition the formula that has gone down into posterity: "The Chorus, in a word, is the idealized spectator." He thus neglects, first of all, to specify that Schlegel proposes this definition in the context of his reflection on Aristotle's theory of catharsis: the chorus conveys to the actual audience the emotions that it feels through music. Second, for Schlegel, the Greek tragic chorus *qua* ideal spectator also represents the poet, and thus constitutes "the spokesman for the whole of humanity" (1846: 76–7). With his universalizing authority, the poet associates himself with the choral voice in order to collaborate with the ideal spectator, disparaged by Nietzsche as a spectator without a spectacle, deprived of any aesthetic sense. Schiller, for his part, appears more worthy to Nietzsche because he compares the chorus to "a living wall that the tragedy erects around itself to isolate it from reality and to preserve its ideal place and its poetic freedom." The dramaturge's conception of the tragic chorus can thus synthesize, in a Hegelian vein, the natural and the fictional. In fact, by transposing a Euripides-like tragedy into medieval, Christian Sicily, Schiller intended his *Braut von Messina* (*Bride from Messina*, 1803) to be a "tragedy with choruses." In his preface, the romantic playwright conflates his representation of the tragic Greek chorus with his self-imposed rule for his own dramatic work.[1] In this normative view, based on the supposed role of the choral group in Greek tragedy, the chorus corresponds to "a general concept," empirically represented by "a powerful, feeling crowd." The function of the tragic chorus, both as a real and ideal entity, would thus be to accompany, and comment on, the dramatic action. It would draw lessons of universal importance from the staged drama.

Levels of Enunciation

Leaving aside these German romantic attempts to define the Greek tragic choral group, and to assign it functions ranging from the reality of an idealized audience to the philosophical ideal of an aesthetic poetics, let us turn to historical conceptions and categories. In the descriptive, genetic, and normative perspective that informs his *Poetics*, Aristotle famously singled out singing (*mélos*) as one of Attic tragedy's constitutive parts. The chorus is thus a part of the whole and, as such, is called upon to contribute to the action (*sunagonízesthai*).[2] With its focus on the *mûthos* as plot and driving force, however, Aristotle's thesis is primarily concerned with the narrative and moral dimension of tragedy. Conversely, in the famous debate between Aeschylus and Euripides portrayed by Aristophanes in *Frogs*, the technical term used for tragic staging is *didáskein*. In the context of the discussion on citizenship, this description in fact summarizes the function of the dramatic poet as he is defined by his contemporaries, as a *(khoro)didáskalos*. Indeed, it appears that the first tragedians, themselves dancers, were responsible for the choreography of the choral group. To participate in the dramatic competition of the Great Dionysia, the poet "requested a chorus" (*khoròn aiteîn*) from the archon-king, who assigned him one (*khoròn didónai*).[3]

In light of their references to the choral group, a good third of the surviving classical tragedies tell of the central role played by the chorus. Certainly it was not by chance that classical Athenians used the term *khoreegós*, the name of the choral group's leader, to define the function of the citizen responsible for constituting and financing tragic and dithyrambic choruses.[4] Through the choral group's chanted interventions, directed by the *coryphaeus*, tragedy thus fits into the "song culture" which was classical Greek civilization. More specifically, it fits into the great tradition of melic poetry, one of whose most illustrious representatives, Alcman, is referred to by the commentators of his Laconian poems as *khorodidáskalos*!

The question of the theatrical roles played by the chorus in the unfolding of the tragic plot – particularly compared with the functions of choral songs for the audience come to celebrate Dionysus in the sanctuary of his theater – leads us to the controversial nature of the "lyrical *I/we*," or rather, of the "melic" subject. The method of discourse analysis adopted here requires that we examine the choral voice's tragic authority from the standpoint of enunciation. As with other genres of melic poetry – paean, threnody, hymenaion, partheneion, and so on – the choral voice, the voice that says *I*, often auto-referentially designates the chanted action in which the choral group is engaged. That is, the chorus refers to the ritual action that it is collectively undertaking, guided by the choregos, through the ritual poetic forms that are the victory song, the song of lamentation and of mourning, the song of marriage, or the cultic song reserved for maidens. This self-referential and performative aspect of the choral melos is connected to its pragmatic dimension; from an enunciative, as well as anthropological perspective, this implies that the choral song forms part of a sequence of ritual gestures, and that it can generally be associated with a cult. The sung and danced enunciations of the choral *I/we* thus include both an internal auto-reference to the song's contents and an external auto-reference to the ritual act that the chorus is accomplishing.

From an enunciative standpoint, then, the insertion onto the tragic stage of the choral group's songs multiplies the choral voice's levels of expression, transforming it into a true polyphony. In this manner, the present of enunciation, inscribed in the chanted choral discourse by such pronominal forms as *I/you*, or by *here* and *now*, can successively and sometimes simultaneously refer to the textual speaker and to the "ideal" author, as well as to the real historical author; it can refer to the textual addressee and to the "virtual" or "implicit" audience, as well as to the real spectators. Furthermore, this mimetic insertion onto the stage of the dramatized choral action involves a mask and costume that in turn refer to a Dionysiac cult. This ritual dramatic mimesis leads to a doubling of the choral voice, with a stage identity determined by the play, on the one hand, and the civic identity of the choristers as members of the Athenian social community on the other. There are thus a large number of internal and external figures, both intra- and extra-discursive, that can employ the enunciative present.[5]

In his seminal study on the choral parts of Greek tragedy, Walther Kranz shows that the chorus facilitates the comprehension of mimed action onstage, both by prolonging it in other areas, and by drawing universal ethical conclusions. At the same time, he recognizes that the chorus members, themselves involved in the action, often express the conflicted feelings which the plot arouses in them, and that these emotions often prod them to ask the gods for their assistance. A more systematic study of the dramatic and semantic functions of choral voices in Greek tragedy reveals that the chorus is called time and time again to participate affectively in the action by voicing the feelings which it provokes, to comment on the action by revealing its narrative antecedents as well as its moral and theological implications, and even to take action by influencing the plot through ritual forms of melic chants addressed to the gods. In terms of content, we can thus distinguish between an "emotive" voice, a "hermeneutic" voice, and a "performative" voice.[6] These voices superimpose themselves inside the reality of choral song, while being carried alternately by the five enunciative positions already defined. In this manner, we can measure the complexity of the polyphonic and polymorphous network that underwrites the authority of the chorus in classical Attic tragedy.

Theatrical Insertion: An Example

According to Aristotle's *Poetics*, Euripides can be distinguished from Sophocles in the following way: in Euripides' tragedies, the chorus does not participate in the action (*sunagonízesthai*). In other words, Euripides' choral songs, like Agathon's, would elude the function mentioned above, and constitute mere interludes (*embólima*) that have no relation to the development of the plot (*mûthos*).[7]

The following example, drawn from one of Euripides' tragedies, illustrates this point. The dramatic action in *Heracles* originates in a complex plot that was probably rewritten by the great tragedian. The action starts with Heracles' return to Thebes, the home he had left to complete the famous labors ordered by King Eurystheus of Argos, and where he had left his mortal father Amphitryon, his wife Megara, and his three young sons. During his absence, Lycos the Euboean has killed Creon, the father of Megara, and assumed the throne. He now plans to attack Heracles' sons, wife, and father, who have sought asylum at the altar of Zeus the Savior. The chorus, composed of 15 elderly men of Thebes loyal to Amphitryon and led by the *coryphaeus*, feels immediately involved in the dramatic action. It does not hesitate to advance its own arguments in the rhetorical debate in the first stasimon between Lycos, who justifies his intention to kill the descendants of Heracles; Amphitryon, who denounces the violence of the usurping king, and Megara, who has come to thank the chorus for its support against the impious and tyrannical insolence of Lycos. In spite of their weakness, expressed in a parodos which assumes the form of a funerary lament, the elders of the chorus, perhaps through the voice of their *coryphaeus*, thus participate in the agon itself. In this particular instance, the chorus does not intervene by chanting, but rather by exceptionally employing the same recited iambic trimeters as the protagonists.[8] While condemning Lycos' hubris, the *choreutai* or the *coryphaeus* nonetheless tell of their inability to intervene practically, in accordance with their status as elderly men. They can therefore have no impact on the usurper's decision to kill Heracles' children, whose father is presumed dead.

The first stasimon begins with a reference to one of the threnody's refrains. The usual invoking of the Muse is replaced by a prayer to Apollo, the god of music who has a lamentation follow the song of success. Then, in the same poetic movement which is found in the prelude to Hesiod's *Works and Days*, the voice of Apollo is swiftly replaced by that of the chorus. Singing in the first-person singular, the choristers describe the choral action of which they are a part; they thus have recourse to the process of auto-referentiality, both intra- and extra-discursive, as we already noted, to express their intention of offering a "hymn." In the purest Pindaric vein, and in the tradition of funereal celebrations (as the choice of metaphors illustrates), this song of praise for Heracles' labors, described in the same terms as the feats of the participants in the Panhellenic games, is compared to the braiding of a crown (*stephánoma*), a crown that becomes a votive statue (*ágalma*).[9] In this manner, the list of the civilizing hero's 12 labors is introduced. From a formal standpoint, this list evokes the enumerative structure of the catalog of ships in the *Iliad*. The narrative character of each summarized episode, as well as the choice of words, points instead to the form of the citharodic nomos, as employed by Stesichorus: heroic narratives such as the *Geryonid*, of which Heracles is precisely the main character, but also lyric, or better melic narratives, with musical accompaniment and a mimetic choral dance.

After a first couple of strophes in an Aeolic rhythm, a second dyad mixes dactylic and trochaic forms, while employing epic diction to evoke the poetic genre of melic narration, which the poet of southern Italy allegedly established. This lovely narrative choral chant is thus self-enclosed, in the manner of a *Homeric Hymn*: when the past narrative shifts to the (dramatic) present, the chorus addresses Heracles, believed to have disappeared during his final underworld labor. Although adapting the invocative structure, which concludes such narrative hymns, by imploring the addressed god to intervene, the chorus cannot fail to acknowledge the hero's absence and to recapitulate its own powerlessness. We may thus understand how the chant narrating Heracles' successes (again, *agálmata eutukhê*, statues of happiness) morphs into a lamentation, as had Apollo's chant, referenced at the beginning of the ode. If the narrative and explanatory voice overpowers the emotive one in this long choral song, the hymnic form's efficiency is obviously diverted and condemned to failure. The tragic genre demands as much: at the end of its long choral intervention, it is the chorus or the *coryphaeus* himself who must announce the arrival on stage of Heracles' children, dressed for their final voyage.

The unexpected appearance of Heracles provokes an unanticipated reversal of fortune. After the protagonists respond to this positive turn of events, the choral group itself reacts – this is quite unusual in the middle of a tragedy – with a beautiful chant in Aeolic rhythm. The first strophe-antistrophe group of the second stasimon almost transports the auditor and the spectator into the context of the symposium. Probably inspired by Delphic wisdom, this web of sententious declarations on the merits of youth evokes the elegiac poems of Mimnermus. It is accompanied by utopian wishes regarding the possibility for mortal men to have a second youth that would distinguish the deserving from the undeserving: critical of the gods, these more personal reflections are often assigned by contemporary critics to the author's sophist voice. Whatever the case, in terms of the plot's unfolding they certainly refer to Heracles who has just returned from Hell and who has been destined to a second life among the gods.[10]

One thus understands better why the second strophic couplet falls entirely under the category of a "performative" chant. This second part of the stasimon finally represents the victory song that the circumstances did not allow the chorus to sing up until now. Not only do the verbs' future performative tense in the choral celebration which punctuates this ode allow the *choreutai*, now under the influence of Dionysus' wine, to join in the dances of the Muses and the Charites, under the sign of Mnemosyne, incarnation of aedic memory; it also engages the chorus in a victory chant, a chant which Pindar explicitly borrows from Archilochus to sing the praises of a victorious wrestler at the Olympic games; a *melos* in which the iambic poet celebrated precisely Heracles and his young nephew Iolaos![11] No longer a threnody, it is a paean, introduced by a wish that it should never end, which recalls the appeals to perpetual memory that open and close, for example, the *Homeric Hymn* dedicated to Apollo. By reaffirming the contrast delineated in the preceding strophes between graceful youth and tiresome old age, the chorus does not hesitate, in conclusion, to rival the Deliades themselves. This celebrated chorus of maidens, already evoked in the same Homeric poem, dedicated its song and dance rituals to the service of Apollo at his sanctuary on the island of Delos. For the spectators of the drama, this large sanctuary had become the religious and economic center of the league of the same name, organized and controlled by the city of Athens. Beyond a strange collusion of gender and age roles, to which we will return shortly, and beyond the intervention of the handsome Apollo after that of Dionysus, one will notice the coincidence between the paean sung by the chorus of the elders of Thebes to celebrate the glorious return of the civilizing hero, and the paean of the young Deliades, known and heard by at least some of the spectators. For a tragedy that was most likely staged during the Peloponnesian War, this coincidence assures one aspect of the expected and complex relation between the heroic story dramatized onstage and the historical context of the representation.[12]

Following this lovely, self-referential choral song, Amphitryon must draw Lycos into the palace, where his own death will replace that of Heracles' sons. However, it is the chorus's responsibility to comment on this bloody turnaround which occurs out of the audience's sight, as required by the rules of tragedy. If Heracles' mortal father sees in his son's murder of Lycos an act of vengeance, as the restoration of justice to a murderer who has lost his sense of moderation, the chorus interprets this just turn of events as a reversal of fortune desired by the gods. Interrupted by cries from Lycos, who has fallen victim to Heracles' plot, the interventions of the chorus and the *coryphaeus* alternate between spoken iambic trimeters and danced dochmii, to express an overpowering emotion.

The third stasimon is introduced by this long iambic and melic prelude. Sung in a mix of iambic and choriambic meter, and concluding in a choreographic development in Aeolic rhythm, this ode aims to include the whole city of Thebes in the lively choral celebration of Heracles' victory. In this repeat of the victory song, already performatively expressed in the second stasimon, the elders' voice no longer mingles with that of the Deliades, who serve Apollo at Delos, but with that of the local nymphs, daughters of the Asôpos, if not of the Helicon Muses of Boiotia. Through the self-referential presentation of the current poetic celebration; through the commentary inspired by the present event; through the sententious affirmation of the moral and lawful lesson that the gods have thus manifested; and finally, through the allusion to the celebrated hero's "mythical" genealogy, this choral chant contains the five components that modern critics have identified as constitutive of Pindar's *Epinikia*, and more generally of almost every melic poem.[13] If the joyful expressions celebrate primarily the reversal of fortune represented by Heracles' return from Hades, it is the hermeneutic voice that, by calling attention to this celebration, dominates the ritual and performative voice.

Just as in Sophocles' *Antigone* or *Trachiniae*, the song of hope and glory immediately precedes the true reversal of fortune: not an announcement of Antigone's or Haemon's death, or the fear of another return of Heracles, but the epiphany of Lyssa (Frenzy), accompanied by Iris, the gods' messenger. The chorus perceives these two divine figures but is unable to identify them; their appearance provokes a short apotropaic appeal to the god Paean, that is, to the Apollo who wards off catastrophes, before the frightened elders of Thebes withdraw. Nonetheless, it is the chorus which reacts when Lyssa announces that she will unwillingly accomplish Hera's revenge: carried away and blinded by Lyssa, Heracles will kill his own sons before his palace crumbles. If Lyssa, in her own concluding words, promises to make Heracles dance "to a flute song that inspires terror," it is the chorus itself that begins a lamentation in dochmiac segments, interspersed with dactylic or iambic elements recalling the third stasimon's prelude. The reversal of evil represented by Lycos' imminent death is thus transformed into a reversal of good fortune, willed by the gods, and which translates into the murder of the children by their father Heracles.[14] The prophetic lamentations of the chorus merge with Amphitryon's moans, before the messenger comes to confirm the death of the hero's sons to a chorus which expresses Amphitryon's agony, all the while claiming second sight. Anticipating events without being able to change their course, the choral group is once again deeply involved in the dramatic action, both from an affective and hermeneutic standpoint. Again, it is the elders who describe a divine epiphany in their chant: after Lyssa and Iris, Pallas Athena herself appears before the ruined palace of Heracles.

After the messenger has related how Heracles, confounded by Lyssa, killed his three children before Pallas herself restrained him from killing his own father, what might be the fourth stasimon presents itself as a lyrical dialogue with Amphitryon; once again, song and dance expressing powerful emotions in dochmii are combined with a few enoplians and some iambic measures. Having mastered its emotions by evoking other tragic murders, such as those committed by the Danaides or by Procne, the chorus wonders which song it should begin next: a moan, a lamentation, the ode to the dead, or the choral chant of Hades. Enunciated in the performative future (*akhéso*), the question recalls the famous doubt expressed by the chorus of elders in *Oedipus the King* about their own choral activity, upon hearing Jocasta question the truth of Apollo's oracles: "Why should I dance in chorus?"[15] Finally, echoing Amphitryon's plaintive and fearful voice, the chorus describes the pitiful scene of the children lying dead at the feet of their chained, sleeping father, before addressing the very master of the gods with a fundamental reproach: "O Zeus, why this excessive hatred toward your own son? Why have you submerged him in this sea of misfortune?"

Apart from the two final, parting lines of the exodos, the chorus does not appear again. The end of the tragedy is given over to Theseus, who, having himself once been saved from Hades by Heracles, offers to shelter the fallen hero in Athens. At the moment of punishing Thebes, the action is thus displaced toward Athens, where King Theseus will share a sanctuary and future heroic honors with the glorious Heracles. All that the unwavering hand of fate and the will of Hera have left standing are the bonds of friendship and of reciprocal aid that can join two mortals.

Before giving way to the wise king who rules over the city of the spectators themselves, the elder Thebans never stopped focusing on the double tragic reversal that they witnessed. Unable as mortals to intervene pragmatically against the pre-destined blows of fate which divinity has sanctioned, they foresee them in their ethical and prophetic comments. This internal and external gaze upon the unfolding action would appear to inscribe an ideal spectator in the text; it indeed corresponds to the view of the real spectators, for the most part citizens and inhabitants of the very town where the dramatic action concludes. But it could also reflect Euripides' own vision of a plot inherited from the heroic tradition; a plot that the tragic author not only reoriented around Athens, with Theseus' final intervention, but also brought down to the level of us mortals who are tormented by the blows of fate and of divine powers beyond our control. Or simply, an invitation to pursue our investigation into the authority of choral voices in classical tragedy.

Emotive Voices

If only because reversals constitute, according to Aristotle, the essential element of tragic plots, the feeling which choral voices most often express is moral pain; this expression of grief can generally assume different ritualized forms of plaintive song. Fear and pity, as Aristotle notes in his *Poetics*; or more precisely, affliction and mercy.

The news of a violent death and the encounter with mortal remains in Attic theater generally provoke a plaintive chant, a threnody – or so they say. In fact, the funerary songs addressed to the public assembled for the Great Dionysia never present in their mode of delivery the formal "model" that scholars have sought to identify in Homeric verse. This model is based on two "prototypical" scenes. The first occurs at the end of the *Iliad*, when the Myrmidons lament the death of Patroclus in a chorus of moans led by Achilles, who then salutes the fallen hero by guaranteeing him a bloody funeral. The second takes place with the return of Hector's corpse to Troy, amidst a more ritualized threnody: professional mourners provoke through their calls the lamentations of the Trojan warriors and the moans of the women, before Andromache the wife, Hecuba the mother, and Helen, the cause of all this grief, praise the dead hero in turn, accompanied by the plaintive cries of those assembled.[16]

In Euripides' *Suppliants*, the chorus is constituted by the women of Argos, mothers of the seven heroes who fell under the walls of Thebes with Polynices. Aided by Theseus, King of Athens, they seek to recover from the Cadmeans the corpses of their sons in order to bury them. As the main characters of the dramatic action, they voice their grief in the fourth stasimon: deprived of their sons, they are condemned in their old age to obey a tearful destiny of mourning. This choral chant of reflective lamentation concludes the scene where, led by a victorious Theseus, the remains of the Argive heroes are returned to Thebes. Introduced by a brief choral song (the third stasimon) announcing the theme of old age without children, which the concluding chant develops, the funeral procession is characterized both by Adrastus' eulogy for the heroes felled in the fight against Eteocles and by the laments of the chorus of Argive mothers. If the funerary catalog of heroic virtues listed by Adrastus recalls the customary funeral speech that the Athenians transposed onto this democratic city, the chorus's plaintive cries echo those of the old Argive king himself. The structure of this song in alternating Aeolic rhythms recalls the Homeric description of heroic threnodies. Before pronouncing the eulogy for those who died in battle, Adrastus, rather like Achilles in the *Iliad*, in fact instigates the plaintive cries that the choral group then develops. But the antiphonic chant of the threnody is here elaborated in the form of a melic dialogue, which, as Aristotle's *Poetics* observes, is characteristic of tragedy. In addition to the prologue, to the parados, to the alternation of episodes and stasima, and to the final exodos, one sometimes finds the *kómmos*, in a characteristically tragic manner.[17]

For this reason, in the central scene of the *Suppliants*, the antiphonic, funeral lamentation cries of Adrastus and of the chorus of Argive women are accompanied by brief plaintive chanted reflections that self-referentially describe the mourning gestures performed in grief. Emotionally voiced both by Adrastus and by the chorus, these performative remarks result in a hermeneutic expression: ultimately, the present despair is blamed on Oedipus' Erinys, a reference to the Theban king's curse on his two sons. If the tragic rearranging of the funeral chant form that Homeric poetry popularized enables the choral group to become a fully-fledged protagonist, the choral voicing of powerful emotions is once again intrinsically linked to auto-referential and interpretative modes. The same holds for an ultimate choral segment, a sort of fifth stasimon, where the chorus responds in melic strophes to the chants of the Argive children bringing onstage the ashes of their cremated fathers. To the reciprocal expressions of mournful pain corresponds the mothers' sense of liberation for sons who can finally access Hades, as their own young sons swear to avenge them.[18]

As in Euripides' *Suppliants*, Aeschylus' *Persians* clearly attributes, through its title, the leading role in the dramatic action to the choral group. The entirety of the conclusive segments of this tragedy, staged at the close of the Persian wars, presents itself as a long plaintive chant. Developed over 150 lines, the exodos is in fact a threnody increasingly stirred by grief and affliction. The tragedy's entire action – the reception at Susa of the news announcing the Persian army's and the Great King's defeat at Salamis – is placed under the sign of suffering and mourning for the lost heroes. At the onset of the tragedy, the fears of the chorus, constituted by the Great King's counselors, and the Queen's premonitory dream are confirmed by the news that the "barbaric" army has been annihilated. After Darius' ghost, invoked onstage, uncovers the *húbris* of a son who, a mere mortal, dared to rival the Greek gods, and after the chorus realizes that the oracle's sudden reversal is desired by the gods, all that remains for Xerxes, when he finally returns to his palace at Susa, is to invoke Zeus and to lament in turn on the twist of fate, which has made him a true Greek tragic hero.

After a third stasimon in which the chorus celebrates Darius and his conquests, in sharp contrast with the present defeat, it falls to the recently arrived Xerxes to instigate a new series of increasingly emotional laments.[19] Following a first "hermeneutic" part in anapests, where the defeat is interpreted by both Xerxes and the chorus in terms of *daímon* and *moîra*, the song of lamentation again adopts the form of melic exchange known as *kómmos*; it is introduced by a series of performative declarations about the grief to come. Beginning with a catalog of the Persian chiefs lost in battle, these mournful complaints traded by Xerxes and the chorus are punctuated by exclamations of profound grief in a crescendo whose culminating point coincides with the tragedy's close. Throughout this plaintive exchange, where iambic meters are interspersed with dochmii, Xerxes eventually assumes the role of the choregus of a choral group made up by his counselors. The agony of defeat and the tragic mourning are thus expressed in a ritualized form that recalls that of a threnody. If on a hermeneutic level, the *choreutai* merely confirm Darius' interpretation of the events, their performative voice helps them convey their collective emotional reactions in a ritual form that assimilates them with ideal spectators. Everything is seemingly designed so that the audience, at the end of the tragedy, will join in the "mournful sobbing" of the chorus and escort (*pémpso*) a Xerxes who, after the interpretative intervention of his father Darius (in the role of an ideal author?), has recognized the power of the Greek gods and the truth of the values they defend.

But it is important to recognize that the chorus is not alone in expressing powerful emotions via different threnodic forms, pursued independently or in exchanges with one of the protagonists. In the final scene of Sophocles' *Antigone*, for instance, it is Creon who, while bringing onstage the corpse of his son who committed suicide after Antigone's death, strikes up a long threnody in dochmii interspersed with a few iambic trimeters. Expressing itself in anapest or iambic rhythms, the chorus of Theban elders, for its part (in an *amoibaion* that ends before the *kómmos*), only comments in terms of blame, justice, and finally fate on the despair of Creon, who still has to face his wife's suicide.[20] Everything is arranged as though, in the threnodic expression of grief and mourning, the chorus and the actors were ultimately interchangeable.

Performative Voices

Often revised on the Attic stage to dramatize the affective, collective, and individual reactions provoked by the plot's unfolding, the threnody's different forms compete with the paean's in the exchanges between choral group and protagonists.[21] If the emotional scope of the chorus's voice is generally expressed through ritual lamentation forms, its performative and pragmatic dimension can mostly be found in different forms of the paean.

Indeed, the chorus of Sophocles' *Trachiniae*, at the onset of the tragedy, chants a paean to celebrate Heracles' return home after his numerous civilizing labors. At the bequest of Deianira, the wife of the victorious hero, the women of Trachis strike up a chant which, in this first stasimon in iambic rhythm, presents all of the formal and traditional features of a victory song addressed to Apollo: a reference to the ritual *ololugé* cry, whose echo will fill the house; the young people's song in unison; a refrain evoking the god Paean; a self-reference to the paean itself; an evocation of the god Apollo and his sister Artemis at Delos. Moreover, this chant adopts the common enunciative gesture characteristic of the more performative melic poems: in an internally self-referential vocal gesture, the women of Trachis who constitute this tragic chorus solicit themselves in the imperative to sing and dance the paean, drawing attention to its important aspects.[22] But in this self-referential and performative gesture, which announces the paean, the chorus members refer to themselves first as maidens then as women; then they participate in the paean in order to address it directly not to Apollo, but to Artemis, and then finally to Dionysus, "the tyrant of my heart." Before pronouncing the ritual paean cry, the young women chant an invocation traditionally addressed to Dionysus, to express their rapture at the sound of the flute.

This choral song is thus once again completely ambivalent: while mentioning Apollo and assuming the choral role generally assumed by men, the young women invoke Artemis, in accordance with their gendered social role, before calling upon the god of theater and of tragic action, by mixing the poetic genres of the paean and of the *evohé* chant. In this choral, ritual, and performative manner, they thereby place the action not only under the auspices of Apollo, the *salvational* god, but also of Dionysus, the god liable to guarantee the plot reversal that will soon take place. From the perspective of the mimetic action, it is under the sign of Zeus, but also under that of Dionysus, that the reversal will occur: Heracles, the triumphant hero, will *morph* into a tragic hero, who meets a disastrous and torturous death.

These performative aspects of a choral intervention adopting the ritual forms of a cult can also be found in the final stasimon of Sophocles' *Antigone*.[23] In an Aeolic rhythm on a choriambic base, the chorus (formed here again by Theban elders) addresses Dionysus in the triadic structure characteristic of every hymnic poem. The invocation of the god in the third person singular, as in the *Homeric Hymns*, is first replaced by a direct invocation that recalls the "cletic," or cultic, hymn structure; Dionysus is addressed via his genealogy, as son of Zeus and the Cadmean Semele. Then the "hymnic" relative pronoun expected in this poetic context introduces the second part of this (as every) hymnic chant, more descriptive than narrative, by listing the different places that Dionysus and his maenads frequent. This "epic" section sets us on a spatial journey that leads from Thebes, where the dramatic action being staged takes place, and where the mention of Semele in the first part of the hymn had already directed us, to southern Italy, then to Eleusis, where the god Bacchus is associated with Demeter, before arriving at the heights of Delphi, and at Mount Nyssa, and then finally bringing us back to Thebes, labeled the "mother-city of the maenads." At the end of this journey, Dionysus almost appears as one of the tutelary divinities of the Cadmeans' city. The mention of the honors given to the god and to his mother Semele by the citizens of the Boiotian town lead us back to the here and now of the choral hymn's chanted performance. In the usual manner of the *do ut des* (I give in order that you give back) ritual that characterizes the third part of every hymn, the chorus again addresses the god directly, to provoke an epiphany: by appearing amongst his maenads, he can purge the city (which amongst all others has always shown him the greatest honors) of its oppressive illness. This third part of the hymn, as dictated by tradition, assumes the form of a prayer.

As opposed to other cultic chants in Attic tragedy which are pronounced in the orchestra, however, this choral hymnic song shows itself to be particularly ineffective with respect to the mimetic action. Indeed, it is immediately followed by the messenger's news of the double disaster afflicting the city of Cadmos: Antigone's death and Haemon's suicide. The expected disaster is thus not averted and everything happens as though the cultic song, with regard to the unfolding of the plot, had lost the practical efficiency with which its performative dimension was endowed.[24] But to assume this is to forget that the Dionysus celebrated in this dramatized hymn is not only the tutelary god of Thebes – the god who provokes the Maenads' nocturnal and frenzied dances – but also the god of theater, who presides over the spectacle of disastrous reversals of fortune experienced by the heroic protagonists of the action staged on scene. In this regard, it is noteworthy that the evocation of the god elicits another confusion in the representation of gender relations: masculine and measured, the chorus members are enjoined to participate in the unrestrained dances of the women caught up in Dionysiac madness. From the parados onward, the choral group of *Antigone*, having lengthily recalled the fatal outcome of the expedition of the Seven against Thebes, places itself under the leadership of Bacchus, who shakes the Theban ground with his dance steps.

Hence in *Oedipus the King*, the basic self-referential question that the choral group performatively poses has an immediate effect on the unfolding of the plot, since at the close of the Theban elders' chant, Jocasta forgets her doubts about the oracles and pleadingly invokes Apollo himself to demand his aid.[25] In *Antigone*, however, the lengthy choral hymn addressed to Dionysus which requests the god's epiphany apparently establishes a performative link, less with one of the gods protecting the city where the plot unfolds, than with the Dionysiac ritual enacted by the Athenian spectators *qua* participants in the tragic performance, allowing for the numerous decenterings and reversals entailed by the heroic action being portrayed.[26] In both cases, the choral group self-referentially describes in its song the ritual action in which it is partaking here and now. In the first case, however, the reference is internal, with respect to the action performed mimetically onstage by masked actors; whereas in the second case, the same self-referential gestures apparently refer beyond the dramatic action to the cultic celebration of Dionysus Eleuthereus in the Athenian Great Dionysia.

Hermeneutic Voices

Moreover, we have already noted how in Sophocles' *Antigone*, in particular, the choral interventions are essentially delivered by a hermeneutic voice that tends to clarify the motives and the different powers involved in the fulfillment of the tragic action.

In Euripides' *Hippolytus*, for instance, the group of young women from Troizen that Phaedra views as her companions are intrinsically tied up in the unfolding of a plot marked by the suicide of the heroine, the death of her young stepson, and the despair of his father Theseus in a triple tragic reversal. If it has often been said, as noted above, that the choral interventions in Euripides are only loosely connected to the dramatic action and to its protagonists, the main chorus of this tragedy is in fact very much involved in the heroic action represented through a palinode. Whether it be the coryphaeus or the entirety of the chorus, the choral voice intervenes not only in its assigned parts, but also in the exchanges between actors, generally in a lyrical dialogue. So if in the parados, the women of Troizen wonder aloud and in unison about the possible causes of Phaedra's lovesickness, evoking a number of exterior divine powers liable to drive women and men mad, doubt and questioning are no longer possible in the choral remarks that punctuate the first episode. Once Theseus' wife has revealed her passion for the young Hippolytus, its origin and cause become clear: it is the will of Cypris, manifested by the goddess herself in the tragedy's prologue. In the wake of the Nurse, it falls to the choregos, whom Phaedra addresses collectively as a community of Troizenian women, to acknowledge that the heroine has fallen victim to an abnormal passion and a disastrous destiny willed by Aphrodite. In a strophe chanted in the dochmiac rhythm of overpowering emotion, the chorus recognizes that Phaedra's ruin is complete. While empathizing with her loss, the chorus interprets her misfortune in terms of *túkhe*.[27]

In the following scene, however, after a famous first stasimon that begins as a hymn to Eros and ends as a denunciation of Aphrodite's power, Phaedra herself recognizes the inevitability of her future ruin. As before in the first stasimon where, following the Nurse's and the chorus's comments, she ultimately ascribes her mad passion to Cypris in order to invoke the goddess's power, the heroine now blames her lust and even the goddess of love for her certain and imminent suicide. This calamitous decision is expressed by the tragic heroine in a short dochmiac chant, which is the exact rhythmic counterpart to the choral chant at the beginning of the first episode. Echoing both the chorus's lament about her own *túkhe*, and the tragic destinies of Semele and Iole that the chorus evoked in its hymn to the fearsome Eros, it comes down to Phaedra to pass comment on the fate which so often awaits Cypris' female victims.[28] In other words, the impact of the choral group's hermeneutic voice is so powerful that, buoyed by a sort of feminine sympathy, it engulfs the heroine, who expresses her own tragic situation in the same terms and sung forms as those employed by the choral group.

Similarly, in the long epirrhematic segment that comprises most of the fifth episode in Aeschylus' *Agamemnon*, the choral group, constituted by the elders of Argos, engages in a long chanted dialogue with Clytemnestra, who has just avenged the sacrifice of her daughter Iphigenia by murdering her husband on his return from Troy. In the course of its different strophic interventions, in dochmiac, choriambic, and iambic rhythms (the latter with anapestic refrains), it is the chorus that singles out the vengeful demon behind all the crimes that, from one generation to the next, plague the Atreidai family. It is the chorus that attributes this perpetual sequence to a merciless vendetta, spurred by this selfsame demon; and the chorus that inscribes this generational chain of vengeful acts within Zeus' order of justice.[29] At the close of the tragedy, furthermore, it is once again the chorus of elders that warns Aegisthus that he, too, will have to pay for his crime, and the chorus that calls attention to Orestes' presence, thereby foreshadowing the conclusion of the trilogy's plot, of which *Agamemnon* is only the first installment.

In its hermeneutic role, the chorus's voice can therefore interpret the meaning of the action unfolding before the spectators' eyes; the chorus explains the tribulations of a tragic destiny in terms of the ephemeral condition of all mortals subjected to a preordained fate willed by the gods. Following these laws of human destiny reflecting Delphic wisdom, this interpretative voice can also predict to a certain degree the future twists and turns, if not the very outcome, of the dramatic action, in which the chorus partakes alongside the spectators, and in which it intervenes more or less manifestly. Finally, it can also enlighten the audience as to what is occurring offstage, both in time and space. Hence in the famous parados of Aeschylus' *Seven Against Thebes*, the chorus of women from Eteocles' city combines emotive, performative, and hermeneutic voices to express their fear and pain at the sight of the approaching Argian army.[30] While collectively expressing worry and distress, and invoking in ritual prayer form the divinities of the Theban pantheon one at a time, the chorus animates the messenger's announcement to Eteocles that the army of the seven is advancing. As is often the case in the choral parts of classical tragedy, it is both through the rhythmic expression of powerful feelings and through the ritual and cultic response given to these feelings that the choral group conveys the importance of this heroic action as the dramatization of tragic destinies. Its physical situation in the orchestra, in between actors and spectators, enables the choral group *qua* decentered entity to perceive what is occurring offstage, not only in time and space, but also in the ethical and theological dimensions of human actions, as they are determined by divine will and inexorable destiny.

But the chorus can only predict, never prophesy. Sustained by emotion and expressed in a performative manner, its knowledge remains that of mortals and does not transcend the human condition. Determined by the specific circumstances of events and by a marginal collective identity, this knowledge is relative and transient.

In Conclusion: Choral Identities

The tragic chorus thus possesses a strange dramatic identity, in particular when the choral group is composed of elders instead of youthful citizens, of Argive or Theban women instead of Athenian men or women, not to mention the counselors of barbarian Persia or enslaved women. If the collective character of the choral group contrasts sharply with the distinct individuality of the heroic actors, its social identity is nonetheless surprising. The chorus in Attic tragedy can therefore not be said to represent the group of citizen-spectators with which it has often been identified, of spectators able to decode the ambiguities of tragic language and to embody the values of the democratic city as opposed to the excessive world of heroes. Indeed, the choral group is often socially and ritually "rooted" in the spatio-temporal context of the dramatic action, or else on the margins of this geohistorical and religious root: a double shift and decentering for the Athenian spectators, emphasized by the traditional Dorian dialect of the chorus's songs, as well as by its social status, which can generally be described as "marginal."[31] Simply perusing the titles of the classical tragedies that survive (such as *Persians* or *Suppliants*) reveals not only a significant drop from Aeschylus to Euripides in titles that assign a lead role in the drama to the choral group even if in a majority of the Euripidean tragedies known to us the chorus is female, but also reveals how the choral group tends to be defined as a "segment" of the given community, a community which is geographically and culturally decentered with respect to the spectators' hometown, Athens.[32]

With respect to both the scenic and fictional community identified in time and space by the heroic action, as well as to the community of participants in the Great Dionysia of fifth-century Athens, the choral group is thus characterized by a generally decentered identity, not only concerned with gender. This peripheral status no doubt explains why the tragic chorus exhibits a constant tension between a powerful emotional implication and a critical distance that allows for universalizing commentary. In this regard, its ritual and performative voice functions as a decisive intermediary; a function underscored by the mask and costume which further mediate between the heroic and fictional action depicted onstage and the sociopolitical sphere of the spectators. The role of masks, which enable the young citizens that constitute the chorus to play young maidens or adult women from a non-Athenian community, has not yet been fully taken into account. These dramatic masks are in fact accompanied by discursive masks, which, for instance, allow the chorus of Theban elders in Euripides' *Heracles* to compare the paean it intends to sing in a performative fashion before the hero's palace, to the paean chanted by the Deliades, in the present tense of dramatic enunciation, honoring the Apollo of Delos.[33] Through the "broken mirror" effect of classical tragedy,[34] the signs of gender reversal are in this instance twofold: not only do the Theban elders identify, in their desire to perform a paean, with a choral group of young maidens serving Apollo at Delos, but the performance of the paean is exceptionally attributed to a feminine choral group, whereas in the reality of the cult, this chanted and danced genre is performed by a masculine chorus, generally accompanied by the ritual cries of a group of women.

The voice of the songs performed by the choral group in Attic tragedy is thus characterized by a remarkable polyphony. This polyphony constantly vacillates between the scenic identity of the chorus members, who as masked actors participate in the heroic and fictional action performed onstage, and their extra-discursive identity, which seems to draw them closer, through their role as implicit spectators, to the actual spectators with different social status grouped together at the Theater of Dionysus. One cannot, therefore, overestimate the authority of the chorus.[35] But one must not forget that this polyphony is in fact arranged by the tragic author who writes both as an individual endowed with his own psychosocial personality, and as a poet invested with an "author-function" by the archon-king, and who, by extension, is at the service of the whole community of the Athenians. Designated by his contemporaries as a *didáskalos*, if not as a *khorodidáskalos*, this master of the chorus also instructs via the staging of the heroic and tragic action. On the other hand, the choreutai (themselves young citizens) are being paid by a wealthy citizen taking on the service of the choregia – another significant term referring to the choral activity, as already mentioned. Hence, the male "author" needs to orchestrate the hermeneutical voice of a male or female chorus in particular, through remarks that often clarify the ethical and theological meaning of the action, and that can thus acquire a universalizing scope. In a polyphony that transcends the action's closure, the tragic choral voice is thus where choral delegation can occur, as can be seen in the great genres of melic poetry such as Alcman's *Partheneia* or Pindar's *Epinikia*. The choral parts of classical Attic tragedy are truly the daughters of the great ritual melic poetry of the preceding and contemporary epoch.[36]

NOTES

1 Significantly, this preface is entitled "On the Purpose of the Chorus in Tragedy." On the controversy that Nietzsche provoked with respect to Schlegel, Schiller, and implicitly Hegel, see Silk (1998b: 195–226).

2 Aristotle *Poetics* 1449b 35, 1450b 15–16, 1456a 25–32.

3 Aristophanes, *Frogs* 1025–62, *Ecclesiazusae* 809, *Knights* 513; other mentions can be found in Pickard-Cambridge (1968: 84–91).

4 On the public service of the *khoregía*, see now Wilson (2000: 3–8, 79–85), with the comments of Foley (2003: 3–8).

5 See the references in Henrichs (1994/5: 55–60) and in Calame (1999: 125–32, 148–53); see also Kaimio (1970: 36–157).

6 See the studies in Kranz (1933: 167–74, 214–25), and Calame (1994/5); see also L. Käppel in Riemer and Zimmermann (1998: 61–88); extended bibliography in Foley (2003: 1 nn. 1, 3).

7 Aristotle *Poetics* 1456a 25–32: see above, n. 2.

8 Euripides *Heracles* 107–37, then 252–74; on the attribution of this *rhêsis*, see Bond (1981: 128–9).

9 Euripides *Heracles* 348–441. See the excellent list of references to Pindar's *Epinikia* and to funeral speeches in Bond (1981: 153–5), as well as his remarks on the canonical sequence of Heracles' twelve labors. See also Hose (1990/1: II.120–2).

10 Euripides *Heracles* 636–700. See the commentary in Bond (1981: 231–3) for similar reflections on other Euripidean tragedies.

11 Pindar *Olympian* 9.1–2, echoing Archilochus fr. 324 West; see also *Nemean Odes* 3, 18 and Euripides *Bacchae* 1161, *Electra* 863–4, 880–1; the different aspects of choral auto-referentiality in the second part of this chant have been flawlessly analyzed by Henrichs (1996: 54–62).

12 On the debated date of *Heracles'* composition, see Bond (1981: XXX–II), who remarks (p. V) that this choral chant was the *Lieblingstück* (favorite piece) of the philologist Richard Porson. On the paean performed by the Deliades, see below, n. 22.

13 Euripides *Heracles* 763–821; for instance, the repetition of *kallínikos* in 180, 681, 789 (see above, n. 10), and then again in 1046 is particularly noteworthy. Fränkel (1962: 511–12, 526–7) defines these five components as *Aktualität* (current events), *Religion, Poesie, Gnomik* (moral, or saying), and *Mythos*.

14 735 (*metabolà kakôn*) should be compared to 885 (*tòn eutukhê metébalen daímon*).

15 Euripides *Heracles* 1016–85; see Sophocles *Oedipus the King* 895–6, and the remarks by Henrichs (1994/5: 65–70), concerning the self-referentiality of this formula; see also below, n. 23.

16 Homer *Iliad* 23.12–29, 24.707–87; see Alexiou (2002: 29–47).

17 Euripides *Suppliants* 955–79, 777–93; for Oedipus' Erinys, see 835–6 as well as 1077. For Aristotle (*Poetics* 1452b 14–24), the *kómmos* is "a threnody performed by both the chorus and the actors onstage."

18 Euripides *Suppliants* 1115–64. Tellingly, Loraux (1990: 57–66) pays little heed to the melic and choral aspect of the lamentations by these "grieving mothers."

19 Aeschylus *Persians* 908–1077; for the historical context, see Broadhead (1960: 294–7, 310–17), as well as Pelling (1997: 14–19).

20 Sophocles *Antigone* 1257–1353; a very useful formal analysis can be found in Griffith (1999: 241–6).

21 See in particular Rutherford (1994/5).

22 Sophocles *Trachiniae* 205–24 (200–4 for Deianira's introduction); for detailed remarks

on this point, see Henrichs (1994/5: 79–85). On the traditional forms of the paean with feminine and masculine refrains, see Calame (2001: 76–9) and Käppel (1992: 81–2, 176–9).

23 Sophocles *Antigone* 1115–52; see Henrichs (1996: 59–60), who lists the numerous interpretations that this paradoxical choral song has inspired.

24 On the structure and irony of this chant, see also Griffith (1999: 313–22). Dionysus' relation with Demeter at Eleusis and with Antigone *qua* "Hades' wife" is well explained by Zeitlin (1993: 154–64); see also Segal (1981: 197–206).

25 Sophocles *Oedipus the King* 892–923; see above, n. 14, as well as Calame (1999: 135–7).

26 On the different aspects of ritual performativity at the festival of the Great Dionysia and in its performances, see most recently Sourvinou-Inwood (2002: 67–120), and, regarding the choral songs in particular, Bierl (2001: 11–64).

27 Euripides *Hippolytus* 267–70, 359–61, 362–72; for a bibliography on the choral hymn to Eros (525–63), see Calame (1999: 144), as well as Hose (1990/1: II.156–9).

28 Euripides *Hippolytus* 415–19, 725–31, 668–79; for a recondite commentary of this chanted dialogue at a distance between the chorus and Phaedra, see Barrett (1964: 224–6, 287–90).

29 Aeschylus *Agamemnon* 1560–6; see the recent study by Judet de La Combe (2001: 604, 704–9), which unfortunately does not address the rhythms employed in these choral interventions.

30 Aeschylus *Seven Against Thebes* 78–180; on the metric structure of this lovely song and for a list of studies, see Calame (1994/5: 139–41).

31 This is the thesis presented by Gould (1996: 215–24), which he opposes to J.-P. Vernant's "model" by drawing on S. Goldhill's nuances and additional comments.

32 On the significance of classical tragedy titles with respect to the role of the chorus, see Sourvinou-Inwood (2002: 265–89) and Foley (2003: 13, 23–5); on the geographical

decentering, see Zeitlin's works, notably 1993: 154–71.

33 Euripides *Heracles* 687–95 (see above, n. 11), and the relevant remarks by Henrichs (1996: 57–60).

34 To quote the title of a recent study by J.-P. Vidal-Naquet, *Le miroir brisé. Tragédie athénienne et politique* (Paris: Belles Lettres, 2002), which only touches upon the chorus's role in the complex relations between Attic tragedy and the political reality of fifth-century Athens.

35 See notably Silk (1998a: 24), who notes: "The different varieties of choral lyric style that a given chorus presents, even perhaps within a single ode, themselves constitute different voices, *de facto*." Silk echoes the thesis advanced by Gould (1996: 219–32), who poses the question of the chorus's identity in terms of fiction and fictionality; see also Foley (2003: 13–25): "In short, choral action in tragedy seems to depend ... on a need for, or duty or inclination to accept, *leadership* or commitment in a range of specific contexts."

36 On these different continuities, see in particular Herington (1985: 103–24) and Calame (1999: 130–2).

REFERENCES AND FURTHER READING

Alexiou, M. (2002). *The Ritual Lament in the Greek Tradition*, 2nd edn. Lanham, MD, Boulder, CO, New York, and Oxford: Rowman & Littlefield.

Barrett, W. S. (1964). *Euripides*: Hippolytos. Oxford: Clarendon Press.

Bierl, A. (2001). *Der Chor in der alten Komödie. Ritual und Performativität* [The chorus in Old Comedy. Ritual and performance]. Munich and Leipzig: K. G. Saur.

Bond, G. W. (1981). *Euripides*: Heracles. Oxford: Clarendon Press.

Broadhead, H. D. (1960). *The* Persae *of Aeschylus*. Cambridge: Cambridge University Press.

Calame, C. (1994/5). "From Choral Poetry to Tragic Stasimon. The Enactment of Women's Song." *Arion* III:3, 136–54.

Calame, C. (1999). "Performative Aspects of the Choral Voice in Greek Tragedy: Civic Identity in Performance." In *Performance Culture and Athenian Democracy*, ed. S. Goldhill and R. Osborne. Cambridge: Cambridge University Press, 125–53.

Calame, C. (2001). *Choruses of Young Women in Ancient Greece. Their Morphology, Religious Role, and Social Functions*, 2nd edn. Lanham, MD, New York, and Oxford: Rowman & Littlefield.

Foley, H. (2003). "Choral Identity in Greek Tragedy." *Classical Philology* 98, 1–30.

Fränkel, H. (1962). *Dichtung und Philosophie des frühen Griechentums. Eine Geschichte der griechischen Epik, Lyrik und Prosa bis zur Mitte des fünften Jahrhunderts* [Fiction and philosophy of the early Greeks. A history of Greek epic, lyric and prose up to the mid-fifth century], 2nd edn. Munich: C. H. Beck.

Gould, J. (1996). "Tragedy and Collective Experience." In *Tragedy and the Tragic: Greek Theatre and Beyond*, ed. M. S. Silk. Oxford: Clarendon Press, 217–43.

Griffith, M. (1999). *Sophocles*: Antigone. Cambridge: Cambridge University Press.

Henrichs, A. (1994/5). " 'Why Should I Dance?': Choral Self-referentiality in Greek Tragedy." *Arion* III:3, 56–111.

Henrichs, A. (1996). "Dancing in Athens, Dancing on Delos: Some Patterns of Choral Projection in Euripides." *Philologus* 140, 48–62.

Herington, J. (1985). *Poetry into Drama. Early Tragedy and the Greek Poetic Tradition*. Berkeley, Los Angeles, and London: University of California Press.

Hose, M. (1990/1). *Studien zum Chor bei Euripides* [Studies of the chorus in Euripides] I, II. Stuttgart: Teubner.

Judet de La Combe, P. (2001). *L'Agamemnon d'Eschyle. Commentaire des dialogues* [Aeschylus' *Agamemnon*. Commentary on the dialogues]. Lille: Septentrion.

Kaimio, M. (1970). *The Chorus of Greek Drama within the Light of the Person and Number Used*. Helsinki and Helsingfors: Societas Scientiarum Fennica.

Käppel, L. (1992). *Paian. Studien zur Geschichte einer Gattung*. [Paian. Studies on the history of a genre]. Berlin: De Gruyter.

Kranz, W. (1933). *Stasimon. Untersuchungen zu Form und Gehalt der griechischen Tragödie* [Stasimon. Investigations into the form and content of Greek tragedy]. Berlin: Weidmann.

Loraux, N. (1990). *Les mères en deuil* [Mothers in mourning]. Paris: Seuil.

Nietzsche, F. (1872). *Die Geburt der Tragödie aus dem Geiste der Musik* [The birth of tragedy from the spirit of music]. Leipzig: E. Frietzch.

Pelling, C. (1997). "Aeschylus *Persae* and History." In *Greek Tragedy and the Historian*, ed. C. Pelling. Oxford: Clarendon Press, 1–19.

Pickard-Cambridge, A. (1968). *The Dramatic Festivals of Athens*, 2nd edn. Oxford: Clarendon Press.

Riemer, P., and Zimmermann B., eds. (1998). *Der Chor im antiken und modernen Drama* [The chorus in ancient and modern drama] *Drama* 7. Stuttgart and Weimar: Metzler.

Rutherford, I. (1994/5). "Apollo on Ivy: The Tragic Paean." *Arion* III:3, 112–35.

Segal, C. (1981). *Tragedy and Civilization. An Interpretation of Sophocles*. Cambridge, MA and London: Harvard University Press.

Schiller, F. (1803). *Die Braut von Messina* = (1980) *Schillers Werke. Nationalausgabe* X [The Bride from Messina = Schiller's works. National edition X], ed. S. Seidel. Weimar: Hermann Böhlaus Nachfolger, 5–125.

Schlegel, A. W. (1846). *Sämtliche Werke V. Vorlesungen über dramatische Kunst und Literatur* [Complete works V. Lectures on dramatic art and literature] I, ed. E. Böcking. Leipzig: Weidmann.

Silk, M. S. (1998a). "Style, Voice and Authority in the Choruses of Greek Drama." In P. Riemer and B. Zimmermann, eds., *Der Chor im antiken und modernen Drama* (*Drama* 7). Stuttgart and Weimar: Metzler, 1–26.

Silk, M. S. (1998b). "Das Urproblem der Tragödie: Notions of the Chorus in the Nineteenth Century." In P. Riemer and B. Zimmermann, eds., *Der Chor im antiken und modernen Drama* (*Drama* 7). Stuttgart and Weimar: Metzler, 195–226.

Sourvinou-Inwood, C. (2002). *Tragedy and Athenian Religion*. Lanham, MD, Boulder, CO, New York, and Oxford: Lexington Books.

Wilson, P. (2000). *The Athenian Institution of the Khoregia: The Chorus, The City and the Stage*. Cambridge: Cambridge University Press.

Zeitlin, F. (1993). "Staging Dionysus between Thebes and Athens." In *Masks of Dionysus*, ed. T. Carpenter and C. A. Faraone. Ithaca, NY, and London: Cornell University Press, 147–82.

14

Women in Greek Tragedy

Sheila Murnaghan

Breaking Silence

Classical Athenian tragedy was composed by men, performed by men, and directed primarily at a male audience. There were no female actors, and it is not certain that women even attended the theater as spectators. In general, women were excluded from most forms of public action and discussion in Athens, where the culture's ideal image of itself was of a world in which women were silent and out of view. Yet women's words and women's actions are essential elements of tragedy. Female characters are at least as prominent as male characters, shaping tragic plots and giving voice to their thoughts and feelings. Only one in our surviving sample of 32 plays, Sophocles' *Philoctetes*, has no female character. Figures like Antigone, Electra, and Medea are as memorable, and as critical to any attempt to understand tragedy, as Oedipus, Agamemnon, or Hippolytus.

As students of tragedy have increasingly focused on issues of gender, making sense of this paradox has become a central challenge. The power and prominence of tragic women have to be understood in the context of a society in which women did not participate in public life and it was considered best for women to be seen and heard from as little as possible.

Our evidence for the lives of actual Athenian women is limited: the male authors who are our main sources were not interested in recording those details of ordinary experience about which we are now curious, and they themselves reflect the culture's reticence about women. But it appears that the ideal of female invisibility was pursued, at least in the wealthiest households, through the maintenance of separate women's quarters and through patterns of life which concentrated women's activities inside the house. In a speech delivered in a court case, the speaker seeks to convey his opponent's licentiousness by telling how "coming to my house drunk one night and breaking down the doors, he went into the women's rooms, where my sister and my nieces were – women who have always lived so decently that they are ashamed to be seen even by relatives" (Lysias *Orations* 3.6). In a fictional dialogue by the philosopher Xenophon, an idealized husband explains to his idealized wife the rationale of their separate lives: since men have been endowed with boldness and endurance, while women have been endowed with vigilance and a love of infants, "for the woman, it is more honorable to stay inside than to be outside; for the man it is more disgraceful to stay inside than to take care of things outside" (Xenophon *Oeconomicus* 7.30–1).

The most famous expression of this premium on female invisibility comes in the words that the historian Thucydides puts in the mouth of the Athenian statesman Pericles in his funeral oration, a speech in which he honors the Athenian men who have died fighting in the first year of the Peloponnesian War. At the very end of the speech, Pericles addresses himself to the widows of these men and says:

> And if I must also say something to those of you who will now be widows on the subject of female virtue, I will put it all in a brief recommendation. There will be great glory for you if you do not fall short of your natural character, and especially for whoever has the least possible reputation, whether good or bad, among the men. (Thucydides 2.45.2)

The strength of this inhibition can be seen in Pericles' own reluctance even to speak about female virtue (in a context in which he stresses spoken praise as compensation for the sacrifices of male warriors) and in the way that positive speech about women is as much to be avoided as negative speech. For a woman to have even a good reputation compromises her value.

Pericles' salute to female anonymity in a speech praising Athens points to the way that the silence of women and silence about women were built into classical ideas of a well-functioning society. In this vision of social life, when women are unheard from and out of view, all is well. Men are doing their job of running things. Women are taken care of, and their interests are protected: they have no need to speak up or to take action. The realms of experience that women are especially identified with – irrationality, religious fervor, and sexual passion – are under control. When women come into view and make themselves heard, that is a symptom of disorder, a sign that something is wrong. It is no accident that what little evidence we do have for actual Athenian women comes largely from courtroom speeches or medical treatises, genres brought into being by conflict or disease.

Tragedy, which uses mythological scenarios to expose the weak points in human society, repeatedly dramatizes the emergence of women into public view. Tragic women come forward, often reluctantly, under painful circumstances created by men's absence or mismanagement. Sophocles' Antigone takes action because her uncle Creon has imposed a dangerously shortsighted prohibition on the burial of her brother Polynices. Jocasta in *Oedipus the King* appears on stage to make peace when her husband Oedipus and brother Creon start to quarrel. In the *Oresteia*, Clytemnestra has taken power in Argos because her husband Agamemnon has been away fighting at Troy for ten years, and her murder of him is motivated by a range of male abuses: Agamemnon's sacrifice of their daughter Iphigenia, his brutal destruction of Troy, and his return with a Trojan concubine, Cassandra; the crime of Agamemnon's father Atreus, who served his brother Thyestes a meal of his own children. The women who appear in Euripides' *Trojan Women* have been displaced by war, so that we see them in transit between their sheltering Trojan homes and the less comfortable obscurity of their future lives as slaves in Greece. The Danaids, the chorus of Egyptian women who are the main actors of Aeschylus' *Suppliants*, appear in the Greek city of Argos because they are in flight, running away from an unwelcome forced marriage to their cousins. Clytemnestra is only one of a number of tragic wives who are moved to act because their husbands violate the bonds of marriage: Medea kills her children to punish her husband Jason for planning a new, more advantageous marriage; Deianira in Sophocles' *Women of Trachis* unwittingly destroys Heracles with what she believes is a love potion when he too brings home a new lover, the captive princess Iole.

The example of Deianira, a modest, tentative, dutiful wife who wishes only to win back her husband's love, illustrates how tragic patterns of female action transcend issues of individual character. Deianira is very different from the self-willed, vengeful Clytemnestra, yet she too is motivated by a betrayal on the part of her husband, and with the same deadly outcome. Because they are often reacting to intolerable offenses, women in tragedy can appear quite noble, as the widely admired Antigone attests. One tragic pattern involves the self-sacrifice of young, unmarried women who become heroic public figures as their deaths are demanded to assure the community's success in war. Iphigenia, who figures in Euripides' *Iphigenia in Aulis*, is the most familiar example; Macaria in Euripides' *Children of Heracles* is another. But as vital links in chains of increasing disaster, women's actions are still a sign of disorder, and we are reminded of Pericles' view that it is a bad thing for a woman to earn even a good reputation.

In their responsiveness to abuse, tragic women are especially associated with revenge and with its tragic excesses, its unstoppable momentum and its disproportionate punishments. Thus in the *Oresteia*, Aeschylus chooses to start his dramatization of cyclic vengeance with the initiative of Clytemnestra; by the end of the trilogy, vengefulness is personified in Clytemnestra's divine champions, the Erinyes or Furies, demonic female sponsors of retaliation, who must be pacified before order can be restored. Some of the most powerful female agents of tragedy engage in extreme forms of revenge: Hecuba, in Euripides' *Hecuba*, lures the Thracian Polymestor into a tent and blinds him because he allowed her daughter Polyxena to be killed; if Hecuba avenges her violated maternity, Medea is willing to be herself the killer of her children to repay Jason for his second marriage. Euripides' *Ion* has a more fortunate outcome, but in it we see the heroine Creusa come very close to poisoning her son Ion because she thinks he is a usurper rather than the lost child for whom she has been longing.

Women's vengefulness is one sign of what was believed to be their greater susceptibility to emotion. Women are the point of entry for the dangerous feelings that can overwhelm social stability, a perspective played out in several plays of Euripides in which vengeful gods exploit human passions for their own ends. In *Hippolytus*, Aphrodite's goal is to punish a young man, Hippolytus, for his neglect of her, but her chosen vehicle is a woman, Hippolytus' virtuous stepmother Phaedra. Aphrodite causes Phaedra to fall in love with Hippolytus, which sets off a chain of events encompassing humiliation and suicide for Phaedra and a gruesome death for Hippolytus, brought about by his furious father Theseus. In *Bacchae*, Dionysus is out to punish his cousin Pentheus, the young ruler of Thebes who denies Dionysus' divinity and prohibits his worship. He begins by inspiring all the women of Thebes to abandon their looms and leave the city for ecstatic rites in his honor; those rites have a horrific culmination when Pentheus' mother Agave tears him apart in the belief that he is a lion cub; in the play's final scene Agave appears on stage to recognize what she has done and to embody the extremes of human destructiveness and human suffering.

The way women's appearance in public signals tragic circumstances is reflected, not only in the construction of the tragic plot, but also in the physical staging of many tragedies. Classical tragedy was performed in open-air theaters; most of the plays we know would have received their original performance in the Theater of Dionysus in Athens, built into a slope of the Acropolis at the heart of the city. Seated on the hillside, the spectators looked down to an *orchestra*, or level dancing-floor, which was occupied by the chorus and some of the time by the actors; the chorus made a formal entrance into this space toward the beginning of the play and departed speaking the final words at the end. But from at least the mid fifth-century on, the *orchestra* had behind it the *skene*, a raised platform with a wooden building placed upon it. This building had a central door, through which actors could enter and exit, and typically represented an enclosed space such as a temple, cave, or house. Many of the surviving plays exploit the dramatic potential of entrances and exits through this door, focusing our attention on the threshold between the public realm of the stage and dancing-floor and the private, unseen world beyond it. As tragic women make their disturbing forays into public space, the crossing of this threshold can become a highly charged event. Thus in *Hippolytus*, Phaedra first appears as she is carried out of the house by her servants. At once passive and mobile, she is consumed by a longing for open space. Exposed in this condition, she is subjected to relentless questioning from her nurse and at last gives voice to the true source of her disquiet: her unrequited and impermissible love for her stepson Hippolytus. The secret that had been kept within her mind and within the house comes out into the open, with ruinous consequences.

A similarly eloquent use of transitions on and off stage is found in Aeschylus' *Oresteia* trilogy. In the first play, *Agamemnon*, Clytemnestra enters from the house to receive her returning husband, then skillfully engineers his departure from the stage on dangerous terms that indicate his subordination to her will. In a momentous exchange, she persuades Agamemnon to trample on precious tapestries as he enters his house. Agamemnon is compelled against his better judgment to enter a realm in which all the things he would like to forget about, to keep hidden at the moment of his triumph, come back to haunt him. Clytemnestra orders Cassandra to follow Agamemnon inside the house, and slaughters them there together. After the murder, the bodies of Agamemnon and Cassandra are wheeled out on the *ekkyklema*, a mobile platform that allows the normally hidden interior to be seen.

When in the second play, *The Libation Bearers*, Agamemnon's son Orestes returns to avenge his father by killing his mother, the crucial action takes place on the same threshold, as Orestes forces Clytemnestra into the house to be killed. This staging underscores the problem raised by the action of this play, the way that Orestes' vengeance is at once an act of necessary justice and a contaminating repetition of the crime to which it responds: in punishing his mother's act Orestes also imitates it, taking on a woman's troubling associations with plotting, deceit, and dark places. In the third play, *Eumenides*, the problem of cyclic revenge is only solved when the action shifts to a new venue, the court of the Areopagus, which is entirely public and in which no actual women appear. Order is restored when a legal decision in favor of male interests is accepted by the Furies, who agree to a new status in which they will occupy a place that is both honored and unseen, ever ready to appear again, but only when the city strays into injustice. The standard formal ending to a tragedy, the exit of the chorus, becomes a procession in which these female spirits are led to their new, hidden homes. This three-play sequence, which begins when a self-willed woman takes matters into her own hands, finally achieves closure as figures representing women in general are removed from view.

Women's association with the physical space of the private house is aligned with a broader association with secrecy in general. Women were seen as possessing unfathomable minds and a special aptitude for deceit – attitudes that can be connected to the ability of the female body to contain new life and to men's anxieties about their dependence on the loyalty of women. This linkage is beautifully illustrated by the way that, when Phaedra is bought out of her house, the terrible desire that she harbors in her mind is also brought to light. Whereas Phaedra struggles with a burdensome secret, Clytemnestra revels in deception, covering her true intentions under manipulative expressions of wifely devotion. But both women, in revealing their true thoughts, perform a similar function as vehicles for normally unspoken truths. The appearance of women on the stage means the disclosing of uncomfortable facts that society might prefer to keep hidden: that a respectable, high-born wife like Phaedra could be attracted to the wrong man, that women's sexual desires might not always coincide with their social circumstances; or that a victorious military leader like Agamemnon might have achieved his victory at the cost of his family, and especially a female member of his family, that his political power is based, not on divine right, but on his father's victory in a bitter fraternal conflict. The silence that is associated with women and broken in tragedy is not just a silence about women's particular concerns; it encompasses the more awkward and troubling aspects of central social and political institutions like marriage or military leadership.

Upholding Women's Values

Tragedy's consistent use of women's appearance in public to signify conditions of suffering and social breakdown does not mean that we find there a single characterization of women or a single set of positions that women invariably adopt. I have already suggested, following Thucydides' Pericles, that the significance of female visibility transcends questions of character. Tragic women are sometimes noble and self-sacrificing, sometimes treacherous and self-serving, and the same behaviors can reflect differently on those who display them. Both Phaedra and Clytemnestra act destructively because of adulterous desire, but in Phaedra's case this desire is a shameful and unwelcome burden; in Clytemnestra's a source of satisfaction that compromises her other, more justifiable motivations. The most interesting female characters in tragedy, like the most interesting male characters, defy easy judgment. Medea is at once a sympathetic abandoned wife and a monster capable of killing her own children in cold blood. Antigone is both a courageous advocate of neglected familial and religious values and a stubborn, self-righteous troublemaker. Sophocles complicates his portrait of Antigone by juxtaposing her with her sister Ismene, who wonders whether it is appropriate or necessary to break the taboo on women's action even under such circumstances. Antigone dismisses her as weak and spineless, and many readers of the play have responded similarly, but it is not clear that we should not view her sympathetically. In his *Electra*, Sophocles similarly pairs Electra with a sister, Chrysothemis, who presses the futility of Electra's insistent focus on revenge for their father's death. Sometimes women in tragedy are pitted against each other by virtue of differing interests and circumstances: Sophocles' Electra also squares off with her mother Clytemnestra in a conflict shaped by the different experiences of a married mother and a virginal daughter. In Aeschylus' *Agamemnon*, we see the temporarily ascendant Clytemnestra lording it over the defeated and enslaved Cassandra.

At the same time, these plays do spring from and respond to a highly polarized world with sharply distinguished male and female spheres of action, and the values that animate female characters reflect their identification with the household and its private concerns. Women in tragedy typically speak and act in defense of interests opposed to those of the public, political realm that is reserved for men, serving as carriers for the conflicts between public and private that afflict men and women alike. Women are thus often associated with family loyalties that could interfere with public purposes. This contrast is drawn starkly in Sophocles' *Antigone*, where Antigone's opposition to Creon stems from her loyalty and sense of obligation to her brother Polynices even though he has died as the enemy of Thebes, leading an army against the city.

Clytemnestra in the *Oresteia* represents the claims of blood kinship so insistently that the issue of their importance has to be addressed in general terms before the trilogy can end. Clytemnestra kills Agamemnon in part because he has sacrificed their daughter Iphigenia to make possible the military expedition against Troy. In the final play, the Furies press Clytemnestra's claim against Orestes because he, in killing her, has imitated his father, also violating a tie of blood. In the trial in which Orestes is freed from punishment for killing his mother, the claims of kinship are explicitly nullified as Orestes' champion Apollo makes two key assertions. The first is that a king is simply more important than a woman: "It is not the same thing for a noble man to die, / one honored by the god-given scepter" (*Eumenides* 625–6). On this argument, the murder of Agamemnon for which Orestes punished his mother was a more serious crime than his own murder of her (and Agamemnon's choice to act as a general rather than a father is implicitly validated). The second, more memorable assertion is that there is no blood tie between mother and child:

> I will tell you this; see how clearly I spell it out.
> The one who is called a child's mother is not
> Its parent, but the nurse of a new-sown seed.
> The one who mounts makes the child, and she, a stranger,
> Protects a stranger's offspring.
>
> (*Eumenides* 657–61)

It is debatable whether this strange argument really reflects views widely held by the Athenian audience, but the episode certainly dramatizes the strength of women's association with ties of kinship, ties so obstructive to such public enterprises as the waging of war and the resolution of disputes that they have to be argued out of existence before a stable order can be achieved.

The claims of motherhood, which provoke so extreme a response in *Eumenides*, are central to women's motivation throughout tragedy. Like Clytemnestra, Hecuba in Euripides' *Hecuba* takes violent revenge on a man who has killed her daughter. In Euripides' *Suppliants*, the mothers of the warriors who fell attacking Thebes with Polynices make a collective appeal to Athens to intervene so that their bodies can be buried; the Athenian king, Theseus, agrees to this risky request at the urging of his own mother, Aethra, who responds with empathy to the suppliants. In Euripides' *Electra*, Electra exploits Clytemnestra's maternal feelings; she lures her mother to the place where she will die on the pretext that she, Electra, has had a baby. In the case of several tragic women, thwarted motherhood inspires vindictive behavior. Creusa, in Euripides' *Ion*, nearly kills Ion when, after years of struggling in a childless marriage, she hears that Ion has been identified as the son of her husband Xuthus (he's actually her own long-lost child, whom she bore and abandoned after being raped by Apollo). In Euripides' *Andromache*, the barrenness suffered by Hermione makes her viciously jealous when her husband Neoptolemus brings home Andromache as his concubine. Hermione accuses Andromache of poisoning her and, with her father, threatens Andromache, insisting that either she or her son by Hector must be killed.

Tragic women also act and speak to uphold women's interests within the institution of marriage. As a vital link in the social order, and as the arena in which the private lives of women and the public lives of men intersect, marriage is a frequent focus of tragedy, and marriage is often the context in which women suffer for men's excesses. In this way, tragedy addresses the defining context for the lives of actual Athenian women. Marriage was envisioned as the sole vocation for women of the citizen class, and entering into marriage was the most significant event in a woman's life. As a formal matter, marriage was a transaction between two men, the woman's father and her husband. The language surrounding marriage suggests that it was seen as a long-term loan, in which the father entrusted his daughter, along with a dowry for her support, to her husband for the purpose of providing him with legitimate heirs; in keeping with this view, Athenian women appear to have retained strong ties to their original families. While the emotional dynamics of Athenian marriages were surely as various and unpredictable as those of any period, in legal terms a woman's husband was her *kurios* or guardian, a role he took over from her father. A husband was responsible for his wife's support and controlled whatever property she brought into the marriage. The children born of a marriage belonged legally to their father and remained with him in the event of a divorce. Divorce was in principle relatively easy to obtain, both for men and for women, who could initiate a divorce with the help of their families, although it may not have been common in practice. Sexual fidelity was required of wives, but not of husbands, who were free to enter into relations with other women and men, including legally recognized unions with concubines.

Highlighting the pitfalls within this institution, tragedy portrays a number of young women whose expected transition to marriage is aborted under circumstances of public turmoil: Antigone, Electra, and Iphigenia. Married women in tragedy register the difficulties imposed by the polarization of gender roles, which sends husbands out on far-flung missions and leaves wives alone at home. Clytemnestra explains herself to Orestes by pointing out that "it is hard for a woman to be without a man" (*The Libation Bearers* 920). Deianira evokes the isolation of her marriage to Heracles:

> Ever since I was chosen to be Heracles' wife,
> I have nursed fear after fear, always agonizing
> Over him. Each night brings some new worry;
> The next night dispels that one with another.
> And we have children, whom he rarely sees,
> Like a farmer with a far-off field
> Who sees it only when he sows and reaps.
> That's his life: it only sends him home
> To send him out again in constant service to another.
>
> (*Women of Trachis* 26–35)

Megara, the wife of Heracles in Euripides' *Heracles*, suffers even more brutally for Heracles' alienation from domestic life. Heracles returns triumphant from his labors and rescues Megara from a vicious tyrant, only to experience a bout of madness in which he attacks and kills his wife and children, turning on them the same irresistible ferocity that has fueled his exploits in the wider world outside.

The women of classical tragedy arrive in their marriages as strangers transferred from their fathers' houses to their husbands', playing out their role as mobile objects of exchange among men. While there is always the danger that this mobility will persist – as Phaedra's restlessness illustrates – tragic women are often committed to a more stable and binding vision of marriage than suits men's interests. A number of women in tragedy take action in response to the double standard that allows their husbands to introduce concubines into the house; to Deianira and Clytemnestra can be added the bitterly vindictive Hermione of Euripides' *Andromache*. Others take their stand against the idea that they could be replaced, treating marriage as an unbreakable tie like blood kinship. Thus Medea insists that Jason is bound to her by oaths that can never be superseded. In Euripides' *Alcestis*, Alcestis is a figure of exceptional nobility because she agrees to die so that her husband Admetus will not have to. But she complicates her sacrifice by insisting that he never remarry, extracting from him a promise that he soon breaks in deference to his male friend Heracles (though by a twist of the plot, the replacement wife is actually Alcestis herself, rescued from death by Heracles). Addressing the same issue from another angle, Antigone distances herself from marriage because of its mutability; she would not have risked her life to bury a husband, she proclaims, because a dead husband can be replaced, while the unique tie that connects her to her brother cannot be replicated.

Finally, tragic women are persistently allied with the obligations imposed by religion. Women's special connection to religion reflects their supposed irrationality, which makes them more receptive than men to the supernatural, and the actual centering of many religious observances in the household. But religion was also the one realm in which women played an active public role in classical Athenian society. Women were expected to come out of their houses to participate in family rituals such as funerals, but also in large-scale civic observances, like the extended procession that marked the Panathenaia, an annual Athens-wide celebration of the city's patron goddess Athena. Women were expected to take particular ritual actions on behalf of the entire city; during a major festival of Dionysus, the Anthesteria, the wife of an important official, accompanied by a group of female attendants, engaged in a ritual sexual union with Dionysus. All citizen wives were required to participate in the Thesmophoria, a three-day festival in honor of Demeter, in which women reenacted Demeter's story to assure the prosperity of the city. Women's actions in tragedy often echo their actions in ritual, and tragic women often ally themselves with proper attention to the gods. Once again, Antigone offers an especially clear and famous example: her burial of her brother is the performance of a religious duty, answering to what she calls "the unwritten laws of the gods" (454–5), in contrast to the decrees of men like her uncle Creon. A more disturbing example is Euripides' *Bacchae*, in which it is the women of Thebes who register first and most powerfully the influence of Dionysus.

Tragic Women's Views on Women

These patterns play out in interesting ways in the comments that women in tragedy make about what it means to be a woman. Generalizations about women abound in tragedy, appearing far more often than generalizations about men, whose characteristics are summed up in accounts of what it means to be human, the broader category that men define. Many of the comments that women make about their sex in general echo the cultural assumptions that both reflect and rationalize their divided world with its limited, invisible role for women. "For a woman, silence and self-control / are best, and staying quietly within the house," says Macaria in *Children of Heracles*, before explaining that only the sound of cries and her concern for her brothers have led her to venture out (476–7). The chorus of Euripides' *Electra* opines that "a sensible wife should yield to her husband in all things" (1052–3); Aethra in Euripides' *Suppliants* that "Wise women / always get things done by men" (40–1). Women's loyalties are connected to their role as mothers. "Childbirth is dreadful and it delivers a powerful drug / so that all women alike fight hard for their children," asserts the chorus of *Iphigenia at Aulis* (917–18); the chorus of *Phoenician Women* makes a similar point: "The pain of giving birth is terrible for women / and so the whole female race loves children"(355–6). Here we might note, lurking within these sympathetic statements, the designation of women as a separate race and the presentation of their love for their children as a form of intoxication, and we might also recall Xenophon's claim that it is women's love of infants that makes their assignment to the indoor realm so fitting. In one of her speeches, Medea interestingly juxtaposes the timidity of women and their jealous intensity. These are contradictory qualities, but they both dictate women's confinement to the house, which is at once a way of protecting them and of keeping them under control:

> Most of the time, a woman is full of fear,
> Too weak to defend herself or to bear the sight of steel;
> But if she happens to be wronged in love,
> Hers is the bloodthirstiest heart of all.
>
> (*Medea* 263–6)

The negative tenor of Medea's comments reflects the darkly self-hating streak found in some women's comments on the nature of their own sex. Such comments suggest, not just acceptance of radically asymmetrical social arrangements, but an internalized misogyny. Tragedy contains some extraordinarily misogynistic statements by men; the most dramatic are the rather similar wishes expressed by Jason, in the face of Medea's resistance to his new marriage, and by Hippolytus, in the face of Phaedra's shocking desire for him, that there could be some other way of getting children so that, as Hippolytus puts it, "we could have lived / in houses free of women's presence" (*Medea* 573–5, *Hippolytus* 616–24). In his sense of women as dangerous contaminants of the most intimate spaces, Hippolytus echoes Creon in *Antigone*, who calls to Ismene as "You, who lurked in my house like a snake, / sucking out its strength without me noticing" (*Antigone* 530–1). But Hippolytus' speech builds to a uniquely bald statement of misogyny, which includes a commitment to its endless perpetuation:

> Women, to hell with you! I'll never get sick of hating
> Women. It's true that I'm endlessly talking about this.
> But that's because women are endlessly evil.
>
> (*Hippolytus* 664–6)

Women in tragedy sometimes echo what is avowedly a male-oriented perspective on women's treachery and licentiousness. Hermione in *Andromache*, voicing a view also expressed by Hippolytus, suggests that women corrupt one another when they get together and recommends:

> Against this
> guard your doors with locks and bolts,
> for women coming in from outside do no good
> and lots of harm.
>
> (*Andromache* 950–3)

To this, the female chorus can only respond that perhaps she would do better not to speak so clearly about women's vices. Earlier in the same play, Andromache portrays women as a curse to all humankind:

> Amazing – that against wild snakes
> A god has given mortals a remedy,
> But against what's worse than any viper or destructive fire–
> I mean an evil woman – there's no cure.
> That's what a plague we are to humankind.
>
> (*Andromache* 269–73)

In other contexts, however, such statements are ironized as women cleverly manipulate traditional views for their own ends. Thus Medea prepares for her revenge by pretending to Jason that she has seen that she should really have embraced, not resisted his plans for a second marriage. "But that's just what we women are like – not exactly wicked, but..." (*Medea* 889–90). Women are also heard at times to critique the social arrangements that define their lives. Medea is famous for a speech in which she complains that men can leave the house for relief from boredom as women cannot, and challenges the claim that women's lot is less taxing than men's: "I would rather stand / three times in the front lines of battle than give birth once" (*Medea* 250–1). In a speech preserved from Sophocles' lost *Tereus*, the wronged wife Procne both expresses dissatisfaction with women's annihilating circumstances and protests the expectation that women should mouth the kinds of compliant sentiments quoted above:

> Now, on my own, I am nothing. I have often
> Thought this about the nature of women,
> That we are nothing. Girls in their fathers' houses
> Live what I think is the sweetest life there is,
> For innocence lets children grow up in happiness.
> But when we're grown and see what's what,
> We are pushed out and sold
> Away from our familiar gods and our parents,
> Some to unknown husbands, some even to foreigners,

Some to joyless households, some even to hostile ones.
And these things, once a single night has yoked us to a husband,
We have to praise and seem to like.

(Sophocles Tereus fr. 583 Radt)

Women in tragedy sometimes protest, not only their own forced acquiescence in an inhumane system, but the skewed perspective behind men's misogynistic comments. On several occasions they point out that women in general are blamed because of the actions of a few bad individuals. Melanippe, in a lost play of Euripides, dismisses men's criticism of women as "worthless twanging of a bowstring and evil talk," and, most radically, the chorus of the Medea points to women's lack of a poetic voice as responsible for their worse reputation; men have told stories to which women could make no answer (*Medea* 418–30, quoted as the epigraph to chapter 9 in this volume).

Women are also portrayed as protesting their depiction in tragedy in the comedies of Aristophanes. To complicate matters, their particular target is Euripides, whose surviving plays include the strongest critiques of women's lot and of traditional attitudes but who was himself often viewed as misogynistic. The plot of Aristophanes' *Women at the Thesmophoria* gives some insight into this paradox. There the women of Athens are angry at Euripides, not because he has portrayed them falsely but because he has revealed their secrets. His unvarnished depiction of their behavior has made it harder for them to pull the wool over their husbands' eyes as they conduct illicit affairs and pass off other men's babies as their husbands'. Before the comedy is over, the women subject Euripides to various forms of humiliation and gain the upper hand, until all is resolved when he promises to stop telling the truth about them. This resolution reinstates the silence about women that tragedy is always breaking and reaffirms, however jokingly, that there are reasons for that silence, that it covers over difficult and painful matters. The danger of breaking that silence is also addressed in Aristophanes' *Frogs*, where in a competition with Aeschylus for the honor of best tragedian, Euripides is accused of having encouraged respectable women to become "Phaedras" and "Sthenoboias" (Sthenoboia fell in love with her husband's guest Bellerophon and, like Phaedra, eventually killed herself). In this case, he is charged not just with reflecting women's licentiousness but actually inspiring it. When Euripides defends himself by asking if his story about Phaedra was not true, Aeschylus responds, "By Zeus, it was! But a poet should conceal what's shameful, / not present it publicly or put it on the stage" (1053–4). Euripides' particular sensitivity to women's passions and to the intolerable confines of their approved roles clearly made him a controversial figure, the tragedian who went furthest to test the limits of tragedy's mission of dramatizing transgressive behavior.

Are the Women of Tragedy Really Women?

We have no way of knowing whether the actual women of classical Athens would have recognized themselves in these portrayals. The poets who wrote the scripts of tragedy (and comedy) and the actors who performed those scripts were certainly all men. In this respect, tragedy itself upholds the social ideal of female silence and invisibility even as it focuses on scenarios in which that ideal breaks down. We are less certain whether women were even present in the audiences of tragedy to engage as spectators with their fictionalized counterparts. This question has been much discussed by scholars, with inconclusive results. We have little evidence to go on and most of it is flimsy, consisting, for example, of a late anecdote about how pregnant women miscarried when the terrifying Furies appeared in *Eumenides* (so they must have been there), or a comic suggestion by the chorus of Aristophanes' *Birds* that the spectators might like to have wings too so they could visit their mistresses while their husbands were at the theater (so they must have been at home). A strong, but not decisive, argument for women's presence is the familiarity with Euripides' allegedly misogynistic portrayals displayed by the incensed women of Aristophanes' *Women at the Thesmophoria*. The question is further complicated by the multifaceted nature of the Great Dionysia, the annual festival at which tragedy was performed. On the one hand, it was a religious festival, held in honor of Dionysus, and thus the kind of public occasion in which women did have a role; on the other hand, it was a political event, incorporating elements of civic ceremonial and rehearsing Athenian power to a large audience, including many foreigners, and so the kind of event from which respectable women, at least, were normally absent (for contrasting views on this question, see Goldhill 1994 and Henderson 1991). Some critics have bypassed the unanswerable question of women's literal presence in the theater to stress that, in a culture in which men dominated public life, in which men alone were fully-fledged citizens, and in which masculinity was equated with fully achieved humanity, men were doubtless construed as the ideal audience of tragedy. On this understanding, tragedy was a conversation, often about women, between men, a conversation on which women might eavesdrop, but in which they did not participate.

Given the conditions of its production, the extent to which tragedy can be said to speak with any authenticity for the women of classical Athens remains a matter of speculation, and of individual opinion about whether it is possible for members of one sex to understand and represent the other. There is no question that tragedy speaks from and about a world of sharply perceived sexual difference and strongly demarcated gender roles, in which the capacities and opportunities of women are diminished compared to those of men. The evidence of tragedy, along with other sources, shows that Athenian men expressed, and attributed to women, no single response to that division. Certainly tragedy does nothing to promote whatever interest women (or for that matter men) may have had in social change. Because it explores the ways in which the social order falls apart, tragedy has much to tell about the pain and dysfunction of a divided world, and it often reveals the fluidity of supposedly gendered identities and interests. But it never suggests that human beings could or should organize their lives in any other way. The resolutions that tragedy is sometimes (but not always) able to find for the conflicts it exposes depend on women disappearing from view and falling silent. At the same time, most readers of tragedy would agree that the female characters found there are, like their male counterparts, too various and too richly characterized to function simply as elements in an ideological argument for the status quo. As Victoria Wohl points out in chapter 9 in this volume, tragedy records the ongoing conflicts of the culture that produced it, rather than any monolithic position on those conflicts.

Students of Greek tragedy are thus faced with the challenge of understanding a genre in which men speak as women. One response to this challenge has been to put aside the question of what the female characters of tragedy can tell us about women and to look instead at what they can tell us about men, to understand them as the men that in one sense they actually are (see especially Zeitlin 1996: 341–74). For the men of classical Athens, the achievement of masculinity meant the denial or suppression of qualities coded as female, such as fearfulness, passion, subordination, and vulnerability to the sufferings of the body. Participation in the scenarios of drama afforded men opportunities to confront those qualities by pretending themselves to be women – or to be men operating under disorienting circumstances of female influence or control. For a man to become a woman signifies the same emergence into view of what is normally hidden that occurs when a woman becomes visible.

The link between men turning into women and tragic disruption and suffering is made explicit at a number of points in the surviving plays. In *Women of Trachis*, the powerful, hypermasculine hero Heracles returns home to a deadly greeting from his wife Deianira, who sends him a cloak smeared with what she thinks is a love charm, but is in fact a caustic poison. Undone by her action, Heracles can no longer withstand the assaults of bodily pain and gives way to his afflictions, crying out to his son:

> Pity me,
> A pitiful sight in many eyes, crying
> And choking like a girl, something no one
> Could ever say he'd seen me do before;
> Always without a sound I followed my arduous path.
> But now, in so much pain, I am found to be a woman.
> (*Women of Trachis* 1070–5)

Euripides' *Bacchae* offers a more literal instance of a man becoming a woman in the crucial episode in which the young ruler Pentheus puts on woman's clothing and disguises himself as a bacchante, a female worshiper of Dionysus. Although Pentheus envisions this as simply a strategic act of disguise, like the costuming of an actor, his change of clothing marks the moment when he loses control and comes under the power of Dionysus. Dionysus, himself a markedly effeminate figure, plays on Pentheus' hidden susceptibilities, finding in him an attraction to Dionysian experiences of ecstasy and license that marks him as truly feminine – and that ultimately spells his destruction.

The Female Voice of Lamentation

Another approach to tragedy's voicing of the female through the male is to look for authentic traces of women's self-expression, not in the sentiments spoken or positions taken by female characters, but in tragedy's stylistic repertoire. Tragedy is a hybrid genre, combining many previous traditions, including epic narrative and multiple forms of lyric poetry, both individual and choral. One type of poetry that makes an especially prominent contribution to tragedy's idiom is lamentation, a form closely identified with women. Throughout the ancient Greek world, women played a major role in funerary ritual, and this included the singing of laments for the dead. We do not have access to the laments that ancient women composed, although we can trace their legacy in the laments that are still sung by contemporary Greek women. But female lamentation is represented in the Homeric epics, especially in the *Iliad*. The *Iliad* memorably closes with three laments for Hector delivered by Hecuba, Andromache, and Helen.

As the incorporation of these women's laments into the *Iliad* indicates, lament was recognized as a necessary response to death, through which women served the community by voicing a shared grief. But it also brought with it an element of danger; lament has the same ambiguous relation to the goals of the community as do the women who perform it, with their closeness to the body, to emotion, and to the eerie realms beyond ordinary life. Lamentation could also be a subversive or disruptive force, incorporating social protest or inspiring vengeance. In Athens, public displays of mourning, including lamentation, were considered so troublesome that legislation was enacted to curtail them. This legislation is attributed in our sources to the sixth-century lawgiver Solon who, according to Plutarch, prohibited "everything disorderly and excessive in women's festivals, processions, and funeral rites" (*Solon* 21.4). The functions of these suppressed laments were appropriated for the city by two state-sponsored literary genres. One was the public funeral oration, of which the one delivered by Pericles and depicted by Thucydides, quoted above, is the most famous example. There a mournful response to death in battle is replaced by patriotic rhetoric that stresses the glory won by such sacrifice and minimizes its cost in individual suffering and, as we have seen, there is little room for women. The other was tragedy, in which women's lamenting voices were preserved, but in a mediated form. Tragedy foregrounds women's expressions of grief, drawing heavily on the traditional vocabulary and phraseology of lament, but also makes them the fictional expressions of mythological characters, inhabitants of a different time and usually of a different city, and gives them to male actors to perform.

In tragedy, lamentation is a leading speech genre of female characters, and the plays contain a large number of laments, in which women's expressions of loss often raise broader, difficult issues or precipitate new catastrophes. In Aeschylus' *Seven Against Thebes* the chorus of Theban women expresses its intense dread of the coming battle by lamenting in advance the fates of women and children in a captured city; for this they are harshly rebuked by Eteocles, who fears their debilitating effect on the morale of the warriors. At the end of the play, when Eteocles and his brother Polynices have both died, the chorus offers a lament for both of them that includes bitter criticism of their polluting mutual fratricide. In *The Libation Bearers*, the chorus and Electra share a long *kommos*, or ritual lament, at the grave of Agamemnon, which helps to precipitate Orestes' revenge on Clytemnestra. In *Antigone*, Antigone goes to her death lamenting for herself, mourning in particular her lost chances for marriage and motherhood, and so underscores the injustice of her punishment by Creon. In *Agamemnon*, the captive prophetess Cassandra uses the language of lament to evoke the whole sequence of past and future disasters infecting the house of Atreus, including her own imminent slaughter by Clytemnestra.

In speaking their grief, the women of tragedy confirm the stereotype that, as Andromache puts it in *Andromache*, "by their nature, / women delight in giving voice / to whatever troubles they have" (93–5). They also confirm tragedy's identity as a genre that is in some sense an expression of the female. Plato's view of tragedy as both inherently female and detrimental to a flourishing city was closely connected to its stress on lamentation, which he saw as an erroneous and ignoble response to life. Troubled by the debilitating effect on actors of playing women "possessed by grief and lamentation" (*Republic* 369 e1) and by the effect on audiences of identifying with characters who surrender to lamentation, he imagines excluding poetry, figured as a woman and identified especially with tragedy, from his ideal city. The Athenians who created tragedy and made it a central, publicly supported institution of their own real city obviously saw it differently. They found it important to place on display those features of human experience that inspire terror, sorrow, and rejection, and they accomplished this mission by giving women visibility and a powerful voice. That voice is not neutral in its significance, for it remains closely bound to the expression of turmoil and grief, as the women of tragedy play out their culturally assigned role as the bearers of news that may not be welcome but cannot always be ignored.

Acknowledgments

My thanks to Rebecca Bushnell and Anne Duncan for comments on an earlier draft of this chapter, and to Deborah H. Roberts for letting me use her unpublished paper, "Generalizations about Women in Euripidean Tragedy." All translations are my own.

References and Further Reading

Alexiou, M. (1974). *The Ritual Lament in Greek Tradition*. Cambridge: Cambridge University Press. A survey, spanning the ancient and modern worlds, of a genre, traditionally authored and performed by women, that helped to shape classical Athenian tragedy.

Bassi, K. (1998). *Acting Like Men: Gender, Drama, and Nostalgia in Ancient Greece*. Ann Arbor: University of Michigan Press. A study of drama in the broader context of gendered performance in classical Athens.

Csapo, E. and Slater, W. J. (1994). *The Context of Ancient Drama*. Ann Arbor: University of Michigan Press. A collection and discussion of the major ancient sources for the production of classical drama.

Foley, H. P. (2001). *Female Acts in Greek Tragedy*. Princeton, NJ: Princeton University Press. A broad discussion of women in tragedy in relation to Athenian social practice and ideology.

Goldhill, S. (1994). "Representing Democracy: Women at the Great Dionysia." In *Ritual, Finance, Politics: Athenian Democratic Accounts Presented to D. M. Lewis*, ed. O. Osborne and S. Hornblower. Oxford: Oxford University Press, 347–96. The question of whether women were present in the audience approached skeptically and within an account of the dramatic festival as a civic institution.

Henderson, J. (1991). "Women and the Athenian Dramatic Festivals." *Transactions of the American Philological Association* 121, 133–47. An argument for women's presence at the dramatic festivals on the grounds that the festivals were primarily religious events.

Holst-Warhaft, G. (1992). *Dangerous Voices: Women's Laments and Greek Literature*. New York: Routledge. An account of ancient Greek culture's responses to the perceived threats of female lamentation, including the incorporation of lamentation into tragedy.

Loraux, N. [1985] (1987). *Tragic Ways of Killing a Woman*, trans. A. Forster. Cambridge, MA: Harvard University Press. An analysis of women's deaths in tragedy as expressions of classical ideas about sexual difference and the female body.

Loraux, N. [1990] (1998). *Mothers in Mourning*, trans. C. Pache. Ithaca, NY: Cornell University Press. An analysis of the connection between maternal grief and female violence in tragedy.

McClure, L. (1999). *Spoken Like a Woman: Speech and Gender in Athenian Drama*. Princeton, NJ: Princeton University Press. A discussion of speech genres associated with women – gossip, obscenity, lamentation, and seductive persuasion – as represented in Athenian drama.

Ormand, K. (1999). *Exchange and the Maiden: Marriage in Sophoclean Drama*. Austin: University of Texas Press. A study of how Sophocles' plays represent women struggling with their role as objects of exchange among men.

Pomeroy, S. B. (1975). *Goddesses, Whores, Wives, and Slaves*. New York: Schocken Books. A pioneering survey of women in ancient Greece, which articulates the discrepancy between women's restricted social roles and their portrayal in drama.

Rabinowitz, N. S. (1993). *Anxiety Veiled: Euripides and the Traffic in Women*. Ithaca, NY: Cornell University Press. A study of women in Euripides with an emphasis on tragedy's affirmation of patriarchal values.

Rehm, R. (1994). *Marriage to Death: The Conflation of Wedding and Funeral Rituals in Greek Tragedy*. Princeton, NJ: Princeton University Press. An examination of women's ritual action in tragedy as an expression of the danger and violence inherent in marriage.

Wohl, V. (1998). *Intimate Commerce: Exchange, Gender, and Subjectivity in Greek Tragedy*. Austin: University of Texas Press. A study of the exchange of women in tragedy as the occasion of male self-definition, female resistance, and ideological conflict.

Zeitlin, F. I. (1996). *Playing the Other*. Chicago: Chicago University Press. A collection of influential essays on gender as a defining feature of individual plays and of tragedy in general.

15

Aristophanes, Old Comedy, and Greek Tragedy

Ralph M. Rosen

In a famous scene at the end of Plato's *Symposium*, after a high-minded philosophical discussion about the nature of love at a festive dinner-party had degenerated into a drunken free-for-all, only three of the guests were sober enough to continue the conversation: the philosopher Socrates, the tragic poet Agathon, and the comic poet Aristophanes. Socrates, it seems, had been trying to get the guests to agree that "the same man is capable of writing both a comedy and a tragedy; that the tragic poet could also be a comic poet." But before the topic could be pursued at any length, Agathon and Aristophanes fell asleep, and Plato's narrator – a devotee of Socrates named Aristodemus who had been up all night drinking with the others – became too sleepy himself to remember any details. It is not entirely clear why Plato chose to end the *Symposium* with this little flourish, especially considering that the work as a whole has nothing explicitly to do with tragedy or comedy, but the issues he fleetingly alludes to here are highly suggestive, and point to a curious relationship between the two genres within the literary culture of fifth century Athens which we will explore in this chapter.

The first thing we may infer from Socrates' discussion with Agathon and Aristophanes is that it was not common for poets of his time to venture outside of their chosen genre. Greek tragic poets may have embellished their plays with touches of comedy here and there,[1] and comic poets, as we will see below, certainly loved to incorporate elements of tragic drama into their own works, if only for the sake of parody; but tragic poets normally stuck to tragedy; comic poets to comedy. One searches in vain for any example suggesting otherwise in the literature that has survived from the period.[2] Why, then, might Socrates have imagined that it could be possible, even desirable, for the same person to compose tragedy and comedy? This question is an appropriate starting point for this chapter because we tend in our own time to share Socrates' assumptions that, despite their obvious differences, Greek tragedy and comedy were nevertheless inextricably bound up with one another. This chapter will be devoted to substantiating such an assumption and demonstrating that in fifth-century Athens, at least, tragic and comic poets often relied upon each other for their own self-definition.

Any discussion of the relationship between Greek tragedy and comedy must begin with a few caveats. The sampling we have of Greek tragedy is already meager enough – a small percentage of plays by a small percentage of known playwrights – but comedy is proportionately even less well represented. We have complete plays by only one comic playwright from the classical period, Aristophanes, and the 11 extant plays account for less than 20 percent of his total output. Although scholars have collected hundreds of fragmentary verses from other contemporary comic poets, serendipitously preserved over the centuries in a variety of sources, only in a few cases can we comfortably extrapolate from these a detailed understanding of the play's plot.[3] Since Aristophanes, therefore, must serve as our main representative of Old Comedy (the comic drama contemporaneous with the great fifth-century tragedians of Athens), we need always to remember that other comic playwrights of the period might well have done things differently at least some of the time. On the other hand, there is plenty of evidence external to Aristophanes to suggest that Athenians could easily conceptualize tragedy and comedy as affiliated genres, even if they expected their poets to compose in only one of them. Aristophanes' interaction with tragedy, in other words, may have been reasonably idiosyncratic in its details, but his audience would have found nothing unfamiliar about a comic poet assuming an almost "natural" relationship with tragedy in the context of Greek theatrical performance.

Occasion and Form

Probably the most obvious point of contact between the tragedy and comedy of classical Athens is the fact that they were each performed at the same two religious festivals in honor of the god Dionysus: the City Dionysia in early spring and the festival at the Lenaia, held in midwinter.[4] The details of these festivals are discussed at greater length elsewhere in this book, but we may note here that audiences would have seen both tragedies and comedies on successive days. Performance traditions were different for each festival: five comedies were produced by five different comic poets at both the Lenaia and the City Dionysia, but at the Lenaia only two tragic poets produced two tragedies each, while at the City Dionysia, three tragic poets produced a tetralogy consisting of three tragedies plus a comedic satyr play.[5] It may well be, as is commonly inferred from this programming, that comedy was more central to the Lenaia, tragedy to the City Dionysia, but the important point to remember is that by the late fifth century Athenians would have watched performances of tragedy and comedy back-to-back on successive days twice a year. A citizen who attended both festivals in a given year, therefore, could have seen up to thirteen tragedies, ten comedies, and three satyr plays. Over a lifetime, this adds up to a substantial number of plays, and it is hardly surprising that audiences would have developed highly sophisticated critical faculties and a well-honed sensitivity to the interaction of the dramatic genres that shared the same stage.

There were more compelling reasons, however, why audiences might conceptualize tragedy and comedy as affiliated genres, quite apart from the mere fact that they appeared at the same festivals. To begin with, by the time of Aristophanes' earliest extant comedy (*Acharnians*, 425 BCE), comedy had evolved to the point where, structurally speaking, it looked a lot like tragedy. Oliver Taplin's fundamental description of tragedy as an alternation of an actor's spoken verse and the singing (and dancing) of a chorus[6] holds equally for comedy, even if comedy tended to have a looser feel.[7] Like tragedy, that is, a typical comedy was composed of episodes in which actors spoke – usually, though not exclusively – in iambic trimeters, punctuated by passages of choral lyric. As Aristophanes' *Frogs* (405 BCE) makes clear, a technical terminology to describe tragedy had already developed by the end of the fifth century,[8] and there is no reason to suppose that people could not speak about the structural features of comedy with the same degree of self-consciousness.

Comedy did certainly display a number of structural devices of its own which served to differentiate it from tragedy. The so-called "parabasis," for example, allowed the chorus leader to step forward (or literally, "aside," from *parabaino*), shed his outer costume in a symbolic gesture of "dropping character," and address the audience in the persona of the poet himself. Some of the examples in Aristophanes indicate that parabases themselves could be embedded within a larger structure that has become known as an "epirrhematic syzygy," a highly formalized choral interlude, in which spoken verses (epirrhemata) were "joined together" (syzygy) with sung passages in carefully balanced alternation.[9] Such highly self-conscious, often metatheatrical, passages would clearly be out of place in a tragedy, where dramatic illusion was considerably less breachable than it was in comedy. Other devices that we have come to associate with Old Comedy, however, had parallels in tragedy as well, such as the formalized contest, or *agon*, in which antagonists played out a central dilemma of the play.[10] Aristophanes' *Clouds* (first produced in 423, but revised as the version we have, ca. 418 BCE), for example, featured an *agon* between two allegorical figures called "Stronger Philosophy" and "Weaker Philosophy," and *Frogs* (405 BCE), to which we will return below, pitted the old-timer Aeschylus against the *outré* Euripides in a debate over poetic style. Tragedy had its own variety of *agon*, and some, such as the debate between Agamemnon and Teucer (with Odysseus interceding) in Sophocles' *Ajax*, or the highly rhetorical quarrel between Jason and Medea in Euripides' *Medea* (446–626), seem every bit as formalized as a comic *agon*. Such formal similarities between the two genres would have easily allowed audiences to regard both as close generic relatives.

Where the two genres differed most was in the matter of plot, and it is perhaps somewhat paradoxical that this difference is what seems most responsible for their close interaction. Tragic plots, as has been discussed elsewhere in this book (see chs. 10-11), deal almost exclusively with mythological narratives – the gods, heroes, famous quasi-historical figures of a distant past, whose actions often had monumental consequences for successive generations. Despite plenty of opportunity for innovation and nuance, tragic poets used inherited plotlines with outcomes often already known to the audience. Comic poets, by contrast, were expected to compose original plots, whether drawn wholly from the imagination or based on themes that had become standard fare for comic treatment.[11] Aristophanes worked with a variety of plot-types: highly topical political plots, such as *Acharnians*, *Knights*, or *Lysistrata*, plots of explicit fantasy, such as the utopian *Birds*, and others aimed at satirizing various aspects of contemporary culture, such as *Clouds*, *Thesmophoriazusae*, or *Frogs*. Usually, in fact, he drew on several plot-types within a single play, and there is no reason to suppose that other comic playwrights of the period (to judge from the many titles and fragments of theirs that survive) did not do likewise.

Despite their wide variation, however, all Aristophanic plots can be characterized as satirical or mocking, in the sense that they were all ultimately directed *against* something – whether a person or an institution. Some plays were explicitly *ad hominem* – *Knights*, for example, directed against the controversial politician Cleon; some more abstract, e.g., *Ecclesiazusae*, a critique of the Athenian political system; others a bit of both, e.g., *Wasps*, a comic send-up of the Athenian judicial system, with barely veiled mockery of Cleon – but very little was off-limits for the comic poets, and it was known throughout antiquity – not always approvingly – as the genre of vituperation, parody, and general scurrility.

In keeping with such literary agenda, Old Comedy frequently sought to deflate with humor anything or anyone with elevated pretensions or an excessive aura of seriousness. It is not surprising, therefore, that tragedy became a favorite target for Aristophanic parody. For tragedy was, after all, a dramatic form with obvious similarities to comedy, performed at the same festivals to the same audiences, but which exuded a kind of piety and solemnity that comedy continually resisted. Its themes were the grandest ones available – man's interaction with the gods, justice, politics, fate, failures of language, to name only a few – but in the hands of a master comic poet, what was in one context tragic profundity could quickly be transformed into mere bombast. Less talented tragedians were easy objects of ridicule, and Athenian audiences, it seems, could be merciless critics. In Aristophanes' *Acharnians*, for example, an otherwise obscure tragic poet named Theognis is ridiculed on several occasions for his "frigid" style (e.g., 138–40). But if we can generalize from Aristophanes, at least, it was far more common for the comic poets to ridicule precisely those tragedians who had been most popular and successful rather than the less illustrious ones who made little impression on the audiences and were quickly forgotten. A hack poet may have been an easy mark for a cheap shot, but Aristophanes seemed to be interested in a more complex type of humor which targeted tragedy that had already become, or was in the process of becoming, canonized.

Aristophanes was obviously intrigued by the comic potential of tragic burlesque, since four of his extant eleven plays have plots explicitly implicated with tragedy or tragic performance (*Acharnians*, *Peace*, *Thesmophoriazusae*, and *Frogs*), and nearly all the others are suffused with parodic allusions to that genre. It is through such "paratragedy," as it has come to be called, that Aristophanes, and, we may presume, his fellow comic poets, offered their most sustained and self-conscious interaction with tragedy.[12] In the next section we will examine this literary relationship, as it is reflected most amply in Aristophanes, and consider some of the larger ramifications of paratragedy.

Aristophanic Paratragedy

We may begin with a simple question: why did Aristophanes parody tragedy so extensively? Was it merely because he knew it would raise a laugh with his audiences, and so would bring him closer to winning the prize at the festival competition? Or did he have in mind some broader, more systematic agenda through which he hoped to articulate some form of "serious" literary criticism? Since Aristophanic paratragedy so often involved *Euripidean* tragedy, moreover, does this mean that he had a particular "problem" with Euripides, as has often been thought?[13] Definitive answers to such questions are difficult to find, since our only evidence must come from the plays themselves, and comic genres are well known for playing fast and loose with fact and reality, but Aristophanes does provide us with a few entry points for discussion.

The first can be found in Aristophanes' earliest extant play, *Acharnians*, produced in 425 BCE. This play is usually classified as one of Aristophanes' "antiwar" plays – its central figure, Dicaeopolis, exasperated by the war between Athens and Sparta, tries to secure a "private peace" of his own – but most of its explicit humor derives from its ongoing parody of a Euripidean play, *Telephus* (438 BCE). The plot of *Acharnians*, in fact, is structured around what must have been the most dramatic and memorable scenes of the Euripides' *Telephus*. Telephus was a king of ancient Mysia (a region in present-day Turkey), who was wounded by Achilles when the Greeks mistook his country for Troy. When his wound would not heal, he learned from an oracle that he must seek a cure from Achilles himself at Argos. Evidently, he appeared at Agamemnon's palace disguised as a beggar, and held the baby Orestes (Agamemnon's son) hostage until his request for a cure was granted.[14] The story contained many of the elements that came to be associated with Euripides: heroic figures reduced to abjection, theatrical spectacle (much seems to have been made of Telephus' beggar costume), and shocking plot twists (the abduction of Orestes was evidently a Euripidean innovation). In Aristophanes' *Acharnians*, when Dicaeopolis realizes that the pro-war Acharnians (a local region of Attica) are after his head for brokering his private truce, he decides to take on the role of the Euripidean Telephus in confronting them. Specifically, he first produces a charcoal basket and treats it comically, as if he is holding a baby hostage. The Acharnians, famous for their production of charcoal, are alarmed at Dicaeopolis' threat and grant him his request to plead his defense to them.

As if there were any doubt by this point that Aristophanes was heading toward a parody of Euripides' *Telephus*, Dicaeopolis then pays a visit to Euripides' house in order to borrow a tragic costume that will make him look especially pitiable when he speaks before the Acharnians. He settles, of course, on the costume that Telephus wore in the original tragic production. The entire scene at Euripides' house (395–479) is laced with lines and phrases either taken directly from Euripides or at least made to sound Euripidean by means of "elevated" language and idiosyncratically tragic diction and meter. Even the staging of the scene itself is self-consciously parodic: Euripides is wheeled out from indoors on that famous emblem of Greek tragedy, the mobile platform known as an *ekkyklema*, reclining and absorbed in the composition of tragedies! Many of the dictional markers of paratragedy are only accessible through the original Greek, but a short passage in this scene will offer perhaps some idea of Aristophanes' paratragic technique. At line 449, Euripides has had his fill of Dicaeopolis' shenanigans, gives him the last piece of Telephus' costume that he had asked for (his little felt cap), and tries once and for all to get rid of him:

> EURIPIDES: Take this, and get thee from these marble halls.
> DICAEOPOLIS: My soul, thou seest how I am thrust from the house, when there's
>   still a lot of props I need. Now then, be clingy, beg and beseech. –
>   Euripides, give me a little basket burnt through by a lamp.
> EURIPIDES: Why needest thou that wicker, thou poor wretch?
> DICAEOPOLIS: I don't need it at all; just the same to have it.
>
> (449–55, trans. Sommerstein)

Philological analysis of the Greek confirms that this is a parody of tragic diction[15] and this translation by Alan Sommerstein (1980) tries to convey some of the comic bombast and bathos of the original with its formal, archaic English. One of the ancient commentators on the passage, preserved in some of the medieval manuscripts of Aristophanes, even identifies the verse from Euripides' *Telephus* which *Acharnians* 454 parodies. By juxtaposing the tragic target text with the comic parody in Aristophanes and translating them very literally, we may catch a glimpse of Aristophanes' technique:

> EURIPIDES: Why, you poor wretch, do you need that wicker?
>   *ti d', o talas, se toud' ekhei plekous khreos?*
>   (*Acharnians* 454)
> What then, you poor wretch? Are you about to obey this one?
>   *ti d', o talas? su toide peithesthai melleis?*
>   (Euripides *Telephus* fr. 717)

If we compare the underlined words in the transliterated Greek above, we can see that both lines sound identical for the first half, though they diverge in sense from the beginning. Aristophanes exploits an ambiguity in the Greek interrogative pronoun *ti* ("why" or "what"), and so completely changes the meaning of his version, but an audience would have recognized the allusion by the phonological similarity between the two verses, and presumably would have found the application of tragic diction to a wicker basket rather amusing. Indeed, it is this persistent, incongruous juxtaposition of tragedy's elevated registers with the rambunctious, often scrappy tones of comedy that made Aristophanic paratragedy so effective.

Now, the first question we may ask is whether Aristophanes' extensive parodies of Euripides in *Acharnians* imply actual "criticism" of the tragedian or of tragedy as a whole. The short answer to this question is certainly "not necessarily," and even a casual consideration of the way parody works throughout literary history will confirm this virtually as a matter of principle. Just to take a modern example: No one hearing the British comedy troupe Monty Python's sketch about an "all-British Proust-writing contest" would conclude that its writers were trying to "repudiate" Proust in any serious fashion. The humor of such a parody lies in the absurd juxtaposition of the highbrow and lowbrow, and in the clever conceit of situating a "classic" novelist in the context of a sporting event.[16] Along the way, whatever "criticism" one might extrapolate from the parody of Proust never really rises above the level of the familiar cliché that Proust wrote long, complicated novels. The same might be said of Aristophanic paratragedy, which relies heavily, as we have seen in some of the examples discussed above, on the immediate comic effect of incorporating grandiose tragic diction within a "lowly" comic context, and often enough does not appear to imply a substantive critique. And yet, in *Acharnians*, at any rate, even though much of the paratragic moments seem to exist for their surface humor – the quick laugh from the audience as they recognize a clever contortion of some known Euripidean line or passage – Aristophanes has also incorporated the figure of Euripides himself so centrally into the plot that one suspects that more is at work here.

If Aristophanes actually intended to criticize Euripides in *Acharnians*, one faces a potential paradox: Dicaeopolis – the play's central character who becomes closely identified with the author himself – goes to Euripides in order to *become* one of his characters, i.e., Telephus. In other words, Dicaeopolis actively seeks out a means of impersonating a *tragic* figure in order to be persuasive within a comedy. Why, if Aristophanes wanted to "criticize" Euripides through parody, would he then have Dicaeopolis "act Euripidean" in order to make what he claims to be a serious point? Many scholars have grappled with this problem,[17] and we cannot here do justice to all the complexities it involves, but one passage in the play will serve to formulate the central issues at stake. After Dicaeopolis leaves Euripides with the costume of Telephus, he prepares to make his case before the hostile Acharnians. At line 497, now "disguised" as the abject, tragic Telephus, Dicaeopolis begins his speech:

> DICAEOPOLIS: Be not indignant with me, members of the audience,
>　　If, though a beggar, I speak before the Athenians
>　　About public affairs in a comedy [*trygoidia*].
>　　Even comedy [*trygoidia*] is acquainted with justice;
>　　And what I have to say will be shocking, but it will be right.
>　　　　　　　　　　　　(497–501, trans. Sommerstein)

Readers have often noticed how oddly Dicaeopolis here fuses details of the fictional plot with a self-consciousness about the play as a theatrical performance in real time. He is supposed to be addressing the fictionalized chorus of Acharnians, after all, but the "members of the audience" turn out to be (as he says in 498) the Athenians watching the play. It soon becomes clear that Dicaeopolis is, in a sense, really speaking in the voice of the poet Aristophanes, and that his defense is as much directed at the Athenians in the theater as to the chorus of Acharnians within the play. At 502–8, Dicaeopolis alludes for the second time in the play (see also 377–84) to a skirmish he had had with the Athenian politician Cleon the previous year, which has convinced most scholars that Aristophanes is using Dicaeopolis here as a thinly veiled mouthpiece for his own attacks on Cleon. The earlier passage claims that Cleon had taken Aristophanes to court for maligning the Athenians in his production of the (now lost) *Babylonians* (426 BCE), and commentators since antiquity have inferred from this that such legal wranglings really did occur. We cannot here enter into the question of the historicity of the alleged quarrel between Aristophanes and Cleon,[18] but it is certainly apparent that in Dicaeopolis' famous speech before the Acharnians, Aristophanes wants us at least to believe that whatever Dicaeopolis says in the play represents the poet's own views.

With this in mind, then, it is worth looking closely at the opening of Dicaeopolis' speech, quoted above, where Aristophanes seems to imply several distinct ways of conceptualizing tragedy, especially in its relation to comedy. The first point Dicaeopolis/Aristophanes makes is that the audience should not hold it against him that he will address them about "public matters" (literally, about the city) by means of a comedy. He reasons that comedy is a legitimate venue for "serious" discourse, because "even comedy knows what is right." Two things are noteworthy here: first, the implied assumption that a character dressed as a beggar could not easily be taken seriously and that such a character was even less credible when speaking in a comedy; second, the comic neologism Dicaeopolis uses to refer to comic drama, *trygoidia*. Now, since Dicaeopolis was dressed up as Telephus, and Telephus was the Euripidean character who pleaded his case originally in a tragedy, when Dicaeopolis (as Telephus) apologizes for his abject state, it is clear that Aristophanes is gently ribbing Euripides here for his notorious practice of investing "low" figures with tragic solemnity. Since such "low" figures (beggars, slaves, laborers, etc.) would have seemed more at home in comedy than tragedy, the implied "critique" of Euripides is that tragic figures such as Telephus are so over the top that they risk becoming comic at the very moments when they are supposed to be the most intensely tragic. It is an odd moment, in fact, since at the same time as Aristophanes seems to be mocking Euripidean tragedy, *Dicaeopolis*, within the fiction of the play itself, is *defending* the practice of using "beggarly" figures for serious ends.

The key to his defense is that *"even* comedy knows what is morally right";[19] that is, no one in the audience should be surprised (implying, of course, that they actually probably are) that Dicaeopolis should plead a "serious" case within a comedy such as they are in the middle of watching. And as if to drive home this point, he does not use the normal word for comedy, *komoidia*, but rather the term *trygoidia*. *Trygoidia* is clearly a pun on the word for "tragedy" (*tragoidia*); whereas *tragoidia* is formed from the combination of "goat" (*tragos*) and "song" (*aoide*), *trygoidia* derives from the combination of *tryx* (new wine/wine-lees) and *aoidé*, and so from "goat-song" we end up with something like "wine-song," along with all the comic associations that such a coinage would conjure up. In other words, *trygoidia* certainly means "comedy," but it sounds a lot like the word for "tragedy," as if it wants to borrow from tragedy, however disingenuously, some of its inherent seriousness of purpose.[20]

It is difficult to know exactly how to read this passage, but recent scholarship tends to favor the idea that Aristophanes was in fact using Dicaeopolis here to make the claim that comedy can be as "serious" as tragedy (see especially Edwards 1991). This may be generally true, although it is a position that requires considerable nuance to maintain in view of Aristophanes' own fondness for undermining it at every turn. To begin with, if we take Aristophanes here at face value and accept that comedy can be as serious as tragedy, it is worth remembering that didacticism was a bona fide trope of Aristophanic comedy, as it almost always is in satiric genres, and it is often difficult to distinguish between generically motivated self-aggrandizement (e.g., a poet's persistent claims that his work benefits the city) and genuine protreptic. These two options, of course, may not necessarily be mutually exclusive (a poet, for example, might assume a conventionally didactic posture in his work in order to advance a serious agenda), but as long as the possibility for comic irony exists, the poet's claims will always remain elusive and unstable.

Further complications arise when we ask why a comic poet would feel compelled to "defend himself" with assertions of didactic self-righteousness in the first place. If we choose to minimize the generic provenance of such apologiae, and accept their sincerity, does this imply that under putatively "normal" circumstances, audiences would *not* be inclined to find much in comic drama to take as seriously as they might a tragedy? When Aristophanes maintains that his comedy has an affiliation with tragedy, as his frequent use of the word *trygoidia* for comedy indicates, does he mean to imply that this affiliation is unusual or idiosyncratic? Or is this constant crowing about the *gravitas* of his comedy ironically tongue-in-cheek, something all ancient audiences might have come to expect of any comedy, and which they would consequently take with a broad grin and a grain of salt? In short, are such passages ironic because no one (including the poet) would ever believe that comedy could have the same effect as tragedy, or do they make the case that Aristophanes was, quite idiosyncratically, reaching beyond the traditional parameters of comedy in an attempt to make comedy behave more like tragedy?

To illustrate just how difficult Aristophanes himself makes it to answer such questions with any certainty, we may consider another passage from *Acharnians*, where the poet again makes grand claims for his *trygoidia*. The following lines come from the play's parabasis (628–64), a section of a comedy which, as we noted earlier, is by nature self-reflective and often assumes a didactic posture:

> ... Ever since our producer has had charge of comic choruses [*khoroisin ... trygikois*],
> He has never come forward to the audience to say that he is clever.
>
> But having been traduced by his enemies before the Athenians, ever quick to make
> up their minds, 630

As one who ridicules our city and insults our people, he now desires to make his
   reply before the Athenians, ever ready to change their minds.
Our poet says that he deserves a rich reward at your hands
For having stopped you being too easily deceived by the words of foreigners,
Taking pleasure in flattery, being citizens of Emptyhead.   635
Previously, when the ambassadors from the allied states were trying to deceive
You, they began by calling you "violet-crowned"; and when someone
Said that, at once that word "crowned" made you sit on the tips of your little buttocks.
And if by way of buttering you up someone called Athens "gleaming",
He could win anything from you by virtue of that word "gleaming", by fastening
   on you an honour fit only for sardines.   640
For doing that our poet deserves a rich reward at your hands,
And also for showing what democracy meant for the peoples of the allied states.
That is why they will come now from those states bringing you their tribute,
Eager to see that superb poet who *took the risk of talking justice* to the Athenians ...
[...]
But if you take my advice, never you let go of him; for in his comedies he'll say
   what's right.   655
He says he will give you *much good instruction* that will bring you true felicity,
Not flattering you nor dangling rewards before you nor diddling you nor playing
   any knavish tricks
Nor drenching you with praise, but *giving you the best of instruction*.
So let Cleon contrive,
Let him devise what he will against me;   660
For *right and justice*
Will be my allies, and never shall I be convicted of being,
As he is, a cowardly and
Right buggerable citizen.

               (trans. Sommerstein; emphasis added and lineation modified)

This passage seems more straightforward than it actually is. It is usually read (as
parabases often are) as a genuine statement of the poet's goals and desires, but exactly
what such desires might be is far from obvious when one actually examines the poetic
dynamics at work here. With its opening reference to comic choruses as *trygikoi*, the
passage implies an affiliation between comedy and tragedy, and so signals that what
follows should be taken as "seriously" as one would tragedy. The "serious" claims that
the parabasis makes, however, ultimately amounts to little more than boasting about
the poet's own greatness. In fact, the chorus leader's attitude to the poet is defensive. It
is high time, he says, that the poet should get some recognition for his cleverness
(629), especially since he has recently been censured (by Cleon) for inappropriately
criticizing the Athenians (631). This is mildly amusing as an opening gambit, but the
speaker rises to a crescendo of hyperbolic (self-) promotion on behalf of his poet,
claiming through it all that whichever of the warring parties had Aristophanes on
their side would be the stronger because they would be able to benefit from his
criticism and mockery! The passage alleges that comedy constantly desires to instruct

by articulating what is just and fair, and so on, a claim that the audience would have associated with tragedy (see next section). This "instruction" here consists in a skillful repackaging of mockery (the Athenians were too quick to make decisions, 630; too quick to change their minds, 631, gullible and easily flattered, 634–40, etc.) as something positive ("mockery may be hard to take, but it's good for you if it originates from a position of self-righteousness").

By the end of the passage, any moral authority that the speaker has implicitly appropriated for comedy from tragedy through such terms as *trygoidia* and *trygikos* has been largely undermined by his own comic narcissism. The scene never offers anything an audience might actually regard as didactic substance, and instead "degenerates" into petty squabbling with his *bête noire* Cleon. Even the diction of the final stanza, which in the Greek offers patterns of rhyming and repetition, seems intended to assure that the audience not miss a note of the irony. We can see, therefore, that in passages such as this Aristophanes indeed adopts a stereotyped posture of tragic seriousness, but this seriousness is soon made to seem disingenuous and self-serving. The "best instruction" (668) claimed for comedy turns out to be either confused or (if one insists on pressing the text for didactic content) simply banal: will the audience really find it profound, after all, to hear the suggestion that war is a bad thing, or that the Athenians ought to work harder to make peace with their Spartan enemies, two obvious "lessons" of *Acharnians?* It is not so much, therefore, that Aristophanes wanted his comedy to "be like" tragedy in any real sense or to transform itself into something less comic than it had been up to that point in its history, but rather that he found ready to hand, in tragedy's hallmark seriousness of purpose, a perfect way to repackage several already established tropes of ancient satirical genres. For long before tragic drama as we know it even existed in Athens, Greek satirical poets had anticipated many of the conceits later worked out on the comic stage of the fifth-century city, such as the poet's stance of self-righteousness and abjection, and a humorous fondness for self-indulgent complaining. Such poetry thrived on a *pretense* of seriousness, even if its seriousness turned out to be just another trick up the poet's comic sleeve. Since tragedy had evolved into (if it had not been from the start) a genre of *genuine* seriousness by Aristophanes' time, it was easily tapped by comic poets as a means of cloaking their conventionally disingenuous claims to seriousness with a veneer of authority and decorum. The veneer, however, was thin, as we have seen, and in the end there was little chance that the audience would ever mistake a comedy for a tragedy.

Euripides in Aristophanes' *Frogs*

In the preceding section we found that Aristophanes' paratragedy is rarely consistent in its effect. He played with the fact that both tragedy and comedy could legitimately claim to be "serious" genres, but the more he insisted on appropriating tragedy for serious purposes, the less credible (and more humorous) he became. This is not to say, of course, that Aristophanes could not communicate anything serious to his audience with his comedies, but only that paratragedy was generally not the most reliable means of doing so. We have seen, also, that Aristophanes' particular attention to Euripides in *Acharnians* was equally complicated: he included many jokes and distorted quotations at Euripides' expense, but at the same time he had Dicaeopolis impersonate Euripides for supposedly respectful reasons. There is little to suggest, in short, that in *Acharnians* paratragedy was intended to repudiate or disparage Euripides.

We turn in this section, however, to another play by Aristophanes, *Frogs*, which has often been interpreted as an *ad hominem* attack on Euripides, or, in a milder variation, an attempt to offer a serious critique of Euripidean tragedy. It is not difficult to see why scholars have often reached such conclusions. First of all, there is the basic plot of the play: the patron god of tragedy, Dionysus, decides to retrieve the recently deceased Euripides from the underworld in order to save Athens from her current wartime troubles. At the end of the play, however, he changes his mind and brings back the older tragedian Aeschylus instead. The focal point of the play is the famous contest between Aeschylus and Euripides, and when Dionysus awards the prize to Aeschylus, it is easy enough to believe that Euripides, and the style of tragedy that he represents in the play, has been repudiated. Certainly, by the end of the play the chorus has become openly hostile to Euripides. At 1482–90, for example, after Euripides leaves the stage in ignominious defeat, it praises Aeschylus for his "accurate understanding," his "good sense" and "intelligence," and contrasts him with Euripides, whom it associates with idle sophists, verbal quibbling, and pretentious diction:

> So it isn't stylish to sit
> Beside Socrates and blabber away,
> Discarding artistry
> And ignoring the most important things
> About the tragedian's craft.
> To spend one's time fecklessly
> On pretentious talk
> And nit-picking humbug
> Is to act like a lunatic.
> (1491–9; trans. Sommerstein, lineation modified)

Aside from the well-known dangers, however, of assuming that the words of a comic chorus necessarily reflect the views of the poet, there are other more compelling reasons to doubt that the point of *Frogs* was to censure Euripides and his tragedy, at least in any simple, unironized fashion. For one thing, both Aeschylus and Euripides are subjected to considerable comic abuse throughout the play, and the formal contest between them, staged between lines 1120 and 1410, hardly points to a decisive winner, despite the fact that Dionysus chooses Aeschylus. In fact, Dionysus himself would be happier if he did not have to choose a winner, since he still likes them both. He articulates, in fact, his inability to decide at 1411–13, where he says to Pluto, the god of the underworld: "These two are friends of mine, and I won't judge between them, because I don't want to become an enemy of either. For I consider *the one* to be wise, and the other – well, I just enjoy!" Aristophanes deliberately has Dionysus avoid clarifying which is "the one," and which "the other," so that we can apply the epithets "wise" and "enjoyable" to either one. Forced by Pluto to make a decision, however, Dionysus explains his mission to the two tragic poets, and poses one final question to each to help him decide:

> ... I came down here for a poet; and why?
> So that the City may survive and go on holding her choral festivals.
> So whichever of you is going to give some good advice to the City,
> That is the one that I think I'll be taking back with me.
> First of all, then, what opinion does each of you have about Alcibiades?
> The City is in travail about him.
>
> (1418–23, trans. Sommerstein, lineation modified)

The answers offered by each tragedian to the Alcibiades question satisfy Dionysus, and once again he is unable to decide. Replicating the ambiguity of 1413, quoted above, he states at 1434 that "One of them has spoken intelligently, the other intelligibly." After offering Aeschylus and Euripides one more chance to make their respective cases for saving the city, Dionysus continues to stall aporetically until Pluto finally forces him to make a decision (1467). In the famous scene that follows, Dionysus strings together a series of (largely) Euripidean quotations (indicated by quotation marks below) in order to explain his choice of Aeschylus:

> DIONYSUS: This shall be my decision between you:
>   "him whom my soul doth wish to choose, him will I choose."
> EURIPIDES: Remember the gods when you choose your friends – the gods
>   by whom you swore that you would take me back home!
> DIONYSUS: "'Twas but my tongue that swore"; I'm choosing Aeschylus.
> EURIPIDES: What ever have you done, you filthy villain?
> DIONYSUS: Me? I've judged Aeschylus the winner. Why shouldn't I?
> EURIPIDES: How can you look me in the face after doing such an utterly shameful thing?
> DIONYSUS: "What's shameful, if it seem not so to those" out there? (*indicating the audience*)
> EURIPIDES: You heartless rogue, will you really stand by and let me ... stay dead?
> DIONYSUS: "Who knows if life is truly death"–
>   and dying is dining, and sleep is a fleecy blanket?
>
> (1467–78, trans. Sommerstein)

In short, Dionysus' decision has no particular rational basis, and he roguishly tries to divert attention from this fact by quoting Euripides back at Euripides![21] The three lines he quotes were famously controversial at the time for their apparent endorsement of perceptual and moral relativism, which Dionysus appropriates in order to disclaim any real responsibility for his decision. It is a fast-paced, over-the-top ending, which does not – nor should it be expected to – hold up to much systematic scrutiny if we try to imagine it in performance.[22] Dionysus had already made it clear in the preceding scene, and indeed throughout most of the play, that he had no particularly deep-seated problems with either Euripides or Aeschylus, and that he could easily see either one of them as a potential "savior" of Athens.

It is this point, however, which raises the larger question of whether *Frogs* can in fact tell us anything about Old Comedy's, or at least Aristophanes', attitude toward tragedy as a cultural force. Does the play suggest that tragedy really had some moral efficacy in the real world, that it could actually "educate" the polis, as Aeschylus and Euripides claim to do with their work at various points in the play? The most we can probably say is that Aristophanes was accurately reflecting contemporary discourse about tragedy as an influential didactic medium.[23] Whether Aristophanes himself believed this himself, and whether he composed *Frogs* in some sense as an attempt to trump tragedy's didacticism with a more effective comic version, must remain an open question. As we noted in the preceding section, Old Comedy thrived on claims of didacticism, but its continual flirtation with disingenuousness and irony rarely allowed an audience to judge these claims with much confidence. What *Frogs* does show, however, for all its own moral indeterminacy, is a sensitivity to aesthetic debates of the period, and a wickedly comic perspective on the various ethical dilemmas to which the different styles of contemporary tragedy gave rise.[24]

Conclusions

The relationship between Athenian tragedy and comedy is often described as one of "rivalry" and "competition." Aristophanes certainly implies that comedy was constantly trying to elbow its way into a part of the audience's mind that seemed already oversaturated with tragedy. Calling their work *trygoidia* was one obvious example of this jockeying for generic supremacy, and Antiphanes' famous complaint (see note 11, p. 266) that comedy was much harder to compose than tragedy may be our most explicit articulation of something resembling a rivalry between the two genres. But if such evidence really does point to a genuine literary rivalry, it is a strangely unidirectional one. It would, of course, be generically inappropriate for a tragedy to break into a disquisition about Athenian literary practices,[25] and so allow us to hear from the "other side" of this alleged rivalry, but one wonders, nevertheless, whether in the end such a rivalry between the two genres was as real as the comic poets wanted us to think it was, or whether it was, rather, constructed as another generically indicated conceit of comic abjection and self-righteous indignation. Are we to imagine, after all, that Sophocles or Euripides lay awake at nights worrying that audiences might come to "prefer" comedy to tragedy? And should we imagine, conversely, that comic poets were jealous of tragedy's "respectability," and genuinely dispirited to suppose that their audiences thought of comedy as "unelevated" in comparison to tragedy? As we have seen in this chapter, there is plenty to suggest that Athenian comic poets were quite comfortable as parodists and satirists of tragedy, and that they cultivated their role as literary underdog, in fact, not so much to correct unjust perceptions of comedy as to highlight how fundamentally different tragedy and comedy were, despite their shared literary forms and performance venues.[26] As a mimetic representation of remote mythological plots, tragedy could offer only very limited literary self-consciousness or commentary on its status as a literary or cultural production. It was, as such, a relatively "closed" system which, while it could mirror well enough contemporary Athenian values and ideologies and even occasionally call attention to its own theatricality,[27] was not dynamic and freewheeling in the ways Old Comedy could be.

Greek comedy, on the other hand, scurried frenetically all around this rather staid, often abstracted, form like a duck snapping at one's feet. Comedy, nibbling away as it did at tragedy's various conceits, doubtless had little effect on how or what tragic poets actually composed, but it did provide an invaluable service for the audience in its ability to compensate for tragedy's own lack of self-reflexivity. Comedy, that is, could lay bare the premises, pretenses, and poetic mechanisms that energized tragedy, but which tragedy had to conceal as much as it could. Aeschylus, Sophocles, or Euripides, after all, were not about to call attention to their literary merits or their social value while busy dramatizing mythological plots. It was left to comic poets, therefore, to serve as public commentators on contemporary tragedy, not so much because any of them – even Aristophanes – necessarily had anything resembling a coherent critical agenda or aesthetic mission, but because it has always been the business of comedy to poke and prod at precisely those aspects of a society which appear to be most stable and authoritative.

Notes

1   See, for example, Seidensticker (1982), Knox (1979), Taplin (1986), Gregory (1999–2000), and Dobrov (2001: 70–85).

2   There remains, of course, the notorious question of what to do with Greek satyr play. Tragic poets in the fifth century composing for the City Dionysia festival normally added a satyr play to their trilogy of tragedies, and there is no question that satyr plays were supposed to be "comic." It is not entirely clear, however, exactly how tragedians (or their audiences) would have conceptualized them in terms of genre, and the single extant complete play, Euripides' *Cyclops*, cannot settle the question on its own. *Cyclops* certainly has many features to distinguish it from a bona fide comedy of the period, but more evidence from other authors might reveal that the line between satyr play and comedy in the fifth

century was more fluid than scholars have usually suspected. The fact remains, however, that no Greek tragedian is known to have composed a comic play (which we might define as a play intended to be performed on the day of the dramatic festival specifically designated for the comic performances; satyr plays were performed on separate days as part of a tragic tetralogy). On the problem of satyr play as a genre, see, e.g., Seaford (1976, 1984: 1–44), Seidensticker (1989), and the remarks of Dobrov (2001: 7).

3   Some notable examples include Cratinus' *Pytine* (wine-flask, frr. 193–217 K–A) and *Dionysalexandros* (frr. 39–51) and Eupolis' *Demoi* (towns, frr. 99–146 K–A), for all of which some form of plot summary has come down to us from antiquity, along with substantial fragments.

4   The Lenaean festival was less prestigious than
    the City Dionysia, and it seems that the
    performance of tragedy was introduced there
    late, toward the last decades of the fifth cen-
    tury. See Wilson (2000: 21–31).

5   On satyr play, see above, n. 2.

6   Taplin (1978: 19–21): "the structural frame-
    work [of tragedy] is based on the interaction
    of (i) the two main modes of delivery (actors'
    speech/choral song) with (ii) the articulation
    of the action through exits and entrances.
    The fundamental form is, then: enter actors
    – act – exeunt actors/strophic choral song/
    enter actors – act – etc." (20).

7   As a rule, Old Comedy allowed for consider-
    ably more freedom and flexibility than tra-
    gedy in matters of diction, plot, and meter.
    On the use of dialect in Aristophanes, see
    Colvin (1999: esp. 1–38); on Aristophanic
    meter, see Parker (1997: esp. 1–17).

8   Aristophanes' *Frogs* dramatizes a contest be-
    tween the tragedians Aeschylus and Euripi-
    des (discussed in detail below, pp. 262–4), in
    which various technical aspects of tragedy are
    considered and compared: "prologues,"
    "monodies," "choral passages," etc.

9   An important early study of the structural
    elements of Old Comedy is Zielinski (1885).
    Two major recent studies of the parabasis are
    Sifakis (1971) and Hubbard (1991).

10 On the *agon* in Aristophanes, see Gelzer
    (1960).

11 For example, plots based on the conflict be-
    tween old and young generations, between a
    paradisiacal past and a corrupt present, be-
    tween the sexes, etc. A famous fragment by
    the fourth-century-BCE comic poet Anti-
    phanes (fr. 189 K–A) complains that comedy
    is much harder to write than tragedy, pre-
    cisely because tragedy has the advantage of
    working with inherited, mythological plots,
    which audiences will readily understand.

12 The foundational study of paratragedy in
    Aristophanes still remains Rau (1967). See
    also Silk (1993). Silk faults Rau for a ten-
    dency to use the terms "parody" and "para-
    tragedy" interchangeably, and suggests that
    "paratragedy" be used for "all of comedy's
    intertextual dependence on tragedy, some of

which is parodic, but some is not," while
"parody" be used for "any kind of distorting
representation of . . . a tragic original" (481).
Silk's distinction seems to me unnecessarily
categorical, but it serves as a useful reminder
that not all parodic language necessarily has
an identifiable "target text" lying behind it.
Plenty of Aristophanic verses, for example,
appropriate tragic diction for comic purposes
without trying to conjure up a specific tragic
passage.

13 As, for example, Hubbard (1991: 217), in
    speaking of the literary contest in Aristopha-
    nes' *Frogs* between Aeschylus and Euripides:
    "In the final analysis Euripides' drama is
    inferior to Aeschylus' because it has lost all
    sense of poetic presence, that is, the notion of
    the poet having a special personal relation-
    ship with his audience thanks to which he
    communicates with them through his
    works." Silk (2000: 52 and *passim*): "Aris-
    tophanes is never hostile to Euripides *tout
    court*, but is content to seem ambivalent
    about the great tragedian's experiments."

14 For details of the Telephus myth and Aris-
    tophanes' particular treatment of it, see
    Olson (2002: liv–lxi). Aristophanes' deploy-
    ment of Telephus has inspired a large bibli-
    ography. See, for example, Foley (1988),
    Dobrov (2001: 37–53), and Slater (2002:
    42–67), through which one can trace the
    earlier scholarship on the topic.

15 See Olson's commentary (2002: 191–3).

16 For parody as a literary phenomenon outside
    of classical literature, see Hutcheon (1985),
    Dane (1988), and Rose (1993).

17 See Olson (2002: xl–lii), with further bibli-
    ography at lxvii n. 23.

18 See now Sommerstein (2004), who traces the
    history of the question, with further bibliog-
    raphy.

19 The phrase "morally right" translates the
    Greek phrase *to dikaion*, "the just thing," or
    "justice." "Presumably intended to remind
    the audience of the hero's name [*Dicaeopolis*,
    mentioned at 406]"; Olson (2002: 201).

20 There is considerable bibliography on the
    term *trygoidia*; see Olson (2002: 200–1) for
    discussion and further bibliography. Notable

studies include Taplin (1983) and Edwards (1991).

21　Line 1471 came from Euripides' *Hippolytus*; 1475 from his *Aeolus* (fr. 19), and 1477 from his *Polyidus* (fr. 638).

22　I should note that this is something of a minority view: classical scholars still generally believe that the defeat of Euripides at the end of *Frogs* reflects a coherent and pointed "message" from Aristophanes about the effects of tragedy on the Athenian polis. Dover (1993: 23) sums up a prevalent view of how the Athenian audience might have seen the contest between Aeschylus and Euripides along broad lines, "[I]t was understandable that by Aristophanes' time Aeschylus had become a symbol of Athenian power, wealth, and success, Euripides a symbol of decline." For a full-scale examination (with extensive bibliography) of *Frogs* that regards the play as an eminently serious work centered on the character of Dionysus and his development during the course of the play, see Lada-Richards (1999). On the contest in *Frogs*, see also Heiden (1991) and Rosen (2004).

23　Certainly Plato in the next century took tragedy very seriously as a genre capable of influencing its audiences in profound ways, for better or worse. See his famous discussion of tragedy at *Republic* 376–92, which repudi-ates most of the tragedy of his day on the grounds that it portrayed characters behaving in morally reprehensible ways. It is often forgotten, however, that this discussion arises out of Plato's attempt to imagine what an ideal education might be for the guardians of a hypothetically ideal state, constructed strictly in accordance with reason. It is less clear what Plato actually thought of Athenian tragedy when he was not explicitly worrying about the philosophical problems of mimetic representation. For a detailed study of tragedy and mimesis in Plato, see Halliwell (2002: *passim*, and esp. 37–71).

24　O'Sullivan (1992) examines the contest between Aeschylus and Euripides in *Frogs* as a reflection of contemporary Athenian debates about stylistic theory, without assuming that Aristophanes was himself necessarily deeply committed to one side or the other.

25　As Oliver Taplin (1993: 63) puts it: "Tragedy would not...acknowledge the rivalry of comedy – it is 'beneath notice.' "

26　See Taplin (1986), who likewise stresses how essentially different Greek tragedy and comedy were despite their many points of affiliation. Taplin (1993: 63–6) amplifies and adds nuance to his earlier discussion.

27　Discussion in Taplin (1986, 1993) and Dobrov (2001).

References and Further Reading

Colvin, Stephen. (1999). *Dialect in Aristophanes and the Politics of Language in Ancient Greek Literature*. Oxford: Oxford University Press.

Dane, Joseph A. (1988). *Parody. Critical Concepts versus Literary Practices, from Aristophanes to Sterne*. Norman: University of Oklahoma Press.

Dobrov, Gregory W. (2001). *Figures of Play: Greek Drama and Metafictional Poetics*. New York: Oxford University Press.

Dover, K. J. (1993). *Aristophanes:* Frogs. Oxford. Oxford University Press.

Edwards, Anthony T. (1991). "Aristophanes' Comic Poetics: *Tryx*, Scatology, *Skómma*." *Transactions of the American Philological Association* 121, 157–79.

Foley, Helene P. (1988). "Tragedy and Politics in Aristophanes' *Acharnians*." *Journal of Hellenic Studies* 108, 33–47.

Gelzer, Thomas. (1960). *Der epirrhematische Agon bei Aristophanes. Untersuchungen zur Struktur der attischen Alten Komödie*. [The epirrhematische 'Agon' in Aristophanes. Investigations of the structure of old Attic comedy]. *Zetemata* 23. Munich.

Gregory, Justina. (1999–2000). "Comic Elements in Euripides." In *Euripides and the Tragic Theatre in the Late Fifth Century*, ed. Martin Cropp, Kevin Lee, and David Sansone. *Illinois Classical Studies* 24–5, 59–74.

Halliwell, Stephen. (2002). _The Aesthetics or Mimesis: Ancient Texts and Modern Problems_. Princeton, NJ: Princeton University Press.

Heiden, Bruce. (1991). "Tragedy and Comedy in the _Frogs_ of Aristophanes." _Ramus_ 20, 95–111.

Hubbard, Thomas K. (1991). _The Mask of Comedy: Aristophanes and the Intertextual Parabasis_. Ithaca, NY: Cornell University Press.

Hutcheon, Linda. (1985). A _Theory of Parody: Teachings of Twentieth-Century Art Forms_. New York: Methuen.

Knox, Bernard. (1979). "Euripidean Comedy." In _Word and Action: Essays on the Ancient Theater_, ed. B. Knox. Baltimore, MD: Johns Hopkins University Press, 250–74.

Lada-Richards, Ismene. (1999). _Initiating Dionysus: Ritual and Theatre in Aristophanes'_ Frogs. Oxford: Oxford University Press.

Olson, S. Douglas. (2002). _Aristophanes:_ Acharnians. Oxford: Oxford University Press.

O'Sullivan, Neil. (1992). _Alcidamas, Aristophanes and the Beginnings of Greek Stylistic Theory. Hermes Einzelschriften_ Heft 60. Stuttgart: Franz Steiner Verlag.

Parker, L. P. E. (1997). _The Songs of Aristophanes_. Oxford: Oxford University Press.

Rau, Peter. (1967). _Paratragodia: Untersuchungen einer komischen Form des Aristophanes_. [Paratragodia: Investigations into Aristophanes' comic form]. _Zetemata_ 45. Munich.

Rose, Margaret. (1993). _Parody: Ancient, Modern and Post-modern_. Cambridge: Cambridge University Press.

Rosen, Ralph M. (2004). "Aristophanes' _Frogs_ and the _Contest of Homer and Hesiod_." _Transactions of the American Philological Association_ 134:2 (forthcoming).

Seaford, Richard A. S. (1976). "On the Origins of Satyric Drama." _Maia_ 28, 209–21.

Seaford, Richard A. S. (1984). _Euripides_: Cyclops. Oxford: Oxford University Press.

Seidensticker, Bernd. (1982). _Palintonos Harmonia. Studien zu komischen Elementen in der griechischen Tragodie_ [Palintonos Harmonia. Studies of/in comic elements of Greek tragedy]. _Hypomnemata_ 72. Göttingen.

Seidensticker, Bernd. (1989). "Das Satyrspiel." In _Satyrspiel_, ed. B. Seidensticker. Darmstadt: Wissenschaftliche Buchgesellschaft, 332–61.

Sifakis, G. M. (1971). _Parabasis and Animal Choruses_. London: Athlone Press.

Silk, Michael S. (1993). "Aristophanic Paratragedy." In _Tragedy, Comedy, and the Polis_, ed. A. H. Sommerstein et al., Bari: Levante Editori, 477–504.

Silk, Michael. (2000). _Aristophanes and the Definition of Comedy_. Oxford: Oxford University Press.

Slater, Niall W. (2002). _Spectator Politics: Metatheatre and Performance in Aristophanes_. Philadelphia: University of Pennsylvania Press.

Sommerstein, Alan H. (1980). _The Comedies of Aristophanes, Vol. 1:_ Acharnians. Warminster: Aris & Phillips.

Sommerstein, Alan H. (1996). _The Comedies of Aristophanes, Vol. IX:_ Frogs. Warminster: Aris & Phillips.

Sommerstein, Alan H. (2004). "Harassing the Satirist: the Alleged Attempts to Prosecute Aristophanes." In _Freedom of Speech in Classical Antiquity_, ed. Ineke Sluiter and Ralph M. Rosen. Leiden: Brill, 145–74.

Sommerstein, Alan H., et al., eds. (1993). _Tragedy, Comedy, and the Polis_. Bari: Levante Editori.

Sutton, Dana. (1980). _The Greek Satyr Play_. Meisenheim am Glan: Hain.

Taplin, Oliver. (1978). _Greek Tragedy in Action_. Berkeley: University of California Press.

Taplin, Oliver. (1983). "Tragedy and Trugedy." _Classical Quarterly_ n.s. 23, 331–3.

Taplin, Oliver. (1986). "Greek Tragedy and Comedy: A Synkrisis." _Journal of Hellenic Studies_ 106, 163–74.

Taplin, Oliver. (1993). _Comic Angels and Other Approaches to Greek Drama Through Vase-Painting_. Oxford: Oxford University Press.

Wilson, Peter. (2000). _The Athenian Institution of the Khoregia. The Chorus, the City and the Stage_. Cambridge: Cambridge University Press.

Zielinski, Tadeusz. (1885). _Die Gliederung der altattischen Komödie_. Leipzig: Teubner.

16

Roman Tragedy

Alessandro Schiesaro

Roman tragedy has the rare, if dubious, distinction of boasting a canonical birthdate. At the *Ludi Romani* held in September 240 BCE Livius Andronicus (a writer of Greek background probably hailing from the Magna Graecia town of Tarentum) put on stage, and acted in, a tragedy translated into Latin from a Greek model. The Romans never looked back. Whether the specific date of 240 is factually correct (ancient sources are not univocal in the matter), such precision[1] should not obscure the fact that theatrical activities of various kinds flourished in Rome and other parts of Italy well before that date (*ludi scaenici* are recorded in Rome as early as 364 BCE (Livy 7.2.1–3), and the development of Roman tragedy should thus be contextualized both within the development of a distinctive local culture, and within the polymorphous vicissitudes of postclassical Greek theater, to which the outlying parts of the Greek-speaking world continued to give their own vital contribution (Greek influence on Roman culture had been developing for centuries). Even so, there is no reason not to credit Livius, as ancient sources do, with the daring decision to stage a play with an organic structure, as opposed to disconnected arias or episodes, and to do so by translating into Latin a Greek model, not necessarily an obvious way to " create" a new genre in Rome.

Restoring some sense of geographical and chronological continuity between the emergence of tragedy at Rome and the world of postclassical Greek tragedy (and drama in general) is essential if we are to appreciate Roman tragedies as a distinctive yet integrated part of a generic and stylistic continuum spanning at least two centuries (Gentili [1977] 1979). From Euripides' death (after 408 BCE) to the end of the third century BCE, tragedy continues to be a living genre in Greece and in other parts of the Hellenistic world. When Livius stages his first tragedy, new ones are still being premiered at the Athenian festival dedicated to Dionysus; third-century-BCE Alexandria is home to an accomplished group of tragedians collectively known as the Pleiad, while in southern Italy Rhinton of Tarentum develops the so-called " phlyax" plays, farces poised between the quotidian and the obscene, into tragicomedies (*hilarotragodiai*) of literary status, which apparently reworked Euripidean themes. Comedy and mythological tragedy must also have flourished in the same cultural milieu. Aristotle himself often refers to fourth-century authors such as Astidamas or Cheremon as accomplished and popular tragedians fully and creatively connected with fifth-century models and practices.

Unfortunately, when we come to reconstruct the evolution of both Greek post-classical tragedy[2] and Republican Roman tragedy, we are severely hampered by the need to rely upon scarce, usually short fragments of what must have been a rich and varied corpus.[3] Indirect tradition – that is, quotation by other authors – has handed down to us a total of approximately 1,700 lines of Roman tragedies written by the great masters of the third, second, and first centuries BCE – Livius Andronicus (?284– after 204), Gnaeus Naevius (active 235–204), Quintus Ennius (239–169), Marcus Pacuvius (220–130),[4] and Lucius Accius (170–186)[5] – plus a number of lines (260) of uncertain attribution, but probably largely penned by the same authors. Since a single play usually included at least a thousand lines, we quickly realize the problematic nature of any attempt to reassemble individual tragedies, not to mention the overall literary or ideological complexion of a playwright, until we reach Seneca's fully preserved tragedies dating to the middle of the first century AD. Very little is known of tragedies written between the death of Accius and Seneca's *floruit*, though Varius wrote a celebrated *Thyestes* in 29 BCE and Ovid (who died in AD 18) a famous *Medea*.[6]

Republican Tragedy

The quantity, quality, and chronological distribution of the extant fragments can suggest flawed perspectives. Many quotations (especially for the oldest tragedians) come from grammatical sources keen to point out and explain linguistic oddities of some kind. It is easy, therefore, to exaggerate the "archaic" tone and stylistic idiosyncrasy of these authors. The paltry number of lines preserved tends to obscure the fact that hundreds of tragedies were written and performed in Republican Rome. Religious festivals with attending theatrical performances lasting one or more days multiply from the second part of the third century, totaling some 11 days by 200 BCE, around 20 half a century later, and a peak of 56 days at the end of the Republic – still not much compared to the 101 days recorded in the mid-fourth century AD – (Polverini 2003; cf. Taylor 1937). As theaters were open to the elements, activity was concentrated between April and November. These calculations exclude the repetitions of *ludi* made necessary for ritual reasons (*instaurationes*), and the performance of tragedies on special occasions such as the dedication of new temples, the celebration of victories in war, or the funerals of important citizens.

Furthermore, while Roman comedy offers a treasure-trove of complete texts which overshadows the more limited remains of contemporary Greek New Comedy, Roman fragmentary tragedies appear to be, at first sight, a very poor relation of the great corpus of Attic fifth-century tragedy. Yet it would be wrong to infer from these accidents of transmission the subordinate position of tragedy *vis-à-vis* comedy in the Roman literary system, or to presume that Roman tragedians failed to innovate or compete with their models. Finally, the near-total loss of plays written in the final years of the Republic and the middle of the first century does not signal the end of the genre, even if restagings of older plays begin to outnumber new productions at this point, and first-rate authors are harder to find.[7] In 55 BCE Pompey inaugurated his new theater in the Campus Martius, the first permanent structure of its kind in stone (as opposed to temporary wooden ones), where huge numbers of spectators (at least 17,000) could watch a Hollywood-style restaging of Accius' *Clytemnestra* (starring – so Cicero informs us – 600 mules), and of Naevius' *Equos Troianus*, featuring 3,000 mixing bowls. Cicero's highbrow criticism of this extravagant *mise en scène* hints at the vitality and continuing popular appeal of such plays (*ad fam.* 7.1.2). Cicero's own abundant use of tragic quotations in his writings also confirms that these texts were actively known and appreciated.

Roman tragedy on mythical subject matter – called *cothurnata* (from *cothurnus*, buskins) – plays a central role in performing and constructing Roman cultural identity by fostering a creative relationship with its Greek archetypes, and also by fulfilling its traditional role as the medium which examines the relationship between men and gods, the boundaries of rationality and self-awareness, virtue and its rewards, the system of core values shared by the body politic. At the same time, Republican tragedy is an active player in the sociopolitical life of Rome,[8] not least through its privileging – as we shall see – of themes more or less directly related to the city's origins and history. Spectators were likely to seek out political overtones in the plays (including the mythological ones), and to react vocally to especially significant allusions (Nicolet [1976] 1980: 361–73; Flaig 1995). Staging itself was a public event involving state responsibility (magistrates commissioned and paid scripts), and taking place in front of a vast public made up of all social orders, women and slaves included. The *ludi* of 240, for instance, followed the conclusion of the First Punic War the year before, and were meant to celebrate a pivotal stage in the transformation of Rome into an international power. The *semigraecus* (half-Greek: Suetonius *de grammaticis et rhetoribus* 1.2) Livius was commissioned by the Senate to sanction Rome's political victory by appropriating for local use a literary genre central to the traditions and civic rituals of Greece (Gruen [1990] 1996: 87–8): the very act of creating Latin versions of hallowed Greek tragedies is an expression of self-confident positioning *vis-à-vis* the hitherto undisputed cultural superpower (as is, for instance, Livius' other inaugural work, his translation of the *Odyssey*). It is also, clearly, a gesture toward a higher degree of cultural and specifically literary refinement, fully understandable in a culture which is now beginning to look well beyond the original boundaries of the central Italian city-state.

Livius', Naevius', and Ennius' biographies testify to the central influence of southern Italian Greek culture on the development of Roman tragedy, and at the same time display the growing civic role of tragedians. They were all born outside

Rome, in parts of Greek-speaking southern Italy, where their education and training must also have taken place, since they all came to Rome as grown men. Livius probably hailed from Tarentum, although there is no firm evidence for the usual assumption that he was brought to Rome as a slave when his hometown fell in 272. Naevius came from Campania, long a thriving center of interaction between Italic, Hellenistic, and Roman culture. Ennius, another *semigraecus*, was born in Messapia, at Rudiae, and according to ancient sources, he was aware of his varied cultural background.[9] Nearby Tarentum might have offered suitable opportunities for the poet's formative years. In the next century, Ennius' nephew and disciple Pacuvius came from Brundisium, not far from Tarentum, where he moved in the last part of his life, while Accius was born in Umbria, at Pisaurum. Whatever the specific accidents of each of these authors' lives, Rome was clearly the thriving hub where theatrical success was to be pursued (Rawson 1985). The creation of an actors' and writers' guild (later known as *collegium poetarum*) toward the end of Livius' life attests the social recognition of the actor's trade, which was put under the aegis of (Roman) Minerva rather than (Greek) Dionysus.

The historian Livy, in his reconstruction of the early literary history of Rome, assigns to his archaic namesake the credit for transforming "medleys full of musical measures" (*impletas modis saturas*, Livy 7.2.7) into organized structures revolving around a plot – *fabulae* (plays) with a coherent *argumentum* (Livy 7.2.8). Livy's summary is teleological and suspiciously neat, but there is no reason to question the idea that Livius was the first to present in Rome a traditional Greek play translated into Latin. In the process, he also managed to render in Latin the complex metrical patterns of Greek drama. His plays alternated recited parts in iambic senarii (a distinctive Latin version of Greek iambic trimeters) with sections sung by actors in other meters (the so-called *cantica*, much like arias in opera), e.g., trochaic septenarii or cretics: in all these cases Livius must have provided original solutions to complex technical issues. The extension and importance of *cantica* in a variety of meters – especially iambic and trochaic, which in Greek were recited, not sung – is a distinctive development of Roman theater, both tragic and comic, *vis-à-vis* Greek models, where the musical element played a relatively more limited role. Conversely, Roman tragedies gave less prominence to the chorus (choral meters modeled on Horatian lyric would be given a new lease of life only by Seneca), whose singing and dancing was restricted. In this respect Roman tragedy develops a trend which is already noticeable in the last comedies by Aristophanes and by Menander, where choral odes are replaced by musical intermezzos (the space in front of the Roman stage was, in any case, smaller than in Greek theaters).

The practice of mixing together different sources (*contaminatio*) was part of a general trend in postclassical Greek theater before it emerged as a trademark of Roman authors (Carrara 1992: 13; Guastella 1988: 11–80). We have titles and fragments from ten tragedies by Livius: *Achilles, Aegisthus, Aiax Mastigophorus* (Ajax the whip-bearer), *Andromeda, Danae, Equos Troianus* (The Trojan horse), *Hermiona, Tereus*, and *Ino* (fragments from the last play have often been considered spurious). While Aeschylus'

Agamemnon, Sophocles' *Ajax, Sinon*, and *Hermione*, as well as Euripides' *Andromeda* and *Danae* could have been used as models for some of Livius' plays, later authors must also have been among his sources, since it is clear, for instance, that his *Tereus* was not directly inspired by Sophocles' tragedy by the same title. The titles and fragments of Ennius' tragedies[10] show a strong attachment to Euripides, though ancient sources also mention the fifth-century tragediographer Aristarchus as a model.[11] Pacuvius' *Armorum Iudicium* (The award of the arms) was based on Aeschylus; his *Chryses, Hermiona*, and *Niptra* (The washing) harked back to Sophocles, *Pentheus* to Euripides' *Bacchae*; but other plots show the probable influence of post-Euripidean authors. As far as we can ascertain the same variety of models characterizes Accius' tragedies, where Homer and the Cyclic tradition also play a significant role.

Within the confines of myth, Republican authors display a definite predilection for topics connected with the Theban saga, the family of the Pelopides, and, first and foremost, the Trojan War and its aftermath. This focused, selective interest is coherent with the civic function of tragic performances. Setting a widespread trend, 6 of Livius' plays focus in various ways on Trojan themes, as do 3 of Naevius' 6 *cothurnatae*,[12] 8 of Pacuvius' 12,[13] and half of Accius' 45.[14]

A distinct, related type of tragic performance, called *praetexta*,[15] takes its name from the type of toga worn by Roman magistrates, and deals with episodes from Rome's legendary past or contemporary history with a clear didactic purpose (Varro *De lingua latina* 6.18). Not many of the *praetextae* survive (and, again, the only complete example is the post-Senecan *Octavia*), although they may have been performed (perhaps in smaller scale) before 240 BCE, and could thus have contributed to transmit historical knowledge in a society where historiography did not emerge until the end of the third century BCE. The lack of evidence for early historical dramas (whether structurally organic or not) may be due to the fact that they were never written down, and thus escaped the inevitably selective attention of the first-century-BCE scholars (chiefly Varro) on whom we rely for much of what we know about Republican tragedy in general. Accounts of early events in classical nondramatic authors can occasionally be seen to preserve traces of what could well have been early dramatic representations.[16]

Praetextae known to us were generally written for a specific patron and occasion – chiefly votive games after a victory or games held to mark the dedication of a temple – which partly explains why they must have focused on controversial episodes and characters (Flower 1995). Naevius, who was also the author of an epic poem devoted to the First Punic War, wrote the first *praetexta* of which a few words survive. *Clastidium* is named after the northern Italian locality where the Roman consul M. Claudius Marcellus decisively defeated the Gauls in 222 BCE. The general import of this victory was clear, but Naevius' play, also known to ancient sources as *Marcellus*, must have centered on the much criticized deeds of the consul. Similarly, Ennius' *Ambracia* celebrates the victory of his patron Marcus Fulvius Nobilior in the eponymous Aetolic town in 189 BCE, just as Pacuvius' only known *praetexta*, *Paullus*, deals with some important episode in the military career of one of the Paullii, perhaps

Lucius Aemilius' victory at Pidna in 168 BCE. Ennius' play must have directly reflected the political discussions surrounding Fulvius' victory, as a result of which the statues of the Muses were transported to Rome, where the temple of Hercules was dedicated to them and became the new venue of the *collegium poetarum*.[17]

Praetextae survive into late Republican and early Imperial times. Cornelius Balbus writes a *De suo itinere* (His journey) on an episode related to the civil war in 48 BCE; the Caesaricide Cassius composes a *Brutus*; in imperial times we know of an *Aeneas* by Pomponius Secundus (consul suffectus in AD 44 and, according to Quintilian (10.1.98), the best tragic poet of his times), and both a *Cato* and a *Domitius* by Curiatius Maternus (who was possibly killed under Domitian), both arguably infused with anti-Imperial sentiment and praise of lost Republican *mores* (Bartsch 1994: 81–2, 98–105). The anonymous *Octavia*, although transmitted as part of the Senecan corpus, should probably be dated toward the end of the first century AD (Ferri 2003: 5–30). In a series of rather disconnected *tableaux*, it stages Nero's repudiation of his wife Octavia in order to marry Poppaea in AD 62, and Seneca appears as a key character in the play. This attempt to restore to *praetextae* concern for recent events is isolated: no evidence survives of later engagements with the genre.

Roman Republican tragedy hosted intellectual enquiry of considerable sophistication, dealing with social, philosophical, and political issues. Ennius' *Hectoris Lytra*, for instance, contrasts an uncritical appreciation of *virtus*, a form of physical prowess which even evil people can possess, with the opposing values of *ius atque aecum* (Jocelyn 1967: 295; Caviglia 2003: 369–70): *melius est virtute ius: nam saepe virtutem mali / nanciscuntur; ius atque aecum se a malis spernit procul* (a better thing than bravery is justice; for bravery the wicked often attain, but justice and fair play do spurn themselves far from the wicked, 160–1 Ribbeck = 155–6 Jocelyn). In a similar contrast proposed by Euripides (*Suppliants* 594–7), the positive pole is represented by the gods' assistance, not by traditional Roman values such as *ius* and *aequum*. Similar reflections on the nature and limits of *virtus* and *imperium*, concepts central to the self-definition of the Roman upper classes and their positioning in a wider social context, occur in other tragic authors as well.[18]

Accius stages a comparable debate when his Achilles, sulking in the tent (in the *Myrmidones*; 4–9 Ribbeck = 108–13 Dangel) refuses the charge of *pertinacia* (stubbornness) leveled against him by his fellow Greeks, and instead describes his behavior as an instance of *pervicacia* (steadfastness). The two concepts are contiguous,[19] and Achilles adroitly distinguishes the positive and negative implications of each. The result is a carefully structured passage of great rhetorical – almost juridical –[20] finesse which in tone and intent anticipates the (often unappreciated) rhetorical elaboration characteristic of Seneca's tragic diction.

Tragedy was the natural forum for discussing religious issues, among which divination attracts considerable attention. A fragment of Ennius' *Iphigenia* (Ribbeck 199–201 = Jocelyn 185–7), for instance, reworks Achilles' tirade against the seer Calchas in Euripides' *Iphigenia in Aulis* (919–74): "what is this peering at the star-readers' constellations in the sky? When the She-goat or the Scorpion rises, or some such name chosen from the beasts, no man looks at what is before his feet; one and all scan the stretches of the sky" (*astrologorum signa in caelo quid sit observationis? / cum Capra aut Nepa aut exoritur nomen aliquod beluarum, / quod est ante pedes nemo spectat, caeli scrutentur plagas*). The intensity of Ennius' polemic (Cicero quotes the lines[21] in the context of an attack against astrologers) ties in with his inclination to privilege rationalistic explanations. In this respect, the tone of the *Iphigenia* fragment may well be seen as an early instance of the all-out attack against the evils of *religio* which Lucretius develops in his own programmatic discussion of the same mythological story in the first book of his Epicurean *De rerum natura* (Ennius' Telamo argues, in orthodox Epicurean terms, against the gods' involvement in human affairs[22]). However, by attacking the emptiness of astrologers – not of official haruspices – Ennius combines his humanistic tendencies with a reaffirmation of the shared civic values threatened by the unwarranted recourse to foreign, uncontrolled, and unsanctioned forms of divination (Paduano 1974: 40–1). As a culture in full and rapid development, forcefully exposed to foreign cultural influences of various kinds, turn-of-the-century Rome shows itself to be particularly sensitive to the threat posed by irrational cults and practices.

The tragedians' noticeable display of interest for Bacchic cults, though perhaps partly motivated by the real or assumed relevance of this myth at the very beginnings of Greek tragedy, and by the lasting importance of Euripides' *Bacchae*, should also be seen as evidence of contemporary cultural (and social) tensions. Naevius' *Lucurgus*, to which belong over half of the 65 surviving lines by Naevius, deals with the downfall of a king horribly punished for his opposition to Dionysus and his bacchants and satyrs. The topic will be revived also in the *Stasiastae vel Tropaeum Liberi* by Accius, also the author of a *Bacchae*; Pacuvius wrote a *Pentheus*; Ennius' *Athamas* contained the description of a Bacchic orgy. The cult of Dionysus had been steadily spreading in Rome toward the end of the third century BCE, and Roman tragedy (and comedy) naturally provide an articulate reflection on the "otherness" of those rituals and their interaction with Roman culture.[23] Political implications were also relevant, since the new cult was soon considered enough of a threat to the stability of the traditional social order to attract the Senate's official ban in 186 BCE. Naevius' and Accius' evaluations of the phenomenon are impossible to establish firmly, though one may perhaps discern a more positive attitude toward it in Naevius than in the conservative Accius.[24]

The Republican tragedies not only established a precedent for political drama, but they also represent an important stylistic model. Accidents of transmission massively condition, to be sure, a full understanding of these authors' style, especially in the case of Livius and Naevius, who are quoted in the context of grammatical discussions.[25] Evaluations by later writers inevitably reflect a change in taste as well as personal preferences. Cicero, for instance, believes that Livius' plays are not worth a second reading (*Brutus* 18.71), but praises Ennius for "not diverting from the ordinary use of words," and Pacuvius' lines appear to him "ornate and elaborate," his style more sober and manly (that is, more "Roman") than Sophocles' (*Orator ad M. Brutum?* 36).

Compared with his Greek models Ennius consistently increases the pathetic appeal of his lines (Traina 1974: 113–65) – a strategy which provides a possible blueprint for Virgil's own approach to Homer. His ability to describe devastating psychological phenomena is noteworthy. A few lines from the *Alcmeo* show the Greek king, whose fate is to certain extent comparable to that of Orestes, persecuted by Furies, a projection of his guilty conscience (25–8 Ribbeck = 22–7 Jocelyn): *unde haec flamma oritur? / . . . adsunt; me expetunt. / fer mi auxilium, pestem abige a me, flammiferam hanc vim quae me excruciat. / caeruleae incinctae igni incedunt, circumstant cum ardentibus taedis* (where from rises this flame? . . . They're here. It's me they seek. Help me! Thrust away this plague from me, this flaming blast which racks me to death! They come on, girdled with snakes of color blue, they stand around me with blazing brands). Alcmeo's words are remarkable for the powerful mixture of referential and metaphoric language: the fire which burns him inside is at the same time the consequence of the "fever" gnawing at his insides (*pestis*) and the product of the Furies' torches which he imagines are upon him. Seneca's description of the Fury torturing Thyestes' ghosts with torches in the prologue of *Thyestes* (96–100) strongly recalls Ennius' imagery, which also finds its way – together with specific linguistic suggestions – into passages by Virgil and Ovid. Here again it is important to underline the thread linking earlier and later tragedy – both share a predilection for intense, graphic descriptions of overpowering feelings and phenomena. But we should also be aware of the more general influence exercised on classical epos by Republican tragedians, especially in the creation of an energic style shot through with pathos. To give but one example, the ancient commentator Servius Danielinus already noticed that Virgil's description of the storm at *Aeneid* 1.87–9 is influenced by Pacuvius' *Teucer* (335–5 Ribbeck) for the image of the *stridor rudentum* (a creaking of ropes) and by Accius' *Clytemnestra* (32 Ribbeck) for the notion that the father of the gods "absconded" on the day during the storm (Pacuvius' use of the rare verb *inhorrescere*, moreover, stands behind Virgil's *inhorrescit mare* at 3.195 – the sea begins to rage). From the very beginning of his poem Virgil declares an admiration for, and affinity with, Roman tragedians which rapidly emerges as a fundamental programmatic intention of the *Aeneid*, an epic poem characterized by situations and modes of expression typical of tragedy. Dido's "tragedy" in book 4 (where echoes of Ennius' *Medea*, for instance, abound) stands as a peculiarly intense instance of Virgil's strategy.[26]

The frequent characterization of Senecan style as "melodramatic" chimes with similar descriptions of (or charges leveled at) early tragedians. Seneca's *Agamemnon*, for instance, is clearly indebted to Livius' *Aegisthus* (the shift in title between Aeschylus and Livius, and then again between Livius and Seneca, is an indication of the different focus which the author privileges). Livius' play, too, must have told the story of the Greeks' difficult journey back from Troy on a hostile sea. Fragment I (2–4 Ribbeck): *nam ut Pergama / accensa et praeda per participes aequiter / partita est* ("for, Pergama being burnt out, the booty shared fairly among the men partaking it")[27] is evoked in Seneca, *Agamemnon* 421–2: *ut Pergamum omne Dorica cecidit face, / divisa praeda est* (when all Pergamum fell under the Doric fire, the spoil was divided).

A particularly graphic section of Seneca's extended description of the sea journey before the apocalyptic tempest (449–55) can be compared to the imagery Livius develops in fragment II (5–6): *tum autem lascivum Nerei simum pecus / ludens ad cantum classem lustratur* (but then the frisky snub-nosed herd of Nereus ranged round the vessels, sporting to our song) – compare Seneca's *tunc . . . ludit* (449), *lascivit chorus* (454), and *lustrat* (455). Well-documented connections also exist between Seneca and Accius (Schiesaro 2003: 30; 84), whose Atreus, in the eponymous play, is already every bit as obsessed with the enormity of his revenge as his Senecan counterpart will be. Both strive to surpass themselves, as both identify *maius*, "more," as the hallmark of their strategy of excess.[28] In Accius, the ethical demarcation between the two brothers is less drastic than in Seneca – both are violent and revengeful. The intertextual memory of Accius' Thyestes will play a significant role in shaping our perception of Seneca's Thyestes, whose flaws are hinted at rather than fully expounded.[29]

Imperial Tragedy

Seneca's plays are the crowning glory of Roman tragedy – and its swan song.[30] Just a handful of lines survive from tragedies composed between the death of Accius and the plays the philosopher-politician-poet writes around the middle of the first century AD, making the numerous, complete tragedies of Seneca's even more of a unique phenomenon. Eight are certainly authentic: *Hercules furens, Troades, Phoenissae* (unfinished by the author), *Medea, Phaedra, Oedipus, Agamemnon*, and *Thyestes*. In addition to *Octavia*, the corpus also contains the unusually long *Hercules Oetaeus*, whose Senecan authorship is generally (though not unanimously) denied.

A masterful example of the expressive powers of Latin poetry, of an aesthetics of excess which has intermittently gripped the Western literary imagination, Seneca's tragedies have attracted over time the most wildly diverging aesthetic judgments. In the sixteenth and seventeenth centuries the plays were considered masterpieces of unsurpassable excellence – Seneca's majestic style was considered superior even to Euripides' (J. C. Scaliger *Poetics* 6.6) – and they exert an extraordinary influence on the whole of Renaissance tragedy[31] and beyond (Corneille is an especially fervent admirer). English tragedians from Marlowe to Shakespeare to the Jacobeans draw from Seneca (or at any rate from the often massaged texts going under his name) crucial situations and images, and, in general, inspiration for a graphic poetics which performs violence and disorder in a troubled cosmos. Shakespeare's *Titus Andronicus* is closest to Seneca in style and content, and shares with *Thyestes* the explicit recognition of Ovid as a common model (*Richard III* is also deeply Senecan).

In our age, the numerous stagings recorded especially after World War II attest the plays' enduring appeal to a contemporary audience – the enormous variety of permissible stage actions readily solving any problems which the text may have posed to ancient directors.[32] Seneca's "theater of cruelty" (Artaud) is a most appropriate medium for portraying and dissecting the horrors of the human psyche in a nihilist world which leaves no room for a regulating divine presence, or for any hope that evil deeds will be punished. T. S. Eliot, an eloquent admirer of Senecan drama, considers the final lines of *Medea* – Jason bids farewell to Medea: "travel up above the high expanses the heavens; bear witness that wherever you go there are no gods" – "unique": "I know of no other play which reserves a shock for the last word" (Eliot 1968: 21). The disturbing, recent play *Phaedra's Love* (premiered in 1996), which the English author Sarah Kane writes "after" Seneca (Euripidean traces are also readily discernible),[33] provides another instance of the creative interest elicited by Seneca's relentless exploration of psychological trauma.

In between these "Senecan ages," the romantic revolution heralds a dramatic reversal of fortune in the appreciation of the tragedies. In 1809 August Wilhelm von Schlegel delivered a violent attack against their shortcomings predicated on an unflattering comparison with Greek tragedy; his momentous, if almost incidental, remark that the plays "were never intended to emerge from the rhetorical schools on to the stage" because they are "turgid and chilly" reveals a very dim view of such schools and, in true romantic vein, of anything having to do with rhetoric and lacking in "natural" charm. Although subsequently refined through detailed analyses of dramatic technique (Zwierlein 1966), the theory that Seneca's plays were intended only for recitation does not emerge from a neutral observation of historical, literary, or dramaturgic elements, but rather from a very negative aesthetic evaluation. As "false," epigonic works, Seneca's plays could not aspire to the direct efficacy of Greek tragedy: it would take almost two centuries to see their theatrical nature reasserted, if far from uniformly.

After Schlegel, Friedrich Leo's canonic edition of the corpus in 1878–9 did much to strengthen the belief in the tragedies' inferior artistic quality. Leo defines the novel category of "rhetorical tragedy" (*tragoedia rhetorica*) to account for a tragedy in which – as he synopsizes it – "*ethos* is nothing, and *pathos* is everything" (1878–9: 148). He traces the origin of this genre to the increased importance of rhetoric in Rome after the civil wars, and the aesthetic dissatisfaction with archaic Roman tragedies. Seneca, however, is not, in Leo's opinion, its founder, since he does not doubt that Varius, Pollio, and Ovid must have written in the same vein before him. Nor is he the best: "I would gladly sell all nine of Seneca's tragedies for Ovid's *Medea*" (1878–9: 149). Seneca, claims Leo, simply imports into his plays the preferred rhetorical strategies of his father's *controversiae* and *suasoriae*. Hence his famous conclusion: "These indeed are not tragedies, but declamations composed in a tragic mould and divided into acts" (1878–9: 145).

Excessively rhetorical, and essentially unfit for "proper" staging, Senecan tragedies have long been confined to a subordinate place in the history of classical drama. The tide has been turning in recent years, partly as the result of a general increase in the appreciation of post-Augustan (so-called "Silver") Latin poetry, and partly through a less Manichaean approach to issues of performability. There are, indeed, intermediate options between full, public staging (even if not on the scale of the 55 BCE extravaganza) and solipsistic reading. Public recitation with no stagings is one possibility, but Seneca's plays, setting aside a limited number of thorny passages where stage actions are indeed problematic, would also be well suited to the kind of intimate performances in private palaces (with a streamlined apparatus) which were well known in Hellenistic and Roman times. It is important, in any case, to decouple any discussion of performability from an evaluation of the aesthetic merits of Senecan drama as a literary form, and to abandon the unspoken – and far from evident – assumption that only performable plays can be aesthetically powerful.

The issue of performability is, in part, kept alive by the important interpretive consequences it entails. Recent studies inspired by the principles and methods of performance criticism have yielded useful insights, for instance, into the issue of the chorus's size, concluding that Seneca most likely presupposes a small, three-sided raised stage with spectators on all three sides: a small chorus of three is probably all such a stage can accommodate without blurring spectators' lines of vision (Marshall 2000). This form of relationship between the stage and the audience better accounts for the metatheatrical dimension of the performance, which is harder to envisage with a full-frontal stage, which heightens the illusionary nature of the plays. In Seneca, the chorus is no longer continuously present on the stage, and its interaction with other characters is limited (Tarrant 1978: 221–8). A small chorus fits well the predominant characterization of Senecan choruses, more often than not the purveyors of a partial, limited, and questionable take on events. Nor should the chorus automatically be seen as voicing the poet's ultimate "truth," the real "message" of the play. The tendency to overestimate the chorus's point of view is a common enough tendency in Senecan criticism; many choral odes, with their Horatian serenity and reassuring common sense, seem to offer a safe haven in the midst of excessive passions and unflinching violence. The chorus is often the repository of a sensible wisdom, the purveyor of more or less orthodox Stoic takes on events and emotions, but there can be no ultimate answer to the question, whether its view of reality should be taken as the true embodiment of the author's own, a sort of "authentic" interpretation of the plays, or, on the contrary, as testimony, with its own faint voice, of well-meaning but impossible aspirations.

Here, though, we should heed a rather different dictum by T. S. Eliot, who points out: "in the tragedies of Seneca the centre of value is shifted from what the personage says to the way in which he says it" (Eliot 1968: 15). Precisely because the chorus is a character with a specific persona, its point of view cannot aspire to a higher level of truth. Indeed, in several plays, but nowhere more prominently than in *Thyestes*, the chorus's inability to grasp the real terms of the situation, to interpret and understand the motives and intentions of the characters on stage, represents the most poignant indication of its narrow and hopelessly moralizing perspective. By promoting certain choral odes to the level of authorial statements we almost automatically eliminate any such view of the chorus, and a crucial aspect of the dialectics which dominate the plays. A small chorus coming and going from the stage, on the other hand, would emphasize that its feelings and thoughts are – like everyone else's – relative. A double chorus, as in *Troades, Phaedra*, and *Agamemnon*, shows further that there is no overarching collective point of view, but events are inevitably focalized by partial spectators with their own prejudices and agendas.

The political dimension of Senecan tragedy is both appealing and elusive, all the more so since the dating of the plays is uncertain,[34] and nothing at all is known about their circulation, if any (they may never have been performed – in whatever fashion – or they could have been seen only by a small coterie of friends of the author, who, after AD 62, left Nero's court and became increasingly disillusioned with his former pupil's politics).[35] Its obsession with the corrupting quality of absolute power – *regnum* – is, of course, easy to picture in a cultural and political context increasingly dominated by the vagaries and excesses of unrestrained rulers. Atreus, the protagonist of *Thyestes*, might look like the quintessential Neronian emperor: overpowering, refinedly cruel, megalomaniac, an irresistible combination of dark wit and evil genius. Political reception of the story of Atreus and Thyestes was well established.[36] At the games organized to celebrate the victory at Actium, in 29 BCE, Varius Rufus had presented a successful *Thyestes*, much appreciated (and rewarded) by Augustus, perhaps pleased by the potential identification between the cruel tyrant Atreus and the defeated Marc Antony suggested by the play (Lefèvre 1976; Leigh 1996). However, this very episode underscores how important the circumstances of representation are in the definition of a political message, and whether Seneca's *Thyestes* can be seen as direct criticism of Nero's rule, or whether the reference to incest in *Phaedra* is a coded condemnation of the emperor's family antics (Lefèvre 1990), must remain uncertain (in the latter case, chronology is also an obstacle).

Seneca's tragedies are actively aware of their positioning in Roman literary history. Their titles and themes hark back to celebrated fifth-century Greek models, as well as to various Roman reincarnations of the same myths, yet they consistently thematize repetition and belatedness. Seneca's relationship with Attic plays cannot be doubted, even if specific instances of verbal coincidence are rare. But, unlike his Republican predecessors, Seneca appears uninterested in "translating" Aeschylus, or Euripides, or their epigones, in bridging the distance separating two very different ages. The essence of Seneca's attitude was famously captured by Wilamowitz-Moellendorf, who quipped that Seneca's Medea must have read Euripides' play by the same name (1919: 3.162). Precisely so. Intertextual awareness plays a central role in the characterization of Senecan characters. Medea is the playwright-cum-director of her own revenge play. While Euripides' prologue had opened on the Nurse's account of the antefacts, Seneca takes this as read, and the Prologue zooms in on Medea's own desire to set in motion a revenge of unprecedented violence, and on her understanding that this new episode in her life will attract the same kind of literary immortality as her actions so far: *paria narrentur tua / repudia thalamis* – "let the story they tell of your divorce be like the one they tell of your marriage" (52–3). Atreus flaunts an impressive knowledge of the poetic tradition, correctly identifies the story of Tereus, Itys, and Procne as the obvious precedent and inspiration for his actions, and actively deploys this knowledge in the pursuit of retribution. The more literal-minded and less learned Thyestes is inevitably outwitted and overpowered. Oedipus enters

Seneca's stage already worn down by a vague and unspoken sense of guilt which is unknown to his Sophoclean counterpart: the Oedipus complex is already at work even before the play unfolds.

Belatedness is thematized in the plot of the tragedies, but is also embodied in their poetics. Seneca's language is shaped by a continuous, even obsessive dialogue with intertextual models, not because of a lack of imagination, but precisely because it is deeply aware that its "coming after" is a reiteration of well-known horrors whose intensity is magnified by repetition (Schiesaro 2003: 221–51). Virgil and Ovid are, unsurprisingly, the predominant stylistic models, but their influence on Seneca is also rooted in thematic and ideological motifs. Seneca appears especially keen to read in the *Aeneid* an authoritative precedent in the exploration of the role of *furor* in human affairs. The Prologue of *Thyestes*, the most sustained metaliterary reflection in the corpus on the connection between *furor* and tragic inspiration, draws unmistakably on the dialogue between Juno and Allecto in *Aeneid* 7, a "second proem" which heralds (again) the beginning of war.[37] The recurrent Senecan motif of the murder-as-sacrifice finds in the closing scene of the *Aeneid* a harrowing archetype whose influence rivals the development of the same theme in Greek tragedy (Putnam 1995: 246).

Scholars have long favored reading Seneca's plays as an illustration of the main tenets of Stoicism[38] – at least after they become reconciled to the idea that both the tragedies and the prose work were written by the one and same author. Stoicism explicitly entertains the possibility of exploiting poetry as a powerful means to express eternal truths, and conveying them more expressively and engagingly than prose would allow. This approach, however, is problematic. There are few instances where Stoic terms of reference and evaluation are directly and explicitly engaged. Moreover, the nature of the tragedies as intricately layered literary products makes it difficult, sometimes impossible, to disentangle moral messages consistent with Stoicism (or even more loosely with conventional Roman morals) from the hopelessly subverted moral chaos that dominates the tragedies. A case in point is *Thyestes*, arguably the most successful of all of Seneca's plays. The tyrant Atreus, bent on punishing his brother Thyestes, commits horrific crimes – he slaughters his nephews and serves them up at dinner to an ignorant Thyestes. The emotional reaction to, and moral evaluation of, Atreus' actions, however, are complicated by two factors. Thyestes himself is far from blameless. Seneca's text hints at *his* earlier attack against Atreus, his attempt to seize the throne, and his adulterous relationship with Atreus' wife Aerope (the doubt about his children's real paternity still torments Atreus). Moreover, from the moment he steps onto the stage Atreus is consistently portrayed as the author's doppelgänger, the playwright of his own revenge tragedy, for which he seeks a poet's inspiration. Without Atreus' artistic creativity, rooted in his thirst for revenge, there would be no *Thyestes* for us to watch – no aesthetic pleasure, if any, to be had. Atreus' "bigger" crime is symbol and reflex of Seneca's own competitive take on tragedy-writing, of his determination to outdo – in style and in horror – the famous models he resuscitates one last time.

Seneca's tragic style is characteristically intense – or "mannerist" and "baroque." A superior control of the expressive power of rhetoric accounts for a large part of the style's strength: rhetorical tropes such as antithesis, brevity, paronomasia, figura etymologica – to name but a few – endow Seneca's language with poignant wit and unexpected depth. Take, for instance, Medea's first unwilling intimation of the horrors to come in the Prologue (23–6): *me coniugem optet, quoque non aliud queam/ peius precari, liberos similes patri / similesque matri – parta iam, parta ultio est: / peperi* (let him long for me to be his wife and – the worst thing that I can pray – let him long for children who resemble their father, and resemble their mother. It's born already, vengeance is born: I have given birth). Still unclear about the shape his revenge against Jason will take, Medea wishes on him hostile and ungrateful children – which she has already borne him. The repetition of the verb *pario* in different forms (and the concurrent shift from metaphorical to referential use) poignantly, if indirectly, conveys to a knowing public the murderous thoughts which are as yet inchoate in Medea's mind. "Let him long for me to be his wife," which was also intended as a destructive wish – Medea is aware of her terrifying magical powers – already conveyed the complexity of her attitude toward Jason: the curse, after all, conceals a desire that he may still long for her as his wife. Like Ovid, an author who plays a central role in shaping Seneca's poetic diction, Seneca excels in the ability to extract unforeseen tragic meanings from an apparently innocuous language.

Seneca's "theater of the word" is animated by such masterful exploitations of the expressive powers of a refined poetic language, schooled, no doubt, in the myriad techniques which rhetoric had perfected. Intense desires, and great horrors, find in this polished and formally impeccable clothing its harshest representation.

NOTES

I am very grateful to Rebecca Bushnell, and to Marco Fantuzzi and Ingo Gildenhard for their helpful comments.

1 Equally problematic is the assumption of 240 BCE as the starting point of Latin literature tout court: Habinek (1998: 34–68, 179–89); Suerbaum (2002: 83–7).

2 About which Xanthakis-Karamanos (1980) offers a realiable survey. See also Sifakis (1967).

3 Fragments are quoted according to the numbering of Ribbeck's second (and third) edition (Ribbeck 1871 = *TRF*). Vols. I (Ennius) and II (Livius, Naevius, Pacuvius, Accius) of Warmington (1935–8) contain almost all fragments with notes and English translation. Noteworthy single-author editions include Jocelyn (1967) for Ennius; D'Anna (1967) for Pacuvius; Dangel (1995) for Accius.

4 The most recent critical study is Manuwald (2003).

5 See most recently the essays collected in Faller and Manuwald (2002).

6 On *Medea* see Nikolaidis (1985). Bardon (1952) provides information on tragedians whose texts are lost: (1952: vol. 1, 52–3; 132–5; 158–66; 326–30; vol. 2, 47–52; 127–32; 213–17).

7 A brief but incisive account of this period of transition can be found in Goldberg (1996).

8 See in general Flower (2004).

9 According to Gellius (17.17.1), Ennius used to say that he had "three hearts, because he could speak in Greek and in Latin and in Oscan."

10 *Achilles, Aiax, Alcmeo, Alexander, Andromacha, Andromeda, Athamas, Cresphontes, Erechtheus,*

Eumenides, Hectoris Lytra (The ransom of Hector), *Hecuba, Iphigenia, Medea Exul* (Medea in exile), *Melanippa, Nemea, Phoenix, Telamo, Telephus, Thyestes.*

11 *Gloss. Lat* 1.568. *Achilles* is quoted as *Achilles Aristarchi* in Fest. p.282.9. No Euripidean model can be pinpointed for *Aiax, Eumenides, Hectoris Lytra, Nemea,* and *Telamo,* and there are doubts about *Athamas, Alcmeo,* and *Cresphontes*: Jocelyn (1967: 45).

12 *Aesiona, Danae, Equos Troianus* (The Trojan horse), *Hector Proficiscens* (Hector's departure), *Iphigenia,* and *Lycurgus.*

13 *Antiopa, Armorum iudicium* (The award of the arms), *Atalanta, Chryses, Dulorestes, Hermiona, Iliona, Medus, Niptra, Pentheus sive Bacchae, Periboea, Teucer.*

14 *Achilles, Aegisthus, Agamemnonidae* (Agamemnon's children), *Alcestis, Alcmeo, Alphesiboea, Amphitruo, Andromeda, Antenoridae* (Antenor's sons), *Antigona, Armorum iudicium* (The award of the arms), *Astyanax, Athamas, Atreus, Bacchae, Chrysippus, Clytemnestra, Deiphobus, Diomedes, Epigoni* (The after-born), *Epinausimache* (The battle at the ships), *Erigona, Eriphyla, Eurysaces, Hecuba, Hellenes* (The Greeks), *Io, Medea sive Argonautae* (Medea, or the Argonauts), *Melanippus, Meleager, Myrmidones* (The Myrmidons), *Neoptolemus, Nyctegresia* (The night-alarm), *Oenomaus, Pelopidae* (Pelops' sons), *Persidae* (Perseus' sons), *Philocteta, Phinidae* (The sons of Phineus), *Phoenissae* (The Phoenician maidens), *Prometheus, Stasiastae vel Tropaeum Liberi* (The rebels or Liber's trophy), *Telephus, Tereus, Thebais* (A tale of Thebes), *Troades* (Women of Troy).

15 On *praetexta*: Zorzetti (1980); Flower (1995); Wiseman (1998); Manuwald (2001).

16 This line of argument has been recently championed especially by Wiseman (1998). See, e.g., Ovid *Fasti* 4.326 on the arrival of the Magna Mater, with the narrator's comment *mira sed et scaena testificata loquar* (amazing events, but the stage is my witness).

17 Other notable Republican *praetextae* include Ennius' *Sabinae,* and Accius' *Aeneadae vel Decius* and *Brutus.*

18 Cf. Livius Andronicus 16–17 Ribbeck, Naevius 17 Ribbeck, inc. 116–17 Ribbeck.

19 Ennius appears to have collapsed them into one (408 Ribbeck = 383 Jocelyn), and Accius may well be seen to be reacting, here, against his predecessor: cf. Degl'Innocenti Pierini (1980: 75).

20 As already acknowledged in antiquity: Quintilian 5.13.43. On the whole issue, and a comparison with similar argumentations in Cato, see Degl'Innocenti Pierini (1980: 74–7).

21 *De republica* 1.30 and *De divinatione* 2.30 (187 only).

22 269–70 Ribbeck = 270–1 Jocelyn: "For my part I have always said, will say, there is no race of gods in heaven; and yet they take no thought, it seems, how fares mankind."

23 See now Flower (2000).

24 On Naevius: Pastorino (1955), a rather extreme view; on Accius: Dangel (1995: 339).

25 The best overall treatment is Lennartz (1994).

26 On Virgil and the Republican tragedians see Wigodsky (1972), with further bibliography, and Hardie (1997: esp. 322–5).

27 Translation from Warmington (1935–8), with modifications, as for all archaic fragments.

28 Cf. 198–201 Ribbeck = 29–32 Dangel with Seneca *Thyestes* 267–70.

29 See later, p. 281.

30 Boyle (1997) is an excellent introduction. Tarrant (1978) a classic account of the structural changes Seneca introduces to his tragedies vis-à-vis earlier plays.

31 See esp. Braden (1985).

32 Information on performances is collected at Oxford by the Archive of Performances of Greek and Roman Drama (www.classics. ac.ox.uk/apgrd).

33 A brief, incisive analysis in Mayer (2002: 85–7).

34 A comparison with another work by Seneca, the *Apocolocyntosis,* invites us to consider a date before AD 54 for *Hercules furens,* while a possible reference to the invasion of Britain in *Medea* 375–9 would point to composition under Claudius (who died in AD 54). Metrical technique, on the other hand, suggests that *Agamemnon, Phaedra,* and *Oedipus* were com-

posed before *Medea, Troades,* and *Hercules,* which in turn precede *Thyestes* and *Phoenissae* (Fitch 1981).

35 Three years later he was ordered to commit suicide after the emperor discovered his involvement in a conspiracy.

36 Garelli-François (1998) argues that Ennius' *Thyestes* displays anti-Macedonian feelings,

and especially an attack against the king, Perseus.

37 Compare esp. *Thyestes* 83–6 with *Aeneid* 7.335–40.

38 On the origins of this method see Mayer (1994).

REFERENCES AND FURTHER READING

Bardon, H. (1952). *La littérature latine inconnue* [Unknown Latin literature], 2 vols. Paris: Klincksieck.

Bartsch, S. (1994). *Actors in the Audience. Theatricality and Doublespeak from Nero to Hadrian.* Cambridge, MA: Harvard University Press.

Beare, W. (1964). *The Roman Stage. A Short History of Latin Drama in the Time of the Republic,* 3rd edn. London: Methuen.

Bilinski B. (1957). *Accio e i Gracchi. Contributo alla storia della plebe e della tragedia romana* [Accio and the *Gracchi.* Contribution to the history of the plebe and Roman tragedy]. Rome: Signorelli.

Boyle, A. J. (1997). *Tragic Seneca. An Essay in the Theatrical Tradition.* London and New York: Routledge.

Braden, G. (1985). *Renaissance Tragedy and the Senecan Tradition: Anger's Privilege.* New Haven, CT: Yale University Press.

Carrara, P. (1992). "Modelli drammaturgici e prassi teatrale greca classica e postclassica nella tragedia romana di epoca repubblicana" [Dramaturgic models and classic and postclassic Greek theater praxis in Republican age Roman tragedy]. *Quaderni catanesi di cultura classica* 10, 9–24.

Caviglia, F. (2003). "Note su alcune strutture ideologico-linguistiche della tragedia romana arcaica" [Notes on some ideological–linguistic structures of archaic Roman tragedy]. In *Teatro greco postclassico e teatro latino. Teoria e prassi drammatica,* ed. A. Martina. Rome: Herder, 367–84.

Dangel, J. (1995). *Accius,* Oeuvres *(fragments).* Paris: Les Belles Lettres.

D'Anna, G. (1967). *M. Pacuvii Fragmenta.* Rome: Edizioni dell'Ateneo.

Degl'Innocenti Pierini, R. (1980). *Studi su Accio* [Studies of Accio]. Florence: CLUSF.

Eliot, T. S. (1968). *Elizabethan Dramatists.* London: Faber & Faber.

Faller, S. and Manuwald, G., eds. (2002). *Accius und seine Zeit* [Accius and his time]. Würzburg: Ergon.

Ferri, R. (2003). *Octavia. A Play Attributed to Seneca.* Cambridge: Cambridge University Press.

Fitch, J. G. (1981). "Sense-pauses and Relative Dating in Seneca, Sophocles and Shakespeare." *American Journal of Philology* 102, 289–307.

Flaig, E. (1995). "Entscheidung und Konsens. Zu den Feldern der politischen Kommunikation zwischen Aristokratie und Plebs" [Decision and consent. Areas of political communication between aristocracy and plebe]. In *Demokratie in Rom? Die Rolle des Volkes in der Politik der römischen Republik* [Democracy in Rome? The role of the people in the policy of the Roman republic], ed. M. Jehne. Stuttgart: Steiner, 118–24.

Flower, H. (1995). "*Fabulae praetextae* in Context: When Were Plays on Contemporary Subjects Performed in Republican Rome?" *Classical Quarterly* 45, 170–90.

Flower, H. (2000). "*Fabula de Bacchanalibus:* The Bacchanalian Cult of the Second Century BC and Roman Drama." In *Indentität und Alterität in der frührömischen Tragödie,* ed. G. Manuwald. Würzburg: Ergon, 23–35.

Flower, H. (2004). "Spectacle and Political Culture in the Roman Republic." In *The Cambridge Companion to the Roman Republic,* ed. H. Flower. Cambridge: Cambridge University Press, 322–43.

Garelli-François, M.-H. (1998). "A propos du 'Thyeste' d'Ennius: tragédie et histoire" [Ennius' *Thyestes*: tragedy and history]. *Pallas* 49, 159–71.

Gentili, B. [1977] (1979). *Theatrical Performances in the Ancient World.* Amsterdam: Gieben.

Goldberg, S. M. (1996). "The Fall and Rise of Roman Tragedy." *Transactions of the American Philological Association* 126, 265–86.

Gruen, E. S. [1990] (1996). *Studies in Greek Culture and Roman Policy.* Leiden: Brill and Berkeley, Los Angeles, and London: University of California Press.

Guastella, G. (1988). *La contaminazione e il parassita. Due studi sulla cultura romana* [Contamination and the parasite. Two studies on Roman culture]. Pisa: Giardini.

Habinek, T. N. (1998). *The Politics of Latin Literature. Writing, Identity, and Empire in Ancient Rome.* Princeton, NJ: Princeton University Press.

Hardie, P. (1997). "Virgil and Tragedy." In *The Cambridge Companion to Virgil*, ed. C. Martindale. Cambridge: Cambridge University Press, 312–26.

Harrison, G. W. M. (2000). (ed.) *Seneca in Performance.* London: Duckworth.

Hine, H. M. (2000). *Seneca:* Medea. Warminster: Aris & Phillips.

Jocelyn, H. D. (1967). *The Tragedies of Ennius. The Fragments Edited with an Introduction and Commentary.* Cambridge: Cambridge University Press.

Jocelyn, H. D. (2000). "Accius' *Aeneadae aut Decius:* Romans and the Gallic Other." In *Indentität und Alterität in der frührömischen Tragödie*, ed. G. Manuwald. Würzburg: Ergon, 325–61.

Lefèvre, E. (1976). *Der Thyestes des Lucius Varius Rufus. Zehn Überlegungen zu Seiner Rekonstruktion* [Lucius Varius Rufus' *Thyestes.* Ten considerations of its reconstruction]. Wiesbaden: Steiner.

Lefèvre, E. (1990). "Die politische Bedeutung von Senecas Phaedra" [The political significance of Seneca's *Phaedra*]. *Wiener Studien* 103: 109–22.

Leigh, M. (1996). "Varius Rufus, *Thyestes* and the Appetites of Antony." *Proceedings of the Cambridge Classical Society* 42, 171–97.

Lennartz, K. (1994). *Non verba sed vim. Kritisch-exegetische Untersuchungen zu den Fragmenten archaischer römischer Tragike* [Non verba sed vim. Critical exegetical investigations into the archaic Roman tragic fragments]. Stuttgart and Leipzig: Teubner.

Leo, F. (1878–9). *Seneca: Tragoediae*, 2 vols. Berlin.

Manuwald, G., ed. (2000). *Indentität und Alterität in der frührömischen Tragödie* [Indentity and alterity in early Roman tragedy]. Würzburg: Ergon.

Manuwald, G. (2001). *Fabulae Praetextae. Spuren einer literarischen Gattung der Römer.* [*Fabulae Praetextae.* Traces of a Roman literary genre]. Munich: C. H. Beck.

Manuwald, G. (2003). *Pacuvius. Summus tragicus poeta. Zum dramatischen Profil seiner Tragödien* [Summus tragicus poeta. The dramatic profile of its tragedies]. Munich and Leipzig: K. G. Saur.

Marshall, C.W. (2000). " 'Location! Location! Location!' Choral Absence and Theatrical Space in *Troades.*" In *Seneca in Performance*, ed. G. W. M. Harrison. London: Duckworth, 27–51.

Martina, A., ed. (2003). *Teatro greco postclassico e teatro latino. Teoria e prassi drammatica* [Postclassical Greek and Latin theater. Dramatic theory and praxis]. Rome: Herder.

Mayer, R. (1994). "Personata Stoa: Neostoicism and Senecan Tragedy." *Journal of the Warburg and Courtauld Institutes* 57, 151–74.

Mayer, R. (2002). *Seneca:* Phaedra. London: Duckworth.

Nicolet, C. [1976] (1980). *The World of the Citizen in Republican Rome*, trans. P. S. Falla. Berkeley and Los Angeles: California University Press.

Nikolaidis, A. J. (1985). Some Observations on Ovid's Lost *Medea. Latomus* 44, 383–7.

Paduano, G. (1974). *Il mondo religioso della tragedia romana* [The religious world of Roman tragedy]. Florence: Sansoni.

Pastorino, A. (1955). *Tropaeum Liberi. Saggio sul* Lucurgus *di Nevio e sui motivi dionisiaci nella tragedia latina arcaica. Tropaeum Liberi.* Text on Nevio's *Lucurgus* and Dionisiac motives in archaic Latin tragedy]. Arona: Paideia.

Polverini, L. (2003). "Tempi e luoghi delle rappresentazioni teatrali a Roma in età repubblicana" [Times and places of the theatrical representations to Rome in the Republican age]. In *Teatro greco postclassico e teatro latino. Teoria e prassi drammatica*, ed. A. Martina. Rome: Herder, 385–95.

Putnam, M. C. J. (1995). *Virgil's* Aeneid. *Interpretation and Influence*. Chapel Hill and London: University of North Carolina Press.

Rawson, E. (1985). "Theatrical Life in Republican Rome and Italy." *Papers of the British School at Rome* 53, 97–113 (now in *Roman Culture and Society: Collected Papers*, Oxford: Clarendon Press, 1991, 468–87).

Ribbeck, O. (1962). *Tragicorum Romanorum* Fragmenta, 2nd edn. Hildesheim: Georg Olms.

Schiesaro, A. (2003). *The Passions in Play. Thyestes and the Poetics of Senecan Drama*. Cambridge: Cambridge University Press.

Sifakis, G. M. (1967). *Studies in the History of Hellenistic Drama*. London: Athlone.

Suerbaum, W. (2002). *Die archaische Literatur von den Anfängen bis Sullas Tod. Die vorliterarische Periode und die Zeit von 240 bis 78 v. Chr.* [Archaic literature from its beginnings to Sulla's death. The pre-literary period and 240 to 78 BCE]. Munich: C. H. Beck.

Tarrant, R. J. (1978). "Senecan Drama and Its Antecedents." *Harvard Studies in Classical Philology* 82, 213–63.

Taylor, L. R. (1937). "The Opportunities for Dramatic Performances in the Time of Plautus and Terence." *Transactions of the American Philological Association* 68, 285–91.

Traina, A. (1974). *Vortit Barbare. Le traduzioni poetiche da Livio Andronico a Cicerone* [Vortit Barbare. The poetic translations from Livius Andronicus to Cicero], 2nd edn. Rome: Edizioni dell'Ateneo.

Warmington, E. H. (1935–38). *Remains of Old Latin*, 4 vols. Cambridge, MA: Harvard University Press.

Wigodsky, M. (1972). *Virgil and Early Latin Poetry*. Wiesbaden: Steiner.

Wilamowitz–Moellendorf, U. von. (1919). *Griechische Tragödien* [Greek tragedies], 4 vols. Berlin: Weidmannsche Buchhandlung.

Wiseman, T. P. (1998). *Roman Drama and Roman History*. Exeter: Exeter University Press.

Xanthakis-Karamanos, G. (1980). *Studies in Fourth-Century Tragedy*. Athens: Akadēmia Athēnōn.

Zorzetti, N. (1980). *La pretesta latina e il teatro latino arcaico* [The Latin pretext and archaic Latin theater]. Naples: Liguori.

Zwierlein, O. (1966). *Die Rezitationsdramen Senecas. Mit einem kritischexegetischen Anhang* [Seneca's "recitation plays." With a critical and exegetical appendix]. Meisenheim am Glan.

Part V
Renaissance and Baroque Tragedy

17

The Fall of Princes: The Classical and Medieval Roots of English Renaissance Tragedy

Rebecca Bushnell

No one can doubt that English Renaissance theater set one of the high-water marks in the history of tragedy's ebb and flow. William Shakespeare, Christopher Marlowe, Thomas Kyd, John Webster, Philip Massinger, and John Ford, among many others, crafted plays unlike any of their predecessors, whether classical or vernacular. Writing for sometimes rowdy, sometimes awestruck audiences that mixed aristocrats and apprentices – and writing for profit – these men and their actors brought to the stage a new tragic language, titanic heroes and villains, and inventive plots that mingled kings and clowns.

Literary historians contend in accounting for the intense explosion of tragic theater. And it was indeed more like an explosion than a flowering, for its life span was relatively brief. What we remember and still teach are a relatively small set of plays performed in England – and mostly in London – from the mid-1580s up through the early 1630s. We tend to begin with Marlowe, Shakespeare, and Kyd, and end with Ford and Massinger, since readers now feel little affection for what came either before or after them. But, while we may have lost the taste for their predecessors, we do want to uncover the prehistory of this phenomenon. What ignited this explosion? What factors happened at this particular place and time to fuel it?

A review of the scholarly debates over the origins of English Renaissance tragedy reveals that this is a loaded question, for how a scholar tells the story is tied to academic politics. Everyone agrees on one point: that English Renaissance tragedy is a mongrel genre, compounded of multiple traditions. But scholars continue to argue about the relative value and influence of the vernacular traditions and new forms of classicism in England.

Twentieth-century literary history periodically adjusted the relative weight of the classical and medieval influences on English Renaissance tragedy. In the earlier part of the century, scholars like T. W. Baldwin and Hardin Craig celebrated the victory of what they saw as new classical values over coarse "popular" medieval theater, with its explicit allegories, crude comedy, and stock characters. As David Bevington describes this perspective:

> Distaste for this popular theater has led too frequently to overemphasis of classical rediscovery as the main line of development in English Renaissance drama: the human-ist experiments of Medwall, Rastell, and Heywood, the early "regular" comedies of the schools and universities, and the erudite plays of the Inns of Court. The preconceived standard of classical scholarship, with its preference for intellect, philosophical probing, and the correspondences of the Aristotelian unities, measures literary progress in the sixteenth century only by the degree to which sophisticated learning freed English drama from the fetters of ignorance and bad taste. (Bevington 1962: 1–2)

One can see from Bevington's tone here that he does not entirely approve of this teleology, which finds the "true" roots of Renaissance tragedy in a renewed classicism, which is also tied to high culture and the world of the grammar schools and universities.

By the mid-twentieth century, the attitude toward classicism in English drama began indeed to change to reflect such critiques of a classicist bias. This shift reflected a swing in academic politics to the left, when as Lorraine Helms notes, "liberal and democratic" scholars of the mid-century "dismissed traces of classical antiquity as a superficial and elitist literariness glossing the robust popular theatricality of medieval mysteries, moralities, and mummers' plays." Studies of classicism were confined to the products of the grammar school, and academics like Alfred Harbage opposed the vital world of the open-air popular playhouse to the "enclosed halls" of the schools, aristocratic courts, and so-called "private playhouses" (Helms 1997: 9–10).

Most influential was Robert Weimann's *Shakespeare and the Popular Tradition in the Theater* (first published in Germany in 1967 and translated into English in 1978). Weimann focused on the social function of the vernacular plays, which he believed defined the essence of the Shakespearean theater, tragic and comic. He had little respect for "the contribution of the humanist drama, its models in Seneca, Terence, and Plautus, the French imitations by Garnier and Jodelle, its classical examples as seen in *Gorboduc* (1561) and the later tragedies by Fulke Greville and Sir William Alexander." What he did appreciate was "the moral vision and the dramatic potency of what humanism – as an approach to art and method rather than as doctrine or philology – gave to the theater" (Weimann 1978: 179).

In recent years some scholars have reevaluated how classicism shaped the sixteenth-century English theater. In *Seneca by Candlelight and Other Stories of Renaissance Drama* (1997) Lorraine Helms explored the theatricality of Senecan rhetoric, and Bruce Smith wrote sympathetically in *Ancient Scripts and Modern Experience on the Stage 1500–1700* (1988) of experiments with classical models, mostly performed in schools and aristocratic households. It may now be possible to discuss without bias how English tragedy developed in this period. We can accept that Renaissance tragedy is the fruit of a multiply grafted stock: part medieval mystery, part morality, part chronicle play, part Seneca, and part of the classical heroic tradition, handed down through medieval epic and discovered anew, in the Renaissance, in its original form, as a genre for representing the passions and values of a society in the grips of political and social change. Weimann observed how in comedy "the popular tradition itself assimilated wholly disparate elements (including classical, courtly, and humanist materials) until it became part of a vastly larger cultural and aesthetic synthesis: the 'mingle-mangle' of which John Lyly spoke when he noted that 'the whole worlde is become an Hodge-podge' " (Weimann 1978: xviii). And such could be said of tragedy as well, although in the case of tragedy, the quality of "hodge-podge" came to threaten the values of generic purity that some took the notion of tragedy to represent.

Even if we do take a side on this matter, at least we can recognize that in so doing, we reenact a debate that took place in the halls, streets, and theaters of sixteenth-century England. Simultaneously defending "poesy" and condemning most English vernacular poets, Sir Philip Sidney's *Defence of Poetry* (1595) strikingly defines the terms of the debate over the status of tragedy in the late sixteenth century. Sidney celebrates tragedy in his defense of the moral claims for "poetry": who, he asks, could condemn

> the high and excellent Tragedy, that openeth the greatest wounds, and showeth forth the ulcers that are covered with tissue; that maketh kings fear to be tyrants, and tyrants to manifest their tyrannical humors; that, with stirring the affects of admiration and commiseration, teacheth the uncertainty of this world, and upon how weak foundations gilden roofs are builded. (Sidney 1966: 45)

Yet when it comes to considering the productions of his own country, Sidney finds them lacking in style:

> Our tragedies and comedies (not without cause cried out against), observing rules neither of honest civility nor skillful poetry excepting *Gorboduc* (again I say of those I have seen), which notwithstanding as it is full of stately speeches and well-sounding phrases, climbing to the height of Seneca's style, and as full of notable morality, which it doth most delightfully teach, and so obtain the very end of poesy, yet in truth it is very defectuous in the circumstances, which grieveth me, because it might not remain as an exact model of all tragedies. For it is faulty both in place and time, the two necessary companions of all corporal actions. For where the stage should always represent but one place, and the uttermost time presupposed in it should be, both by Aristotle's precept and common reason, but one say, there is both many days, and many places, inartificially imagined. (Sidney 1966: 75)

He presents a withering description of the defects of the plays of his contemporaries, which have "Asia of the one side and Afric of the other" and portray a prince's life from birth to death, thus transgressing the limits of time and space (Sidney 1966: 65). Tragedy, he claims,

> is tied to the laws of poesy, and not of history; not bound to follow the story, but having liberty either to feign a quite new matter or to frame the history to the most tragical

conveniency . . . Again, many things may be told which cannot be showed, if they know the difference betwixt reporting and representing. (Sidney 1966: 66)

The tragic poets are free, in short, to follow what Sidney poses as the new tragic artifice, which demands a new decorum.

In praising the high style of *Gorboduc*, with its stately speeches and shows, and yet condemning it for neglect of the neo-Aristotelian unities of time and place (see chapters 3 and 21 in this volume), Sidney draws on two distinct notions of "classical tragedy" in his time: "English Seneca" and the relatively recent intro-duction of the notion of the unities of time, place, and action. When Greek tragedy resurfaced in southern Europe in the fourteenth century, and much later in England, Seneca had already begun to exercise a strong influence on both English and French Renaissance drama (Braden 1985: 101–2). By the mid-sixteenth century, however, Italian and French commentators on Aristotle's *Poetics* were busy con-structing the neoclassical theory of the unities, which burst into full flower in France in the seventeenth century.[1] But the truth is that, outside of "closet" or purely academic tragedy, very few English tragedies of the sixteenth and seven-teenth centuries ever exactly fit either the Senecan or the neoclassical model. Cross-breeding a strong vernacular tradition of theater of the hall, school, and street with the voices of Seneca and the classical dramatic conventions, English playwrights developed a startling hybrid species, in defiance of the complaints of Sidney and his followers.

The Fall of Princes: The Vernacular Traditions

The writers and actors of the sixteenth century did inherit from the preceding centuries' scholars and divines a definitive notion of what "tragedy" is, which was as much a political as an ethical concept: the fall of those of high estate or rank. Chaucer's translation of Boethius offered a simple definition: "What other thing bywalen the cryinges of tragedyes but oonly the dedes of Fortune that with unwar strook overturneth the realmes of great nobleye? (Glose. Tragedye is to seyn a dite of a prosperite for a tyme, that endeth in wrecchidnesse)" ([1951] 1964: 44). In his *Troy Book*, Lydgate had also written:

> But tragedie, who so list to knowe,
> It begynneth in prosperite,
> And endeth ever in adversity;
> And it also doth the conquest trete
> Of riche kynges and of lordys grete,
> Of mighty men and olde conquerou[ri]s.
> Whiche by fraude of Fortunys schowrris
> Ben overcast and whelmed from her glorie.
> (Cunningham [1951] 1964: 46–7)

The three themes of this conventional image of tragedy almost always thus occur together: the fall from a prosperous or "high" condition to a wretched or low one; the role of "Fortune" in causing that fall; and the idea that the tragedies only happen to "mighty men" – kings, conquerors, and those of "great nobility" – and not common people, and thus they are fundamentally political. Absent from this idea of tragedy is the notion of *hamartia*, whether understood as a misjudgment or a flaw of character. The tragic fall was considered as inherent to nobility or political power, when the wheel of Fortune ground through its inexorable turns.

This medieval conception of tragedy was fundamentally a critical concept, not a theatrical reality. Before the sixteenth century, tragic drama as we know it was not played in the streets and halls of medieval England. What were performed, the mystery plays of the medieval cities and the morality plays of schools and aristocratic households, did leave their mark on the unique form of tragedy that emerged in London in the sixteenth century. The mystery plays contributed to the performative style of later tragedy, while also carving out a space for tragic theater in the market-place and city space. The allegorical morality plays, the stuff of school and court theaters, with their core of moral conflict and homilies of fall and redemption, reinterpreted the medieval theory of tragedy for "everyman" and helped to define a new tragic political drama.

The vernacular mystery (or miracle) cycle plays had a long life span, extending from the twelfth century right up through Elizabeth's reign. Thus, when English tragedy came to flower in the third decade of the sixteenth century, their influence was still active. The mystery plays were a pan-European phenomenon, a mode for performance of biblical events often focusing on the life of Christ. In England, we know that in the mid-twelfth century, clerics in elaborate costumes acted a mixed Latin–French play, *Mystère d'Adam*, on a scaffold outside a church (Woolf 1972: 49–50). While still religious in theme, in later centuries the English plays became detached from the liturgical year, occurring mostly during the festivals of Whitsun-tide and Corpus Christi (and hence they are sometimes referred to as Corpus Christi plays) (Woolf 1972: Ch. 4). In succeeding centuries the mysteries also shifted their playing space from the church porch to the streets and marketplaces of London and provincial towns. In the fourteenth and fifteenth centuries, the town guilds took over the sponsorship of the mystery plays, which had now become extensive "cycles" or long, episodic processional performances of up to forty-eight distinct plays with laymen playing all the roles. In these towns each of the guilds would have its play to perform on a wagon that processed through the town, and citizens enacted roles ranging from angels to tyrants to shepherds, unfolding the high drama of the Old and New Testaments. Lawrence Clopper argued that the transition from church porch to city street suggests a conflict over authority between the secular and religious spheres of English society. While the plays may have been religious in their content, representing the events in the Old Testament that prefigured those of the New, their origin and purpose were closely linked to the guilds and concerns of late medieval civic life (Clopper [1999] 2002: 759–83). As such, they shaped a place for a public tragic theater in England and for a theater played by and for the people of the city.

The mystery plays also developed a mixture of sacred and profane that would also come to distinguish English tragedy. Their scope was wide, enacting events from the rebellion of the angels to the last judgment, and their form was episodic (see Woolf 1972: 55). The style could be rough, characterized by a mixture of piety and humor, devotion and violence: for example, in the Wakefield cycle the Second Shepherd's Play interweaves a comic plot about a stolen sheep with the mystery of the Nativity. The mystery plays were also remembered well after their height for their representation of kings and knights, who, as Clopper notes, "are almost universally represented as tyrants and thugs" (Clopper [1999] 2002: 762). The mystery cycles' vain Herods and Pilates bluster about on stage, threatening to punish anyone who defies them (see Bushnell 1990: 84–8); their knights are at once ineffectual and cruel. The mystery plays thus licensed the parodic representation of secular figures alongside sacred ones, juxtaposing the high and low in society, in public, and in the context of serious drama.

The other late medieval dramatic genre that shaped Elizabethan tragedy, the morality play or moral interlude, was peopled not by biblical characters but by abstractions, allegorical figures who met in battle over the destiny of a hero who stands for us all. The morality play emerged in the late fourteenth century, just when the mysteries were flourishing, but today the ones we know best are *The Castle of Perseverance* (early fifteenth century), *Mankind* (from the mid-fifteenth century), and *Everyman* (late fifteenth century). Such plays apparently made use of a fixed stage with scaffolding, rather than the mysteries' procession of wagons (although there is no evidence that *Everyman* was ever acted in its own time). The manuscript of *The Castle of Perseverance* is rife with stage directions that imply performance in a large open-air space surrounded by scaffolds representing the realms of God, the World, and the Devil. We can also see that the audience enjoyed riveting special effects, for example, that the actor playing Belial the devil had "gunne-powdyr brennynge in pipys in hys handys and in his erys and in his ars whenne he gothe to the batayle" (Happé [1979] 1987: 78). From the fifteenth century on, however, it is more likely that the morality plays would have been performed in the great halls of universities, schools, and aristocratic households, either by groups of traveling professional players or by students. By the sixteenth century, the morality play was more typically a short, more secular drama referred to as a moral interlude; these were a mixed bag of plays that often mingled allegorical characters with historical or mythological types. The interludes covered themes suitable to the groups of students and aristocratic families that were often their audiences. Favorite topics were the value of education, political virtues, and general moral doctrine (see Happé 1999: ch. 9).

What binds together this heterogenous group of plays is not only their habit of allegory or personification; it is also the plot pattern of a temptation, fall, and redemption, often centered on the fate of a single protagonist, who may be a figure of mankind, a king, or a youth whose soul is at stake. The morality play is a drama with a crisis at its core, whether played out in comic violence and action or high-flown rhetorical debate. In *Everyman* the crisis is the coming of death. God summons Everyman to prepare to die, and so he seeks help from Fellowship, Kinsmen, Goods, and Riches, all of whom betray him. He finds aid in Good Deeds and Knowledge, as well as his Five Wits, but when the angel of death comes he is left with Good Deeds alone to bear him to his maker. *The Castle of Perseverance* model is the more prevalent one: there vices and virtues battle for the soul of Humanum Genus. Encouraged by his Malus Angelus, or bad angel, Humanum Genus decides to embark on a life of sin, but his Bonus Angelus persuades him to repent, and leads him to the Castle of Perseverance. There the powers of evil lay siege to the Castle: when war fails, Avaricia tricks Humanum Genus, who then confronts his death in sin. He dies praying, and after a debate before God among Misericordia (Mercy), Veritas (Truth), Justicia (Justice), and Pax (Peace), Humanum Genus is forgiven. *Mankind* is a sparer version of the same conflict, with seven characters as opposed to the thirty-five of *Perseverance*. It is also more comical. When Mischief conflicts with Mercy over the control of Mankind, a farmer, he is tempted away from his work and godly life by Nought, New-Guise, and Nowadays. When Mankind is brought to account, it appears it is too late, but Mercy finds him, and he is saved. The morality plays thus characteristically bring their heroes to the brink of damnation through their sin but allow for their salvation through mercy or grace.

In establishing this scheme for ethical drama, the morality thus defined a paradigm that both overlapped and conflicted with that of classical tragedy. Fundamentally, the conflict lay in the clash between Christian and classical ethics, between the image of a hero who confronts his own often inexplicable fate and a story of sin and death that finds its fulfillment in grace and redemption. In his study of *Ancient Scripts and Modern Experience*, Bruce Smith describes the two ethics as in fact informing each other in the creation of Renaissance tragedy:

> In the world of classical tragedy, larger-than-life heroes with an awesome capacity for action, for suffering, and for eloquence are destroyed by external forces – often very unjust forces – over which they nonetheless triumph in the very act of dying. In the world of medieval morality plays, on the other hand, heroes with the life-size homeliness of Everyman are faced with moral choices and are rewarded by a providential God when they choose rightly and are punished when they choose wrongly. Classical tragedies, Seneca's in particular, make no claims for the justice of the universe; morality plays assume a sometimes inscrutable yet always certain providence. It is, perhaps, the interplay between these polarities, pagan and Christian, that defines the imaginative power of modern tragedy. (Smith 1988: 202).

What this comparison implies, also, is that, in contrast with the mysteries, classical tragedy and the moralities share a focus on the reversal of fortune of a single protagonist. The allegory of the moralities reinforced the message that the protagonist's experience stands for more than his own life: somehow, that hero, that Everyman's fate either mirrors that of the spectator or takes us with him.

This focus on the career of a single protagonist also explains how the morality might come to define political tragedy. The medieval idea of the tragic as the unfortunate fall of princes paved the way for the allied genre of the "mirror for magistrates," didactic poems that recounted the disastrous careers of historical and legendary figures meant as warnings to presumptuous men and women in power. The political moralities blended a medieval message of inevitable disaster under the rule of Fortune with the implication of moral responsibility, conflating the fate of Everyman with that of the ruler and the state. The best developed example of such a play is John Skelton's *Magnificence* (ca. 1515), which stages the downfall of the prince, Magnificence, who is dragged into degradation when he follows Fancy's advice that he banish Measure and free the figure of Liberty. The false courtiers Cloaked Collusion, Counterfeit Countenance, and Crafty Conveyance lead him to a state when he confronts Adversity and Poverty. At the end, he is redeemed by the efforts of Good Hope, Redress, and Circumspection. *Magnificence* thus attributes responsibility to the prince for his own downfall. The message is clear to those who would aspire to rule: avoid excessive consumption and beware the flattery of false counsel, a timely message at its historical moment under the reign of Henry VIII.

In a different way, Thomas Preston's notorious *Cambyses* shows in spectacular fashion what the title page describes as

> a lamentable tragedy mixed ful of pleasant mirth, conteyning the life of Cambises king of Percia, from the beginning of his kingdome unto his death, his one good deed of execution, after that many wicked deeds and tirannous murders, committed by and through him, and last of all, his odious death by Gods Iustice appointed. (Preston 1570: title page)

This play represented a new direction for English theater, in mixing history with the morality's focus on the career of a single overweening protagonist. In his lamentable career Cambyses is abetted by the traditional morality "Vice" figure Ambidexter, who is both a type of the devil and a figure of the corrupt counselor who is a double-dealer. Ambidexter urges Cambyses to follow what appear to be his own violent instincts in murder and treachery, thus suggesting that he is at once a personification of Cambyses' own evil and an image of bad counsel. Cambyses' death comes unexpectedly, in a fall from a horse. It appears unmotivated but is moralized by the onstage spectators, and the whole play is offered as an object lesson for Elizabeth and her council. By the middle of the century, with plays like *Cambyses* as well as other hybrid plays that mixed chronicle or classical myth or history with morality, such as George Whetstone's *Promos and Cassandra* (1578), Richard Edwarde's *Damon and Pithias* (1571), John Pikering's *Horestes* (1567), and R. B.'s *Appius and Virginia* (1575), the school and aristocratic audiences of the moral interludes would be prepared to appreciate the stage career of tyrant or hero torn between half-allegorized, half-realistic antagonists who draw him toward a destiny of damnation or salvation. The career of king and hero is inseparable from the fate of the country and the lives of his subjects, and ultimately, a mirror for a audience of state.

Classical Models

English readers and audiences who would come face to face with Greek or Roman tragedy in the early sixteenth century would not have necessarily found it entirely foreign – and indeed, they might have been fully prepared to assimilate it to existing dramatic structures and values. The story of Greek tragedy's reception in the English Renaissance is both less well known than that of Seneca and ultimately less productive. The sixteenth century saw the production of some Latin translations of Greek tragedy (including Erasmus' two influential translations of *Hecuba* and *Iphigenia at Aulis* written when he was living in England from 1501 to 1506). The humanist and royal schoolmaster Roger Ascham was said to have translated *Philoctetes*, and Thomas Watson translated *Antigone* (see Cunliffe 1912: xlxxx; also Smith 1988: 224–6). Only one English translation of Euripides and one of Sophocles (Watson's) were published before 1600 (see Bolgar 1954: Appendix II), and a manuscript of Lady Lumley's translation of *Iphigenia at Aulis* survives to this day. For the most part these translations were purely literary and not done for the stage, although George Gascoigne's and Francis Kinwelmershe's *Jocasta* was performed at the Inns of Court in 1566[2] (see Smith 1988: 217), and the colleges of Oxford and Cambridge recorded stagings of Greek classical tragedy. Several scholars also adapted Euripidean models for biblical drama. The Scottish Humanist George Buchanan composed *Jepthes* and *Baptistes*, two Latin imitations of Euripides based on biblical themes and acted in French schools in the mid-1540s. Later in 1576 Buchanan informed his young charge James VI that *Baptistes* turns young people from popular theatrical fictions (*a vulgari fabularum scaenicarum*) toward the imitation of antiquity (*ad imitationem antiquitatis*) (Buchanan 1983: 97).

But, as Bruce Smith puts it, "Sophocles may have had academic snob appeal; Seneca pleased audiences" (Smith 1988: 204). The peak of the reception of Seneca was Thomas Newton's 1581 edition of the *Tenne Tragedies* of Seneca, translated into English by several different authors (the translations themselves date from 1559– 66). Seneca certainly had the potential to stultify Renaissance European tragedy, insofar as, in Gordon Braden's words, "the attempt to imitate Senecan drama directly at the level of the play as a whole, is still essentially a dead end; the general result is a static collection of formal speeches ... The rediscovery of tragedy through Seneca threatens to be its ossification" (Braden 1985: 104). Braden does see Seneca powerfully defining a rhetorical drama, when freed from "its treacherous dramaturgical casing," a liberation that allowed "its hyperbolic strain" to flourish (Braden 1985: 182).

Even in the sixteenth century, feelings about the value of Seneca's impact on the development of Elizabethan tragedy differed. Late Tudor writers also saw high-flown rhetoric as the hallmark of Seneca, but associated with it a grim presentational style. The Senecan stage is imagined as haunted by ghosts, dripping with blood, and sounding with cries to revenge. In his preface to Thomas Greene's *Menaphon*, Thomas

Nashe mocked English meddling with Seneca. He dismissed most English translators as poor Latin scholars, admitting

> yet English Seneca read by candle light yeeldes manie good sentences, as *Blood is a beggar*, and so foorth: and if you intreate him faire in a frostie morning, he will afford you whole *Hamlets*, I should say handfulls of tragical speeches: But o griefe! *tempus edax rerum*, what's that will last alwaies? The sea exhaled by droppes will in continuance be drie, and *Seneca* let bloud line by line and page by page, at length must needes die to our stage. (Greene 1589: 3r)

The *Hamlet* that Nashe refers to is not Shakespeare's, but certainly Shakespeare's *Hamlet* bears the marks of that bloody English Seneca, with its good "sentences" or pithy apothegms and florid speeches, not to mention the ghost of Hamlet's father who stalks the battlements of Elsinore.

Another significant feature of English Seneca was its obsession with the excesses of power. Like the original, with its typically Roman or historical subject matter, European neo-Senecan drama glories in the representation of tyranny and the violent exercise of power (see Braden 1985: 107–8). Thomas Newton was quite aware of this element of Seneca in the translations he brought together in his *Tenne Tragedies*. In his dedication he expressed his fear that his Seneca might at first be misread, as "literally tending (at the first sight) sometime to the prayse of Ambition, sometyme to the mayntenaunce of cruelty, now and then to approbation of incontinencie and here and there to the ratification of tyranny." Thus he worried that Seneca "cannot be digested without great daunger of infection." But he reassured his readers that one should not fear

> the direct meaning of Seneca himselfe, whose whole wrytinges (penned with a peerlesse sublimity and loftinesse of style, are so farre from countenauncing Vice, that I doubt whether there bee any amonge all the Catalogue of Heathen wryters, that with more gravity of Philosophicall sentences, more waightynesse of sappy [*sic*] words, or greater authority of sound matter beateth down sinne, loose lyfe, dissolute dealinge, and unbrydaled sensuality: or that more sensibly, pithily, and bytingly layeth doune the gue[r]don of filthy lust, cloaked dissimulation, and odious treachery: which is the dryft whereunto he leveleth the whole issue of ech one of his Tragedies. (Seneca 1927: 4–5)

Thus, like the morality plays, Seneca was seen as an antidote to unbridled power and the excess of vice, while it was posed a danger in so vividly representing them.

While one strain of interpretation of Seneca led to revenge tragedies, beginning with Thomas Kyd's *The Spanish Tragedy* (ca. 1584; see chapter 19 in this volume), another thus led to the shaping of political tragedies. The first notable example in this line was Thomas Norton's and Thomas Sackville's *Gorboduc, or Ferrex and Porrex*, acted at the Inn of Court in 1561 and before Queen Elizabeth at Whitehall in 1562 (see chapter 18 in this volume for an extensive discussion of this play). Indirectly modeled on Euripides' *Phoenician Women*, Thomas Hughes's *The Misfortunes of Arthur* (printed in 1587) used all the elements of Senecan rhetorical debate, the image of tyranny, and the theme of revenge, to stage the story of the defeat of Arthur and his tyrannical son Mordred (like *Gorboduc*, this play was performed before the queen). Arthur is introduced as the child of Uther Pendragon's adultery, while Mordred is the child produced by Arthur's incest with his sister Anne. Mordred arises as a tyrant when Arthur is away at war and takes Guinevere as his lover. As the play opens, the ghost of Gorlois, the betrayed husband of Uther Pendragon's lover, calls for revenge when Arthur returns. After attempts to reconcile them, Mordred and Arthur kill each other in a bloody civil war. Mordred himself is a composite of every Senecan tyrant (Hughes gives him all the best tyrant lines from Seneca), but Arthur, too is tainted by his descent from Uther Pendragon's adultery. The play is imbued with the kind of dark ambivalence and conflict that is the strongest expression of English Senecanism (see also Bushnell 1990: 103–5).

Whether read in the study or aristocratic "closet" or performed in the schools, universities, or Inns of Court, classical tragedy in its purest form remained "private" and not public drama, produced as a self-consciously literary and didactic genre for a limited audience. All of the dramatic genres discussed in this chapter so far were meant in some way to teach as well as to entertain: the mysteries, to unfold the events of the Bible and relate them to the lives of the citizens; the moralities, to reveal the evils that we must resist in order to be saved – or at least be virtuous; and the classical tragedies, to display the dangers of excess. Bruce Smith has argued that

> For all its fiery poetry, for all its fierce portrayal of social disaster and intense human suffering, classical tragedy was produced so as to confirm, not challenge, the values of the closed societies, the private sixteenth- and seventeenth-century households, who watched it. Seneca's Phaedra and Oedipus, Euripides' Creon and Eteocles, Sophocles' Antigone, Euripides' Orestes – the insistent individuality of these heroes was seen as a threat to established social values of moderation, obedience, and rationality and thus was not allowed to engage an audience's sympathy for long. In the hands of the earliest English producers, performance of Greek and Roman tragedy became a ritual in which indomitable individuals were ceremonially exorcised from the social order. (Smith 1988: 239)

It is significant that in their own time the popular audiences were understood to have little taste for such elevated fare. Ben Jonson often complained that his audiences were like pigs that preferred acorns to the pure wheat of classical drama (see his "Ode to Himselfe"). John Webster, in his preface to *The White Devil*, admitted that his play was "no true Drammaticke poem," but he protested that it was so intentionally, since his audience would not suffer it:

> for, should a man present to such an Auditory the most sententious Tragedy that ever was written, observing all the critticall lawes, as heigth of style; and gravety of person, inrich it with the sententious Chorus, and as it were, life'n Death, in the passionate and waighty Nuntius: yet, after all this divine rapture,...the breath that comes from the uncapable multitude, is able to poison it. (Webster 1612: A2r–A2v)

Since both men wrote wonderfully complex and sophisticated plays for the public stage, seen by people of many different ranks, one must be cautious of interpreting these statements as marking a clear distinction between the classical and vernacular that also matches an opposition between aristocratic and popular audiences. However, such a distinction certainly had some cultural significance in its time, and it continued to shape the profile of the English tragic theater, balanced between the sometimes conflicting drivers of commercial appeal, academic values, and aesthetic exploration.

The New Tragedy: Marlowe's *Tamburlaine* and *Doctor Faustus*

All this distributed theatrical energy of the school play, mystery cycle, inn-yard performance, and household entertainment continued to surge in the second half of the sixteenth century. Yet matters changed in London, first in 1567 with the building of the Red Lion Theater in Whitechapel, and then, more significantly, with the construction of the spectacular open Theater in Shoreditch in 1576 (see Gurr [1987] 1996: 13). In his massive history of *Early English Stages 1300–1660*, Glynne Wickham called the construction of this theater "a point towards which everything seems inexorably to move and after which those same things are never quite the same again" (Wickham 1959: I.xxix; see commentary by De Grazia 1997: 17–18). Built by James Burbage and John Brayne, the Theater in Shoreditch, with its polygonal structure and open galleries, set the model for the later amphitheatres that to at least one observer, Johannes De Witt, appeared to be in a Roman style (Gurr 1992: 132). While it echoed the older inn-yards and scaffold stages of the early moralities, it was also an imposing structure that could be seen as alluding to the classical past.

This theater thus situated the performance of English tragedy and comedy in a unique space that was very much its own while echoing both the vernacular and classical traditions. Its creation signaled a new freedom for professional playwrights and actors: as Margreta De Grazia puts it, "In 1576, it might be said, the theater became free to occupy its own time and space" (De Grazia 1997: 13). What the construction of this theater meant for the development of English tragedy is far more than can be explored in this short chapter. But it is crucial to note that the location of the theater in this space disentangled the plays performed there from the world of church, on the one hand, and that of the state and city on the other (while its relationship with the latter two institutions remained complex). While their companies still nominally operated under aristocratic or royal patronage, they were preeminently commercial, thriving on the attendance of all ranks of city folk and flourishing outside the halls of the universities, schools, and the aristocratic households that had defined the audiences and ends of the moral interludes. The acting companies were bound by the constraints of censorship, but their commercial orientation also pulled them toward the tastes and desires of this new audience. This new theater was also freed from any associations with the liturgical year and from any obligation to represent biblical material. The Shoreditch Theater, and those venues that replaced it, including the Swan, Rose, and Globe, while they competed with the bearbaiting pits and taverns that offered alternative city entertainment, encompassed an astonishing variety of theatrical themes and styles.

The early fortunes of these theaters are linked with that of their first great tragic playwright: Christopher Marlowe, whose own spectacular death from stab wounds received in a tavern brawl echoed the scandal of his plays. Consideration of Marlowe's *Tamburlaine* (1587) and *Doctor Faustus* (ca. 1590) offers a fitting conclusion for this chapter, which also serves as an introduction to the chapters on English Renaissance revenge tragedies and tragedies of state that follow. In calling his influential study of early sixteenth-century drama *From Mankind to Marlowe*, David Bevington marked a direct line from the morality tradition to the new tragedy of Marlowe, linking his "tragical" work to the tradition of the *Mankind*-style Psychomachia play and the hybrid chronicle of the *Cambyses* type (Bevington 1962: 198). But the plays of Marlowe also bore the marks of a new English classicism: a lofty rhetoric that owes far more to both Seneca and Ovid than to Skelton; and a hero whose aspirations to fortune, fame, or love far exceed the morality heroes' desires, both in magnitude and depth.

The two parts of *Tamburlaine* are advertised on the title page as the story of Tamburlaine the Great, "who from a Scythian Shepherde, by his rare and wonderfull Conquests, became a most puissant and mightye Monarque, And for his tyranny, and terrour in Warre was tearmed, The Scourge of God. Divided in two Tragicall Discourses, as they were sundrie times shewed upon Stages in the Citie of London" (the play's author was not named, as was typical at this time). The printer's preface, too, calls it a "tragical discourse," and also notes that in printing so "stately a history" the printer took care to leave out "some fond and frivolous gestures . . . far unmeet for the matter." This confession implies that the printer was aware that, at least in print, some lapse in decorum or "disgrace" would result from "mixing" high and low content.

In judging what was understood to be "tragic" in *Tamburlaine* we can look to the clues given by the prologue, which proclaims, in introducing the first part:

> From jigging veins of rhyming mother wits,
> And such conceits as clownage keeps in pay,
> We'll lead you to the stately tent of war,
> Where you shall hear the Scythian Tamburlaine
> Threatening the world with high astounding terms,
> And scourging kingdoms with his conquering sword.
> View but his picture in this tragic glass,
> And then applaud his fortunes as you please.
>   (Marlowe 1969: 109)

The qualities of *Tamburlaine* defined as tragic are primarily stylistic: both metrical (blank verse, not the "jigging veins of rhyming mother wits") and rhetorical ("high astounding terms"). Content also matters, for the prologue boasts of its display of the "stately tent of war" and Tamburlaine's relentless rise from base shepherd to world conqueror, subjecting mighty princes to defeat and humiliation.

But what does the reader/spectator see in "the tragic glass"? It depends on whether you are looking at Part One, Part Two, or the arc of both plays seen together. While scholars debate whether both plays were composed at once, the prologue to Part Two tells us that "the general welcomes Tamburlaine receiv'd / When he arrived last on our stage, / Have made our poet pen his Second Part" (Marlowe 1969: 183). Thus it would seem that, in fact, Marlowe originally intended his story of Tamburlaine to end, not with Tamburlaine's fall, but with his violent subjection of the kings of Arabia and Turkey and his marriage to the fair Zenocrate. What is "tragic" about that? Tamburlaine's upward trajectory proceeds without a pause, and the fall we witness, if any, is of the arrogant Turk Bajazeth, not of Tamburlaine.

The second part of *Tamburlaine* does follow its hero to his unanticipated death. Part Two traces his career of conquest (and his disappointment in his third son), climaxing in his siege of Babylon and burning of the Koran. Shortly thereafter he is stricken by a fatal illness. Some readers feel that we are to understand this end as precipitated by Tamburlaine's hubris, expressed in his defiance of the gods. Even in his sickness he cries out against them:

> Come, let us march against the powers of heaven
> And set black streamers in the firmament
> To signify the slaughter of the gods.
> Ah, friends, what shall I do? I cannot stand.
> Come, carry me to war against the gods,
> That thus envy the health of Tamburlaine.
>   (Marlowe 1969: *Tamburlaine*, 5.3.48–53)

Yet at the same time this breathless speech offers no indication of any clear cause of this sudden turn of fortune, other than his burning of the Koran. In Marlowe's time, any retribution for this act would surely be seen as ironic. There is little sense that either Marlowe or his audience condemned his hero (and indeed, the play was evidently wildly popular then). As an example to later playwrights, it had the power to define a secular tragedy that transcended simple moral formulae and played to an audience's desire to witness the shepherd triumphant, defeated only by death, "where death cuts off the progress of his pomp, / And murderous Fates throws all his triumphs down" (Marlowe 1969: *Tamburlaine* prologue, 4–5).

The Chorus of *The Tragical History of Doctor Faustus* self-consciously presents this play as a different sort of performance. It is not one where you will see the hero "sporting in the dalliance of love / In courts of kings where state is overturned, / Nor in the pomp of proud audacious deeds." Rather, as the Chorus says with wonderful ambiguity, it is the staging of "the form of Faustus' fortune, good or bad" (Marlowe 1969: Chorus, prologue 18–22). *Doctor Faustus* is a history of a man low born like Tamburlaine, who rose to the heights of scholarship and theology "excelling all," "till swol'n with cunning of a self-conceit, / His waxen wings" (Marlowe 1969: *Faustus*, prologue). In this sense, unlike *Tamburlaine*, *Doctor Faustus* set up the trajectory of its hero in terms of the tragic paradigm of Icarus, displaying a heroic ambition that soars above human limits – and which is punished by the "heavens." But the moral resonance of the play is far more complex than the Chorus would suggest.

The architecture of the play, which sets Faustus caught between the realms of Heaven and Hell, and the influences of Good and Bad angels, does set that classical plot motif of Icarus and a figure of Senecan ambition in an explicitly Christian universe. As Ruth Lunney comments on the division of critical opinion on the play, this generic hybridity can generate contradictory meanings:

> From one perspective of course Faustus remains just another conventional figure: readily typed (fool, "insatiable speculator"), his career an old-fashioned cautionary tale. Then again, the character is complex enough to satisfy the "commonsense" expectations of the 1590s audience. But his presentation before an audience is by no means coherent: when Faustus makes important choices, the action ranges from the up-to-date Senecan set-speech which opens the play, methodically surveying his career options like Gaveston or Richard of Gloucester; to the routine psychomachia late in the play where Mephistopheles threatens arrest and Faustus submits like a typical morality character; to the complex debate with himself in the final soliloquy. (Lunney 2002: 132–3)

This constant change in dramatic convention in the representation of Faustus's character, crossed with the shifting frame in which one scene is a tavern and the other the world overseen by Satan, results in proliferating interpretations, whereby one reader can claim that the play is severely Christian in outlook, true to its morality model, and another reader aver that it is daringly subversive, observing Faustus' excess and defiance (see Bluestone 1969; Dollimore [1984] 1989: ch. 6).

The interpretation of *Doctor Faustus* and our characterization of it as a tragedy is further complicated by the existence of two quite different texts of the play, neither of which has undisputed priority or authority: the A-text published in 1604 (ten years after Marlowe's death), which is sparer, and the B-text printed in 1616, which includes not only a great deal of comic business not in the 1604 version but also extra appearances by Lucifer and Beelzebub. Readers continue to debate about which is more "tragic." J. B. Steane expresses his preference for the A-text on the grounds that it

> has everything essential to the presentation of "the tragical history"; the B-text . . . adds, for the most part, light, simple-minded comedy, innocuous enough except that it distracts the mind from what is serious and valuable in the play; or rather, it fails to occupy the *mind* at all and so lessens the poetic and dramatic intensity. (Marlowe 1969: 261)

It can, however, be argued that the B-text's comic business, where Faustus's servants adapt his magic and manage to call forth Mephistopheles, brilliantly parodies Faustus's career and thus offers ironic commentary on it. In this sense, the B-text's mixture of modes, which evokes vernacular traditions, serves to define the style of English tragedy, and especially Shakespearean tragedy, where comic scenes complement and comment on the main plot. The world of English tragedy that *Doctor Faustus* defines, where popes and emperors are chased off the stage by hostlers and serving men, and where the specter of Helen of Troy shares a stage with Mephistopheles and Wagner the servant, is one that is rich in irony, even while it stretches to the very limits of belief. It is a world that is as much this world, a world of the historical present and the lives of the audience, as it is of myth and providence.

By the time Marlowe died in 1593, after writing *Edward II*, *Dido, Queen of Carthage*, *The Massacre of Paris*, and *The Jew of Malta*, in addition to *Faustus* and *Tamburlaine*, the audience of the London theaters had gained a taste for such tragedies that charted the spectacular careers of men – and women – who clawed their way to a victory that was also their disaster. In particular, they had learned, through Marlowe, Shakespeare, and the works of playwrights whose names we have now lost, how history could be staged as tragedy. In 1591, the anonymous *True Tragedy of Richard III* was performed; it was followed, near the time of Marlowe's death, by Shakespeare's *Richard III*, which was significantly named a tragedy and not a history play when it appeared in print in 1597. *Richard III* reeks far more of English Seneca than *Doctor Faustus*, in its formal structure, multiple ghosts, and set speeches, all drenched in the blood of Richard's murders. However, like *Faustus*, it is very much a story that an English audience would see as real – and as their own, even when it challenged the boundaries of the real. Like *Faustus*, too, *Richard III* was indebted to the conventions of the morality play, and its obsession with the moral downfall of a protagonist who in this case was the sovereign prince of England. English Seneca and moral interludes thus met to define a uniquely political tragedy in the English Renaissance.

In the end, then, we can see in these plays of the 1590s that, even while some might have felt compelled to take a side on the classics or vernacular, in fact, tragic playwrights, eager to please an audience that ranged from a queen to apprentices, borrowed from multiple sources and models. In this feverish time, a new tragic art was generated from the energy of a culture and society on the move, painfully conscious of the weight of the past but also with a growing confidence in the future of England. Tragedy was to become one of the arts of the new age that at once expressed its deepest anxieties and recorded its greatness.

Notes

1 The key texts were Francesco Robortello's *In Librum Aristotelis De arte poetica explications* (1548), Giambattista Giraldi's *Discoursi* (1554), the *De poeta* of Sebastiano Minturno (1559), and the *Poetice libri septem* (1561) of Julius Caesar Scaliger (Sidney's source was Lodovico Castelvetro's *Poetica De'Aristotele vul-garizzata e sposta* from 1570) (see Cunliffe 1912: xliv–xlvii).

2 This *Jocasta* was a version of Euripides' *Phoenician Women* based on Ludovico Dolce's Italian *Giocasta*, adapted in turn from a Latin translation of Euripides' play.

REFERENCES AND FURTHER READING

Bevington, David M. (1962). *From Mankind to Marlowe: Growth of Structure in the Popular Drama of Tudor England*. Cambridge, MA: Harvard University Press. A comprehensive study of the morality plays and their influence on later Tudor tragedy and comedy.

Bluestone, Max. (1969). "Libido Speculandi: Doctrine and Dramaturgy in Contemporary Interpretations of Marlowe's *Doctor Faustus*." In *Reinterpretations of Elizabethan Drama*, ed. Norman Rabkin. New York and London: Columbia University Press, 33–88. A survey of conflicting interpretations of Marlowe's plays.

Bolgar, R. R. (1954). *The Classical Heritage and its Beneficiaries*. Cambridge: Cambridge University Press. A survey of the influence of Greek and Roman literature on later European culture.

Braden, Gordon. (1985). *Anger's Privilege: Renaissance Tragedy and the Senecan Tradition*. New Haven, CT and London: Yale University Press. A study of Seneca's tragedies and their influence on European drama.

Buchanan, George. (1983). *George Buchanan: Tragedies*, ed. P. Sharratt and P. G. Walsh. Edinburgh: Scottish Academic Press. The Latin versions and translations of Buchanan's neoclassical tragedies.

Bushnell, Rebecca W. (1990). *Tragedies of Tyrants: Political Thought and Theater in the English Renaissance*. Ithaca, NY and London: Cornell University Press. A study of the complex development of the image of the tyrant in English Renaissance theater.

Clopper, Lawrence W. [1999] (2002). "English Drama: From Ungodly *Ludi* to Sacred Play." In *The Cambridge History of Medieval English Literature*, ed. David Wallace. Cambridge: Cambridge University Press, 739–66. An essay on development of the mystery plays.

Cunliffe, John W., ed. (1912). *Early English Classical Tragedies*. Oxford: Clarendon Press. A thorough survey of early English imitations of classical tragedy.

Cunningham, J. V. [1951] (1964). *Woe or Wonder: The Emotional Effect of Shakespearean Tragedy*. Chicago: Swallow Press. Provides a helpful background on the medieval and classical notion of the tragic.

De Grazia, Margreta. (1997). "World Pictures, Modern Periods, and the Early Stage." In *A New History of Early English Drama*, ed. John D. Cox and David Scott Kastan. New York: Columbia University Press, 7–21. An essay on the significance of the new Shoreditch Theater and theater in general in London.

Dollimore, Jonathan. [1984] (1989). *Radical Tragedy: Religion, Ideology and Power in the Drama of Shakespeare and his Contemporaries*. New York: Harvester Wheatsheaf. A cultural materialist interpretation of the politics of English Renaissance tragedy.

Greene, Robert. (1589). *Menaphon*. London: Printed by T[homas] O[rwin] for Sampson Clarke.

Gurr, Andrew. (1992). *The Shakespearean Stage 1574–1642*. Cambridge: Cambridge University Press. A comprehensive history of the development of the English Renaissance theatrical space.

Gurr, Andrew. [1987] (1996). *Playgoing in Shakespeare's London*. Cambridge: Cambridge University Press. A study of the nature and habits of the early modern English theatrical audience.

Happé, Peter, ed. [1979] (1987). *Four Morality Plays*. Harmondsworth and New York: Penguin. Includes *The Castle of Perseverance*, Skelton's *Magnyfycence*, Bale's *King Johan*, and Lindsay's *Ane Satire of the Thrie Estaitis*.

Happé, Peter. (1999). *English Drama before Shakespeare*. London and New York: Longman. A survey of all forms of early English drama.

Helms, Lorraine. (1997). *Seneca by Candlelight and Other Stories of Renaissance Drama*. Philadelphia: University of Pennsylvania Press. An exploration of the performative dimensions of Senecan rhetoric.

Lunney, Ruth. (2002). *Marlowe and the Popular Tradition: Innovation in the English Drama Before 1595*. Manchester and New York: Manchester University Press. A new approach to Marlowe's adaptation of popular and morality tradition.

Marlowe, Christopher. (1590). *Tamburlaine the Great*. London: Richard Ihones.

Marlowe, Christopher. (1969). *Christopher Marlowe: The Complete Plays*, ed. J. B. Steane. Harmondsworth and New York: Penguin.

Preston, Thomas. (1570 [date conjectured by the Short Title Catalogue]). *A lamentable tragedy mixed ful of pleasant mirth, conteyning the life of Cambises king of Percia*. London: John Allde.

Seneca, ed. Thomas Newton. [1581] (1927). *Seneca: His Tenne Tragedies*, translated into English. Bloomington and London: Indiana University Press.

Sidney, Sir Philip, ed. J. A. Van Dorsten. [1595] (1966). *A Defence of Poetry*. Oxford: Oxford University Press.

Smith, Bruce R. (1988). *Ancient Scripts & Modern Experience on the English Stage 1500–1700*. Princeton, NJ: Princeton University Press. A reconsideration of the significance of imitation of classical drama in Renaissance England.

Webster, John. (1612). *The White Devil*. London: Printed by N[icholas] O[kes] for Thomas Archer.

Weimann, Robert. (1978). *Shakespeare and the Popular Tradition in the Theater: Studies in the Social Dimension of Dramatic Form and Function*, ed. Robert Schwartz. Baltimore, MD and London: Johns Hopkins University Press. An influential Marxist study of the popular dramatic tradition.

Wickham, Glynne. (1959). *Early English Stages 1300 to 1660*, 2 vols. London: Routledge & Kegan Paul. An all-inclusive survey of the development of medieval and Renaissance English theatrical practice.

Woolf, Rosemary. (1972). *The English Mystery Plays*. Berkeley and Los Angeles: University of California Press. A survey of the life span of the English mystery plays.

18

Something is Rotten: English Renaissance Tragedies of State

Matthew H. Wikander

"Something is rotten in the state of Denmark," Marcellus famously murmurs as Hamlet goes off to confer in private with the Ghost (*Hamlet* 1.4.90). In this remark, as in Horatio's speculation that the Ghost bears a primarily political message, Shakespeare refers to a long tradition in early modern English drama in which the state, often "gored" (*King Lear* 5.3.326), "tottering" (*Richard III* 3.2.37), and "practiced dangerously against" (*2 Henry VI* 2.1.174), is personified as fully human, having a body, with "nerves" (*Measure for Measure* 1.4.53), a "navel" (*Coriolanus* 3.1.126), an "ear" (*Hamlet* 1.5.37) and, of course, a head. Subject to disease, *corruption* in a medical sense of the word, the state can sicken, languish for want of a cure, and die. Mismanaged and erring, the state can hurl itself into self-destruction and disaster. The state, the realm, the kingdom, can turn on itself, dismember itself, and die.

In the early morality plays, the state could indeed appear as a character, like the allegorized figure of *Respublica* in the play of that name by Nicholas Udall (1553). A widowed, female character, Respublica is tempted by Avarice and his fellow Vices. These are indeed, as A. P. Rossiter would have put it, "flat Abstractions masking as characters" (Rossiter 1946: 9), and the eventual "squeezing" of Avarice by the People is straightforward both as political propaganda and as morality drama. A more complex representation of the body politic, with an expressly tragic as well as political agenda, can be found in the very first English verse tragedy, Sackville and Norton's *Gorboduc*.

Gorboduc

In a recent study, Greg Walker declares:

> *Gorboduc* is rightly considered a landmark in English literary history. . . . As the earliest extant five-act verse tragedy in English, the earliest attempt to imitate Senecan tragic form in English, the earliest surviving English drama in blank verse, and the earliest English play to adopt the use of dumb-shows preceding each act, it offers itself as a

point of departure for much of the Renaissance dramatic experimentation of the following decades. (1998: 201)

The play was performed at Christmas 1561, in the Inner Temple at the Inns of Court, and received a repeat performance in January 1562, before Queen Elizabeth I, at Whitehall. Its two authors, Thomas Sackville and Thomas Norton, were powerful courtiers, with political as well as literary aspirations, though Sackville was also well known as a contributor to the *Mirror for Magistrates*, a series of cautionary, *de casibus*, or fall-of-princes tales for rulers that was a bestseller through the Elizabethan period. Recent scholarship, by Walker and by Marie Axton, has emphasized the very specific ways in which *Gorboduc* spoke directly to the issue of the Queen's reluctance to marry and championed her English favorite, Robert Dudley, Earl of Leicester, over the Swedish suitor, King Erik XIV, whose representative, Lord Nils Gyllenstjerna (the original Guildenstern), had led marriage missions to England in 1560 and 1562 (see Walker 1998; Axton 1977). *Gorboduc* has long been studied for its position of generic primacy and its importance as an extremely early English tragedy, but its performance at a pivotal moment in Elizabeth's and Leicester's careers marks how deeply embedded English drama was in the life of the polity.

The play's plot is derived from Geoffrey of Monmouth's *Historia Regium Britanniae* (*History of Britain*, ca. 1137); it treats an episode that is one of several tragic errors reported by Geoffrey, in which the ruler of Britain foolishly divides the island into separate kingdoms. The first of these rulers in Geoffrey's account is Brut, according to legend the great-grandson of Aeneas, the founder of Rome. Unlike Aeneas, Brut determined that the future of empire lay elsewhere, and took his party to the island which he named after himself, as Brutoyne or Britain. At his death, he sought to divide the kingdom fairly among his three sons – Albanius, Logris, and Camber, identified with Scotland, England, and Wales. The result was civil war. Gorboduc, the king who retires at the beginning of the play and parts the realm between his two sons Ferrex and Porrex, is a direct descendant of Brut and an ancestor to King Leir (or Lear), who reenacts this fatal family mistake, angrily splitting the kingdom between his two sons-in-law after his favorite, unmarried daughter, Cordelia, disappoints him by refusing to declare her love with sufficient fervor.

Gorboduc thus by happy coincidence enjoys originary status, both as the first of its kind, but also as a tragedy of origins, a play that dramatizes the fall of Britain from an imagined paradisal unity to civil war and division. The play's authors clearly intended its royal audience member to draw the appropriate lesson from its presentation before her of a primal British monarch who arranged the succession foolishly, and to avoid his error by marrying prudently and promptly. *Gorboduc*'s way of teaching this lesson is closely connected with the morality tradition, as the dumb shows before each act indicate. Each plays out the allegorical significance of the scenes that follow, and the published versions of the play (an unauthorized edition in 1565 and a corrected version in 1570) are particularly insistent. For example, in the dumb show (panto-mime) before the first act, six wild men enter and attempt unsuccessfully to break a bundle of sticks; then they take each stick separately and break them one by one. "Hereby was signified that a state knit in unity doth continue strong against all force, but being divided is easily destroyed; as befell King Gorboduc dividing his land to his two sons, which he before held in monarchy, and upon the dissension of the brethren to whom it was divided" (83). The first dumb show points, as does the Brut legend, to the appropriation of Roman legends and motifs to British folk material, as wild men of the woods attack the Roman *fasces*.

Inflamed by ill counsel and ambition, Ferrex kills Porrex; he in turn is killed by his mother, and she and Gorboduc are slain by a popular rebellion. The lords who remain face the threat of imminent conquest by Fergus, "the mighty Duke of Albany" (5.2.76), and they vow to resist. But more saliently, with a view to Queen Elizabeth's succession, the lords swear, once they have "with armed force repressed / The proud attempts of this Albanian prince" (5.2.137–8) to "have pity of the torn estate" and "help to salve the well-near hopeless sore" by meeting "in parliament" and awarding the crown to a "chosen king...born within your native land" (148, 150, 158, 169–70). Before such a wished-for end, however, Britain must suffer, as Eubulus, one of the sage advisors whom the king has disregarded, points out:

> Thus shall the wasted soil yield forth no fruit,
> But dearth and famine shall possess the land.
> The towns shall be consumed and burnt with fire,
> And peopled cities shall wax desolate;
> And thou, O Britain, whilom in renown,
> Whilom in wealth and fame, shalt thus be torn,
> Dismembered thus; and thus be rent in twain,
> Thus wasted and defaced, spoiled and destroyed.
> These be the fruits your civil wars shall bring.
> Hereto it comes when kings will not consent
> To grave advice, but follow willful will.
>
> (5.2.225 35)

Eubulus prophesies a future of civil war, with Britain personified as a dismembered, torn, and barren body politic.

Such a future is envisioned, too, by the Chorus at the end of Shakespeare's *Henry V*. After the marriage and peace that conclude that play, the Chorus reminds the regular theatergoers of Shakespeare's London:

> Henry the Sixth, in infant bands crowned King
> Of France and England, did this king succeed;
> Whose state so many had the managing.
> That they lost France and made his England bleed,
> Which oft our stage hath shown; and for their sake.
> In your fair minds let this acceptance take.
>
> (*Henry V* Epilogue, 9–14)

Here the playwright alludes to the highly popular sequence of plays dealing with the loss of France and the Wars of the Roses in England, the three parts of *Henry VI* and *Richard III*. Just as *Gorboduc* grounds early modern English tragedy in the sufferings of the common weal, the English history plays represent the realm as victim and protagonist playing out a tragic fate.

Tragical History

Shakespeare's early histories

In categorizing the genres of Shakespearean drama as Comedy, Tragedy, and History, the editors of the First Folio paid tribute to the prominence in the late sixteenth century and first decade of the seventeenth of plays that drew their stories (or fables) from the enormously popular narrative chronicles of Edward Halle and Raphael Holinshed. These sources were characterized by twentieth-century scholars as propagating a "Tudor myth," a version of English history which runs something like this: the deposition of Richard II by Henry Bolingbroke (later Henry IV) was a kind of original sin, an act which ushered in a period of uncertainty for Henry IV, whose troubles included not only civil unrest in the North and in Wales, but also the drunken and riotous behavior of his son. A brief period of glory ensued with the reign of Henry V, who reformed his manners when he took the throne and restored England's dominions in France. Henry's untimely death, leaving a son "in infant bands," led to the Wars of the Roses, as the houses of York and Lancaster contended for power. Finally, England's suffering reached a nadir with the emergence of Richard III, whose tyrannous abuse of the people came to an end with the victory of Henry Tudor, earl of Richmond (later Henry VII) at the Battle of Bosworth Field. The power of this coherent narrative led A. P. Rossiter to argue that "it may be said that one way at least of composing a history-play in the XVIth Century was to read chronicle with a preconceived or ready-made moral in mind," and that this moral was one that ratified the current Tudor regime (Rossiter 1946: 8).

More recent critics have taken issue with the idea that the chronicle plays merely served the power structure as homilies on obedience. The New Historicist critics have seen the history plays as part of a dynamic of subversion and containment, functioning to express anxieties about the government's absolutist tendencies while participating, as part of the institution of theater, in the government's strategies of marginalizing, distracting, and containing political dissent (see Greenblatt 1980). The refusal of the plays fully to dramatize the Tudor myth has long been noted.

The generic uncertainty that accompanied the publication (and no doubt performance) of the early English history plays has been obscured by the Folio's classification of them as a separate genre. In reality, the situation was a "Polonian nightmare," to borrow Steve Longstaffe's terms, in which tragical–historical–comical–pastoral merged and diffused in wildly unstable combinations (Longstaffe 1997: 35). The version of Shakespeare's *Henry VI, Part Two* that appeared in 1594 was called *The First Part of the Contention betwixt the two famous Houses of Yorke and Lancaster, with the death of the good Duke Humphrey: And the banishment and death of the Duke of Suffolke, and the Tragicall End of the Proud Cardinall of Winchester, with the notable Rebellion of Jack Cade: and the Duke of Yorkes first claime unto the Crowne.* The unwieldiness of this title is in part a function of the printer's desire to touch on all the play's features that might make this book a quick seller, but it also shows an uncertainty about where to place the emphasis, not least with regard to the problem of tragedy: of all the deaths mentioned, only one is singled out as "tragicall." The 1595 version of what we now call *Henry VI, Part Three* appeared as *The True Tragedie of Richard Duke of Yorke, and the death of the good King Henrie the Sixt, with the whole contention between the two Houses Lancaster and Yorke, as it was sundrie times acted by the Right Honourable the Earle of Pembroke his Servants.* In their *Original-Spelling Edition* of Shakespeare's works, the Oxford editors Stanley Wells and Gary Taylor have restored these old titles.

The Contention plays (as these two are sometimes called) show tragedy emerging out of the historical matrix. In these plays, as in *Gorboduc,* the realm is personified, and it is difficult to see by what criteria some deaths are tragic and some are not. York meets his end, in *The True Tragedie,* at the end of the first act, set upon a molehill, crowned with a paper crown, taunted by Queen Margaret, in a scene reminiscent of (and parodic of) the plays of the mocking of Christ in the medieval mystery cycles. The scene is mirrored later in the play by a scene in which King Henry, likewise on a molehill, witnesses the sad spectacle of a "Son that hath killed his father" entering "at one door," and, entering "at another door, a Father that hath killed his son." The pathos of these generic, allegorized figures comments on and amplifies the agony of York, whom Margaret torments with a napkin dipped in his son's blood and who is killed by Clifford to avenge Clifford's father's death. As King Henry comments on the scene, it becomes a metaphor for civil strife:

> O, pity, pity, gentle heaven, pity!
> The red rose and the white are in his face,
> The fatal colors of our striving houses.
> The one his purple right resembles;
> The other his pale cheeks, methinks, presenteth.
> Wither one rose, and let the other flourish;
> If you contend, a thousand lives must wither.
> (*2 Henry VI* 2.5.96–102)

At the end of the play, King Edward sits in the throne and describes his victory as a harvest: "What valiant foemen, like to autumn's corn, / Have we mowed down in tops of all their pride!" (5.7.3–4). Edward marks his own overweening pride as he arrogates to himself the function of mowing down the proud, a function reserved to the divine order in the *de casibus* tradition. "I'll blast his harvest," mutters the king's younger brother, Richard of Gloucester, as Edward presents his son to the court (21).

Richard III

Richard's own play, published in 1597 as *The Tragedy of King Richard the Third* (but classified among the Histories in the Folio), marks the appearance in Shakespeare's work of a powerful central character whose actions precipitate the tragic plot. The overreaching protagonists of Christopher Marlowe's plays contributed to the emergence of such characters, as David Riggs has pointed out (see Riggs 1971). But Richard is composed of a variety of elements, in addition to being a Marlovian overreacher. Like the morality-play Vice, Iniquity, Richard can "moralize two meanings in one word" (*Richard III* 3.1.83); he can "set the murderous Machiavel to school" (*3 Henry VI* 3.2.193); his physical deformities derive from Thomas More's life of Richard III incorporated within the chronicle sources of the play. It is hard to overestimate the full impact of the emergence of this charming monster upon the development of English tragedy. Shakespeare faced a particular problem in adapting this figure to the demands of the historical narrative the play needed to follow. For the play's political agenda requires that Richard be a monstrous tyrant, and the earl of Richmond's victory at Bosworth Field a providential deliverance of the suffering realm; yet Shakespeare imbues the character with such energy, wit, and exuberance that audiences, like Lady Anne in the wooing scene at the beginning of the play, find him almost irresistible.

Through a sequence of sub-tragedies – the deaths of Clarence, Hastings, the little Princes in the Tower, and Buckingham – Shakespeare surrounds Richard with choric utterances proclaiming his inevitable doom in this great harvest of death. The murder of the Princes marks a turning point in Richard's career, as he ascends the throne only to overreach in seeking to control the succession and stifle Edward's line. Buckingham, his alter ego, refuses the assignment, and Richard enlists the aid of Tyrrel, who himself subcontracts the murder to Dighton and Forrest, "fleshed villains, bloody dogs." "The tyrannous and bloody act is done," Tyrrel announces, "The most arch deed of piteous massacre that ever this land was guilty of" (4.3.6, 1–2). Richard's worst crime becomes by metaphoric extension one of the land's many massacres, engulfed in the Wars of the Roses. The little Princes figure peace and reconciliation forestalled and denied in Forrest's account of their sleep,

> girdling one another
> Within their alabaster innocent arms.
> Their lips were four red roses on a stalk,
> Which in their summer beauty kissed each other.
> (9–12)

The evocation here of white (alabaster) and red roses looks back to Henry VI's meditation on the Father and the Son, and the seasonal imagery, picking up from Richard's famous description of the Civil Wars as a "winter of our discontent" (1.1.1), anticipates Richmond's oration at the end of the play, which predicts a return to "smiling plenty, and fair prosperous days" (5.5.34–5). Richmond offers a narrative in which the Wars of the Roses can come to a final end with his marriage to Elizabeth of York, and in which the realm can finally come to its senses:

> England hath long been mad, and scarred herself;
> The brother blindly shed the brother's blood,
> The father rashly slaughtered his own son,
> The son, compelled, been butcher to the sire.
> All this divided York and Lancaster,
> Divided in their dire division.
>
> (5.5.22–7)

The imagery presents the country's return to health as part of a natural process of healing and harvest.

Yet this is a language that Richard repeatedly mocks as he sabotages Edward's harvest and arranges his brother Clarence's demise. Edward himself proposed his reign as a restoration of natural balance at the end of *3 Henry VI*; so we are entitled to see Richmond's declaration of closure as provisional, with the language of nature leaving open the possibility of another cycle of the seasons. One way Shakespeare works to suggest that Richard's end really *is* the end of the vicious round of violence is to contrive it so that Richard self-destructs as soon as he gains the throne. The murder of the Princes loses him his one ally, Buckingham; and subsequent events in the play are marked by blundering and stumbling, carelessness unthinkable in the conniving Proteus of the play's first acts. His wooing of Elizabeth by proxy through her mother is a pale imitation of his triumphant suit to Lady Anne, and he seems not to realize that the Queen has no intention of surrendering her daughter to him (she immediately arranges the match with Richmond). A series of Senecan ghosts menace him with threats in the scene of the night before the battle. Shakespeare splits the stage, with Richard's tent on one side and Richmond's on the other. Richard's victims both enter, each intoning "Despair, and die!" to Richard and each offering words of encouragement to Richmond.

The split stage evokes the divided realm, but the vengeful ghosts remind us of Richard's private wrongs, his crimes against them personally. And the split is further dramatized as a split within Richard himself, as he awakes from his sleep:

> What do I fear? Myself? There's none else by.
> Richard loves Richard; that is, I am I.
> Is there a murderer here? No. Yes, I am.
> Then fly. What, from myself? Great reason why:
> Lest I revenge. What, myself upon myself?
> Alack, I love myself. Wherefore? For any good
> That I myself have done unto myself?
> O, no! Alas, I rather hate myself
> For hateful deeds committed by myself!

I am a villain. Yet I lie, I am not.
Fool, of thyself speak well. Fool, do not flatter.

                                        (5.3.182–92)

This representation of Richard's splintering psyche is almost comical in its explicit-
ness, as Richard virtually comes to blows with himself. The riddling self that Richard
reveals in his soliloquies and asides becomes here a self-contradictory self; not a Vice
moralizing two meanings in a single word, but an "I" that cannot recognize or
acknowledge any integrity of self.

Richard is indicted by a multiplicity of tongues: "a thousand several tongues"
testify against him in his conscience, "and every tongue brings in a several tale, / And
every tale condemns me for a villain" (193–5). Through this internalized juridical
process, Richard's conscience links the ghosts' vengeance for their private wrongs to a
communal, public justice. The play works both as Tudor myth, shoring up the polity
by dramatizing Richmond's rise to power as inevitable and just, and as tragedy, by
dramatizing Richard's fall as the inevitable consequence of his divided, unstable, self-
loathing self.

Sad Stories of the Deaths of Kings

Richard II

Shakespeare's Richard II, unlike Richard III, is not a usurper or a Marlovian overreacher. He sees his fall as fully within the *de casibus* tradition, and urges his
supporters to join him:

> For God's sake, let us sit upon the ground
> And tell sad stories of the death of kings–
> How some have been deposed, some slain in war,
> Some haunted by the ghosts they have deposed,
> Some poisoned by their wives, some sleeping killed,
> All murdered. For within the hollow crown
> That rounds the mortal temple of a king
> Keeps death his court, and there the antic sits
> Scoffing his state and grinning at his pomp,
> Allowing him a breath, a little scene,
> To monarchize, be feared, and kill with looks.
> Infusing him with self and vain conceit,
> As if this flesh which walls about our life
> Were brass impregnable, and humored thus,
> Comes at the last with a little pin
> Bores through his castle wall, and – farewell king!
>
>   (*Richard II* 3.2.155–70)

There is a delightful reference here to the previous stage triumph of *Richard III*, haunted by the ghosts of his predecessors, and to his scoffing, grinning, antic ways. But more characteristic of mature Shakespeare is the development of a pattern of imagery through the whole play that allows us to see in the second Richard a complex dramatic evocation of the political doctrine of the king's two bodies, a mortal body which can die, and a body politic, which lives on in the kingdom.

In this speech we hear an echo of John of Gaunt's famous "sceptr'd isle" speech. The walls of the impregnable body that Richard describes in the speech cited above are celebrated as the country's walls in Gaunt's invocation of England as a

> fortress built by Nature for herself
> Against infection and the hand of war,
> This happy breed of men, this little world,
> This precious stone set in the silver sea,
> Which serves it in the office of a wall
> Or as a moat defensive to a house,
> Against the envy of less happier lands,
> This blessed plot, this earth, this realm, this England
> This nurse, this teeming womb of royal kings . . .
> Is now leased out – I die pronouncing it –
> Like to a tenement or pelting farm.
>   (*Richard II* 2.1.42–52, 59–60)

Both speeches are rich with references to containment, to enclosure: the hollow crown and the castle walls in Richard's; the wall, the moat, the ring-setting in John of Gaunt's. Emptiness awaits the Duchess of Gloucester when she returns to her castle at Pleshey: "empty lodgings and unfurnished walls / Unpeopled offices, untrodden stones" (1.2.68–9). The Queen's complaint of an "unborn sorrow ripe in Fortune's womb" that she senses "coming towards me" (2.2.10–11) links up with the "teeming womb" of Gaunt's speech. The enclosing castle walls, bodies, theaters, islands, wombs, oscillate in a kaleidoscopic vision in which King Richard both is and is not contiguous and coterminous with his own body, the body of his kingdom, and the body of his wife.

Recent feminist criticism, especially the work of Coppélia Kahn, Phyllis Rackin, and Jean E. Howard, has seen the conflict between Richard and Bolingbroke in *Richard II* as a clash of gendered opposites (see Kahn 1981 and Howard and Rackin 1997). Richard is effeminately self-dramatizing, kneeling to mother earth; Bolingbroke phallically ascendant, taking the crown from the vain, weeping king. The conflation of crown, kingdom, womb, theater, castle, and farm in this particular cluster of images tends to support an identification of Richard as slipping elusively from male to female roles, playing the king and playing the "mockery king of snow" (4.1.261), being himself both the wearer of the hollow crown and the antic death grinning within it.

Imprisoned at the end of the play, Richard fantasizes tearing "a passage through the flinty ribs / Of this hard world, my ragged prison walls" (5.5.20–1). In the context of his attempt to "people this little world" (9) with a "generation of still-breeding thoughts" (8), Richard imagines himself giving birth to himself, a doubling of himself into "king," "beggar," and then, finally, "nothing":

> But whate'er I be,
> Nor I, nor any man that but man is,
> With nothing shall be pleased till he be eased
> With being nothing.
>
> (38–41)

Richard's prison soliloquy offers a vision of teeming barrenness that looks back to all the enclosures ranging through the play's imagery – the sceptered isle, the hollow crown, the empty rooms of Pleshey and the Queen's empty womb – to figure his deposition and death within a large scheme of dispossession and containment that alienates him from both his body politic and his physical body. "Exton, thy fierce hand / Hath with the King's own blood stained the King's own land," he charges his murderer. "Mount, mount my soul! Thy seat is up on high, / While my gross flesh sinks downward, here to die." Richard's last words triumphantly recall the doctrine of the king's two bodies, so shattered, fragmented, and unstable (like the mirror he breaks in the deposition scene) throughout the play. And the land, feminized and bloody, continues to haunt his successor Henry IV at the beginning of his first play. Carlisle's prophecy in the deposition scene – "The blood of English shall manure the ground / And future ages groan for this foul act... And in this seat of peace tumultuous wars / Shall here inhabit, and kin with kin and kind with kind confound" 4.1.138–9, 141–2) – strikes home as Henry's desire to end civil war proves bootless. "No more the thirsty entrance of this soil / Shall daub her lips with her own children's blood," he wishfully intones in the first scene of *1 Henry IV*; "No more shall trenching war channel her fields / Nor bruise her flowerets with the armèd hoofs / Of hostile paces" (1.1.4–8). No, as in *Gorboduc*, peace is not to come; the English hold "the knife" at their "own mother's throat" (*Gorboduc* 5.2.151).

In *Richard III*, Shakespeare reconciles tragedy to history by conflating private vengeance and public justice in Richard's indictment by conscience. In *Richard II* he makes of Richard's fall and Bolingbroke's ascent a ravaging assault upon the female body of the land. By the end of the second tetralogy, this feminized land, "this best garden of the world" (*Henry V* V.2.36), has become France. Gaunt's fantasy of English Christian knights teeming forth on crusades, Henry IV's fantasy of an expedition to the Holy Land, turn England's "opposed eyes" outward, but the conquest of France sounds like another mutilation, an extension of England's civil wars out to her annexed conquest, and the Chorus compounds the irony with its prophetic reminder to the audience that what it has just seen is a prequel to the agonies of the first tetralogy.

Marlowe's *Edward II*

The relationship between Christopher Marlowe's *Edward II* (first published in 1598 as *The Troublesome Raigne and Lamentable Death of Edward the Second, King of England: with the tragicall fall of proud Mortimer*) and Shakespeare's first and second tetralogies is a complicated one (see Forker 1994: 18). Many early critics of Marlowe found the play to be anomalous: most of Marlowe's overreachers were felt to enact their crimes on a cosmic rather than national scale. Harry Levin's assertion that in *Edward II* Marlowe "was to bring the chronicle within the perspective of tragedy, to adapt the most public of forms to the most private of emotions" (quoted by Forker 1994: 90–1) assumes a primacy for Marlowe's play that the available evidence cannot support. Examining the relationships among *Edward II*, the first tetralogy, and the anonymous *Woodstock* (also known as the first part of *Richard II*), A. P. Rossiter, like Forker and other recent editors, notes a matrix of borrowings and lendings that, if not precisely collaboration and not exactly plagiarism, confounds older notions of authorship and current notions of intellectual property.

Nor is it accurate to say that Marlowe's dramatic output, with the exception of *Edward II*, was generally apolitical. Tamburlaine, after all, aspires towards "that perfect bliss and sole felicity / The sweet fruition of an earthly crown" (*Tamburlaine the Great I* 2.7.28–9). Faustus imagines walling "all Germany with brass," transforming Wittenberg into a Protestant island by circling it with the "swift Rhine," and "chas[ing] the Prince of Parma from our land," and his magician friend Valdes covets "from America the golden fleece / That yearly stuffs old Phillip's treasury" (*Doctor Faustus* 1.1.90, 91, 95,133–4). The Doctor works his magic in the Emperor's and Pope's courts. Lisa Hopkins has showed how deeply Marlowe's plays engage issues of immediate political concern to his audiences. Tamburlaine's conquests mark a kind of European imperialism in reverse, as his troops encroach on Christendom and as he dies looking "westward from the midst of Cancer's line": "And shall I die, and this unconquerèd?" (*Tamburlaine the Great II* 146, 150.) The Malta in which the Jew practices his Machiavellian schemes is, Hopkins points out, a very specifically historical Malta; and *The Massacre at Paris* is firmly grounded in the atrocities of the French religious wars (see Hopkins 2000).

Whichever way the influence went, *Edward II* participates in the tradition of *Gorboduc*, in which the King's crimes lead to suffering in both the body politic and the King's own private body. "England, unkind to thy nobility, / Groan for this grief; behold how thou art maimed," Mortimer proclaims as Warwick and Lancaster are taken off to "speedy execution" (*Edward II* 3.2.66–7). The conflict between Edward and the powerful nobles in the play over Edward's dependency on his favorites is recast in terms of a maiming of the body politic. Similarly, Queen Isabella, landed in England, moralizes the conflict: "a heavy case,

> When force to force is knit and sword and glaive
> In civil broils makes kin and countrymen

> Slaughter themselves in others, and their sides
> With their own weapons gored. But what's the help?
> Misgoverned kings are cause of all this wrack;
> And Edward, thou art one among them all,
> Whose looseness hath betrayed thy land to spoil
> And made the channels overflow with blood.
> Of thine own people patron shouldst thou be,
> But thou—

"Nay, madam, if you be a warrior," Mortimer interrupts, "Ye must not grow so passionate in speeches" (4.4.4–15). In both these instances, speeches whose homiletic content might be choric are ironically undercut by Mortimer's ambition and the Queen's own ruthless quest for power. The language of civil broils and internecine slaughter is here exposed as propagandistic, just as Henry IV's repeated invocation of this language serves to remind us of his unsteady, shaken grasp on power.

Edward's terrible death, by means of a red-hot spit forced into his bowels (see Forker 1994: 306–7 for discussion of the sources and possible staging), has been the source of much critical controversy. There are those who see it as a horribly appropriate end for a sodomite and a moral lesson taught on the king's body, but appropriate as well to the "unnatural state of the realm" (W. L. Godschalk, quoted by Forker 1994: 93). Stephen Greenblatt takes issue with such moralistic readings, and argues that "in *Edward II* Marlowe uses the emblematic method of admonitory drama, but uses it to such devastating effect that the audience recoils from it in disgust" (quoted by Forker, 1994: 94). Kept in "the sink / Wherein the filth of all the castle falls" (5.5.55–6), Edward acknowledges the connection between his loves and his fate: "O Gaveston, it is for thee that I am wronged; / For me, both thou and both the Spencers died,/And for your sakes a thousand wrongs I'll take" (5.3.41–3). No longer a king, he accepts his fate as a private man, asking Lightborn to give him a chance to make his peace with God: "let me see the stroke before it comes, / That even then when I shall lose my life, / My mind may be more steadfast on my God." "O spare me! Or dispatch me in a trice!" are the last words he utters before the terrible "cry [that] will raise the town" (5.5.75–7, 110). The brutality of the scene is enhanced by the emphasis upon Edward's isolation and vulnerability.

No choric prophecy of the misery of civil war follows this end. Rather, such utterances in the play are ironically undercut by the blatant self-interest of their speakers. Where a figure like Carlisle in *Richard II* may speak out with authority on the country's impending torment (and be arrested for it by Bolingbroke), the moralizing of Marlowe's characters rings hollow. When the new king, Edward III, hears the news of his father's death, he "vows to be revenged" on Mortimer and his mother; with the "aid and succour of his peers" he commands the hanging and quartering of Mortimer (5.6.18, 20). Mortimer meets his death with a thoroughly conventional invocation of fortune's wheel:

> Base Fortune, now I see that in thy wheel
> There is a point to which, when men aspire,
> They tumble headlong down. That point I touched,
> And seeing there was no place to mount up higher,
> Why should I grieve at my declining fall?
>
> (5.6.58–62)

But is this Stoic resignation or arrogance, a final sneer at the "paltry boy" (56) who now occupies the throne? While Edward III's reputation as a great warrior-king certainly precedes him in this play, are we to see his seizure of Mortimer (with the counsel of his peers) as a heroic counterpoint to his father's dismissal of his peers' advice and blatant preference of his favorites? And what are we to make of his insistence, in the play's final lines, that his tears are "witness of my grief and innocency" (101)? Like all the Marlowe plays, *Edward II* offers a plot that is moralistic, pious, and conservative, but lavishes sympathy upon its transgressive agents. The protracted and sometimes vehement critical disagreement about his plays is a reflection of this divisive dramaturgy. Marlowe leaves the problem with the audience.

Radical Tragedy

It has not gone unnoticed that the problems Marlowe asks his audiences to wrestle with are problems that are central to most recent criticism of early modern drama: race, class, and gender. Postcolonial approaches have opened new ways of thinking about *The Jew of Malta* and *Tamburlaine*, and queer theory has devoted much attention to *Edward II* and the representation of male–male desire. Mortimer Senior urges his son not to oppose Edward and invokes the classical precedents:

> The mightiest kings have had their minions:
> Great Alexander loved Hephestion;
> The conquering Hercules for Hylas wept;
> And for Patroclus the stern Achilles drooped.
> And not kings only, but the wisest men,
> The Roman Tully loved Octavius,
> Grave Socrates, wild Alcibiades.
>
> (1.4.390–6)

But Mortimer rejects this argument, claiming not to be "grieve[d]" by Edward's "wanton humour" (401) but rather by the challenge to class barriers that Gaveston's promotions mount. The powerful barons in the play also stigmatize Edward's other favorites, the Spencers, in class terms, seeing them also as upstarts, dapper Jacks.

Marlowe has indeed been seen, by Jonathan Dollimore, as the proponent of a "radical tragedy" that challenges the premises of Western essentialist humanism.

While American New Historicist criticism has tended to see early modern English tragedy as representing social mobility and challenges to political orthodoxy primarily within the containment and license of the institution of theater, Dollimore's cultural materialist criticism sees in the plays calls for revolutionary rethinking of and action against the social structure. In Dollimore's argument, *Doctor Faustus* "is important for subsequent tragedy" because, like *Edward II*, it features "the inscribing of a subversive discourse within an orthodox one, a vindication of the letter of an orthodoxy while subverting its spirit" (Dollimore 1984: 119). Thus *Edward II*, in this view, does not merely dramatize transgressive behavior; it anticipates a Brechtian alienation-effect by forcing an audience to consider what kind of social system makes Edward's behavior transgressive. What notions of "nature" make certain kinds of sexual conduct "unnatural"?

Such interrogation of *nature* and *the unnatural* is characteristic not only of Marlowe but of Shakespeare in his mature tragedies. In these plays, strange perturbations to the state reach out into the natural world. Ghosts walk in *Hamlet* and, as Horatio points out in that play, before the death of Julius Caesar as well. Duncan's horses eat each other in *Macbeth*. And in *King Lear* the storm on the heath mirrors the perturbations in the kingdom and in Lear's own "little world of man" (3.1.10).

Macbeth

The parallel between the little world of an individual and the larger world of the state finds explicit expression in terms of bodies and diseases in all the mature tragedies. In *Macbeth*, for example, Shakespeare presents a "Doctor of Physic" as a character, commenting on the illness that besets Lady Macbeth. After witnessing her guilt-ridden sleepwalking, the Doctor connects her troubles with Scotland's:

> Foul whisperings are abroad. Unnatural deeds
> Do breed unnatural troubles. Infected minds
> To their deaf pillows will discharge their secrets.
> More needs she the divine than the physician.
> God, God forgive us all!
>
> (5.1.71–4)

A little later, Macbeth himself interrogates the Doctor about his patient and also about Scotland: "What rhubarb, senna, or what purgative drug / Would scour these English hence?" he asks (5.3.57–8). Parodically, Macbeth seems unaware that he is himself his realm's disease. Malcolm and his English allies envision themselves as offering a laxative cure for the bloated king: "He cannot buckle his distempered cause / Within the belt of rule," says Caithness in an image that links Macbeth's usurpation with bilious flatulence. "Meet we the med'cine of the sickly weal," he urges as the troops proceed to their rendezvous with Malcolm, "And with him pour we in our country's purge / Each drop of us" (5.1.15–16; 27–9).

Under Macbeth's tyranny all Scotland has fallen ill. "It cannot / Be called our mother, but our grave," Ross says, echoing the imagery of *Richard II*. "What's the newest grief?" asks Malcolm; "Each minute teems a new one," replies Ross (4.1.167, 175, 176). Scotland is fertile only in horrors, and the childless Macbeth breeds heirs only for "blood-boltered Banquo" (4.1.123). In this Scottish play, England, ruled by "the most pious Edward" (3.6.127), is itself a medicine, its monarch a physician. Edward cures with his touch the "wretched souls" that suffer from scrofula, the king's evil, and he can pass on the gift: "to the succeeding royalty he leaves / The healing benediction," Malcolm tells Macduff (4.3.156–7). When Macduff learns that his wife and children have been massacred by Macbeth's agents, Malcolm urges him to join the rebellion against Macbeth: "Let's make us medicines of our great revenge / To cure this deadly grief" (4.3.215-16). Marlowe's exposure of the use of the language of the body politic by self-interested agents allows us to question whether Malcolm really is the cure, whether he offers Scotland a return to a time when, as Macbeth wistfully puts it, "humane statute purged the gentle weal" (3.4.77). The historical fact that Banquo's heirs must succeed Malcolm's undercuts the purgative, curative rhetoric of the play's close.

King Lear

"Is there any cause in nature that makes these hard hearts?" Lear asks as he presides over a mad imaginary anatomy – dissection – of Regan (3.6.75–6).

This inquiry reaches beyond the political, but it too has a dimension of state: for if the monarchical polity is mandated by God, a mirror in little of the divine hierarchy, then action that disrupts the social order is unnatural, a defiance of God's will. But, as J. F. Danby pointed out, when Lear rebukes his daughters as unnatural and calls down Nature's curses on them, "Lear is tacitly condemning the social order in which they stand" (Danby 1968: 30). What is appalling in Goneril and Regan is not that their Machiavellian self-seeking rends the body politic and drives their royal father mad, but that their ways are the ways of the world. In *Gorboduc* and in the history plays civil war's self-inflicted wounds are seen as terrible retributions, the working-out of crimes against the state; in *Edward II* and in *King Lear* the horror is that the state of nature is a state of war.

To a great degree the warfare is class warfare, as Lear shows when he dissects Regan's gorgeous clothing (just before he is shut out for the stormy night):

> Our basest beggars
> Are in the poorest thing superfluous.
> Allow not nature more than nature needs,
> Man's life is cheap as beasts. Thou art a lady;
> If only to go warm were gorgeous,
> Why, nature needs not what thou gorgeous wear'st,
> Which scarcely keeps thee warm.
>
> (2.4.267–72)

A strand of vehement satire about clothing runs through the whole play, and it is of course gorgeous clothing, protected by sumptuary laws, that marks the upper classes. Mortimer resents the "short Italian hooded cloak / Larded with pearl," that Gaveston, "dapper jack" that he is, wears; "and in his Tuscan cap / A jewel of more value than the crown." Worse, Gaveston and his cronies "flout our train and jest at our attire" (1.4.411–14; 417). In *Woodstock*, the king's uncle is mistaken for a groom and handed a horse to care for: his clothing is warm, not gorgeous. "You cowardly rascal, nature disclaims in thee," Kent snarls at Oswald. "A tailor made thee" (*King Lear* 2.2.55–6).

It is in terms of clothing that Lear arrives at his famous moment of empathy with the homeless and dispossessed:

> Poor naked wretches, wheresoe'er you are,
> That bide the pelting of this pitiless storm,
> How shall your houseless heads and unfed sides,
> Your looped and windowed raggedness, defend you
> From seasons such as these? O, I have ta'en
> Too little care of this! Take physic, pomp;
> Expose thyself to feel what wretches feel,
> That thou mayst shake the superflux to them
> And show the heavens more just.
>
> (3.4.28–36)

Moving though Lear's prayer is, it is laced with ironies. Lear experiences the miseries of the homeless poor not as a king, but as one of their number, locked out and houseless. The fairy-tale motif of beggar and king – exchanging places with an inevitable reversal, so that the king can know what beggars feel and become more just – is alluded to here, but the play's refusal to restore Lear to his throne (as the sources do) contradicts that motif. Lear takes physic – medicine – here, but since he is no longer king, the cure has no effect. No more than does the discovery that Regan's hard heart has a natural cause.

The state in *Lear* mirrors the natural world not, as in the orthodox political theory of Hooker and other Tudor thinkers, by being hierarchical and well ordered, but instead by virtue of its chaotic violence. A perverse arbitrariness divides the world into rich and poor, kings and beggars, as Lear perceives in his madness:

> Through tattered clothes small vices do appear;
> Robes and furred gowns hide all. Plate sin with gold,
> And the strong lance of justice hurtless breaks;
> Arm it in rags, a pygmy's straw does pierce it.
> None does offend, none, I say, none.
>
> (4.6.164–8)

From setting himself and his kingdom up as objects of a grotesque love-auction in the first scene, Lear descends to poverty and sees a world where everything is for sale, especially justice. The body politic in *Lear* is feminized, as in the history plays and in *Macbeth*: "To't luxury, pell-mell, for I lack soldiers," Lear cries. The teeming womb of John of Gaunt's dying vision becomes Lear's nightmare vision of Goneril and Regan's voracious sexuality: "But to the girdle do the gods inherit; / Beneath is all the fiend's" (4.6.117, 126–7). While at the end of the play the "gored state" is sustained by Albany and Edgar (with Kent slipping quietly away to die), a dim memory of *Gorboduc* stirs (was it not Albanius who threatened the maimed state then?) and undercuts any consolation, any sense of order restored.

John Turner has pointed out that *King Lear*'s return to origins has special reference to the chronicles deriving from Geoffrey of Monmouth. At Dover Cliff, where mad Lear and blind Gloucester meet, one of the original Brut's retinue, Corineus, wrestled with the giant Gogmagog and threw him off. Thus, to Turner, the play "depicts the history of its country as nightmare...The play is *dangerous*... it *initiates* its audience into the injustice, confusion, and violence of the past which become in performance the injustice, confusion and violence of the present" (Turner 1988: 117, emphasis in original). The act of Corineus is what René Girard would call an act of "foundational violence or foundational murder," an original scapegoating that grounds the state in collective violence (Girard 1991: 201). In *King Lear*, the state's collapse into internecine chaos is predetermined from its very beginnings.

Tragedies of Rome

Girard posits the assassination of Julius Caesar in Shakespeare's play of that name as such a "foundational murder": it establishes the Roman state as a state of almost constant civil war. Coining the phrase "tragedy of state" in 1970, J. W. Lever took another angle, and proposed that with these early modern English plays we are dealing with "modes of tragedy unrelated to Aristotle's familiar definitions":

> They are not primarily treatments of characters with a so-called "fatal flaw", whose downfall is brought about by the decree of just if inscrutable powers. The heroes may have their faults of deficiency or excess; but the fundamental flaw is not in them but in the world they inhabit; in the political state, in the social order it upholds, and likewise, by projection, in the cosmic state of shifting arbitrary phenomena called "Fortune".
> (Lever 1971: 10)

Lever goes on to consider in detail the way in which Roman history encouraged dramatists to explore "the workings of power, the concept of freedom, and the bearings of history itself upon the fortunes of the individual. More specifically," he continues, "they recognized as the period of maximum tension the years which marked the rise of Caesar and the civil wars leading to the replacement of the republic by the empire" (Lever 1971: 60).

Julius Caesar

As Lever and Rebecca Bushnell have demonstrated, Julius Caesar occupied a major place in Renaissance European debates about tyrants and tyrannicide. This was a confused issue, as Caesar was both revered as a precursor of the age's absolutist monarchies and reviled as an arrogant usurper of his people's ancient liberties. Bushnell points out that James I's "fondness for the high Roman style" gave him "a way of styling himself as a god," while "for his antagonists, the comparison would suggest a less complimentary association with depravity and cruelty" (Bushnell 1990: 149-50). As Shakespeare's *Julius Caesar* and Ben Jonson's *Sejanus* demonstrate, the preferred dramatic mode for approaching the paradoxes of Rome, as republic or empire, was irony.

The irony is both historical and theatrical in *Julius Caesar*. As the conspirators stoop to "bathe [their] hands in Caesar's blood," they imagine the effect upon posterity of their great act and propose a motto of "Peace, freedom, and liberty!" (3.1.107, 110):

> CASSIUS: How many ages hence
>   Shall this our lofty scene be acted over
>   In states unborn and accents yet unknown!
> BRUTUS: How many times shall Caesar bleed in sport
>   That now on Pompey's basis lies along
>   No worthier than dust!
> CASSIUS: So oft as that shall be,
>   So often shall the knot of us be called
>   The men that gave their country liberty.
>
> (113–20)

While Brutus and Cassius envision a future in which their act will be replayed in places (England?) and languages (English?) that they do not know, they do not anticipate the contests that will erupt in the early modern period over the word *liberty*, which they claim as their own here. As Catherine Belsey points out, in these Roman tragedies, "Freedom is only an idea, popular sovereignty no more than a momentary possibility." And she makes the connection between stage representations of Roman struggles and the English political context: "The civil war is still forty years off." "Absolutism, the plays imply," she continues, "produces precisely the resistance it sets out to exclude. And the dramatization of absolutism gives birth, however tentatively, to the concept of the autonomous subject" (Belsey 1985: 109).

Historical Parallels

The frequent use of historical parallels in early modern English drama analogizes contemporary events to precedents in the past, often the British past, as in *Gorboduc*, but more frequently in the late Elizabethan and early Stuart period the Roman or recent French past. Increasingly vigilant government censorship and a clearer sense of the absolutist Stuart agenda on the part of officials seem at least partly responsible for the scarcity in the 1610s and 1620s of plays in which the gored state was nominally English. In George Chapman's Byron and Bussy plays (*The Tragedy and Conspiracy of Byron*, *The Tragedy of Bussy d'Ambois*, and *The Revenge of Bussy*) a corrupt French court stands in for a corrupt Jacobean polity, and Italian courts in John Marston's and John Webster's plays appear to perform the same function. In Jonson's *Sejanus* (1605), for which the playwright claims he was hauled before the Privy Council and charged with treason and "popery" by his old enemy Northampton, censorship itself is a major issue, as the historian Cremutius Cordus gets into trouble for writing "annals of late, they say, and very well" (76). "Those times are somewhat queasy to be touched," says Natta (an informer for the tyrannical Tiberius) thoughtfully (82). "These our times are not the same, Arruntius," comments Silius, provoking this outburst from his friend:

> Times? The men,
> The men are not the same! 'Tis we are base,
> Poor and degenerate from th'exalted strain
> Of our great fathers!
>
> (85–9)

In this interchange, Jonson not only offers a glimpse of life under an oppressive regime, but also anticipates the uses that can be made of historical applications under such regimes. The Germanicans (to whose party Arruntius belongs) invoke a glorious past to shame the present, while the agents of the government seek to suppress Cordus' annals.

An autonomous subject is perhaps a dream in Jonson's Roman tragedy, in which the emperor Tiberius simply replaces the overweening favorite Sejanus with an even more dangerous, because more efficient and less self-absorbed, agent of tyranny, Macro. Cordus's annals are suppressed (with the ironic consequence that they become more sought after) and the opponents of the regime are caught in their own nostalgia for the Republican past, with no hope for the future.

"O world, no world but mass of public wrongs," exclaims Hieronymo in Thomas Kyd's *Spanish Tragedy* (3.2.2): the chaotic worlds of the Roman, French, and Italian plays of the English Renaissance show characters hemmed around by oppressive systems, betrayed and exploited by lustful tyrants (as in Beaumont and Fletcher's *The Maid's Tragedy*), excluded from any remedies of civil justice. Their only recourse is to oppose this "mass of public wrongs," this "sea of troubles" (*Hamlet*, 3.1.60) with strategies of misdirection and concealment, pursuing private agendas of revenge. The blood of English may cry out for justice as it manures the ground, but who will hear?

REFERENCES AND FURTHER READING

Axton, M. (1977). *The Queen's Two Bodies: Drama and the Elizabethan Succession*. London: British Historical Society. Discusses the political context of English Renaissance tragedies.

Barish, J., ed. (1965). *Ben Jonson's* Sejanus. New Haven, CT: Yale University Press.

Belsey, C. (1985). *The Subject of Tragedy: Identity and Difference in Renaissance Drama*. London: Methuen. Discusses the rise of the idea of the "autonomous subject" in English Renaissance tragedies.

Bevington, D., ed. (1992). *The Complete Works of William Shakespeare*, 4th edn. New York: HarperCollins.

Bushnell, R. (1990). *Tragedies of Tyrants: Political Thought and Theater in the English Renaissance*. Ithaca, NY: Cornell University Press. Discusses transformations of the tyrant figure from early to late Renaissance English tragedy.

Cox, J. D. and Kastan, D. S., eds. (1997). *A New History of Early English Drama*. New York: Columbia University Press. A collection of essays stressing the material and cultural contexts of medieval and Renaissance English drama.

Danby, J. F. (1968). *Shakespeare's Doctrine of Nature: A Study of* King Lear. London: Faber & Faber. Discusses *King Lear* in a context of early modern ideas about nature, with emphasis on Hooker and Hobbes.

Dollimore, J. (1984). *Radical Tragedy: Religion, Ideology, and Power in the Drama of Shakespeare and his Contemporaries*. Chicago: University of Chicago Press. Discusses English Renaissance tragedy as a critique of essentialist humanism.

Forker, C. R., ed. (1994). *Christopher Marlowe: Edward the Second*, The Revels Plays. Manchester: Manchester University Press.

Fraser, R. A. and Rabkin, N., eds. (1976). *Drama of the English Renaissance, Volume I: The Tudor Period*. New York: Macmillan. *Gorboduc* and *The Spanish Tragedy* are cited from this edition.

Girard, R. (1991). *A Theater of Envy: William Shakespeare*. New York: Oxford University Press. Offers a reading of Shakespeare's plays with emphasis on mimetic rivalry, foundational murder, and scapegoating.

Greenblatt, S. (1980). *Renaissance Self-Fashioning: From More to Shakespeare*. Chicago: University of Chicago Press. A New Historicist classic which examines the idea of the self in the early modern period.

Hopkins, L. (2000). *Christopher Marlowe: A Literary Life*. New York: Palgrave. A reading of Marlowe that stresses the political and historical contexts of his plays.

Howard, J. E. and Rackin, P. (1997). *Engendering a Nation: A Feminist Account of Shakespeare's Histories*. London: Routledge. Discusses the English history plays with special emphasis on issues of gender differentiation.

Kahn, C. (1981). *Man's Estate: Masculine Identity in Shakespeare*. Berkeley and Los Angeles: University of California Press. A feminist/psychoanalytical reading of Shakespeare's comedies, tragedies, and histories.

Lever, J. W. (1971). *The Tragedy of State*. London: Methuen. Discusses revenge tragedies and political tragedies primarily of the Stuart period.

Longstaffe, S. (1997). "What is the English History Play and Why Are They Saying Such Terrible Things about It?" *Renaissance Forum* 2 (http://www.hull.ac.uk/renforum.v2no2/longstaf.htm). Questions the idea that Shakespeare's histories stand apart from run-of-the-mill chronicle plays.

Rackin, P. (1990). *Stages of History: Shakespeare's English Chronicles*. Ithaca, NY: Cornell University Press. Discusses Shakespeare's history plays as history and as theater.

Riggs, D. (1971). *Shakespeare's Heroical Histories: Henry VI and its Literary Tradition*. Cambridge, MA: Harvard University Press. Locates early Shakespearean tragedy within its cultural context.

Rossiter, A. P., ed. (1946). *Woodstock: A Moral History*. London: Chatto & Windus. Offers a useful introduction to the relationship between morality drama and the English history play.

Steane, J. B., ed. (1969). *The Complete Plays of Christopher Marlowe*. Harmondsworth: Penguin. All Marlowe's plays except *Edward II* are quoted from this edition.

Turner, J. (1988). "King Lear." In *Shakespeare: The Play of History*, ed. G. Holderness, N. Potter, and J. Turner. Iowa City: University of Iowa Press. A collection of essays that highlights recent cultural materialist criticism of Shakespeare.

Walker, G. (1998). *The Politics of Performance in Early Renaissance Drama*. Cambridge: Cambridge University Press. Discusses the topicality of Tudor interludes and early tragedies.

19
English Revenge Tragedy

Michael Neill

Justice, Revenge, and Law

In Henry Chettle's *Tragedy of Hoffman* (1602), the outlawed protagonist, driven to lead "a savadge life...amongst beasts" (sig. B3) whilst he seeks vengeance for his murdered father, forms a living picture of the contradiction that lies at the heart of English revenge tragedy: as a man seeking justice for unpunished crime he is an agent of the very principles on which the civil society depends for its survival; yet his wild appearance bespeaks a social alienation that will drive him to extremes of destructive violence. "Caught in a double bind," as Katharine Maus puts it, "the revenger seems simultaneously an avatar and enemy of social order" (Maus 1995: xiii; Neill 1983: 39). This is the contradiction that Francis Bacon sought to define when, in a celebrated oxymoron, he wrote of revenge as "a kind of wild justice" (Bacon 1906: 13). Revenge, Bacon implied, was simply justice in its primitive, undomesticated condition; but because it remained wild, it constituted a danger to the order of the state, threatening to overrun and choke it like an invasive weed in some formal garden. Himself a jurist of distinction and later to be James I's Attorney General and Lord Chancellor, Bacon recognized in the ethos of revenge a fundamental challenge to the rule of law: "[f]or as for the first wrong, it doth but offend the law; but the revenge of that wrong, putteth the law out of office." This is why, in the harmonious resolutions of comedy, the man with revenge in his heart, like Malvolio or Shylock, however cruelly wronged, must be expelled from the reordered community.

Even Bacon, however, admitted the existence of "wrongs which there is no law to remedy"; and these, he felt, invited "the most tolerable sort of revenge." By conceding the possibility of circumstances in which usurpation of the law might be tolerated, Bacon pointed to the very tension that energizes revenge tragedy in its exploration of irreconcilable conflicts between the private desire for revenge, and the public constraints of law. As Fredson Bowers long ago demonstrated, revenge had become an increasingly political issue in early modern England, where the centralizing ambitions of the Tudor monarchy led to an insistence upon the state's absolute monopoly of justice (Bowers 1940; Maus 1995: xiii–xiv). Endlessly reinforced in the propaganda of sermons, homilies, and pious tracts, this doctrine put the institution of law in conflict with the traditional code of chivalric honor.[1] Fastening on those scriptural texts which proclaimed that the right of vengeance belonged to God alone, official dogma asserted an absolute ethical divide between justice and revenge, insisting that, barring direct intervention from on high, only the King, as God's vicegerent, could inflict punishment. Under this dispensation, private retribution constituted, as Bacon recognized, an implicit challenge not merely to the authority of the state, but to its very legitimacy.

In its emphasis upon the potentially catastrophic consequences of putting the law out of office, revenge tragedy paid due regard to official doctrine; but at the same time it invested most of its emotional energy in the predicament of the revenger. Typically it chose to explore the conflict between law and revenge by imagining some crisis in which the state proved either unable or unwilling to satisfy an individual's demand for retribution. To this extent it was well calculated to speak to the resentments of those who, whether for political, religious, or social reasons, felt themselves victimized by what Hamlet calls "Th'oppressor's wrong, the proud man's contumely... the law's delay, / The insolence of office" (*Hamlet* 3.1.79–81). The generality of Hamlet's indictment draws attention to the thoroughly generic nature of his dilemma: more often than not the revenger finds himself pitched against the very authority that should be responsible for the implementation of justice. In Hamlet's case, his father's murderer is the King himself; in *Titus Andronicus* (ca. 1588–93), it is the Emperor who stands in the way of retribution against Tamora, her lover, and her vicious sons; in Thomas Kyd's *Spanish Tragedy* (ca. 1587), Hieronimo's only son is treacherously butchered by the King's nephew and presumptive heir, Lorenzo; in Marston's *Antonio's Revenge* (ca. 1601) it is Duke Piero, the ruler of Venice, whom the hero is bound to punish for his father's death; in the anonymous *Revenger's Tragedy* (1606–7),[2] the killing of Vindice's father and his betrothed mistress pitches the hero against the whole ruling family; while in *Hoffman* (1602) the outlawed protagonist becomes the enemy of the entire princely caste.

Katharine Maus has written of the way in which revenge drama, by presenting the delicious spectacle of subjects hoodwinking and finally annihilating their superiors, addressed the "repressed frustrations" of a society in painful transition – one still highly stratified along feudal lines, but exposed to sudden changes of economic and political fortune (Maus 1995: xi–xii); and it is clear that in some respects the revenger corresponds to the type of the "social bandit," that paradoxical "revolutionary traditionalist" whom Eric Hobsbawm has described as a characteristic phenomenon of popular resistance in periods of rapid social transformation. Like the social bandit, the revenger sometimes adopts a distinctive mode of dress as the sign of the alienation that drives him to "right wrongs and avenge cases of injustice"; like the bandit, he too feels himself committed to "the defence or restoration of the traditional order of things 'as it should be' (which... means as it is believed to have been in some real or mythical past)";[3] and insofar as he provides a kind of fantasy surrogate for all those elements in society whose powerlessness puts them beyond the solutions of law and reason, he becomes the scourge not just of his personal enemies, but of all those who (in Hoffman's words) "wring the poore, and eate the people up . . . such as have rob'd souldiers of / Reward, and punish true desert with scorned death" (*Hoffman*: sig. I2v). Something of this largeness of social scope is implicit in the sweeping satire of courtly mores that informs Vindice's tirades in *The Revenger's Tragedy* – reminding us that in Florio's dictionary "Vendice" is glossed as "a revenger of wrongs, a redresser of abuses, a defender, one that restoreth unto liberty and freeth from dangers, a punisher" (Florio 1611: 592). More speculatively, we might imagine that in its preoccupation with suppressed histories of crime, its pervasive use of Fall mythology, and its nostalgia for a vanished pre-lapsarian order, revenge tragedy provided a way of indirectly address-ing the repressed guilts and anxieties arising from the crises of Reformation and Counter-Reformation and the oscillating political fortunes with which they were associated (Neill 1997: 245–7).

The exceptional power of the genre to compel the early modern imagination, then, had much to do with its ability to mobilize conflicting attitudes toward the subver-siveness of personal vengeance. In several of the plays the process by which revenge puts the law out of office is rendered remarkably explicit. The action of *The Revenger's Tragedy*, for example – after the extended exposition that establishes Vindice's role as revenger – effectively begins with a trial scene: here the Duchess's youngest son is found guilty of raping Antonio's wife, only for the Duke to intervene, deferring judgment at his wife's behest (1.2.83). In turn, this spectacle of aborted justice is set against a scene in which Antonio and his faction, anticipating that "judgment [will] speak all in gold, and spare the blood / Of such a serpent," vow revenge for his wife's degradation and suicide.[4] In thus highlighting "the insolence of office" and "the law's delay" as motors for revenge, the playwright must have been inspired as much by the example of *The Spanish Tragedy* and *Titus* as by *Hamlet*. The protagonist of Kyd's play is the kingdom's principal judge, yet is humiliatingly unable to obtain justice for himself, even as he dispenses it to others:

> Thus must we toil in other men's extremes,
> That know not how to remedy our own,
> And do them justice, when unjustly we,
> For all our wrongs, can compass no redress.
>   (3.6.1–4)

The main action of *The Spanish Tragedy* is framed by a dramatized Prologue and Epilogue in which questions of justice are debated by the ghost of Andrea and the spirit of Revenge. In the Prologue Andrea's Ghost describes his arraignment before the three judges of the classical underworld, Aeacus, Rhadamanth, and Minos, who, failing to arrive at a decision, refer his case to Pluto, their "infernal king," for judgment (1.1.52–3). In his turn, however, Pluto yields the right of sentence to his consort Proserpine, who, with an enigmatic smile, whispers her decision in Revenge's ear. The precise terms of her "doom," with its ominous delegation of authority from a court of law to the private jurisdiction of Revenge, are not explicitly revealed, but are left instead to be worked out in the tragedy for which Revenge and his ghostly companion are to serve as "chorus" (1.1.91).

The play proper then begins with its own judgment scene, in which the King apportions reward between Lorenzo and Horatio, the rival captors of the Portuguese Prince Balthazar. The judicious balance of the King's decision ("You both deserve and both shall have reward," 179), combined with Hieronimo's praise for his sovereign's wisdom and justice (166), suggest a perfect consonance between law and power. However, the murder of the ambitious Horatio, as a result of his erotic rivalry with Balthazar, drives a wedge between the protagonist and his avocation, between the judge and the regal fount of justice. Stiffening his resolve with reminders that vengeance belongs only to God and his royal deputy (3.13.1–5, 3.7.69–70), Hieronimo continues to perform his judicial duties, even presiding over the trial and execution of Lorenzo's tool villain, Pedringano (3.6); but he is increasingly maddened by his own inability to secure punishment for his son's killers. What results is a progressive destabilization of the image of authority, in which the King's indifference to the old man's frantic appeals for justice (3.12) seems mirrored in the deafness of the gods to all his "soliciting for justice and revenge":

> they are plac'd in those empyreal heights
> Where, countermur'd with walls of diamond,
> I find the place impregnable, and they
> Resist my woes, and give my words no way.
> (3.7.15–18)

As a result, Hieronimo's mind is increasingly filled with dreams of private vengeance and inspired by fantasies of the very underworld from which the play's vengeful chorus first emerged:

> Though on this earth justice will not be found,
> I'll down to hell, and in this passion
> Knock at the gates of dismal Pluto's court . . .
> Go back my son, complain to Aeacus,
> For here's no justice: gentle boy be gone,
> For justice is exiled from the earth . . .
> Thy mother cries on righteous Rhadamanth
> For just revenge against the murderers.
> (3.13. 108–10, 138–43)

When Hieronimo speaks of Justice as "exiled from the earth" he invokes a classical myth that will be cited again in Shakespeare's *Titus Andronicus*:[5] allegorizing a world of radical inequity, it concerns Astraea, goddess of justice and last of the immortals to leave the earth after the onset of the impious and violent Age of Iron. *"Terras Astraea reliquit,"* declares the despairing Titus, quoting Ovid's *Metamorphoses* (i.150), "She's gone, she's fled . . . If you will have Revenge from hell, you shall; / Marry, for Justice, she is so employed, / He thinks, with Jove in heaven, or somewhere else" (4.3.4–5, 39–41). In the case of Kyd's tragedy, although the changing fortunes of the plot persuade Hieronimo that "heaven applies our drift, / And all the saints do sit soliciting / For vengeance on those cursed murderers" (4.1.33–4), the ending amply confirms the pessimism of this pagan myth: the linguistic "confusion" of the play through which Hieronimo accomplishes his revenge against Lorenzo and Balthazar, followed by the senseless butchery of the innocent Castile, and his own suicide, far from restoring the order of law and justice, presents a spectacle of chaos that belongs to the antisocial wilderness of revenge; and it is the figure of Revenge himself who, together with Andrea's vindictive ghost, assumes the ultimate right to fierce and partial judgment in the final chorus:

> *Andrea:* Then, sweet Revenge, do this at my request.
>   Let me be judge, and doom them to unrest . . .
> *Revenge:* Then haste we down to meet thy friends and foes
>   To place thy friends in ease, the rest in woes:
>
> (4.5.29–30, 45–6)

"Blood Cries for Blood": The Scales of Revenge

"Revenge," according to one of its most recent exponents, "means seeking a kind of cosmic, primal balance, restoring equilibrium" (Blumenfeld 2002: 61). In the proem to Book 5 of Edmund Spenser's Elizabethan epic, *The Faerie Queene*, we learn how Artegall, the Knight of Justice, was tutored in his infancy by Astraea: in order that he might combat the excesses of "wrongfull powre," she taught him "to weigh both right and wrong / In equall ballance with due recompence, / And equitie to measure out along" (canto 1, stanza 7). Astraea's "equall ballance" will be familiar from the iconography of modern law courts, but it has an ancient history; and revenge might even be said to have owned the scales of justice long before they were usurped by law. Indeed, the earliest attempts to formulate a legal system, such as the Babylonian Code of Hammurabi (ca. 1780 BCE), were in many respects barely distinguishable from the primitive tit-for-tat code of revenge which they sought to displace; and the justice of God himself was often asserted in the language of vengeance, as Hieronimo reminds us when he quotes the biblical *Vindicta mihi* (3.13.1) – "Vengeance is mine, saith the lord, I will repay" (Romans 12.19).

In a famous scriptural episode, the great feast ordered by Belshazzar, King of Babylon, is interrupted by a fearful portent: the fingers of a man's hand appear and write three mysterious words on the palace wall; as interpreted by the prophet Daniel, these graffiti announce God's revenge against the iniquity of the King, and the imminent destruction of his kingdom: "God Hath numbered thy kingdom and finished it . . . Thou art weighed in the balances and found wanting" (Daniel 6. 26–7). Not only did this episode provide a template for the murderous banquets at which the corrupt rulers of such plays as *Titus Andronicus, The Revenger's Tragedy, Antonio's Revenge*, and even *Hamlet* meet their ends; in its stress upon numbering and weighing it encodes an essential principle of the revenge ethic. Revenge, as the popular idiom expresses it, is about "getting *even*"; its satisfactions depend upon the ironic calculus of exchange announced by Iago when, his innards gnawed by the "poisonous mineral" of jealousy, he determines to be "evened" with Othello "wife for wife" (*Othello*, 2.1. 297). Its aesthetic of "proportion" is expounded in remarkably similar terms by characters in Chettle's *Hoffman* and Chapman's *The Revenge of Bussy D'Ambois*. "Revenge should have proportion," declares Chettle's Mathias, for "Then the revenge were fit, just, and square" (sig. I4v); while the Ghost of Bussy proclaims that

> To be [God's] image is to do those things
> That make us deathless, which, by death, is only
> Doing those deeds that fit eternity;
> And those deeds are the perfecting that justice
> That makes the world last, which proportion is
> Of punishment and wreak for every wrong,
> As well as for right a reward as strong.
> (*The Revenge of Bussy D'Ambois*, 5.1.89–95)

For all the high Renaissance solemnity of his rhetorical style, Bussy's idea of "proportion" expresses the same primitive notions of justice embodied in the biblical *lex talionis*, with its precise balancing of crime and requital: "thou shalt give eye for eye, tooth for tooth, hand for hand, foot for foot, burning for burning, wound for wound, stripe for stripe" (Exodus 21.23–5). Here and elsewhere in the Old Testament (Leviticus 24, 17–20), the languages of justice and revenge are virtually indistinguishable – as they are for Hieronimo, the frustrated justicer of *The Spanish Tragedy*: "For blood with blood shall, while I sit as judge, / Be satisfied, and the law discharg'd" (3.6.35–6). The same remorseless symmetries are invoked again and again in the world of Elizabethan and Jacobean revenge tragedy: "Blood cries for blood, and murder murder craves," proclaims the hero of John Marston's *Antonio's Revenge* (ca. 1601), as he sprinkles the tomb of his murdered father with the blood of the murderer's child (3.1.216).

Like Othello when he revenges himself on Desdemona's supposed infidelity, or Hamlet when he forces the poisoned chalice to Claudius' lips in a grisly parody of communion, Antonio turns murder into "sacrifice" (*Othello*, 5.2.65); and the ritualized nature of the gesture is a reminder that in the accomplishment of revenge more is at stake than simply the revenger's private grievance. In fact, so long as the original crime goes unpunished, society as a whole was felt to be contaminated: significantly, in Greek mythology, the "upholders of honour and vengeance," known as the Furies, were also responsible for "keep[ing] categories clear, which is to say unmixed, unpolluted" (Visser 2002: 52). Thus revenge becomes an act of purgation, making the revenger "another Hercules," whose role it is to "rid ... huge pollution from our state" by cleansing the Augean stables of the court (*Antonio's Revenge*, 5.3.129–30). This is why, for Bussy's Ghost, revenge is godlike: by perfecting justice, it "makes the world to last." Implicit in his claim is the notion that certain crimes (especially those against one's family, one's honor, or one's person) upset the proper balance of creation, rendering it, in Hamlet's phrase, "out of joint," so that only the application of an exactly proportionate vengeance can "set it right" (1.5.210–11). The crime that thus disjoints the world amounts to an act of radical disintegration, a dismembering of the body politic, whose "scattered limbs" it is the business of the revenger's "plot" to reunite (*Antonio's Revenge*, 5.1.12); for only when revenge is accomplished can the survivors (as Marcus expresses it in *Titus*) set about knitting "This scattered corn into one mutual sheaf, / These broken limbs again into one body" (*Titus Andronicus* 5.3.70–1).

This way of thinking about revenge appears to be widely dispersed across human cultures, and is closely linked to notions of "price" and "reward" (each of which can denote retribution as well as recompense). Thus in ancient Greece, for example, revenge was *poinē* (recompense), while the word for revenger was *timōros* (one who exacts a price, reciprocates, enforces an exchange) (Kerrigan 1996: 21). At the other end of the world, in New Zealand Maori the word commonly translated as "revenge," *utu*, is better rendered as "reward," "price," or "(re)payment." Vindice, in *The Revenger's Tragedy*, appeals to the same structure of ideas when he calls vengeance "Murder's quit-rent" (1.1.39), playing on the complex meaning of "quittance" as both "final repayment" and "reprisal," as well as "release from obligation," to express the relentless moral accountancy on which the ethos of revenge is constructed (Maus 1995: x).

Because the revenger can free himself from his burden of deadly obligation only by an action that precisely counteracts the original offense, revenge drama is characterized by a relish of witty symmetries, like that exemplified in Vindice's manipulation of Gloriana's poisoned skull to bring about the death of her poisoner: "Those that did eat are eaten," he exults, as the Duke's teeth are consumed by her corrosive kiss. This play of wit explains why, as John Kerrigan puts it, the best revenge often resembles "a form of practical joke" (Kerrigan 1996: 204). "The *sport*," as Hamlet puts it, is "to have the enginer / Hoist with his own petard" (3.4.229–30; emphasis added); and this is precisely how Macbeth, as though remembering Claudius' involuntary draft from his own poisoned cup (*Hamlet* 5.2.356–60), imagines the irony of his own destruction: "This even-handed justice / Commends the ingredients of our poison'd chalice / To our own lips" (*Macbeth* 1.7.10–12).

In early plays especially, such wit often extends from the ingenuities of the plot to a style marked by figures of antithesis and chiasmus, elaborate stichomythia, and self-conscious use of rhyme. So, in *The Spanish Tragedy*, the Viceroy's lament for his dead son lays down a remorseless chain of cause and effect that supplies a rhetorical pattern for the plotting of vendetta, even before Horatio's murder sets the main plot in train:

> My late ambition hath distain'd my faith,
> My breach of faith occasion'd blood wars,
> Those bloody wars have spent my treasure,
> And with my treasure my people's blood,
> And with their blood, my joy and best belov'd,
> My best belov'd, my sweet and only son.
>
> (1.3.33–9)

In a similar fashion, the chiastic balance of Hieronimo's couplets seems to anticipate the witty structural "rhymes" of the revenge plot – its dance of action and vindictive counteraction – at the very point when retribution seems to him most frustratingly elusive:

> O sacred heavens! if this unhallow'd deed...
> Shall unreveal'd and unrevenged pass,
> How should we term your dealings to be just,
> If you unjustly deal with those that in your justice trust?
>
> *   *   *   *
>
> This toils my body, this consumeth age,
> That only I to all men just must be,
> And neither gods nor men be just to me
>
> (3.2.5–11, 3.6.8–10)

But even as rhetorical devices of this kind seem to articulate the ironic proportion by which revenge will ultimately perfect itself, they can also serve to highlight its dangerously recursive potential. At the end of *Titus Andronicus* (ca. 1593), the patness of the hero's sardonic rhyming points up the witty aptness of the revenge whereby he tricked Tamora into a perfect expression of her barbarous nature by making her feed upon her own sons: "Why here they are, both baked in this pie, / Whereof their mother daintily hath fed, / Eating the flesh that she herself hath bred" (5.3.59–61).

However, if Tamora is the deserving victim of Titus' fury, she herself is also a bereaved mother, seeking retribution for the butchery of her own son, Alarbus; and in the strangely masque-like 5.2 it is in the person of Revenge that, accompanied by her surviving sons in the suitable guise of Murder and Rape, she visits her adversary. This show, which constitutes a kind of ex post facto justification of her atrocities against the Andronici, is also a reminder of the extent to which their shared obsession with revenge reduces Tamora and Titus to a common savagery in which "barbarous Goth" and "pious" Roman are barely distinguishable. Thus the self-consuming savagery of Tamora's fate serves as an ironic pointer to the ultimately self-destructive character of Titus' rival passion: her feasting on her own flesh and blood is uncannily mirrored in Titus's "unnatural" butchery of his own daughter in the midst of the cannibal feast. A similarly self-annihilating logic is played out in a grim knockabout scene from *The Revenger's Tragedy* where Vindice, having been hired to kill his own alter ego, Piato, performs his burlesque butchery on the Duke's corpse, dressed up in the same clothes that once disguised his own identity: "Brother that's I: that sits for me...And I must stand ready here to make away / myself yonder; I must sit to be killed, and stand to kill myself" (5.1.4–6). The eldritch humour of the scene perfectly anticipates the wry self-mockery with which, at the end of the play, Vindice will identify himself as his own undoer: "'Tis time to die when we are ourselves our foes" (5.3.112). Earlier in the play Vindice has commented sardonically on the scheming of his antagonist Lussurioso: "How strangely does himself work to undo him" (4.1.61); but his own plotting has had exactly the same effect – each proves to be like the silkworm of Vindice's misogynistic satire, expending "her yellow labours...[to] undo herself" (3.5.71–2).

The process of self-undoing revealed by the ironic symmetries of revenge tragedy is generally inseparable from the ironies that force the revenger to imitate the methods of the very adversary he seeks to destroy. Thus, in *The Spanish Tragedy*, there is a painful appropriateness in the casting of Hieronimo's "Soliman and Perseda" playlet, where Hieronimo takes the part of the Bashaw, whose murderous treachery resembles Lorenzo's, while Lorenzo himself is made to play the Horatio-like victim, Erasto. In *Hoffman*, the hero initiates his revenge by hanging up a second skeleton beside the "anatomy" of his murdered father, their skulls identically seared with burning crowns; but this ironic doubling will be turned against him at the end of the play when a third cadaver, etched with the same scar, is sentenced to join them – that of Hoffman himself. In *Hamlet* the principle of uncanny duplication is apparent not just in the way that Hamlet dispatches his father's killer with the murderer's own weapon, poison, but also in the weird doubling of bereaved sons, which turns both of Hamlet's rivals (the man who kills him, and the man who takes his throne) into mirrors of his own predicament – as the Prince himself recognizes when he says of Laertes that "by the image of my cause, I see the portraiture of his" (5.2.87–8).

What is encoded in these recursive symmetries is more than simply an ironic comment on the folly of personal revenge: it is the fear that the desire for vengeance, unbounded by the restraints of law, will begin to operate like the "universal wolf," Appetite, as Ulysses describes it in *Troilus and Cressida*: a creature whose ravenous demand for "universal prey" will drive it in the end to "eat up [it]self" in a "chaos" of social disintegration (*Troilus and Cressida* 1.3.121–5). Revenge, as the familiar metaphor has it, is "sweet," something that human beings long to "taste"; but revenge, like Vindice's corrosive poison, can also eat. The vicious reflexivity of revenge is what underlies the farcical confusion at the end of *The Revenger's Tragedy*, where two identically clad groups of masquers, one consisting of the hero and his supporters, the other of his arch-enemies Ambitioso, Supervacuo, and Spurio, compete to murder Lussurioso and his banqueting courtiers, before rounding on one another (5.3.41 ff.); but it is perhaps most explicitly spelt out at the cannibal banquet in *Titus Andronicus*, when Marcus, fearing that his entire society may be caught up in the apocalyptic firestorm of revenge and counter-revenge that culminates in his brother's suicide, imagines how Rome, too, may become "bane unto herself" and "Like a forlorn and desperate castaway / Do desperate execution on herself" (5.3.72–5).

The hunger for payback, then, rests on deeply felt principles of natural reciprocity which reflect the need to preserve a prescribed equilibrium in the order of things; and it is on this ideal of balance that the vexed relationship between revenge and justice can be seen to turn. Yet the ironic mirror-effects displayed in episodes such as those we have just examined are a reminder of the fatality by which the symmetrical compulsions of revenge are liable to convert the revenger into the image of what he most abhors, turning the action back on himself in self-consuming fury.

"Wild Justice": The Garden State and the Wilderness of Revenge

When Bacon imagined revenge as a wild, undomesticated form of justice – a weed which "the more man's nature runs to [revenge], the more ought law to root it out," he drew on one of the most well-used political tropes of the day – one that imaged the state as a garden, tended by a ruler who must strive by constant discipline to return it to the ideal condition of the First Garden, the prototypical Adamic state (Wilders 1978: 137–8; Mack 1973: 83–4). This is the figure famously elaborated by Shakespeare in the garden scene of *Richard II*, whose Gardener the Queen addresses as "Old Adam's likeness" (3.4.73). The Gardener and his men expressly contrast Richard's feckless rule to the careful husbandry with which they preserve "law and form and due proportion" in their horticultural "commonwealth" by "root[ing] away / The noisome weeds which without profit suck / The soil's fertility" (3.4.35–46). Hamlet turns to this same figure when, brooding on his father's unrequited killing, he imagines Denmark as "an unweeded garden / That grows to seed," a wasteland possessed by "things rank and gross in nature" (1.2.135–6). Rendered uncannily literal in the Ghost's account of how he was murdered when sleeping in his "orchard" (1.5.46), this violated garden is twice brought to life on stage in the play-within-the-play when the Player King is "poison[ed] i'th'garden for his estate" (3.2.261).

In symbolic terms the garden / orchard *is* the King's estate, a model of the realm in its ideal perfection, which the "primal, eldest curse" of murder (3.3.37) has reduced to a wilderness governed only by revenge. This is the wasteland that Shakespeare placed at the symbolic center of his first essay in revenge tragedy, *Titus Andronicus* (ca. 1589–93). In act 2, scene 3 Tamora's savage longing for vengeance transforms the paradisal *locus amoenus* where she makes love to Aaron into the "barren detested vale" of her savage revenge against Titus – a place of death where

> nothing breeds
> Unless the nightly owl or fatal raven . . .
> A thousand fiends, a thousand hissing snakes,
> Ten thousand swelling toads.
>
> (2.3.93–101)

The accursed landscape Tamora evokes is the domain of the "ravenous tiger" she herself has become (5.3.194), the desert which, in her guise as Revenge, she will

identify as the "lurking place" of Murder and Rape (5.2.35–8), and the wilderness to
which her own body will be consigned at the end of the play (5.3.197–9). At its heart
lies the "detested, dark, blood-drinking pit" that will devour Titus' sons as though it
were the mouth of hell itself (2.3.224, 236); and just as this "fell devouring
receptacle" (235) symbolically displaces that "sacred receptacle" of Roman piety
(1.1.91), the family tomb of the Andronici which dominates act 1, so Rome itself
will be transformed into the "wilderness of tigers" denounced by Titus (3.1.54). By
the same token, just as the barbarous Tamora becomes "incorporate in Rome"
(1.1.462), so Titus, the former "[p]atron of virtue, Rome's best champion" (1.1.65),
who imagines himself "Environed with a wilderness of sea" (3.1.94), will shortly feel
that wilderness of passion drawn into himself:

> When heaven doth weep, doth not the earth o'erflow
> If the winds rage, doth not the sea wax mad,
> Threat'ning the welkin with his big-swoll'n face? . . .
> I am the sea.
>
> (3.1.220–4)

Nowhere perhaps is the idea of revenge as a force calculated to reduce the order of
civilization to the chaos of wild nature more powerfully expressed than in the play
that exerted such a formative influence on English revenge drama, Kyd's *The Spanish
Tragedy*. At the emblematic center of its action is the garden where (in a scene
displayed on the title page of successive editions) Hieronimo discovers the body of
his murdered son. Represented by the same stylized stage property that would be used
for the murder of *Hamlet*'s Player King,[6] this garden appears again in the quasi-
allegorical scene (4.2) that ushers in the apocalyptic climax of the tragedy. Here
Isabella, driven mad by Hieronimo's failure to avenge their son's death, lays waste this
formerly "sacred bower" (2.5.27), transforming it into a snake-infested wilderness, in
an action that not only replays the loss of Eden but symbolically prefigures the
sanguinary chaos into which Hieronimo will plunge the Spanish state:

> Fruitless forever may this garden be,
> Barren the earth, and blissless whosoever
> Imagines not to keep it unmanured!
> An eastern wind commix'd with noisome airs
> Shall blast the plants and the young saplings,
> The earth with serpents shall be pestered . . .
>
> (4.2.14–19)

The evocative power of the garden icon as an image of political order was further
enhanced by its metaphoric association with language, reflected in such titles as
Richard Taverner's *Garden of Wysdom* (1539) and Henry Peacham's *Garden of Eloquence*
(1593). Thinkers since Aristotle had recognized speech as the enabling instrument of
human society: it was what ultimately distinguished the *polis* from the wilderness –

the world of barbarians, whose very name connoted the confused "ba ba" of their meaningless babble. In addition to its echoes of the Fall, Isabella's apocalyptic imagery identifies the destruction of her garden with the laying waste of Babylon envisioned by the prophets Jeremiah (51.1–2, 37–43) and Isaiah (13.19–22); and Hieronimo in turn conflates that devastation with the destruction of the Tower of Babel in Genesis 11.1–9 (Johnson 1963: 23–36): looking forward to the performance of the revenge-play in which his purpose will be accomplished, he announces the imminent "fall of Babylon, / Wrought by the heavens in this confusion" (4.1.195–6). The "confusion" he anticipates is represented by the babel of "unknown languages" in which, to his victims' dismay, his play is to be performed (4.1.172–83). Frequently identified as the Second Fall of Mankind, the destruction of Babel, when God "confound[ed] all the language of the earth," scattering its people abroad so that "they left off to build the city,' is the archetypal symbol of social distintegration. In Kyd's play Hieronimo's Babel-performance climaxes a series of episodes in which the failure of civil order is figured in the collapse of language. The first of these occurs in 3.12, when driven to fury by the King's deafness to his cries for justice, the old Knight Marshall abandons himself to frenzied gesture:

> Away! I'll rip the bowels of the earth,
> *He diggeth with his dagger.*
> And ferry over to th'Elysian plains,
> And bring my son to show his deadly wounds.
>
> (71–3)

This is followed in the next scene by an even more eloquent gesture of linguistic repudiation in which the instrument of speech itself, the mouth, becomes the agent of violence. Surrounded by petitioners who look to him for "equity" (54), Hieronimo is accosted by an old man whose bereavement mirrors his own, and who complains that the "distressful words" of his petition "With ink bewray what blood began in me" (75–7). Proclaiming the old man his "Orpheus" (a figure for the magical power of language to bring order to nature), Hieronimo suddenly seizes their legal papers from his petitioners and rips them to pieces in a ferocious mimicry of revenge, rending and tearing the words as though they were his enemies, "shivering their limbs in pieces with my teeth" (123). In a last variation upon this trope, those same teeth become the instrument by which his speech is permanently silenced, when, following the performance of his babel-play, Hieronimo bites out his own tongue (4.4.191) in a gesture designed (according to the gloss supplied by the play's reviser) "to express the rupture of my part" (5th Addition, l. 47).[7]

Linguistic breakdown is likewise a symptom of the social disintegration attendant upon revenge in *Titus*, where Aaron's description of the imperial palace as "full of *tongues*, of eyes and ears" and the woods as "ruthless, dreadful, *deaf* and dull" (2.1.128–9; emphasis added) figures the contrast between the eloquent world of the city, and the inarticulate wilderness whose only mouth is that of the "blood-drinking pit" where Bassianus meets his end (2.3.224, 236). The excision of Lavinia's tongue and the amputation of those other instruments of eloquence, her hands,[8] by Tamora's sons, consigns her father to a world of mute semiotics in which he dreams of "cut[ting] away our hands" or "bit[ing] our tongues, and in dumb shows / Pass[ing] the remainder of our hateful days" (3.1.130–2). Scanning Lavinia's "map of woe," he seeks to "interpret all her martyred signs," assuring his "speechless complainer" that he will perfect his mastery of her "dumb action" to the point where he can "wrest an alphabet" from her repertory of frantic gesture (3.2.12, 36–45).

If speech is the faculty that distinguishes men from beasts, then the loss or abandonment of language becomes a potent metaphor for the anarchy produced by the lonely frenzy of the revenger: "Where words prevail not," declares Kyd's Lorenzo, "violence prevails" (2.1.108). That is why the figure of Lavinia as "speechless complainer" is charged with a horror that goes beyond the mere shock of mutilation and violated innocence; it is also what gives a particular edge of menace to Hamlet's gathering contempt for "Words, words, words" (2.2.210, 614), and what seems to charge the wild, disordered "nothing" of Ophelia's mad speech (4.5.9 ff.) with a murderous power beyond the reach of rational discourse: "Hadst thou thy wits and didst persuade revenge, / It could not move thus . . . This nothing's more than matter" (4.5.192–8).

"Endless Tragedy": Dramatic Structure
and the Rhetoric of Excess

The moral and emotional contradictions from which revenge tragedy draws its ferocious energy also have a structural equivalent in a recurrent tension between the tightly contained formal patterns dictated by the revenge ethic and its appetite for chaotic excess. Revenge tragedy is the most remorselessly plot-driven and end-directed of dramatic genres: indeed, it might be said that the hero's sole *raison d'être* is to drive the plot to its conclusion, to accomplish the ends of revenge. When Hamlet, after killing Polonius, resolves to "draw [him] towards an end" (3.4.239), this is the destiny he punningly enacts as he drags the old man's corpse from the stage; and however much the Prince may recoil from the obligations of his role into the labyrinths of ratiocination, it is as the instrument of an ineluctable plot that he is finally compelled to see himself: "There's a divinity that shapes our ends, / Rough-hew them how we will" (5.2.11–12; Neill 1997: 237–442).

In the play that established the generic mold for later dramatists, Kyd's *The Spanish Tragedy*, the overwhelming agency of plot is represented by two supernatural figures, the Ghost of Andrea and the spirit of Revenge, who place themselves on stage at the beginning of the play to "serve for Chorus in this tragedy" (1.1.91). Their silent presence throughout the action serves (together with the commentary they supply at the end of each act) as a constant reminder of the characters' subjection to the predetermined pattern of revenge; and although the Ghost is repeatedly frustrated by seemingly retrograde twists in the plot, Revenge reassures him as to its true direction. At last, after the murderous catastrophe has consumed his enemies in the Spanish court, Andrea declares his satisfaction: "Ay, now my hopes have *end* in their effects, / When blood and sorrow *finish* my desires" (4.5.1–2; emphasis added). The rhetorical stress on ending in these lines, complementing the ceremonial gestures of closure in the funeral procession that ends scene 4, appears to announce a perfect resolution of the plot. However, the succeeding dialogue undercuts this comforting sense of finality, as Andrea assigns "endless" punishments to the victims of Hieronimo's vengeance (31–44) while Revenge insists that, although on earth "death hath end their misery," in the underworld the dead will be compelled to play out "their endless tragedy" (47–8). What is especially chilling about Revenge's promise is not so much its (quite orthodox) confirmation of eternal punishment, as the way in which his theatrical metaphor threatens to turn the afterlife into an infinitely protracted repetition of the drama of retribution we have just witnessed – a repetition which, because of the unspecified referent of "their," disturbingly threatens to encompass friend as well as foe, good and bad alike.

This is an ending that promises no end, withdrawing the satisfaction of aesthetic closure in the very couplet that should seal it; and the paradox it entails was one to which later dramatists repeatedly returned – notably the author of the 1602 additions to Kyd's play, whose remarkable "Painter Scene" extends the queasy *mise en abîme* of Revenge's "endless tragedy." Here Hieronimo commissions a painter to prepare a revenger's memento – a work not unlike the Darnley Memorial,[9] the painting through which the infant King James was adjured to seek vengeance for his murdered father. Outlining the program for his own revenge painting, Hieronimo begins with an extravagantly colored description of the scene in which he discovered Horatio's boy; but then, to the puzzlement of his interlocutor, he suddenly breaks off:

> {*Hieronimo:*} . . . make me curse hell, invocate heaven, and in the end, leave me in a trance – and so forth.
> *Painter:* And is this the end?
> *Hieronimo:* O no, there is no end: the end is death and madness . . . . reason abuseth me, and there's the torment, there's the hell. At the last, sir, bring me to one of the murderers: were he as strong as Hector, thus would I tear and drag him up and down.
> (4th Addition, ll. 160–9; emphasis added)

At this point, in a frenzy of grief and frustration, Hieronimo assaults the luckless painter: thus the revenger's attempt to write a proleptic *finis* to his plot through the agency of art collapses, as fiction breaks its boundaries to engulf the real world. Much the same thing will happen, of course, in the final scene of the play, where the metatheatrical conceit created by the onstage audience of Andrea and Revenge, is mirrored in the theatrical performance staged by Hieronimo for the edification of the court: his tragedy enables the "acting" of his "plot . . . of dire revenge" (4.3.28–30), dispatching his son's killers by maneuvering them into a witty reenactment of their original crime. "See here my show," Hieronimo urges his audience, gesturing at his motive in the suddenly revealed form of Horatio's butchered carcass, "look on this spectacle: / Here lay my hope, and here my hope hath end" (4.4.89–90). He follows this with an elaborate explanatory epilogue, climaxing in the offer to "conclude his part" in suicide: "And gentles, thus I end my play: / Urge no more words, I have no more to say" (4.4.146–52). The carefully orchestrated closure announced in this couplet is delusive, however, proving the artifice of the hero's theatrical design inadequate to contain the savagery of revenge: instead of the terminal silence he promises, Hieronimo becomes embroiled in a bitter debate with the onstage audience, which culminates in a fresh explosion of violence, as he bites out his tongue and then stabs the Duke of Castile to death, before killing himself.

Commentators are often puzzled by the excess of violence in this scene: what, after all (apart from fathering Lorenzo), has the wretched Castile done to merit death – let alone the eternal torture reserved for him by Andrea? Why should Hieronimo, whose epilogue constituted a full and frank confession, chose to devour his own tongue rather than reveal the mysterious "thing which I have vow'd inviolate" (188)? But of course excess – the breach of proper bounds – is precisely what is encoded in Hieronimo's violent repudiation of speech, and in the other episodes we have been considering, with their repeated frustration of aesthetic closure (Neill 1997: 211–15). The fondness for excess was part of the Elizabethan inheritance from the Roman dramatist Seneca, who, in revenge dramas like *Thyestes*, with its ferocious cannibal banquet, provided an unimpeachable classical model for their violent sensationalism. But the dramatists display a self-consciousness about the debt which suggests that something more than simple mimicry was involved. Kyd, for example, openly signals his indebtedness in the motto drawn from Seneca's *Agamemnon* – *Per scelus semper tutum est sceleribus iter* (the safest route for crime is always through more crime) – which Hieronimo uses to refute the quietism enjoined in the biblical claim that vengeance belongs only to God (3.13.1–6); "Seneca cannot be too heavy" for Hamlet's tragedians of the city (2.2.424); and in *Hoffman* the protagonist is made to boast that the murder with which he has initiated his revenge is only "the prologue to a Tragedy" that will surpass the bloodiest of Seneca's murderous extravaganzas: "Thyestes, Tereus, / Jocasta, or Duke Jason's jealous wife" (sig. C2v).

Metatheatrical allusions of this kind help to extend the function of excess beyond mere narrative sensationalism, to the level of rhetoric and psychology. It is the destiny of every revenge-hero to produce a holocaust – one in which the ends of justice are swamped in a savage mini-apocalypse of blood; but what is striking about Elizabethan and Jacobean revenge plays is the way in which their heroes and villains openly embrace an ethos of excess, triumphantly rejecting all constraints of law and custom: "They reck no laws that meditate revenge," declares the bereaved Viceroy in *The Spanish Tragedy* (1.3.48), acknowledging that to embark on revenge, is to commit oneself to a course of extremity that knows no limit. "Revenge," declares Claudius, in response to Laertes' maddened undertaking to cut Hamlet's throat in the church, "should know no bounds" (*Hamlet* 4.7.100). In *The Revenger's Tragedy*, one of Vindice's co-conspirators proclaims "our wrongs are such, / We cannot justly be revenged too much" (5.2.9), while Vindice himself, not content with killing the old Duke who murdered his beloved, crows with satisfaction at the extermination of a whole "nest of dukes" (5.3.128). In *Antonio's Revenge*, Piero and Andrugio, villain and victim, are similarly at one in their insistence that their vindictive appetites are "boundless," and therefore to be satisfied only by a piece of "topless villainy" or "peerless... revenge," which, because it cannot be "equalled," excels any conceivable response (1.1.79, 85, 102, 3.5.29). By the same token, Antonio, still unsatisfied after his murder of the infant Julio, compares himself to "insatiate hell, still crying 'More!'" (3.1.212–13). Blood for blood is no longer enough: Antonio claims "large interest for blood" (5.6.22). Beginning in a frustrated desire for condign punishment, revenge becomes a kind of competition in atrocity, where the revenger's greatest satisfaction is not to match but to outstrip his opponent as bloodily as possible – as Vasques gloatingly does in John Ford's *'Tis Pity She's a Whore* (ca. 1629–33), when he boasts of how "a Spaniard outwent an Italian in revenge" (5.2.145–6).

There is a point to all of this reveling in excess, of course; for it once again draws attention to the fundamental contradiction at the heart of early modern revenge narratives – the conflict between the revenge hero's longing to restore order and balance to the world, and the self-confounding extravagance of the method he employs.[10] By exploiting and probing such contradictions, revenge tragedy became a vehicle for exploring deeply felt anxieties about the very possibility of justice in a fallen world. But the tendency of revenge to generate "endless tragedy" also served to point up a crucial paradox in the genre's treatment of memory and time.

"Remember Me": The Time of Revenge

In accordance with the patterns of ironic duplication so characteristic of revenge tragedy, the action of *Hamlet* sets two bereaved sons, each seeking requital for a father's murder, in opposition to one another. The resemblances between them go well beyond their common thirst for justice, however; for each seems haunted as much by the contemptuous neglect of his father's memory as by the murder itself. When we first meet him, Hamlet – set apart from the gaudy court by his "customary suits of solemn black" and by the "mourning duties" and "obsequious sorrow" that keep him seeking "his noble father in the dust" (1.2.81, 91–6) – rails against the scanting of the dead king's funeral rites, and the shameless impropriety by which "[t]he funeral baked meats / Did coldly furnish forth the marriage tables" (187–8). Later we will hear Laertes lamenting not merely the "means" of Polonius' death, but the public insult of his hugger-mugger interment – "his obscure funeral, / No trophy, sword, nor hatchment o'er his bones, / No noble rite, nor formal ostentation" (4.5.238–40) – an insult that will be compounded in his mind by the shrunken obsequies allowed to his sister Ophelia (5.1.230–52). The intense emotional significance that both characters attach to funeral ceremonies in *Hamlet* can be illuminated by comparison with two particularly striking scenes in a play closely modeled on *Hamlet*, *Antonio's Revenge*. The second act of Marston's drama opens with an unusually lengthy stage direction, detailing the ornate funeral procession of Duke Andrugio, the murdered father whom the hero will be bound to avenge. This display of pageantry is complemented by a second, equally elaborate dumb show at the beginning of the third act, where Andrugio's widow and son enter to perform their mourning obsequies at Andrugio's tomb. These two shows, with their shared display of knightly achievements – helmet, sword, and banners – represent successive phases of a single ritual. Like any of the great heraldic funerals that announced the passing of the rich and powerful, while simultaneously proclaiming their triumph over death, Andrugio's is designed both as an act of ceremonial closure and a rite of memory, whose lavish parade of the dead man's fame will reach its designated "end" in the monument where his memory is to be enshrined forever (Neill 1997: ch. 8). Andrugio's rites, however, are deliberately violated by his murderer, who concludes the funeral procession by consigning the corpse to oblivion, in a parodic inversion of the conventional funeral oration with its proclamations of immortal renown:

> Rot there, thou cerecloth that enfolds the flesh
> Of my loathed foe; moulder to crumbling dust;
> Oblivion choke the passage of thy fame!
> Trophies of honoured birth drop quickly down;
> Let naught of him, but what was vicious live.
> (2.1.1–5)

Determined to extend his "snaky Vengeance" beyond the grave (6–8), Piero goes on to woo Maria as she kneels at her husband's "honoured sepulchre," beneath the streamers bearing his arms (3.1.0, 5, 12) – an insult which, combined with Antonio's pious invocations of his father's "mighty spirit" (27), is sufficient to summon Andrugio's ghost from his coffin to demand revenge (32–51).

By virtue of their spectacular character and structural prominence, these two episodes serve to highlight the crucial importance of memory in this form of drama, where the protagonist and antagonist find themselves locked in a battle for the control and disposition of time. In his drive to control the future, the usurping villain of revenge tragedy seeks, like Macbeth, to annihilate the past, to make the death-blow of murder "the be-all and the end-all" so that nothing can "return / To plague th'inventor" (*Macbeth* 1.7.4–5, 9–10). The revenger, by contrast, is wedded to the past: his role is that of a "remembrancer" in both senses of that formerly potent word – one who exacts payment for past debts, and one whose task it is to rescue the past from the grave of oblivion. The badge of this function is the memento or relic that he treasures, both as a covert warning to his enemies and as a proof of the guilty history that tyrannical power seeks to erase. In *The Spanish Tragedy* Hieronimo hides away Horatio's body, but carries with him a handkerchief besmeared with the youth's blood as a constant incentive to revenge; in *Antonio's Revenge*, Pandulpho produces the corpse of his murdered son and "*lay{s} it thwart Antonio's breast*" to spur his fellow-revenger to his duty (4.5.0.2); in *Hoffman*, the hero has carefully preserved the "dead remembrance of [his] living father" in the form of the skeleton hanging in his arbor; while in *The Revenger's Tragedy*, Vindice has spent nine years sighing over the skull of his poisoned mistress, awaiting the moment of retribution. By contrast, the more civilized Hamlet carries only the portrait of his dead father, but even he will find its symbolic surrogate in the graveyard, where, as a prologue to the achievement of his task, he broods over the skull of poor Yorick. Revenge, as we are reminded when Horatio's corpse, the "bare bones" of Hoffman senior, or Gloriana's skull become essential properties in the conduct of revenge, is merely remembrance continued by other means (Kerrigan 1996: ch. 7; Neill 1983; 1992: 316–20; 1997: chs. 7–8; Blumenfeld 2002: 34–49, 53–64).[11] The crime which the hero seeks to avenge lies beyond the reach of the law precisely because authority denies its very existence, casting it into the shameful "oblivion" which Piero reserves for his victim.

When Claudius cynically erases the memory of "our dear brother's death" by appealing to the more pressing need for "remembrance of ourselves" (*Hamlet*, 1.2.1–7), the subtext of his smooth oration is a contemptuous reproof to his nephew, whose defiant exhibition of mourning constitutes a wordless insistence on the claims of the past. But, as the anguish of Hamlet's ensuing soliloquy ("Must I remember," 147) immediately demonstrates, this lonely commitment to the preservation of memory constitutes an almost intolerable burden. To insist upon it in the teeth of the bland oblivion to which his whole society subscribes is to appear mad. Moreover, it has the potential to destroy him: the revenger's virtuous desire to rejoint the *membra disjecta* of the violated past – even to making it live again through the conduct of a plot that, like Hieronimo's "Soliman and Perseda," Hamlet's "Murder of Gonzago," or Vindice's puppet play, replicates the original scene of murder – is proof of his integrity; but it is also the source of his corruption. This was what Bacon had in mind when he wrote of "vindictive persons liv[ing] the life of witches" (Bacon 1906: 14) – being possessed, as it were, by the evil spirit of the past, which must in the end undo them. Although at the level of convention they can be explained away as survivals from Senecan drama, the restless, unappeased ghosts of revenge tragedy are the manifestations of that fearful incubus – representations of a past that refuses to be buried: "The time has been," agonizes Macbeth, haunted by Banquo's ghost, "That when the brains were out, the man would die, / And there an end; but now they rise again" (3.4.77–9).

In Kyd's "endless tragedy," the Ghost of Andrea might be read as a figure of historical destiny, representing the way in which the dead hand of the past exercises a grip on the present of which its denizens are not even conscious. But more typically it is the tormented imagination of the living that summons these specters of history: so in *Antonio's Revenge*, as Antonio vows his nightly ritual of mourning, his father's spirit rises from his tomb to command vengeance: "Thy pangs of anguish rip my cerecloth up; / And lo, the ghost of old Andrugio / Forsakes his coffin. Antonio, revenge!" (3.1.32–4). In *Hamlet*, when the "canonized bones" of the dead king, "hearsed in death," similarly "burst their cerements," it is to the mourning Prince alone that the

Ghost reveals its meaning – though (like some shadow of a forgotten past) it troubles the minds of his fellow-watchers on the battlements. Unlike Andrugio's ghost, or its own more primitive predecessor in Shakespeare's putative source, the lost Ur-*Hamlet*, however, this Ghost seems less pressingly concerned with revenge than with remembrance itself. Where the Ur-*Hamlet* ghost was notorious for its shriek of "Hamlet, revenge!," this Ghost is notable for its preoccupation with the story of its silenced past and for the plangently yearning "Remember me" (1.5.98), which Hamlet makes his watchword:

> Remember thee?
> Ay, thou poor ghost, whiles memory holds a seat
> In this distracted globe. Remember thee?
> Yea, from the table of my memory
> I'll wipe away all trivial fond records
>
> *   *   *   *   *   *
>
> Now to my word.
> It is "adieu, adieu, remember me."
>
> (1.5.102–18)

When the Ghost reappears in the closet scene to whet Hamlet's "almost blunted purpose," it does so with stern reproof: "Do not forget" (3.4.126). However, this shift from the rhetoric of revenge to that of remembrance does not, in the end, signal any abatement in the violence of the narrative: despite his intellectual disposition and propensity for melancholy introspection, the Hamlet who longs to "drink hot blood" (3.2.423), who refrains from assassinating Claudius only because he seeks to extend his revenge beyond the grave (3.3.92–100), who stabs Polonius to death with no more compunction than if he had killed a rat (3.4), and who takes a gloating satisfaction in tricking his old schoolfellows, Rosencrantz and Guildenstern, into carrying their own death warrant, proves to be no less ruthless than other revenge heroes. Rather, the difference is one that enables Shakespeare to shift the ethical attention of the play from debate over the morality of private retribution, to an extended meditation on the ambiguous function of memory in the mythos of revenge.

The result is that *Hamlet* focuses to an unprecedented degree upon the inner life of a revenger who, condemned to sweat under the burden of memory in a world of "bestial oblivion," finds himself tormented by the disparity between the truth of the past and the lying version propagated by official history. If the Ghost is Hamlet's "cherub" of remembrance (4.3.58), then the King is a spirit of oblivion; and to Hamlet, not only Gertrude with her scandalously hasty remarriage, but Polonius, Rosencrantz and Guildenstern, and even Ophelia ("I have remembrances of yours, / That I have longèd long to redeliver", 3.1.102–3) are pliant accessories in Claudius' conspiracy to deny the past. Hamlet's obsession with remembering (1.2.96) – dismissed by Claudius, with a contemptuous quibble, as "obsequious sorrow" (1.2.96) – commits the Prince (who represents the future of a past that Claudius has "cut off") to "follow" the Ghost in an enactment of due sequence that answers the claims of memory, consequence, and succession (1.4.70, 76, 87, 96). What he inevitably discovers, however, is that such a commitment to the rejointing of time also embroils him in an all-too-familiar kind of plot, one which, because its only imaginable end is death, threatens the radical undoing of self represented by the anonymous skulls of the graveyard: "Imperious Caesar, dead and turned to clay, / Might stop a hole to keep the wind away" (5.1.220–1).

Hamlet escapes the net of Claudius's narrative, only to become entangled in that of the Ghost. If it is true that those haunted by the wrongs of the past "live the life of witches," then it is with good cause that Horatio fears that the Ghost may draw Hamlet into insanity, despair, or suicide (1.4.77–86). The Prince himself suspects that "the spirit that I have seen / May be a devil" (2.2.627–8), and there is an uncanny congruence in the way its tale of poison-through-the-ear itself acts like a kind of "leprous distilment" poured in Hamlet's own ear and then coursing "through / The natural gates and alleys of the body" (1.5.71–4), before breaking out in the canker of revenge. Thus the Ghost appears to contain in itself the contradictions by which the revenger is typically destroyed: on the one hand, as the embodiment of the obliterated past, an uncanny return of the repressed, it represents the indestructible power of memory to contest the dispensations of tyrannous usurpation; on the other, as it takes possession of Hamlet's mind, it too becomes a kind of usurper, not only (in Horatio's resonant metaphor) "usurping" both the night and the "fair and warlike form" of the dead King (1.1.54–7), but acting upon Hamlet like the poison that "usurps" the "wholesome" life of the Player King (3.2.286).

Hamlet's ambiguous feelings about the role to which he is committed by the Ghost's narrative and his own vow of remembrance are revealed in his anxious "scourge and minister" speech, with its sense that the killing of Polonius amounts to a punishment that is fated to rebound upon himself (3.4.194–6). This deep ambivalence is what underlies the inability to match actions to words or thoughts to ends, which becomes a recurrent theme of his self-tormenting soliloquies; and it helps to explain the curiously indecisive use to which he puts the play-within-the-play in the Murder of Gonzago, where (in contrast to the perfect concatenation of memorial and vengeance in Hieronimo's or Vindice's theatrical performances) the reenactment of Claudius's crime serves a purely diagnostic function. Thus Hamlet's play, like the fantasy of blood-revenge in the Player's Hecuba speech, is reduced to a mere "fiction, [or] a dream of passion" (2.2.579). Yet (as critics have often observed) the metatheatrical satisfactions so frustratingly deferred by the abortive "Mousetrap" are brought to a kind of consummation in the self-consciously theatrical "play" of Hamlet's exhibition bout with Laertes – another scene of pretended violence that becomes the real thing, and that concludes in a properly ironic compacting of past and present, as the Prince forces his uncle to drink the poisonous instrument of his own treachery. One reason for the extreme importance which the revenger attaches to symmetrical schemes of "balance" and "proportion" is that, by producing a kind of reversed reenactment of the past crime, they magically cancel out its power to hurt. In this case, however, the accomplishment of revenge is shorn of the triumphant swagger with which the traditional revenger invited the simultaneous admiration and horrified recoil of the audience; for, unlike the ingenious Machiavellian designs of a Hieronimo or a Vindice, the plot worked out here is conspicuously not of the hero's own composition. Instead, as Hamlet's fatalistic surrender to the shaping hand of "providence" emphasizes, it is as though he had now become the merely passive instrument of memory, abandoning himself to a "special providence" whose script is barely distinguishable from those hoary old revenge dramas that his temperament seemed most inclined to resist. Like the revengers described by Laura Blumenfeld who "try to rewrite history by reliving it," Hamlet "get[s] stuck inside a story" (Blumenfeld 2002: 45).

It is not perhaps surprising that, after the probing inquisition to which *Hamlet* subjected the conventions of revenge tragedy, dramatists like Chettle, Marston, and Middleton should have approached the genre in a style increasingly inflected by ironic burlesque and satiric exaggeration; or that Chapman in *The Revenge of Bussy D'Ambois* (ca. 1610) and Tourneur in *The Atheist's Tragedy* (ca. 1609), should have turned the genre on its head by crafting what Katharine Maus has called "anti-revenge plays" (Maus 1995: xxiii). But possibly the most interesting response to Hamlet's agonizing over the ambiguous seductions of memory and revenge was provided by Shakespeare himself in his last independently written work; for *The Tempest* is a drama that artfully converts the conventions of revenge tragedy to the benevolent ends of tragicomic romance (Neill 1983: 45–9; Kerrigan 1996: 211–16). Here once again, in a play whose patterns of conspiracy and betrayal, possession and dispossession, shipwreck and rescue, suggest a past constantly reimposing itself upon the present, the words "remember," "remembrance," and "memory" are repeated with almost incantatory insistence. *The Tempest* is dominated, however, by a reformed revenger, for whom "the rarer action is / In virtue than in vengeance" (5.1.27–8) – one whose talisman is a living daughter rather than the revenger's deathly memento, and whose very name suggests hope for the future (*Pro-spero*) rather than obsession with the past. The protagonist, like Hamlet, is a "minister" of remembrance whose mission is to those, like his usurping brother, Antonio, and King Alonso, who have "made . . . sinner[s] of [their] memory" (1.2.101); but, although Prospero's patience must struggle to contain his fury, in his scheme of renewal compassion will supplant passion, and repentance displace revenge. "That which is past is gone, and irrevocable," Bacon wrote at the end of his essay on revenge, "and wise men have enough to do, with things present and to come; therefore they do but trifle with themselves, that labor in past matters" (1906: 14). *The Tempest* does not dismiss the "labor" of remembering quite so lightly: at the beginning of the play Prospero (like Hamlet, weighed down by the "fardels" of agonized recollection) continues to groan under the "burden" of his past (1.2 156); but (as if in extended meditation upon John Donne's luminous aphorism that "the art of *salvation*, is but the art of *memory*" – Donne 1952ff.: 2, 73) this play imagines a process by which human beings, through a full remembrance of their past errors, can free themselves from the cycle of revenge – allowing them to move through a series of unburdenings (both literal and metaphorical) toward the blessed oblivion envisaged by a forgiving Prospero: " Let us not burden our remembrance with / A heaviness that's gone" (5.1.199–200).

NOTES

1 On revenge as a function of honour societies, see Visser (2002: 43–5).

2 Thanks to the work of David Lake and Mac Jackson, this play, formerly attributed to Cyril Tourneur, is now widely regarded as an early work by Thomas Middleton – for a summary of the arguments see R.A. Foakes's introduction to his edition of the play (Anon.: 1996).

3 Hobsbawm (1972: 29, 35–6).

4 All citations from *The Revenger's Tragedy* are to Brian Gibbons' New Mermaid edition (Anon.: 2000).

5 Recent work by Mac Jackson, Brian Boyd, and Brian Vickers makes it clear that *Titus* was the result of collaboration with George Peele, who seems to have written at least the first act; but Shakespeare was clearly the principal partner in this enterprise, and it seems reasonable to grant him responsibility for the overall design. The authorship arguments are extensively rehearsed in Vickers (2002: 148–243).

6 The stage direction in the First Quarto (1603), which, despite its notorious textual deficiencies, is a mine of information about original stage practice, indicates that Player King "sits down in an Arbor" before his murder.

7 The 1602 quarto of *The Spanish Tragedy* contains five significant additional passages by an unknown hand. The case for Ben Jonson's authorship is powerfully stated by Anne Barton (Barton 1984: 13 28).

8 On the hand as a primary vehicle of meaning in early modern culture and its significance in *Titus Andronicus*, see Neill (2000).

9 George Vertue's engraving of the memorial is reproduced in Frye (1984: figs. 11.3–11.5).

10 The paradox is perhaps already implicit in the *koros* of revenge as understood by the Greeks: this could mean either "satiety" (sufficiency) or the excess that produced *ate* (disorder, confusion) – Visser (2002: 59).

11 On the importance of memory in revenge drama in general and *Hamlet* in particular, see Kerrigan (1996: ch. 7) and Neill (1983: passim; 1997: chs. 7–8, and in n. 11).

REFERENCES AND FURTHER READING

Anon. (Middleton, Thomas?). (1996). *The Revenger's Tragedy*, ed. R.A. Foakes. Revels Plays. Manchester: Manchester University Press.

Anon. (Middleton, Thomas?). (2000). *The Revenger's Tragedy*, 2nd edn, ed. Brian Gibbons. New Mermaids. London: A & C Black.

Bacon, Francis. (1906). "Of Revenge." In *Francis Bacon's Essays*, intro. Oliphant Smeaton (London: Dent), 13–14.

Barton, Anne. (1984). *Ben Jonson: Dramatist*. Cambridge: Cambridge University Press.

Blumenfeld, Laura. (2002). *Revenge: A Story of Hope*. New York: Simon & Schuster.

Bowers, Fredson. (1940). *Elizabethan Revenge Tragedy*. Princeton, NJ: Princeton University Press.

Chettle, Henry. (1631). *The Tragedy of Hoffman, or A Revenge for a Father*. London: Hugh Perry.

Donne, John. (1952ff.). *Sermons*, 10 vols., ed. George R. Potter and Evelyn M. Simpson. Berkeley: University of California Press.

Florio, John. (1611). *Queen Anna's New World of Words*. London: Edward Blount and William Barrett.

Ford, John. (1975). *'Tis Pity She's a Whore*, ed. Derek Roper. Revels Plays. London: Methuen.

Frye, R. M. (1984). *The Renaissance Hamlet: Issues and Responses in 1600*. Princeton, NJ: Princeton University Press.

Hobsbawm, Eric. (1972). *Bandits*. London: Weidenfeld & Nicolson.

Johnson, S. F. (1963). "*The Spanish Tragedy*, or Babylon Revisited." In *Essays on Shakespeare and Elizabethan Drama*, ed. Richard Hosley. Columbia, MO: University of Missouri Press, 23–36.

Kerrigan, John. (1996). *Revenge Tragedy: Aeschylus to Armageddon*. Oxford: Clarendon Press.

Kyd, Thomas. (1959). *The Spanish Tragedy*, ed. Philip Edwards. Revels Plays. London: Methuen.

Mack, Maynard, Jr. (1973). *Killing the King: Three Studies in Shakespeare's Tragic Structure*. New Haven, CT: Yale University Press.

Marston, John. (1986). *The Selected Plays of John Marston*, ed. Macdonald P. Jackson and Michael Neill. Cambridge: Cambridge University Press.

Maus, Katharine Eisaman, ed. (1995). *Four Revenge Tragedies*. Oxford: Oxford University Press.

Neill, Michael. (1983). "Remembrance and Revenge; *Hamlet*, *Macbeth*, and *The Tempest*." In *Shakespeare and Jonson*, ed. Ian Donaldson. Basingstoke: Macmillan, 35–56.

Neill, Michael. (1992). "*Hamlet*: A Modern Perspective." In Barbara A. Mowat and Paul Werstine, eds, *Hamlet*. New Folger Library. New York: Washington Square Press, 301–26.

Neill, Michael. (1997). *Issues of Death: Mortality and Identity in English Renaissance Tragedy*. Oxford: Clarendon Press.

Neill, Michael. (2000). " 'Amphitheaters in the Body': Playing with Hands on the Shakespearean Stage." In *Putting History to the Question: Power, Politics and Society in English Renaissance Drama*, ed. M. Neill. New York: Columbia University Press, 167–203.

Shakespeare, William. (1974). *The Riverside Shakespeare*, ed. G. Blakemore Evans. Boston: Houghton Mifflin.

Shakespeare, William. (1984). *Titus Andronicus*, ed. Eugene M. Waith. Oxford Shakespeare. Oxford: Oxford University Press.

Shakespeare, William. (1992). *Hamlet*, ed. Barbara A. Mowat and Paul Werstine, New Folger Library. New York: Washington Square Press.

Shakespeare, William. (1997). *Othello*, ed. E. A. J. Honigmann. Arden Shakespeare. Walton-on-Thames: Thomas Nelson.

Vickers, Brian. (2002). *Shakespeare, Co-Author: A Historical Study of Five Collaborative Plays*. Oxford: Oxford University Press.

Visser, Margaret. (2002). *Beyond Fate*. Toronto: Anansi.

Wilders, John. (1978). *The Lost Garden*. Totowa, NJ: Rowman & Littlefield.

20

Spanish Golden Age Tragedy:
From Cervantes to Calderón

Margaret R. Greer

Tragedy is only possible to a mind which is for the moment agnostic or Manichean. The least touch of any theology which has a compensating Heaven to offer the tragic hero is fatal. (Richards 1924: 246)

The two rocks on which the whole ideological system of the comedia is built are *la honra* and *la fe* . . . Spiritually, *la fe* has the answers to all conflicts and, for Spanish *integralismo* between the divine and the human, heaven is never far away. (Reichenberger 1959: 308, 311)

It may be that tragedy itself first emerges when a civilization is caught between fate and freedom . . . in some twilight zone between politics and myth, civic and religious allegiance, ethical autonomy and a still cogent sense of the numinous. (Eagleton 2003: 107–8)

Despite allegations of critics like Richards and Reichenberger, Spanish Golden Age tragedy is not an oxymoron. Reichenberger shared with Richards and many others the view that tragedy is incompatible with the supposedly fundamental optimism of Christian faith and the promise of perfect justice in a life after death, a faith fervently defended in Counter-Reformation Catholic Spain. That faith, however, did not immunize Spain against competing pressures generated by religious alterity, absolutism, empire, and socioeconomic change. Eagleton's suggestion of tragedy's emergence in societies caught between belief systems is a more accurate description of the wellspring of tragic drama in early modern Spain. My difficulty in writing a chapter surveying tragic drama in the age of Cervantes, Lope de Vega, Tirso de Molina, and Calderón de la Barca is not that of locating tragedy, but of selecting just which works to highlight.

Tragedies do constitute only a minor proportion of early modern Spain's immense theatrical production, however. The generic term used to designate all three-act dramas was *comedia*, whether the work was comic or tragic, although dramatists or their publishers qualified some works as tragicomedies or tragedies in titles or final lines. Even in the case of Pedro Calderón de la Barca, the dramatist who most cultivated the tragic mode, tragedies constitute at most 10 to 15 percent of his approximately 100-plus *comedias*, and a much smaller percentage of his total dramatic output.

In Madrid and other Spanish cities, the *corrales de comedias* (public theaters) were the principal performance venues from about 1580 onward. The theater arrangement and audience composition were similar to those of the Elizabethan public theaters.[1] The rectangular open-air patio was surrounded on three sides by galleries and viewing boxes, with the stage and multistory acting structure on the fourth side. Seating arrangements for viewing reflected the hierarchical structure of the society of the time, and the wide range of prices allowed at least occasional attendance by diverse sectors of the society, male and female, from artisans, soldiers, and servants to clerics and the wealthiest nobility. The owner-manager of a theater company paid play-wrights for new plays and later sold them for publication, generally without inter-vention by the dramatist. Consequently, plays were frequently misattributed and many can only be dated by circumstantial evidence. Since the playbill was changed every few days, demand for plays was great and production by favored playwrights correspondingly large. Even the most prolific playwright could not live solely by his pen, however. Lope, Calderón, and Vélez de Guevara supplemented their income by serving wealthy noblemen, while Tirso was a Mercedarian friar, and Calderón and Lope became priests late in life.[2] Although between the last decades of the sixteenth century and the end of the seventeenth, scores of dramatists wrote *comedias* for the *corral* audiences, I will concentrate on the five most significant tragedians of the period: Miguel de Cervantes (1547–1616), Lope de Vega Carpio (1562–1635), Tirso de Molina (pseudonym of Gabriel Téllez, 1579–1648), Luis Vélez de Guevara (1578/9–1644) and Pedro Calderón de la Barca (1600–81).

As Raymond Williams points out, "tragedy attracts the fundamental beliefs and tensions of a period," and in its tragic theory, the fundamental shape of a culture is realized (Williams 1966: 45). The tragic form developed by these five dramatists never rigidly followed classical precepts such as unity of time and space, as we shall see. But a more significant departure from classical form, given the nexus between the shape of a culture and its tragic form, is that Spanish tragedies often involve collective responsibility and suffering rather that the destruction of a single hero. The fundamental beliefs and tensions they manifest involve the legitimacy of imperialism, religious and cultural antagonism, political ambition and tyranny, sexual aggression and repression, class conflict, and competing demands of state and family, of society and the individual will, articulated as crises of honor. While the majority are grounded in Iberian history or legend, the conflicts at their center are part of a general early modern crisis in Europe. In the pages that follow, I intertwine consideration of those themes with that of the developing shape of tragic form in Spain, as both relate to the larger collective tragedy of early modern Spain itself.

Beginnings; Imperialism

Since the first performances of the works of Juan del Encina (ca.1468–ca.1530), traditionally (albeit debatably) called the "father" of Spanish drama, took place about 1495, the birth of Spanish drama coincided in time with Columbus' voyages to America. Its early development, however, was nourished by Spanish expansion in Italy and contact there with efforts to revive, translate, and imitate classical comedy and tragedy. Bartolomé de Torres Naharro (ca.1485–ca.1520) wrote several *comedias* while serving in Rome and published his collected works, the *Propalladia* (1517), in Naples. Naharro's preface to that volume is one of the earliest statements of dramatic theory in Renaissance Europe, before the general rediscovery of Aristotle's *Poetics*, and it marks out the independent path Spanish drama would follow. He summarizes certain classical dramatic precepts – the distinction between comedy and tragedy; Cicero's definition of drama as an imitation of life, a mirror of customs, an image of truth; six types of comedy, the Horatian recommendation of five-act works, and the importance of decorum – "All of which," he concludes, "seems to me longer in telling than necessary to hear" (Sánchez Escribano and Porqueras Mayo 1972: 63). Naharro calls the acts "jornadas," the length of a day's travel or work, or of an audience's attention, a label that would become standard in later *comedias*.

In the latter half of the sixteenth century, various members of humanist and university circles in Spain tried their hands at creating tragedy in the vernacular, by translating or imitating Greek or Senecan tragedies.[5] The influence of Seneca, born in the Iberian peninsula and hence often claimed as a Spanish rather than Roman forebear, was all-pervasive. The earliest tragedy that has earned lasting favor, however, was Miguel de Cervantes' *El cerco de la Numancia* ("The siege of Numantia"). That play, written at the height of Spain's imperial power, dramatizes the peninsula's history not as subject but as the object of imperial expansion, in the fall of the holdout Celtiberian city Numantia to imperial Roman troops. The Roman conquest of Iberia began in 218 BCE and by 133 BCE the Romans controlled the majority of the peninsula, but repeated attempts to take Numantia had failed. Scipio Aemilianus finally accomplished it in 133 BCE, not by direct attack but by hunger, laying an eight-month siege to the town. According to Appian of Alexandria's second-century-AD account, the Numantians had resorted to cannibalism before their final surrender, first consuming their dead, then the sick, and finally the weakest inhabitants. Appian reported that many of the Numantians chose to commit suicide rather than surrender, and an alternate history developed, according to which not a single inhabitant survived the siege, and Scipio was therefore denied a triumphal celebration and reward for his victory. Numantia came to symbolize the independence of the Iberian spirit, and many of the ingredients Cervantes employs circulated in the rich Spanish ballad tradition.

Cervantes dramatized the conflict in four acts with an episodic structure that alternates between the Roman forces and the besieged Numantians, beginning with

Scipio's disciplinary harangue to the Roman troops for devoting themselves not to war but to the pleasures of Bacchus and Venus. Scipio concludes his exhortation to defeat these "rebellious, barbarous Spaniards" with the assertion that every person forges his own destiny. He curtly dismisses the Numantians' request for a peace accord, calling them caged beasts whom he will tame without losing a single Roman soldier. The Numantian women dissuade their desperate men from a suicidal plan to break through the Roman fortifications and die fighting, pleading that they would thus leave their wives and children prey to Roman rape and slavery. Vowing to leave nothing from which the Romans might profit, the Numantians elect to burn all their goods and to die at each other's hands.

Before this collective suicide is carried out, however, Cervantes performs a double sublimation of the memory of Numantian cannibalism. First, he makes it a weapon of battle turned against the enemy and carried out in an egalitarian fashion to nourish the community; they kill their Roman captives and distribute their flesh equally among all. Second, he turns it into a lover's sacrifice that prefigures the celebration of that of Christ in the Catholic mass. The young Marandro vows that he will die before allowing his fiancée Lira to die of hunger, scales the Roman walls to steal their bread, kills six Roman soldiers, and returns with a basketful of bread drenched with his own blood, to die in Lira's arms. Despite her hunger, she cannot eat such bread; she only brings his offering to her mouth to kiss it, and her starving young brother dies before he can partake of it. The transformation of the memory of a society reduced to the extreme of cannibalism to one characterized by heroic sacrifice for the good of the community is further underlined in the final scene. A youth, named Bariato after a famous hero of the Celtiberian resistance, hides in a tower as the Numantians turn their swords on one another, but when the Romans discover the carnage and destruction within the suddenly quiet city, he emerges and, rejecting Scipio's offer of pardon and riches, jumps to his death to deny Scipio his triumph over Numantia.

In this sublimation and other aspects of *Numantia*, I read a striking validation of Timothy Reiss's concept of tragedy in *Tragedy and Truth* (1980: 2–38; 283–4) as the discourse that in periods of profound political and social change serves to grasp the inexpressible, to fill in the absence of meaningfulness in the transition from one dominant discourse to another, to enclose that hole of unmeaning in an ordered discourse that creates a new signified and contributes to the consolidation of a new episteme. It affords the spectator the knowledge the tragic characters cannot possess, experiencing both the fear of disorder and the pleasure in seeing it overcome (27). Surely if there is a prospect of disorder that excites that fear, it is the thought of cannibalism, here twice sublimated and redeemed by heroic sacrifice.

The sixteenth and seventeenth centuries were, for Spain, in ways sometimes akin to, sometimes distinct from, the rest of Europe, a period of profound political and socioeconomic change. Spain's was a lengthy and incomplete transition, from a semifeudal society periodically battling to "reconquer" its territory from centuries of Arab control, to an imperial power engaged in multiple wars to maintain its wide-flung dominions. The issue of imperialism was particularly current when Cervantes wrote *Numantia*, sometime between 1581 and 1587. After a decade occupied with what today would be called "homeland security" – a rebellion by the *moriscos* (Arabs converted to Christianity) in Andalusia, Turkish aggression in the Mediterranean, and rebellion in the Low Countries – Philip II had renewed Charles V's policy of active imperialism. In 1579–80 he incorporated Portugal into Spain when the throne was left vacant by the death of its king, Sebastian, on an ill-fated campaign in Africa, a move that met with substantial criticism even within Spain. Hermenegildo (Cervantes 1994: 11) argues that Cervantes meant to associate Spain both *with* the besieging Roman forces *and* with their victims, akin in his day to the *moriscos*, the Dutch rebels, the Portuguese, and the indigenous civilizations of America. Cervantes put on stage a number of allegorical figures (Spain, the Duero River, War, Sickness, Hunger, and Fame) to make sense for his audience of this tragic history and the moral ambiguity the action posed for imperial Spain. The figure Spain laments her continual history of invasions, from the Phoenicians and Greeks to the menacing Romans. The Duero then foresees the Roman Empire crumbling under the invading Goths and Huns, the 1527 invasion of Rome by the troops of Charles V, papal baptism of Spain's monarchs as "Catholic Kings . . . insignia of Gothic union," and the "blessed" imperial rule of Philip II who will unite all Spain's realms, including the "Portuguese strip," and bring a thousand foreign nations under her flag and sword (77–8). Nowhere in the play do these allegorical prophets allude to the Arab conquest, however, or the seven centuries of Arab rule in Iberia, equal in duration to the Roman presence. This despite the fact that Cervantes himself had just returned from five years of captivity in Algiers, and drew on that experience for other works. Rather, in the sense-making discourse of this tragedy, the Arab invasion is repressed and in Spain's lament, its proximate cause – division among the Visigoths and the resentment of their rule by the more urban Roman Hispanic and Jewish peoples of the Peninsula – is transferred back in time to the Celtiberians.

The tragic ambiguity of a Spain both imperial victim and victimizer is thus both performed and contained within the work. Debates over the identity of the tragic hero of the work underline that ambiguity. Critics who look for the presence of an Aristotelian *hamartia* and *anagnorisis* consider Scipio the tragic hero; as he surveys the ashes and blood of Numantia, he acknowledges his arrogance and lack of pity and accords the glory of victory to Bariato. Others argue for considering the population of Numantia a collective tragic hero, synecdochically present in the body of Bariato, carried off at the end of the play to the acclaim of white-robed Fame. Significantly, the debate over whether to consider the victim or the surviving victimizer the tragic hero is repeated for a number of Spanish Golden Age tragedies.

Numantia and its place in the tradition of Spanish tragedy also supports another Reiss theory (1980: 41–2), that Renaissance tragedy moved through three stages: first that of language, of working out texts with their own rhetorical patterns; second, that of relating them to a generic order, tragedy; and third, that of playing out the imitation of external order beyond the mere concerns of literary genre. Early efforts to create tragedy in Spanish were associated, as in England and France, with the desire to ennoble the "vulgar" language to make it a medium of communication of a dignity comparable to Latin or Greek (Arellano 1995: 30). Cervantes wrote on the path between the second and third stage and, reflecting back on his later lack of success as a dramatist, proclaimed pride in his early contributions to the development of the genre, that of reducing the number of acts, and of supposedly being the first to represent on stage the hidden imagination and thoughts of the soul by the use of "moral," i.e., allegorical figures (Cervantes 1994: 9).

Comedia Form and Honor (I)

A decade later, Alonso López Pinciano published his *Philosophia antigua poética* (1596), an important commentary in dialogue, much less strict in its adherence to classical rules than preceding Italian commentaries on Aristotle's *Poetics*. By the time "El Pinciano" published his treatise, however, Lope de Vega had already developed the *comedia* form that would make it *the* popular entertainment for more than a century. As he explained his art in an ironic but fundamentally serious treatise, *Arte nuevo de hacer comedias en este tiempo* (The new art of crafting drama in this age) (1609), Lope locked classical precepts under seven keys when he wrote, preferring the variety of nature to the artificial unities prescribed by academic followers of Aristotle's *Poetics*. In action-filled plots divided into three acts that could cover wide swaths of space and time, the *comedia* combined elements of high and popular culture, as it mixed kings and commoners, saints and sinners, and included comic scenes even in high tragedy. Lope, a supremely gifted poet, gave the *comedia* a supple polyrhythmic texture, changing the verse form to suit the character and to set the mood of the scene for a public still close to oral culture, who came to "hear" a play.

Lope recommended plots centered on questions of honor as the most moving, and defined honor in *Los comendadores de Córdoba* (ca.1596) as "that which resides in another" from whom one receives honor. Although a variety of slights, from disrespectful address to the accusation of lying or cowardice, were offenses against honor, the key issue in theater is usually sexual, a man's capacity to ensure his wife's fidelity and the purity of other family females. The conjunction between female chastity and masculine honor thus functions, as Jonathan Dollimore observes regarding Jacobean tragedy, as "the ideological imposition and self-representation of the male ego in a male-dominated world" (Dollimore 1984: 141). Much ink has been devoted to the nature and role of honor in the *comedia*, by those who condemn the genre as barbarous because it supported a cruel concept of honor, and those who argue that the most notorious "wife-murder" tragedies served to criticize that code, between those who say that it reflected a social reality, and those who maintain that it was nothing more than a convenient literary convention. It was, at the very least, an important structuring device, particularly in tragedies, in which many protagonists engage the topic in an anguished monologue with honor as an inflexible and all-seeing superego. Dopico-Black (2001: 110–17) links it to a newly urgent instability of signs and practices of reading both texts and bodies, and the literalization of three sacraments in Catholic Counter-Reformation theology – the transubstantiation of the communion bread and wine, the literal merger of two bodies and wills into one in marriage, and the conversion of the religious (and racial) Other through baptism. Spanish expulsion and forced conversion of Jews and Muslims was followed, she says, by an anxious and futile attempt to read in the bodies of the converted any telltale sign of impurity, in body and blood as well as religious practice. Pressure to fashion a perfect (Old Christian) masculine subject combined with the one-flesh marriage sacrament led to obsession with any trace of adulterous (i.e., independent) feminine desire (Dopico-Black 2001: 117–64). The historic setting Lope gives his bloody *Comendadores*, just after the fall of Islamic Granada to Christian forces, lends support to her thesis. The protagonist, returning from success as a soldier to possible adultery in his house, conducts a minute analysis of honor's laws before killing not only his wife and niece and their lovers but also the whole household – servant, dogs, cats, and even a monkey and a parrot who did not warn him of his dishonor.

Honor (II), Tyranny and Political Ambition

Given the reality of absolutism and the lingering Senecan heritage within Spanish tragedy, tyrannical abuse of power is central to a number of tragedies. Questions of honor therein serve to personalize philosophical debates over the nature of political power. Castillo and Egginton (1995: 422, following Lacan via Žižek) call the code of honor a "quilting point" – the empty signifier that anchors a whole constellation of meaning, creating an illusory private sphere of autonomy for the subject while anchoring his honor in the king, thus stabilizing a system under severe tension, the ideology of absolutism. In tragedies, however, it serves to critique rather than to stabilize the system. In *La Estrella de Sevilla*, a play variously attributed to Lope, Andrés de Claramonte (ca.1580–1626), and Vélez de Guevara, the king's drive to seduce Estrella traps her brother Busto between the conflicting demands of political loyalty and honor, and her fiancé Sancho between those of loyalty to the king, love for Estrella, and friendship with Busto. When Sancho chooses obedience, kills Busto and refuses the king's offer of immunity, the judges of Seville, resisting the king's pressure to pardon Sancho, condemn him to death, thus forcing the king to admit his own guilt. Juan Oleza (cited in Arellano 1995: 199) describes the tragedy as a far-reaching exploration of the right of rebellion, individual and collective, against monarchical injustice, and deems it the equivalent of a "moral lynching" of the monarch.

Few dramas go that far, however, since the monarch was considered God's representative on earth, however humanly imperfect; improper delegation of effective sovereignty to a *privado* (royal favorite) painted as unscrupulous and ambitious was a less risky theme, and one with great relevance to the widespread critique of the reliance of Philip III on the Duke of Lerma and Philip IV on the Count-Duke of

Olivares. Lope's *El duque de Viseo* (ca.1608–9), loosely based on an occurrence in the reign of John II of Portugal, is a drama of the abuse of power by a paranoid king and of envy – over love relations and prestige – at court. The king, a supremely ungracious and ungenerous man, envies the great popularity of his brother-in-law and cousin, the Duke of Viseo, as well as Elvira's love for him. The flames of his envy are fanned by a revengeful and manipulative *privado*, Egas, who convinces him that Viseo and his brothers conspire against him. The king has Viseo's brother Guimarans executed and kills Viseo with his own dagger. When Viseo's loyal servant Brito stabs Egas to death, the king concludes that Brito has delivered God's punishment to a flattering traitor, the cause of the tragedy. But this is a patently hypocritical invocation of Providence, for as McKendrick's (2000) analysis shows, the king himself is guiltier than Egas. Thus, Lope makes the work a tragedy of the divorce of power and ethics.

A *privado* is also key to disaster in Calderón's consummately crafted dramatization of Henry VIII and the English Reformation, *La cisma de Ingalaterra* ("The English schism") (ca.1627), in which the twin demons are Cardinal Thomas Wolsey and Anne Boleyn, both driven by unrestrained ambition. In contrast, Calderón presents Henry VIII as a complex and fundamentally sympathetic character whose passions overpower his good intentions. In this tragedy as elsewhere, Calderón uses history with great poetic license, not chronicling but telescoping events to dramatize a lesson to be learned from them. Calderón brings the drama to a climax with a scene in which Mary appears in mourning for her mother Catherine and is shown Anne's corpse, and an anguished and repentant Henry summons Parliament to declare Mary his heir, arguing against her resolute dedication to Catholicism that, for reasons of state, she should promise her subjects freedom of conscience. Ruiz Ramón (1984: 11–13, 62–76) sees in this drama a tragic confrontation between freedom and destiny, citing Calderón's characteristic use of prophetic foreshadowing of the fate of Henry, Anne, and Wolsey, prophecies whose misinterpretation leads to actions intended to avoid the fate they in fact produce. Parker reads it as a Christian tragedy operating both at an individual and political level. Whereas the sins of Wolsey and Anne are coldly calculated, "Henry sins through a physical passion that cannot be suppressed . . . in his weakness, [he] bears the tragic burden of all humanity" (Parker 1988: 255). Henry's incapacity despite his repentance to alter the damage done dramatizes the danger of absolute power when combined with fallible human judgment. There was a private palace performance of *Cisma* for Philip IV, in 1627, shortly after the 1623 surprise visit to Madrid of the Prince of Wales, the future Charles I, and the subsequent failure of negotiations for his marriage to Philip's sister Mary, a marriage which Spaniards had hoped would reverse the schism produced by Henry's divorce. With Spain then engaged in a long and ultimately futile battle against Protestant rebels in the Low Countries and newly embarked on the Thirty Years War over larger European schisms, Parker concludes "Everything in the action and the tone of *La cisma de Ingalaterra* points to the message that crusades cannot succeed, and that it would be better for public policy not to be governed by intransigence" (287). It is a lesson that, at the beginning of the twenty-first century, we have yet to learn.

Religious and Cultural Difference

Although rarely foregrounded as in *Cisma*, other religious and cultural tensions lurk within many Spanish tragedies. In Lope's *Viseo*, the whole disastrous web of envy and revenge that brings about the death of Viseo, Guimarans, Elvira, and Egas is launched by the question of "impure" blood. Guimarans' brother, pressed by Inés for the reason why he advises against her marrying Egas, reluctantly admits that it is because Egas had a Moorish grandmother. When Egas learns this, he vows revenge, using the same weapon that has wounded him: the tongue.

An apparently extraneous discussion of religious and cultural difference stands as the axis on which Lope's *El caballero de Olmedo* (ca.1620) shifts from comic to tragic mode. This lyrical and moving play is built on two triangles: that of love, fate, and death that enmeshes the lovers Inés and Alonso and his rival and assassin, Rodrigo. The play takes its clue from a 1521 nocturnal assassination between the towns of Olmedo and Messina, and Lope uses both historical and literary traditions rather as Greek dramatists used familiar myths to impart a sense of impending fate. Building tension on dramatic irony, he reminds the audience at key moments of a popular *seguidilla* about that ambush: "Que de noche le mataron / al caballero, / la gala de Medina, / la flor de Olmedo" (They killed by night the noble knight, glory of Medina, flower of Olmedo) (Vega 1992: 139, 141, 197, 199). The lovers' go-between Fabia recalls the fatal end of Francisco de Rojas' *Celestina* and other characters call each other Melibea, Calisto, and Sempronio, who all die in that work (F. Rico in Vega 1992: 6, 25–9). And before the trip to Olmedo, Alonso bids farewell to Inés with a gloss on a familiar refrain of lovers' deathly pain at separation: "Puesto ya el pie en el estribo / con las ansias de la muerte, / señora, aquesta te escribo, / pues partir no puedo vivo, / cuanto más, volver a verte" (One foot already in the stirrup, with the anguish of death, I write you this, my lady, for I cannot leave alive, nor yet return to see you); (Vega 1992: 33, 190 2). Lope builds on these ominous signs with supernatural omens: Alonso's dark dream of a goldfinch killed by a hawk; a black-masked shadow that blocks his departure for Olmedo; a song that relates his fate, sung by a mysterious *labrador* whose footsteps are soundless. Alonso ignores them, condemning his fears as unworthy of a nobleman. Parker and other critics propose that Alonso's tragic error is his recourse to the sorceress Fabia as a go-between, but I find it instead in his unquestioning faith that the feudal code of honor by which he lives will also deter revenge by Rodrigo, whose life he saved in a bullfight before the king (Vega 1992: 194). Cohen (1985: 372–4) sees his death by shooting as a symbol of the supersession of medieval aristocratic warfare whose demise Lope intuits and mourns.

Although there are no charges of "impure blood" in *Caballero*, the issue appears enigmatically within it. At midpoint in this apparently private tragedy of rivalry in love, we find a curious political intermission in which the king discusses a change in the habits of the religio-military orders of Calatrava and Alcántara, his plan to award a habit to Alonso, and an order requiring that Spanish Jews and Moors wear distinctive dress so that Christians will be able to avoid contamination of their nobility by contact with them. This discussion, and the setting of the play in the era of Juan II, a period of political and religio-racial tumult, of episodically virulent antisemitism driven partly by resentment of an old nobility against a newer nobility admixed with wealthy *conversos*, associates the private catastrophe with Spain's public tragedy of hatred, accusations, and recriminations related to those divisions (Fothergill-Payne 1984).[4]

Incest, Sexual and Political

A frequent critique of the *comedia* is that it is peopled by flat stock types, not "rounded" characters of psychological depth. As an overall commentary, that is at least partly true, as it is of another eminently popular medium, American cinema, also designed to satisfy mass demand and constructed on formulas that produce thousands of predictable works – and a much smaller number of memorable jewels. More importantly, however, the nature of dramatic characterization in Spanish drama reflects a different conception of the individual than that in early modern French and English drama. Spanish tragedies are not entitled *Hamlet, Othello, Phèdre*, or *Andromaque*, but *The Knight from Olmedo, The Surgeon of his Honor*, or *Punishment without Revenge*, titles that identify the protagonist in relationship to an apparently transcendent signifier or to his position or function within the social order (Sullivan 1990: 40). The essence of the individual in the *comedia* is not located within an "inner" self but between the individual and other members of the social group. When in the throes of an honor crisis that provokes a private monologue, a character makes the classic declaration, "Soy quien soy" (I am who I am), the self-definition that follows is not dedicated to psychological analysis, but is based on gender and social position and the obligations they impose (e.g., Calderón 1970: 81–2, 153–7). Character in the best Spanish tragedies therefore is most frequently revealed not in self-analytical monologues, but through interaction with other characters; thus, identity is shown as constituted by social process (cf. Dollimore 1984: 18–19).

Tirso's mastery of such interactive character development is marvelously illustrated in *La venganza de Tamar* (1620–4), a tragedy of the illicit desire, fratricidal rivalry, and revenge that ravaged the biblical House of David. From the play's first lines, as David's heir-apparent Amón wearily removes his boots and spurs, the obsessive and sensuous character that will lead him to incestuous love and rape of his half-sister Tamar emerges as he complains about continuous military campaigns and seemingly rejects the amorous conquests savored by the narcissistically handsome Absalón. Tirso builds the biblical storyline (Samuel 2:13) of Amón's melancholy, David's anxious love, and the self-serving duplicity of Absalón into a persuasive familial psychodrama. In a consummately constructed third act, the raped and rejected Tamar clamors for revenge and David, remembering his own guilt with Bathsheba and Uriah, vacillates between justice and mercy, his role as father and king. Absalón, happy to use Tamar's honor as a pretext to replace Amón as heir to the throne, stabs him to death at a banqueting table during a sheep-shearing festival. Tirso stages this in a pastoral setting interwoven with floral omens and rustic invocations of water that washes away stains, set against Tamar's demand for bloodletting revenge, turning the climax into a perverted Last Supper–communion scene in which Absalón invites Tamar to drink her brother's warm blood. Thus, Tirso gives us again the specter of anthropophagy, in a spectacular dramatic metaphor of destructive human passions in the quintessential Judeo-Christian family. The last words of this tragedy are those of a weeping David, reciting Jacob's lament in Genesis 37:33 for his beloved son, devoured by a "fiera pésima" (fierce beast). As Paterson puts it, "In David's divided family, we are offered an allegory... of man's failure to redeem himself by law; guilt generates fresh guilt, and any finer aspirations meet with shattering failure" (in Calderón 1991: 20).

Calderón reworked that history in *Los cabellos de Absalón* (1633–5), a tragedy that Rodríguez Cuadros compares to Euripides in marking the distance between language and being, and Ruiz Ramón to Aeschylus' trilogy of Thebes in its portrayal of the tragic curse on David's house (Calderón 1969: 3:20). Calderón incorporates Tirso's third act almost verbatim as his second act, an extreme example of Spanish dramatists' common practice of reworking earlier plays, their own and those of others (see Sloman 1958). He reorients it, however, with his first and third acts, into a play centered on the lust for power, as Tamar and ambitious courtiers second Absalón's rebellion. Individual will and predestination come to grips through Calderón's use of a black Ethiopian prophetess, Teuca, whose ambiguous predictions display each character's nature as they interpret her words to suit their own desires. Absalón reads her words "ya veo / que te ha de ver tu ambición / en alto por los cabellos" (I now see that your ambition will see you on high by your hair) (Calderón 1989: 166) as a prediction that a people who love his beauty and compete to buy his hair will one day acclaim him king. Since Calderón's public knew the biblical history, as Greek audiences knew classical history and myth, they could savor the dramatic irony of recognizing his narcissistic misreading, and anticipate his literal "on high" end, his hair caught in a tree as he pursues David to kill him, and the classic *anagnorisis* in his dying repetition of the prediction: "¡Yo muero / puesto, como el Cielo quiso, / en alto por los cabellos, / sin el Cielo y sin la Tierra, / entre la Tierra y el Cielo!" (I die, as Heaven willed, held high by my hair, without Heaven and without earth, between earth and Heaven!) (278). Nevertheless, other prophecies – for Joab, Adonías, and Salomón – remain at most half-fulfilled; Calderón here, as in other tragedies, leaves the drama open-ended, inviting an audience to recognize that for the House of David, if not for all humankind, the cycle of sexual violations and political violence extends into the future, so that as David returns to Jerusalem "más que vencedor, vencido" (more conquered than conqueror) (281), the tragedy's end is an unspoken "to be continued."

The aging Lope, having learned tighter dramatic construction from Calderón's early work, in 1631 penned a more contemporary tale of paternal love, incestuous passion, and monarchical power, his best tragedy: *El castigo sin venganza* ("Punishment without revenge"). A libertine Duke of Ferrara compares himself and the illegitimate son Federico he loves to David and Absalón as he forces Federico to kill his young stepmother Casandra and has Federico slain for the crime. The Phaedra-like Casandra, neglected by the Duke, nourishes the instinctive attraction she and Federico felt at first sight of each other, and they surrender to that passion when the Duke leaves to serve in a papal war in Italy. Lope puts his lyrical gifts to superb use in developing these characters; most notably, he spins out Federico's obsessive, self-destructive nature in an extended gloss on a traditional motif:

> En fin, señora, me veo
> sin mí, sin vos, y sin Dios:
> sin Dios, por lo que os deseo;
> sin mí, porque estoy sin vos;
> sin vos, porque no os poseo.
> (Vega 1970: 318–21)
>
> (In all, my lady, I am / without myself, without you, without God:/ without God, for so desiring you; without my self, because I am without you; without you, because I do not possess you.)

All three engage casuistically in monologues with the laws of honor, God, and man to rationalize breaking those laws. In the network of intertwined imagery in which Lope enfolds them, the most telling is that of mirrors that reflect their specular entanglement and their sins; Aurora, the Duke's niece and Federico's rejected love, with "the wall-piercing eyes of jealousy," sees Federico and Casandra's affair reflected in a dressing-room mirror as "el conde las rosas mide / de Casandra con los labios" ("as the Count measures the roses of Casandra's cheeks with his lips") (Vega 1970: 326–7). And the Duke himself, scolded by an actress in the nocturnal opening scene, develops the classic Ciceronian metaphor of drama as a mirror:

> un espejo
> en que el necio, el sabio, el viejo,
> el mozo, el fuerte, el gallardo,
> el rey, el gobernador,
> la doncella, la casada,
> siendo al ejemplo escuchada
> de la vida y del honor,
> retrata nuestras costumbres,
> o livianas o severas,
> mezclando burlas y veras,
> donaires y pesadumbres . . .
> (Vega 1970: 242)
>
> (a mirror / in which the fool and the wise man, the old man, / the youth, the strong, the gallant, / king, governor, / maid, and wife, / heeding the example / of life and of honor, / portrays our customs, / be they fickle or severe, / mixing tricks and truths, / graces and sorrows . . .)

Castigo may have been too telling a mirror, politically, given the similarity between the libertine Duke and the womanizing for which Philip IV was criticized; it was performed just one day on the *corral* stage, Lope reported in the preface of the 1634 *princeps*. However, it was approved for publication, and stage censorship in Spain generally focused on questions of religious doctrine or decorum and oaths rather than political critique, if the latter was sufficiently veiled.

Honor and Patriarchy, Microcosm and Macrocosm

Even in the theoretically private realm of Spain's notorious wife-murder tragedies, political implication of the monarch is the rule, dramatizing the inseparability of injustice in the familial microcosm and political macrocosm in the patriarchal order, when honor has displaced Christianity as the dominant code. A classic illustration is Calderón's powerful tragedy *El médico de su honra* (The surgeon of his honor) (ca. 1629), in which Prince Enrique's pursuit of Mencía provokes her suspicious husband Gutierre to apply a fatal bloodletting "cure" to his ailing honor. Enrique is half-brother to Pedro I of Castile (1334–69), alternately known in historical and literary depictions as Peter the Just or the Cruel. Calderón sets the climate of suspicion and fear that Pedro's rule provokes in the opening scene. Don Arias criticizes the king's "fiera condición" (cruel nature) when Pedro continues toward Seville, leaving his brother "in the arms of death" after he has fallen from a horse, but another courtier quickly silences him, warning that "si oyen las paredes, los troncos . . . ven" (if walls hear, trees see). Pedro is doubly implicated in the tragic events, as he attempts to remedy complaints of dishonor by the rich and powerful of his realm: first, by Leonor, whom the wealthy Gutierre had courted but abandoned on unfounded suspicion of dishonor, and second, by Gutierre, who makes a veiled charge against Enrique, whose dagger he has found in his bedroom. Pedro's imprudent actions aggravate both cases, and as he returns the dagger to Enrique, the latter accidentally cuts his hand, foreshadowing Enrique's assassination of Pedro at Montiel in the civil war that would implicate Spain in the Hundred Years' War and elevate Enrique's Trastámara faction to the throne. Hence, when he orders Gutierre to give his still-bloody hand in marriage to Leonor, whom Arias now pursues, Calderón does not give us an order-restoring support of the honor code, but another provocative open ending.

Parker described Calderón's tragic conception as one of diffused responsibility, a collective *hamartia* operant alike in *La devoción de la cruz* (Devotion to the Cross), *El pintor de su deshonra* (The painter of his dishonor), *Las tres justicias en una* (Three justices in one), and *El médico*, in which every character operating according to the aristocratic code of conduct contributes to disaster (202). Pedro, Gutierre, Leonor, and their kin achieve no on-stage enlightenment, no tension-releasing *anagnorisis*; rather, the open ending called upon the audience to achieve their own recognition of the generalized location of tragic guilt (234).

Audiences do have an onstage guide, however, in the person of Coquín, the *gracioso*, Gutierre's comic servant who stands to lose his teeth in a wager over making the severe Pedro laugh. He alone, on the one hand not thoroughly castrated into the Symbolic order as are Mencía and Gutierre, and on the other, aware that he is an empty signifier configured by power (of the king and of language), can act outside the code of honor, risking his life and teeth to warn Pedro that Gutierre is bleeding Mencía to death. He and other *graciosos*, operating in the audience-oriented downstage *platea*, critique the action played out by center-stage aristocrats in the same manner that Weiman describes for Shakespeare's interrogation of the dominant institutions of Elizabethan England.

Who, then, is the tragic hero? In *Médico*, as in Lope's *Castigo* and Vélez de Guevara's *Reinar después de la muerte* (Reigning after death), the opposing poles are always external obligations versus private desire or pleasure. The woman condemned is always associated with interiority, both in the metaphorical structures of the works and in crucial stage directions, the most spectacular of which is the exposure of the innocent Mencía, bled to death, in the curtained backstage discovery space in *El médico*.[5] Critics singling out a tragic hero often choose the husband who survives rather than the woman who dies, a hair-raising judgment that, within the structure of diffused responsibility, has some validity. Tragedy in early modern Spain, as in the Greek tragedy Zeitlin (1990) describes, was a means by which men thought about their place in a society dominated by men. Feminine "interiority" represented not only the pleasure of the flesh condemned by Counter-Reformation dogma, but also a threat to aristocratic male dominance. The illusive pursuit of a unified subjectivity in Counter-Reformation Spain required a complete submission of noble males to the paternal signifier, however flawed that patriarchal order might be (El Saffar 1989). Hence, it is women or noncompliant sons who are sacrificed in tragedy, leaving the tragic hero alive to suffer that loss.

In another superb and philosophically complex Calderonian tragedy, *El pintor de su deshonra* (ca.1648–50), Juan Roca, the aging painter-husband unable to render in a portrait the beauty of his young wife, ends by painting her in blood, shooting to death both Serafina and her abductor Álvaro, each of whom die in their fathers' arms. The setting is significant, moving between Naples and Barcelona, for it traces out both the path of art between Italy and Spain (Paterson in Calderón 1991: 16–17) and the important Italy–Barcelona trade route, which Álvaro traveled on family business. Hence, to Paterson's reading that the drama is a study of "the ultimately violent nature of male dominance" (16), Bass (2004) adds that in its conclusion, with youth lying dead in the arms of fathers who sanction Roca's revenge, we can read Calderón's awareness of the crushing hand of the dominant institutions on two of the three orders of social production: economic and biological. Only the artist survives, and Roca's death-wish points toward the decline of that order as well.

Honor (III), Class, and Gender Divisions

Class division is a visible and structural constant in the *comedia*, in the standard separation of aristocratic protagonists and the servants who serve as their confidants, critics, or comic foils. But some dramas problematize that separation by creating non-noble protagonists who defend their own claim to honor. Honor as social reputation is linked to Spain's long period of socioeconomic and political change, from a hierarchical society rooted in a feudal concept of inherited worth that conferred "vertical honor" on the nobility, toward an increasingly court-centered society in which urbanization had loosened traditional social bonds. That process, on the one hand, allowed some upward mobility and made honor depend on external displays of the trappings of wealth and power and, on the other, opened the way for defense of a proto-bourgeois honor not based on inherited blood but on individual merit. Calderón's *El alcalde de Zalamea* (The mayor of Zalamea) (ca.1640–4?), set in 1581 as Spanish troops march toward Portugal to secure Philip II's claim as monarch, also pits civilian against military authority, figured respectively by a wealthy farmer, Pedro Crespo, and military general Lope de Figueroa. Crespo, who has refused to purchase a title of nobility, tells Lope, "Al Rey la hacienda y la vida / se ha de dar; pero el honor / es patrimonio del alma, / y el alma sólo es de Dios" (My life and wealth belong to the king, but honor is the soul's patrimony, and the soul belongs only to God) (Calderón 1981: 187–8). But the patrimony of his honor – materially and ideologically centered not in the soul but in the body of his daughter Isabel and in his capacity to protect her chastity – is attacked by the captain of troops billeted in Zalamea, who abducts and rapes her. Her brother Juan tries to kill her to cleanse the family honor, but Crespo, just elected mayor of the town, jails both Juan and the Captain. He offers the Captain all his wealth if he will marry Isabel, but when that offer is haughtily refused, institutes judicial procedures and the Captain is garroted. Philip II arrives and, approving the justice of the sentence, accepts Crespo's defense that the king's justice is one body with many hands, one of which can as well apply a just sentence as another, and names him lifetime mayor. In this tragedy, then, Calderón does portray the king as the ultimate guarantor of justice, and the linchpin that sustains the sociopolitical hierarchy.[6] That administration of poetic justice, however, only slightly mitigates the tragedy of the destruction of Crespo's family, as he sends Isabel to a convent and Juan departs as a soldier with Lope de Figueroa.

Luis Vélez de Guevara's *La serrana de la Vera* (The mountain-maid of Vera) (1613) also opens with a dispute between Giraldo, a prosperous farmer who protests soldiers being billeted in his house and a captain who demands it as his obligation. That class disputes should take this form is logical, because the nobility's right to preference was grounded in the medieval concept that they provided the defense of the realm. In early modern Spain, however, with professional armies and an aristocracy revolving around an absolutist court and increasingly reluctant to leave it for military service, that justification was undermined. The class issue is complicated by Gila, Giraldo's daughter, a manly woman of prodigious beauty who sends the captain packing at gunpoint.[7] His masculine and class superiority challenged, he vows revenge, which he works by returning to seduce her under promise of marriage. She had earlier rebelled against the idea of marriage, saying that it degraded her sex, but within *comedia* conventions and reigning gender rules, such female independence is always overruled. When the Captain then abandons her, she turns to banditry and kills 2,000 men, including the Captain, whom she throws to his death from a precipice, repeating the town crier's knell at executions and inviting Heaven to fall as she does so. Caught between forces from above and below, she is then captured – without resisting, having secured her revenge. She is condemned and executed as Fernando and Isabela – the powerful queen Gila sought to imitate – look on. Women in tragedy, whether or not they submit to patriarchal law that dictates their obedience and confinement, are sacrificed to its demands.

Mythological Court Spectacle

Aside from *corral* performances, *La serrana de la Vera* was performed in the palace for Philip IV and Isabel in 1623,[8] and all the above tragedies were likely to have been performed in palace theaters for the private entertainment of king and court. The mythological spectacle, however, was specifically crafted for court theaters, to celebrate occasions of state. Such drama spread from the courts of northern Italy across Europe beginning in the late fifteenth century, encouraged by humanists' interests in reviving ancient Greek drama and by the rise of absolute monarchs eager to employ spectacle to enhance their prestige and power. Calderón ranks as the consummate dramatist of the European court spectacle play not only because he most effectively synthesized its polyphonic medium of poetic text, music, dance, stage scenery, and machinery, but also because he crafted his works polysemically. His court spectacle plays, availing themselves of the flexibility of classical mythology, while effectively transmitting the requisite message of Habsburg glory and power, also included a tactful criticism of specific royal policies (Greer 1991). Several of Calderón's court mythological plays are works of tragic shape and import, despite the artificial concluding rescue by metamorphosis.

Most accessible to a modern audience is Calderón's *Eco y Narciso* (Echo and Narcissus), first performed in 1661 to celebrate the tenth birthday of Margarita, the princess who appears at the center of Velázquez's famous painting *Las Meninas* (ca. 1656). She is linked to Eco in the opening scene, a pastoral celebration of Eco's birthday that includes the curious note that she is not immortal, that every year completed marks one year less to live in beauty and fortune. To the basic Ovidian myth, Calderón adds an all-containing mother who has crippled Narciso's development, making him one of many Calderonian variants of the Segismundo figure of his most famous drama, *La vida es sueño* (Life is a dream). Narciso, schooled in his mother's fear of the prediction that a voice and a beauty would cause his death, drowns in his own self-absorbed beauty. Eco, his specular opposite, is so dependent on the accustomed adoration of others that when Narciso spurns her, her very being dissolves. The counterposed staging of aristocratic and skeptical plebian discourses in Spain permeates even this court production. The *gracioso* Bato, presumably downstage and speaking directly to the audience, concludes *Eco y Narciso*. As the hero and heroine are transformed into flower and star for the requisite spectacular "happy" ending for a court play, Bato says sardonically to the audience, "¡Y habrá bobos que lo crean!" (And some fools will believe it!).

I suggest that this drama, like Velázquez's painting, is a study of the problematic of being – its constitution and representation – in a court society. At the pragmatic level of a discrete political lesson for the royal spectators, it is a warning of the danger of raising and (not) educating royal children in a pampering, circumscribing court, a reminder that they are all too mortal. More generally, it is a study of the circumscribing pressure on all subjects of absolute monarchy, Counter-Reformation doctrine, and the re-aristocratization that drastically postponed if not derailed Spain's sixteenth-century movement toward a more open and progressive society. We might even take *Eco y Narciso* as a critical allegory for the larger tragedy of late seventeenth-century Spain, narcissistically absorbed in its own world, ideologically bounded by a powerful mother Church, fearful of contamination by its own internal others (racial, religious, and sexual) as well as external difference, falteringly ruled by a kind of absent father in the weak kings biologically diminished by intermarriage, with the overall consequence that its voice on the world stage was reduced to an echo of its former power.

NOTES

1 A significant difference, however, is that women's roles on the Spanish stage were played by actresses, not, as in England, by boys.

2 For a brief survey of early modern Spanish theater, see Greer, forthcoming; see Arellano (1995), Cohen (1985), and McKendrick (1989) for good book-length studies.

3 Early authors of such tragedies include Rey de Artieda, Cristóbal de Virués, Juan de la Cueva, Jerónimo Bermúdez, and Leonardo Lupercio Argensola.

4 Calderón did make religious and cultural clash central to one tragedy, *Amar después de la muerte* (To love after death; ca. 1632–3), a sympa-

thetic presentation of the uprising of *moriscos* in the Alpujarras in 1569.

5 Vélez's lyrical dramatization of the oft-told tragedy of Inés de Castro, mistress or wife of crown prince Pedro of Portugal, assassinated for reasons of state, makes splendid use of this vulnerable interior feminine space, both on stage and in the reader/spectator's imagination, as Inés is portrayed multiply mediated by the vision of others.

6 The complex character Calderón creates in Crespo complicates reading the play as a defense of the legitimacy of sociopolitical mobility. He is a man of principle and loving father, but also an astute negotiator and

chameleon-like in adjusting his deportment to the situation and the treatment he receives.

7 Vélez wrote this play for Jusepa Vaca, an actress renowned for playing manly woman roles.

8 Bolaños 2001: 25 n.30, citing Hugo Rennert. It might, however, have been a play by the same name by Lope de Vega; the documentation of the performance does not name the author.

REFERENCES AND FURTHER READING

Appian. (1696). *The history of Appian of Alexandria: in two parts: the first consisting of the Punick, Syrian, Parthian, Mithridatick, Illyrian, Spanish, and Hannibalick wars: the second containing five books of the civil wars of Rome*. London: John Amery.

Arellano, I. (1995). *Historia del teatro español del siglo XVII*. Madrid: Cátedra. The best survey in Spanish.

Bass, L. (2004). "To Possess Her in Paint: (Pro)creation and Crisis in *El pintor de su deshonra*." In *Writing for the Eyes in the Spanish Golden Age*, ed. F. A. De Armas. Lewisburg, PA: Bucknell University Press.

Bolaños, P. (2001). "Introducción." In L. Vélez de Guevara, *La serrana de la Vera*, ed. P. Bolanos. Madrid: Clásicos Castalia, 9–89.

Calderón de la Barca, P. (1963). *Eco y Narciso*, ed. C. Aubrun. Paris: Centre de Recherches de l'Institut d'Études Hispaniques.

Calderón de la Barca, P. (1969). *Tragedias I*, ed. F. Ruíz Ramón, 3 vols. Madrid: Alianza.

Calderón de la Barca, P. (1970). *El médico de su honra*, ed. D. W. Cruickshank. Madrid: Clásicos Castalia.

Calderón de la Barca, P. (1981). *El alcalde de Zalamea*, ed. J. M. Díez-Borque. Madrid: Clásicos Castalia.

Calderón de la Barca, P. (1989). *Los cabellos de Absalón*, ed. Evangelina Rodríguez Cuadros. Madrid: Espasa Calpe.

Calderón de la Barca, P. (1991). *The Painter of His Dishonour. El pintor de su deshonra*, ed. and trans. A. K. G. Paterson. Warminster: Aris & Phillips. An excellent bilingual edition, thoughtfully introduced and annotated.

Castillo, D. and Egginton, W. (1995). "All the King's Subjects: Honor in Early Modernity." *Romance Language Annual* 6, 422–7.

Cervantes, M. (1994). *El cerco de Numancia*, ed. A. Hermenegildo. Madrid: Clásicos Castalia. A good edition with substantial bibliography, by an expert on sixteenth-century Spanish tragedy.

Cohen, W. (1985). *Drama of a Nation: Public Theater in Renaissance England and Spain*. Ithaca, NY: Cornell University Press. An excellent comparative history and analysis, from a Marxist perspective.

Dollimore, Jonathan. (1984). *Radical Tragedy: Religion, Ideology and Power in the Drama of Shakespeare and His Contemporaries*. Chicago: Chicago University Press.

Dopico-Black, G. (2001). *Perfect Wives, Other Women: Adultery and Inquisition in Early Modern Spain*. Durham, NC: Duke University Press.

Eagleton, T. (2003). *Sweet Violence. The Idea of the Tragic*. Oxford: Blackwell.

El Saffar, R. (1989). "Gutierre's Anxiety of Identity in *El médico de su honra*." In *Studies in Honor of Bruce W. Wardropper*, ed. D Fox, H. Sieber, and R. TerHorst. Newark, DE: Juan de la Cuesta, 105–24.

Fothergill-Payne, L. (1984). "*El caballero de Olmedo* y la Razón de Diferencia." *Bulletin of the Comediantes* 36, 111–24. Discusses historical drama and the treatment of race.

Greer, M. R. (1991). *The Play of Power: Mythological Court Dramas of Calderón de la Barca*. Princeton, NJ: Princeton University Press.

Greer, M. R. (forthcoming). "The Development of National Theater." In *Cambridge History of Spanish Literature*, ed. D. Gies. Cambridge: Cambridge University Press.

López Pinciano, A. (1953). *Philosophia Antigua poética*, ed. A. Carballo Picazo, 3 vols. Madrid: Consejo Superior de Investigaciones Científicas.

McKendrick, M. (1989). *Theatre in Spain, 1490–1700*. Cambridge: Cambridge University Press. The best survey in English.

McKendrick, M. (2000). *Playing the King: Lope de Vega and the Limits of Conformity*. London: Tamesis.

Molina, Tirso de. (1969). *La venganza de Tamar*, ed. A. K. G. Paterson. Cambridge: Cambridge University Press. A bilingual edition with a good introduction and notes in English.

Parker, A. A. (1988). *The Mind and Art of Calderón: Essays on the Comedias*, ed. D. Kong. Cambridge: Cambridge University Press.

Reichenberger, A. (1959). "The Uniqueness of the *Comedia*." *Hispanic Review* 27, 301–16.

Reiss, Timothy J. (1980). *Tragedy and Truth: Studies in the Development of a Renaissance and Classical Discourse*. New Haven, CT: Yale University Press.

Richards, I. A. (1924). *Principles of Literary Criticism*. New York: Harcourt, Brace.

Ruíz Ramon, F. (1984). *Calderón y la tragedia*. Madrid: Alambra.

Sánchez Escribano, F. and Porqueras Mayo, A. (1972). *Preceptiva dramática española del Renacimiento y el Barroco*, 2nd. ed. Madrid: Gredos.

Sloman, A. E. (1958). *The Dramatic Craftsmanship of Calderón*. Oxford: Oxford University Press.

Sullivan, H. W. (1990). "Lacan and Calderón: Spanish Classical Drama in the Light of Psychoanalytic Theory." *Gestos* 10, 39–55.

Vega, Lope de. (1609). *Los comendadores de Cordova*. In *Segunda parte de las comedias de Lope de Vega Carpio*. Madrid: Iuan Maurizio. Electronic edition in Chadwyck-Healy, *Teatro español del Siglo de Oro*. ProQuest Information and Learning Company.

Vega, Lope de. (1966). *El duque de Viseo*, ed. F. Ruíz Ramón. Madrid: Alianza.

Vega, Lope de. (1970). *El perro del hortelano. El castigo sin venganza*, ed. D. Kossoff. Madrid: Castalia. Well annotated and introduced.

Vega, Lope de. (1971). *El arte nuevo de hacer comedias en este tiempo*, ed. J. de José Prados. Madrid: Consejo de Investigaciones Científicas.

Vega, Lope de. (1992). *El caballero de Olmedo*, ed. Francisco Rico. Madrid: Cátedra. A good edition by one of Spain's most respected Golden Age scholars.

Vega, Lope de. (1999). *Fuente Ovejuna; The knight from Olmedo; Punishment without revenge*, ed. and trans. G. Edwards. Oxford: Oxford University Press.

Vélez de Guevara, L. (2001). *La serrana de la Vera*, ed. P. Bolaños. Madrid: Clásicos Castalia.

Weiman, R. (1992). "Representation and Performance: The Uses of Authority in Shakespeare's Theater." *Proceedings of the Modern Language Association* 107, 497–510.

Williams, R. (1966). *Modern Tragedy*. Stanford, CA: Stanford University Press.

Zeitlin, F. (1990). "Playing the Other: Theater, Theatricality and the Feminine in Greek Drama." In *Nothing to Do with Dionysos: Athenian Drama in its Social Context*, ed. J. Winkler and F. Zeitlin. Princeton, NJ: Princeton University Press, 63–96.

Part VI
Neoclassical and Romantic Tragedy

21

Neoclassical Dramatic Theory in Seventeenth-Century France

Richard E. Goodkin

Overview

The classical period in France, roughly speaking from about 1630 until the end of the seventeenth century, is preoccupied with theories of drama, and more particularly theories of tragedy, by far the most prestigious theatrical form of the day. While the strong interest in dramatic theory at this time is not new – the rediscovery and dissemination of Aristotle's *Poetics* in the sixteenth century helped fuel a great deal of theorizing, especially in Italy, long before 1630 – what is particular to the classical period in France is the development of a highly codified set of rules that is generally held to apply to all serious dramatic output, including not only tragedy but also other theatrical genres, albeit less strictly. By the time the classical period reached its height under Louis XIV, whose independent reign began in the early 1660s, composing "irregular" tragedies that did not conform to these rules – which had been, in fact, in existence in some form for nearly a century at the outset of the classical period but had been sketchily applied – became unthinkable.

The rules that came to govern French classical theater in the seventeenth century did not spring fully fashioned from the mind of a single theoretician; rather, they were refined and codified over a long period of time. The two greatest ancient influences on French classical theories of tragedy were Aristotle's *Poetics* and, to a lesser extent, Horace's *Ars Poetica*. Horace was already well known in France in the sixteenth century, and starting in the mid-sixteenth century, quite a number of published commentaries on Aristotle's treatise, mostly but not exclusively Italian, gained currency in France. These commentaries include (but are not limited to) those of Robertello (1548), Scaliger (1561), Castelvetro (1570), and Heinsius (1611), the latter being particularly influential in disseminating Aristotelian thought in the decades leading up to French classicism – although the precise attitude of French theoreticians toward Aristotle's theory of tragedy is far from simple.

Toward the end of the sixteenth century the French humanist Pierre de Ronsard emphasized the importance both of following in the footsteps of the ancient tragedians and of writing tragedies in French rather than in Latin, but it was not until the early seventeenth century that French theoreticians began to participate fully in the discussions about tragedy that had already been taking place in Italy for decades. Among the theoreticians of tragedy writing in France from the 1630s through the 1650s, the first decades of French classicism, particularly influential are Jean Chapelain, Jules de la Mesnardiere, and the Abbé d'Aubignac. Although tragedies were written and produced in France in the second half of the sixteenth century and the first three decades of the seventeenth, these plays are not today considered part of the classical repertoire, which is generally held to begin in the 1630s, the period corresponding to the codification of the rules of theater.

While the influence of Greek and Latin theoreticians is indisputably one of the chief components of French classical theories of tragedy, it is quite difficult to generalize about the precise role played by the works of the Attic tragedians and their Roman counterparts in the formation of the French classical aesthetic. Euripides and Seneca are probably the most influential and best-known ancient tragedians of the French classical period, although other Greek and Latin playwrights also have some influence, direct or indirect, upon particular French tragedians. Even before the production of the first tragedy written in French, Jodelle's *Cléopâtre captive* (1552), several Greek plays were translated into French, including Sophocles' *Electra* (Lazare de Baïf, 1537) and Euripides' *Hecuba* and *Iphigenia at Aulis*; many Greek tragedies were known in their Latin translations (Lanson [1895] 1951: 412). But the only French classical tragedian of note who read Greek well enough to make extensive use of the Greek tragedians in the original language was Jean Racine, who was not active until the second half of the seventeenth century.

As for the most important Latin model for French classical tragedy, Seneca's plays were quite widely read throughout the period. They were much admired for their rhetorical dexterity and their moral vigor, both of which traits would be central to the French classical aesthetic. The extreme, violent nature of Senecan tragedy also had a certain appeal in the period leading up to the beginnings of French classicism, although this element was to be increasingly frowned upon or at least driven underground as the classical aesthetic, which places a premium on propriety and decorum, developed (Tobin 1971; Levitan 1989).

While the principal rules that came to govern tragedy in France in the seventeenth century are mutually reinforcing and form a coherent unit, the concerns raised by writers about tragedy are actually quite diverse; they are not only theoretical but can also be practical and concrete. The principal rules are largely based on abstract, difficult-to-quantify problems such as believability, decency, and the moral impact a play might have, but far more mundane issues are also touched upon: for example, the number of hours appropriate for a theatrical production, the number of scenes that should be in each act, and the most effective way to carry out the transition between two scenes. Theoreticians write extensively both about what they see as the elements of an ideal tragedy and about the flaws and strengths – with an emphasis on the former – of particular plays. The theoretical issues raised are generally of greatest interest to today's readers; in my subsequent discussion I will focus on these.

Aristotle and Descartes, Authority vs. Reason

Although it is difficult to characterize French neoclassical writing about tragedy in any global way, dramaturgical texts do fall into certain meaningful patterns that reflect some of the deep-seated tensions and contradictions of the period. One of the central conflicts fueling debates about the theory of tragedy can be understood in terms of the distinction between descriptive and prescriptive (or proscriptive) discussions of theater. Descriptive treatments take the plays themselves as a starting point, and try to describe what they do: how they operate, their different elements, and the patterns into which they fall. Prescriptive or proscriptive treatments, by contrast, take theoretical and/or ideological concerns as their starting point, and explain what plays ought to do: how they should function, what different elements should (prescriptive) or should not (proscriptive) be included, and the patterns or rules to which they must conform.

Descriptive treatments of drama generally lead to an inductive approach to the theory of tragedy, while prescriptive treatments tend toward a more deductive approach (a given theoretician may, of course, alternate between the two). On the one hand, descriptive treatments take the plays as objects of scrutiny, describing how they function in an attempt to infer dramatic theory from dramatic practice. This is essentially an inductive process: the theoretician studies the dramatic corpus and seeks out a set of principles that might help to account for this or that aspect of the plays. On the other hand, the kind of rule-making, both positive and negative – musts and must-nots – that characterizes much seventeenth-century dramatic theory reverses the process, as theoreticians, motivated by various ideological and aesthetic concerns, formulate rules which should provide a starting point for any playwright setting out to compose a drama. This is essentially a deductive process: the theoretician posits an idealized set of principles, applies it to existing plays, and judges the plays accordingly; or, in terms of future productions, the playwright reads the rules of dramaturgy and keeps them in mind while writing new plays.

The danger of the deductive approach to the rules of theater is that applying previously established, inflexible rules to theatrical productions does not necessarily lead to the composition of good plays, a problem memorably evoked in a hilarious passage of "De la tragédie ancienne et moderne" (Of ancient and modern tragedy) by Saint-Évremond. Saint-Évremond reports (spuriously) on the reaction to a play presented by the Abbé d'Aubignac – who also happens to be the author of one of the century's most important dramatic treatises – a play written strictly according to the rules: " 'I am grateful to Monsieur d'Aubignac,' said Monsieur le Prince [le Grand Condé], 'for having followed Aristotle's rules so well; but I cannot forgive Aristotle's rules for making Monsieur d'Aubignac write such a bad Tragedy' " (Saint-Évremond 1962: 4: 170–1).[1]

Not surprisingly, playwrights like Pierre Corneille and Jean Racine, who also write about theater,[2] often seem to resent deductive approaches to tragedy, at times defending their plays on an empirical basis by pointing out that the acid-test of theatrical practice must be audience reaction. A writer like Corneille, who often feels more constrained than assisted by the rules of theater, is adamant in his position that within reasonable limits, a playwright must be free to use whatever he discovers from experience will move and please the audience.

This tension between descriptive, inductive approaches to the plays and prescriptive, deductive ones results in part from the complexities of neoclassical interpretations of Aristotle, whose influence, both direct and indirect, is very great indeed: his *Poetics* provides the foundation of neoclassical dramatic theory in France. Aristotle himself straddles descriptive and prescriptive approaches in his treatment of tragedy. While he deals with issues like the length of time of tragic action – a question that would inspire much controversy in seventeenth-century France – in a descriptive way, stating that most tragedies take place within a single revolution of the sun or slightly beyond, he does not hesitate to pass aesthetic judgments on the relative worth of different forms of reversal (peripeteia) and recognition (anagnorisis), for example.

Interpretations of Aristotle's work in this period are far from uniform. An ongoing subject of debate is whether the Greek philosopher is to be considered as an authority simply to be respected and followed or, on the contrary, as an outmoded theoretician whose ideas, while useful, no longer fully apply to the present day. This debate in fact anticipates the literary quarrel of the ancients and the moderns later in the seventeenth century.

Indeed, an important cultural trend that greatly affects theories of tragedy in the neoclassical period is the conflict between authority and, for lack of a better word, "reason." The ongoing movement toward the apotheosis of human reason in an era imbued with the work of French philosopher and mathematician René Descartes (1596–1650) is concomitant with the gradual breakdown of various kinds of orthodoxy, especially religious, but also scientific and philosophical, Aristotle being both a key authority figure for traditionalists and a prime target for iconoclasts. Cartesian rationalism is a major influence on the neoclassical period in France, including drama and theories of drama. Descartes' seminal *Discours de la méthode* (Discourse of the method) dates from 1637, contemporary with Pierre Corneille's *Le Cid*, a play whose premiere in January 1637 is sometimes taken as the starting point of the classical period in France. In the primordial importance Descartes gives to the analytical breakdown of questions into their constituent parts, he formulates a method that requires the freedom to question authority and orthodoxy – the often unreflective acceptance of traditional models – in the name of reason. Whether influenced by Descartes or affected by the same intellectual context as he is, theoreticians of tragedy often demonstrate a willingness to question authority, especially that of Aristotle and other ancient models like Horace, and also show an eagerness to analyze and systematize tragedy – sometimes in reductive or spurious ways – that resonates with many of Descartes' ideas.

The Rules of Theater

Let us turn now to a discussion of the principal rules of theater, as formulated by theorists of the classical period in France. They are: (1) *vraisemblance*, verisimilitude or plausibility; (2) *bienséance*, propriety or decorum; and (3) the three unities: unity of time, place, and action.

Vraisemblance

The most important of the rules is *vraisemblance*,[3] variously translated as "verisimilitude," "plausibility," or "likelihood"; neoclassical theoreticians saw the other rules as the natural result of respecting *vraisemblance*.[4] The rules of French classical tragedy are formulated partly in reaction to popular theatrical genres influenced by the novel, such as tragicomedy and pastoral, forms that are little concerned with the internal logic of either characters or events and which draw their most striking effects from variety, heterogeneity, and surprise. By contrast, classical tragedy takes as gospel the idea of presenting characters and events that make *sense*. Characters are asked to act coherently and not in contradictory ways. If possible, all events and plot developments are internally motivated – they should seem inevitable, the logical outcome of the situation at hand – and at the very least they must not appear out of nowhere or offer inconsistencies that might distract the viewing or reading public from the play's central action.

Theoreticians of theater take great pains to distinguish *vraisemblance* from *vérité*, truth: the truth might be something quite difficult to believe; it might entail events so extraordinary that the viewing public would not be able to see them as sufficiently motivated by the dramatic context. Conversely, a chain of events that spectators might believe likely or even inevitable might be one that would never happen in real life. Verisimilitude deals neither with what actually happened nor with what could happen or is likely to happen in some theoretical sense, but rather with what the theatergoing public of the time believes could happen or is likely to happen; verisimilitude is a function not only of reason, but also of belief. To take a twenty-first-century example, people who believe in the traditional division of labor between men and women might not find a female construction worker *vraisemblable*; even as the world changed around them and more and more construction workers came to be female, their belief would not necessarily change, and they could be introduced to any number of actual female construction workers and still find some way to think of them all as aberrations, as *invraisemblable*, or implausible.[5]

Thus verisimilitude, which is presented by many as a tool of pure reason, actually has a strong ethical component. In his highly influential 1570 commentary on Aristotle's *Poetics*, Castelvetro defines "the possible" in a fairly straightforward way, as anything that can be carried out or can happen without any objections or obstacles preventing it from occurring; by contrast, he defines verisimilitude as the state of something that, given the circumstances, had to happen as it happened (Bray [1945] 1983: 195). But that only raises further questions: what do people believe had to happen, and why? In the end one can only *believe* that something had to happen as it did; one cannot prove it. And what one believes had to happen owes as much to one's ethical principles and assumptions about the world as to one's power of reasoning. Still elaborating on Aristotle, Castelvetro points out that an event that is possible is not suitable for tragedy unless it is also *vraisemblable*, whereas one that is *vraisemblable* is suitable, whether it is possible or not, a sentiment echoed by a number of seventeenth-century French commentators, including Jules de la Mesnardière in Chapter 5 ("La Composition du sujet") of his *Poétique*: "Although truth is everywhere adored, plausibility [*Vraisemblance*] still wins out over it; and *something false but plausible*, must be accorded greater esteem than strange, miraculous, and unbelievable true things" (La Mesnardière [1640] 1972: 34). Thus in the end verisimilitude is a profoundly conservative principle: it speaks to the necessity of respecting and conforming to the audience's beliefs rather than shaking up their ideas about the world.

One strong defender of verisimilitude (among many) is the Abbé d'Aubignac, whose *Pratique du théâtre* (Practice of the theater), commissioned by Louis XIII's Prime Minister, Cardinal Richelieu, in the early 1640s but not completed and published until 1657, is a particularly painstaking and complete statement of classical doctrine. Here is d'Aubignac's discussion of verisimilitude:

> But when the playwright scrutinizes his tragedy as a true story [*Histoire véritable*] or one that he assumes to be true, the only thing that concerns him is to keep the verisimilitude of things, and to compose all the Actions, Discourses, and Incidents, as if they had truly [*véritablement*] happened. He creates a harmonious relation between people and their thoughts, time and place, consequences and general principles. Indeed he is so attuned to the Nature of things that he is unwilling to contradict either their state, or their order, or their effects, or their conventions; and in a word he takes as his sole guide verisimilitude, and rejects everything that does not have its character. (d'Aubignac [1657] 1971: 31–2)

A playwright well-versed in verisimilitude does not treat events and characters as being true in themselves; rather, he treats them as if they were true, which gives a particular slant to the word "true": in trying to get to the "nature of things," the playwright is free, up to a point, to transform his sources, whether historical or mythological, not only to conform to his audience's beliefs but also to show them profound truths. The dramatist makes everything hang together: characters' thoughts and words are appropriate to their personality, their station in life, their situation; causes lead to expected effects. In other words, he gives to the representation of the *véritable* the kind of coherence that true events rarely enjoy.

It may seem astonishing to us today, but this kind of transformation of "true" into "believable" applies indifferently to plays based on historical sources and ones based on mythological sources; in fact, there is no hard-and-fast distinction between the two meanings of the word *histoire*, history and story, in the seventeenth century. This doesn't mean that people believe in the actual existence of mythologically based characters like Phaedra or Oedipus as much as they believe in the existence of historically based characters like Nero or Augustus, but from the point of view of verisimilitude – of seeing events played out in a way that is plausible and makes sense to the audience – the difference between historical and mythological sources is minimal. Racine, in his second preface to *Andromaque* (1676), justifies having modified Euripides' *Andromache*, one of his main sources, by making Andromaque's endangered son be her child by Hector rather than by her captor, Neoptolemos/Pyrrhus, for the extraordinary reason that this is how his audience sees the myth of Andromache:

> In this I believed I was conforming to the idea that we have nowadays of this princess [Andromaque]. Most of those who have heard of Andromaque know her only as Hector's widow and Astyanax' mother. People do not believe that she is to love [*On ne croit point qu'elle doive aimer*] another husband or another son. (Racine 1999: 297–8)

What is the value of the word *doive* – from *devoir*, "must" or "to have to" – that Racine uses to characterize how his audiences believe Andromaque should be? Does the verb here connote supposition (it must be raining, since the pavement is wet) or obligation (it must rain, or the crops will fail)? I would argue that in this case in particular, as with verisimilitude in general, we are in a gray area between supposition and prescription: Racine seems to be saying that his public either doesn't know about versions of the story in which Andromache has a child by her captor ("she *must not* love another husband" as a supposition), or would not like them ("she *must not* love another husband" as an obligation); or perhaps that they would forget or ignore those other versions because they would not like them. If verisimilitude may be used to justify Racine's revisionism (he was indeed attacked for having modified the myth in his *Andromaque*), this is because the term itself straddles perception (our suppositions about what does happen in the world) and moral judgment (our ideas about what should happen in the world).

Many theoreticians, including d'Aubignac, present verisimilitude as something universal and natural (*la Nature des choses*), as a kind of reasonableness with which sane spectators in any culture or era would agree. But with the benefit of three-and-a-half centuries of hindsight we would likely conclude otherwise; it seems hard to overlook the importance of cultural differences in viewer and reader expectations, and expectations, of course, reflect beliefs. Rather than calling verisimilitude an example of universal reason, we would be more accurate in saying that it reflects the classical era's mythification of the power of reason. To say that all reasonable spectators ought to object to this or that contradiction, or would appreciate the cohesiveness and inevitability of the plot in a given play, is to make audience reaction itself an object of verisimilitude. It is as if the theoreticians were saying: this is how the viewing public will most likely reason, or how they ought to reason about the situation. We might conclude, then, that at the center of the complex principle of verisimilitude is a *belief* in *reason*.

At times, concerns for verisimilitude and the assumption that spectators will "naturally" question certain conventions of theater as illogical – or, more to the point, that all conventional aspects of theater could ever be eliminated, yielding plays that are a perfect mirror of the "nature of things" – are taken so far they might be said to impoverish rather than enrich the classical aesthetic. The rhetoric of French classical tragedy, for example, is closely scrutinized by theoreticians, whose eagerness to point out incoherent metaphors and distasteful images is one of the main reasons why the language of French tragedy becomes abstract, almost disembodied: striking physical images run the risk of being unsettling, so that once the rules become deeply ingrained, original concrete imagery comes to be avoided by playwrights like Racine. A highly developed system of conventional metaphorical language that borrows heavily from the language of preciosity – *flamme* for passion, *courage* for heart, and so on – allows tragedians to play it safe, steering clear of an excessive physicality that might be deemed degrading and of jarring combinations of words or concepts that might be criticized on the grounds of incoherence.

Another example of the rather censorious effect of verisimilitude is the criticism of conventional theatrical devices like soliloquies and overheard speech that are used to great effect by Shakespeare and other tragedians but that, largely because of verisimilitude, are used relatively sparingly by French classical dramatists. As d'Aubignac puts it:

> When a speaker who thinks he is alone is overheard by another person, he ought to be speaking quietly: all the more so as it is not *vraisemblable* that a man alone would scream at the top of his lungs, as actors must do in order to be heard. . . . And even though it sometimes happens that a man says out loud something that he thought he was saying or that he should have been saying to himself, we still cannot put up with it in the theater, where human foolishness should not be so roundly represented. (d'Aubignac [1657] 1971: 231–2)

It is not that what d'Aubignac is saying is untrue; it is rather that he seems to be implying that it would be possible and desirable to eliminate all conventions such as those governing soliloquies, whereby speakers say aloud what is going on in their heads.

Ironically, while this kind of extreme rationalization sometimes hinders playwrights as much as it helps them, it can also lead writers to find ingenious ways around the rules. In reaction to the problem of soliloquies, for example, Jean Racine, whom most consider to be France's greatest tragedian, develops the role of the confidant in complex, compelling ways. He thereby fends off objections about characters orating alone, but more importantly also creates pivotal figures like Oenone, Phèdre's nurse and confidante, whose role in *Phèdre* is key to the development of the play's titular character.[6]

And yet, while verisimilitude may indirectly goad playwrights into creating characters, one could argue that more often than not, it limits their freedom to develop them. Jean Chapelain, for example, one of the most influential theoreticians of the early decades of classicism, implies that a character must never fundamentally change, stating that "within the work each character must act in conformity with the habits that have been attributed to him; a bad person must not, for example, form a good plan" (Chapelain 1936: 162–3). While a concern for consistency is understandable, the idea that bad characters cannot have good intentions implies that character is quantifiable and fully graspable by reason and that people do not change or contradict themselves; both in earlier tragedy and in real life numerous examples of people at odds with themselves might be conjured up to challenge this stance. While the contradictions inherent in a tragic situation – the opposing forces, demands, or allegiances such as duty and love, or filial love and conjugal love, that create tension within characters – could not be completely disallowed without eliminating the tragic conflict, characters' responses to these contradictions are subjected to close scrutiny lest they do something other than what they say they will do in a given situation. One of the results of this aesthetic of rationality and coherence is that playwrights have to find clever ways of showing characters' conflicting thoughts and feelings. Ironically, it is possible that the preoccupation with rationality is one of the factors that drives Racine to create so many characters who seem to be teetering on the edge of madness, a state that at least can be used to explain voicing contradictory or conflicting feelings and ideas.

Bienséance

Another rule of classical theater that is so closely linked to verisimilitude that it is often difficult to distinguish from it is *bienséance* (sometimes used in the plural, *bienséances*), decorum or propriety. While verisimilitude may apply to either events or individual actions, *bienséance* tends to be used of characters, both their actions and their feelings. The basic idea of *bienséance* is that characters must behave in a manner that is fitting, appropriate, and seemly, this in spite of the need for actions of doubtful moral value in tragedy – Aristotle's *hamartia*, tragic error or flaw, is widely acknowledged and accepted in this period and is generally interpreted to mean a crime or moral failing of some sort. Although the audiences who attended performances of French classical tragedies were not exclusively aristocratic, especially for productions staged in Paris rather than at the court in Versailles, the plays were written essentially for and about the nobility, and playwrights were highly conscious of maintaining a certain level of propriety, however extreme the tragic situation might be. Thus tragedians deal with characters who are noble both in the social sense and in the moral sense of the word: they are not perfect, but they should never seem debased, undignified, or truly wicked.

For this reason violence is generally banned from the stage, except in the form of speeches reporting on offstage events. In the case of warfare, the justification for not showing violence onstage is as much *vraisemblance* and the unities as it is *bienséance*, but even the kind of familial or self-directed violence that is not uncommon in Shakespeare, for example, is strongly frowned upon in French classical tragedy. Corneille's *Horace* (1640), one of the first classical tragedies, originally staged the death of the female protagonist, Camille, at the hands of her brother; Corneille, in response to criticism, simply moved the murder *derrière le théâtre*, i.e., behind the theater, or offstage. In Corneille's *Rodogune* (1644), Cléopâtre takes poison and begins to feel its effects onstage in the final scene, but she is discreetly led away to die. Racine's *Phèdre* dies onstage, although the act of taking the poison that kills her takes place offstage; in fact Racine resorts to only one clear-cut onstage suicide, Atalide in the final scene of *Bajazet* (1672).

The concern for *bienséance* is apparent in the strong moralizing bent apparent in much theoretical writing about French classical tragedy, itself a reflection, in part, of the doubtful moral light in which theater is still seen in this period. Although Louis XIV was a great patron of the arts and the Catholic Church had little choice but to tolerate the grandiose theatrical productions he so enthusiastically supported, theater was still officially condemned by the Church, and its practitioners were excommunicated – in 1673 Molière received a Christian burial only after the King's intercession. While the Aristotelian and Horatian notions that tragedy is or should be morally beneficial are well known, many classical theoreticians seem to share to some extent Plato's mistrust of tragedy as a potential corrupter of morals and are consequently vigilant about its dangers. The Jansenist Pierre Nicole, who wrote about the arts, including theater, is an extreme example of this strain, as is pointed out by Béatrice Guion:

> In the end the Platonic influence [on Nicole] is revealed by the very status he accords art. He recalls . . . [Plato's] condemnation banishing poets from the ideal city. If Nicole points out the excessiveness of Plato's action, it is not, apparently, without a certain regret: "it would be too great an undertaking to attempt to persuade people to give up completely an art for which they have such a powerful inclination." (Guion 1996: 32)

Few writers about the theater are as extreme as Nicole, whose objections to theater are motivated by religious conviction, but even those who are quite accepting of tragedy keep a close watch on it. The vast majority of theoreticians agree with the Horatian notion that tragedy aims both to please and to instruct the audience, but most believe that tragedy must be carefully monitored so that the necessary ethical component is not subordinated to the pleasurable aspect.

It could be argued that the greatest French tragedies are as morally ambiguous as the greatest tragedies of Sophocles or Shakespeare, and yet a tragedian like Racine goes to great lengths to present his works as exercises in public instruction. In defense of what, in the eyes of history, will become his greatest tragedy, *Phèdre et Hippolyte* (today generally referred to as *Phèdre*), Racine, in a tone of moral outrage, fends off criticisms that his play is immoral:

Moreover, I cannot yet ascertain that this play is in reality the greatest of my tragedies. I leave it up to readers and to history to decide what it is truly worth. What I can ascertain is that I have never written a tragedy in which virtue is so clearly revealed as it is in this one. In it, the slightest faults are severely punished. The very thought of a crime is viewed with as much horror as the crime itself...Passions are made manifest only to show the great disorder they lead to. And vice is depicted, from beginning to end, in a light that reveals it as something deformed and hateful. That is, strictly speaking, the goal that any man working for the Public must give himself. And that is what the earliest tragedians had in mind on all matters. Their theater is a school in which virtue is no less well taught than in the philosophers' schools...It would be worthwhile if our own works were as solid and full of useful lessons as theirs. (Racine 1999: 819)

Independently of one's interpretation of the play itself, it is interesting to observe Racine's eagerness to present himself as a protector of public morality, an upstanding purveyor of *bienséance*.

Bienséance is also one of the rules invoked to purify the form of tragedy. Language must be lofty and formal; all classical tragedies use the extremely stylized Alexandrine verse, with its unremitting twelve-syllable line, neatly divided into two equal hemistiches of six syllables each, and a strict alternation between "feminine" rhymes, those whose last syllable includes a mute "e," and other types, "masculine" rhymes. The vocabulary must be suitable to personages of noble birth and character; individual words may be criticized by theoreticians on the grounds of being inappropriate. Comedy has a great deal more leeway on this score than does tragedy; mixed genres like tragicomedy, however, which were quite popular at the beginning of the classical period, were not long tolerated once the rules were in place. *Bienséance* requires that a funny play be funny and that a serious play be serious. A mixture of tones is seen as inappropriate, and the kind of comic relief that one sometimes finds in Aeschylus or Euripides is not deemed acceptable in French classical tragedy.

A representative discussion of *bienséance* comes from René Rapin's 1674 *Réflexions sur la poétique d'Aristote*:

People sin against this rule either because they confuse seriousness with humor..., or endow characters with manners disproportionate to their station..., or are not careful to carry through people's characters..., or are not modest..., or talk about everything under the sun without discretion...In a word everything that is against the rules of time, morals, feeling and expression is against *bienséance*. (Bray [1945] 1983: 215)

If *bienséance* is designed, like verisimilitude, to avoid shocking the audience, it apparently does not take all that much to shock the audience: having nobles use even a single term more appropriate to their lackeys or chambermaids can draw criticism on the grounds of a violation of *bienséance*. Rapin's observations are not untypical of the period in that the list he draws up does not consist of examples of *bienséance* but of counterexamples, infractions against the rule. This in itself is not insignificant: if the rules of theater work properly, the audience should not even be aware of their existence; they act as a kind of buffer against the audience's potential reaction of indignation at something distasteful.

As is the case with verisimilitude, *bienséance* is also presented as so important that if need be it should take priority over raw truth, as Jean Chapelain points out:

> If the playwright is forced to adapt historical material of this sort [i.e., material that includes shocking elements, like Corneille's *Le Cid*], he must reduce it to the terms of *bienséance*, even at the expense of truth. Under those circumstances it is preferable to change the entire story rather than to leave a single blemish incompatible with the rules of his art, which seeks out the universal aspect of things and purifies them of the flaws and particular irregularities that history, because of the severity of its laws, is forced to put up with. (Chapelain 1936: 165)

Here again, as with verisimilitude, a doctrine based on the actual tastes and values of the culture of a particular place and era is presented as ideal, universal, and general.

The unities: time, place, action

The unities of time and place, which elicit great controversy and a good deal of heated discussion, can be seen as a logical extension of verisimilitude. Theoreticians reason that if a playwright sets the action at a particular time and place in the first scene of a play, it strains the audience's belief to move to another time or place in the course of the five acts. Writers about the theater stress repeatedly the importance of establishing and maintaining an illusion of reality as part of the theatergoing experience. An excellent example of this position is Jean Chapelain's letter to Pierre Godeau of 1630 entitled "Lettre sur la règle des 24 heures" (Letter on the twenty-four-hour rule) in which the theoretician states:

> One of the fundamental principles is that imitation in all works of art must be so perfect that no difference appears between the thing imitated and the thing that is imitating it, for the main source of effectiveness for the representation is to proffer objects to the mind as if they were true and present...; something that, although it holds for all genres, seems particularly applicable to the art of theater, in which the person of the playwright is hidden simply to have a greater impact on the viewer's imagination and to eliminate obstacles so as to lead viewers more effectively toward the kind of faith in what is being represented that one wishes to instill in them. (Chapelain 1936: 115)

The playwright's absence commented upon here is emblematic of the viewers' necessary acceptance of the premise that they are observing a series of events actually unfolding; anything that breaks that illusion is seen as weakening dramatic impact. And in the eyes of many theoreticians – indeed, by about 1640 in the eyes of nearly all of them – a change of scenery or a discontinuity in time frame do just that.

The unity of time, generally referred to in the seventeenth century as unity of day (*unité de jour*), is an issue with a very long history. Aristotle observes that most plays take place within one turn of the sun, or slightly longer (*Poetics* 5), although the Greek text has been variously interpreted, including by some who exclude the possibility of ever going beyond 24 hours. While many scholars and critics today seem to go on the assumption that the unity of time limited the action to 24 hours, at least three distinct interpretations of this rule held currency in the sixteenth and seventeenth centuries: 24 hours; 12 hours; and the same length of time as the play itself took to stage, usually 2 or 3 hours, but sometimes as much as 8.

The notion of a 12-hour unity of time apparently originates from a particular interpretation of Aristotle's text whereby a turn of the sun is construed to mean the time between sunrise and sunset, or, conceivably, sunset and sunrise. As early as 1548, the Italian commentator Robertello hypothesizes that Aristotle is referring to the daylight hours: he argues that people don't act at night but during the day, so that at any rate the additional 12 hours would be superfluous (Bray [1945] 1983: 254).

In 1570 Castelvetro, in his commentary on Aristotle, compresses the unity of time even further by stating that if the playwright wishes to create an illusion of reality, the play ought to last no longer than the spectators actually spend in the theater. Since 12 hours is too long for a single production, the action would have to be limited even further chronologically in order for the audience to believe in what is happening onstage.

The three interpretations of the rule – 24 hours, 12 hours, or what we might today call "real time" continued to be aired by theoreticians in the seventeenth century, and some refinements are brought to the debate, but nothing that fundamentally questions or alters the fundamental principle of having the action limited to, at most, a single day. For example, intermissions are said to provide a bit of flexibility in that the temporal break makes a jump of a few hours in the time of the action somewhat palatable, as Jean Chapelain notes:

> I do see your objection that it is just as difficult to imagine that one has spent twenty-four hours at a performance that has lasted a mere three as it is to think that a story that lasts ten years might take place within the bounds of those very same three hours . . . But I believe the separation of the acts and the time when the theater empties of actors, and the audience is entertained with music or interludes, must take the place of some time such that one can imagine the time stretching out to twenty-four hours. (Chapelain 1936: 121–2)[7]

A musical interlude might last just a short while, but because it leaves the framework of the representation of action, Chapelain argues that the audience experiences the temporal break between acts in a different way than it experiences the passage of time during the play itself.

By the 1650s the unity of time is no longer a matter of great debate in itself, which leaves the Abbé d'Aubignac free to indulge in a miniature lesson in astronomical geography:

> We mustn't interpret [Aristotle's] *single turn of the sun* too loosely to mean the time of its presence on the horizon; for it is known that there are places that are sunlit continuously

for five or six months a year; or else one would have to limit the meaning of these words to the city of Athens, as if the philosopher had not written for other places. What remains to be said is that *a single turn of the sun* means its daily movement; but as the day can be considered in two different ways, one being... what we call *natural day*, or *twenty-four-hour day*; and the other, by the presence of its light between its rising and its setting, being what we call *artificial day*, we must observe that Aristotle is speaking only about artificial day. (Abbé d'Aubignac 1971: 108)

I would argue that this passage is more interesting as an illustration of the pervasiveness of Cartesianism in neoclassical theoretical discussions of theater than as a discussion of the unity of time.

Two main principles emerge from the century of controversy about the unity of time: (1) in France, from about 1640 on, the need for unity of time in tragedy and other theatrical forms is well established and little questioned; (2) in terms of how the rule is applied, although there continues to be some disagreement, the general principle is: the shorter the better, and no longer than 24 hours. There are voices of dissent; Pierre Corneille, who sometimes has difficulty fitting his action-laden plots into the space of 24 hours without eliciting satirical commentaries, points out as late as 1660 that novelists, not constrained by the unities, have all the luck:

We are bothered in theater by place, by time, and by the inconveniences of the performance... The novel has none of these constraints: it gives the actions it describes all the leisure they need to unfold... Theater tells us nothing except through people onstage viewed by the public in a short space of time. (Corneille 1963: 837)

Corneille's frustration at limiting himself to a single day and place is almost palpable, and yet after the quarrel set off by *Le Cid* (see below), even he does his best to conform to rules about which he seems to have harbored some doubts. Concentration and economy of language and action ultimately win out and become central not only to classical theater in France, but also to the French aesthetic long after classicism has died out.

To some extent unity of place follows logically from unity of time – one cannot travel very far afield in the space of a few hours – but here again the French carry things to quite an extreme, ultimately presenting as an ideal – not always reached, however – no change of scenery at all, not even different parts of a single building. The problem of unity of place is complicated by seventeenth-century performance practices. A popular stage configuration at the beginning of the classical period is to have two or three settings onstage simultaneously, and to vary the scenes between or among them, thus adding excitement and visual interest to the production. The purveyors of the unities see this as undermining the spectators' belief in the veracity of events and work to stamp it out.

One important consequence of the unity of place is the increased need for reported action in the form of speeches narrating offstage happenings. As we have seen, events like battles would be unsuitable at any rate on other grounds, particularly *vraisem-*

blance, but unity of place would also condemn them, as it would popular uprisings, meetings of the Senate, and many of the events routinely occupying the kind of political tragedy popular in the period. Some of the most famous passages in the entire repertoire of French classical tragedy are in fact reports of actions or scenes taking place offstage, occasionally in the distant past, particularly in the works of Racine: to name only a few examples, Andromaque's narration of the fall of Troy in *Andromaque*, the murder of Narcisse and the rescue of Junie by the people of Rome at the end of *Britannicus*, and the death of Hippolyte in *Phèdre*.[8]

Of the three unities, unity of action, which Aristotle also touches upon (*Poetics* 8), excites the least controversy in the classical period, which is quite easy to understand if one views classical theater in counterpoint to what precedes it: the open-ended, complex plots of the Baroque, including tragicomedy, pastoral, and even nontheatrical genres like the novel. Here is how unity of action is defined by d'Aubignac:

> From the vast material available our playwright will choose a notable action, and, so to speak, a point of history that is striking in its recounting of the joy or misfortune of some illustrious figure and in which the playwright can include the rest in an abridged form, and while limiting himself to the representation of a single part, make everything take place skillfully before the public's eyes, but without putting too much into the main action, and without leaving out any of the beauties necessary for the carrying out of his work. (d'Aubignac 1971: 74)

Unity of action, a matter of effective framing, is intimately linked with the other two unities: the playwright must know when and where to begin the action and what characters and events to include. Subplots might be interesting and promising in themselves, but insofar as they distract from the main story, they cannot be allowed.

The Process of Codification

Although the play generally considered to be the first tragedy written in French, Jodelle's *Cléopâtre captive* (1552), alludes vaguely to the unity of time, at that early date it is unclear where the playwright would even have come into contact with the concept (Bray [1945] 1983: 260). And indeed, one consequence of the nearly century-long gestation period between the presentation of the first French tragedies in the mid-sixteenth century and the codification of the rules of theater in the seventeenth is that dramatists and theoreticians are to varying degrees aware of the debate about the rules of theater long before those rules become codified in the 1630s and 1640s. The problem of "regular" and "irregular" theater is one of the central issues upon which discussion of theater focuses in the century or so preceding the classical period in France. Most of the basic elements of what would in the seventeenth century become the rules of theater are already being discussed in the sixteenth century, and some quite early playwrights hold to some of the rules. But they are not systematically formulated or applied in France until at least the 1630s.

This decade sees such an intense transformation of attitudes that it could fairly be considered the period in which the basic groundwork for the rules and their application were laid. Two nearly simultaneous events are key to this development, both affecting changes in themselves and reflecting changes that have gone on in the minds of the theatrical community, playwrights, theoreticians, and the theatergoing public. These events are the founding of the Académie française in 1634 and the 1637 theatrical sensation, Pierre Corneille's tragicomedy (later dubbed a tragedy) *Le Cid*, and the explosive debate about theater that it fuels.

The Académie française, which still today remains one of the most prestigious institutions in France, has rather humble origins. It began as a discussion group, nine individuals who met weekly to discuss current events, the arts, and other matters. When Richelieu got wind of the existence of the group, he decided to use it as the kernel of a French Academy, an organization officially sanctioned and supported by the government to oversee matters related to the French language and to books written in French (Adam 1962: 220–5). The Academy, founded in 1634, took a few years to get off the ground, but when in 1637 Pierre Corneille presented *Le Cid*, one of the great theatrical sensations of the century, the Academy used the production of this controversial play as a taking-off point to launch Richelieu's plan to impose order and authority on French theater.

Le Cid was an enormous success – the public loved it. As well as being one of the masterpieces of French theater, the play can be read as a cultural artifact that reenacts the birth pangs of classicism. Corneille, aware of the debate about the rules of theater, does actually try to respect some of them at least, but even though the play is a great success on its own terms, Corneille's efforts at following the rules are so clumsy and heavy-handed that often we are simply made aware of the attempt to conform to regularity, rather than any real integration or assimilation of the rules into the playwright's aesthetic.

Le Cid almost immediately drew attacks and counterattacks: Georges de Scudéry, one of Corneille's rivals, wrote his scathing "Observations sur *Le Cid*," complemented soon thereafter by "Les Sentiments de l'Académie française sur la tragi-comédie du Cid" penned, under pressure from Richelieu, by Jean Chapelain, a member of the new Academy. The two men take Corneille to task on a number of issues. If he has tried to respect the unity of time, it is only at the expense of plausibility. In the space of a day or so – the exact chronology of the play is not completely clear – the young lovers, Chimène and Rodrigue, lay the groundwork for their engagement, helped along by the King's daughter, who is also in love with Rodrigue; the King names a new tutor for his son; the fathers of the two lovers argue over the King's choice; Rodrigue challenges Chimène's father to a duel; the two men fight, and Chimène's father is killed; Chimène demands revenge; Rodrigue demands Chimène's forgiveness; the Moors attack; Rodrigue raises an army to repel them, and defeats them; he returns to court and fights a duel for the hand of Chimène; and finally the King orders Chimène to let enough time pass for her to accept Rodrigue, her father's killer, as her husband. Corneille himself was undoubtedly not unaware of the problem; when in act

4 he is running out of time and still has to have Rodrigue fight for Chimène's hand, he gives us the following exchange among Don Diègue (Rodrigue's father), Chimène, and the King, Don Fernand:

DON FERNAND:	Chimène, will you entrust your feud to his [Rodrigue's adversary's] hand?
CHIMÈNE:	Sire, I have promised.
DON FERNAND:	Be ready to fight tomorrow.
DON DIÈGUE:	No, Sire, we mustn't put it off:
	A man is always quite ready when he has heart.
DON FERNAND:	Just off the battlefield, how can he fight immediately?
DON DIÈGUE:	Rodrigue caught his breath while he told you about the battle.

(Corneille 1963: 237; *Le Cid* 4.5.1443–8)

It is difficult to know what the tone of these lines is meant to be; perhaps the scene was performed with no hint of humor, but the allusion to the problem of an overcharged plot does risk compromising the solemn, austere atmosphere of the tragic situation.

In addition to the problem of unity of time, *Le Cid* is also criticized for being disunified in action and in genre. The character of the King's daughter, l'Infante, is seen as a distraction from the love story between Rodrigue and Chimène, all the more so as l'Infante is a member of the royal family and cannot properly disappear into the background. When Corneille presents *Le Cid* he calls it a *tragi-comédie*, and that, too, is part of the problem: as we have seen, classical dramaturgy avoids mixed genres as being indecorous, the combination of tones and the division of interest undermining the concentration and purity so central to the classical aesthetic.

Perhaps more than anything else, however, the play is found morally shocking, an affront to *bienséance* as well as to *vraisemblance*. This is how Scudéry characterizes the dilemma of Chimène, caught between allegiance to her slain father and love for the man who killed him:

> *Le Cid* gives a very bad example: in it we see a denatured daughter who speaks only of her folly when she ought to be speaking only of her misfortune; who complains about the loss of her suitor when she ought to be thinking only of the loss of her father; who loves the person she must abhor; who allows the murderer and the poor body of his victim into the same house at the same time; and – the height of impiety – joins her hand to one that is still dripping with her father's blood. (Scudéry [1637] 1980: 787)

Scudéry's moral indignation at Chimène's tragic plight exemplifies the central paradox of the corpus of tragedies that are composed and produced for the next half-century under the censorious eye of the Académie and other theoreticians preoccupied with consistency, clarity, and decorum. From its origins in ancient Greece, tragedy deals with contradictions; with problems that cannot be satisfactorily resolved; with conflicting desires, allegiances, and obligations; and with violence, physical and/or spiritual. Classical French playwrights are invited to practice the form as an exercise in prestige for the monarchy, but only if they conform to a set of principles that, taken to an extreme, can be at odds with the very works they are intended to govern and enhance.

Conclusion: The Legacy of French Classical Tragedy

One of the most puzzling aspects of French classical tragedy is the way that it combines a hyperawareness of clarity, coherence, and logic with plays that deal with irrationality, blind passion, and contradiction and paradox. And yet it could be argued that this peculiar combination is precisely the legacy of French classical tragedy. Tragedians are enjoined to compose plays that are clear, regular, and harmonious, and yet the plays deal with violent stories full of emotion; they are performed by actors whose acting style is so extreme that it is not unheard of for them to do themselves harm or even to die during a performance;[9] and a successful production will stir the audience to impressive fits of weeping. This kind of melding of strong emotion with hyperrationalism – and, more specifically, hyperrationalism about strong emotion – is to be found in many of the greatest works of French literature, both in theater and in other genres, from later centuries as well. Indeed, the codification of the rules for theater during the classical age has ramifications that go far beyond the period, deeply informing the subsequent history of French theater. While less restrictive dramatic forms like the eighteenth-century *drame bourgeois* do develop, French playwrights remain keenly aware of and in many cases constrained by neoclassical dramaturgy well into the twentieth century. It has been observed by more than one critic that subsequent French tragedy in particular is stunted by the legacy of the classical period, with its restrictive rules and the daunting model of perfection offered by virtually all of Racine's remarkable tragedies, as well as many by Pierre Corneille. And yet, an aesthetic favoring an intense, often streamlined dramatic action that comes to a head in a short period of time – a notion that originates in the neoclassical rule of the unities of time, place, and action – is central to postclassical French literature, extending far beyond theater into narrative forms and, later, cinema. This taste for austere minimalism is one of the reasons why Shakespeare, whose aesthetic is quite different, did not begin to be appreciated in France until the romantic period. Perhaps the ultimate paradox of French classical tragedy is that the principal beneficiaries of its legacy are neither subsequent tragedy nor other theatrical forms, but rather French literary tastes in a much more general sense.

NOTES

1   All translations from the French are my own.

2   In addition to prefaces, Pierre Corneille composed a series of treatises on tragedy entitled "Discours de la tragédie," published in 1660. Racine wrote thought-provoking prefaces to his plays, in some cases revising the prefaces to respond to criticisms of the works in question.

3   See, among others, Bray ([1945] 1983: 191).

4   I mean this in a logical rather than a chronological sense, i.e., without implying that *vraisemblance* preceded the other rules chronologically.

5   To this day a French person who finds a situation bizarre will use this theatrical metaphor and say, "C'est invraisemblable" – loosely translatable as "that's hard to believe" – about something that has indisputably occurred but that the speaker finds hard to fathom or displeasing; what the word expresses is not so much doubt as disapproval.

6   Another play of Racine's in which the role of confidant is key is *Britannicus* (Narcisse); several other Racinian tragedies feature characters who have confidant-like roles, including *Bérénice* (Antiochus) and *Iphigénie* (Eriphile).

7   In fact this argument does not originate with Chapelain, but comes from sixteenth-century Italian commentators.

8   The passages are, respectively, *Andromaque* 3.8.996–1012, *Britannicus* 5.9.1721–64, and *Phèdre* 5.6.1498–1570.

9   One actor is said to have died shortly after performing the scene of Orestes' madness at the end of Racine's *Andromaque*. Molière had a stroke while playing the character of Argan in his comedy *Le Malade imaginaire* and died shortly after the end of the performance.

REFERENCES AND FURTHER READING

Adam, Antoine. (1962). *Histoire de la littérature française au XVIIe siècle 1: L'Epoque d'Henri IV et de Louis XIII*. Paris: Editions mondiales. A detailed and well-documented study of the Baroque period of French literature and the first decade of French classicism.

Adam, Antoine. (1968). *L'Age classique 1: 1624–1660*. Paris: Arthaud. A fairly general overview of the first decades of French classical literature.

Aristotle. (1958). *Poetics*, trans. G. M. A. Grube. In *On Poetry and Style*. Indianapolis, IN: Bobbs-Merrill. The most influential writing on tragedy in the Western canon is also the most influential theoretical work for French classical tragedy.

Boileau-Despréaux, Nicolas. [1674] (1966). *Art poétique*. In *Oeuvres complètes*, ed. Françoise Escal. Paris: Gallimard, Bibliothèque de la Pléiade. An influential treatise on classical aesthetics, written in verse.

Bray, René. [1945] (1983). *La Formation de la doctrine classique*. Paris: Nizet. A detailed study of the rules of theater governing French classicism.

Chapelain, Jean. (1936). "Lettre sur la règle des vingt-quatre heures" (1630) and "Les Sentiments de l'Académie française touchant les observations faites sur la tragi-comédie du *Cid*" (1637). In *Opuscules critiques*. Paris: Droz, 114–26, 154–97. Both of these texts are crucial to the development of the rules of theater.

Chappuzeau, Samuel. [1674] (1876). *Le Théâtre françois*, ed. Georges Monval. Paris: Jules Bonnassies. An influential treatise on French theater.

Corneille, Pierre. (1963). *Oeuvres complètes*, ed. André Stegmann. Paris: Seuil, L'Intégrale. One of the two most admired French tragedians of the classical period, Pierre Corneille also wrote a number of influential comedies.

d'Aubignac, François Hédelin, Abbé. [1657] (1971). *La Pratique du théâtre*, ed. Hans-Jörg Neuschäfer. Munich: Wilhelm Fink. One of the most thorough and detailed treatises of French classical dramatic theory and practice, commissioned by Richelieu and composed over a period of more than a decade.

Guion, Béatrice, ed. (1996). "Introduction." In *La Vraie beauté et son fantôme et autres textes d'esthétique*, ed. Pierre Nicole. Paris: Honoré Champion. An analysis of the impact of the aesthetic writings of an influential Jansenist writer of the period.

Horace. [1965] (2000). *The Art of Poetry*, trans. Penelope Murray and T. S. Dorsch. In *Classical Literary Criticism*. London: Penguin. The most influential Latin treatise in the French classical period.

La Mesnardière, Jules de. [1640] (1972). *La Poëtique*. Geneva: Slatkine. An influential early discussion of the rules of theater.

Lancaster, Henry Carrington. (vol. 1, 1928; vol. 2, 1932.) *A History of French Dramatic Literature in the Seventeenth Century*, 2 vols. Baltimore, MD: Johns Hopkins University Press. An authoritative critical text that details the history of the French classical period.

Lanson, Gustave. [1895] (1951). *Histoire de la littérature française*, ed. Paul Tuffrau. Paris: Hachette. A highly influential critical work synthesizing the history of French literature, including the French classical period.

Lanson, Gustave. (1916–17). *Esquisse d'une histoire de la tragedie en France*. New York: Columbia University Press. Published lecture notes on the history of tragedy in France.

Levitan, William. (1989). "Seneca in Racine." *Yale French Studies* 76, 185–210. An analysis of the subtle influence of the Latin tragedian Seneca on Racine, focusing on Racine's most famous tragedy, *Phèdre*.

Lyons, John D. (1999). *Kingdom of Disorder: The Theory of Tragedy in Classical France*. West Lafayette, IN: Purdue University Press. A recent critical work on theories of French classical tragedy, highlighting the tensions and even contradictions among various theories of tragedy.

Morel, Jacques. (1964). *La Tragédie*. New York: McGraw Hill and Armand Collin. An overview of French tragedy of the sixteenth and seventeenth centuries, including a wide variety of theoretical texts about tragedy and representative selections from tragedies of the period.

Racine, Jean. (1999). *Oeuvres complètes 1*, ed. Georges Forestier. Paris: Gallimard, Bibliothèque de la Pléiade. This revered playwright, a generation younger than Pierre Corneille, wrote fewer than a dozen tragedies but is generally considered the greatest of all French tragedians.

Saint-Évremond, Charles de Marguetel de Saint Denis, seigneur de. (1962). *Oeuvres en prose*, 4 vols., ed. René Ternois. Paris: Marcel Didier. Includes diverse prose pieces about theater, religion, and other topics of interest for French classical tragedy.

Scudéry, Georges de. [1637] (1980). "Observations sur *Le Cid*." In Pierre Corneille, *Oeuvres complètes 1*, ed. Georges Couton. Paris: Gallimard, Bibliothèque de la Pléiade. One of the texts that helped launch the famous quarrel of *Le Cid*, a critique of Pierre Corneille composed by a rival playwright.

Tobin, Ronald. (1971). *Racine and Seneca*. Chapel Hill: University of North Carolina Press. An analysis of the importance of the Latin playwright for the greatest of the French tragedians.

22

French Neoclassical Tragedy: Corneille/Racine

Mitchell Greenberg

For a span of just over fifty years (1637–91), two dramatists dominated the stage of French classical tragedy. Pierre Corneille (1606–84) and Jean Racine (1639–99), while espousing radically different views of the tragic genre, appeared to their contemporaries and to succeeding generations intimately locked in artistic rivalry. This competition opposed two widely opposed ethical views of the tragic universe (one open and "political," the other, claustrophobically intimate and "personal"). From La Bruyère's first critically opposite judgments of the two ("Corneille represents mankind as it should be, Racine as it is") to our own day the competition for public validation between France's two greatest tragic playwrights extends beyond the theater into the world of French (Parisian) cultural life, forming an integral part of the ongoing debates about national identity.

Although the Third Republic and its heirs have created for us a rather static, if not to say marmoreal, image of the French seventeenth century, current research presents a rather different picture of this tumultuous period. The France over which Louis XIII and Louis XIV presided was a society in epochal transition. The French social order was undergoing momentous changes in its religious, economic, sexual, and political structures. The gradual but relentless drive of a mercantilist economy was fomenting radical social changes as a waning feudal aristocracy saw its wealth and influence recede before the onrush of the newly empowered third estate. At the same time the very notions of "family" and therefore of the confused imbrication of sexual and political economies were undergoing a radical reformation. In this sense the seventeenth century mediates those changes that will eventuate in the eighteenth as the emergence of a new, "modern" subjectivity. This subjectivity, however, is given its first adumbration in the cauldron of classical France, where elements of a dying order mingled and mixed with those still inchoate forces of the new that were struggling to emerge. It is at this point of mediation that the theater appears as the most enchafed locus of social experimentation. For the theater, more so than any other form of representation, proves to be the most ample space on and through which this new subject is essayed and triumphs.

The new tragic subject of the French seventeenth-century stage emerges at the conflicted juncture of several interrelated forces. For our present purposes, however, and limiting ourselves to the subject of tragedy, we must at least ask, if not answer, several important questions. In this century which has become synonymous with the expansion of Absolutism across Europe, the first question that comes to mind is: why does the theater, and tragedy in particular, become the privileged form of representation of all the emerging Absolutist nation-states (England, France, Spain)? Why is it that this theater that produces some of the greatest tragic dramas of the Western tradition is almost exclusively a familial one? And finally, why do the family and the subject formed within the family emerge at this historical juncture in direct relation to, if not reflection of, a political system, Absolutism, that is subtended by and inseparable from a patriarchal ideology whose influence pervades every aspect of social life? For it would be fruitless as well as more than a little naïve to attempt to separate a political system structured around the image/imaginary of the king – an image of unity, integrity, and closure – from an aesthetics and an ethos of tragedy that is at the same time constructing on the stage, and under the gaze of this adulated monarch, the parameters of subjectivity inside of which the subject of seventeenth-century tragedy plays out his or her personal (that is, sexually politicized) fate.

Although Corneille had been an active playwright since the early 1630s, those plays of his that were produced on the Parisian stages were primarily convoluted comedies where plot still ruled over character. It was only in 1634 that Corneille's first tragedy, *Médée*, was performed. It is interesting that Corneille chose to enter the tragic universe through the door of myth, a universe he was to abandon in all his later tragedies. In choosing to center his first tragedy on the matricidal fury of betrayed love, Corneille reveals a penchant for a particular type of the tragic he will later, in his "great" plays, eschew. In the *Discours*, written almost thirty years after *Médée*, Corneille specifically states that politics, not love, must be the motivating force of tragedy. Tragedy's true nature demands a plot in which major questions of state – the end of a dynasty, the death of a great king, the destruction of an empire – are hanging in the balance. Love can only be allowed into the tragic universe as incidental to these events. It must take an ancillary role and leave the main spotlight on political concerns.[1]

Quite clearly *Médée* does not do this. Although we are aware of a political undercurrent in its plot, the crux of this tragedy is sexual desire, jealousy, and revenge. It is a tragedy of excess, a play of unbridled emotions. It is probably not for nothing that in this, his first tragedy, Corneille chose to follow Seneca (perhaps the leading influence, not just in French but in Elizabethan dramaturgy as well) in his depiction of the passions, fears, and murderous powers of a woman scorned. In this he was most probably following the reigning "baroque" theatrical style that dominated the Parisian stage in the first third of the century. This "baroque" drama was replete with twisted plots, dramatic misprisions, cross-dressing disguises, and last-minute plot reversals, and was dripping with blood and gore. The leading practitioners of the genre (a genre in which "tragedy" was actually almost abandoned in favor of the more contemporary "tragicomedies") – Garnier, Rotrou, du Ryer, and others – were embroiled in an ethical and aesthetic battle for the redefinition of the role and function of the theater in general and of tragedy in particular. It is from the heated debates, first in Italy, then in France, that the "classical dicta" would emerge and triumph in France in the 1630s, signaling the end of "baroque excess" and the imposition on the theater of classical propriety. With *Médée*, Corneille is still very much writing in a tradition that he will soon abandon. He presents us, however, with an "original" drama, a prototypical "family romance" in which the conflicting tensions are so great, the resolution so utterly traumatic to the political universe, that its violence and more specifically the fear of a particular type of female violence will cast a long shadow over the "classical" tragedies to come.

Although formally *Médée* belongs to the major current of baroque "blood and gore" tragedies that had so large a role on the French stage in the 1620s and early 1630s, there is no attempt to make the play fit into those neoclassical parameters that are being debated in "avant-garde" literary circles – no unity of time, place, or plot, no respect paid to the *bienséances* of language – it is not for that unworthy of our attention. For although the rather florid "baroque" style of the play will be promptly abandoned (at the same time that Corneille leaves the world of myth for the stage of history), the enigmatic presence of its eponymous heroine – a fantasy, we might suggest, of a feminine power inimical to life in the polis, inimical to all stable political formations (first and foremost the family), inimical to what is perceived to be the masculine domain of reason and restraint – will haunt the universe of Corneille's greatest tragedies. When in the last scene of this tragedy, Medea, the Scythian sorceress admitted into the clear light of Corinth, flies off in her dragon-drawn chariot, she leaves behind her the destruction not only of the political base of the city-state (its king is dead; his daughter and Medea's rival burned to death in her poisoned robes), but also of the family (Medea has murdered her two sons and her husband is left, suicidal), and the future is deemed utterly desolate. Leaving the scene of the carnage her fury and powers have wreaked, Medea disappears back into the fantasies that spawned her, ready to be reincarnated in those proper Corneillean heroines entangled in sexual / political imbroglios that will continue to dominate Corneille's tragic universe.

If *Médée*, despite its all-consuming violence, did not evoke a loud public outcry, such was, as we know, not the case with Corneille's next tragedy (actually, in its first version, a "tragicomedy"), *Le Cid*. The public's reaction to *Le Cid* was in its vehemence, passion, and division unique in the annals of the French stage. No other theatrical debut was to have such a momentous impact on its contemporaries and on successive generations of admirers as Corneille's new play. From its premiere to this day, *Le Cid* is marked as *une pièce à scandale*. Scandalous because of the predicament of its protagonists – will the heroine, whose father has been killed by her "lover," seek his death, or will she give in to her passion and marry him? – scandalous because of its enormous "popular" success which flies in the face of classical dicta regarding the three unities; and, finally, scandalous because of the playwright's haughty refusal to respond to his "learned" critics.

Corneillean tragedy, and in this *Le Cid* is just the first example, is always situated at a moment of historical crisis, at a moment of momentous change where an old order is in its death throes and a new order is struggling to emerge. In *Le Cid*, for example, we are present at the birth of the (Absolute) Castilian monarchy. The king, Don Fernand, is the "first King of Castile"; his position is still shaky and his power is threatened both internally (the potentially rebellious great feudal nobles, of whom Don Gomes, Chimène's father, is the most obvious example) and externally by the ever present threat of the Muslim invaders. It is this historico-political setting that serves as the backdrop for the more "intimate" plot of the play, where the personal situation of the young protagonists (their "passion") is informed and deformed by the ambient social tensions. There is, in other words, no "love" in Corneille that is not also an overly invested political structure. It is perhaps for this reason that in all the great Corneillean tragedies, "marriage" – that strangely convoluted institution where the strands of sexuality, desire, politics, and economy meet and are entangled – is not only the plot device driving each tragedy on to its conclusion, but is also in each (except in *Polyeucte*) always left hanging. Marriage, with its promise of happiness and its constant deferral, becomes the tragic vortex of the plays, uniting politics, history, and sexuality in a downward spiral toward death.

Briefly stated, the plot of *Le Cid* (with Corneille's heavy borrowings from Guillén de Castro's *Las mocedades del Cid*) turns around what we will come to know as the inextricable tragic dilemma in Corneille – the opposition of personal desire and civic (familial, clanic) "duty" (*devoir*): the two young protagonists who love each other and wish to marry, whose love is presented as "unproblematic," are suddenly and irrevocably sundered by a "political" crisis that descends on them and forever changes the course of their life/love. Rodrigue, the young hero and happy "lover" of Chimène, is summoned by his father (the family patriarch and thus the embodiment of all those masculine values – duty, honor, self-sacrifice – that preside over the Corneillean universe) to revenge an insult that sullies his and his family's reputation. The man responsible for the insult is Chimène's father. Rodrigue takes up the defense of his family's honor, challenges the Count to a duel, and slays him. It now becomes Chimène's "duty" to defend her dead father by demanding Rodrigue's death.

By staunchly defending her dead father, Chimène, as a woman, is clearly made a surrogate for all that her father represented, politically and metaphysically, for the sociohistoric battle that the play also adumbrates: Chimène becomes the representative of a regressive, feudal order that refuses the march of history, the progress toward a new absolutist state. Rodrigue, on the other hand, having eliminated the Count, now takes his place as the leading warrior of the Castilian state. In a rather opportune invasion, the Moors are defeated by Rodrigue, who, in the battle and victory, is reborn as an immortal legend – the Cid ("leader" in Arabic). As the new mainstay of the Castilian throne, Rodrigue has become essential for the triumph of the monarchic hegemony. It is against this *raison d'état* that Chimène, always torn between love and duty, must be made to conform.

As we have seen with Medea, the women in Corneille are also sundered – that is their defining mark – and always potentially retrograde. For this reason the love of Chimène and Rodrigue is an overdetermined political scenario where the resistant woman must be appropriated into a patriarchal schema (marriage to the hero) that would contain her and her fantasized erotic/destructive powers. At the denouement of the play, Chimène is tricked by the king into admitting her passion – even as this passion will define her as scandalous to Corneille's contemporaries.[2] Although "history" tells us that Chimène and Rodrigue did marry, the play ends with the marriage deferred, put off for another time and another stage.

Although *Le Cid* was a great success, it was also the target of a heated debate among the leading intellectual and political figures of the day. Corneille seemed, by his silence, impervious to the attacks he and his play were forced to endure. The Académie Française was finally summoned by Cardinal Richelieu to put an end to the quarrel with its own definitive judgment on the merits of the play. The Académie's judgment was rather wishy-washy, both accusing Corneille for not really producing a work that strictly followed the "rules," but excusing him nevertheless for the great pleasure his play had brought the audience. Corneille, as I have said, remained aloof to the attacks and counterattacks. His only response came in 1640 with his new tragedy, *Horace*, which marks an epiphanous moment in the history of the French stage. In this, Corneille's first *tragédie régulière*, classicism, full-blown and triumphant, emerges as the paragon of a new aesthetic. Suddenly, a work captures and perfects those laws of harmony, symmetry, and *bienséances* that, up to this point, the French theater had only stumbled toward blindly. The term *tragédie régulière* that Corneille's contemporaries used to describe this new mode of representation refers both to an ethos and to an aesthetic. In a first sense, *régulière* designates a work which follows the rules. A regular tragedy obeys the Law. This obedience, reproduced as spectacle, continually serves as a new production of the Law's origin, the founding act of society. Second, *régulière* defines the aesthetic parameters of such a representation. By following the rules classicism achieves a wholeness, an integrity of being in which the various parts of the work are subsumed in a unified, total structure. This shining image of perfection is, of course, subtended by an entire ideology which, at the same time that it is espousing the triumph of the unitary Cartesian "ego," is defining this unity as male, along a metaphoric axis that equates unity, masculinity, and power with ideality, and femininity with emotions, dispersion, materiality, and death.

Certainly this dyadic opposition is the ruling paradigm presiding over the world of *Horace*. The very first lines of the play introduce us into a universe that is split along sexual (male/female) and political (Rome/Alba) lines. The verses themselves are beautifully cadenced counterpoints whose antithetical rhetoric prefigures all the other divisions that inform this universe; male is opposed to female, family to state, passion to reason, Rome to Alba. Once again we are present at a tremulous historic moment: Rome and Alba, although "ethnically" identical, are political antagonists, currently at a hostile standoff to see which will triumph militarily over and subjugate the other. We are, in other words, present at a conflict the results of which will establish the foundations for Roman hegemony. The political stakes, which are enormous for the course of Western history, are transformed and focused on the personal, familial drama in which the two warring states are reduced to two archetypal families, the Horatii and the Curiae. The drama opposes Horace, the stoically unflinching Roman patriot, with his less dogmatic brother-in-law Curiace. Horace is the husband of Curiace's sister, Sabine, while Curiace is engaged to Camille, Horace's younger sister. Thus the political quarrel becomes inextricably entangled in the amorous/familial ties binding these members of the two emblematic families together. At the center of this imbroglio stands the ever promised and ever deferred marriage of Camille and Curiace, a marriage that would join Rome and Alba in a union that ostensibly would eradicate political divisions.

The tragic space becomes ever more confined as the political confrontation is reduced to this decisive familial conflict. In this, as in all of Corneille's great tragedies, the intimate space of family condenses in itself all the tensions of the greater political sphere and exacerbates them to the point of patricide (in the seventeenth-century sense of the term as a "crime committed against a close family member"). Tragedy in Corneille, although politically motivated, always needs to be anchored in the family, because it is in the family, in the words of the French psychoanalyst and critic, André Green, that "the ties of love and therefore of hate, are the earliest and most important" (Green 1969: 69). The two sets of brothers representing each family are called to fight to the death on the battlefield that separates the two massed armies. This experience of death is, of course, in accordance with the dictates of classical decorum, kept out of representation. We are never allowed to see what was depicted on the frontispiece of the play's first edition – the actual presence of blood and death. What we do see is the reaction of the women who are kept prisoners inside their home. We experience the battle, with its peripeteia and slaughter, in a scene of the distressed wives and sisters.[3] In a sense, we might conclude, therefore, that in Corneille the female characters stand in for, represent, "death" for the tragic audience.

Of the six combatants in this battle, only Horace – thanks to his physical prowess and psychological shrewdness – survives. He thus becomes the hero responsible not only for Rome's victory over its rival, Alba, but also and at the same time the origin of Rome's imperial destiny. From this point forward Rome will, we know, consolidate its hold over the Italian peninsula and go on to colonize the greater part of the known world, establishing, among other things, the language and institutions that will eventually give birth (at least in official royal propaganda) to the French nation.

While Horace's victory is a political and ideological triumph for nascent Roman hegemony it is a familial disaster for the women, most pointedly for his sister, Camille. Just as Chimène can be seen as the mirror image of Rodrigue in sexual reversal, Camille's self-righteous indignation is the direct counterpart of her brother's unquestioning dedication to Rome. In this case, once more, the woman is shown to be, by her passionate indignation and revolt, an obstacle to the unproblematic unfolding of the historical "progress." By her passionate outburst of "anti-Roman" sentiment with which she greets her brother upon his return from his heroic combat – an outburst that not only undermines her brother's clear-cut, but, we must assume, fragile sense of himself as a Roman and as a man, Camille shows herself situated on the side of passion, of the claims of the body, and by so doing plunges herself into the center of the tragic vortex. Her grief, her taunts, and her invective against Rome prove too much for Horace who, in the heat of passionate indignation, kills her with the same sword he had used in his duel against the Curiae.

Once again, a tragic blood crime of the most overinvested type (parricide) throws the entire political structure into disarray. And once again, it is a political solution that must be found to paper over this rift in the social fabric. The entire last act of the tragedy is devoted to what many see as a verbal jousting that smacks too much of the law courts, for it requires an entire act to move Horace from his new place as a social pariah to a more politically acceptable situation that recognizes his status as initiator of Roman hegemony. Horace has to be cleansed of his sin, in such a way that his homicidal act is, if not forgiven, at least repressed. We are made to understand that the origins of the polis (Rome) are always both a sacrifice and a repression of that sacrifice. As we are reminded by the king, Tulle, of the scandal at the origin of Rome, the murder of Remus by Romulus, a parricidal crime marks and hides the violence of all beginnings. In *Horace*, where the family and the state are complicitous, a new beginning is announced by Tulle, who decrees, as if to reestablish a broken harmony, that Camille and her lover, Curiace, at last be joined in the constantly deferred "marriage" that Camille knew was not to be her lot in life. The king orders, by way of an expiation, but also certainly as an appropriation, that this recalcitrant woman and her slain lover be laid to rest in a common grave. *Horace* ends therefore with a "legal" blurring of the "original sin" of all political foundational acts – the murder/ sacrifice of woman to the Law that must contain her excess in order for the new social order confirmed by this sacrifice to triumph.

This Machiavellian importance of *raison d'état* takes on an even more central role in Corneille's next, "bloodless," tragedy, *Cinna*. Perhaps no other of Corneille's major tragedies was greeted with such unanimous praise as this one. It would seem that to Corneille's contemporaries the play's supremacy over his other works was due mostly to its technical perfections. *Cinna* was judged a triumph principally because the laws of verisimilitude are made to function so well that form and content are intimately fused, creating a gleaming, shining mirage of theatrical illusion. Since the end of the eighteenth century *Cinna* has been seen as an essentially political tragedy. Whether or not Napoleon was a good judge of the theater, and whether or not he was correct in interpreting Auguste's inviting Cinna to be his "friend," as the "ruse of a tyrant," his judgment is emblematic of the trend that interprets *Cinna* as a study in totalitarianism. Curiously, for Corneille's contemporaries the political import of the play was its least compelling aspect. For them the heart of *Cinna* was passion. They were moved by the love of Cinna and Emilie and by the threats to that ardor. The play's title, *Cinna, ou la clémence d'Auguste*, seems to reflect, in its own ambivalence, these contradictory visions of the play; either "Cinna," that is the story of a love affair set against the backdrop of the intrigues of imperial Rome, or "Auguste," the *mise en scène* of the Machiavellian workings of tyranny.

That these two visions of the tragedy are not mutually exclusive, that they are, in fact, reflected in the copula (*ou*) that joins them, should not surprise anyone familiar with the typical imbrication of Corneillean dramaturgy. Neither in his theoretical writings nor in his previous practice had Corneille allowed the political to be separated from the passional, nor for the passions to exist outside the limits of the polis. What is new in *Cinna*, and what is perhaps so unsettling, is the greater subtlety Corneille brings to this, his second "Roman," tragedy. When we consider, for instance, that Cinna was composed at the same time as *Horace*, that both plays were worked on simultaneously, it does seem shocking that the two plays project a glaringly different representation of the tragic. Compared to *Horace*'s white-hot fury, with its descent into the abyssal sacrifice of familial blood, *Cinna* appears as a strikingly "pallid" tragedy. For the first time in Corneille's dramatic *oeuvre* we are spectators at a tragedy that appears to skirt around the "tragic": there is no blood shed in this play, and no expiatory victim dies so that a new state may rise from this immolation.

It would, however, be an error to judge the tragic of *Cinna* on this basis. For here, in the most conflictual of plays, we witness Corneille's audacious redefinition of tragedy. *Cinna* presents an insidiously clever articulation of a new tragic vortex. It is a vortex of rhetorical illusion which draws into its center the diverse demands of sexuality and politics. It produces a violence so shattering yet so subtle that death can be omitted without diminishing the effect the play exercises on its audience. In *Cinna*, Corneillean tragedy truly becomes *cosa mentale*.

Although there is no physical violence in the play, the entire historical backdrop to the dramatic action, the "origin" of this new play, is bathed in blood. All the main characters are products of the fiercely traumatic history of the end of the Roman Republic and the birth of Imperial Rome. In that tumultuous history the new Emperor Auguste (whose name during the civil wars was still "Octave") triumphed over the major families of the Republic. He was directly responsible for the death of Emilie's father, the destruction of Cinna's family, and the destitution of Maxime's. These latter three, despite the generosity they have since received from Auguste, cannot forget their familial/political tragedies. Despite the newly established peace and prosperity that Rome now enjoys, these three lead a plot to overthrow Auguste, who is considered by them and their co-conspirators a "tyrant," and to reestablish the Republic.

These political plans are, as usual, complicated by the amorous imbroglio. Cinna and Emilie are in love and plan to marry. Emilie, however, uses the promise of marriage to keep a wavering Cinna in line. Cinna is torn between his desire for Emilie and his duty and gratitude to the Emperor. He wavers in his determination. Emilie, who is described as a Republican "fury," does not. Her duty, as she sees it, is to revenge her slain father. Despite her feelings for Cinna, she will give herself only to the man who slays Auguste, revenging her father and restoring her family to its rightful place in the Roman Republican hierarchy. The third conspirator, Maxime, friend of Cinna, is secretly in love with Emilie. When he learns of the weakening of Cinna's resolve, of his wavering in carrying out the assassination plot, he uses this knowledge to betray Cinna in an attempt to convince Emilie to flee Rome with him.

When the plot is revealed to Auguste he summons the three conspirators to him in order to mete out their punishment. Although deeply affected by the betrayal of these young people for whom he has, he thinks, done so much (Auguste has "adopted" Emilie and treated her as his own daughter), he nevertheless wants their punishment to be exemplary. Each of the conspirators in turn admits to his/her betrayal and asks for death. In a moment of supreme self-mastery Auguste – having eradicated the negative passion that was left in him of "Octave" the murderous general – decides to abandon his first impulse of revenge. Instead of punishment, he pardons each of the conspirators, heaps them with gifts and honors, and lets them get on with their lives. It is at this point that, faced with such overwhelming generosity, each of the conspirators, in turn, falls on his knees, acknowledges the indelible debt to the emperor and swears fealty to him and to the new state he embodies.

At the start of the play, Auguste was merely the master of his subjects: he ruled over their bodies but not their minds. At the play's end he has found a way to be master of their hearts. This move, the most totalitarian of gestures, is presented paradoxically, as the most progressive. Auguste breaks out of the system of repetition that had condemned Rome to constantly replay her internal strife in dissension and fragmentation. He has constituted a new order of history where all is sacrificed to the monarch, and where the supreme pleasure of the citizen is to die so that the Law may live. Is it not the ultimate ruse of a tyrant, the ultimate tragedy for his subjects, to give these subjects a sense of their subjectivity that is inseparable from the repressions of his law, and to have them articulate this repression as their supreme pleasure?

Polyeucte, Corneille's last canonical play, although cast as a "Christian tragedy," is, like *Cinna*, firmly grounded in political history. *Polyeucte* lies on the threshold of a new world order. As the play begins, at the far corners of the Roman Empire, in Armenia, the Christians are an ever more present menace to the internal stability of the Roman world. On the border of that world, the Persians, although contained for the moment, are a threat to its integrity. The atmosphere in which *Polyeucte* evolves is one of malaise, of instability. A moment of historical becoming is the backdrop, here as in the preceding plays, of the tragic action.

Despite, however, its involvement in a problematic that remains essentially identical in all the great tragedies, *Polyeucte* also differs radically from its predecessors. For however different the plays that preceded *Polyeucte* were from each other, they had in common a central underlying sexual tension that served as the impetus to tragic action. The desire that propelled the protagonists toward each other was forever exacerbated in its own frustration. In them, the marriage that engages the sexuality of Corneille's protagonists in an elaborate sociopolitical network is always forestalled. Desire and politics are shown to be inextricably interwoven, and in this interweave dramatic tension is maintained. *Polyeucte* fundamentally alters this situation. It is the only major tragedy to be situated on the other side of what was posited as an impossible divide. For the first time in classical tragedy we are given the marriage as a *fait accompli*. The consequences of this radical change in tragic structure are at once subtle and far-reaching.

Like all the major tragedies *Polyeucte* begins on a note of conflict. Here, however, the focus of discord has shifted. Instead of beginning with a woman sundered by the alienating demands of a male-dominated universe, *Polyeucte* presents us with a divided hero. Polyeucte is torn between two irreconcilable claims on him: the exigency of spiritual salvation and the imperious demands of sexual gratification; between Christianity and Pauline. The new creed that Polyeucte ardently desires to embrace is just as ardently held beyond his grasp by his own sexual pleasure. Polyeucte has strayed from his manly role and is ensnared, as his confidant Néarque makes clear, by the Devil in the guise of Pauline.

The difficulty in creating a "Christian" tragedy goes to the very paradox that is at the heart of the theater. Although the *theatrum mundi* topos was an ever present commonplace in seventeenth-century discourse, Corneille uses this commonplace as the pivot of his new tragedy. The problematics of "seeming and being" so essential to both sociability and theatricality are brought to bear on the very heart of *Polyeucte*'s tragic dilemma. What is perceived as illusion (Pauline's dream that prefigures Polyeucte's martyrdom) becomes reality, just as that reality (his death) is shown to be, in Christian terms, true, immortal "life." It is this vision of the truth that functioning as "grace" descends upon the recalcitrant Pauline and her even more retrograde father, Félix, converting them to the path of Christ.

In the play this conversion, of course, radically shifts both the political and amorous position of all the major characters. For, as we learn, and as the plot thickens, Pauline, although recently married to Polyeucte, is a woman with a past. In that past she was passionately in love with and loved by Sévère, a noble but poor Roman soldier. Despite her love for Sévère, she, like all great Corneillean heroines, follows her duty to her father. Seeing in Polyeucte a much better match for his political ambitions, her father insists on her marriage to him. She, therefore, as she says, sacrifices herself to her duty by entering Polyeucte's bed, thus "giving to him by duty what the other had by love." In other words, Pauline's desire is, like Chimène's, like Camille's, like Emilie's, sacrificed on the altar of patriarchal necessity. When, however, Sévère, whom everyone believes killed on the battlefield, returns from the dead, enriched and honored by the emperor, Pauline and her father's world, for very different reasons, is thrown into panic: Pauline because she fears her passion, Félix because he is afraid of Sévère's retribution.

Against this background of worldy *vanitas*, Polyeucte follows his path to the Truth: secretly baptized, he decides to demonstrate his faith by interrupting a public sacrifice in honor of Sévère. Because they have knocked down the Roman deities, Polyeucte and Néarque are imprisoned for sacrilege, Néarque is executed, and Polyeucte is threatened with death if he does not renounce his new faith.

Polyeucte becomes, therefore, the spectacular center around which swirl the tormented passions, political and amorous, of the other characters. Félix, blinded by his life as a courtier in the imperial court, cannot see Sévère's generosity. Sévère cannot understand Pauline's virtuous refusal of the possibility of rekindling their love. Pauline, trapped between all the men, each of whom use her as an object of exchange, passing her metaphorically from father to husband to lover, cannot understand her abandonment by Polyeucte, cannot see the Truth. They are all trapped in the illusion of the material world. It is only through the shattering experience of witnessing Polyeucte's martyrdom and being spattered with his blood that the scales fall from Pauline's eyes ("I see, I know, I believe"). Through the intervention of her martyred husband, she too now receives the grace necessary for her conversion. And at the very end of the play, even Félix, led by his daughter's example, sees the error of his life and becomes a Christian. Invested by the tolerant Sévère with his former administrative duties and power, Félix, with Pauline by his side, now form a new "Christian couple." The tragedy ends with this moment of grace as Pauline and Félix are summoned to go forth and bear witness to the universal Truth of Christianity.

With *Polyeucte*'s epiphany French classicism is transformed into a vision of divine transcendence. This vision is both a mystery and, of course, a mystification. In *Polyeucte* sexuality and politics, individual desire, and *raison d'état* continue their spiraling ascension. After *Polyeucte* something changes in Corneillean dramaturgy. Although Corneille's theatrical career lasted well into the century, never again does he create a tragedy of the overwhelming power and grace of the four canonical plays. One could almost think that the tragedies produced in the latter part of Corneille's dramatic career offer, in negative reversal, a captivating image of the world so minutely elaborated in the "great" plays. These later plays are peopled not with heroes but with the hero's Other, the monsters of classicism's nether side.

Could it be that Corneille was turned away from the classical clarity he had almost single-handedly introduced upon the French stage because he felt challenged by the ever greater success of his young rival Racine? Certainly the rivalry between France's two greatest tragic playwrights divided seventeenth-century society, as that society moved from the values and aspirations of the court of Louis XIII and Richelieu through the more imperial(ist) strivings of Louis XIV's personal reign. Although this reign, especially in its early stages, has often been associated with a thirst for pleasure and an opulent display of royal largesse, Racine's tragedies plunge us into a universe of dark passions, murderous rivalries, and familial obsessions, where even more intimately than in Corneille the personal desires of the protagonists and the ever present demands of politics are shown to be the inextricable nexus from which emerge the seductive monsters of Racinian tragedy.

What makes Racinian tragedy particularly compelling is perhaps the ease with which Racine functioned within the confines of classicism's aesthetic parameters. Unlike Corneille, Racine seems to have used those unities of time, place, and action to his advantage, seems to have been able with no trouble at all to fit his dramatic vision into the very straitened limits of neoclassical conventions. The resulting plays inhabit a tragic locus novel in its intensity and narrowness of focus. This tightly organized, compressed tragic arena is always represented in Racine as the space of the family. Racinian tragedy is always a family affair. In the world of classical dramaturgy, this tightening represents one more suffocating twist of the tragic knot that condemns the subject of this tragedy to ever more violent efforts to escape his/her fate, a fate that seems to close ever more forcefully around him/her with harrowing consequences.

The narrowing of the tragic familial locus allows us to speculate on the very major differences between Racinian and Corneillean dramaturgy and on the subjectivity this dramaturgy inscribes. Corneillean tragedy would seem to correspond to that historical passage that Michel Foucault has hypothesized as "the moment of the great enclosure": that is, that moment when those structures defining self and other gradually but inexorably shift European civilization out of the order of the analogous and into the world of classical representation (1966: "Introduction"). Corneille would represent this moment of passage by figuring it in the clearly delineated sexual/political divisions that legislate his dramatic universe: the importance of symmetry – sexual, political, and aesthetic – is worked out in his plays against the larger canvas of a social conflict that pits the individual against the family/state. Nevertheless there is still, in the Corneille of the great tragedies, a separation, if only the separation of the mirror, between family and state: the one reflects and stands in a homologous relation to the other. In Racine, however, we have moved to a world already on the other side of that great divide, a world that is firmly entrenched in the episteme of classical representation. On the one hand, what this means for Racinian tragedy is that there is no longer any separation between family and state; dramatically from the beginning in *La Thébaïde* the family *is* the state. There is no longer any division possible between the political dimension of the tragic and the private/sexual world of the protagonists. The "origin" of tragedy, the "origin" of family are one. On the other hand, what this also means is that once reduced to its most intimate dynamic, once there is no longer any outside at all; once we are trapped in the suffocating space of this family/state the clear boundaries of sexual symmetry are blurred. As the exacerbation between characters and desires is turned inward, it becomes internalized as conflict and doubling, contradiction and bad faith. As Roland Barthes has remarked, this new dynamic signals a profound change in seventeenth-century sexuality, for what happens in Racine, as opposed to Corneille, is that sexuality, as a supposed "natural," biological distinction, is confounded: "nature" is shown to be a play of forces, a play that determines, by pitting the strong against the weak, the executioners against the victims, a redistribution of sexual roles (1963: 25). Sexuality now becomes a production, the production of political forces rather than the unmediated fiat of biology. The essentialization of masculinity and femininity, so firmly articulated in the Corneillean canon, is no longer operative in Racine.

In Racine's internalization of difference the remarkably stable "sexual essentiality" of Corneille's great plays is inverted, confounded, and confused. While in Corneille difference is imposed from the outside – the hero's dilemma is conventionally an impossible option between his/her sexual desire and the correct political choice that is antithetical to it – that dilemma is external to those desires. In Racine, however, the difference is already a "difference within." The characters suffer first and foremost because they struggle with an internal division that they seem incapable of suturing, that refuses a compromise with the omnipresent social gaze that envelops them and increases their sense of always being somehow lacking, guilty.

Significantly, Racine's step forward in tragic complexity is manifested as a backward movement in representation. Racine retreats from the stage of history and returns to the more archaic cosmology of myth for his greatest creations – *Andromaque, Iphigénie, Phèdre*. All of these different scenarios are affiliated in their genealogy, as Phillip Lewis has demonstrated, to the overriding myth of Oedipus, his family, his descendants, and the consequences of his fate (1986: 58–9). Even those historically based tragedies, *Britannicus, Bajazet,* and *Mithridate,* or the biblical tragedy of *Athalie,* can be seen, conjuring up as they do forces of an "unconscious" familial–sexual terror, to supersede the merely picturesque qualities of the historical and to plunge back into the mysterious, sacred world of Oedipal fantasies. Could we offer as a hypothesis that the entire Racinian endeavor apppears to rescript, in an obsessive return of the past, the story of Oedipus as it intersects with a newly emerging subjectivity in seventeenth-century France?[4]

We know that of all the major writers of the classical age, Racine had the most thorough knowledge of ancient Greek literature. Schooled at Port-Royal, he benefited enormously from the radical reforms in education offered in this Jansenist environment. Although his direct and intimate knowledge of the Greek classics allowed Racine to range broadly over the major authors of the Greek tradition, his major influence, the writer to whom he returned the most often, was Euripides. Even if we learn of his interest in following in the footsteps of Sophocles and writing his own version of *Oedipus Rex,* the closest Racine came to the Oedipus legend itself was in his first tragedy, *La Thébaïde, ou les frères ennemis,* where, of course, Oedipus is not present among the cast of characters, but where his fate presides over the unfolding tragedy of his children.

From the beginning, then, and as if creating his own tragic origins, Racine's first drama plunges us into a world predetermined by the unspeakable crimes of one's ancestors, the results of which doom his protagonists in the present, to incest, fraternal hatred, and political chaos. Although *La Thébaïde* is generally considered both the most Corneillean of Racine's tragedies and also the least successful dramatically speaking, it is interesting for delineating some of the major dramatic themes and conventions that will become ever more present in Racinian tragedy. The sins of the parents are visited, here in Racine's adaptation of *Seven Against Thebes,* on the children. But since these children are also the embodiment of the state, the entire political edifice risks being thrown into total disarray. The twin brothers, Polynices and Eteocles, are monstrous in their visceral hatred for each other, a hatred, we are told, that begins in the incestuous womb of their mother, Jocasta. It is this hatred, the result of a family taint, a sexual crime that goes back through the generations and that can never be expiated, that always condemns its carriers to a tragic death. Further-more, although the monstrosity that wreaks havoc on Theban society is the result of transgressive parental sexuality, this excessive, unnatural sexuality is – because of the text's insistent focus on the pathetic expiatory rhetoric of the mother, Jocasta, and by echoing the hollow absence of the father – coded as feminine. In Racine, Jocasta remains onstage as a constant reminder of the reality of the flesh, of its dangerous potential constantly to exceed any of the bounds with which society would constrain it. Oedipus, on the other hand, has vanished from the world. The father is gone; he has become an immaterial abstraction. It is only (the myth tells us, not Racine) at the end of his wanderings when he is welcomed at last by Theseus, King of Athens, that Oedipus is freed of his sacred suffering. The sovereignty of his fate is transferred to Theseus. In return for Athens' hospitality Oedipus' secret, the secret of "kingship," remains with the kings of that city. It is a secret passed from king to king, forming an Oedipal legacy of sovereignty.

Metaphysically, that is, "politically" speaking, the entire movement of Racinian tragedy will be to flee the sinful flesh of the mother and come into the place of Oedipus the King. Racine's task will be to concretize, through the tragic narration, precisely the absence the father has become, the father no longer condemned to the passions of the body, but freed from physicality, become pure "essence," finally the Law (the God of *Athalie*). But, of course, the only way tragedy can move us toward this absolute moment of the Law is by embodying this movement as a turn away from the material, from the flesh, that is, by constantly reinscribing the passions of the body, in each of the succeeding plays, as the major dramatic vehicle propelling tragic action.

Although Racine's next play, *Alexandre le Grand*, had considerably more success than *La Thébaïde,* it was the triumph of *Andromaque* that catapulted Racine into the same empyrean as Corneille. At the same time it announced that a new form of tragedy had emerged, a tragedy where, contrary to the Corneillean, amorous passion, no longer relegated to the secondary role, took center stage. From *Andromaque* onward, through all of his great creations, it is the combination of the protean thematics of desire with the incantatory seduction of his verse that makes Racine the unequaled master of the French stage.

Andromaque presents us with what will be, *mutatis mutandis*, the principal dynamics of Racinian tragedy: the impossibility of reciprocal love among a cast of characters divided into masters and slaves, victims and executioners. All the characters in *Andromaque* live in the shadow of that greatest of all epics – the Trojan War, and of the larger-than-life heroes – their own parents – who played so large a role in the destruction of Troy. They are all the products of a traumatic past which clings to them and inhibits any of their attempts to lead noncontingent, independent existences. All are condemned to love precisely that person who, because of history, can never love them in return. In the classic Racinian paradigm: Oreste loves Hermione, who loves Pyrrhus, who loves Andromaque, who loves Hector, who is dead. This first great tragedy posits, first of all, the impossibility of desire ever being satisfied, at the same time that it presents as a structural necessity the particular pleasure that locks the Racinian protagonists in a sadomasochistic dialectic between the (usually young) defenseless victim (here Andromaque, but later, Junie, Bajazet, Britannicus, Monime, Hippolyte, Joas, and so on) in a struggle to the death with a powerfully aggressive suitor/rival (Hermione, Agrippine, Roxane, Mithridate, Phèdre, Athalie). The love/lust of the master is precisely enflamed through its frustration: the victim's refusal to offer any reciprocation. In other words, the essential dynamic of the Racinian tragic is a spiraling whirlwind of desire and aggression that reaches its climax in the destruction of what we can only define as the expiatory victim of this theater of beauty and cruelty.

While Racine's dramatic plots focus on the tragic predicament of his protagonist, this predicament is always brought to the foreground by a political crisis. All the tragedies are situated on the fault line separating the death of an old political regime and the birth of another, as yet unfocused, order. This crisis, internalized in the Racinian hero as a passionate, guilt-ridden rift in his/her own emotional world, is exacerbated by being presented against a background of impending political chaos. What we hear echoing across the Racinian world, at the beginning of each play, is that something in the order of that world has been irrevocably changed. Racine constructs his tragedies so that we are plunged from the very beginning into a familial crisis that is also a political turning point threatening the entire world order of the play.[5]

Quickly, however, Racine moves from the political instability of the outer world into the psychological turmoil of the play's protagonist. In an extremely subtle play of inversions, the tragic plot will work itself out, resolving the political crisis by and through the sacrifice of the tragic hero (Pyrrhus, Britannicus, Bajazet, Phèdre, and so on). In a sense, therefore, Racine moves from the larger political stage of an empire in crisis to the narrower, but analogous, ferment of the tragic hero who, becoming the victim of that world's crisis, is immolated to expiate the sins of society, and, by so doing, restore order to it.

Although space does not permit even a cursory analysis of each of the nine tragedies (Racine was also the author of one comedy, *Les Plaideurs*), following the lead of Roland Barthes, who studied the Racinian tragic world as one large, multifaceted canvas, we can draw some general conclusions regarding Racine's tragic vision. Among the innovations he brought to the seventeenth-century theater, Racine was the first to place a child on the stage. This novelty transforms the world of classical dramaturgy into a compelling scenario of sacrifice and horror; for this child, led out into the public's embrace, is brought forth upon the scene of classicism as its victim. Racine puts children on his stage to immolate them, or at least to keep the threat of immolation suspended over their heads. From his first triumphant tragedy *Andromaque* to his last, *Athalie,* the tragic dilemma turns around the figure of the child who is to be sacrificed (Astyanax, Britannicus, Hippolyte, Joas). The central importance of the child corresponds to the conflicted familial scenarios that form the frame inside of which Racinian tragedy plays out one of the most conflicted dilemmas of seventeenth-century subjectivity as it is informed by the ideological parameters of absolutism. For this society, what is unacceptable is precisely what makes Racine's characters so compelling – heterogeneity. The sign of the other, of the "monstrous," is precisely to be a heterogeneous being. In a world that aspires to an integrity of being, all that represents division, a splitting of the subject will be termed "monstrous."

Monsters, as we know, populate the Racinian universe, either mythological monsters – the bull from the sea in *Phèdre* – or actual "psychological" monsters – Neron, Agrippine, Roxane, Athalie. And it is precisely Neron who is paradigmatic of those hybrid Racinian children who are monstrous precisely because they are not one, but two. Phèdre, "daughter of Minos and Pasiphae," is, of course, the most famous, the most pathetic of Racine's heroines. She, like Neron, like the other children (and of course, all the characters are also always "children"), bears the internal duality of the darkness of the underworld and the blinding light of day: granddaughter of the sun, her father, "in Hell, judges the pale shades of mortals." She too is the product of a mixture of bloods, of histories, of old debts that become her internal division, the victim of a curse she inherits in her being, a being that is monstrous because it is not pure, not one but two.

We are beginning to see the pattern of internal contradiction that emerges in Racine's theater and that focuses on the child. For in an obvious sense all Racine's characters are children and therefore all are monstrous. All bear the burden of a heterogeneous past that strives to free itself from its own heterogeneity that strives for the realm of the absolute. It is this impossible denial, a denial that resurfaces in the violence of murder, of incest, of sexuality that makes these children the victims of their secret monstrous origin and coterminously makes this origin always the result of an even more primeval violence.

Of all the children who are actually sacrificed in Racine – Iphigénie/Eriphile, Hippolyte, and Phèdre – the last two in the dyad they form are the most riveting. Although it may first strike us as odd to see Phèdre and Hippolyte as but two differently gendered variations of the same, a figuration of a two-headed "monster" of recalcitrant sexuality because of the very obvious difference in the plot of the tragedy, these differences should not blind us to the structural similarities that ally them to each other as victims of the familial order that destroys them. Each is condemned to the role of the victim by the internal, inalienable difference that they bear as children of a tainted lineage. Phèdre's predisposition to victimization is, as we have already seen, double: daughter of Pasiphaë and Minos, she bears all the weight of the familial curse, the curse of excessive, transgressive sexuality. Hippolyte, likewise, is the tainted product of the cross between "nature and culture," between the world of his father, Theseus, the world of politics and order, and the savage universe of Antiope, his Amazon mother. From his mother comes his aversion to sexuality. But with such an antecedent this aversion can only interpreted as a refusal of the sexuality of the Father, the refusal to assume a sexuality that is inscribed in a patriarchal political network. When Hippolyte falls in love with Aricie he falls outside of the paternal order. His passion is "transgressive," just as is, for different reasons, Phèdre's.

Both Phèdre and Hippolyte represent, therefore, two valences of sexuality that are directly inimical to the (patriarchal) polis. Combined, they form a hybrid sexual being, a monster that must be eradicated despite, and perhaps because of, the pity they inspire in the audience. Thésée, as the representative of civilization, must intervene, must call down the gods' wrath and destroy his family, lest that family, as monstrous sexuality, destroy civilization.

Finally, we should not forget that before Oedipus murdered his father, that father tried to kill him. This initial attack by the father, his turning on his own child to save himself, to save his rule, is the fearsome fantasy of Racine's tragic heroes. They are all the children of Oedipus and bear his heavy debt and blinding insight. And insofar as Racinian tragedy can be seen to inaugurate the reign of the modern, the impossible era of the divided self, our participation in that theater, our pleasure and terror that the sacrifice and reinscription of ambivalence conjures up in us, suspending its awesome power of hatred and passion over our heads, prove that we continue to act out Absolutism's conflicted legacy. On the inner stage of our own desirous fantasies, we remain the victims of Racine: we are all his children.[6]

NOTES

1 "[La] dignité [de la tragédie] demande quelque grand intérêt d'Etat, ou quelque passion plus noble et plus male que l'amour... il faut qu'il [l'amour] se contente du second rang dans le poème, et laisse [à la politique] le premier" (Tragedy's dignity calls for either an important political crisis where the fate of the nation is at stake, or a more noble and more virile passion than love, which must be happy with secondary role in the play while leaving to politics the primary one) (Corneille 1963: 13).

2 In the French Academy's judgment of the play – caught as it was in an aesthetico-political debate – Chimène is defined as an

Amante trop sensible et fille trop denaturée. Quelque violence que luiy peust faire sa passion, il est certain qu'elle ne devait point se relâcher dans la vengeance de la mort de son père et moins encore se résoudre à epouser celuy qui l'avoit fait mourir. En cecy il faut avouer que ses moeurs sont du moins scandaleuses, si en effet elles ne sont pas dépravées. (Chapelain 1637: 39).

(Too sensitive for a young lady in love and too "unnatural." For however violent her passion might be, it is certain that she should not slack off in her quest for revenge for the death of her father and even less to decide to marry the man who killed him. In this we must admit that her morals are at the least scandalous if not, in fact, depraved.)

3 Remarkably, in Corneille's canonical familial dramas, there are, at least since Medea's disappearance, no mothers.

4 The preceding paragraphs are borrowed with slight alterations from the chapter "Racine's Children," in my *Subjectivity and Subjugation in Seventeenth-Century Drama and Prose: The Family Romance of French Classicism* (Cambridge: Cambridge University Press, 1992).

5 As Mauron has pointed out (1969: 26–31) in his reading of Racine, in the tragedies leading up to *Mithridate* the political crisis is precipitated because the place of the father is vacant, creating turmoil in the universe of the drama. From *Mithridate* on, the father returns, only to find his place usurped or in danger of being usurped.

6 For a more detailed account of Racine's tragic universe, especially in reference to the dynamics of paternity, sacrifice, and infanticide, see "Racine's Children" (from which much of the above is drawn), 141–73.

REFERENCES AND FURTHER READING

Barthes, Roland. (1963). *Sur Racine*. Paris, Seuil.

Chapelain, Jean. (1637). *Les Sentiments de l'Académie Française sur la tragi-comédie du* Cid. Paris.

Corneille, Pierre. (1963). *Œuvres complètes, "Discours de l'utilité et des parties du poème dramatique."* Paris: Seuil.

Foucault, Michel. (1966). *Les Mots et les choses, une archéologie des sciences humaines*. Paris: Gallimard.

Green, André. (1969). *Un Oeil en trop: Le complexe d'Œdipe dans la tragédie*. Paris: Minuit.

Greenberg, Mitchell. (1992). *Subjectivity and Subjugation in Seventeenth-Century Drama and Prose: The Family Romance of French Classicism*. Cambridge: Cambridge University Press.

Lewis, Phillip. (1986). "Sacrifice and Suicide: Some Afterthoughts on the Career of J. Racine." In *Actes de Baton Rouge*, ed. Selma A. Zebouni. *Biblio 17*, Tübingen, Germany, Series No. 25. Paris: Papers on French Seventeenth Century Literature.

Mauron, Charles. (1969). *L'Inconscient dans l'œuvre et la vie de Racine*. Paris: Corti.

23

Romantic Tragic Drama and its Eighteenth-Century Precursors: Remaking British Tragedy

Jeffrey N. Cox

The Death of Tragedy

In his *Defence of Poetry*, Shelley surveys the repertoire of new tragedies inherited from the eighteenth century and finds it wanting:

> Tragedy becomes a cold imitation of the form of the great masterpieces of antiquity, divested of all harmonious accompaniment of the kindred arts; and often the very form misunderstood, or a weak attempt to teach certain doctrines, which the writer considers as moral truths; and which are usually no more than specious flatteries of some gross vice or weakness, with which the author, in common with his auditors, are infected. Hence what has been called the classical and domestic drama. Addison's "Cato" is a specimen of the one; and would it were not superfluous to cite examples of the other! (Shelley 1821. 285)

While eighteenth-century scholars might want to dispute this bleak assessment of a century's work in the drama, Shelley points to two main lines of development, long noted by scholars,[1] that preceded romanticism's own experimentation with tragedy: first, classicizing tragedies that follow French models in seeking inspiration from antiquity; and, second, personal or domestic tragedies developing out of a line of affective realism that runs from Thomas Otway through Nicholas Rowe to George Lillo, and that, by Shelley's time, had yielded what we might see as the anti-tragic melodrama. For Shelley, neoclassical tragedy strives to reanimate the dead body of traditional dramatic form, while the domestic drama claims to offer a new tragic vision while merely staging clichéd morality. Shelley wants to remake both the form and vision of tragedy.

Shelley and other playwrights of his day were seeking an equivalent for their time of an inherited notion of tragedy that involved not only a set of (often disputed) formal features, but also an exploration of Western notions of man's greatness and destruction.[2] The body of traditional tragedy against which romantic drama defined itself included the works of the Greeks, the Elizabethans, and the Baroque writers of Spain and France such as Calderón and Racine. It is not that the romantics were unaware of the differences between, say, Sophocles and Shakespeare; long before Walter Benjamin (1977) argued that there is an insurmountable gap between Greek tragedy and the "sorrow" drama or *Trauerspiel* created by Shakespeare and his contemporaries, A. W. Schlegel [1846] (1861) had offered the very influential distinction between "classical" or Greco-Roman culture and the "romantic" culture that he saw arising with the advent of Christianity, chivalry, and new notions of love and honor. Still, there remained then and there remains in critical discourse now a sense that the gap between, say, Shelley and Shakespeare is greater than that between Shakespeare and Sophocles, with the two earlier writers sharing a tragic vision lost to romanticism. The tradition of tragedy that eighteenth- and nineteenth-century playwrights looked back to staged a confrontation between a heroic figure and the gods, fate, or God's Providence, between a man of "high estate," who expands our sense of human greatness by suggesting that humanity, confronting the chaos that typically marks the tragic world, can find within itself a new order for life and a nonhuman force that finally insists upon the limits to humanity's knowledge and power. Whether we think of Oedipus, solver of the riddle of the Sphinx, coming forth at the beginning of his play to proclaim that he alone can heal the plague that besets Thebes, or Hamlet, who proclaims that "the time is out of joint," and that he was born "to set it right," the tragic hero offers himself as the solution to his world's woes. For a moment, the hero seems capable of remaking the cosmos. Of course, Oedipus must learn that no matter what he does to escape the curse upon him, however hard he struggles to heal himself and his world, he is doomed to murder his father and marry his mother; Hamlet finds that for all the frenzied action undertaken by himself, Laertes, and Fortinbras all must bow before "a divinity that shapes our ends / Rough-hew them how we will" (5.2.10–11). The hero most often dies in coming face to face with the powers that limit man, but out of the destructive confrontation between man's assertion of his own order and the reimposition of an extra-human and perhaps inhuman order arises an expanded sense of both man's power and of the forces that exceed it. Traditional tragedy, then, seems to lie in a tense balance between free will and fate, the destruction of the supremely human and the revelation of a divine order. The difficulties facing writers of tragedy in the eighteenth century and romantic era can be gauged in part by noting that there was a sense that the two poles of tragedy had come to organize different classes of drama, as the heroic drama of the Restoration can be seen to exalt the hero at the expense of any containing order, and as the so-called tragedy of fate often reduces man to a pawn in an ironic game played by an inscrutable cosmic order. In particular, romanticism – arising in the era of democratic revolutions, when the hierarchies that defined the hero as sitting atop society were challenged, and in a time of a deep questioning of providential models – has been seen by many (e.g., Steiner 1961) as incapable of producing tragedy because it cannot, it is argued, depict a hero or delineate a supernatural order.

While it is true that eighteenth-century and romantic playwrights could not reproduce Sophocles or Shakespeare, the drive to create a new form of tragedy might be seen as marking British serious drama (a term often used to suggest that tragedy no longer stands alone as the serious alternative to comedy) from the Restoration on. The hiatus in London theatrical life enforced by the Commonwealth, though less drastic than we once assumed (see Wiseman 1998), did open a gap between Elizabethan and Jacobean tragedy and what came afterward. Of course, earlier plays did survive and thrive on stage, with Jonson, Beaumont and Fletcher, and particularly and increasingly Shakespeare, providing much of the regular reper-toire, but dramatic culture had surely changed, as is suggested in little by the reworkings of Shakespeare's plays — whether in Dryden's reimagining of *Antony and Cleopatra* as *All for Love* (King's Company, 1677) or Nahum Tate's revision of the end of *King Lear* (1681), so that Lear lives to retire and Cordelia enjoys wedded bliss. The culture and society at large that shaped and were shaped by the drama had changed even more, and thus it was necessary in the eighteenth century, and even more strongly during the romantic period, to reimagine tragedy or to find an alternative form of serious drama.

There were various efforts to create a new version of tragedy or an alternative to it; we might think of the heroic drama, the bourgeois *drame*, the Gothic drama, and even serious opera. It is important to stress the sheer proliferation of tragic forms, with J. Douglas Canfield (2002), for example, dividing Restoration and eighteenth-century serious drama into heroic romance, political tragedy, personal tragedy, and tragical satire, and Allardyce Nicoll (1925) finding that the early eighteenth century offers heroic dramas, pseudo-classic tragedies, Augustan tragedies, and domestic tragedies, not to mention translations and Elizabethan survivals; the situation in the romantic period is, if anything, more complex, with the addition of mixed forms such as the melodrama and with playwrights exploring the entire history of tragic drama, from Shelley's imitations of Aeschylus to Byron's turn to medieval mystery plays, from Elizabethanizing turns to calls to return to neoclassical rules. Simplifying a complex period of dramatic development, we might see the drama of the eighteenth century as seeking a "modern" form of British tragedy, that is, a kind of serious drama that would neither simply replicate the "old" English drama of Shakespeare and his contempor-aries nor slavishly imitate French neoclassical theory, and the classical models that it claimed to codify. Moreover, it would provide the power of Greek tragedy but within a Christian moral framework. This final point is crucial (and it is perhaps here where Benjamin's move to divorce Greek tragedy from Christian *Trauerspiel* has the most force). Classical tragedy might be seen to offer an amoral superman — Oedipus as heroic victor over the Sphinx, but also the man who killed his father and married his mother — and an inhuman order of things — the gods will that Oedipus kill his father and marry his mother, no matter what he or his parents do to avoid this awful fate. This version of tragedy must be made to conform to a Christian providential vision in which God orders the world, and thus we see various attempts to moralize Greek tragedy through notions such as the tragic flaw, where the Gordian knot of inter-linked power and excess in the tragic hero is untied to reveal a nearly perfect man brought low by a single moral flaw, and even more strongly poetic justice, where, unlike the conclusions of *Antigone* or *King Lear*, the evil characters must be punished and the good rewarded at the play's end. While individual plays may explore various solutions, the critical consensus was that tragedy had to be made moral.

Following Shelley, I want, first, to examine two eighteenth-century attempts to create such a modern, moral tragedy. Addison's *Cato* (Drury Lane, 1713) is the exemplary neoclassical drama, and its prestige can help us to understand the power that the neoclassical formula for tragedy would continue to hold long into the romantic period, still drawing the allegiance of Alfieri and Byron, for example. The domestic drama, best represented by George Lillo's *The London Merchant; or, The History of George Barnwell* (Drury Lane, 1731), and particularly its descendant, the melodrama, turn from classical models to offer modern characters and modern situations, but they too work to establish a conventional moral vision. Where the neoclassical drama won critical prestige, the domestic melodrama won over popular audiences. Shelley and his fellow romantics battled against both the critical establishment and popular taste to create a new form of tragic drama.

Addison's *Cato*: Re-creating Classical Tragedy

Looking back at the eighteenth century from the early nineteenth, one would have found writers across the century – including key poets such as James Thompson (*Sophonisba*, Drury Lane, 1729; *Agamemnon*, Drury Lane, 1738; and *Tancred and Sigismunda*, Drury Lane, 1744) and Samuel Johnson (*Irene*, Drury Lane, 1749) – seeking a classical drama. There were translations of Greek plays, as well as modern-izations and transformations, but the most powerful models were French, and of the French tragedians it was Voltaire rather than Corneille or Racine who had the greatest influence.[3] What unites these plays is the belief in the efficacy of a set of formal rules: the unities of time, place, and action; decorum; for some, poetic justice. Shakespeare, of course, was the great example of success through violation of these rules, and many playwrights would break them when it suited them, but there still was a strong critical consensus that the formula for great tragedy lay in restricting the action to approximately one day and one locale, in ordering the action around a single plot, in preserving a decorous sense of style and of the classed nature of heroes, and in meting out awards and punishments on moral grounds.

Nicoll (1925: 85) has argued that these neoclassical plays were never particularly popular on the eighteenth-century British stage, despite a critical climate that favored them (see also Faller 1988). The dominant tragedies on the early eighteenth-century stage, beyond Shakespeare, were either Restoration plays such as Otway's *Venice Preserv'd* (1682) and Dryden's *All for Love* (1677), or the affective tragedies of Rowe. The one exception is Addison's *Cato*, which won both critical success and popular acclaim. *Cato* is a key play because it demonstrated the continuing power of the classicizing drama while being able to draw upon the affective appeal that marked modernizing plays.

Addison's tragedy takes up Cato's resistance to Caesar in northern Africa after the defeat of Pompey. Caesar is closing in on Cato's last stronghold at Utica, where plots swirl around Cato, until he finally commits suicide in order to declare his allegiance to the republican liberty he sees Caesar destroying. Decorum is strictly observed as all violence is placed offstage, including Cato's climactic suicide. The play takes place in a single locale, Utica, moving only from the governor's palace for one scene when the Senate meets in exile. Addison creates unity in time by collapsing various historical events, for example, having Juba (the historical Juba II) already an adult and a follower of Cato, while in fact he was a child at the time the play takes place, and displacing Syphax from his place in history, 150 years before the play begins. We see the advantages of these unities in providing a sense of tragedy, for the restriction of place contributes to the feeling that Cato and his allies are inevitably trapped, while the time limit provides a sense of urgency to the actions of those around Cato who, for very different reasons, wish to prevent him from committing heroic suicide.

The central action leading up to Cato's death is announced in the very first speech of the play, when his son Portius notes, "Our father's death / Would fill up all the guilt of civil war / And close the scene of blood" (Addison 1713: 1.1.4–6). In one sense, the play invites us simply to admire Cato as he prepares to die for his beliefs rather than submit to the inevitable triumph of an Imperial Rome. Addison provides through Cato the modern moral figure he had called for in his *Spectator* essay on tragedy when, in criticizing Otway's otherwise admired *Venice Preserv'd* for making "Rebels and Traitors" into heroes, he says, "Had the Hero of his Play discovered the same good Qualities in the Defence of his Country, that he shewed for its Ruin and Subversion, the Audience could not enough pity and admire him" (*Spectator*, No. 39, April 14, 1711).[4] Addison uses the neoclassical rules to create a sense of Cato's inevitable entrapment by, if not fate, then Caesar as the force of historical necessity, and then he allows Cato to rise above his entrapment to assert a moral vision greater than the force that destroys him.

However, such a description hardly does justice to the experience of the play, for if Cato remains a strong, solid point fixed within the tight circle of neoclassical unities, those around him engage in feverish action as everyone is driven by passion. Cato's sons, Portius and Marcus, love the same woman, Lucia; Marcus, in particular, is unable to control his emotions, for example, "tortured, ev'n to madness" at the thought of Caesar's victory (1.1.16). Sempronius, on the surface a violently passionate defender of republican Rome, joins with Syphax to betray Cato; Sempronius is angry because Cato "has refused / His daughter Marcia to my ardent vows" (1.1.167), with Marcia in fact in love with Juba. These conflicts provide Addison with the opportunity to stage a range of violently emotional moments, as Lucia faints over a dispute with Portius, Sempronius incites an unsuccessful rebellion of Roman troops whom he then betrays, Syphax seeks to lead his Numidian troops to Caesar only to die in the attempt while Marcus is killed stopping him, and Sempronius seeks to rape Marcia while disguised as Juba. While Cato may remain the great stoic in the midst of crisis, the other characters rage in love and anger and continuously burst into tears. As Julie

Ellison notes: "Tears, shed seven times in *Cato* by men for brothers, fathers, sons, and friends, and only three times by women, make weeping a ritual of male bonding that combines shared feelings with civic virtue" (1999: 52). We thus get collective scenes of passion as well: captured rebel leaders weep when confronted by Cato, and, finding his attempts to arrange a truce dashed, Decius proclaims, "All Rome will be in tears" (2.1.183). Even Cato cries, though famously it is not for his dead son but for the death of the Roman Republic (4.2.99–108).

The play still might be seen as contrasting the passionate excesses of lovers and rebels with the calm moral control of Cato, but from another perspective Cato seeks to block not only the future Caesar would impose but also the future the younger generation would create. As Portius suggests, the "scene of blood" will only "close," the curtain will be drawn on the civil war only when Cato dies, and only then can the younger generation turn to love. Cato will not allow his daughter Marcia to think of love while war still wages, and Lucia puts aside her love for Portius for she believes it will bring "thy sister's tears, / Thy father's anguish, and thy brother's death" (3.1.95–6). Only in his death speech does Cato release the lovers into marriage (5.1.188–91).

There is a divorce finally between Cato the moral hero and any plausible course of action in the play. As Cato himself says, "Justice gives way to force; the conquered world / Is Caesar's: Cato has no business in it" (4.3.26–7). This contrasts with the sentiments of perhaps the key survivor of the play, Juba, whom Cato praises as a true Roman but who also proclaims, "Let Caesar have the world, if Marcia's mine" (4.2.134). Even if Caesar wins, Juba, sacrificing all for love, can imagine a satisfactory life, but Cato's moral stand sets him beyond the possibilities of his world. In a sense, Addison's play re-creates a traditional moral hero but then imagines a future in which domestic passion rather than heroic morality will rule the day. In an odd way that perhaps contributed to the play's success, Addison dramatizes the end of the world of classicizing tragedy and the victory of the world of emotional, domestic drama. While romantic playwrights will face the same problem Addison did – how do you find heroic action in an increasingly unheroic world – and while they will learn from his solution in identifying heroism with a refusal to act in a corrupted world, they will attempt to reconnect the idealist with the political actor, the visionary with the revolutionary. If Addison wanted to convert Otway's rebel hero into a patriot, Shelley and the romantics will transform the solitary moralist dying for a lost past into the idealistic rebel dying for a hoped-for future.

Lillo's *London Merchant*: Creating Modern Melodrama

One might trace Shelley's second eighteenth-century form, the domestic drama, back to Elizabethan and Jacobean plays such as Heywood's *A Woman Killed with Kindness* (1607) and even into Shakespearean tragedies such as *Romeo and Juliet* (1599), more concerned with private rather than public catastrophes. Restoration plays of personal distress such as Otway's *The Orphan* (1680) and Southerne's *The Fatal Marriage* (1694) are often cited as precursors of later, more clearly domestic, plays. Nicholas Rowe, famous for his "she-tragedies" focused on the woes of central women characters, announced in the Prologue to his *Fair Penitent* (Lincoln's Inn Fields, 1703) that his play would offer "A melancholy tale of private woes: / No princes here lost royalty bemoan, / But you shall meet with sorrows like your own" (Rowe 1703: ll. 16–18). The anonymous *Rival Brothers* (Lincoln's Inn Fields, 1704) is said to be the first tragedy with a bourgeois hero, and plays such as *The Fatal Extravagance* (Lincoln's Inn Fields, 1721), attributed to Aaron Hill, offered middling characters in modern settings, but it is Lillo's *The London Merchant* that is seen by most scholars as defining the domestic drama for the eighteenth century.

Lillo's dedicatory preface makes clear his design: noting the worth of plays such as *Cato*, Lillo still claims for himself the desire "to enlarge the Province of the graver Kind of Poetry":

> Tragedy is so far from losing its Dignity, by being accommodated to the Circumstances of the Generality of Mankind, that it is more truly august in Proportion to the Extent of its Influence, and the Numbers that are properly affected by it ... If Princes, &c. were alone liable to Misfortunes, arising from Vice, or Weakness in themselves, or others, there wou'd be good Reason for confining the Characters in Tragedy to those of superior Rank; but, since the contrary is evident, nothing can be more reasonable than to proportion the Remedy to the Disease. (Lillo 1731: 151, 152)

Lillo makes it clear that this tragedy for the "Generality of Mankind" works toward a moral end through "the exciting of the Passions," but only to pursue "the correcting such of them as are criminal" (151). If *Cato* offers an extraordinary moral hero who stands above the order of his world, the domestic drama turns to ordinary protagonists who find themselves subordinated to a plot that resolves itself in moral judgment.

Lillo's *London Merchant* tracks the destruction of a young apprentice, George Barnwell, who serves an excellent master, Mr. Thorowgood, who is not only wealthy and moral but who also helped defeat the Spanish Armada as part of a group of "honest Merchants" who "may sometimes contribute to the Safety of their Country, as they do at all times to its Happiness" (Lillo 1731: 1.1.12–14). Barnwell falls under the spell of Millwood, a seductress who leads him into a world of sensual pleasures as a prelude to a life of crime, as she urges him on to theft and then murder. Offering characters from the lower orders living in the modern world, the play, quite unlike the neoclassical *Cato*, is episodic, made up of very short scenes that cover an extended period of time and a variety of locales in London and in a nearby village, where Barnwell kills his uncle. These scenes allow for a wide display of emotion, from Barnwell's desire to his remorse, from Millwood's cynical eroticism, to Maria's tearful concern for Barnwell. The play closes with Barnwell repentant and Millwood despairing as they are led to the scaffold, in a scene not staged at the time, as even this modernizing domestic play had to bow to a sense of decorum. Barnwell sounds the appropriately moral note when he hopes that "From our Example may all be taught to fly the first Approach of Vice" (5.11.56–7). While Barnwell interests us as an ordinary man who seems able to tap the powerful emotions we might identify with a Macbeth or an Othello, in the end these emotions are simply a trap. More than that, for all the interest in the motivations of both Barnwell and Millwood, the play suggests that there is something fated in their fall, that once they are tainted by uncontrolled passion they are inevitably led to crime. While the play offers Millwood scope to argue that her sins are simply a rational reaction to a male-dominated world, and provides Barnwell with a series of scenes in which we can see his essentially good nature as he struggles with passions beyond his control, in the end sociological and psychological interest are subordinated, as it will be in the melodrama, to moral certainty.

The London Merchant, even though it was praised internationally by everyone from Pope to Rousseau, Diderot to Goethe, and Schiller, prompted few immediate successful imitators. Lillo himself would offer *Fatal Curiosity: A True Tragedy of Three Acts* at the Haymarket in 1736, and there were plays such as Charles Johnson's *Caelia; or, The Perjur'd Lover* (Drury Lane, 1732), John Hewitt's *Fatal Falshood; or, Distress'd Innocence: A Tragedy in Three Acts* (Drury Lane, 1734), and later Edward Moore's important *The Gamester* (Drury Lane, 1753), that seem to be under Lillo's influence. Still, theater historians have seen this line of drama dying out, with A. H. Scouten, for example, concluding his account of eighteenth-century domestic drama with the pronouncement that the novel had displaced the drama and that "There was nothing to do but stand around and wait for Ibsen" (Scouten 1976: 287). Shelley, however, clearly sees the domestic drama as thriving ("would it were not superfluous to cite examples" of the domestic drama, he complains) because he identifies, correctly I believe, the domestic drama with the melodrama that came to become a dominant force on stages across Europe by the end of the eighteenth century.

While the first melodrama so identified on the British stage was Thomas Holcroft's *Tale of Mystery* (Covent Garden, 1802), melodrama was created in the 1790s in France by René-Charles Guilbert Pixérécourt, in Germany by Friedrich von Kotzebue and August Wilhelm Iffland, and in England by writers such as George Colman the Younger and Thomas Morton. The term *mélodrame* was coined by Rousseau for his *Pygmalion*, which as an attempt to reform opera does remind us that the "melo-drama" is literally "music-drama." The increasing presence of music in serious dramas – the use of nearly continuous music such as we hear in movie scores – was seen as an innovation in these plays, and one often decried by critics who felt that these pieces relied upon music – and other special effects such as pantomime, striking stage sets, crowd scenes, and spectacular lighting – to the detriment of the power of the word. The melodrama, which drew upon forms that sprang up in popular theaters and fairgrounds, became a dominant form of mass entertainment, with Pixérécourt seeing 30,000 performances of his plays between 1797 and 1834, with Kotzebue and Iffland filling German stages more often than the more admired works of Goethe and Schiller, and with the London stage given increasingly over to melodrama, as 17 plays by Pixérécourt were translated; as a rage for Kotzebue produced such adaptations as Elizabeth Inchbald's *Lover's Vows* (Covent Garden, 1798), which famously reappears in Austen's *Mansfield Park*; and as English writers such as Holcroft, Morton, William Dimond, and Isaac Pocock offered melodrama after melodrama. If we are to understand romantic drama, we need to set it against not only the neoclassical plays that were held up by conservative critics as models of aesthetic perfection, but also the melodrama that, for most audiences, became the key form of modern serious drama.

Part of the melodrama's appeal clearly came from its use of music and other sensational effects, but we need to see that it also offered a vision that, while reactionary, fitted these revolutionary times. Pixérécourt, the so-called "father" of French melodrama, asserted that the melodrama offered "religious and providential ideals" in opposition to the revolutionary sentiments of the time (1841–3: 4.493). As Peter Brooks has demonstrated, "the melodrama becomes the principal mode for uncovering, demonstrating, and making operative the essential moral universe in a post-sacred era" (1976: 15).[5] The preface to Pixérécourt's collected plays by Charles Nodier argues further that the melodrama arose with the French Revolution and engaged its violence only to assert in the end that the old order was right, that moral stability – grounded on the patriarchal family, the nation, and the Church – must win out over political innovation. In the era of Wollstonecraft, Paine, and Godwin, the melodrama was a reactionary form, reasserting a system of relations that had, perhaps, worked in the past, but which is now embraced solely sentimentally. If neoclassical tragedies such as *Cato*, tying themselves to ancient traditions and history, assert a moral standard that seemingly had lasted across the ages, the melodrama, arising in the midst of great upheaval, reasserts traditional morality even when it had been thrown deeply into doubt, even when it could be revealed only through the violence that is so central to these plays. It is this image of terror as the guarantor of restored virtue that I believe horrifies Shelley about the domestic drama which, in the shape of the melodrama, had come to dominate the British stage.

The Birth of Romantic Tragedy from the Spirit of Revolt

While Shelley hoped that romantic writers would revive tragedy, romanticism is often seen, by George Steiner (1961), for example, as having led to the "death" of tragedy. The massive political, economic, and social changes we identify with the romantic era[6] – the American and French Revolutions, the Napoleonic wars, the Industrial Revolution, the challenges to established religion that took many forms from Unitarianism to Deism to atheism, and the threat to conventional gender norms we identify with Mary Wollstonecraft's creation of a modern feminism – have been seen to destroy the aristocratic, sacralized world many believe is essential to tragedy. Can the era of the rights of man still portray the extraordinary men and women we identify as heroes? Can a period which challenged man's relation to the state, woman's relation to man, and humanity's relation to God still imagine an overarching providential order to give shape and meaning to tragic loss? Simply put, did the French

Revolution, with its execution of the king and its disestablishment of the Church, symbolically destroy the tragic world?

As the eighteenth century wore on, there certainly were strengthening concerns about the state of tragedy. The repertoire system kept Shakespeare, some heroic plays, some affective and domestic tragedies, *Cato*, and *The London Merchant* (often performed on Boxing Day) on stage, but few new tragedies succeeded. John Home's *Douglas* (Edinburgh, 1756; Covent Garden, 1757) was thought by at least the Scots to rival "Wully Shakespeare" and did manage to hold the stage for years; Robert Jephson showed in his *Count of Narbonne* (Covent Garden, 1781), based on Walpole's *Castle of Otranto*, that there was potentially tragic material in the Gothic, and Walpole himself penned the interesting *Mysterious Mother* (1768), but it was never performed owing to its treatment of mother–son incest; Hannah More combined classical form and Gothic appeal in her successful *Percy* (Covent Garden, 1777); but prologues, prefaces, and pamphlets all attest to a sense that the tragic muse could no longer hold the London stage.

The writers we identify with romanticism offered a new kind of tragedy to fill this vacuum. There are two striking bursts of dramatic activity, which can be located within the two generations of British romantic writers. When Coleridge and Wordsworth met, for example, they shared a hope of capturing the London stage, with Wordsworth failing to have the *Borderers* staged but with Coleridge, after Sheridan rejected *Osorio*, finally having a major success with the revised *Remorse* on January 23, 1813. Others identified with first-generation romanticism also penned tragedies: Charles Lamb, for example, wrote *John Woodvil* (1802), and Sir Walter Scott published a translation of Goethe's *Götz* in 1799 and also attempted a number of unacted plays. William Godwin saw both *Antonio* in 1800 and *Faulkener* in 1807, staged at Drury Lane. There were also some minor successes for tragedy by less well-known writers such as William Sotheby (*Julian and Agnes*; Drury Lane, 1801) and James Tobin (*The Curfew*, Drury Lane, 1807), and Matthew Lewis, the most successful playwright of the day, not only offered such Gothic smash hits as *The Castle Spectre* (Drury Lane, 1797) but also two tragedies, *Alfonso, King of Castille* (Covent Garden, 1802) and *Adelgitha; or, The Fruits of a Single Error* (Drury Lane, 1807).

The most respected playwright at the time was, however, neither a writer for the popular stage nor a poet linked to the Lake School, but instead the Scottish woman writer Joanna Baillie. Baillie, the author of more than 25 plays, was believed by Scott (1894: 1.99) to be "the best dramatic writer since the days of Shakespeare and Massinger," and Byron (1973–94: 3.109) claimed her as "our only dramatist since Otway and Southerne"; Anna Laetitia Barbauld would praise "loved Joanna" in *England in Eighteen Hundred and Eleven* (1812), and Elizabeth Inchbald (1808: 24.3) called her "a woman of genius." When the first, anonymous volume of her *Series of Plays: In Which It is Attempted To Delineate The Stronger Passions of the Mind Each Passion Being The Subject of A Tragedy and a Comedy* (usually referred to as the *Plays on the Passions*) was published in 1798, it was met with praise, securing twenty-five reviews and five reprintings in six years. While it is often said that her plays did not succeed on stage, seven of her plays were performed during her lifetime, with both Kemble and Kean acting in *De Monfort* and with at least *The Family Legend* providing Baillie with a hit when it was produced by Scott in Edinburgh in 1810.

Baillie's example of devoting a play to a central passion perhaps shaped Coleridge's reworking of *Osorio* as the admired *Remorse*, and the success of Coleridge's *Remorse* — it was the most popular new tragedy since More's *Percy* and had a quite successful run of 20 nights — spurred a second burst of dramatic activity that can be identified with the second generation of romantic poets. Byron worked on the drama throughout his career, from *Manfred* (1817) through his neoclassical history plays, *Marino Faliero, Doge of Venice* (Drury Lane, 1821), *Sardanapalus*, and *The Two Foscari* (both 1821), and his "mystery" plays, *Cain* (1821), *The Deformed Transformed* (1824), and *Heaven and Earth* (1822, 1824), to the melodramatic *Werner* (1823). While only *Marino Faliero* was performed during Byron's lifetime and only with limited success, his plays became a force on the stage later in the century, with *Sardanapalus* receiving a spectacular staging at Drury Lane in 1834, *The Two Foscari* reaching the stage at Covent Garden in 1837, and *Werner* entering the repertoire in 1830, first at Drury Lane. The drama also occupies a central place in Shelley's work. He wrote perhaps the greatest play of the era, *The Cenci*, which was not staged until 1886 owing to its treatment of incest, and its controversial author used a dramatic form for his masterpiece, *Prometheus Unbound* (1819; finally performed in Austin, Texas in 1998), and wrote the satirical *Swellfoot the Tyrant* (1820) and the "Lyrical Drama" *Hellas* (1822). He left unfinished at his death the "Fragment of an Indian Drama," owing something to the Sanskrit drama *Sakuntala*, and a second history play, *Charles I*; he had earlier contemplated a drama on Tasso. He translated Euripides' *Cyclops*, the only extant Greek satyr play, as well as scenes from Calderón and Goethe's *Faust*. We might note the dramatic efforts of other second-generation romantics: Keats tried his hand at historical drama in *Otho the Great* (composed 1819; published 1848); Leigh Hunt responded to the fall of Napoleon with a masque, *The Descent of Liberty* (1815), an important influence on *Prometheus Unbound*; Horace Smith successfully adopted Hunt's and Shelley's mythological mode in *Amarynthus the Nympholept* (1821); and Bryan Proctor, or "Barry Cornwall," wrote several dramatic works including *Mirandola* (Covent Garden, 1821). The years after Waterloo saw a number of other successfully staged tragedies with ties to romanticism, including Charles Robert Maturin's enormously popular Gothic tragedy, *Bertram; or, The Castle of St. Aldobrand* (Drury Lane, 1816), Richard Lalor Sheil's *The Apostate* (Covent Garden, 1817) and *Evadne; or, The Statue* (Covent Garden, 1819), and Henry Hart Milman's *Fazio* (Covent Garden, 1818). There was also fascinating work done by women writers in these years, including Mary Shelley's *Proserpine* (1820, 1832), Barbarina Wilmot's *Ina* (Drury Lane, 1815), and Felicia Hemans's intriguing *Vespers of Palermo* (Covent Garden, 1823) and *The Siege of Valencia* (1823).[7]

One of the striking features of this gathering of romantic plays is the wide range of dramatic models they engage as they seek to revitalize the form of tragedy that Shelley saw as moribund. If the eighteenth century witnessed a struggle between an attempt to preserve a neoclassical style and a turn to a "modern" domestic drama, the romantic era sees an explosion of experiments with the shape of tragedy. Shakespeare and his contemporaries, embraced for example by Lamb and Beddoes, provided an inspiration for Shelley's *Cenci* as well as works by Sheil and Milman, but Byron argued that the Elizabethans were the wrong model for modern drama and urged instead a return to the classical unities as he wrote history plays that owed much to Dryden and Otway. Shelley himself sought inspiration in Greek tragedy, turning in particular to Aeschylus for his revisionary *Prometheus Unbound* and for his *Hellas*, based on *Persians*. Drawing on the Greeks, Calderón, Goethe, Shakespeare, Indian drama, and the popular theater, Shelley sought inspiration in all available dramatic forms, old and new, including the masque (*Prometheus Unbound* as well as "The Mask of Anarchy"), the burlesque (*Swellfoot the Tyrant*), and even the harlequinade (*Prometheus, Swellfoot*). Byron would draw not only upon the medieval mystery plays in *Cain* but also upon the contemporary melodrama in *Werner*. If we think of nineteenth-century architecture as going through a series of revivals from Greek to Gothic, then we can find the same tendency to range over the entire Western dramatic inheritance in the romantics' drive to remake the form of tragedy.

These playwrights also faced a challenge as they looked to the vision of traditional tragedy. Arising as we have seen after the French Revolution's execution of the king and disestablishment of the Church, these plays could no longer rest easily upon the hierarchical, providential order of traditional tragedy. Addison's *Cato* could still in many ways be a traditional hero, standing at the summit of his society and embodying at the same time its heroic qualities and a tragic inability to control its future. The heroes of romantic tragedy can never be social exemplars; even when they are rulers such as Byron's Sardanapalus, they are rebels against a limiting world. Both *Cato* and *The London Merchant* still relied upon a sense of underlying providential order: that, whatever happens in man's world, God is in his heaven and will finally establish a moral regime. The world of romantic plays lacks a providential order and instead threatens a fall in chaos halted only by man's efforts to reenvision life.

The collapse of traditional social order is often enacted directly in these plays as they engage historical crises. We might note how many of them are placed in moments of civil war, revolt, or social and cultural transformation. For example, Coleridge's *Remorse*, which traces Alvar's return to Spain, where he hopes to regain his beloved Teresa and to awaken remorse in his brother Ordonio, who has attempted fratricide, takes place at a time of social, cultural, and religious upheaval, as Spain is both conducting an internal campaign against the remnants of Moorish cultural and religious practice and fighting a war against Protestant rebels in the Netherlands; at the play's conclusion, as Ordonio seems ready to repent, a band of Moors rushes onstage and Alhadra, the wife of a man murdered by Ordonio, slays him in turn, as we see a contrast between a Christian notion of remorse and repentance and an ethic of revenge. Felicia Hemans's *Siege of Valencia*, set during an imaginary Moorish siege of a Spanish city in the thirteenth century, takes up a different moment in the struggle between the Moors and Christian Spain, and her *Vespers of Palermo* treats the Sicilian revolt against the French. Joanna Baillie's *Count Basil*, which explores the destructive impact of Basil's overpowering infatuation with Victoria as it enables her father the Duke of Mantua to distract Basil from his military obligations, occurs at a moment when the Holy Roman Emperor and the King of France battle for control of Italy. Again, Wordsworth's *Borderers* takes place at the time of the barons' wars against Henry III (around 1265), and is set in an unruly borderland between England and Scotland where robbers hold sway, with this rather anarchic situation forming the backdrop to Wordsworth's tale of intellectual temptation, as the Iagoesque Oswald convinces the heroic Marmaduke to murder an old man as an act of mental liberation. Byron offers spectacles of rulers in revolt against their own societies, as Faliero, though Doge of Venice, sides with the people in a rebellion against the tyranny of the aristocratic families and as Sardanapalus, who rules Assyria but who rejects his ancestors' devotion to war and conquest, seeks to transform his culture from one of war to one of love and peace, only to be confronted with a revolt against his reforms. Shelley's *Hellas*, his reworking of Aeschylus' *Persians* in which Mahmud comes to understand the futility of tyrannical rule even as his forces appear victorious, unfolds in the midst of the Greek rebellion against Turkey, while his unfinished *Charles I* takes up the English Civil War itself. His *Cenci* would seem to be an exception, for in that play, the patriarchal powers of God the Father, of the Pope, and of Count Cenci as lord and father stand oppressively secure. The play opens upon Count Cenci as he finds he can escape a murder charge by bribing the Pope and as he details his sadistic vision of life in which he "love[s] / The sight of agony, and the sense of joy, / When this shall be another's, and that mine" (Shelley 1819: 1.1.81–3), a vision he believes he shares with a vengeful God. Cenci exults in the death of two of his sons and imprisons and tortures his family until he works himself up to a deed "Whose horror might make sharp an appetite / Duller than mine" (1.1.101–2), the rape of his daughter Beatrice. Seeking to avoid her father's attempt to corrupt her soul as he assaults her body, Beatrice forms a plot to murder her father; upon his death, she and her fellow plotters are arrested and executed, as the Pope sides with the father "In the great war between the old and young" (2.2.38). While this would seem to a world in which there is no hope of displacing the interlocking oppressive authority of God, Pope, Lord, and father, Shelley makes it clear that this tyrannical order is what he elsewhere calls "anarchy," the misrule of those who seek to use social, cultural, and religious institutions to enforce a demonic parody of a providential, hierarchical order that in fact merely exalts the most destructive urges of the self.

These plays also engage moments in which the security offered by a traditional religious order is threatened. Coleridge's and Hemans's depiction of the wars between Christianity and Islam offer glimpses in this clash of civilizations of views of the divine different from that of the Christian West. In *Remorse*, while the Inquisition remains a powerful force, the two central characters – Alvar and Teresa – both have Protestant leanings, as Alvar has left his homeland for the Protestant revolt in "The Belgic states: there join'd the better cause" (Coleridge 1813: 1.1.75) and as Teresa "has no faith in Holy Church, 'tis true, / Her lover school'd her in some newer nonsense" (1.2.55–6). Alvar makes use of the confused, contested religious climate to play a trick on his brother Ordonio in whom he wants to provoke remorse. Disguised as a Moor, Alvar is hired by Ordonio to act as a wizard capable of communicating with the dead so as to convince Teresa that her beloved Alvar is indeed deceased. Alvar turns the tables on Ordonio, using the spectacular conjuration scene, complete with solemn music and special lighting effects, to display a portrait of the attempted fratricide. Where in earlier plays – in *Oedipus*, say, with its oracle, or *Macbeth* with its witches – such moments might provide a supernatural revelation, here it is all just a trick, a series of human plots within plots. Throughout romantic drama, we see key moments where the providential order that structured traditional tragedy is found either absent, as here; or in Schiller's *Wallenstein* (which Coleridge translated), where the general consults the stars to chart a future that is upon him before he can understand it; or deeply questioned, as in *The Cenci*, where the papacy can be bought and where God is invoked by the sadistic Count to justify his crimes. Even Byron's *Cain*, based on the biblical story of the first murder, does not focus on the divine but instead depicts life in the "Land without Paradise," as Cain mourns being cut off from God, as he complains that his father's religion is merely oppression, and as he receives, like Goethe's Faust, not a divine but a demonic revelation in the form of Lucifer, who takes him on a cosmic journey designed to impress upon him the insignificance of human life. Also paralleling *Faust*, Byron's *Manfred* provides a pervasive critique of providential order, staging a world that is now Catholic, now Greek, now Zoroastrian, where nature spirits, the Witch of the Alps, Nemesis, Arimanes, and the God of the Abbot all inhabit the same universe, suggesting that no one religious model is adequate to life. If Byron's play engages an eclectic array of religions, Shelley's *Prometheus Unbound* offers a summary image in Jupiter of all religious and political tyrannies that can be overthrown, the

> Thrones, altars, judgement-seats, and prisons, . . .
> Sceptres, tiaras, swords, and chains, and tomes
> Of reasoned wrong, glozed on by ignorance,

all that

> imaged to the pride of kings and priests
> A dark yet mighty faith, a power as wide
> As is the world it wasted, and are now
> But an astonishment.
>   (Shelley 1820: 3.3.164, 166–7, 173–6)

Faced with the collapse of external hierarchical and providential orders, the protagonist of romantic tragedy turns within for a vision of order that s/he then promulgates as a plan for revolutionizing the world of the play. The inward turn of the romantic hero is perhaps the best known feature of these plays, which are often seen to operate as psychological case studies under, as it were, the sign of Hamlet and to offer characters "without the strength of nerve which forms a hero," as Goethe says of Hamlet himself (Goethe 1899: bk. 4, ch. 13, vol. 23.282). A well-known example is Byron's *Manfred*, with a motto – "There are more things in heaven and earth, Horatio, / Than are dreamt of in your philosophy" – from *Hamlet*, which opens with the hero proclaiming "these eyes but close / To look within" as he pursues "a continuance of enduring thought" (Byron 1817: 1.1.6–7, 4); later telling the Witch of the Alps that "My spirit walk'd not with the souls of men" (2.2.52), and that his only love has been an apparently incestuous one for his sister, Manfred seems to many to move through the play conducting an inner dialogue with himself in which the other characters are merely manifestations of his own thoughts. It is important, however, to see that such intense self-consciousness – such "enduring thought" – is not the goal of a character such as Manfred who, after all, longs for "self-oblivion" (1.1.144), but a problem to be solved. Like Faust, Manfred has mastered all branches of human knowledge but he finds they offer him little solace, as "The Tree of Knowledge is not that of Life" (1.1.12). He thus turns to various supernatural figures who might offer him some solution to the problem of man's divided nature, "Half dust, half deity, alike unfit / To sink or soar" (1.2.40–1), but he refuses to bow to any external force – he rejects both God and the devil – because he sees them as offering not a resolution but a reduction of man's complexity. At the close of his play, as devils come to haul him, like Faust, off to Hell, he asserts his human independence:

> Thou didst not tempt me, and thou couldst not tempt me;
> I have not been thy dupe, nor am thy prey—
> But was my own destroyer, and will be
> My own hereafter. – Back, ye baffled fiends!
> The hand of death is on me – but not yours.
>
>   (3.4.137–41)

Manfred dies asserting his own humanity as the only source of meaning in a world bereft of traditional order.

As in *Manfred*, the world of romantic drama is marked by what Shelley's Orsino in *The Cenci* defines as "self-anatomy," but Shelley makes it clear that while such an inner turn can grant power, it is also a trap:

> . . . 'tis a trick of this same family
> To analyse their own and other minds.
> Such self-anatomy shall teach the will
> Dangerous secrets: for it tempts our powers,
> Knowing what must be thought, and may be done,
> Into the depth of darkest purposes.
>   (Shelley 1819: 2.2.108–13)

Here we see the dangers of an unrestricted journey into the interior. Shelley argues that a turn to the self and away from others results in a loss of true self-knowledge and self-control. The free intellect, unchecked by external rules or by ties to others, would seem to offer the only true autonomy, a way of finding the absolute self-definition that marked the traditional hero. This is certainly the argument of Rivers/Oswald in Wordsworth's *Borderers*, who urges Marmaduke to cast aside conventional notions of good and evil, to eschew all ties of love and loyalty, even to commit murder, in order "to enlarge / Man's intellectual empire" (Wordsworth 1842: 4.1854–5). Coleridge's fratricidal Ordonio makes a similar claim, arguing that "Nature had made him for some other planet... In this world / He found no fit companion" (Coleridge 1813: 4.1.100, 102–4), and contending that this isolation has enabled him to gain an enormous intellectual freedom, as "Something within would still be shadowing out / All possibilities" (107–8). That these two characters are the nominal villains of their plays (and one could add here numerous villain-heroes from Gothic plays allied to romantic efforts in tragedy, such as Osmond in Lewis's *Castle Spectre* or Bertram in Maturin's play) suggests that romantic tragic drama is not as enamored of the isolated self as is sometimes believed. What Shelley's Orsino suggests is that this isolated intellect, murdering its links to others in order to dissect the self, ends up under the power of our deepest fears and desires, the "dangerous secrets" within.

A key instance of this examination of a dangerous inner life comes in Baillie's *Plays on the Passions*, where her central characters are trapped within a powerful central emotion, as hatred comes to dominate De Monfort, love to obsess Basil, and fear to subdue Orra. Again depicting a world in which the old orders no longer hold sway, *Orra* opens with a contested tournament which has been won by Theobald, a "Nobleman of Reduced Fortune," and now a burgher or bourgeois office-holder, "mixture most unseemly / Of base and noble" (Baillie 1812: 1.1.10–11). Glottenbal, the son of a count, cannot believe he has lost to a man of lower rank and thus is easily convinced that magic must have ruled the day, with the introduction of a Gothic element here and elsewhere offering a sign that religious authority too is being questioned. Opening with a scene where the "witchy north" rather than providence rules and where class order seems confused, Baillie offers a world in which the traditional regime of social rules and religious order no longer organizes human life. The resultant turn to the interior can be tracked in the play's central character, Orra, who is freed from direct patriarchal control through the death of her father and inheritance and who, in defiance of convention and the opinions of those around her, prefers not to marry, not to "consign myself / With all my lands and rights into the hands / Of some proud man" (2.1.3–5). Her guardian, who might provide her with a father figure and stand as an emblem of order, selfishly wishes her to marry his son Glottenbal. She is also secretly pursued by the Iagoesque Rudigere, a bastard, another figure without a home in the conventional system of rules and roles: "The laws have cast me off from every claim / Of house and kindred, and within my veins / Turn'd noble blood to baseness and reproach" (1.2.16–18). Refusing to marry Glottenbal and at least attracted to Theobald, Orra is condemned by Hughobert to be imprisoned under Rudigere's control in a remote and supposedly haunted castle. Theobald attempts to rescue her by teaming with a band of Schillerian robbers, another sign of the collapse of political order, and by entering the castle disguised as the ghost who supposedly haunts it, with his flaunting of superstition suggesting the collapse of supernatural order. In the absence of order, Orra and her fellow heroes in Baillie's other plays project an inner vision that appears to make sense of a confused, corrupted world. In Orra's case, this vision arises from her terrified fascination with ghost stories. We learn that she and the women in her entourage enjoy telling each other tales of terror as a form of female bonding. Orra goes further, however, drawing upon these stories to read the world around her, as when she interprets what Cathrina sees as an ordinary cloud as "Some air-clad spirit – some portentous thing" (4.1.36), or when, alone in her chamber, she transforms every sound and sight according to the legend of the ghostly huntsman who haunts the castle, seeking revenge upon her ancestor who killed him. When Theobald makes use of this story of the ghost to enter the castle, Orra believes him to be a real spirit and goes mad. In the final act, she completely reimagines her world in private terms, transforming the world into her vision of fearful monstrosities. Insofar as she is clearly insane, she is defeated by the world around her, but insofar as her insane vision is the only one that makes sense of her world in which she is tortured by even those who love her, she suggests a possible order beyond that found within her society ruled by rapacious men.

All of which suggests that the turn to the self is an essential but not sufficient aspect of the definition of the romantic tragic hero. Where the villainous characters in these plays, such as Count Cenci, remain trapped in the self, the tragic heroes such as Beatrice turn outward to seek either in love or in revolt a community to set against their oppressive, chaotic world. Even Manfred has sought love, though a forbidden one with his sister soul Astarte. Coleridge's Alvar has lived a life of exile and sought a new intellectual independence in Protestantism, but returns in the play to claim the love of Teresa. Less successful upon his return, Maturin's Bertram demands his beloved Imogen join him in an adulterous union, through which he seeks to image a community set against that dominated by those within the Church and State who would confine him.

Love, then, can embody a kind of revolt, and other tragic figures move more clearly to embrace collective action against the limits of their worlds. Where melodrama reasserts the power of family, State, and Church, in the romantic drama revolt becomes the means by which these characters seek to create order in a post-providential world. As Camus would write much later:

> The rebel is a man who is on the point of accepting or rejecting the sacred and
> determined on laying claim to a human situation in which all the answers are human
> ... Is it possible to find a rule of conduct outside the realm of religion and its absolute
> values? This is the question raised by rebellion. ([1954] 1956: 20–1)

This quest for a new order is what inspires the intellectual villains of Wordsworth and Coleridge, and Byron's Cain offers a heroic version of the same move to, in Lucifer's words, "form an inner world / In your own bosom – where the outward fails" (Byron

1821a: 2.2.463–4). Revolt is also the project of figures such as Beatrice Cenci and Elmina in Hemans's *Siege of Valencia*, who offer counter-visions to oppressive patriarchal worlds. Beatrice is the one figure in her play who can stand up to her demonic father, as is seen, for example, at the end of the first act, when everyone but Beatrice cowers as the Count gloats over the death of two of his sons. Cenci's incestuous rape of Beatrice is an attempt both to tame this rebel and to corrupt the one person in his world able to withstand the destructive allure of self-anatomy. Most commentators have found Count Cenci victorious,[8] but Cenci himself admits, "I must give up the great point, which was / To poison and corrupt her soul" (Shelley 1819: 4.1.44–5). Shortly after her nightmare vision in the last scene of an eternity ruled by an evil patriarchal God, Beatrice proclaims, "'Tis past / Whatever comes my heart shall sink no more" (5.4.77–8). More than that, she moves beyond the Christian vision she shares with her father and that has underpinned her claims for innocence, as she responds to Lucretia's reminder of the "tender promises of Christ" (5.4.76) by saying, "your words strike chill" (79). She then calls upon death, which, in striking contrast to the image of eternity ruled by her father, is conceived in maternal terms:

> Come, obscure Death,
> And wind me in thine all-embracing arms!
> Like a fond mother hide me in thy bosom
> And rock me to the sleep from which none wake.
> (5.4.115–19)

As she exits to the place of execution, she and her mother bind up each other's hair in a final act of female bonding set against the masculine bondage that has defined the world of the play. Hemans's Elmina also searches out a womanly vision to pit against a masculinist regime of honor and death. The central conflict of the play arises when Elmina's and Gonzalez's two sons are captured by the Moorish leader, Abdullah, who threatens to kill them unless Gonzalez surrenders the city. While Elmina offers to betray the city to save her children and while their daughter, Ximena, rouses the populace to issue forth from the city, the two sons are executed, Ximena dies, confessing her heart was broken when earlier her beloved was killed in battle, and Gonzalez receives mortal wounds trying to rescue his sons. While the play ends with the Christians triumphant, as the king enters with an army able to overwhelm the siege force, and while the play closes with many pious paeans to God's power, feminist scholars (i.e., Wolfson and Fay 2002: 26–8) have argued that the play's real focus is not on victorious religious might but upon the losses felt by the city, particularly the losses experienced by women such as Elmina and Ximena. Again, we might point to the harsh religiosity of the priest Hernandez, who feels that God delights most in blood, to suggest that the play offers no simple endorsement of God and King. Like Beatrice or Orra, Elmina can be read as calling for a revolt against a masculine world that preaches morality but practices death.

Such figures also suggest the difficulty in arriving at some sort of collective revolt. Beatrice does, in a sense, offer a kind of collective resistance in joining with her family and two hired assassins to murder her father, and Elmina attempts direct action in going to the enemy, while her daughter Ximena even manages to spur a collective effort by the people of Valencia, but all these efforts fail. One way in which to offer an image of collective action is through the inclusion of Schillerian bands of noble robbers, as are found in Wordsworth's *Borderers*, Baillie's *Orra*, and even Maturin's *Bertram*, but the fact that the rebel is often a robber suggests his/her confused status. Perhaps the most interesting accounts of collective rebellion are found in Byron's history plays. Sardanapalus, for example, seems an unlikely rebel, since he rules Assyria, but he rejects the violence that has marked Assyrian rule, embracing instead a life of love and pleasure: "I thought to have made my realm a paradise, / And every moon an epoch of new pleasures" (Byron 1821b: 4.1.517–18). A revolutionary on the throne, he sparks a conservative revolt that finally leads to his spectacular death on a funeral pyre, which he hopes will be "a light / To lesson ages" (5.1.440–1). In *Marino Faliero*, the Doge finds that his heroic identity, founded on fighting for Venice, becomes compromised as the city changes, as the social order which he had aspired to climb in order to prove himself is subverted by the power of an aristocratic oligarchy: the "hundred-handed senate rules, / Making the people nothing, and the prince / A pageant" (Byron 1821c: 1.2.269–71). The Doge decides to join a revolt against the aristocracy, even though this means he must betray his own class and his own friends and acquaintances. He joins the revolt in the hopes of remaking Venice – "We will renew the times of truth and justice, / Condensing in a far free common-wealth / Not rash equality but equal rights" (3.2.168–70) – but he finds his revolt caught up in contradictions. First, Faliero must fight against those who have honored him in the past; his identity is bound up with the very class he must destroy, a fact he recognizes when he proclaims, "Each stab to them will seem my suicide" (3.2.472). Second, here as throughout romantic drama, the rebellion is fought in the name of a more perfect world, but must be conducted with the tools available in the fallen realm inhabited by the hero and his opponents. The Doge and his fellow rebels must perpetrate the kind of violence they have opposed, and this proves to be too much for one of the conspirators, who betrays the revolt to an aristocratic friend he does not wish to see killed. Beatrice committing parricide to free herself from her father's oppression, Ordonio seeking a liberation of thought and action through fratricide, the Doge having to will the destruction of the city he has loved – all are images of the double bind in which the romantic hero finds him- or herself as s/he, seeking an order grounded in the human imagination rather than divine providence, must stoop to horrible violence in the name of remaking the world.

Such double binds mark the tragic impasse that confronts the protagonists of romantic drama. In a sense, what they find is that there is no place for heroes in a world in which there are no longer hierarchical markers of the heroic, no longer gods and monsters against which to prove oneself great. Oddly, their heroism rests in their impossible attempt to prove themselves heroic, as Sardanapalus tries to discover a heroism of love not war, or Cain seeks an intellectual heroism, or Beatrice a heroism of feminist resistance. We can agree with those who have found that romantic tragic drama could not re-create the world of Aeschylus, or Shakespeare, or Racine, and yet still find that they offer a modern equivalent to traditional tragedy in finding greatness in the attempt to discover within the human self a model for a chaotic, oppressive world and to use that model to transform that world through revolt. Simply put, these heroic attempts fail because these would-be heroes must betray two key values within romanticism, imagination and love, as they try to create their vision in the here-and-now and not in some imaginative space, and as this commitment to transformation in the present forces them to turn to the violence available in their world rather than to the power of love the romantics espouse elsewhere. Romantic tragic drama arises, then, through an exploration of the failure of the move to an imaginative, loving transformation of the world, a failure of the romantic vision itself.

NOTES

1 Accounts of the drama and theater of the eighteenth century include: Backscheider (1993), Bernbaum [1915] (1958), Bevis (1988), Brown (1981), Kavnik (1995), Loftis (1963), Nicoll (1925, 1927), O'Brien (2004), Price (1973), and Van Lennep et al. (1960–2).

2 For a fuller account, see Cox (1987: 1–25).

3 On neoclassical theory, see chapter 21 in this volume. There were attempts to follow the Greeks across the century, from John Dennis, who adapted Euripides in *Iphigenia* (Lincoln's Inn Fields, 1699), to John Delap, who turned to the same author for his *Royal Suppliants* (Drury Lane, 1781). Corneille was imitated by, for example, Colley Cibber in *Ximena* (Drury Lane, 1712) and by W. Whitehead in *The Roman Father* (Drury Lane, 1750). Ambrose Philips's popular *Distrest Mother* (Drury Lane, 1711) was an adaptation of Racine, as were Abel Boyer's *Achilles; or, Iphigenia in Aulis* (Drury Lane, 1699), Edmund Smith's *Phaedra and Hippolitus* (Haymarket, 1707), and Charles Johnson's *The Victim* (Drury Lane, 1713) and *The Sultaness* (Drury Lane, 1717). Aaron Hill was a key adapter of Voltaire, staging the French dramatist's reworking of *Othello* as *Zara* (Drury Lane, 1736), *Alzira* (Lincoln's Inn Fields, 1736), and *Mérope* (Drury Lane, 1749). Later in the century, Smollett and Francklin's edition of *The Works of M. de Voltaire*, begun in 1761, would spur a number of productions of Voltaire's works, including *Orestes* (Covent Garden, 1769), *Tancrède* as *Almida* (Drury Lane, 1771), and *Sémiramis* (Drury Lane, 1776).

4 *The Works of Joseph Addison*, 1.71; The *Works of the Right Honourable Joseph Addison*, 2.307. On Racine and Corneille, see chapter 22 in this volume.

5 For other accounts of the melodrama, see, for example, Booth (1965), Evans (1947), Hadley (1995), and Rahill (1967).

6 Among other overviews of the romantic period in relation to its context, see Butler (1982), Gaull (1988), and Stabler (2002).

7 On this body of romantic plays, see, for example, Burroughs (1997), Carlson (1994), Cox (1987), Donohue (1970), Moody (2000), Richardson (1988), Simpson (1998), and Watkins (1993).

8 Antonin Artaud, in his adaptation of the play, even has Beatrice state, "I fear that death may teach me that I have ended by resembling him" (1970: 52).

REFERENCES AND FURTHER READING

Addison, Joseph. (1713). *Cato*. In *The Broadview Anthology of Restoration and Eighteenth-Century Drama*, ed. J. Douglas Canfield, Peterborough, Ont.: Broadview Press, 2002; *The Works of Joseph Addison*, 3 vols., New York: Harper & Brothers, 1850, vol. 2; *The Works of the Right Honourable Joseph Addison*, 6 vols., ed. Richard Hurd and Henry G. Bohn, London: George Bell & Sons, 1877, vol. 1; and *The Miscellaneous Works of Joseph Addison*, 3 vols., ed. A. G. Guthklech, London: G. Bell & Sons, 1914, vol. 1.

Artaud, Antonin. (1970). *The Cenci*, trans. Simon Watson Taylor. New York: Grove Press. (*Les Cenci* first published in 1935.)

Backscheider, Paula R. (1993). *Spectacular Politics: Theatrical Power and Mass Culture in Early Modern England*. Baltimore, MD: Johns Hopkins University Press. Covering drama from the Restoration to the rise of the Gothic in the late eighteenth century, Backscheider offers a powerful account of drama's place in power politics.

Baillie, Joanna. (1812). *Orra*. In *A series of plays: in which it is attempted to delineate the stronger passions of the mind: each passion being the subject of a tragedy and a comedy*, vol. 3. London: Longman, Hurst, Rees, & Orme; also in *The Broadview Anthology of Romantic Drama*, ed. Jeffrey N. Cox and Michael Gamer. Peterborough, Ont.: Broadview Press, 2003.

Barbauld, Anna Laetitia. (1812). *Eighteen Hundred and Eleven*. In *The Poems of Anna Laetitia Barbauld*, ed. William McCarthy and Elizabeth Croft. Athens, GA: University of Georgia Press, 1994, 152–62.

Benjamin, Walter. (1977). *The Origins of German Tragic Drama*, trans. John Osborne. London: NLB. (*Ursprung des deutschen Trauerspiels* first published in 1928.) The great literary and culture critic Benjamin explores the ways in which the Baroque broke from classical tragedy grounded in myth to create the modern "sorrow play" of man's entrapment in history.

Bernbaum, Ernest. [1915] (1958). *The Drama of Sensibility*. Gloucester, MA: Peter Smith. Bernbaum's book was an early attempt to track the impact of the rise of sentimentality/sensibility on comedy and tragedy.

Bevis, Richard M. (1988). *English Drama: Restoration and Eighteenth Century*. London: Longman. Bevis surveys the drama and theater of the period in this volume from the Longman Literature in English series.

Booth, Michael. (1965). *English Melodrama*. London: Jenkins. Booth penned the standard account of the melodrama on the London stage.

Brooks, Peter. (1976). *The Melodramatic Imagination*. New Haven, CT: Yale University Press. Brooks places the nineteenth-century novel in relation to the stage, offering an important account of the political and epistemological import of the melodrama.

Brown, Laura. (1981). *English Dramatic Form, 1660–1760*. New Haven, CT: Yale University Press. Brown tracks the development of dramatic genre in relation to changes in the cultural, social, and political context.

Burroughs, Catherine. (1997). *Closet Stages: Joanna Baillie and the Theater Theory of British Romantic Women Writers*. Philadelphia: University of Pennsylvania Press. Burroughs offers the most thorough account we have of Baillie as a dramatist and theater theorist.

Butler, Marilyn. (1982). *Romantics, Rebels and Reactionaries: English Literature and its Background 1760–1830*. Oxford: Oxford University Press. Butler provides a magisterial overview of the literature of the romantic period in relation to cultural, social, and political developments.

Byron, George Gordon, Lord. (1817). *Manfred*. In *Complete Poetical Works*, 7 vols., ed. Jerome McGann. Oxford: Clarendon Press, 1980–93, vol. 4.

Byron, George Gordon, Lord. (1821a). *Cain*. In *Complete Poetical Works*, 7 vols., ed. Jerome McGann. Oxford: Clarendon Press, 1980–93, vol. 6.

Byron, George Gordon, Lord. (1821b). *Sardanapalus*. In *The Broadview Anthology of Romantic Drama*, ed. Jeffrey N. Cox and Michael Gamer, Peterborough, Ont.: Broadview Press, 2003; *Complete Poetical Works*, 7 vols., ed. Jerome McGann. Oxford: Clarendon Press, 1980–93, vol. 6.

Byron, George Gordon, Lord. (1821c). *Marino Faliero, Doge of Venice*. In *Complete Poetical Works*, 7 vols., ed. Jerome McGann. Oxford: Clarendon Press, 1980–93, vol. 6.

Byron, George Gordon, Lord. (1973–94). *Byron's Letters and Journals*, 13 vols., ed. Leslie Marchand. London: John Murray.

Byron, George Gordon, Lord. (1980–93). *Complete Poetical Works*, 7 vols., ed. Jerome McGann. Oxford: Clarendon Press.

Camus, Albert. [1954] (1956). *The Rebel*, trans. Anthony Bower. New York: Random House. (*L'Homme révolté* first published in 1951.)

Canfield, J. Douglas, ed. (2002). *The Broadview Anthology of Restoration and Eighteenth-Century Drama*. Peterborough, Ont.: Broadview Press. Canfield and his coeditors provide the most thorough collection of Restoration and eighteenth-century drama to date.

Carlson, Julie. (1994). *In the Theater of Romanticism: Coleridge, Nationalism, Women*. Cambridge: Cambridge University Press. Carlson provides a subtle, influential account of the romantic drama's role in shaping gender and national identities.

Coleridge, Samuel Taylor. (1813). *Remorse*. In *The Broadview Anthology of Romantic Drama*, ed. Jeffrey N. Cox and Michael Gamer, Peterborough, Ont.: Broadview Press, 2003; *The Collected Works of Samuel Taylor Coleridge, Poetical Works, Part III: Plays*, ed. J. C. C. Mays, Princeton, NJ: Princeton University Press, 2001.

Cox, Jeffrey N. (1987). *In The Shadows of Romance: Romantic Tragic Drama in Germany, England, and France*. Athens: Ohio University Press. Cox argues that romanticism remade tragedy in keeping with its concerns with subjectivity and revolt.

Cox, Jeffrey N. and Gamer, Michael, eds. (2003). *The Broadview Anthology of Romantic Drama*. Peterborough, Ont.: Broadview Press. This collection brings together plays by Coleridge, Shelley, and Byron with key works by women playwrights and major stage successes of the period.

Donohue, Joseph. (1970). *Dramatic Character in the English Romantic Age*. Princeton, NJ: Princeton University Press. A groundbreaking study of romantic drama, Donohue's book also connects the work of romantic playwrights to a dramatic tradition running back to Beaumont and Fletcher.

Ellison, Julie. (1999). *Cato's Tears and the Making of Anglo-American Emotion*. Chicago: University of Chicago Press. Ellison excavates the history of emotion in the formation of Anglo-American liberalism and libertarianism.

Evans, Bertrand. (1947). *The Gothic Drama From Walpole to Shelley*. Berkeley: University of California Press. While somewhat dated, Evans's book is still the standard survey of Gothic drama.

Faller, Lincoln B. (1988). *The Popularity of Addison's* Cato *and Lillo's* The London Merchant, *1700–1776*. New York: Garland. Faller focuses on these two popular plays and their place in the repertoire.

Gaull, Marilyn. (1988). *English Romanticism: The Human Context*. New York: W. W. Norton. Gaull provides a wide range of contexts for the understanding of romantic literature, including material on the theater of the day.

Goethe, Wolfgang von. (1899). *Wilhelm Meister's Apprenticeship*, trans. Thomas Carlyle. In *The Works of Thomas Carlyle in Thirty Volumes*, New York: AMS Press, 1969 (*Wilhelm Meister's Lehrjahre* first published in 1795–6.)

Hadley, Elaine. (1995). *Melodramatic Tactics: Theatricalized Dissent in the English Marketplace, 1800–1885*. Stanford, CA: Stanford University Press. Hadley establishes the impact of melodrama on a wide range of nineteenth-century discourses.

Inchbald, Elizabeth, ed. (1808). *The British Theatre*, 25 vols. London: Longman, Hurst, Rees, & Orme.

Kavnik, Frances M. (1995). *British Drama, 1660–1779: A Critical History*. New York: Twayne. Kavnik surveys the drama from the Restoration through the age of Garrick, offering readings of exemplary plays.

Lillo, George. (1731). *The London Merchant*. In *The Dramatic Works of George Lillo*, ed. James L. Steffensen. Oxford: Clarendon Press, 1993; *The Broadview Anthology of Restoration and Eighteenth-Century* Drama, ed. J. Douglas Canfield, Peterborough, Ont.: Broadview Press, 2002.

Loftis, John. (1963). *The Politics of Drama in Augustan England*. Oxford: Clarendon Press. Loftis treats the political valence of the drama up to the Licensing Act of 1737.

Moody, Jane. (2000). *Illegitimate Theatre in London, 1770–1840*. Cambridge: Cambridge University Press. Moody explores the impact of the "illegitimate" theater found on minor stages and in new dramatic forms during the romantic period.

Nicoll, Allardyce. (1925). *A History of Early Eighteenth Century Drama 1700–1750*. Cambridge: Cambridge University Press. Nicoll offers the traditional account of English drama, with an invaluable handlist of plays from each period.

Nicoll, Allardyce. (1927). *A History of Late Eighteenth Century Drama 1750–1800*. Cambridge: Cambridge University Press. Nicoll offers the traditional account of English drama, with an invaluable handlist of plays from each period.

O'Brien, John. (2004). *Harlequin Britain: Pantomime and Entertainment, 1690–1760*. Baltimore, MD: Johns Hopkins University Press. O'Brien provides a breakthrough account of the popular harlequinade and its place in eighteenth-century British culture.

Pixérécourt, René-Charles Guilbert (1841–3). *Dernières reflexions sur le melodrama* [Last reflections on the melodrama]. In *Théâtre choisi* [Selected theater], 4 vols. Paris: Tresse, vol. 1.

Price, Cecil. (1973). *Theatre in the Age of Garrick*. Oxford: Basil Blackwell. Price provides an overview of acting styles, costuming, stage sets, audiences, criticism, and plays during the mid-eighteenth century, a period dominated by the actor David Garrick.

Rahill, Frank. (1967). *The World of Melodrama*. University Park: Pennsylvania State University Press. Rahill provides a good overview of European melodrama.

Richardson, Alan. (1988). *A Mental Theatre: Poetic Drama and Consciousness in the Romantic Age*. University Park: Pennsylvania State University Press. Richardson argues strongly for the view that romantic plays comprise a mental or closet drama.

Rowe, Nicholas. (1703). *Fair Penitent*, ed. Malcolm Goldstein. Regents Restoration Drama Series. Lincoln: Nebraska University Press, 1969; also in *The Broadview Anthology of Restoration and Eighteenth-Century Drama*, ed. J. Douglas Canfield, Peterborough, Ont.: Broadview Press, 2002.

Schlegel, August Wilhelm. [1846] (1861). *Course of Lectures on Dramatic Art and Literature*, trans. John Black. London: H. G. Bohn. (*Vorlesungen über dramatische Kunst und Literatur* first published in 1808.) Schlegel's seminal examination of the differences between "classical" and "romantic" culture was popularized in Madame de Staël's *D'Allemagne* (1810) and had a European-wide influence.

Scott, Sir Walter. (1894). *Familiar Letters*, 2 vols., ed. David Douglas. Edinburgh: Douglas.

Scouten, A. H. (1976). "Tragedy." In *The Revels History of Drama in English*, ed. John Loftis, Richard Southern, Marion Jones, and A. H. Scouten. London: Methuen, vol. 5: 1660–1750, 256–87. The "Revels" history updates Nicoll's overview, with Scouten's essay covering Restoration and early eighteenth-century tragedy.

Shelley, Percy Bysshe. (1819). *The Cenci*. In *The Broadview Anthology of Romantic Drama*, ed. Jeffrey N. Cox and Michael Gamer, Peterborough, Ont.: Broadview Press, 2003; *Shelley's Selected Poetry and Prose*, ed. Donald Reiman and Neil Fraistat, 2nd edn., New York: W. W. Norton.

Shelley, Percy Bysshe. (1820). *Prometheus Unbound*. In *Shelley's Selected Poetry and Prose*, ed. Donald Reiman and Neil Fraistat, 2nd edn., New York: W. W. Norton.

Shelley, Percy Bysshe. (1821) *A Defence of Poetry*. In *Shelley's Prose; or The Trumpet of a Prophecy*, ed. David Lee Clark. Albuquerque: University of New Mexico Press, [1954] 1966, 275–97.

Shelley, Percy Bysshe. (2002). *Shelley's Selected Poetry and Prose*, ed. Donald Reiman and Neil Fraistat, 2nd edn. New York: W. W. Norton.

Simpson, Michael. (1998). *Closet Performances: Political Exhibition and Prohibition in the Dramas of Byron and Shelley*. Stanford, CA: Stanford University Press. Simpson explores the political context for romantic dramatists' experimentation with closet drama.

Stabler, Jane. (2002). *Burke to Byron, Barbauld to Baillie, 1790–1830*. New York: Palgrave Macmillan. Stabler provides a contextualized overview of the period that takes into account recent developments in the field such as the focus on women writers.

Steiner, George. (1961). *The Death of Tragedy*. London: Faber & Faber. Steiner's is the classic argument for the inability of the modern world to create tragedy.

Van Lennep, W., Avery, E. L., Scouten, A., Stone, G. W., Jr., and Hogan, C. B., eds. (1960–2). *The London Stage, 1660–1800*. Carbondale: Southern Illinois University Press. An invaluable calendar of theatrical performances during the Restoration and eighteenth century, these volumes also include excellent prefaces to each year's work in the theater.

Watkins, Daniel. (1993). *A Materialist Critique of English Romantic Drama*. Gainesville: University Press of Florida. Watkins surveys the successes and failures of romantic drama from a Marxist perspective.

Wiseman, Susan. (1998). *Drama and Politics in the English Civil War*. Cambridge: Cambridge University Press. Wiseman corrects earlier accounts, which had assumed that the drama had more or less vanished during the Civil War until being restored under Charles II.

Wolfson, Susan and Fay, Elizabeth. (2002). "Introduction." In Felicia Hemans, *The Siege of Valencia*, ed. Susan Wolfson and Elizabeth Fay. Peterborough, Ont.: Broadview Press, 7–28.

Wordsworth, William. (1842). *The Borderers*. In *The Borderers*, ed. Robert Osborn. Cornell Wordsworth Edition. Ithaca, NY: Cornell University Press, 1982.

24

German Classical Tragedy: Lessing, Goethe, Schiller, Kleist, and Büchner

Simon Richter

The difference between the words tragedy and *Trauerspiel* may seem negligible at first, a matter of translating the word used in many European languages (including German) into the German idiom, or vice versa. In fact, *Trauerspiel* (literally the play of mourning) names a rival conception of classical tragedy, namely, that of the Baroque *Trauerspiel*, evocatively explored in Walter Benjamin's study, *The Origin of German Tragic Drama* (1928). German classical tragedy, on the other hand, takes place as a comparatively short episode in the eighteenth and early nineteenth centuries, wrested, in a sense, from a Baroque tradition of world theater (*theatrum mundi*) that includes the German plays of Benjamin's study, but also Shakespeare and most especially Calderón. The experiment with classical tragedy presupposes a resolute rejection of this tradition – often figured as the expulsion of Hans Wurst (the German Harlequin) from the stage – and an abrupt and dogmatic turn to French classical theater under the auspices of Johann Christian Gottsched (1700–66). Convinced that the imposition of the model of French classical tragedy missed the point, Gotthold Ephraim Lessing set in motion an effort to domesticize tragedy for Germans and the German language that resulted, finally, in a return of the repressed. Along the way, German classical tragedy would enjoy remarkable triumphs and see the concurrent development of a radical artistic doctrine by Johann Wolfgang von Goethe and Friedrich Schiller in the 1790s, known as the theory of aesthetic autonomy. Still, the greatest work of German tragic theater, Goethe's *Faust*, completed shortly before the author's death in 1832, finds its way back to a thoroughly mediated and self-reflexive form of theater antithetical to any classical notion of tragedy. Throughout the period of German classical tragedy, *Trauerspiel* is never far away.

For the purposes of this chapter, "German classical tragedy" will refer to an engagement with and practice of tragic theater in the period between roughly 1750 and 1832 by Gotthold Ephraim Lessing, Johann Wolfgang von Goethe, Friedrich Schiller, Heinrich von Kleist, and Georg Büchner.[1] Even though the classical traged-ies that come into our purview were written over a period of eight decades, and across an array of literary periods, there are deeper discursive continuities that we should note at the outset. For one thing, the handful of tragedians that will occupy our interest wrote their plays in an intense and critical awareness of the tradition of classical tragedy stretching from the Greeks, by way of the French (Racine, Corneille), the English (Shakespeare), and the Spanish (Calderón), to themselves. Their tragedies were composed in the conviction that they spoke to and intervened in this tradition. Their theater is literate, intertextual, self-reflexive, and ambitious. Not only did most of them contribute substantial theoretical and critical essays on tragedy; their plays themselves are infused with theoretical self-awareness. This observation goes hand in hand with a second: German classical tragedy reads like an intense and almost compulsive revision of Aristotle's *Poetics*, partially enabled by developments in classical philology in Germany, and in the service of a critique of French classicism and its understanding of the three unities, but more in the spirit of returning to Aristotle and the origins of tragedy. Such a return should be understood in the context of the immense influence exerted by Johann Joachim Winckelmann's project of neo-Hellenism – an influence felt in art, literature, and culture throughout Europe. Winckelmann's *Gedanken über die Nachahmung der griechischen Werke der Malerei und Bildhauerkunst* (Reflections on the imitation of Greek works of painting and sculpture, 1755) reads like a manifesto and broadly asserts that the only way for moderns to become inimitable (i.e., classical) is through imitation of the Greeks. Precisely what such imitation would entail was up for grabs, but in any event a fresh look at Aristotle was definitely called for.

Lessing, Goethe, and Schiller were convinced that if they got Aristotle right, if they succeeded in becoming inimitable in Winckelmannian fashion, Germany would finally get the national theater it both needed and deserved. By national theater they meant not only the contribution of high-quality German plays to an otherwise largely European (French, Italian, British, and Spanish) and/or insipid domestic repertoire, but also actually getting their hands dirty in the business of theater: Lessing in Hamburg as dramaturge and theater critic, Goethe (as actor and director) and Schiller (as dramaturge) separately in Weimar and Mannheim, respectively, and then together as directors of the National Theater in Weimar. Lessing and Goethe introduced numerous reforms, educating their actors in what Lessing called "corporeal eloquence" (Gustafson 1995: 51–63) and in the declamation of blank verse. In response to and in the aftermath of the Weimar project, Kleist and Büchner write for a theater that does not exist – not because Lessing, Goethe, and Schiller failed in the attempt – a more differentiated judgment is called for – but because the political and cultural tenor of their times was not in accord with their radical vision of tragic theater. Goethe's *Faust, Part Two* (despite the recent production by Peter Stein[2]) should also be regarded as straining the limits of theater, in addition to returning to an alternate conception of tragedy as *Trauerspiel*. The plays of these authors have competed for and sustained international interest among theorists and practitioners of theater for many years, into our own day. Of course, Kleist and Büchner had to wait a century or more before receiving the attention they deserved, and Lessing, Schiller, and Goethe had to be rescued from the nationalistic excesses of the nineteenth century, not to mention the Nazis. For better or worse, these are the authors of German classical tragedy.

Pain, Terror, and the Origin of German Classical Tragedy

Classical tragedy in Germany begins with a muted scream and a mistranslation. Appropriately, the mistranslated word is from Aristotle's definition of tragedy: "The tragedy is an imitation of an action . . . arousing *phobos* and *eleos*" (*Poetics* 1449b 27–8). For decades, the German, French, and English had alternately translated *phobos* as *Schrecken*, *terreur*, terror and *Furcht*, *crainte*, fear. As Lessing approaches the scene, he calls for a revision: Aristotle, after all, used only the one word and certainly terror and fear are different things.[3] Under terror, Lessing will come to imagine the atrocities of a Richard III, a character not likely to win an audience's *Mitleid* (sympathy), to refer to the preferred (mis)translation of the second term in Aristotle's definition. In other words, terror so understood cannot readily be assimilated to sympathy, and Lessing will place his entire emphasis on the latter. The terror and horror, the profound shudder of *phobos*, are therefore categorically excluded and systematically replaced with fear: "Das Wort, welches Aristoteles braucht, heißt Furcht: Mitleid und Furcht, sagt er, soll die Tragödie erregen; nicht Mitleid und Schrecken" (Lessing 2003: 2.374; The word Aristotle uses is fear: the tragedy, he says, should arouse sympathy and fear; not sympathy and terror). The fact that Lessing has forced the issue is confirmed by the reversal of Aristotle's terms. Not only has *phobos* been mistranslated, but it has also sacrificed its priority, and now stands as fear in the service of sympathy. As we will see, for Lessing, everything comes down to sympathy. And it is the audience's sympathy with the tragic hero that is the result aspired to by the tragedy.

The muted scream is also Greek – or at least Hellenist – in origin. I am referring to the description of the Laocoön statue in Winckelmann's *Reflections on the Imitation of Greek Works in Painting and Sculpture*. In a famous passage in which he singles out the Laocoön as the perfect instance of *edle Einfalt* (noble simplicity) and *stille Größe* (quiet grandeur), he goes on to write:

> Der Schmerz, welcher sich in allen Muskeln und Sehnen des Körpers entdecket, und den man ganz allein, ohne das Gesicht und andere Teile zu betrachten, an dem schmerzlich eingezognen Unterleibe beinahe selbst zu empfinden glaubet; dieser Schmerz . . . äußert sich dennoch mit keiner Wut in dem Gesichte und in der ganzen Stellung. Er erhebet kein schreckliches Geschrei . . . Der Schmerz des Körpers und die Größe der Seele sind durch den ganzen Bau der Figur mit gleicher Stärke ausgeteilet, und gleichsam abgewogen. (Winckelmann [1755] 1982: 20)

> [The pain is revealed in all the muscles and sinews of his body, and we ourselves can feel it as we observe the painful contraction of the abdomen alone without regarding the face and other parts of the body. This pain, however, expresses itself with no sign of rage in

his face or in his entire bearing. He emits no terrible screams . . . The physical pain and the nobility of soul are distributed with equal strength over the entire body. (Winckelmann 1987: 33–4)]

Here we encounter a new tragic body in the person of an Homeric hero, grounded in physiological discourse, and minutely analyzed as a surface on which two forces of representation are locked in dynamic tension: the powerful contorting power of pain and the equally powerful ability of the soul to contain the pain. The hero, writes Winckelmann, does not erupt in a terrified and terrifying scream.

The predisposition to view the tragic body in almost medical terms comes from new developments in the discourse of physiology. Albrecht von Haller, professor of anatomy and physiology at the University of Göttingen, and literary author in his own right, published the results of his extensive laboratory experiments in *De partibus corporis humani sensilibus et irritabilibus* (1753; entitled *A Dissertation on the Sensible and Irritable Parts of Animals* in an English translation of 1755). In a virtual duplication of the Laocoön statue, Haller applied painful stimuli to living animals of various species. "I then observed whether the animal were brought out of its calm and silence [its quiet grandeur, so to speak] by touching, splitting, cutting, burning, or ripping; whether it threw itself back and forth, or drew the limb into itself, and twitched with the wound, whether a cramped twitching showed in this limb, or whether nothing of all this occurred" (Haller 1922: 15). Those body parts that involve the registration of pain in the brain were designated *empfindlich* (sensitive). *Empfindlich* is the medical counterpart of the contemporaneous aesthetic term *empfindsam* (sensible), which names the culture (*Empfindsamkeit* or age of sensibility) in which works of literature and tragedy were tearfully and sympathetically received. In both instances, physiological and literary, it is a question of *Wirkung*, the effect on the body of representations of pain. This new concept of the body is connected with the equally new discipline of aesthetics established by Alexander Baumgarten (1983). In *Briefe über die Empfindungen* (Letters on Feelings), Lessing's friend Moses Mendelssohn provides a nexus for reflection on aesthetics, tragedy, and the body (1974). All of our playwrights respond to this new conception of the physiology of the human body, in particular its relevance to any notion of catharsis and affect.

Lessing picks up on Winckelmann's image in his major aesthetic treatise entitled *Laokoon, oder über die Grenzen der Malerei und Poesie* (1984). He argues for a media-based aesthetics, according to which each medium determines its conditions and limitations for optimal representation. The visual arts (e.g., sculpture) depend on visible signs rendered spatially and therefore can only imply movement. The visual representation of Laocoön's cry, a moment of terror rendered timeless in stone, would be abhorrent and violate the propriety of the visual medium. The poetic arts, on the other hand, depend on linguistic signs rendered temporally and can only imply bodies. This explains Virgil's license to represent Laocoön's terrified scream. Although Lessing does not expressly treat the dramatic arts in this text, it is evident that from this perspective drama would be a hybrid art, operating in both media (visible and linguistic signs), and able to represent bodies and movement. To what extent the expression of the terrified/terrifying scream is legitimate for theater remains to be seen.

For Goethe and Schiller the Laocoön becomes an emblem of their classical project. The key moment in their response to Winckelmann's description is the idea of aesthetic containment. No matter what the medium, they are interested in the moment in which a sudden, unexpected pain is inflicted on the body and in art's ability to contain and transmute that pain into beauty. In the statue, containment is not attributable to the moral character of the hero, but rather to the formal composition of the figures enabled by the encircling snakes. As Goethe writes: "Durch dieses Mittel der Lähmung wird, bei der grossen Bewegung, über das Ganze schon eine gewisse Ruhe und Einheit verbreitet" (MA 4.2: 78; Through this medium of paralysis, a certain sense of tranquility and unity pervades the group despite all movement). The snakes are the means through which the artist stifles the terrifying cry and transforms pain into a work of art. A new kind of aesthetic formalism is summoned as an antidote against pain and terror. "Es ist," writes Goethe, "ein grosser Vorteil für ein Kunstwerk, wenn es selbständig, wenn es geschlossen ist" (MA 4.2: 78; it is a great advantage for a work of art to be autonomous, closed in itself).

It would fall to Schiller to formulate the process of aesthetic containment specifically for tragedy. In the foreword to one of his last plays, *Die Braut von Messina*, entitled "Über den Gebrauch des Chors in der Tragödie" (On the use of the chorus in tragedy), Schiller defends his anachronistic use of the ancient chorus in an early nineteenth-century play. The chorus, he argues, heightens the artificiality of the play so that no one will mistake it for nature – in other words, it is in the service of aesthetic autonomy: "So sollte er [the chorus] uns eine lebendige Mauer sein, die die Tragödie um sich herumzieht, um sich von der wirklichen Welt rein abzuschließen, und sich ihren idealen Boden, ihre poetische Freiheit zu bewahren" (NA 10–11; The chorus should be a living wall that the tragedy draws around itself in order to cut itself off completely from the real world and to preserve its ideal ground, its ideal freedom). The chorus, like the snakes in the statue, encircles and contains the tragic plot and the passions it arouses: "So wie der Chor in die Sprache Leben bringt, so bringt er Ruhe in die Handlung – aber die schöne und hohe Ruhe, die der Charakter eines edeln Kunstwerkes sein muß" (NA 10.14; Just as the chorus brings life to the language, it also brings tranquility to the plot – but the beautiful and grand tranquility, which must be the character of a noble artwork). There is no mistaking the language of Winckelmann's description of the Laocoön. The difference, however, is that such tranquility and grandeur are achieved by formal means. Schiller's own play certainly calls for aesthetic containment. One of the few plots of his own invention, it consists of a brutally tragic plot of Oedipal proportions, with scenes of fratricide and incest. The chorus, Schiller writes, "reinigt also das tragische Gedicht" (NA 10.13; the chorus thus purifies the tragic poem). It makes pain and terror bearable for the viewer, even as it abstracts the play and the viewer from the real world.

Now the point of calling attention to the mistranslation of terror and the terrifying/terrified cry of Laocoön is to underscore a fateful thread that runs through German classical tragedy. For all its apparent influence – German editions of the *Poetics* would for years to come continue to substitute *Schrecken* with *Furcht*, on Lessing's authority – Lessing's substitution and reversal are unable to expel terror. From the repression – or abjection – of terror in Lessing, through its aesthetic formalization in Goethe and Schiller, to the profound terror-related representations and meditations in Kleist and Büchner, it is terror that presents itself as a crux for tragedy and aesthetic thought. With sufficient abstraction it becomes possible at times to glimpse the rudiments of a theater of cruelty already at work in German classical tragedy. Such abstraction, however, should not delude us about pressing horrors contemporary with the authors under consideration. For Lessing, it was the Seven Years War that showed him the face of terror. For Goethe, Schiller, Kleist, and Büchner it was terror itself – the *Terreur* of the French Revolution – that stared them in the face and would not go away.

Lessing and the Theater of Sympathy

Lessing came onto the theatrical scene in Berlin as a young man, in 1749. Like the German nation – fragmented and scattered within the dissolving Holy Roman Empire, a fond idea without reality – the German theater was in a desultory state. Perched between two or more conceptions of theater – the court-sponsored theater of royalty and the rising bourgeois theater associated with urban centers, not to mention itinerant theater and puppet troupes – the most recent attempt at reform, oriented to the imitation of French theater associated with the playwright Gottsched and theater director Christiane Neuber, struck Lessing as a cultural and national disaster. Gottsched's error lay in a misinterpretation of the German national character – not the French, but rather the British, Shakespeare in particular, were the appropriate models for emulation and appropriation. "Das Große, das Schreckliche, das Melancholische, [wirkt] besser auf uns als das Artige, das Zärtliche, das Verliebte" (Lessing 2003: 2.624; the magnificent, the terrifying, the melancholy affect us more than the polite, the delicate, and the lovelorn). He famously concludes his condemnation of Gottsched with the prophetic promise of a German Faust. Though Lessing does not deliver, Goethe will.

Lessing's theatrical interventions amount to a handful of both well-known and all but forgotten tragedies and comedies, a lively and significant three-way exchange of letters about tragedy conducted with Moses Mendelssohn and Friedrich Nicolai in 1757 (Lessing et al. 1972), the translation into German of Diderot's essays on theater, and a considerable amount of reflective theater journalism (the *Hamburgische Dramaturgie*), written over a period of one year (1767–8), when he was the dramaturge of the publicly funded National Theater of Hamburg, the latest, unsuccessful attempt to give the nonexistent nation a nonexistent theater. In all of these interventions we readily identify a lively, polemical intelligence, hugely dedicated to the theater, with a remarkable erudition in European drama, past and present.

Lessing was the first to move German audiences to tears with a bourgeois tragedy of Aristotelian proportions, *Miss Sara Sampson* (1755) – the title alone reveals its English provenance. Sara has been seduced by Lord Mellefont and resides with him in a hotel. Realizing that he has lost the succor of his old age, her father resolves to forgive her, despite moral reservations. A conspiring former lover, Lady Marwood, tracks down Mellefont, hoping through a battery of stratagems to win him back. In the process, a wavering Mellefont decides in favor of bourgeois marriage, a reluctant Sara accepts her father's forgiveness, and an increasingly enraged Marwood grasps a last opportunity at revenge: having revealed the existence of her illegitimate daughter by Mellefont to Sara only to find her disposed to accept the child, Marwood resorts to poison. Sara dies a painful and protracted death (almost ten pages in length), explicitly referenced in terms of *Schrecken*, and orchestrated to achieve a maximum tearful effect. Her efforts to contain the waves of pain are heroic; failing to suppress the grimaces of pain, she covers her face with her hand. Mellefont stands in for the audience and finds himself confronted with a female Laocoön: "Warum verbirgt mir diese neidische Hand (*indem er sie wegnimmt*) so holde Blicke? – Ach es sind Mienen, die den grausamsten Schmerz, aber ungern, verraten! – Und doch ist die Hand neidisch, die mir diese Mienen verbergen will. Soll ich Ihre Schmerzen nicht mit fühlen, Miß?" (Lessing 2003: 1.378; Why does this envious hand (*as he removes it*) conceal such fair glances from me? – Oh, these are expressions that reluctantly betray the most horrible pain! And yet is this hand envious that desires to conceal these expressions. Should I not feel your pains with you, Miss?). As she finally expires, Mellefont grasps a dagger and fatally stabs himself.

The twenty-first-century reader of *Miss Sara Sampson* is necessarily struck by the tragedy's almost Jamesian prolixity. Affects suffered by the characters are described or self-described in minute detail – no main character, not even Marwood, fails to shed tears. These affects correspond precisely to those the tragedy is bent on arousing in the audience: tears of sympathy, fear, and terror. Indeed, through the actualization of theoretical terms in the play's discourse, *Miss Sara Sampson* doubles as a meta-text, a text about itself as an instance of bourgeois theater understood as theater of cruelty. We encounter the discourse of torture on the first page: Sara's father asks his servant to refrain from memories that martyr and rip him apart (*zerfleischen*). His point of vulnerability – and this obtains for all the characters – is his imagination. As Sara says at another point: "Diese eingebildete Qualen [sind] doch Qualen, und für die, die sie empfindet, wirklich Qualen" (Lessing 2003: 1.307; imagined torments are still torments, and for her, who feels them, really torments). To the extent that these imagined torments correspond to the audience's apprehension of the play, the audience is assumed to be affected mimetically.

A *mise-en-abyme* at the conclusion of the second act discloses the calculated, physiology-based logic of Lessing's tragic practice. Marwood has just revealed the depths of her malice to Mellefont: "Sieh in mir eine neue Medea!" (Behold in me a new Medea!) – thus referencing the terrifying renewal of Greek tragedy in bourgeois guise. She then minutely fantasizes the manner in which she would torture Mellefont and their common child:

> Durch langsame Martern will ich in seinem Gesichte jeden ähnlichen Zug, den es von dir hat, sich verstellen, verzerren und verschwinden sehen. Ich will mit begieriger Hand Glied von Glied, Ader von Ader, Nerve von Nerve lösen, und das kleinste derselben auch da noch nicht aufhören zu schneiden und zu brennen, wenn es schon nichts mehr sein wird, als ein Empfindungsloses Aas. (Lessing 2003: 1.329)
> [Through slow torture I will rearrange, distort and eradicate every feature that she has from you. With eager hand I will separate limb from limb, artery from artery, nerve from nerve, and will not cease to cut and burn even the smallest of these when she will have been reduced to no more than an insensitive carrion.]

When Mendelssohn objected to the excess of this passage, Lessing responded instructively: Had he intended only to strain the actress's abilities to their limit, he would have stopped with "verstellen, verzerren und verschwinden" (Lessing 1757). However, since he wanted to achieve certain exquisite effects of rage in her face that were beyond her control, he went a step further and attempted to arouse her imagination through sensate images. In other words, he deliberately sought to torture her imagination in order to produce desired effects in and on her body. Who is the torturer now? And how does this square with Lessing's stated commitment to a theater of sympathy?

Tragedy, in Lessing's considered opinion, should improve its audience. For all his theatrical innovation, Lessing remained an Enlightenment conservative in this regard. The vehicle for the moral betterment of his audience was sympathy: "*Der mitleidigste Mensch ist der beste Mensch*, zu allen gesellschaftlichen Tugenden, zu allen Arten der Großmuth der aufgelegteste" (Lessing et al. 1972: 55, emphasis in original; The most sympathizing person is the best person, most disposed to all social virtues, to all manner of generosity). Tragedy is the best means to practice sympathy (Lessing et al. 1972: 80; *Mitleiden üben*). The transformation of a theater of cruelty into a theater of sympathy is explained with reference to a physical phenomenon. Lessing asks us to consider two equally taut strings (Lessing et al. 1972: 102–3). One of them is plucked (*berührt*) – and such plucking may be imagined as painful. The second vibrates sympathetically (*bebt*) without having been painfully plucked. Transfer the situation to the theater and we have an actress who suffers a painful affect and an audience who is mimetically and pleasantly moved, but without the pain. This painless affect, predicated on the pain or representation of pain of another, is best defined as sympathy. In this way Lessing as playwright is licensed to practice an almost Sadean torture on stage, confident of its beneficial effects on a morally improving audience.

Lessing's next major tragedy, *Emilia Galotti* (1772), repeats the father/daughter constellation. Pitting rural, domestic virtue against courtly desire and lust, Lessing interrupts an imminent marriage by having the Prince and his conniving courtier murder the fiancé and waylay Emilia at the Prince's *Lustschloβ* (pleasure palace) for his delectation. Although the constellations in many respects are similar to *Sara Sampson* – we readily identify Marwood's counterpart in the jilted Lady Orsina – *Emilia Galotti*'s distinction is to have brought sexual desire as a force of terror onto the stage. Sexual desire not only motivates the Prince's machinations, but also Orsina's terrifying rage, and, finally, even the bizarre murder/suicide of Emilia at her father's hands. Referring to her blood and senses as metonyms of her sexual desire, despite her moral resolve, she challenges her father to repeat the classical murder of Virginia who rather died than become the plaything of a tyrant. In an incestuous *tableau vivant*, he obliges, with the dagger originally intended for the Prince, and she dies kissing his hand.

Goethe, Schiller, and the Containment of Terror

Fast on the heels of Lessing, a younger generation of playwrights briefly takes the theater by storm. Known as the *Sturm und Drang* (storm and stress), a handful of brash young writers around Goethe took up Lessing's challenge and upped the ante. Reveling in the apparent dramatic freedom appropriation of Shakespearean theater afforded them, they assaulted the audience with unheard of and unseen representations of sexual desire. The most infamous instance of what Peter Handke would later term *Publikumsbeschimpfung* (insulting the audience) occurs in Goethe's *Götz von Berlichingen* (1773). The audience sees Götz, a free knight at odds with the new rational administration of the Empire, at a window, responding to an official summons. Goethe expressly mutes the offstage messenger, so that the audience hears (and sees) only Götz's response: "Sag deinem Hauptmann: Vor Ihro Kaiserliche Majestät hab ich wie immer, schuldigen Respekt. Er aber, sag's ihm, er kann mich am Arsch lecken (*Schmeiβt das Fenster zu*)" (FA 4.349; Tell your captain: for his majesty the emperor I have as always due respect. But as for him – tell him – he can kiss my ass [*Slams the window shut*]). This scene is an emblem of the storm and stress play's confrontation with the audience. Moral improvement is still on the agenda, but through an in-your-face encounter with sexual desire and the body. No one pressed the limits more than Jakob Michael Reinhold Lenz (1751–92). In a bizarre comedy of tragic proportions, *Der Hofmeister* (The private tutor, 1774) sexuality and the discipline designed to repress it jointly produce the circumstances under which the tutor decides to castrate himself as a last, and finally unsuccessful resort to bring his sexual desire under control. For all their youthfulness, and their staging of sexuality in coarse language, the storm and stress playwrights are strangely melancholic, convinced that human (and sexual) desire stands in irresolvable and terrifying conflict with society. The play that gives the movement its name, Friedrich Maximilian Klinger's *Sturm und Drang* (1777), is marked by a dreamy aimlessness that anticipates the anticlassical response of Kleist, Büchner, and Goethe himself, even as it pays early homage to Calderón's *La Vida es sueño* (Life is a dream).

At this point we must leap over several intermediate tragedies by Goethe and Schiller (e.g., the latter's *Don Carlos*, 1787, and the former's *Egmont*, 1788, both of which set a vision of human politics – the idea of the Dutch Republic – in tragic opposition to the terror of the Inquisition), in order to arrive at the classical tragedy of their "classical" period. Separate trajectories bring Goethe and Schiller together in 1794. While Goethe basks in the afterglow of his extended Italian sojourn (1786–8), convinced that he has gained access to an immediacy of life, experience, and perception, Schiller negotiates a position vis-à-vis Kant's critical philosophy with specific reference to tragedy and its effects. In a series of essays based on lectures he gave at the University of Jena,[4] Schiller appropriates Kant's concept of the sublime to explain tragedy in terms of the triumphant resistance of the moral aspect of humanity as it withstands the onslaught of terror understood as the infliction of life-threatening, corporeal pain. Revising Lessing, Schiller readmits *Schrecken*, indeed requires terror, in order to assure the optimal quality of tragic resistance and to prevent descent into sentimentality in the form of easy tears. Schiller recognizes and responds to the terror-bound core of Lessing's plays – the Marwoods and Orsinas, the barely submerged Medeas, Medusas, and bacchants – while rejecting the sentimentality associated with a poetics of sympathy. Aspects of the bourgeois tragedy are retained, specifically the dynamics of the intimate family, but an elevated tone is sought by the use of blank verse and a return to courtly settings. Despite these modifications, Schiller's concept of tragedy continues to operate within a moral register, involving the opposition of two contradictory forces (pain and the superior will of the hero), essentially continuous with Winckelmann's description of the Laocoön.

It is the encounter with Goethe that changes all that. From this point on, Schiller and Goethe jointly develop a third, mediating instance between these two forces. Containment of pain (of *Schrecken*) continues to be the focus, but the responsibility for doing this is shifted from the hero and what s/he represents (will, reason, virtue) to art itself. A thoroughgoing concept of aesthetic autonomy, some fifty years in the making (from Baumgarten, over Mendelssohn and Kant, to Schiller), attains its full expression here. In his *Briefe über die Aesthetische Erziehung* (Letters on aesthetic education, 1795), Schiller theorizes this third instance in terms of what he calls the *Spieltrieb* ("play drive"). Although he seems to understand this drive primarily in psychological and anthropological terms, there is nothing to prevent us from acknowledging the second meaning of play, i.e., drama, especially since the play, i.e., theatrical practice, would prove to be a crucial part of the project of Weimar Classicism (Brown 2004). In other words, containment is accomplished aesthetically within the work itself. The work becomes a virtual, self-sufficient world in its own right, a place that sustains the free play of the imagination. It no longer desires to affect the audience, to arouse feelings of sympathy and fear. It is divested of its moral office. As Schiller reads Aristotle's *Poetics* for the first time in 1797, he ignores the definition of tragedy and the concept of catharsis. Instead, he writes in a letter to Goethe, "Daß er bei der Tragödie das Hauptgewicht in die Verknüpfung der Begebenheiten legt, heißt den Nagel auf den Kopf getroffen" (May 5, 1797: 389; that in relation to tragedy he places the main emphasis on the knotting together of the occurrences which means hitting the nail on the head). In subsequent years, Goethe would restate their core insight more provocatively. In a short essay entitled "Nachlese zu Aristoteles' Poetik" (A gleaning from Aristotle's *Poetics*, 1827), he returns to Aristotle's key definition, but paraphrases it in such a fashion as to be consistent with notions of aesthetic autonomy: Tragedy is an imitation of an action "[die] nach einem Verlauf aber von Mitleid und Furcht mit Ausgleichung solcher Leidenschaften ihr Geschäft abschließt" (1962: 10.581; that after a course of sympathy and fear concludes its business with a balancing-out of such passions). For Aristotle, Goethe writes, catharsis "ist diese aussöhnende Abrundung, welche eigentlich von allem Drama, ja sogar von allen poetischen Werken gefordert wird" (1962: 10.583; is this reconciling rounding off), a formal balance, achieved by formal means. As for the spectator: "Die Verwicklung wird ihn verwirren, die Auflösung aufklären, er aber um nichts gebessert nach Hause gehen" (1962: 10.584; The complications will confuse him, the solution enlighten him, he will, however, go home unimproved in any regard). Catharsis and the terror or fear that promote it are strictly formal affairs.

Seen in this light, the various tragedies Goethe and Schiller wrote during the period of their mutual friendship may be seen as a series of formal experiments – the word should remind us once again of Albrecht von Haller and his laboratory. While Schiller tries his hand at a range of subjects drawn from history and legend (*Maria Stuart*, *Wallenstein* [a general in the Thirty Years War], *Wilhelm Tell*, and *Die Jungfrau von Orleans* [The maid of Orléans], concluding with the *Braut von Messina*, Goethe is more interested in epic forms – the novel *Wilhelm Meisters Lehrjahre* (Wilhelm Meisters' apprenticeship, 1795 /6) – as well as epic poems in a Homeric style (e.g., *Herrmann und Dorothea*, 1797). Only two tragedies from this period achieve a condition resembling completion: *Die Natürliche Tochter* (The natural/bastard daughter, 1804), the first play of a trilogy which was never completed, and *Faust, Part I*, explicitly, though very problematically, not to say provocatively, subtitled *Eine deutsche Tragödie*, and not published until 1808. Since Goethe would continue to work on *Faust* until shortly before his death in 1832, I shall reserve my comments for below. As for *Die Natürliche Tochter*, a *Trauerspiel* of an almost allegorical nature, set against the background of the French Revolution as a figure of terror, this is a play in which Goethe, as so often, experiments with the limits of genre. Eugenie is a young noblewoman suddenly bereft of her father and any other protection within a milieu of brutal court intrigue. Her tragic fate is to choose between certain death and marriage to an upright bourgeois city counselor. After a protracted rhetorical skirmish, she resigns to the latter. Her final words – "Hier meine Hand: wir gehen zum Altar" (MA 6.393; Here, my hand: we'll go to the altar) – recalling the happy resolution of comedy, ring ominously as we realize that the altar also figures the place of tragic and ritual sacrifice. In this sense, *Die Natürliche Tochter* is the inverse mirror image of Goethe's earlier *Iphigenie auf Tauris*, whose story begins with an altar and ends (happily) with the refusal of marriage.

While Goethe's versions of terror are subtle,[5] Schiller allows his imagination to run loose. In *Maria Stuart*, he stages a magnificent scene in which Maria's offstage execution is represented through the traitorous and double-dealing Leicester, who is assailed by its sounds. Initially intending to observe her death, steeling himself by quashing any vestige of *Mitleid*, he is overcome by the thought of seeing "das Schreckliche" and unsuccessfully seeks an exit from this "Haus des Schreckens und des Todes!" ("house of terror and death"). He reports each noise as though it has assaulted his body, collapsing on the stage "mit einer zuckenden Bewegung" (with a convulsive movement) as the fatal blow strikes (Schiller FA: 5.141). In *Wilhelm Tell*, only peripherally a tragedy, the eponymous hero is spared tragic blame for the cold-blooded assassination of a representative of tyranny by the introduction of a true tragic figure, the entirely marginal Parracida, a role that seems to stray onto the stage from another set. However, terror is evoked in association with the legendary apple shot and once again thematized in terms of seeing and not seeing. As the trembling Tell prepares to shoot the apple from his son's head, a heated conversation between the tyrant and a mutinous soldier distracts and obstructs our gaze and substitutes for the shot we fail to see. In *Die Braut von Messina*, Schiller represents and contains terror with the chorus he has anachronistically reintroduced. As the incestuously motivated fratricide is revealed to the perpetrator and his sister, the chorus confronts the terror in ritual and purgative song: "Brechet auf ihr Wunden! / Fließet, fließet! / In schwarzen Güssen / Strömet hervor ihr Bäche des Bluts!" (FA 5.370; Break open, you wounds! / Flow, flow! / In black gushes, / flow forth, you rivers of blood!"). Schiller self-consciously stages the catharsis in physiological terms. In every instance unabashed terror is admitted, but contained: mediated, obstructed, transformed into song.

Kleist, Büchner, Goethe, and the End of German Classical Tragedy

The fantasy of the aesthetic containment of rampant terror and pain within a classicizing program could not be maintained. Goethe's restrained and harmoniously poised tragic heroines in particular, his Iphigenie and Eugenie, seemed to invite, rather than ward off further assault. A lack of credibility set in. One of the most telling challenges to Goethe's vision with respect to tragedy came from Heinrich von Kleist (1777–1811). His *Penthesilea* amounts to a programmatic assault on Goethe and Schiller's classical aesthetics of tragedy. Penthesilea is an Amazon queen who unaccountably leads her Amazon warriors in battle against Greek and Trojan alike. Soon, it appears, she has singled out Achilles for a murderous/erotic encounter. His manly interest piqued, Achilles sidelines Homer and the Trojan War in order to learn more. A series of combative trysts leads to a final misunderstanding and a confrontation in which a meek and defenseless Achilles is ripped apart and cannibalized by Penthesilea and her dogs. When, later, Penthesilea emerges from mute stupor and slowly comes to realize what terror she unleashed on Achilles' body, she confesses that she merely "misspoke": "So war es ein Versehen. Küsse, Bisse, / Das reimt sich, und wer recht von Herzen liebt, / Kann schon das eine für das andre greifen" (Kleist 1987:

1.425; So it was a mistake. A kiss, a bite, / The two should rhyme, for one who truly loves / With all her heart can easily mistake them). Taking Achilles' severed head in her hands, she asks his forgiveness: "Ich habe mich, bei Diana, bloß versprochen, / Weil ich der raschen Lippe Herr nicht bin" (Kleist 1987: 1.426; By Artemis, my tongue pronounced one word / For sheer unbridled haste to say another). With Achilles' dismembered classical body, not to mention Homer's and Goethe's texts in tatters, *Penthesilea* introduces a new tragic language that calls into question the distinction between words and deeds. Terror infects language, renders it into an instrument of terror's own realization. The play's conclusion bears this out. Fearing her suicide, her friend has stripped her of her weapons. Penthesilea unfolds an elaborate metaphor comparing her breast to a smithy, where she forges a dagger with which she stabs herself and falls dead to the ground. Kleist has a High Priestess utter summary words from the Greek classical tradition that vainly attempt to contain the horror that has been witnessed. These are trumped, however, by Prothoe's rejoinder and the final words of the play: "Sie sank, weil sie zu stolz und kräftig blühte! / Die abgestorbene Eiche steht im Sturm, / Doch die gesunde stürzt er schmetternd nieder, Weil er in ihre Krone greifen kann" (Kleist 1987: 1.428; Because she flowered with too much pride and spirit, / She fell. The dead oak stands against the storm, / The healthy one he topples with a crash / Because his grasp can reach into its crown). Storm and tree correspond to the hero and the snakes of Winckelmann's description of the Laocoön – two unmediated forces in extreme opposition with only one possible result.

If *Penthesilea* marks the end of German classical tragedy and the triumph of terror, Kleist's last play, *Prinz Friedrich von Homburg* (1807), as well as Georg Büchner's *Dantons Tod* (Danton's death, 1834), amount to meditative, even melancholic responses to terror and a return to anticlassical, baroque modes of tragedy and theatrical representation. Kleist's *Friedrich* returns to Calderonian principles of symmetry and dream. In a wonderful play of contingencies, Kleist has his Prussian prince, whose love-inspired distractedness caused him to disobey orders and therefore win the decisive battle, placed in a position where he must loyally accept his own execution. As, blindfolded, he awaits the fatal blow, he is suddenly asked to rise. Reassured that he will not face anything that would terrorize him (Kleist 1987: 1.708; "Nichts, das dich erschrecken dürfte"), he is suddenly confronted with his sovereign who not only awards him with a medal and wreath, but presents him with his daughter. The scene repeats the bizarre sleepwalking scene of the first act and Friedrich falls unconscious to the ground. "Die Freude tötet ihn" (The joy is killing him). Whisked off and into further battle, he asks, "Ist es ein Traum?" (Is this a dream?), to which the response is: "Ein Traum, was sonst?" (A dream, what else?). The dream, with its own logic, and *not* the mimetic representation of terror and its overcoming through voluntary or aesthetic means, becomes the preferred and necessary mode.

Büchner's *Dantons Tod* deals directly with the Terror. All pretense of action, of containment, of strategic effect on a sensitive audience is abandoned. The theatrical and aesthetic universe is reorganized. The Revolution and Terror take the stage. The basic opposition of terror and virtue that structured the bourgeois tragic drama has been compromised. Terror and virtue are now aligned – as Robespierre says: "Der Schrecken ist ein Ausfluß der Tugend, er ist nichts anders als die schnelle, strenge und unbeugsame Gerechtigkeit" (Büchner 1984: 16; Terror is an extension of virtue; it is nothing other than swift, stern and unbendable justice). Danton and the other protagonists of the play are idle, hapless, prolix fodder for the guillotine and the appetite of the people. Penthesilea's isolated cannibalism has been generalized: "Unsere Weiber und Kinder schreien nach Brot, wir wollen sie mit Aristokraten- fleisch füttern" (Büchner 1984: 13; Our women and children cry for bread, we'll feed them with the flesh of aristocrats), calls one citizen. All that remains is to wait for death.

> Wie lange soll die Menschheit im ewigen Hunger ihre eignen Glieder fressen? oder, wie lange sollen wir Schiffbrüchige auf einem Wrack in unlöschbarem Durst einander das Blut aus den Adern saugen? oder, wie lange sollen wir Algebraisten im Fleisch beim Suchen nach dem Unbekannten, ewig verweigerten X unsere Rechnungen mit zerfetz- ten Gliedern schreiben? (Büchner 1984: 29) [How long shall humanity consume its own limbs in eternal hunger? Or, how long shall we shipwrecked sailors suck the blood from each other's veins in unquenchable thirst? Or, how shall we algebraists inscribe our calculations into our flesh with dismembered limbs in our search for the eternally denied unknown x?].

The repetition of ineffectual words and the repetition of the guillotine remain as one and the same possibility. As a student of medicine whose published work includes essays on anatomy and physiology, Büchner returns us to Haller's laboratory and the practice of vivisection.[6] Distinctions, however, no longer matter. There is only terror and pain.

Although Goethe died two years before Büchner completed *Dantons Tod*, and famously misjudged Kleist, his post-classical efforts in connection with theater confirm that he shared Kleist's and Büchner's assessment to a considerable degree. In fact, after Schiller's death, Goethe wrote no significant tragedy or play, except for the second part of *Faust*. Puzzlingly subtitled "A German tragedy" and begun in his *Sturm und Drang* days, *Faust, Part One* does contain a bourgeois tragedy – the so-called Gretchen story – but not as its main feature, despite common perceptions to the contrary. A succession of highly self-reflexive frames seems to enclose the Gretchen story, except that even this story is interrupted to become a frame to the Walpurgis Night, a scene of demonic revelry that thematizes constant deviation from any linear path and winds up, finally, at a small theater where Faust and Mephistopheles take in an entirely unmotivated amateur masque in lieu of the apotheosis of Satan Goethe had originally planned. If this is not enough, the tragic heroine of part one is declared saved, just as Faust himself at the conclusion of the cosmos-embracing part two will likewise be saved. If there is anything classical (and tragic) about Goethe's *Faust*, it is the desire of the main character. Summarized in a wager made with Mephistopheles (and not a pact), what Faust desires is a kind of corporeal perfection, a contingent moment in time so shot through with the qualities of the absolute and eternal as to be entirely beautiful and self-complete – we sense the presence of the doctrine of aesthetic autonomy. But this wager is framed within the play of illusions and every scene of *Faust* rings with artifice, self-consciousness, and, increasingly, an almost operatic excess. When Faust dies in old age he is blinded, somewhat like the young Friedrich in Kleist's play, and savors a vision of utopian government and mastery over nature, while, in fact, he stands in front of his grave. He appears to utter the fateful words that confer possession of his soul on Mephistopheles, but the statement and circumstances are so riddled with ironies and contingencies that Mephistopheles' claim is not ironclad. As Mephistopheles is distracted by the sensuous form of dancing angelic posteriors, Faust's soul is wordlessly whisked toward the heavens and the eternal feminine.

Goethe may have subtitled his play "A German tragedy" – the fact of the matter is that *Faust*, as Jane Brown has repeatedly and brilliantly argued, is world theater, and, as such, thoroughly non-illusionist.[7] This is *Trauerspiel* in its most profound and philosophical form. Calderón and a certain Baroque disposition stand as warrants for this new kind of tragedy. The terror of modernity, its effects on body, soul, and nation, call for a different response than Lessing initially imagined. The cry of terror has to be staged. From Büchner, Kleist, and the late Goethe to the great twentieth-century innovators of tragic theater in Germany (Wedekind, Brecht, and Heiner Müller), German tragedy will never be the same.

Notes

I would like to acknowledge my intellectual debt to two scholars who have devoted much of their career to thinking about German classical drama: Jane K. Brown, whose work on Goethe's *Faust* has shaped my own, and Benjamin K. Bennett, whose *Modern Drama and German Classicism: Renaissance from Lessing to Brecht* (Ithaca: Cornell University Press, 1979) was in the back of my mind as I wrote this essay. All translations, unless otherwise indicated, are my own.

1 For much of the nineteenth century and well into the twentieth, "German classicism" was unquestioningly and nationalistically applied to the same historical span, conveniently mapped onto Goethe's birth (1749) and death (1832), essentially comprising the literary accomplishments of Lessing, Goethe, and Schiller as world-class authors, while exclud-

ing the Romantics and others (including Kleist and Büchner). The problem, of course, is that the German romantics (August and Friedrich Schlegel, Ludwig Tieck, and E. T. A. Hoffmann, to name a few) were active from at least 1798 on. The hesitation to include the romantics in German classicism derived from the circumstance that, for all concerned, classicism (more narrowly conceived) and romanticism were understood to be opposed terms. Reluctant to forfeit Germany's apparently sole opportunity to lay claim to the status of "classical," and wanting to preserve the classicism/romanticism distinction at the same time, German literary historians gave Lessing back to the Enlightenment, identified pre-classical periods in Goethe and Schiller's output (e.g., *Sturm und Drang*), and staked out a period confined both temporally (beginning with Goethe's Italian journey in 1876 and ending with Schiller's death in 1805) and geographically (to the small town of Weimar, where Goethe and later Schiller resided). Known as Weimar classicism to Germans and Germanists, this reduced claim now strikes most literary historians as even more preposterous. Not only are the Jena romantics and idealist philosophers (Fichte, Schelling, etc.) just a few kilometers down the road, but Goethe and Schiller's "classical" efforts are perfectly consistent with and even exemplary of the broader and far more legitimate phenomenon of European romanticism.

2   For an intelligent account of this rare event, see Hamlin (2002).

3   There are two periods of intense preoccupation with Aristotle: the correspondence with Mendelssohn and Nicolai about tragedy in 1756–7 and again in the *Hamburgische Dramaturgie* in 1768. The former can be found in Lessing et al. (1972). For the latter see any edition or trans-

lation of the *Hamburgische Dramaturgie*, specifically sections 74–83. For the clearest account of Lessing's mistranslations and misunderstandings and their consequences, see Schadewaldt (1966).

4   Among the essays are "Über den Grund des Vergnügens an tragischen Gegenständen" (On the basis for pleasure in relation to tragic objects, 1792), "Vom Erhabenen" (Of the sublime, 1793), and "Über das Pathetische" (On the pathetic, 1793).

5   Goethe has sometimes been accused of avoiding tragedy. For a version of this argument, see Heller (1957). A subtle rejoinder to this assertion can be found in Szondi (2002: 25–7).

6   For a thoughtful account of the connections between his medical and literary work, see Müller-Sievers (2003).

7   The finest introduction to Goethe's *Faust* is Brown (2002). For those interested in a more substantial engagement, I recommend Brown (1986).

REFERENCES AND FURTHER READING

Baumgarten, A. G. (1983). *Texte zur Grundlegung der Ästhetik*. Hamburg: Meiner.

Brown, J. K. (1986). *Goethe's* Faust: *The German Tragedy*. Ithaca, NY: Cornell University Press.

Brown, J. K. (2002). "*Faust*." In *The Cambridge Companion to Goethe*, ed. L. Sharpe. Cambridge: Cambridge University Press, 84–100.

Brown, J. K. (2004). "Drama and Theatrical Practice in Classical Weimar." In *The Literature of Weimar Classicism*, ed. S. Richter. Camden House History of German Literature, 10 vols. Rochester, NY: Camden House, vol. 7.

Büchner, G. (1984). *Werke und Briefe*. Munich: Deutscher Taschenbuch Verlag.

Goethe, J. W. von. (1962). *Werke*, 10 vols. Zurich and Stuttgart: Artemis.

Goethe, J. W. von. (1985–98) *Sämtliche Werke* (Frankfurt edition, hereafter FA), 40 vols. Frankfurt am Main: Deutscher Klassiker Verlag.

Goethe, J. W. von. (1985–98). *Sämtliche Werke* (Munich edition, hereafter MA), 21 vols. Munich: Carl Hanser Verlag.

Gustafson, S. (1995). *Absent Mothers and Orphaned Fathers: Narcissism and Abjection in Lessing's Aesthetic and Dramatic Production*. Detroit, MI: Wayne State University Press.

Haller, A. von. (1922). *Von den empfindlichen und reizbaren Teilen des Menschlichen Körpers* [On the sensitive and irritable parts of the human body]. Leipzig: Johann Ambrosius Barth.

Hamlin, C. (2002). "Faust in Performance: Peter Stein's Production of *Faust, Parts 1 and 2*." *Theater* 32, 117–36.

Heller, E. (1957). "Goethe and the Avoidance of Tragedy." In *The Disinherited Mind: Essays in Modern German Literature and Thought*. New York: Farrar, Straus, & Cudahy, 37–63.

Kleist, H. von. (1987). *Sämtliche Werke und Briefe*, 2 vols., ed. Helmut Sembdner. Munich: Deutscher Taschenbuch Verlag.

Lessing, G. E. (1757). Letter to Moses Mendelssohn, September 14.

Lessing, G. E. (1984). *Laocoön: An Essay on the Limits of Painting and Poetry*, trans. E. A. McCormick. Baltimore, MD: Johns Hopkins University Press.

Lessing, G. E. (2003). *Werke in drei Bänden* [Works in three volumes]. Munich, Deutscher Taschenbuch Verlag.

Lessing, G. E. et al. (1972) *Mendelssohn, Nicolai: Briefwechsel über das Trauerspiel*, ed. J. Schulte-Sasse. Munich: Winkler.

Mendelssohn, M. (1974). *Ästhetische Schriften in Auswahl*, ed. Otto F. Best. Darmstadt: Wissenschaftliche Buchgesellschaft.

Müller-Sievers, H. (2003). *Desorientierung: Anatomie und Dichtung bei Georg Büchner* [Disorientation: anatomy and poetry in Georg Büchner]. Göttingen: Wallstein Verlag.

Schadewaldt, W. (1966). Furcht und Mitleid [Fear and sympathy]. *Antike und Gegenwart: Über die Tragödie* [Antiquity and the present: on tragedy]. Munich: Deutscher Taschenbuch Verlag, 16–60.

Schiller, F. (1943–). *Werke* (National Edition, hereafter NA), 42 vols. Weimar: Hermann Böhlaus Nachfolger.

Schiller, F. (1988). *Werke und Briefe*, 12 vols. Frankfurt am Main: Deutscher Klassiker Verlag.

Szondi, P. (2002). *An Essay on the Tragic*, trans. P. Fleming. Stanford, CA: Stanford University Press.

Winckelmann, J. J. [1755] (1982). *Gedanken über die Nachahmung der griechischen Werke der Malerei und Bildhauerkunst* [Reflections on the imitation of Greek works of painting and sculpture]. Stuttgart: Reclam.

Winckelmann, J. J. (1987). *Reflections on the Imitation of Greek Works in Painting and Sculpture*, trans. E. Heyer and R. C. Norton. La Salle, IL: Open Court.

25

French Romantic Tragedy

Barbara T. Cooper

In the highly charged and frequently unstable political and social environment of post-Revolutionary France, the definition of tragic drama, like so many of the fundamental values and cultural practices of earlier times, came under question. Institutional authority, aesthetic conventions, and the towering achievements of authors such as Corneille and Racine no longer held universal sway over the genre – if, indeed, they ever had. Playwrights and literary theorists, government officials, elite and popular audiences, performers and theater managers all participated, to varying degrees and in various ways, in the search for the forms and subjects of tragedy best suited to a new, post-providential age. Their productions and pamphlets, edicts, and individual responses did not lead to a broadly shared understanding of the shape and substance of tragic drama, however. Instead, melodrama, neoclassical tragedy, and romantic drama, each proposing a different vision and expression of the tragic experience in the modern world, existed side by side.

In fact, the genealogy and character of French romantic tragedy are vastly more complex than is generally recognized. Some of the elements that would lead to its birth were already present in the eighteenth century. These include the introduction of national historical subject matter by such playwrights as Voltaire (e.g., *Adélaïde du Guesclin*, 1734) and Marie-Joseph Chénier (e.g., *Charles IX, ou l'Ecole des Rois*, 1789), and the development of bourgeois tragedy conceived and illustrated by Diderot in *Le Fils naturel* and the *Entretiens sur "Le Fils naturel"* (Conversations about *Le Fils naturel*, 1757) and by Beaumarchais in his *Essai sur le genre dramatique sérieux* (Essay on serious drama, 1767) that served as a preface to his play, *Eugénie*. Both Diderot and Beaumarchais called for the use of prose rather than verse, emphasized the role of sentiment and tableaux in appealing to audiences, and focused on their protagonists' character (morality, virtue, personality). It was not until the beginning of the nineteenth century, however, that a new sense of the role of history and society in human destiny, a new understanding of the importance of individual genius, ambition (as opposed to rank and privilege), and temperament, and a new regard for the dramatic works of Shakespeare, Schiller, and other European playwrights would create the conditions that would lead to the birth of romantic tragedy in France.[1]

Early French Neoclassical Drama: Lemercier and Pixérécourt

Some of the first signs of that transition are clearly discernible in the theatrical compositions of Louis-Jean-Népomucène Lemercier. One of Lemercier's earliest works, *Agamemnon* (1797), is a traditional neoclassical tragedy both by virtue of its form and its subject matter. Written in alexandrine verse, with the limited range of vocabulary, periphrastic style, and a concern for propriety (*bienséances*) typical of the genre since the seventeenth century, the play respected the unities of time, place, and action and had only a handful of aristocratic protagonists. The universal and eternal nature of the story was highlighted rather than any particular elements of local color, whether defined in terms of customs, costumes, or sets. In performance, its blocking, gestures, and declamation were all highly stylized and might be likened to the hieratic world depicted in Jacques-Louis David's painting *The Oath of the Horatii* (1784).

Lemercier's adherence to the tenets of French neoclassicism was far less apparent in a work that premiered in 1800: *Pinto, ou La Journée d'une conspiration* (Pinto, or the day of a conspiracy). The piece, which Lemercier saw as the foundation of a new dramatic genre – historical comedy – was written in prose instead of verse. Rather than being drawn from the annals of ancient or biblical history or legend, the story was set in "modern" Portugal (modern designating any era from the Middle Ages on) and described the efforts of the titular character, a commoner who is secretary to the Duc de Bragance, to liberate his country from Spanish occupation. Seconded by a socially diverse and colorful cast of characters, Pinto does in fact succeed in reestablishing the Duc as the legitimate ruler of Portugal. What is more, designated prime minister at the play's conclusion, Pinto is in a position to determine the course of the nation's future. This attribution of political agency to a person of ordinary birth was unusual outside of the propaganda pieces written during the Revolution and seems to anticipate such romantic tragedies as Victor Hugo's *Ruy Blas* (1838), albeit with a more positive outcome.

Despite *Pinto*'s designation as a comedy, Stendhal – an important theorist of French romantic drama – would later write, in his essay *Racine et Shakespeare* (1823–5), that "Notre tragédie nouvelle ressemblera beaucoup à *Pinto*, le chef-d'œuvre de M. Lemercier" ([1823–5] 1970: 75; Our new [romantic] tragedy will be very much like Lemercier's masterpiece, *Pinto*). Lemercier's play appealed to Stendhal as a model for romantic tragedy for several reasons. In *Racine et Shakespeare*, Stendhal rejects alexandrine verse as a vehicle for dramatic expression because it calls attention to itself and to the beauty of language rather than allowing for the realistic and straightforward representation of ideas and actions. He contended that "[s]i la police laissait jouer *Pinto*, en moins de six mois le public ne pourrait plus supporter les conspirations en vers alexandrins" (Stendhal [1823–5] 1970: 97; if the police allowed *Pinto* to be performed, in less than six months the public would no longer be able to tolerate conspiracies in alexandrine verse). Stendhal also believed that tragedy must be relevant to the concerns of contemporary audiences, reflecting their historical experiences and worldviews rather than those of previous generations. Racine's plays might have been 'modern' in the seventeenth century (suited to the tastes of that day), Stendhal averred, but they were no longer meaningful in the nineteenth century. Neither were more recent tragedies written in line with seventeenth-century aesthetic models. He declared: "Je ne vois que *Pinto* qui ait été fait pour des Français modernes" ([1823–5] 1970: 96–7; As far as I can see, *Pinto* is the only work that has been made for modern Frenchmen).

Pinto did not meet another of Stendhal's criteria for modern, romantic tragedy, however: the abandonment of the unities of time and place. Historical events, Stendhal held, could not be understood in all their complexity if a drama were allowed to show only the final hours before the resolution of a crisis and was limited to a single location. Lemercier was less persuaded of this than Stendhal would be, and thus did not abandon the temporal and spatial constraints typical of the French neoclassical dramatic aesthetic until he wrote *Christophe Colomb* (Christopher Columbus, 1809), a three-act verse drama designated a "Shakespearean comedy." Declaring the unities of time and place uniquely incompatible with the story of Columbus's attempt to discover the New World, Lemercier apologized in advance for his break with French neoclassical tradition and cautioned other dramatists not to imitate his formal "irregularities" in their plays. The playwright's repudiation of dramatic innovation and its generic label notwithstanding, *Colomb* surely deserves to be seen as a proto-romantic tragedy not only because it violates the unities of time and place, moves beyond the usual stylistic and metrical restrictions of French neoclassical drama, and mixes comic and serious elements together, but also because it prefigures the romantic preoccupation with the isolation and alienation of those individuals whose status or genius sets them apart from society. What is more, if we read Lemercier's account of Columbus's journey as a failed quest – as the temporary frustration of the explorer's dreams of renown and prestige at the end of the piece invites us to do – we can see that Columbus clearly announces "the Romantic character who must struggle to create himself a hero in opposition to an unheroic world" (Cox 1994: 157). The suicide of the eponymous poet-hero at the conclusion of Alfred de Vigny's *Chatterton* (1834) and the death of the titular character in Musset's *Lorenzaccio* (1834) will underscore, with even greater finality than Lemercier suggests here, the inevitable outcome of such an endeavor in romantic tragedy.

Not all of Lemercier's plays displayed the same innovative tendencies as those found in *Pinto* and *Christophe Colomb*, however. *La Démence de Charles VI* (The madness of Charles VI, 1820) is far more typical of the playwright's work and better reflects his public pronouncements in favor of the French neoclassical tragic aesthetic. This five-act verse tragedy is "modern" to the extent that its subject is drawn from the history of medieval France, but its daring is otherwise limited. In contrast to Shakespeare's

King Lear, Lemercier uses only conventionally decorous language to allude to Charles's mental state and limits the external representation of the king's infirmity to his decently disheveled, nonregal clothes. Royal dignity and power and the traditional social order are shown to be under attack in the play, but Lemercier is careful to describe these using *récits* rather than to display the chaos that results from the king's inability to govern. By respecting the formal norms and traditions of French neoclassical tragedy, the playwright may have hoped to contain the signs of political and familial disorder at an intellectual distance and thus diminish their potential to undermine the current (ninetenth-century) regime. The government's theater censors were not, however, persuaded that the dangerous potential of the play's subject had been sufficiently attenuated, and thus banned its performance.

While Lemercier's chosen subject ran afoul of authority on this as well as other occasions, the use of "modern" history in his plays illustrates one of the distinguishing features of French romantic tragedy: its preoccupation with moments of social or political tensions and transformations in the creation of national and/or individual destiny. Of course, Lemercier was neither the first nor the only playwright who sought to renew French tragedy via the introduction of modern historical subjects. Neither did he fully exploit, as French melodramatists and romantic dramatists would do, the elements of local color and spectacle inherent in his chosen topics. For early examples of the emotional and pictorial components and the more dynamic style of *mise en scène* that further differentiate romantic tragedy from neoclassical tragedy, we can look to the works of Lemercier's contemporary, René-Charles Guilbert de Pixérécourt.

Pixérécourt is widely regarded as the father of French melodrama and his works set the initial standards for that genre. Like Lemercier, Pixérécourt repeatedly declared his respect for, and belief in, the value of the neoclassical unities of time, place, and action and rarely failed to apply them in his works. And like Lemercier, Pixérécourt, too, frequently wove modern historical subjects into his plays. Pixérécourt's melodramas differed from both neoclassical tragedies and romantic drama, however, by their emphasis on pathos, sensationalism, and spectacle, as well as by their depiction of a Manichaean universe in which the persecution of innocence inevitably leads, at the play's conclusion, to the exclusion of villains from a community of virtue and to the recognition and restoration of other characters' legitimate moral, social, or political status. The importance of pantomime, music, and the expressive, "breathless" style presented as characteristic of moments of intense emotion (*le style haletant*) likewise set many early melodramas apart from tragedy and romantic drama, but would later disappear more or less entirely from the genre's aesthetic code.

Pizarre, ou La Conquête du Pérou (Pizarro, or the conquest of Peru, 1802) is the first melodrama that Pixérécourt seems to have labeled as *historique* (historical), but it is another work so designated, *Tékéli, ou Le Siège de Montgatz* (Tékéli, or the siege of Montgatz, 1803), that provides a more typical and commercially successful model of the genre. A three-act prose drama enhanced by music, dance, and special effects, *Tékéli* recounts the efforts of the Hungarian Count Tékéli to return home from exile and imprisonment to reclaim his sovereign rights and embrace his beloved wife,

Axelina. To do this, he must escape detection by the Austrian forces occupying his country and arrive at the walled city of Montgatz in time to lead a group of besieged patriots (headed, in his absence, by his wife) in a final battle against the Austrians. Although the play recalls real historical events, Pixérécourt is less concerned with the faithful reproduction of facts than with ideology, emotion, and vivid spectacle. Loyalty, integrity, love of and respect for legitimate (political and familial) authority, and compassion are modeled and rewarded in the play whose action is limited to a single day and to one – geographically broad – location. Moments of comedy occasionally relieve the tensions inherent in the drama's serious subject matter and are often associated with the introduction of characters drawn from the lower ranks of society. Language is simple and straightforward and, like the action, reflects a Manichaean rather than a psychologically and morally complex world. Picturesque sets and distinctive costumes and customs bring local color to the incidents showcased in the drama, while an emotionally compelling performance style and spectacular stage effects draw the viewer into sympathetic engagement with the (virtuous) characters and events. Some of these features, especially those that contribute to the immediacy and *present*ness of time, place, and action, announce important dimensions of romantic tragedy rarely, if ever, apparent in nineteenth-century French neo-classical plays.

It is primarily from a formal and thematic perspective that another of Pixérécourt's plays, *La Fille de l'exilé, ou Huit Mois en deux heures* (The exile's daughter, or eight months in two hours, 1819), best serves to highlight both the similarities and the differences between romantic tragedy and melodrama. This historical melodrama, whose subject matter had already been fictionalized by sentimental novelist Sophie Cottin, is the first work in which Pixérécourt completely abandons both the unities of time and place. He even goes so far as to include an onstage scene change (*changement à vue*) in the midst of the play's final act. Like Lemercier before him, however, Pixérécourt argues that it is the specific nature of the events he recounts in this drama – 16-year-old Élisabeth's months'-long journey on foot from Siberia to Moscow to seek a pardon for her unjustly exiled father, Count Potoki – that requires this break with the unities, and he urges others not to follow his example. Each of the work's three acts is set at a time and place quite distant from the others and is labeled a *partie* (part) rather than an *acte* in order to signal Pixérécourt's departure from his usual practice of limiting the spatial and temporal discontinuities between internal textual divisions. Such nontraditional nomenclature as *partie* and *tableau* – Pixérécourt used both words on rare occasion but would reuse them in his *Dernières Réflexions de l'auteur sur le mélodrame* (Final thoughts on melodrama, 1841) – would later be adopted by romantic dramatists, who also used terms such as *journée* (day) to designate the major sections of their plays. In addition to the shift away from the conventions of temporal continuity and spatial contiguity between acts practiced by neoclassical dramatists, this change of terminology underscores the emphasis on stagecraft (i.e., spectacle, the multiplication of practicable stage sets and props, the active occupation of the playing space, and a more energetic performance style) found in the works of most romantic

dramatists and their melodramatic forebears. Reflecting a more dynamic and physically and socially diverse world than that found in court- and castle-centered neoclassical tragedies with their single, indistinguishable *palais à volonté* (antechambers), this
preoccupation with plural settings announces a changed vision of story and history
and a significant expansion of the personnel and places that contribute to the making
of both. Victor Hugo would later articulate this altered perception in the "Preface" to
his play, *Cromwell* (1827), where he wrote that the depiction of the place in which an
action occurred made the representation of that action appear more genuine. Hugo
was not, however, the first or the only one to sense that drama needed to account in
new, concrete ways for past and present social and political realities.

If Pixérécourt's *La Fille de l'exilé*, like his *Latude, ou Trente-Cinq Ans de Captivité*
(Latude, or thirty-five years in captivity, 1834), bears some similarity to romantic
drama in a formal way, it clearly differs from romantic tragedy on an ideological level.
While the *topoi* of exile, imprisonment, and abuse of power are present in *La Fille* (and
later, in *Latude*), as they frequently are in romantic tragedy, they are inflected in a
more positive, providential way in melodrama. In *La Fille*, although Count Potoki
endures cruel deprivations and harassment in Siberia at the beginning of the play, he
does have the consolations of family, virtue, and faith in God to sustain him. Thus he
bemoans his fate, but does not actively rebel against it as a romantic hero might.
What is more, by the end of the play, thanks to his daughter, whose filial devotion
and compassion are recognized and rewarded at every turn, and thanks to the
generosity of the new Czar, Potoki and his wife return to Moscow where their fortune,
position, and honor are fully and publicly restored. Such an outcome is totally at odds
with the denouements of romantic drama where the (re)integration of marginalized
figures, if achieved at all, proves to have been ephemeral and illusory. To be sure, not
all melodramas ended on a positive note – Victor Ducange's plays generally did not –
but it is fair, I think, to suggest that writers of romantic tragedy offered viewers and
readers a darker, more pessimistic view of the world than most early melodramatists
did. For the romantics, there is no redemption or reward, no joyful "homecoming" for
those who have been excluded from the centers of power or from society.

Influences on and Theories of French Romantic Drama

There are other playwrights – including Casimir Delavigne, Prosper Mérimée, and
Ludovic Vitet – whose role in the evolution toward romantic drama deserve recognition. But it is just as important to acknowledge, however briefly, the role of a number
of essayists, including Germaine de Staël, Benjamin Constant, François Guizot,
Alessandro Manzoni, and Stendhal, who helped to shape romantic tragedy. It is
impossible to detail here the arguments they advanced in their pamphlets and
prefaces, but each of these writers, in her or his own way, helped to spark discussion
and debate over the forms, the subjects, and the significance of tragedy in the modern
world. Whether through translation and commentary (Constant adapted and

commented on Schiller's *Wallenstein*; Guizot presented Shakespeare) or analysis of foreign dramatic models (Staël wrote about German playwrights; Stendhal about Shakespeare), each challenged the continuing pertinence and hegemony of French neoclassical dramaturgy and offered suggestions or guidelines for a new type of tragedy more suited to the times. Their writings, together with the translation of the novels of Walter Scott and the performances of British actors and actresses in Paris in 1822 and 1827, served both as a stimulus and a justification for change. Indeed, there are many examples of early nineteenth-century French plays based on or derived from the texts of Goethe, Schiller, Shakespeare, and Scott, including Lemercier's *Richard III et Jeanne Shore* (Richard III and Jane Shore, 1824), Pixérécourt's and Benjamin Antier's *Guillaume Tell* (William Tell, 1828), and Alfred de Vigny's *Le More de Venise* (The Moor of Venice [Othello], 1829). The goal of writers like Staël, Constant, and Stendhal was not to substitute a German or an English model for the traditional French one. Instead, they highlighted the value of "modern" (especially national historical) subjects and proposed a range of politically and aesthetically liberal options (including the freedom to reject the unities of time and place, to ignore the stifling constraints of decorum and alexandrine verse, to benefit from the inclusion of local color, and so on).

It was, however, Victor Hugo's "Preface" to *Cromwell* (1827) that most famously sought to redefine tragedy for modern times. Like his predecessors, Hugo, too, wished to free drama from the unities of time and place, from an arbitrary sense of decorum, and from past limits on subject matter. Anything that was in nature could be in art, he insisted. Rejecting conventional distinctions between comedy and tragedy, which he deemed incompatible with modern experience and Christianity's vision of the dual nature of human beings, Hugo proposed mixing together the (morally and/or physically) sublime and the grotesque to create a drama that offered a richer, more realistic picture of life. Local color, he felt, further contributed to that end. If the times, places, and circumstances that gave rise to events were represented in all their specificity, drama would no longer set forth an abstract image of the past, but would illuminate and explain the relationship between individuals and the world in which they lived. Hugo also believed that verse, provided it was freed from the constraints of lexical and metrical tradition, was fully compatible with modern tragic expression. It could heighten and intensify the theatrical experience rather than stultify it.[2] The (then) unperformable *Cromwell* provided a perfect illustration of his description of modern drama.

Major Romantic Dramatists

Alexandre Dumas *père* never elaborated a theory on the forms, purpose, or pertinence of French romantic drama to the modern world. He was, however, the most prolific and popular writer of French romantic dramas. Influenced by his readings of the works of foreign playwrights and by the performances of the British actors who toured in Paris, Dumas helped to transform serious drama in France by combining the dynamism and spectacle of melodrama with the gravity of tragedy. His plays were generally grounded in "modern" history or treated contemporary social issues.

Dumas's path-breaking national historical drama, *Henri III et sa cour* (Henri III and his court, 1829), opened the doors of the Comédie-Française to romantic tragedy. Written in prose, the play violated the unities of time and place, made dramaturgically effective use of several practicable sets that contributed to the action of the play, emphasized local color in customs, costumes, props, and decor, disregarded conventional rules of decorum by showing scenes of violence on stage, and took full advantage of dynamic pacing and emotionally intense dialogue. Indeed, the play's energetic and vivid portrayal of the past made it quite unlike any other French drama previously staged at the Comédie.

The plot of the play highlights the intersection of political passions with amorous ones at a time of civil and religious unrest. The seemingly ineffectual King Henri finds his reign challenged by his powerful and ambitious cousin, the Duc de Guise. As a result, the Queen Mother, Catherine de Médicis, long the real power behind the throne, fears losing control over her son and matters of state. Hoping to weaken the influence of both Guise and Saint-Mégrin, one of the king's favorites whom she sees as a rival for Henri's affections, Catherine uses the Duchesse de Guise as a pawn. She arranges an involuntary meeting between the Duchesse and Saint-Mégrin, whose love for one another has gone unspoken and remains unconsummated. This later leads to a confrontation between the duchess and her husband and, at the play's conclusion, to the traitorous assassination of Saint-Mégrin. Meanwhile, Henri manages to undermine his cousin's political ascendancy by declaring himself, rather than Guise, the head of the Holy Catholic League.

This tale of ambition, abuse of power, and the victimization of lovers reveals a world filled with menace and hostility. It is a world governed by human passions and actions rather than by the abstract forces of fate or divine providence. By naming himself head of the League, Henri reclaims his role as head of State and Church and thereby reaffirms the existing order. By using violence against his wife and Saint-Mégrin, Guise reestablishes the primacy of patriarchal authority over love. Through deception and manipulation, Catherine eliminates the challenge to her control and restores the *status quo ante*. Thus Saint-Mégrin and the Duchesse de Guise, who dared dream of emotional fulfillment, are caught in the middle of a larger struggle for power they cannot control and from which there is no escape. Our sympathy goes out to them rather than to those who do battle for supremacy over the affairs of state or society. The unequal contest between personal happiness and political forces set forth in *Henri III* was powerfully portrayed in Dumas's piece but is not unique; it would become a frequent subject of French romantic tragedy and would be treated in a variety of periods and settings.

Dumas depicted another type of tragic conflict in what is today his most famous romantic drama, *Antony* (1831). In this five-act prose piece, Dumas again violated the unities of time and place and the conventions of neoclassical decorum (intent on possessing her, Antony breaks into Adèle d'Hervey's hotel room in full sight of the audience in act 3; he kills her on stage at the end of act 5 to save her reputation). Once again, the playwright displayed a keen sense of modern stagecraft and used emotionally powerful language. But whereas *Henri III* was set in the past (the sixteenth century) and focused on characters of unquestioned identity and aristocratic status, *Antony* was set in the present (the nineteenth century) and featured a titular character of unknown parentage and uncertain rank, despite his exceptional merit.

Unable to marry his beloved Adèle because he could not elucidate his origins, the somber and embittered Antony fled a society from which he felt excluded. Now, returning to Paris after a lengthy absence, he is determined to reclaim Adèle who, in the meantime, has been forced by her family to wed Colonel d'Hervey (he has both name and position), and has borne him a daughter. As is made clear by both this expository information and by Adèle's conflicted feelings (duty vs. passion) after seeing Antony again, the lovers in this play fall victim to social rather than political pressures. Public condemnation of their relationship at a ball and the play's tragic conclusion further emphasize the impossibility of rebelling against or living outside of society. Indeed, Dumas and other French romantic playwrights would frequently reiterate the message that the recognition of personal merit and true love is impossible in the rigidly enforced (but nonheroic) social order that defines the modern world.

If the passions, pessimism, and defeat displayed in *Antony* and *Henri III et sa cour* are representative of much of French romantic tragedy so, too, is the richly detailed portrait these works offer of the universe their protagonists inhabit. Apposite costumes, props, and set designs lend an aura of authenticity and historical accuracy to the action. They serve to abolish distance and to create a feeling of physical and temporal proximity between the audience and the characters on stage. What is more, the multiplication of settings – an astrologer's laboratory, the Louvre, the Duchesse de Guise's oratory in *Henri III*; Adèle's home in Paris, an inn on the route to Strasbourg, the reception rooms in the home of Adèle's friend, the Vicomtesse de Lacy, in *Antony* – brings layers of geographical and social dimension to the action, thereby enhancing its realism. Not only does this scenic diversity allow for the introduction of characters who could not plausibly meet in a single location, it also underscores the significance of the action (e.g., the ostracism of Antony and Adèle takes place in a space whose social character is clearly apparent) and its temporal duration (e.g., Adèle's flight from Paris, the lovers' brief period of withdrawal from society, their return, condemnation, and demise). Emotionally charged language; blocking, gestures, and pacing that emphasize dynamism and heighten intensity; and scenes of onstage violence (the Duc de Guise's torture of his wife, Antony's assault on and, later, killing of Adèle) likewise make the fictional universe come alive in a manner totally at odds with the decorous abstraction of neoclassical tragedy. While melodramatists had already exploited some of the techniques described here, romantic dramatists like Dumas generally assigned them greater complexity and meaning.

Like *Antony*, another of Dumas's works, *Kean, ou Désordre et Génie* (Kean, or disorder and genius, 1836), seems to extol passion and self-fulfillment as important values and to suggest that they cannot survive in a world where rigid social conventions exclude certain classes of people and dictate behavior. *Kean*, a five-act drama in prose written for and performed by the celebrated French Boulevard theater actor, Frédérick Lemaître, offers a fictional account of the life of the English stage star, Edmund Kean. Beguiled by Kean's superior skill in such roles as Romeo and Othello, Éléna de Koefeld, the wife of the Danish ambassador to England, has fallen in love with the actor, who loves her in return. What neither of these individuals has yet understood, but what we can already guess, is that their relationship, founded on an illusion, has no future. And indeed, the real-world forces that will separate the aristocratic Éléna from the socially marginalized Kean are made apparent from the beginning of the drama, set in the *salon* of the Danish ambassador's London residence. The conversation at a social gathering there makes it clear that Kean, who has been sent an invitation to attend the event, is considered by everyone but Éléna to be a mere entertainer rather than an equal of the elite class of guests (including the Prince of Wales) who are present. Imbued with a sense of his own genius, deluded by the apparent friendship of the Prince – their relationship is based on little more than a shared passion for pleasure and debauchery – and confident of Éléna's affections, Kean sees his position altogether differently. The action in the rest of the play, set in a variety of locations in London ranging from the Drury Lane theater to a low-class bar beside the Thames, will serve to dispel his error. In the end, after publicly insulting the Prince and the rest of the theater audience from the stage, Kean will leave for New York (a space of both exile and opportunity) with the young Anna Damby, an orphaned heiress who likewise seeks to flee the constraints London society would impose on her future.

While love is still an important theme in *Kean*, that emotion is neither of the same intensity nor of the same nature as in *Henri III* and *Antony*. Éléna's and Kean's feelings for one another seem less persuasively rooted in the heart than was true in those earlier dramas. What is more, as the subtitle of the play suggests, the true focus of this piece lies elsewhere. At issue is the question of genius or, more specifically, of society's failure to honor genius with the (elevated) status that is its due regardless of an individual's origins and its unwillingness to accord genius the freedom from the bounds of ordinary rules that it needs to flourish. For some, Kean's exile may not appear as fully tragic as Saint-Mégrin's assassination or Antony's implied execution since there is a future for him in (a democratic) New York. However, like Lemercier's Columbus, what Kean really seeks is recognition of his personal worth – a recognition English society is unwilling to provide. This makes the actor's involuntary departure from the center of artistic and social distinction (London) just as pitiable as those more traditional tragic outcomes.

Alfred de Vigny's *Chatterton* (Comédie-Française, 1835) – the story of a young, impoverished poet who falls victim to English (and, implicitly, French) society's capitalist values and indifference to genius and art – tells a similar tale. Vigny is far more respectful of neoclassical norms in *Chatterton* than Dumas was in his plays. Perhaps that is because he did not wish to detract attention from the didactic message of this work by multiplying settings or to diminish the intensity of the poet's suffering by repeating the indignities he suffered over an extended period. Still, while clearly adhering to the unities of time and place (the home of the heartlessly utilitarian industrialist John Bell, where Chatterton has taken up temporary lodgings) in this piece, Vigny nonetheless includes a few limited touches of local color. As the story evolves, the struggling poet's alienation from society is tempered only by the compassion of an elderly Quaker who also lodges at Bell's home and by the industrialist's timid, bullied wife, Kitty – a role played to great effect by Marie Dorval. In the end, unable to pay his debts or to find a place in society that honors his gifts and his pride, Chatterton commits suicide in his room after burning his manuscripts. Kitty, who has loved the young man without acting on her feelings, dies from shock after finding his inanimate body sprawled on the bed in his room. Dorval's dramatic fall down the staircase before the curtain rings down on the dying Kitty packed the same kind of emotional punch as her character's death in Dumas's *Antony*, where she played Adèle. Both scenes viscerally reinforced their respective drama's philosophical message about the frustration of individual merit or genius by a society whose values (economic worth in *Chatterton*, birth in *Antony* and *Kean*) closed the door to love and self-realization and became indelibly fixed in the imagination of audiences who saw the works performed.

Despite Dumas's popular success and aesthetic innovations and the drama of Vigny's Chatterton, it is Victor Hugo who is most often held up as the exemplar of French romantic tragedy. Hugo's recognized status as a poet and novelist, together with his theoretical pronouncements in the "Preface" to *Cromwell* and the controversy surrounding the form and performance of *Hernani* (Comédie Française, 1830), no doubt contributed to his designation as the putative head of the romantic school of drama. As the head of a literary circle known as the Cénacle and as a defender of theatrical liberty – he most notably took issue with the censorship of his drama *Le Roi s'amuse* (The king's jester, 1832) – Hugo further solidified his position as the head of that artistic movement.

With Hugo's *Hernani*, the commingling of political and amorous affairs already seen in *Henri III et sa cour* is once again apparent. In contrast to Dumas's prose piece, however, Hugo's drama, set principally in Spain in the early sixteenth century, was written in alexandrine verse – a traditional form the playwright revolutionized by violating metrical conventions and earlier standards of linguistic propriety. In accord with the views he outlined in his Preface to *Cromwell* several years before, Hugo also violated the unities of time and place in *Hernani*. Each act of the drama, to which the playwright assigned a separate title, is set in a different location whose pertinence to the action is clear (e.g., the family portrait gallery where don Ruy Gomez de Silva invokes his ancestors' honor when refusing to betray the laws of hospitality and surrender his guest, the outlawed Hernani, to don Carlos, king of Spain; Charlemagne's tomb in Aix-la-Chapelle where don Carlos, awaiting his election as Holy Roman emperor, reflects on the role and meaning of power and undergoes a moral change that leads him to pardon Hernani, restore his aristocratic titles, and allow him to marry doña Sol). Hugo likewise weaves local color into the action, costumes, and settings of the play and combines elements of the comic and the tragic, the sublime and the grotesque. As a result, despite echoes of works ranging from Corneille's *Cinna* and *Le Cid* to Shakespeare's *Romeo and Juliet* and from comedy to melodrama, the play is distinctively romantic, tenderly lyrical, and darkly dramatic. The battle between partisans of the neoclassical and romantic aesthetics that took place at the time of the play's premiere, while scarcely the first or the most dramatic of its kind – the battle surrounding Lemercier's *Christophe Colomb* had earlier resulted in injuries and a death – nonetheless seemed to announce the triumph of the romantic conception of tragic drama.

The love story at the heart of Hugo's play finds three men competing for the hand of the orphaned doña Sol: her elderly uncle and guardian, don Ruy Gomez, to whom she is betrothed and who offers her security and profound affection; the young and handsome outlaw, Hernani, who offers her intense passion but no security; and don Carlos, King of Spain, who offers her the possibility of elevated status and wealth, but whose feelings may well prove less enduring than those of his rivals. The first acts of the play make it clear that the young woman's heart belongs to Hernani. The son of an aristocratic rebel put to death by don Carlos's father, Hernani lives under an assumed name (he was born Jean d'Aragon) and is himself a political outcast pursued by the authorities. The amorous rivalry that pits the outlaw against the king is thus paired with a political contest that sets the two men at odds with one another at critical moments in the drama (most notably in acts 2–4). Carlos's transformation in Charlemagne's tomb in act 4 appears to mark the conclusion of the piece. But while act 4 resolves the Hernani–don Carlos conflict and seems to signal the (political and social) reintegration of the outcast/bandit, it does not settle the debt Hernani owes his other rival for doña Sol's hand, don Ruy Gomez. Thus, the young lovers' marriage festivities, celebrated with lyrical expansion under the stars at the d'Aragon family castle in act 5, turn tragic when don Ruy, disguised in a black domino, arrives uninvited and sounds a horn, symbol of the debt of honor that the then-outlawed Hernani had promised to pay him in exchange for his hospitality in act 3. The payment don Ruy now demands is his rival's death. In the end, both the newlyweds drink the poison don Ruy presents to Hernani and the old man is left alone. The couple's onstage demise, reminiscent of Romeo's and Juliet's tragic deaths, violated the laws of neoclassical propriety which normally banished such unseemly sights behind the scenes, and highlights once again the substitution of human action for divine intervention.

Politics and passion clash again in Hugo's *Ruy Blas* (1838), a play set in late seventeenth-century Spain and the first work performed at the Théâtre de la Renaissance, an enterprise owned jointly by Hugo and Dumas and meant to feature their works. Disguised and presented at court by his master (don Salluste) as that nobleman's cousin (don César), the valet Ruy Blas (played with great success by Frédérick Lemaître) will unwittingly serve Salluste's plan for vengeance against the Spanish queen who has banished him. Six months later, the valet, long in love with the queen – he is "un vers de terre amoureux d'une étoile" (an earthworm in love with a star) – has risen in rank on his own merits, but under his assumed name. Now prime minister, he is critical of those aristocrats who would put personal profit above the nation's well-being. After overhearing "don César"/Ruy Blas's speech condemning the noblemen, the queen reveals her love for him and asks him to save the state from collapse. The married queen's feelings, if publicized and/or acted upon, would forever compromise her in the rigid moral and social environment of the Spanish court and that, of course, is exactly what Salluste hoped all along his plan would accomplish. Returned to Madrid in disguise, Salluste orders Ruy Blas from court and arranges a rendezvous between his valet and the queen in a mysterious house. After a series of twists and turns, Ruy Blas kills Salluste, drinks the poison the queen threatened to take when she saw her position and honor endangered, and dies in her arms. In this play, then, as in other romantic dramas, the present proves impermanent, past actions inescapable, and the future closed to superior individuals who seek personal happiness and other rewards. The political advancement of a member of the lower class, possible only by means of a borrowed identity, is shown to be ephemeral and without long-term effect.

Les Burgraves (The burgraves, 1843), a three-part (*partie*) verse drama, is set at a medieval German court. Its theatrical failure is usually cited as marking the demise of French romantic drama, even though some tragedies in the romantic mode continued to be written and performed after that date. Crimes of violence and other forms of moral and political corruption lie at the heart of this work that focuses on four generations of the ruling family. Epic in scale and tone, the piece reaches beyond the scope of Hugo's other historical dramas. It is almost as if the playwright were seeking to combine elements of the story of Cain and Abel with those of the house of Atreus and to suffuse both with the atmospherics of German legend and the "modern" aesthetic of the sublime and the grotesque. Love is present here, as always, as are the themes of injustice and imprisonment which are so frequently found in Hugo's works and in those of other French romantic dramatists. The conclusion of the play is, however, more optimistic than that of most of Hugo's dramatic writings from this period.

Alfred de Musset's best-known drama, *Lorenzaccio* (1834), also tries to paint a broad tableau, but is far more pessimistic, examining the frustrations of political idealism and reform in a corrupt world. Written as a closet drama (*spectacle dans un fauteuil*), the work, freed from the limits imposed by contemporary stagecraft and censorship, is kaleidoscopic in form and content. Set primarily in Florence during the reign of Alexandre de Médicis, the five-act piece multiplies decors, features a broad range of secondary characters taken from all ranks of society, and entertains discussions on politics and art, morality and religion, ambition and love, purity and degradation. Filled with depravity and violence, the action centers on the titular character whose once-pure being has fused with the mask of debauchery he habitually wears while pursuing his (ultimately quixotic) dream of ridding Florence of tyranny and corruption. Political freedom proves as elusive as personal freedom and in the end, as he had anticipated, Lorenzo's assassination of his cousin Alexandre does nothing to restore liberty to Florence or purity to his own soul. Weighed down by a sense of the hollowness of rhetoric and idealism, seeing no acceptable future for himself or his country, Lorenzo/Lorenzaccio allows himself to be killed by assassins attracted by the monetary reward offered for his death.

The corruption of one's truest, most innocent nature by external forces is set in an altogether different context in Musset's three-act dramatic proverb, *On ne badine pas avec l'amour* (Don't trifle with love, 1833–4). There, the affection that the young, orphaned Camille bore her cousin Perdican as a girl is expected to result in their marriage now that the two have completed their studies and grown to adulthood. But Camille's convent education has given her a perverted idea of men and love – an idea that has grown not from Christian doctrine, but from the experience of the betrayed women at her convent school who have filled her mind with their tales of woe. Stung by her refusal of his hand, Perdican soon turns his attentions to Rosette, a young peasant woman and Camille's *sœur de lait* ("sister" because the two were suckled together), whose unschooled trust and innocent affection he uses as a means to prick Camille's ego and spark feelings of jealousy. The naïve Rosette at first believes Perdican's professions of love and proposal of marriage. Later, after overhearing the aristocratic couple confess their true feelings for one another, she dies. Her death creates a permanent obstacle to their nuptials and sends Camille back to the convent with her own bitter story to tell about men and love. Alongside this tragic tale of misprized and misrepresented emotions, Musset has placed "grotesque," one-dimensional secondary characters (*fantoches*) who figure in scenes of comic absurdity that, by contrast, intensify the drama of love lost.

Les Caprices de Marianne (Marianne's whims, 1833) also treats the subject of love and life lost. A two-act prose piece filled with passages of lyrical beauty and sharp wit, it tells the story of Coelio, an Italian youth passionately and idealistically in love with his elderly cousin's young wife, Marianne, but too timid and inexperienced to overcome her objections to his suit. In a moment of despair, he enlists his friend Octave, a man who seems to live for pleasure and is never at a loss for words, to speak on his behalf. Octave and Marianne engage in several verbal jousts, following which she agrees to an assignation. Believing that his words have won Marianne's heart for Coelio and unaware that the young woman's husband, having overheard their plans, intends to attack her lover, Octave sends his friend to the arranged rendezvous. There Coelio, imagining himself betrayed by Octave, allows himself to be killed. Like *Lorenzaccio* and *Badine*, this play was not written for performance. All three works, however, have been staged with regularity since the twentieth century and have come to be regarded as the finest and most enduring examples of French romantic drama. Their portrayal of frustrated idealism and innocence, of a world-wariness and world-weariness that lead to an ironically bitter end, today seem to embody most fully the tragic Angst of the romantic generation.

Edmond Rostand, who is often considered a late romantic dramatist, did not write his plays until the end of the nineteenth century. While Rostand's best-known piece, the five-act heroic comedy *Cyrano de Bergerac* (1897), shares with other romantic dramas a modern historical setting (the action takes place in seventeenth-century France), a preoccupation with local color and dynamic staging, a concern for the social and political factors that impinge on the protagonists' lives, and a willingness to violate the unities of time and place and to mix tragedy with comedy, his play is not altogether like those earlier works. Cyrano may be just as loath as Chatterton is to compromise his poetic gifts and his pride, but he does not succumb to despair as Vigny's hero does. Instead, he is a man of action willing to challenge those who would humiliate him or attempt to limit his independence. The juxtaposition of these very different protagonists may be unusual, but it helps to make the point that French romantic tragedy cannot be described solely by means of its formal departures from neoclassical dramaturgy. As important as they were, the liberalization of language and style; the introduction of prose or a metrically freer form of alexandrine verse; the lifting of temporal and spatial limits on action; the promotion of "modern" history, local color, and spectacle; and the rejection of a decorum inherited from earlier times and of generic boundaries that compartmentalized the representation of human existence, do not completely explain what makes romantic drama distinctive. To understand its uniqueness, one must also note the importance of a secularized, purely human causality that, directly or indirectly, grew out of the French Revolution. In the post-Revolutionary, post-providential era that saw melodrama, romantic drama, and neoclassical tragedy exist side by side, political, economic, and social forces brought forth new ideas and aspirations, created new opportunities for and obstacles to success, and prompted new means of expression and new definitions of the tragic.

Stendhal, as we have seen, saw literature as an expression of society as it is, not as it was. He believed that if tragedy were to be relevant in the modern world it would have to be human and historical rather than legendary, mythological, or divine; specific rather than universal; national and individual rather than universal. Others – Hugo, Staël, Constant among them – expressed similar thoughts in different ways. French romantic tragedy is thus both the moral and the aesthetic product of its age: an age of uncertainty where past institutions, values, beliefs, and forms no longer won automatic acceptance or held universal appeal. There is often a note of despair, a sense of frustration in French romantic dramas. That is because playwrights and audiences understood that they were living at a time when personal and collective aspirations might not be realized, when rewards and recognition might be withheld, and when passions could be thwarted or traversed by political or social forces beyond their control.

Changed forms, subjects, and performance styles are an important part of the romantic redefinition of tragedy in early nineteenth-century France. They signal a new understanding of the forces that shape individual stories and shared histories, and as such are deserving of our attention. The energy and despondency that many romantic heroes display, the ideals they pursue, and the respect that they seek but are rarely granted are just as significant. They reflect the struggles and vicissitudes experienced by a generation living in a period of turmoil and transition and offer a key to the *mentalité* of those times.

Notes

1   French literature specialists almost never use the term "tragedy" in connection with French romantic drama, although a few works, including Alexandre Dumas's *Charles VII chez ses grands vassaux* [Charles VII at the home of his principal vassals, 1831], were labeled tragedies. I shall at times use tragedy and drama interchangeably to designate works under discussion here, although the two terms are not equivalent. *Drame* in French means both drama in the general sense and a particular genre of serious plays. See Thomasseau (1995: *passim*) for further clarification on the subject.

2   See Thomasseau (1999: *passim*) on the importance of the debate over prose vs. poetry in romantic drama.

References and Further Reading

Brooks, Peter. [1976] (1995). *The Melodramatic Imagination: Balzac, Henry James and the Mode of Excess*. New Haven, CT and London: Yale University Press. An important study that rehabilitated melodrama and its aesthetic code.

Cooper, Barbara T., ed. (1998). *Dictionary of Literary Biography*, Vol. 192: *French Dramatists, 1789–1914*. Detroit, MI: Gale Research. Essays on Lemercier, Pixérécourt, Staël, Dumas, Hugo, Vigny, Musset, et al.

Cox, Jeffrey N. (1987). *In the Shadows of Romance: Romantic Tragic Drama in Germany, England, and France*. Athens: Ohio University Press. A general study of romantic tragedy that includes studies of individual authors/works.

Cox, Jeffrey N. (1994). "Romantic Redefinitions of the Tragic." In *Romantic Drama*, ed. Gerald Gillespie, Amsterdam and Philadelphia, PA: John Benjamins, 153–65. Draws on previous work but with slightly different focus, greater condensation.

Daniels, Barry V., ed. (1983). *Revolution in the Theatre: French Romantic Theories of Drama*. Westport, CT: Greenwood Press. A compilation of theoretical writings on French romantic drama from the period.

Daniels, Barry V., ed. (2003). *Le Décor de théâtre à l'époque romantique: Catalogue raisonné des décors de la Comédie-Française, 1799 1848* [Stage sets in the romantic era.] Paris: Bibliothèque nationale de France. A *catalogue raisonné* of the sets used at the Comédie-Française between 1799 and 1848.

Dumas, Alexandre. (1974—). *Théâtre complet* [Complete theatrical works], ed. Fernande Bassan. Paris: Lettres modernes/Minard. The most recent edition of Dumas's complete theatrical works, with introductions, notes, etc.

Frantz, Pierre and François Jacob, eds. (2002). *Tragédies tardives* [Late tragedies]. Paris: Honoré Champion. A collection of essays on late tragedy from several eras/countries, including France.

Gengembre, Gérard. (1999). *Le Théâtre français au 19e siècle* [French theater in the nineteenth century]. Paris: Armand Colin. A general study of nineteenth-century French theater, covering all genres.

Hugo, Victor. (1967–9). *Œuvres complètes, édition chronologique* [Complete works, chronological edition]. Paris: Club Français du Livre. The standard reference edition of Hugo's works, with introductions, notes, variants, etc.

Le Hir, Marie-Pierre. (1992). *Le Romantisme aux enchères: Ducange, Pixérécourt, Hugo* [Romanticism on the auction block: Ducange, Pixérécourt, Hugo]. Amsterdam and Philadelphia, PA: John Benjamins. Explores similarities and differences in the works of authors named in the title.

Lemercier, Louis-Jean-Népomucène. [1800] (1976). *Pinto*, ed. Norma Perry. Exeter: University of Exeter Press. The only recent edition of any of Lemercier's plays, this also has an introduction.

Lemercier, Louis-Jean-Népomucène. (1809). *Christophe Colomb* [Christopher Columbus]. Paris: L. Collin.

Musset, Alfred de. (1990). *Théâtre complet d'Alfred de Musset* [Complete theatrical works of Alfred de Musset], ed. Simon Jeune. Paris: Gallimard. The most recent Pléiade edition of Musset's theater, including introduction, notes, etc.

Naugrette, Florence. (2001). *Le Théâtre romantique* [Romantic theater]. Paris: Editions du Seuil. A study of the history, staging, and aesthetics of French romantic drama.

Pixérécourt, René-Charles Guilbert de. [1841–3] (1971). *Théâtre choisi* [Selected plays], ed. Charles Nodie. Geneva: Slatkine Reprints. Includes texts, plus some contemporary reviews and commentaries.

Rostand, Edmond. (1998). *Cyrano de Bergerac*, ed. Jacques Truchet and Jean-Denis Malclès. Paris: Imprimerie nationale. A comprehensive, centennial edition of the play.

Stendhal [pseud. Henri Beyle]. [1823–5] (1970). *Racine et Shakespeare*. Paris: Garnier-Flammarion.

Thomasseau, Jean-Marie. (1995). *Drame et tragédie*. Paris: Hachette. A study of two closely related genres, *drame* and tragedy, over several centuries in France.

Thomasseau, Jean-Marie. (1999). "Le Vers noble ou les chiens noirs de la prose?" [Noble verse or the black dogs of prose?]. In *Le Drame romantique: Rencontres nationales de dramaturgie du Havre* [Romantic drama: a national conference on dramaturgy in Le Havre]. Paris: Editions des Quatre-Vents, 32–40. A study of the importance of the prose vs. poetry conflict, published with conference papers by others on various aspects of French romantic drama.

Ubersfeld, Anne. (1993). *Le drame romantique* [Romantic drama]. Paris: Belin. A general introduction to French romantic drama.

Vigny, Alfred de. (1986). *Œuvres complètes* [Complete works], ed. François Germain and André Jarry. Paris: Gallimard. (Original edition of *Chatterton* published 1835). Volume 1 of this Pleiade edition of the complete works contains all of Vigny's theater.

Zaragoza, Georges, ed. (1999). *Dramaturgies romantiques* [Romantic dramaturgies]. Dijon: Editions Universitaires de Dijon. Collection of essays on dramaturgy (aesthetics, stagecraft, etc.) in French and other romantic dramas.

Part VII
Tragedy and Modernity

26

Modern Theater and the Tragic in Europe

Gail Finney

Prelude

The term "modern" is a controversial one. Its ambiguity may be traced to its etymology: deriving from the Latin *modo*, meaning "lately, just now," the word has had a relative definition since its beginnings. Literary and cultural historians have nonetheless sought to define it in absolute terms, seeking variously to locate the origins of "the modern" in Europe in the post-medieval era, the Renaissance, or the years around 1800; "high modernism" in fiction, poetry, and the plastic arts is usually defined as the period from 1910 to 1930. Where European theater is concerned, however, there is general agreement that modernism begins with the work of Ibsen; the location of its endpoint depends on how (or whether) one defines postmodern theater – whether beginning with World War II or later. My treatment of modern European theater and the tragic will focus on the years from roughly 1880 to 1910, a period that can be said to represent modern theater at its apex. In the broadest terms – terms that will be elaborated and qualified in the course of this chapter – the "modernism" of tragic theater in this era lies in the increased heterogeneity of its form and in the heightened extent to which it explores the influence of gender, sexuality, and socioeconomic factors in determining human lives. I will therefore concentrate on four parameters through which modern European tragic theater may usefully be examined: class, gender, sexuality, and form. The plays I focus on are meant to be not exhaustive but representative.

Before discussing modern European tragic theater itself it will be helpful to look at its origins, which extend at least as far back as the eighteenth century. Many of the formal features that characterize modern theater originate in the rejection of classical conventions that is generally termed "anti-Aristotelian." Although some of these traits are evident in the theater of Shakespeare, they are more self-consciously and systematically advocated in the drama and dramatic theory of several of his German-language champions writing in the eighteenth century, above all Gotthold E. Lessing and Jakob M. R. Lenz. Both were motivated by a reaction against seventeenth-century neoclassical French tragedians like Pierre Corneille and Jean Racine and their followers in Germany, notably Johann C. Gottsched, whose theater Lessing calls "Frenchified theater" (Lessing, "Siebzehnter Brief, die neueste Literatur betreffend" [The seventeenth letter concerning the newest literature, 1759], in Herzfeld-Sander 1985: 2). Both Lessing and Lenz attack the stilted, pompous speech characteristic of neoclassical theater, advocating instead a language produced by feeling. Both attack the unities of time, place, and action prescribed by Aristotle's *Poetics* and artificially observed, in their opinion, by neoclassical dramatists; as Lessing writes, "As far as I am concerned Voltaire's and Maffei's *Merope* may extend over eight days and the scene may be laid in seven places in Greece! If only they had the beauties to make me forget these pedantries!" (Lessing, *Hamburgische Dramaturgie* [Hamburg dramaturgy, 1769], in Herzfeld-Sander 1985: 12). Lenz is even more vociferous in his *Anmerkungen übers Theater* [Notes on the theater, 1774]:

> I must still fire back at one of [Aristotle's] fundamental laws which makes so much noise simply because it is so small, and that is the dreadfully and lamentably famous edict of the three unities. And what, my dears, are the names of these three unities? . . . I want to mention to you a hundred unities, all of which, however, always remain the one. Unity of country, unity of language, unity of religion, unity of morals – well, what is it going to be? Always the same, always and eternally the same. The poet and the public must feel but not classify the one unity. (Herzfeld-Sander 1985: 21)

The nationalistic dimensions of these aesthetically driven debates, reflecting the age-old enmity between Germany and France as well as Germany's eighteenth-century political affiliations with England, are evident throughout, as when Lenz employs the differences between the English and the French garden to illustrate the open and closed forms of the drama, respectively. But the contrast Lessing and Lenz draw between the rigid formality of French neoclassical theater and the emotional power of Shakespeare's drama endures in aesthetic writing for decades, finding perhaps its culmination in Stendhal's *Racine et Shakespeare* (1823). In some ways, the debate between the neoclassicists and those advocating a move toward looser, more open forms in the theater is reminiscent of "la querelle des anciens et des modernes," the aesthetic war waged in seventeenth-century France between those arguing in favor of the imitation of Greek and Latin models and those defending contemporary French literature in the name of progress. That some of the same authors – notably Racine and Corneille – were viewed as progressive in the first instance and as retrograde in the second underlines the relative nature of aesthetic debate. Yet the anti-Aristotelian impulse, comprising a revolt against conventions which had dominated Western theater for some 2000 years, became so powerful and widespread that it not only endured but formed the foundation of modern theater.

Lessing's use in his *Hamburgische Dramaturgie* of the term *bürgerliches Trauerspiel* (domestic or bourgeois tragedy) points to one of the major innovations on the path to modern tragic drama. The first major bourgeois or domestic tragedy is conventionally identified as George Lillo's *The London Merchant* (1731), which treats the fall of a young merchant's apprentice. In his lengthy dedication of the play to a member of Parliament, Lillo justifies the appearance of middle-class characters in tragedy for the common-sense reason that the middle class is larger than the nobility:

> [T]ragedy is so far from losing its dignity by being accommodated to the circumstances of the generality of mankind that it is more truly august in proportion to the extent of its influence and the numbers that are properly affected by it, as it is more truly great to be the instrument of good to many who stand in need of our assistance than to a very small part of that number. (Lillo 1965: 3)

Similarly, overthrowing Aristotle's well-known convention specifying that the protagonist of tragedy "must be one who is highly renowned and prosperous" (Aristotle 1961: 76) – a dictum embodied in the princes and heroes of the French neoclassical tragedies – Lessing argues in his *Hamburgische Dramaturgie* that we are moved by what we know. As bourgeois citizens, we are familiar not with the nobility but with other members of the middle class, above all with our families. To highlight this point Lessing quotes the *Poétique française* (French poetics, 1763) of the French writer and encyclopedist Jean François Marmontel:

> We wrong the human heart, we misread nature, if we believe that it requires titles to rouse and touch us. The sacred names of friend, father, lover, husband, son, mother, of mankind in general, these are far more pathetic than aught else and retain their claims forever. What matters the rank, the surname, the genealogy of the unfortunate man whose easy good nature towards unworthy friends has involved him in gambling and who loses over this his wealth and honour and now sighs in prison distracted by shame and remorse? (Herzfeld-Sander 1985: 7)

To be sure, tragic drama has focused on the family since the beginnings of Western theater; one need think only of the Theban plays of Sophocles or of Aeschylus' *Oresteia* trilogy. As Bennett Simon observes, "war against the outside world in epic becomes war within the family in tragedy" (1988: 21). But in contrast to the royal purview of classical, Renaissance, and neoclassical tragedy, in which the fate of nations often hangs in the balance, from the eighteenth century onward the scope of tragedy can generally be said to shrink and its characters to descend in social standing. Today's audiences have become so accustomed to commonplace characters onstage that it is difficult to appreciate the revolutionary importance of this development for modern tragic theater.

In discussing the term *bürgerlich* (bourgeois or domestic) in the eighteenth century, Karl Guthke notes that the bourgeois defines himself in relation to the community, to which he is bound by virtue of duties and responsibilities, and at a distance from the larger world of nations, rulers, and politics (1994: 10). Yet the domestic tragedy often has sociocritical implications, insofar as the family can function as a microcosm for society at large. This is more the case in Lessing's bourgeois tragedy *Emilia Galotti*

(1772) than in his play modeled on Lillo's *The London Merchant, Miss Sara Sampson* (1755). In an updating of the Roman story of Virginia, the character of the title, who belongs to the affluent middle class, is abducted with her aristocratic fiancé by the lustful local prince with the help of his amoral and devious chamberlain, who has the fiancé killed. The virtuous but vulnerable Emilia Galotti persuades her father to stab her to death rather than see her lose her innocence to the prince. That the play critiques *in nuce* the impotence of the middle class vis-à-vis the absolute monarchs ruling German principalities in the eighteenth century was forcefully underlined two years after its premiere by the conclusion of Goethe's popular novel *Die Leiden des jungen Werthers* (The sorrows of young Werther, 1774), in which a copy of *Emilia Galotti* is found lying open on the desk of the character of the title after he shoots himself, a victim (among other things) of rejection by the local court.

The emphasis on social criticism constitutes another major contribution of the domestic or bourgeois tragedy to the evolution of modern tragic theater. To present things schematically, classical tragedy can be described as the tragedy of fate, and Shakespearean and romantic tragedy as the tragedy of character. In the words of Walter Benjamin, in *"Trauerspiel* and Tragedy" (1916), "[C]lassical tragedy is characterized by the ever more powerful eruption of tragic forces. It deals with the tragedy of fate, Shakespeare with the tragic hero, the tragic action. Goethe rightly calls him Romantic" (Benjamin [1916] 1996: 56). I would extend this schema by suggesting that in modern tragedy, the role of fate is taken over by socioeconomic forces – attitudes toward class, gender, and sexuality – as these affect or interact with character.

All these forces come to the fore in the play often called the first modern European tragedy, Georg Büchner's unfinished drama *Woyzeck* (written in 1836–7). Based on an actual ex-soldier who was executed for killing his mistress, the simple barber Woyzeck is depicted as a creature without free will, exploited by a series of caricatured figures. Portraying his social, economic, and psychological disintegration, the play is an appropriate vehicle for assessing the usefulness of a Marxist approach to literature and theater, particularly in view of Büchner's other writings and activities opposing class oppression. Much in the drama attributes Woyzeck's victimization to his poverty. When the Captain persists in making fun of him and in lambasting his actions as immoral, Woyzeck himself responds that money is the key to everything and that the lower classes are correspondingly doomed:

> When you're poor like us, sir... It's the money, the money! If you haven't got the money... I mean you can't bring the likes of us into the world on decency. We're flesh and blood too. Our kind doesn't get a chance in this world or the next. If we go to heaven they'll put us to work on the thunder. (Büchner [1836–7] 1971: 108)

Similarly, Woyzeck functions as a guinea pig in inhumane scientific experiments for the sake of the pittance the Doctor pays him. A physician himself, Büchner was in an excellent position to satirize the scientific zeal of the medical profession.

The markedly existential dimensions of the play, however, encapsulated by Woyzeck's observation that "Every man is a bottomless pit; you get dizzy when you look down" (Büchner [1836–7] 1971: 120), thwart a one-sidedly Marxist interpretation. In the course of the drama Woyzeck's actions become increasingly nervous and harried, his demeanor more and more hunted and desperate. Yet mental cruelty, exploitation, and privation hurt him far less than does his lover Marie's betrayal of him with the virile drum major, since she is the only thing that gives his life meaning. Like so much else in the play, the motives behind Marie's infidelity with the drum major are ambiguous: does Büchner intend to make a negative statement about female sexuality or to portray her as a victim of circumstance comparable to Woyzeck? On the one hand, she expresses clear sexual admiration for the drum major, describing him as "Broad as an ox and a beard like a lion" (Büchner [1836–7] 1971: 116), yet on the other hand she laments that "The likes of me have only a hole like this to call our own, and a bit of broken mirror. But my lips are as red as madame's with her mirrors down to the floor and her fine gentlemen to kiss her hand. And I'm just a poor girl" (Büchner [1836–7] 1971: 114).

The complex heterogeneity of his characters' motivation is a reflection of Büchner's modernity. As a quasi naturalistic case study of a working-class man driven by jealousy to murder his beloved, *Woyzeck* is far ahead of its time. Its formal features also point forward to twentieth-century theater: its scenic structure, which is so nonlinear that the order of the scenes cannot be definitively established; its elliptical, at times illogical dialogue, much of which consists of characters talking past one another; its use of dialect and the inclusion of songs; its employment of unnamed types as featured characters; its strikingly graphic imagery. It is little wonder that the play has invited adaptation by artists from Alban Berg, who transformed it into an opera, to Werner Herzog, who reworked it for the cinema.

Class

Büchner's serious treatment of the proletariat in tragic theater, representing a far cry from the Aristotelian dictum that the personages of tragedy should be illustrious and affluent, found followers, though not immediately (it should be noted that the text of *Woyzeck* was lost until 1879, when it was discovered and published for the first time as *Wozzeck*; the play was not performed until 1913). The working-class tragedy does not come into its own in Europe until the end of the nineteenth century, which was the great period of the middle class in theater and literature. One of the dramatists best known for his treatment of the working class is the German naturalist writer Gerhart Hauptmann, who created a lasting monument to the proletariat in *Die Weber* (The weavers, 1892), based on the historical revolt of the Silesian weavers in 1844. Hauptmann also focuses tragic attention on lower-class characters in his plays *Hanneles Himmelfahrt* (Hannele, 1893), which features an abused child dying in a poorhouse; *Florian Geyer* (1896), which deals with the peasant wars; *Fuhrmann Henschel*

(Drayman Henschel, 1898); and *Rose Bernd* (1903), a latter-day treatment of the infanticide motif in its depiction of the sexual victimization of a peasant girl.

More consistent attention to the peasantry is found in the plays of Irish dramatist John Millington Synge. Several of these are dark comedies, such as *The Shadow of the Glen* (1904), *The Well of the Saints* (1905), *The Tinker's Wedding* (1907) – and *The Playboy of the Western World* (1907), the humorous elements of which are countered by the play's anti-comic ending, in which the girl – Pegeen Mike – does not win her man – the "playboy" and self-proclaimed father-killer Christy Mahon – but rather famously "loses" him. This conclusion is especially illustrative of what Arthur Ganz has called "the essential sadness lying beneath even the brightest of Synge's plays" (1980: 28).

But Synge's fatalistic vision of the Irish peasantry is more fully realized in his two tragic plays, *Riders to the Sea* (1903) and *Deirdre of the Sorrows* (1910). *Riders to the Sea* was Synge's most successful work during his lifetime and is probably still the most frequently performed of his one-act dramas. The setting is desolate – a peasant cottage on one of the Aran Islands, located off the west coast of Ireland. The play presents an extremely economical dichotomy between turn-of-the-century naturalism and mythic timelessness: on the one hand, a lower-class milieu, a bickering family, and the use of dialect; on the other, a stark fatalism centering on a latter-day Niobe in the person of Maurya, who has already lost her husband and four sons to the sea. The dominant mood of the play is one of waiting for the inevitable, as Maurya's two daughters are confronted with the arrival of some clothing from a drowned man and must determine whether it belongs to their absent brother, at the same time that another brother, Bartley, sets off for the coast. In contrast to Beckett's *Waiting For Godot* (1956), however, in *Riders to the Sea* that which the characters are waiting for actually arrives: by the play's end the family learns not only that the dead man is their brother but that Bartley has drowned as well.

The play's one-act structure allows the tension produced by dread to be sustained and intensified throughout. The fatalistic atmosphere of impending doom and death, given clearest voice in Maurya's repeated direful predictions that her two surviving sons will go the way of the other four, is enhanced by frequent references to the elements – the wind, waves, and rocks that have been so powerful in determining this family's destiny. While people of all classes live under the sway of natural forces, the peasant background of this family both underlines their victimization and foregrounds the fact that the lower classes are worthy subjects of tragedy. The extreme degree of loss in the play – the family father and six sons by its end – seems to epitomize the lack of control human beings have over their fates and allies Synge's brief play with classical tragedy. The play's determinism is further emphasized through reference to the impotence of Christianity, manifested in the insistence of the local priest that God will not leave Maurya alive without any of her sons, although this is precisely what occurs.

Deirdre of the Sorrows moves expressly into the realm of myth, in this case the same Irish legends treated by William B. Yeats, with a cast of characters including Fergus and his friend Conchubor, the elderly King of Ulster. As in Synge's other plays, however, the main character is from the lower classes: in an Irish version of the Cinderella story, the beautiful peasant girl Deirdre is promised to Conchubor, who offers her jewels and other elegant gifts in place of the nuts and twigs that she is fond of gathering in the hills. But she willfully thwarts him to marry the young and handsome Naisi, despite the frequently intoned prophesy that her union with him will bring disaster on him and his two brothers – the explanation of the "sorrows" associated with her name. When Fergus succeeds seven years later in convincing Deirdre and Naisi that Conchubor wants peace and that they should return to his realm, the prophesy is fulfilled, as Conchubor has Naisi and his brothers killed to avenge his marriage to Deirdre. True to her oath that she will not live without Naisi, Deirdre stabs herself and falls into his grave.

Such a brief summary does justice neither to the lyrical quality of the play's language nor to the psychological complexity with which Synge endows the transmitted Irish legend. The true tragedy of the play can be said to be the transience of beauty and of life in general – a favorite theme of turn-of-the-century artists. Yet Synge's characters approach this theme from another angle, not lamenting the finite nature of life but rather recognizing that it is precisely in the brevity of treasured experience that its value lies; as Deirdre tells Naisi, "It should be a sweet thing to have what is best and richest if it's for a short space only" (Synge 1968: 209). The actual reasons for their return to Conchubor's realm belie their trust in his offer of peace: their awareness that the perfect love they experienced for seven years cannot be extended and can never be replicated, and their concomitant dread of seeing each other grow old. Hence through the mythic veil of the play's setting it is possible to read a comment on the institution of marriage in Synge's own day – not only on the dire consequences of a mismatch, but on the tedium that can ensue even in the most promising of unions.

Gender

The topic of marriage leads us to one of the most perceptive analysts of this institution, Henrik Ibsen. Ibsen's importance in the history of theater cannot be overestimated. He has been called the father of modern drama, and all subsequent dramatists have had to come to terms with him either directly or indirectly. He was the first major playwright to deal convincingly with highly controversial, topical subjects, for example syphilis (in *Ghosts*, 1881), and he was one of the first European dramatists after Büchner to use theater as an expression of social revolt. He was a pivotal figure in the movement of tragedy from the sphere of royalty to the living rooms of the middle class, and in his refinement of close psychological analysis in the drama he did a great deal to render prose dialogue more natural and verisimilar.

Few issues receive more serious attention in Ibsen's *oeuvre* than the situation of women. At a time when women throughout the world were fighting for equal rights, above all for the right to vote, it was virtually impossible for serious writers and artists to ignore them. While women's assertion of their right to equality made some male artists nervous and inspired a vivid array of antifeminist and even misogynist images in turn-of-the-century European culture, a small number of men jumped onto the feminist bandwagon. Ibsen's own statements on the subject vary. In a speech made to laborers in Trondheim in 1885 he pledged his intention of working to improve the status of workers and women, yet in a speech given in 1898 at a banquet in his honor by the Norwegian Women's Rights League he avows: "I . . . must disclaim the honour of having consciously worked for the women's rights movement. I am not even quite clear as to just what this women's rights movement really is. To me it has seemed a problem of humanity in general" (Ibsen 1972: 65). Thus although Ibsen was widely perceived to be a supporter of the feminist cause, a belief especially fueled by *A Doll House* (1879), at the conclusion of which Nora Helmer leaves her oppressive husband and small children to educate and discover herself, in fact he eschewed ideological labels and held views that were more nuanced and ambivalent than those at either end of the feminist/antifeminist spectrum.

Ibsen's nuanced views on women are memorably reflected in his tragic drama *Hedda Gabler* (1890). On one level this middle-class drawing-room drama is a study of what can happen when a spirited woman marries a pedantic, scholarly man unsuited to her. More broadly, it explores the clash between a woman whose temperament exceeds the bounds of conventional femininity at the time – conditioned as she is by factors of heredity and environment – and the circumstances within which she is confined. Hedda Gabler has frequently been viewed as a termagant, embodying a highly negative conception of femininity. She appears spoiled and self-centered, and her behavior is often downright bitchy: she financially manipulates her husband Tesman and treats him with belittling sarcasm; deliberately hurts the feelings of his elderly aunt, Juliana Tesman; is physically cruel to her old friend Thea Elvsted when she suddenly turns up from out of the past; and burns the sole copy of the most recent book by Løvborg, her former admirer and her husband's rival.

Yet much in Hedda's temperament is explained by looking, as Ibsen so often encourages his audiences to do, at the circumstances in which she grew up. The dominant influence on the young Hedda is intimated even before the action of the play begins, in the reference in the stage directions to "a portrait of a handsome, elderly man in a general's uniform" (Ibsen 1965: 695). Her upbringing without a mother and under the influence of a military father produces an independent, strong-willed young woman who is more interested in horses, pistols, and competition than in the occupations typical for girls at the time. That Ibsen titles his play with her maiden name, although it deals with her life after marriage, reflects his desire "to indicate thereby that as a personality she is to be regarded rather as her father's daughter than as her husband's wife" (Ibsen 1966: 500).

Hedda's tragedy, however, is that she is nonetheless Tesman's wife, a role that in turn-of-the-century Europe was severely restrictive. Riding and shooting are the only men's activities available to her, since as a woman she is excluded from the realm of public activity. To a considerable extent, she lives through the men she knows. Already as a girl she took vicarious pleasure in hearing Løvborg's stories of drinking and womanizing, things she was officially forbidden to know about. The gender division of the day is poignantly evident in her response to family friend Judge Brack's question about whether there is no goal in life she can work toward; she replies that she is thinking of getting Tesman to go into politics. When Brack, disturbed by her freewheeling hand with the pistols she has inherited from her father, asks her what she is shooting at, her response can be read as symbolic of her activity in general: "Oh, I was just shooting into the sky" (Ibsen 1965: 722). Her motivation in sending the alcoholic Løvborg off to Brack's drinking party is telling: "For once in my life, I want to have power over a human being" (Ibsen 1965: 745).

The extent to which Hedda is restricted because of her position as a middle-class wife is epitomized in her pregnancy, which is alluded to obliquely several times in the play. In contrast to Juliana Tesman, who delights in the role of caretaker, and Thea Elvsted, who happily acts as midwife to Løvborg's books, Hedda is wholly unmaternal and has no desire to have a child. She is a consummate embodiment of the process Michel Foucault has described as the "hysterization" of the female body, one of the mechanisms of knowledge and power centering on sex that he believes to have intensified during the nineteenth century. The import of hysterization, or the reduction of the woman to her bodily femininity, was to tie women to their reproductive function (Foucault [1976] (1978): 103–4). Exemplifying Foucault's claim that "the Mother, with her negative image of 'nervous woman,' constituted the most visible form of this hysterization" (Foucault [1976] (1978): 104), Hedda manifests hysterical behavior throughout the play, constantly pacing the floor, opening the curtains, raising her arms and clenching her fists; her pinching, slapping, and dragging of Thea Elvsted can likewise be regarded as hysterical actions.

The contrast to Nora Helmer of *A Doll House* is illuminating. Nora too is portrayed as suffocating in a marriage to an oppressive husband, is confined by conventional expectations for women, and exhibits hysterical symptoms, most graphically manifested in the tarantella she dances. (Hélène Cixous and Catherine Clément have argued that the tarantella, danced by women in southern Italy in simulation of a reaction to the spider's bite, functions as a kind of hysterical catharsis; Cixous and Clément [1975] 1986: 19–22). Yet Nora ultimately has the courage to leave her restrictive environment and strike out on her own. Hedda Gabler, by contrast, is for all her independent thinking much more concerned with propriety, with what people think. She confides to Brack that she married Tesman because her "time was up" (Ibsen 1965: 725) – in other words, because she had reached the limit of the age where people expected her to marry. She is throughout concerned with doing what is "proper" and with avoiding public humiliation. Ultimately, when faced with the choice between an adulterous relationship with Brack and the scandalous revelation that she gave Løvborg the pistol with which he accidentally shot himself, she can tolerate neither alternative. Trapped on the one hand by her status as a female and on the other by her social conditioning, she faces a tragic impasse. Where Nora moves from hysteria to feminism, Hedda remains trapped in hysteria and its extreme consequence, self-destruction.

Sexuality

Alongside male dramatists like Ibsen, who were at least partially sympathetic to the women's cause, a number of female dramatists make their mark on the modern theater in both the United States and Europe. Although not part of the canon of world theater, one play by a woman worth singling out for mention because of its unusually candid treatment of sexuality is Else Lasker-Schüler's *Die Wupper* (The Wupper River, 1909). Lasker-Schüler is one of the more colorful figures in the German literary tradition. Her second husband was the editor of one of the leading expressionist literary journals in Germany, and she produced some of the finest expressionist poetry in the German language. Following her second divorce she cultivated a self-consciously bohemian way of life, living on a pittance, spending her days in bars, circuses, and cafés, frequently wearing Middle Eastern garb, and often cross-dressing.

Die Wupper reflects Lasker-Schüler's unconventional attitudes toward sexuality, class, and dramatic form. The play is formally too loose to be called a tragedy per se, but its entire worldview is tragic: it is pervaded by a sense of life as incomprehensible and pointless that points forward to the theater of the absurd. Set in one of the most industrialized regions of Germany, the textile-producing area along the Wupper River in northern Westphalia, the play juxtaposes workers with members of the managerial class in a virtually unprecedented manner. The interaction between the classes, especially of an erotic nature, is microcosmically depicted in the relationships between two families, the Pius clan, who are factory workers, and the family of Frau Sonntag, a factory owner. In the course of the play we witness sadomasochistic games between Carl Pius and Frau Sonntag's daughter Marta, Frau Sonntag's son Heinrich joking about kissing Carl's grandmother, this same grandmother attempting to interest Carl in Marta by showing him a nude photograph of her and seeking to arouse his passion for the lower-class girl Lieschen, Carl's confession that he was fond of doing needlework as a boy and the concomitant homosexual overtones in his relationship with Marta's brother Eduard, and a relationship between Lieschen and Heinrich that leads to Heinrich's demise. These transnormative sexual activities openly thwart the traditional patriarchal family structure dominant in Imperial Germany, in which – officially speaking – father knows best, women know their place, and sex occurs only between married partners and is not to be talked about.

But the play's most striking challenge to traditional sexual norms is posed by the three vagrants who hover around the edges of the action, appearing at critical moments in the play: Tall Anna, a transvestite who wears articles of women's clothing, speaks in a high voice, whimpers like a woman, and plays on his harmonica a melancholic melody that is heard at other points in the play as well: "Oh, dear Augustine, everything is lost, lost, lost" (Lasker-Schüler 1997: 35 *et passim*);

Pendelfrederech, who wears a patch over his oozing eye, mutters constantly, and exhibitionistically displays his genital *Pendel* (pendulum); and Glassy Amadeus, an androgynous figure who can interpret dreams. These three characters are completely marginal, living in nature and outside the world of work, yet with their oblique commentary on the play's action their function is analogous to that of the chorus in Greek tragedy.

The sexual and class heterogeneity of *Die Wupper* is paralleled by a highly mixed form. Its treatment of the proletariat in an industrial milieu – here, the dyers and weavers of the Wupper valley – links it to the naturalist drama of the 1890s, as does its candid portrayal of the harshness of the workers' lives – their poverty, alcoholism, and the earthy details associated with their labor. Also classically naturalistic is Lasker-Schüler's replication of the Low German dialect of the region. And yet her talent as an expressionist poet is evident in the play's lyrical language, graphic imagery, striking use of color, and visionary sets. Like much later expressionist drama, the play contains little conflict or suspense and consists of a series of episodic scenes, although it maintains formal division into acts.

Following the period in which naturalist theater flourished and preceding the true era of expressionist drama, then, *Die Wupper* manifests features of both modes and is stylistically unclassifiable. Critics in Lasker-Schüler's day, baffled by the play's eclecticism and aware of the identity of its author, labeled its style "feminine." Yet in view of the drama's subversion of conventional attitudes toward sexuality with an eye to revealing the degree to which they are socially constructed, it is more accurate to call the play modern.

Form

Language

The extent to which Anton Chekhov's dramas are tragic has been debated. On the one hand, it is noted that the plays do not end with the death(s) of the main character(s), although deaths do occur; two of the plays are subtitled "Comedy." On the other hand, it has been suggested, given the dismal view of existence conveyed by the plays, that the characters' real tragedy is the fact that they survive. Yet all the plays contain a great deal of black humor, and the most appropriate term for their genre is probably tragicomedy. Already in Chekhov's day a theater critic claimed that the development of modern drama begins with the fusion of tragedy and comedy (Friedell 1906: 543), whereby "modern" has its relative meaning of "recent." In any case, after Chekhov tragicomedy becomes the dominant mode of theater in the twentieth century.

Much of the tragicomedy of Chekhov's plays stems from the fact that his characters are deadened by the ennui of provincial life, ache with love for someone who does not love them in return, are plagued by the gap between intention and action, experience a resulting sense of frustrated ineffectualness, speak and are misunderstood or unheard. In their dazed helplessness Chekhov's men and women often resemble somnambulists, a comparison that is verbalized again and again. To mention only a few instances, near the beginning of *The Sea Gull* (1896) Sorin remarks that he feels as if he were "in a nightmare" (Chekhov 1960: 82), and his sister Arkadina's insistence at the opening of her son Treplev's play that "We are asleep" (Chekhov 1960: 90) figuratively fore-shadows the listlessness with which she and her entourage will drift through the drama in which *they* are featured. Similarly, in *The Cherry Orchard* (1903), both the landowner Madame Ranevskaya and the merchant Lopakhin express incredulity by claiming that they are dreaming (Chekhov 1960: 295, 338).

Chekhov conveys the experiences of his characters – unrequited love, provincial ennui to the point of feeling dazed, unrealized intentions – through a form of dialogue that is in fact no dialogue at all but rather a talking past, a language of misunder-standing and misdirection. One especially extensive and graphic example occurs at the beginning of *The Three Sisters* (1900), where two of the sisters' nostalgic comments about returning to Moscow and about their missed opportunities are punctuated by rude exclamations from the officers in the next room:

> OLGA: I remember perfectly that by this time, at the beginning of May in Moscow, everything was in bloom, it was warm, all bathed in sunshine. Eleven years have passed, but I remember it all as though we had left there yesterday. Oh, God! This morning I woke up, I saw this flood of sunlight, saw the spring, and joy stirred in my soul, I had a passionate longing to go home again.
>
> CHEBUTYKIN: Like hell he did!
>
> TUZENBACH: Of course, that's nonsense . . .
>
> IRINA: To go to Moscow. To sell the house, make an end of everything here, and go to Moscow . . .
> OLGA: Yes! To go to Moscow as soon as possible.
> (*Chebutykin and Tuzenbach laugh.*) . . .
>
> OLGA: It's all good, all from God, but it seems to me that if I had married and stayed at home all day, it would have been better. (*Pause*) I should have loved my husband.
> TUZENBACH (*to* SOLYONY): You talk such nonsense I'm tired of listening to you.
>
> (Chekhov 1960: 207–9)

Rather than responding to the women's words, the men's lines serve as an indirect commentary on them, intimating the futility of the desires they express. Another striking example of the technique of talking past is found in *The Cherry Orchard*, in the preoccupation of Madame Ranevskaya's brother with billiards; most of his lines, describing shots he imagines himself taking, have little to do with the surrounding dialogue or action and point up instead the aimlessness of his life and his isolation in his obsession.

The technique of characters talking past, rather than to, each other is found in much of modern drama, reflecting the degree to which the theater of the late nineteenth and early twentieth centuries is concerned with the difficulties and limitations of verbal communication. Chekhov's use of the technique highlights his portrayal of a malaise that transcends the social problems of a specific era and can therefore be termed existential. In both these features, his drama anticipates the postmodern theater of Beckett, Pinter, Genet, and others.

Space

In modern theater Else Lasker-Schüler is an early practitioner in a wide range of experiments in dramatic form. In the course of the twentieth century theatrical space takes on increasingly symbolic dimensions, a development previewed in realistic drawing-room drama. Ibsen exploits the potential of his one-room settings by concentrating the action in the room the audience can see but extending the room beyond its physical dimensions through references to conversations and other sounds heard in surrounding rooms, as well as to places offstage. In a notable example, in *Ghosts* (1881), Mrs. Alving's overhearing the struggle and dialogue in the next room between her son Osvald and her servant girl alerts her to the presence of "ghosts" – insofar as Osvald is repeating with the servant the behavior of Mrs. Alving's deceased husband with the girl's mother. In Ibsen's *The Wild Duck* (1884) the outside world is microcosmically brought indoors: the attic room in which the duck is kept is so resonant with elements from the outdoors – poultry, pigeons, rabbits, a straw basket and trough of water for the duck, and skylights that literally allow part of the outside world to enter – that it resembles a kind of miniature indoor forest. The tension between the visible spaces and those evoked audially or verbally adds considerably to the dramatic power of Ibsen's settings.

But the most radical use of spatial symbolism in modern theater is found in the drama of August Strindberg, above all in *A Dream Play* (1901), in which the products of the unconscious mind are made visible onstage. In the use of this technique, the play can be seen to launch expressionist theater. Other features that would become typical of expressionist theater are the play's episodic structure, poetic imagery, and highly lyrical language (the play even introduces musical notation into the text), and the use of character types – in this case, the Officer, the Lawyer, the Doorkeeper, the Quarantine Master, the Schoolmaster, the Poet, and so on – rather than individualized characters. This last trait reflects the fact that, like Lasker-Schüler's *Die Wupper*, *A Dream Play* portrays the tragedy of human existence rather than the tragedy of a single individual character(s).

When Strindberg's German translator, Emil Schering, expressed consternation upon reading the play, the author wrote him a letter containing a concise explanation of its project:

How to understand *A Dream Play*?

Indra's daughter has descended to Earth to find out how human beings have it. And there she learns how difficult life is. And the worst is: having to injure or do harm to others if one wants to live. The form is motivated in a preface: the conglomeration out of a dream in which, however, there is a definite logic. Everything *irrational* becomes believable. Human beings appear at several points and are sketched, the sketches flow together; the same person splits into several persons only to form into one again.

Time and place do not exist; a minute is equal to many years, etc. (Strindberg 1973: 3)

Since the scope of dreams is cosmic, the sky is literally the limit of the play's purview. It begins in the clouds, the home of Indra and the other gods, from which Indra's daughter descends to earth, the "densest and heaviest / of the spheres wandering in space" (Strindberg 1973: 20). In her search to learn whether the complaints of human beings are justified, the Daughter witnesses or participates in a series of human experiences in synthetic form – the pursuit of knowledge, love, marriage and its difficulties. Settings change without transition and with stunning vividness, moving from a castle crowned with a flower bud to the deathbed of the Officer's mother to the corridor of the opera house, where the Officer has waited for his beloved for seven years, to the Lawyer's office to Fingal's Cave (an actual cave on an island in the Hebrides west of Scotland) to the suffocating apartment where the Daughter lives as the wife of the Lawyer to Foulstrand and Fairhaven. Although the play's cosmic scope would seem to present an enormous challenge to any set designer, Strindberg's stage directions provide for considerable spatial economy, making frequent suggestions about how to adapt one set for use as the next one.

The rich symbolism of the play's dream settings is virtually mythic in its universal resonance. The air hole in the shape of a four-leaf clover in the door at the opera house, for example, can be read as symbolic of the key to the meaning of life – hope – such as that necessary to sustain the Officer in his long wait for his beloved. By contrast, the shawl worn by the doorkeeper is heavy with the agonies of people she has encountered during her 30 years there. Foulstrand and Fairhaven can be read as anxiety dream and wish-fulfillment dream, respectively, the former a place containing quarantine buildings for the sick and a gymnasium "in which people are exercised on machines resembling instruments of torture" (Strindberg 1973: 46) designed to counteract their physical deformities brought on by excessive eating and drinking, the latter a felicitous spot featuring sunshine, children, flowers, singing and dancing, lovers in a sailboat on a beautiful bay, flags on docks, white handkerchiefs of greeting, and a lovely melody in the background. Like many of our dreams, both terrifying and pleasant, Foulstrand and Fairhaven are grotesquely exaggerated, and, significantly, the boundary between them is a thin one; the lovers on the sailboat glide from Fairhaven inexorably to Foulstrand, where they are condemned to a 40-day quarantine.

Just as the seeds of Strindberg's expressionist drama lie in the symbolism of his earlier realist and naturalist plays, *A Dream Play* abounds in realistic elements. To cite a single, telling example: the hairpins which the Lawyer finds on the floor of the apartment he shares with the Daughter are emblematic of the Daughter's slovenliness, which is one of the major causes of his discontent in their marriage. Yet typically for the complex symbolic structure of this play, Strindberg does not leave things at that. Rather, a conversation about hairpins between the Lawyer and the Officer points to another level of significance:

LAWYER: Look at this one. It has two prongs but is one pin! There are two, but it's one! If
    I straighten it out, there's only one! If I bend it, there are two without ceasing to be
    one. That means: the two are one! But if I break it – here! Then they're two! Two!
    (*Breaks the hairpin and throws the pieces away*)
OFFICER: You've seen all this . . . But before you can break them off, the prongs have to
    diverge. If they converge, it holds up.

(Strindberg 1973: 46)

It is not difficult to interpret the hairpin in this dialogue as a symbol of romantic
partnership. Hence in Strindberg's ingeniously economical rendering the same object
symbolizes both marital strife and marital unity, and yet is effective in both functions.
Furthermore, insofar as this scene occurs just after the Officer has invited the
Daughter to go away with him and immediately before the Lawyer leaves her, it
also serves as a symbolic transition from one relationship to the next.

In the end, however, the Daughter is disappointed in this as in every earthly
experience in which she takes part, again and again observing that "Human beings
are to be pitied": joy has to be paid for doubly with sorrow, life is filled with
repetition and tedium, doing good for one person means bringing misery to others.
The essence of what she learns about human life – its split nature – is compellingly
captured in the last words she speaks before leaving the earth:

> Now I feel all the agony of being,
> that's how it's to be a human being , , ,
> One misses even what one has not valued,
> one regrets even what one has not broken . . .
> One wants to leave, and one wants to stay . . .
> So the halves of the heart are torn apart,
> and feelings are torn as between horses
> by contradiction, indecision, disharmony . . .
> (Strindberg 1973: 85–6)

The play's consummate symbol of the fundamental duality of existence is the first and
last station the Daughter encounters: the castle crowned by a flower bud is, significantly, surrounded by manure and litter from the stables; when the castle catches fire
at the play's end, a wall of human faces, "asking, sorrowing, despairing" (Strindberg
1973: 86), is illuminated, yet the flower bud bursts into a gigantic chrysanthemum.

In the wake of Strindberg much of twentieth-century drama is enriched by the
presence of figures from dream and fantasy existing onstage alongside realistic
characters. Following his expressionistic use of space, reflecting his awareness of the
power of the unconscious mind over our daily lives, theater could never be the same
again.

REFERENCES AND FURTHER READING

Aristotle (1961). *Poetics*, trans. S. H. Butcher. New York: Hill & Wang. Primary text.

Benjamin, Walter. [1916] (1996). "*Trauerspiel* and Tragedy," trans. Rodney Livingstone. In *Selected Writings*, vol. I, ed. Marcus Bullock and Michael W. Jennings. Cambridge, MA: Harvard University Press, 55–68. Contains the seeds of some of the main ideas in Benjamin's landmark book *Ursprung des deutschen Trauerspiels* (1925; translated as *The Origin of German Tragic Drama*, 1977), which he was outlining at the time this essay was written.

Bennett, Benjamin. (1990). *Theater as Problem: Modern Drama and Its Place in Literature*. Ithaca, NY: Cornell University Press. Investigates the disruptive effects of drama and of dramatic theory from Ibsen to Dürrenmatt.

Büchner, Georg. [1836–7] (1971). *Woyzeck*, trans. Victor Price. In *Danton's Death, Leonce and Lena, Woyzeck*. Oxford: Oxford University Press, 105–32. Primary text.

Chekhov, Anton. (1960). *Plays and Stories*, trans. Ann Dunnigan. Garden City, NY: International Collectors Library. Primary text.

Cixous, Hélène and Clément, Catherine. [1975] (1986). *The Newly Born Woman*, trans. Betsy Wing. Minneapolis: University of Minnesota Press. This pivotal text of new French feminism discusses ways in which women have been oppressed and silenced, as well as their modes of resistance.

Finney, Gail. (1989). *Women in Modern Drama: Freud, Feminism, and European Theater at the Turn of the Century*. Ithaca, NY: Cornell University Press. Explores the dynamics of gender identity and family relationships in major plays by nine playwrights writing between 1880 and 1920.

Foucault, Michel. [1976] (1978). *The History of Sexuality. Vol I: An Introduction*, trans. Robert Hurley. New York: Vintage. Overthrows conventional thinking about the history of sexuality, notably about its supposed repression during the Victorian era.

Friedell, Egon. (1906). "Das Ende der Tragödie" [The end of tragedy]. *Die Schaubühne* 2, 541–5. Suggests that tragicomedy is the dominant mode of modern drama (the drama of his time).

Ganz, Arthur. (1980). *Realms of the Self: Variations on a Theme in Modern Drama*. New York: New York University Press. Studies the theme of the quest for self-fulfillment in drama from Wilde to Pinter.

Guthke, Karl. (1994). *Das deutsche bürgerliche Trauerspiel* [The German bourgeois tragedy]. Stuttgart: Metzler. Seminal work on the genre, dealing not only with canonical figures but touching on lesser-known dramatists as well.

Herzfeld-Sander, Margaret, ed. (1985). *Essays on German Theater*. New York: Continuum. English translations of key texts in history of German theater from Lessing to Heiner-Müller, including excerpts from Gotthold E. Lessing's "Siebzehnter Brief, die neueste Literatur betreffend" (The seventeenth letter concerning the newest literature) and *Hamburgische Dramaturgie* (Hamburg dramaturgy) and from Jakob M. R. Lenz's *Anmerkungen übers Theater* (Notes on the theater).

Ibsen, Henrik. (1965). *The Complete Major Prose Plays*, trans. Rolf Fjelde. New York: Farrar, Straus & Giroux. Primary text.

Ibsen, Henrik. (1966). *The Oxford Ibsen*, vol. VII, ed. James W. McFarlane. London: Oxford University Press. Primary text.

Ibsen, Henrik. (1972). *Speeches and New Letters*, trans. Arne Kildal. New York: Haskell House. Primary text.

Lasker-Schüler, Else. (1997). *Die Wupper* [The Wupper River]. In *Werke und Briefe: Kritische Ausgabe*, vol. II. Frankfurt/Main: Suhrkamp. Primary text.

Lillo, George. (1965). *The London Merchant*, ed. William H. McBurney. Lincoln: University of Nebraska Press. Primary text.

Simon, Bennett. (1988). *Tragic Drama and the Family: Psychoanalytic Studies from Aeschylus to Beckett*. New Haven, CT: Yale University Press. Psychoanalytically informed analyses of family dynamics in tragic plays from ancient Greece to contemporary theater.

Strindberg, August. (1973). *A Dream Play and Four Chamber Plays*, trans. Walter Johnson. Seattle: University of Washington Press. Primary text.

Synge, J. M. (1968). *Plays*, Book II. In *Collected Works*, vol. IV, ed. Ann Saddlemyer. London: Oxford University Press. Primary text.

27

Tragedy in the Modern American Theater

Brenda Murphy

In 1886, referring to Dostoevsky's *Crime and Punishment*, the major nineteenth-century American critic and cultural arbiter William Dean Howells wrote that "whoever struck a note so profoundly tragic in American fiction would do a false and mistaken thing," inviting American writers to "concern themselves with the more smiling aspects of life, which are the more American" (Howells 1993: 35). In the decades since then, Howells's words about the "smiling aspects," taken out of context, have become a cultural shorthand for the putative inability of Americans to fully understand the tragic vision of human experience, and therefore, for the failure of American literature to encompass fully developed tragedy as a genre.

Although none of them remain in the contemporary repertoire, there were in fact a number of tragedies written by Americans in the eighteenth and nineteenth centuries. Many had native subjects, such as the demise of the "noble savage." Several raised the historical figures of the new nation to tragic status. The most popular, from Thomas Godfrey's *The Prince of Parthia* (1767) to George Boker's *Francesca da Rimini* (1855) and William Young's *Pendragon* (1881), focused on subjects that were remote from the audience, both chronologically and geographically. By the end of the nineteenth century, however, eclipsed by popular melodrama and, later, the domestic realism favored by Howells and other Progressive critics, contemporary tragedy was hard to find on the American stage.

In 1949, when Arthur Miller wrote *Death of a Salesman*, he felt it necessary to explain his chosen genre in the *New York Times*. "In this age few tragedies are written," he said, and offered his account of the cultural explanations for the near-absence of tragedy in the mid-twentieth-century American theater:

> It has often been held that the lack is due to a paucity of heroes among us, or else that modern man has had the blood drawn out of his organs of belief by the skepticism of science, and the heroic attack on life cannot feed on an attitude of reserve and circumspection. For one reason or another, we are often held to be below tragedy – or

tragedy above us. The inevitable conclusion is, of course, that the tragic mode is archaic, fit only for the very highly placed, the kings or the kingly, and where this admission is not made in so many words it is often implied. (Miller 1996: 3)

It is true that American playwrights who chose tragedy as their genre were writing against cultural expectations in the twentieth century, but the absence of tragedy was not quite so complete as this account suggests. In fact, a revival of the genre was taking place during the period from 1925 to 1960, which produced the United States' most distinguished tragedies, including *Death of a Salesman* and several other plays by Miller. It began with Maxwell Anderson's intense interest in reviving verse drama on the modern stage and the renewed interest in tragedy among modernist playwrights like Eugene O'Neill, who were influenced by Nietzsche's *The Birth of Tragedy* (1872).

Maxwell Anderson

A poet, critic, and former college professor, Maxwell Anderson did not shy away from making pronouncements on literary matters. In several essays, he clarified his decision to write in verse for the contemporary theater and his application of Aristotle to modern tragedy. He wrote in "Poetry in the Theatre" that "the best prose in the world is inferior on the stage to the best poetry" (1939: 34). Anderson wrote several verse tragedies on historical subjects, including *Elizabeth the Queen* (1930), *Mary of Scotland* (1933), and *Anne of the Thousand Days* (1948), which enjoyed both critical and popular success, and were made into successful Hollywood movies. It was the verse plays he wrote on contemporary subjects, such as *Night over Taos* (1932), *Winterset* (1935), and *Key Largo* (1939) that he thought more difficult and more daring, however. He wrote that he was attempting to "establish a new convention" by treating a contemporary tragic theme in verse, "more of an experiment than I could wish, for the great masters themselves never tried to make tragic poetry out of the stuff of their own times" (1939: 38). There is no denying that Anderson was unsuccessful at establishing a convention for the modern theater, but many critics attest that he succeeded in creating contemporary tragedy with *Winterset*, and the popular success of his historical verse plays paved the way for playwrights like T. S. Eliot and Christopher Fry.

In describing his approach to tragedy, Anderson left no doubt that he followed Aristotle. He described his fundamental rule for the writing of a serious play in an essay entitled "The Essence of Tragedy" (1938): "A play should lead up to and away from a central crisis, and this crisis should consist in a discovery by the leading character which has an indelible effect on his thought and emotion and completely alters his course of action" (1939: 7). For Anderson the hero's discovery of "some element in his environment or in his own soul of which he has not been aware – or which he has not taken sufficiently into account" was "the mainspring in the mechanism of a modern play" (1939: 6). What's more, he thought that the hero's discovery must lead to his personal redemption through suffering. In a revised version of the essay published in 1947, Anderson personalized the experience of the tragic hero even further, declaring that "the story of a play must be conflict, and specifically, a conflict between the forces of good and evil within a single person." Along with the personalization of the tragic experience went its moralization. Anderson explained that, in a modern play, the protagonist "must represent the forces of good and must win, or, if he has been evil, must yield to the forces of the good, and know himself defeated" (Anderson 1947: 25).

For Anderson, then, tragedy was essentially a moral genre, based on the redemption of the hero through suffering. Like Aristotle, Anderson thought that "the hero who is to make the central discovery in a play must not be a perfect man. He must have some variation of what Aristotle calls a tragic fault . . . and he must change for the better" (1939: 8–9). The reason Anderson consistently gave for his insistence on the protagonist's being on the side of the good was the audience. He insisted that

> what the audience wants to believe is that men have a desire to break the moulds of earth which encase them and claim a kinship with a higher morality than that which hems them in . . . the theatre at its best is a religious affirmation, an age-old rite restating and reassuring man's belief in his own destiny and his ultimate hope. (1939: 13–14).

For Anderson, modern tragedy presupposed the same conjunction of desire for spiritual transcendence with striving for ethical behavior as modern Christianity. It must affirm both humankind's essential sinfulness and the promise of redemption and union with the divinity that Christianity affirms. His essentially Christian understanding of the genre is reflected in his essay "Yes, by the Eternal": "The last act of a tragedy contains the moment when the wheel of a man's fate carries him simultaneously to spiritual realization and to the end of his life" (1939: 51–2).

The execution of Anderson's ideas is clear in *Winterset*, his tragedy based on the notorious 1927 execution of anarchists Nicola Sacco and Bartolomeo Vanzetti for the murder of a paymaster they were supposed to have robbed. Anderson was consumed by the miscarriage of justice in the case, and had treated it more directly in his realistic play *Gods of the Lightning* (1928), but in *Winterset* he wrote a verse tragedy about a chain of events that might have occurred after the execution. In the play, 17-year-old Mio Romagna has dedicated his life to proving what he believes to be the truth, that his father was wrongfully executed for robbery and murder. The play centers on Mio's interaction with the Esdras family, when he comes to ask them about new evidence suggesting that there was a witness to the crime. The family consists of the son Garth, who did witness the murder by members of the gang he belongs to, but, in order to save his own life, did not speak up to save Romagna; his father, who has taught him that it is "better to tell a lie and live" (20); and his young sister Miriamne, who falls in love with Mio and must eventually choose between telling the truth and saving Mio from the gang, or telling a lie and saving her brother from the law.

Anderson sets Mio and Miriamne against a group of characters who represent degrees or gradations of evil. At one end of the scale is Trock Estrella, who actually killed the paymaster. Trock represents an unthinking evil, formed by a youth spent in the hands of the criminal justice system. Motivated by pure self-interest, Trock is determined to kill anyone who would put him in danger of being locked up again. The next degree of evil is represented by the moral relativism of two old men, the Jewish intellectual Esdras and Judge Gaunt, who presided over the trial that sent Bartolomeo Romagna to his death. These men have been so jaded and corrupted by experience that they reject all moral absolutes. Esdras counsels his guilt-ridden son Garth to keep silent about the murder, saying, "you bear no guilt at all – / unless you wish" (19), for guilt does not exist until he names it. Garth's instinctive moral sense will not allow him to accept his father's rationalization. But he has fallen into a suicidal despair, feeling that he is damned anyway and "dying inside" every day because he "sat here and let [Romagna] die instead of me / because I wanted to live!" (17). Garth has concluded that life is worthless and means "to get it over" and "take some scum down with me" (17), but he is paralyzed by weakness and fear when he has the chance.

The conflict between good and evil that Anderson said must take place within the hero is divided between the two young people, Miriamne and Mio. Forced to choose between saving her brother by supporting his lie or telling the truth that will keep Mio out of danger, Miriamne supports Garth, telling Mio, "he's my brother. / I couldn't give them my brother" (109). While Miriamne cannot sacrifice her brother's life, she can give up her own. When Mio is killed by Trock Estrella's gang, Miriamne is driven to walk into the gang's machine-gun fire. Acting out of her rudimentary understanding of morality, Miriamne succeeds only in showing the pathos of her desire to cancel her guilt for endangering Mio's life by giving her own. It is only the hero Mio who is allowed to learn anything in the course of the tragedy. When Mio hears the truth about the trial from Judge Gaunt and Trock Estrella, it is salvific, as is his love for Miriamne. But his redemption comes with his real understanding of the values his father lived for. His realization is of the transcendent and eternal nature of love. As Mio is dying, he repeats to Miriamne his father's last words to him, "I love you, and will love you after I die" (131). After both of them have died, Esdras, acting as a choral figure, calls on them to forgive him and Garth, and to "forgive the ancient evil of the earth / that brought you here" (133).

By affirming the transformational and transcendent character of love, Anderson elevates the virtue of *caritas* over that of justice, which, he implies, is inevitably corrupted in its human execution by the base desire for revenge or the human frailty of those who administer it. The tragic universe that he represents is a Christian one in which suffering is inevitable and death is inescapable, but redemption is possible. He wrote that the theater has the capacity to bring all the arts together "in a communal religious service. Any other art, practiced separately, can be either moral or amoral, religious or pagan, affirmative or despairing. But when they come together in the theater they must affirm, they cannot deny" (1947: 32). Anderson's tragedy affirmed a belief in a definable good and evil and the possibility for salvation, even for those who have succumbed to evil in various guises.

Eugene O'Neill

While Anderson's tragedy is fundamentally grounded in Aristotle, this is not the case with that of the United States' greatest playwright, Eugene O'Neill. In 1928, when O'Neill was asked by an interviewer who his literary idol was, he replied: "The answer to that is in one word – Nietzsche" (Estrin 1990: 81). This had been true since 1907, when O'Neill was first introduced to Nietzsche's work. The most important of Nietzsche's books for O'Neill was *Also Sprach Zarathustra* (1883–5). In 1927, he wrote to fellow Nietzschean Benjamin DeCasseres that the book had "influenced me more than any book I've ever read" (Bogard and Bryer 1988: 246). But this was by no means the only one of Nietzsche's works O'Neill studied carefully. He read and made copious notations in several of Nietzsche's works during his Greenwich Village period, most importantly *The Birth of Tragedy*, and the presence of Nietzsche's ideas in O'Neill's work has been well documented. Gerhard Hoffman articulates the consensus of critics: "Nietzsche's influence on Eugene O'Neill was probably greater than on any other English-speaking playwright" (1995: 197). The influence of Nietzsche on *Desire Under the Elms* (1924), *Strange Interlude* (1928), *Mourning Becomes Electra* (1931), *The Fountain* (1925), and other plays has been noted, but it is most evident in two tragedies written during O'Neill's most intense period of modernist experimentation: *The Great God Brown* (1926) and *Lazarus Laughed* (1928).

O'Neill wrote in 1942 that he considered *The Great God Brown* "one of the most interesting and moving" plays he had written because it succeeded "in conveying a sense of the tragic mystery drama of Life revealed through the lives in the play" (Commins 1986: 205). The play centers on a fundamental Nietzschean division. Defining realms of art, Nietzsche suggests, Apollo is "the transfiguring genius of the *principium individuationis*," while "under the mystical cry of exultation of Dionysus the spell of individuation is burst apart and the path to the Mothers of Being, to the innermost core of things, lies open" (2000: 86). O'Neill's play is an enactment of the tragic myth that Nietzsche describes as "a transformation of the wisdom of Dionysus into images through the artistic means of Apollo," ending in "the fraternal bond between both artistic deities in tragedy" which produces "the highest original artistic joy in the womb of the original Unity" (2000: 118–19). In *The Great God Brown*, Dion Anthony is a Dionysian artist, while Bill Brown is an Apollonian architect. O'Neill explained that his characters reflect Nietzsche's idea of the self and the anti-self:

> Dion Anthony – Dionysus and St. Anthony – the creative pagan acceptance of life, fighting eternal war with the masochistic, life-denying spirit of Christianity as represented by St. Anthony – the whole struggle resulting in this modern day in

mutual exhaustion – creative joy in life for life's sake frustrated, rendered abortive, distorted by morality from Pan into Satan, into a Mephistopheles mocking himself in order to feel alive; Christianity, once heroic in martyrs for its intense faith now pleading weakly for intense belief in anything, even Godhead itself. (Clark 1929: 160–1)

While Dion is an artist tortured by the division of his soul, Bill Brown "is the visionless demi-god of our new materialistic myth – a Success – building his life of exterior things, inwardly empty and resourceless, an uncreative creature of superficial preordained social grooves, a by-product forced aside into slack waters by the deep main current of life-desire" (Clark 1929: 161). In the play, Dion as a boy puts on a mask which is *"a fixed forcing of his own face – dark, spiritual, poetic, passionately supersensitive, helplessly unprotected in its childlike, religious faith in life – into the expression of a mocking, reckless, defiant, gayly scoffing and sensual young Pan"* (O'Neill 1982: 1.260). O'Neill said that this mask is "not only a defense against the world for the super-sensitive painter-poet underneath it, but also an integral part of his character as the artist" (Clark 1929: 161). The world not only is blind to the artist beneath the mask, but "sneers at and condemns" the Pan mask it sees.

After this, "Dion's inner self retrogresses along the line of Christian resignation until it partakes of the nature of the Saint while at the same time the outer Pan is slowly transformed by his struggle with reality into Mephistopheles" (Clark 1929: 161). After Dion dies, leaving "Dion Anthony to William Brown – for him to love and obey – for him to become" (299), Brown appropriates his mask, hoping to capture the creative power with which he has enlivened his architectural designs and the sexual passion that has bound the two women for whom the men are rivals, Margaret and Cybel, to Dion rather than to Brown. He buries Dion in the garden, and, in putting on his mask, thinks, "I am drinking your strength, Dion – strength to love in this world and die and sleep and become fertile earth, as you are becoming now in my garden" (307). As O'Neill explains:

> Brown has always envied the creative life force in Dion – what he himself lacks. When he steals Dion's mask of Mephistopheles he thinks he is gaining the power to live creatively, while in reality he is only stealing that creative power made self-destructive by complete frustration. This devil of mocking doubt makes short work of him. (Clark 1929: 161)

He kills off "William Brown," the successful face that was presented to the world, and becomes "Dion Brown," a temporary union of the Dionysian and Apollonian forces, but he is quickly killed by the "people." As the earth-mother character Cybel says: "They must find a victim! . . . They've got to absolve themselves by finding a guilty one! They've got to kill someone now, to live!" (320). In the moment of death, Brown experiences the temporary lifting of the veil of Maya that Nietzsche describes as a seeing past the phenomena of the world into Unity. As Cybel says her prayer, "Our Father Who Art!," Brown has his momentary ecstatic vision:

I know! I have found Him! I hear Him speak! "Blessed are they that weep, for they shall laugh!" Only he that has wept can laugh! The laughter of Heaven sows earth with a rain of tears, and out of earth's transfigured birth-pain the laughter of Man returns to bless and play again in innumerable dancing gales of flame upon the knees of God! (322)

Having seen this vision of truth, he dies, leaving Cybel articulating a version of the myth of eternal recurrence. As O'Neill puts it, "out of this anguish his soul is born, a tortured Christian soul such as the dying Dion's, begging for belief, and at the last finding it on the lips of Cybel" (Clark 1929: 162).

While the Christian myth is somewhat buried in *The Great God Brown*, O'Neill made it the central framework for *Lazarus Laughed*, which has been called "the most thoroughly Nietzschean play ever written" (Bridgwater 1972: 189). O'Neill's play is a development of the Lazarus story in the Gospel of John, and its title is an allusion and an answer to the verse that is known for being the shortest in the Bible: John 11.35, "Jesus wept." In the Bible, Jesus is asked to come to Bethany to cure his friend Lazarus, but finding that he is dead and has already been entombed when he gets there, Jesus raises him from the dead. O'Neill called the play "Lazarus Laughed" in answer to "Jesus wept," but the more important verse for him was what Jesus says to Lazarus' sister Martha in John 11.25: "I am the resurrection and the life; he who believes in me, even if he die, shall live; and whoever lives and believes in me, shall never die."

The play is a representation of the "second life" of Lazarus as O'Neill envisioned it, the result of having been raised from the dead after being privileged to see beyond the veil of Maya. The experience has made him into a Nietzschean *Übermensch*, capable of the affirmation and laughter Nietzsche describes at the end of *Also Sprach Zarathustra*. A witness to the miracle in the play says that "Jesus looked into his face for what seemed a long time and suddenly Lazarus said, 'Yes,' as if he were answering a question in Jesus' eyes" (O'Neill 1982: 3.277). After smiling sadly, Jesus had blessed Lazarus, called him "My Brother," and gone away, but Lazarus, "looking after Him, began to laugh softly like a man in love with God! Such a laugh I never heard! It made my ears drunk! It was like wine! And though I was half-dead with fright I found myself laughing too" (277). When Lazarus appears, he explains, "I heard the heart of Jesus laughing in my heart; 'There is Eternal Life in No,' it said, 'and there is the same Eternal Life in Yes! Death is the fear between!'" (279). And so begins the mystical cult of Lazarus, whose followers chant:

> Laugh! Laugh!
> There is only life!
> There is only laughter!
> Fear is no more!
> Death is dead!
>   (281)

Laughter is the Gospel of Lazarus, but human beings are not ready to hear it, because, as soon as they are out of touch with Lazarus' living spirit, they forget and begin to fear death, which causes them to kill and behave in other hateful ways. "That is your tragedy," he tells them, "You forget! You forget the God in you!" (289).

The play is an elaborately staged pageant, meant to reflect the classical culture that Nietzsche writes about in *The Birth of Tragedy*. Like Nietzsche, O'Neill placed a great emphasis on the chorus, with a choral scheme based on 49 different masks, typifying both genders in "seven periods of life" and seven "general types of character" in each scene (273). The major conflict of the play is between Lazarus, representing the force of life, and the young Caligula and the Emperor Tiberius, representing the force of death. Caligula, a small monkey-like figure, falls in love with Lazarus, and is constantly attracted by his Gospel, but is unable to escape his fear, finally having to kill Lazarus, "Who taught the treason that fear and death were dead! But I am Lord of Fear! I am Caesar of Death!" (370). Afraid of dying, the elderly Tiberius wants Lazarus to give him hope, "for me, Tiberius Caesar," but Lazarus responds, "What is – you? But there is hope for Man! Love is Man's hope – love for his life on earth, a noble love above suspicion and distrust" (351–2). Tiberius is unable to get beyond the belief that "all laughter is malice, all gods are dead, and life is a sickness" (352). He kills Lazarus, but allows him his last affirmation for the crowd/chorus. When they ask him "What is beyond," he responds, "Life! Eternity! Stars and dust! God's Eternal Laughter!" (367–8), and *"his laughter bursts forth now in its highest pitch of ecstatic summons to the feast and sacrifice of Life, the Eternal"* while *"the crowds laugh with him in a frenzied rhythmic chorus"* (368). This ecstasy is momentary, of course, for it is Caligula who has the last word: "All the same, I killed him and I proved there is death! . . . Forgive me, Lazarus! Men forget!" (371). The momentary lifting of the veil allows for a glimpse into the eternal Unity, but it is the human tragedy that the moment of enlightenment cannot be sustained.

O'Neill wrote to the critic Arthur Hobson Quinn what he thought to be "the deep underlying idea" of *Lazarus Laughed*:

> The fear of death is the root of all evil, the cause of all man's blundering unhappiness. Lazarus knows there is no death, there is only change. He is reborn without that fear. Therefore he is the first and only man who is able to laugh affirmatively. His laughter is a triumphant Yes to life in its entirety and its eternity. His laughter affirms God, it is too noble to desire personal immortality, it wills its own extinction, it gives its life for the sake of Eternal Life (patriotism carried to its logical ultimate). His laughter is the direct expression of joy in the Dionysian sense, the joy of a celebrant who is at the same time a sacrifice in the eternal process of change and growth and transmutation which is life of which his life is an insignificant manifestation, soon to be reabsorbed. And life itself is the Self-affirmative joyous laughter of God. (Bogard and Bryer 1988: 245)

Egil Törnqvist observed a generation ago that "O'Neill considered Greek tragedy (including Euripides) the unsurpassed example of art *and* religion" and that "O'Neill's *oeuvre* is in itself a gigantic endeavor to recapture the spirit of Greek tragedy within a modern framework" (1968: 102). This is particularly evident in *Desire Under the Elms* and *Mourning Becomes Electra*, two plays in which O'Neill used Greek myths familiar from the great tragedies to dramatize one of his most compelling modernist preoccupations, the conflict between the Dionysian spirit of vitality expressed in sexual passion and what he saw as a repressive and puritanical American culture in the twentieth century.

Desire Under the Elms is based primarily on the myth of Hippolytus and Phaedra, but it is combined with others. It focuses on the sexual love between stepson and stepmother, in this case, Eben Cabot and his father Ephraim's newly married young wife, Abbie. O'Neill also draws on the Oedipus myth in his allusion to Eben's attachment to his dead mother, and his famous description of the set in which two enormous elm trees "bend their trailing branches down over the roof" of the house, appearing "to protect and at the same time subdue. There is a sinister maternity in their aspect, a crushing, jealous absorption" (O'Neill 1982: 3.202). This maternal force is represented in the play by the ghostly presence of Eben's "Maw" in the parlor, *"a grim, repressed room like a tomb in which the family has been interred alive"* (241). This blends with the allusion to Phaedra in Abbie when she first makes love to Eben in the parlor: *"In spite of her overwhelming desire for him, there is a sincere and maternal love in her manner and voice – a horribly frank mixture of lust and mother love"* (243). And finally, O'Neill alludes to Medea, as Abbie kills the baby that has resulted from her union with Eben in order to prove that she is not trying to get the farm away from him by producing another heir for Ephraim. As in *Lazarus Laughed,* O'Neill combines the Greek references with Christian ones – in this case Ephraim's version of the "hard" God of the Puritans that hovers over his rocky New England farm: "God's hard, not easy! God's in the stones! Build my church on a rock – out o' stones an' I'll be in them! That's what He meant t' Peter!" (237).

In *Desire Under the Elms*, the recuperation of these fragmented myths to tell a story of modern "primitives" serves a modernist function, the construction of a myth that might serve to explain the contemporary human predicament. O'Neill makes the link between his characters and elemental humanity by suggesting their closeness to the earth and the animals. The plot proceeds from elemental human drives and emotions. But Abbie and Eben are elevated by selfless feelings. After turning Abbie in to the sheriff for murdering their baby, Eben comes to her and asks her forgiveness. Abbie forgives him, and rather than run away as Eben proposes, is determined to stay and take her punishment, "t' pay fur my sin" (266). She makes it clear that the sin was killing the child, not their sexual union: "I don't repent that sin! I hain't askin' God t' fergive that!" (266). Eben insists that he must share her guilt and her punishment: "I got t' pay fur my part o' the sin! . . . I want t' share with ye, Abbie – prison 'r death 'r hell 'r anythin'!" (267).

At the end of the play, the two walk off hand in hand toward the sunrise, an image that has been identified with that of Adam and Eve as they leave the garden in *Paradise Lost*. In embracing justice and a selfless love as they go off to jail, they transcend the greedy self-interest that dominates the rest of the play, leaving behind Ephraim, who has been unable to set himself free by turning the animals loose and setting fire to the farm as he had intended. Ephraim, alone on his farm with his God, sees that "it's a-goin' t' be lonesomer now than ever it war afore ... Waal – what d'ye want? God's lonesome, hain't He? God's hard an' lonesome!" (268). The most important aspect of transcendence in the ending for O'Neill is the achievement of "belonging," as he would put it, the sense that one is not alone in the universe. Abbie and Eben achieve this through their love. As Eben says, "If I'm sharin' with ye, I won't feel lonesome leastways" (267). Through their connection to each other, proven by a surrendering of self-interest, Eben and Abbie achieve a momentary glimpse of Unity, which elevates them from the various forms of desire that have enslaved the Cabot family throughout the play.

In his trilogy *Mourning Becomes Electra*, O'Neill made a more overt use of Greek myth, joining the story of the *Oresteia* to the Nietzschean theme of Dionysian vitality through the symbolism of the "Blessed Isles." Frederick Carpenter has pointed out that O'Neill follows the Greek versions of the myth in the first two plays, translating "classical myth into modern psychological terms; in the third, he created his own myth" (1979: 127). In the first play, *The Homecoming*, General Ezra Mannon (Agamemnon) returns from the Civil War and is murdered by his wife Christine (Clytemnestra) at the urging of her lover, Adam Brant (Aegisthus). The play ends with a confrontation between Christine and her daughter Lavinia (Electra), who accuses her of the murder and vows to avenge her father. In the second play, *The Hunted*, Christine's son Orin (Orestes) returns from the war, and, urged on by Lavinia, shoots Adam Brant. In a departure from the myth, Orin does not kill Christine; instead he drives her to suicide. The third play, *The Haunted*, centers not on Orin, but on Lavinia, placing Electra at the center of the myth. Like his mother, Orin commits suicide, driven by his guilt and despair, but the central conflict of O'Neill's play, between the repressive Puritan heritage of the Mannons and the passion and vitality represented by Christine, plays itself out within Lavinia.

In the first two plays, Lavinia is closely allied with the Mannons, who, as Ezra says, "went to the white meeting-house on Sabbaths and meditated on death. Life was a dying. Being born was starting to die. Death was being born" (O'Neill 1982: 2.54). Denying as far as possible her strong physical resemblance to her sensual mother, who "*has a fine, voluptuous figure*" and "*moves with a flowing animal grace,*" Lavinia exemplifies the puritanical, military look of the Mannons: "*Her movements are stiff and she carries herself with a wooden, square-shouldered, military bearing*" (10). The symbolism of the Mannons is built around their mansion, which dominates the play's setting. An imitation Greek temple, it appears to Christine like a "sepulchre": "the 'whited' one of the Bible – pagan temple front stuck like a mask on Puritan gray ugliness. It was just like old Abe Mannon to build such a monstrosity – as a temple for his hatred" (17). The symbolism for the other side of Lavinia's nature, proceeding from her mother, is the Blessed Isles, which are referred to throughout the trilogy by various characters. Adam Brant says they are "as near the Garden of Paradise before sin was discovered as you'll find on this earth" (24). For the guilty and doomed Christine and Adam they are the much desired but unattainable place of "peace and forgetfulness" (112). To Orin, the Islands "came to mean... everything that was peace and warmth and security" (90), a womblike place where he could be alone with his mother. Finally, in the third play, they become Lavinia's Islands, as only she and Orin actually go there. The Islands awaken Lavinia to the awareness that she is "only half Mannon" and she shares her mother's sensual nature (146). The Islands give her a momentary glimpse of the Unity behind the veil of Maya. She says they "finished setting me free. There was something there mysterious and beautiful – a good spirit – of love – coming out of the land and sea. It made me forget death" (147). Lavinia's experience in the Blessed Isles makes for *"an extraordinary change in her... She now bears a striking resemblance to her mother in every respect"* (137). The conflict in the final play is Lavinia's struggle to embrace the part of her that comes from her mother, and the values that are figured in the image of the Blessed Isles, in the face of the rigid Puritanism of the Mannons.

At the end of the second play, Lavinia accepts the pistol shot that ends her mother's life with the words, "It is justice! It is your justice, Father!" (123). At the beginning of the third play, she tells Orin that their business with their parents "is all past and finished. The dead have forgotten us! We've forgotten them!" (138), and she proclaims to the Mannon portraits that she's done her "duty" by them (146), but she is to learn that the claim of the Mannons is not so easily dismissed. As she struggles to evade the reality of her brother's imminent suicide, she tells her fiancé, "nothing matters but love, does it? That must come first! No price is too great, is it? Or for peace!" (167). After Orin shoots himself, she is determined to free herself from the Mannons: "I'm through with you forever now, do you hear? I'm Mother's daughter – not one of you! I'll live in spite of you!" (168). But she finds that she is more Mannon than not. After a last desperate attempt to get her fiancé to play Adam Brant to her Christine, she gives up, saying *"(in a dead voice)* I can't marry you, Peter... Love isn't permitted to me. The dead are too strong!" (177). She drives him away, accepting the fact that she is "bound here – to the Mannon dead." She will not commit suicide, but shuts herself up in the house that symbolizes the Puritanism of the Mannons: "Living alone here with the dead is a worse act of justice than death or prison!... It takes the Mannons to punish themselves for being born!" (178). Lavinia's last act is to order the shutters closed up and nailed shut and the flowers, the last vestige of her mother's vitality, thrown out. Despite the momentary freedom provided by her glimpse of the Blessed Isles, she is unable to deny the past that has shaped her and her present reality. The Mannon heritage is the stronger force, and its Puritanical standard of justice demands expiation.

Mourning Becomes Electra was the last full-blown tragedy that O'Neill would write. The great autobiographical plays that he wrote at the end of his career contain fragmented expressions of his tragic sense of life, but they lack the Dionysian element of the tragedies. In *Long Day's Journey Into Night* (1940), for example, there is no recognizable protagonist. Each of the four members of the Tyrone family makes what could be a transformative discovery during the play, but it is too late for them to realize it. James tells his son Edmund that he sold his gift for acting for the promise of easy money from a play that ruined him as an actor while it made him rich. His son Jamie warns Edmund against the part of himself that hates his brother and will destroy him if he can, but despairs of his own redemption. Edmund himself is a poet who has seen behind the veil of Maya to "the moment of ecstatic freedom... the peace, the end of the quest, the last harbor, the joy of belonging to a fulfillment beyond men's lousy, pitiful, greedy fears and hopes and dreams" (O'Neill 1955: 153), but he can only "stammer" when he tries to articulate his vision, and he finally feels that "it was a great mistake, my being born a man . . . who can never belong, who must always be a little in love with death!" (153–4). Most pitiful is the mother Mary, whose addiction to morphine keeps her from remembering "something I need terribly. I remember when I had it I was never lonely nor afraid. I can't have lost it forever, I would die if I thought that. Because then there would be no hope" (173). What she has lost is her faith, a loss she cannot confront, because she despairs of forgiveness.

Arthur Miller

The most important statement about tragedy made by an American in the twentieth century was the brief newspaper article published by Arthur Miller a few days after the premiere of the country's defining tragedy, *Death of a Salesman* (1949). In "Tragedy and the Common Man," Miller set out to explain why, "in this age" when "few tragedies are written," he believed that "the common man is as apt a subject for tragedy in its highest sense as kings were" (1996: 3). He dismissed rank "or nobility of character" as requisites for the tragic protagonist, proposing that "The tragic feeling is evoked in us when we are in the presence of a character who is ready to lay down his life, if need be, to secure one thing – his sense of personal dignity... tragedy, then is the consequence of a man's total compulsion to evaluate himself justly" (1996: 4). Miller wrote that what separated tragic heroes from the rest of us was their compulsion to "act against the scheme of things that degrades them" and that "from this total onslaught by an individual against the seemingly stable cosmos... comes the terror and the fear that is classically associated with tragedy" (1996: 4). More importantly, from "this total questioning of what has previously been unquestioned, we learn" (1996: 4). He found no reason why a common person like Willy Loman should be less capable of tragic action than a citizen who was more prosperous or had greater social stature than he. The most radical aspect of Miller's statement came in his definition of good and evil, however. In two concise paragraphs, he laid out his view of a tragic moral order for the twentieth century:

> Now if it is true that tragedy is the consequence of a man's total compulsion to evaluate himself justly, his destruction in the attempt posits a wrong or an evil in his environment. And this is precisely the morality of tragedy and its lesson... The tragic right is a

condition of life, a condition in which the human personality is able to flower and
realize itself. The wrong is the condition which suppresses man, perverts the flowing
out of his love and creative instinct. Tragedy enlightens – and it must, in that it points
the heroic finger at the enemy of man's freedom. The thrust for freedom is the quality in
tragedy which exalts. The revolutionary questioning of the stable environment is what
terrifies. (1996: 5)

Miller thus defined good and evil, not in terms of a transcendent moral order, but in
terms of human beings themselves. The right is that which enables human self-
actualization; the wrong is that which inhibits it. In this moral scheme, striking out
against more powerful forces that inhibit the protagonist becomes a righteous act, not
a guilty rebellion against a higher order. For Miller, modern tragedy cannot come
about if its author "fears to question absolutely everything," when he regards any
"institution, habit or custom" as "everlasting, immutable or inevitable" (1996: 6). He
held that in modern tragedy, "the need of man to wholly realize himself is the only
fixed star, and whatever it is that hedges his nature and lowers it is ripe for attack and
examination" (1996: 6). In such a scheme, there is no place for resignation or
submission, but Miller believed strongly in the capacity for enlightenment. In his
view, it is to come not through the hero's suffering, but through the process of his
"thrust for freedom," his rebellion against the forces that are repressing him. It is from
this total questioning of what has previously been unquestioned that "we learn"
(1996: 4).

Miller had *Death of a Salesman* immediately in mind when he wrote this statement,
but it also describes the conception of tragedy that informs *The Crucible* (1953) and
A View from the Bridge (1955). Each of his heroes, Willy Loman, John Proctor, and
Eddie Carbone, is fighting to secure his "sense of personal dignity" against forces that
threaten to destroy it. In Willy's case, it is the real conditions of the business world
that threaten his dream of the way it should be: "Be liked and you will never want"
(1949: 33). He fights the truth that his son Biff flings at him with a furious insistence
on his worth: "I am not a dime a dozen! I am Willy Loman" (132). John Proctor is on
the verge of submitting to the superior forces of the Church and the State when he
finally balks at signing a false confession that will be nailed up on the church door.
When Judge Danforth demands an explanation, he explodes *"with a cry of his whole
soul*: Because it is my name! . . . How may I live without my name? I have given you
my soul; leave me my name!" (Miller 1953: 143). Eddie Carbone echoes him when he
demands that Marco take back the accusation of betrayal he has made against him:
"I want my good name, Marco! You took my name!" (Miller 1955: 159).

While each of these men is ultimately destroyed by the powerful forces he is up
against, Miller notes that "the flaw, or crack in the character" of the modern tragic
hero "need be nothing but his inherent unwillingness to remain passive in the face of
what he conceives to be a challenge to his dignity, his image of his rightful status"
(1996: 4). Each of his heroes destroys himself through his compulsion to act. Willy
Loman commits suicide in order to get the insurance money that he thinks will enable

his son Biff to fulfill the destiny he imagines for him: "Can you imagine that magnificence with twenty thousand dollars in his pocket?...I always knew one way or another we were gonna make it, Biff and I!" (Miller 1949: 135). John Proctor goes to his death, unwilling, finally, to bargain his life for a false confession. Eddie Carbone is killed fighting Marco for his sense of his own righteousness against the truth that he is guilty.

The enlightenment that comes from these tragedies is not, except perhaps in John Proctor's case, a greater degree of wisdom for the character. It is enlightenment for the audience. As we have already noted, Miller says: "from this total questioning of what has previously been unquestioned, we learn" (1996: 4). It is through the hero's "thrust for freedom" against institutions, customs, and economic forces that are commonly viewed as inevitable, permanent, and unassailable that the audience is led to see them in relation to Miller's conception of good and evil, to weigh their economic, social, religious, and familial institutions and values against the standard of human freedom and self-actualization. In Miller's plays, they are often found wanting.

Reprinted many times, Miller's brief essay proved to be a seminal document in the discussion of twentieth-century tragedy, as *Death of a Salesman* has come to be seen as the United States' defining play. A salesman who was born to be a carpenter, Willy Loman embodies a fundamental condition that Miller saw as endemic to twentieth-century life in the United States. Willy's tragedy is that he is born to a kind of bad faith. His talent is working with his hands – as Biff says, "there's more of him in that front stoop [that he constructed] than in all the sales he ever made" (Miller 1949: 138). But he can't be a carpenter, because, as he tells Biff, even his father was better than a carpenter. In America, everyone has to be better than his father. Willy has to pursue the goal of "Success." This concept of success is what Miller calls "Willy's law – the belief, in other words, which administers guilt to him ... a deeply believed and deeply suspect 'good' " (1996: 149), which severely limits his self-conception and his freedom. As his son Hap says, Willy had "the only dream you can have – to come out number-one man" (Miller 1949: 139).

Miller, who was aware of the suicides of many broken businessmen during the Great Depression, wrote that Willy's tragic death proceeds from the fact that he "has broken a law without whose protection life is insupportable if not incomprehensible to him and to many others; it is the law which says that a failure in society and in business has no right to live" (1996: 149). And, what's more, his death is

the wage of his sin, which was to have committed himself so completely to the counterfeits of dignity and the false coinage embodied in his idea of success that he can prove his existence only by bestowing "power" on his posterity, a power deriving from the sale of his last asset, himself, for the price of his insurance policy. (Miller 1996: 147)

There is learning in the play, on the part of Biff, who comes to realize that Willy had "the wrong dreams" (1949: 138) and rejects them for himself. The tragic irony is that

Willy sees the revelation of Biff's love for him not as an alternative to the "law of success," as Miller says it is (1996: 149), but as an incentive to trade his life for a $20,000 insurance policy. It is too late for Willy to be enlightened, but not, Miller suggests, for the audience. Miller sees the United States as a nation that has the wrong dreams, that is in thrall to the law of success. His hope is to provide a vision of the opportunity for "a thrust for freedom" by the audience, for "in the tragic view the need of man to wholly realize himself is the only fixed star" and "the final result" of a tragedy "ought to be the reinforcement of the onlooker's brightest opinions of the human animal" (1996: 6).

While Miller insisted on his modern understanding of the nature of tragedy, he did not by any means reject classical tragedy wholesale. In fact, he said in an interview that when he began to write plays, "one assumed inevitably that one was in the mainstream that began with Aeschylus and went through about twenty-five hundred years of playwriting" (1996: 265). Asked what playwrights he had admired when he was young, he replied, "first, the Greeks, for their magnificent form, the symmetry... that form has never left me; I suppose it just got burned in" (1996: 265–6). Writing *The Crucible* led him to a larger view of the Greek tragedies. He thought that they must have had a "therapeutic effect" on the community by "raising to conscious awareness the clan's capacity of brutal and unredeemed violence so that it could be sublimated and contained by new institutions, like the law" (1987: 342).

This is most evident in *A View from the Bridge*, which is consciously constructed according to Miller's understanding of a classical Greek tragedy. It is a "vendetta story," about people who have "a blood debt" to pay (Roudané 1987: 262). The story of an uncle who has an illicit passion for his niece, and is driven to kill the man who accuses him of it in order to avoid facing his guilt, had a "myth-like resonance" for Miller, who did not feel he was "making anything up, but rather recording something old and marvelous" (Roudané 1987: 192). The play was deliberately written in one act, and made use of the convention of the chorus in the lawyer Alfieri, who is able to see the course of Eddie's inevitable self-destruction, but is unable to stop it. Eddie, the hero, is "as good a man as he had to be, / In a life that was hard and even" (Miller 1955: 96). Miller sets civilization, in the person of the lawyer Alfieri, in opposition to the primal demands of nature and blood. These are dramatized in Eddie, who violates the taboos of his culture while acting on a passion he neither wants nor understands, and Marco, who is driven to kill Eddie because he has harmed his family. By making Alfieri the chorus, Miller allies the audience with his point of view, placing them on the side of civilization while at the same time being awestruck by the power of nature and blood.

Although no other modern American playwrights have taken on the question of modern tragedy as directly as Anderson, O'Neill, and Miller did, significant tragedies such as Tennessee Williams's *A Streetcar Named Desire* (1947), Archibald MacLeish's *J. B.* (1958), Edward Albee's *Who's Afraid of Virginia Woolf?* (1962), and Marsha Norman's *'night Mother* (1983) have been written, mostly modeled along Aristotelian lines. During the late twentieth century, several playwrights experimented with the conception and conventions of tragedy. A. R. Gurney wrote his *Another Antigone* (1988), which has the form of classical tragedy, and which Gurney has said "is about, and should constantly remind us that it is about, both its similarity to and difference from its Greek counterpart" (1989: viii). David Mamet wrote *Oleanna* (1992), which he called a "tragedy about power" (Kane 2001: 125). Several of August Wilson's plays, including *Ma Rainey's Black Bottom* (1984) and *Fences* (1987), integrate traditional tragic structure with what Wilson sees as a uniquely African-American worldview, juxtaposing supernatural experience with everyday reality.

It is one of the ironies of American theater history that, while the tragic vision is not generally considered to characterize the American view of life, the most significant plays in the classic American repertoire are tragic in vision even if they do not exemplify all of the conventions associated with the genre. *Death of a Salesman, A Streetcar Named Desire, Long Day's Journey Into Night, The Crucible, Who's Afraid of Virginia Woolf?* – for contemporary playwrights, there is no escaping the influence of these great works and the tragic vision they embody. David Mamet may call his *Glengarry Glen Ross* (1988) a "gang comedy," but its vision of the American businessman's dark predicament echoes that of *Death of a Salesman*, as does the tragic mutual misunderstanding of the generations in August Wilson's *Fences* (1986). While the family and the business world provided the focus for mid-twentieth-century American tragedy, the playwrights at the end of the century were forced to face the failure of the American dream of the "Great Society." The pervasive issues of identity politics, such as racism, sexism, and homophobia, pointed to the failure of the democratic ideal to produce a society that embodied the values of equality, justice, and human dignity. Tony Kushner's two-part *Angels in America* (1993) is perhaps the defining play of this period. It exemplifies the conjunction that characterizes American tragic vision at the beginning of the twenty-first century: a realization of the United States' failed social and political policies with a mythically transcendent hope inspired by a vision of its ideal possibilities.

REFERENCES AND FURTHER READING

Anderson, Maxwell. (1939). *The Essence of Tragedy and Other Footnotes and Papers*. Washington, DC: Anderson House. A collection of Anderson's critical writing.

Anderson, Maxwell. (1940). *Winterset*. In *Eleven Verse Plays 1929–1939*. New York: Harcourt Brace. Anderson's most important play.

Anderson, Maxwell. (1947). *Off Broadway: Essays about the Theater*. New York: William Sloane. A collection of Anderson's critical writing.

Bogard, Travis and Bryer, Jackson L., eds. (1988). *Selected Letters of Eugene O'Neill*. New Haven, CT: Yale University Press. The standard edition of O'Neill's letters.

Bridgwater, Patrick. (1972). *Nietzsche in Anglosaxony: A Study of Nietzsche's Impact on English and American Literature*. Leicester: Leicester University Press. A critical study of Nietzsche's influence, including that on O'Neill.

Carpenter, Frederick I. (1979). *Eugene O'Neill*. Boston: Twayne. A biocritical study of O'Neill.

Clark, Barrett H. (1929). *Eugene O'Neill: The Man and His Plays*. New York: McBride. The earliest critical book on O'Neill.

Commins, Dorothy, ed. (1986). *"Love and Admiration and Respect": The O'Neill–Commins Correspondence*. Durham, NC: Duke University Press. An edition of O'Neill's correspondence with his editor, Saxe Commins.

Estrin, Mark, ed. (1990). *Conversations with Eugene O'Neill*. Jackson: University Press of Mississippi. A collection of interviews with O'Neill.

Hoffmann, Gerhard. (1995). "Eugene O'Neill: America's Nietzschean Playwright." In *Nietzsche in American Literature and Thought*, ed. Manfred Pütz. Columbia, SC: Camden House, 197–221. A thorough study of Nietzsche's influence on O'Neill.

Howells, William Dean. (1993). *Selected Literary Criticism. Vol. II: 1886–1897*. Bloomington: Indiana University Press. The standard edition of Howells's works.

Gurney, A. R. (1989). *The Cocktail Hour and Two Other Plays: Another Antigone and The Perfect Party*. New York: Plume. Three plays by Gurney.

Kane, Leslie, ed. (2001). *David Mamet in Conversation*. Ann Arbor: University of Michigan Press. A collection of interviews with Mamet.

Miller, Arthur. (1949). *Death of a Salesman*. New York: Viking. The defining tragedy of the American repertoire.

Miller, Arthur. (1953). *The Crucible*. New York: Viking. Miller's tragedy based on the Salem witch trials and the McCarthyism of the 1950s.

Miller, Arthur. (1955). *A View from the Bridge*. New York: Viking. Miller's tragedy based on the Italian-American community in Brooklyn.

Miller, Arthur. (1987). *Timebends: A Life*. New York: Viking. Miller's autobiography.

Miller, Arthur. (1996). *The Theater Essays of Arthur Miller*, ed. Robert A. Martin and Steven R. Centola. New York: Da Capo. The standard collection of Miller's critical writing.

Nietzsche, Friedrich. [1872] (2000). *The Birth of Tragedy*, trans. Douglas Smith. Oxford: Oxford University Press. Oxford's most recent edition of Nietzsche's seminal work.

O'Neill, Eugene. (1955). *Long Day's Journey Into Night*. New Haven, CT: Yale University Press. O'Neill's play about his family.

O'Neill, Eugene. (1982). *The Plays of Eugene O'Neill*, 3 vols. New York: Modern Library. A standard edition of O'Neill's plays.

Roudané, Matthew. (1987). *Conversations with Arthur Miller*. Jackson: University Press of Mississippi. A collection of interviews with Miller.

Törnqvist, Egil. (1968). "Nietzsche and O'Neill: A Study in Affinity." *Orbis Litterarum* 28, 97–126. The earliest study of Nietzsche's influence on O'Neill.

28

Using Tragedy against its Makers: Some African and Caribbean Instances

Timothy J. Reiss

In January, 1995, the Royal Shakespeare Company performed *Macbeth* in William-sport, Pennsylvania, "with a nearly all-black cast." In a review, S. Ekema Agbaw wrote of the director's and company's strained efforts to emphasize similarities, even iden-tities, of medieval Scotland and contemporary Africa. The director Stephen Raynes told of a Scotland subject to "supernatural forces," "in the grip of tribal and international war, suffering from famine and disease, where extremes of good and bad ('fair and foul') are at play." "Africa today," he wrote,

> is a continent of similar extremes: hope and despair, wealth and poverty, . . . reeling under economic and political instability, with the world's highest birth rates, lowest life expectancy, and half the world's refugees. Africa is riddled with corruption alongside indescribable poverty, creating at the same time extremely wealthy politicians and entire generations dying of malnutrition. It is a place of overcrowded cities and drought-stricken deserts, tribal carnage and international wars. In a world of such physical and spiritual conflict what is moral or immoral? Right or wrong? Fair or foul? (Agbaw 1996: 104)

Ignoring the nasty inability to take sides and the offense of conflating utterly different historical situations – the supposals, notes Agbaw, "that you can still learn all you need to know about Africans by reading Shakespeare," that the ubiquity of "human experiences" makes "medieval Scottish kings and contemporary African leaders . . . in-terchangeable," and that "Africans are at a point in their social development where Europeans were eight or nine hundred years ago" – and ignoring the production's failure to "capture [the] contemporary African nuances" it claimed to, what are "the historical, political, and cultural implications of presenting a medieval Scottish murderer as a contemporary African dictator" (1996: 102, 108–9)?

What does it mean to claim to grasp *any* African reality, for example, in a wholly familiar European tragedy? How can tragedy be used by non-Europeans to figure their own realities? (The question has been asked by writers like John Pepper

Clark-Bekederemo, 'Zulu Sofola, and Wole Soyinka in the course of using tragedy as a way to render home experiences, issues, and debates.) Does the mere fact of using tragedy in different ways and contexts represent a "speaking-back" to a colonizing Europe of which tragedy has been a principal and unique cultural form?

Tragedy and Its "Others"

I limit this chapter to two arguments. One, the briefer, while imbuing the other, answers the first question (and to a degree the third – which the whole hopes to answer), using bits of a longer argument (Reiss 2002). This shows tragedy to embody, from the Greeks, Western cultures part of whose self-image was of being riven with insuperable divides, scissions evinced as the essence of human life. Humans were split from the divine, other human groups, often each other, surely from the material world.[1] Given as universal, this condition of human actions and their consequences limited human responsibility for them, even as some singular charge could be heroically assumed. Of this, the Oedipus of *Oedipus the King* remains an archetype:

> Apollo, friends, Apollo—
> he ordained my agonies – these my pains on pains!
> But the hand that struck my eyes was mine,
> mine alone – no one else—
> I did it all myself!
>
> (Sophocles 1984: 1329–33)

Oedipus is archetypal because he now grounds a usual Western view of the relation of "self" to, or *against*, divine, social, or some other totality. This is not limited to tragedy, even if it began there. Franz Kafka, in a notorious letter to his father, protested: "My writing was all about you; all I did there, after all, was to bemoan what I could not bemoan upon your breast. It was an intentionally long-drawn-out leave-taking from you, only although it was brought about by force on your part, it did take its course in the direction determined by me" (1954: 177).[2] In Western tragedy, this sensibility is lauded. That the experience was ancient is doubtful, but it is basic to a modern Western sense of "self" as individually facing a greater divine, social, or political whole; indeed, facing-*off* with it in some more or less anguished conflict.

Even as tragedy offers this scythed sense of human life, its aesthetic form in time gave a standard of judgment both within Western culture (as to who and what merited moral respect) and between cultures; a scale of analogy, even a way to possess – naming "tragic" the victims of some impersonally noble "tragedy" of cultural clash, for which, it being a universal state of life, no one was responsible, far less guilty – the "tragic Indian," "tragic mulatto," or anthropological indigene irrevocably doomed to iron night by a golden dawn of civilization's march. Of this standard and scale, the director's survey of the Royal Shakespeare's 1995 *Macbeth* is near-parody. I shall suggest at the end that a different experience of tragedy produces a different "tragic" reading of life. For, as 'Zulu Sofola writes, for African cultures, all things, including humans, are "endowed with the same Supreme Energy, all creatures are essentially one and the same." If the scissions of tragedy offer a "negative" view of human life, it differs utterly from an "African world view [that], *ab initio*, is positive, [no one] perceiv[ing] himself in essence as a negative force. It is within this cosmic view of life that the African defines the artist and his role in the society" (1994: 4–5).[3]

My second argument, using a few plays by African and Caribbean writers, shows how they have used tragedy, the dramatic form, to reject the cultural implications Agbaw spurns apropos of the *Macbeth* performance and write back against such seizures.[4] Here a caveat: African tragedies are in many languages, many more directly accessible to popular audiences than the English and French of which I write here. Whether some traditional drama is "tragedy" and what split there is between popular and "elite," African- and European-language drama, are 50-year-long debates that this chapter eludes. I perforce refer to few plays; and these target a small elite of European language-speakers. (The African plays do. The Caribbean case differs.) These plays are those most concerned to "turn" *tragedy*, targeting a public knowing the theoretical history and the genre. At issue are uses of what is *called* tragedy in places outside the cultural tradition to which *tragedy* as a genre is historically tied. These uses make tragedy, as a dramatic genre (setting aside the word's spread to wider emotional, ontological, and social feelings, practices, and concepts), so powerful an aesthetic and political tool for developing and renewing embattled cultures.

Colonialism, Racism, and Their Turning

A third into *The Birth of Tragedy from the Spirit of Music*, Friedrich Nietzsche wrote of satyrs, monkeys, and then flute-playing Marsyas, flayed alive by Apollo for daring to vie with the god in music. To represent the cultural transition marked by tragedy, Nietzsche took the satyr, whom the Greeks "did not confound . . . with the monkey. Quite the contrary, the satyr was man's true prototype, an expression of his highest and strongest aspirations": Dionysus *with* Apollo (1956: 52). But the contrast is equivocal. The satyr was intimately bound to music. Many stories tell that Marsyas was the first to play the flute, which he got from Athena when he said that playing it twisted her face. This may be why Nietzsche added his rider about *dem Affen* (apes / monkeys) – the two were not otherwise tied. Playing the flute gave the satyr a fearful mask, like the look associated with the ape, taken as evil, foolish, vain, and lecherous: connotations lasting into the European Middle Ages and Renaissance, to say nothing of later racisms. For Nietzsche, man's satyr prototype, not ape, was apelike. But why, save possibly for the flute, did Nietzsche relate either satyr or ape to tragedy and the transition he took it to signal between Dionysus and Apollo, representing a last moment of union? Was he cued by remarks Aristotle made near the end of the *Poetics* on corrupt performances of tragedies, and ham actors, like "flute players whirling about" exaggeratedly, or the player Callipides, whom his older contemporary Mynniscus "dubbed an 'ape'" (Aristotle 1995: 1461b30–5)? Was he was cued, more, by a racist sensibility as to what was "outside," different from, the "other" of a European civilization of which tragedy was always a notably sophisticated and sublime evidence? Of the difference between an advanced culture *with* tragedy and others without, the monkey / ape became the very figure.

Aristotle's remarks may have stirred Nietzsche's second remark about a monkey a few pages later, after he writes of "the Heraclean power of music, which reached its highest form in tragedy" (Nietzsche 1956: 68). Accusing Euripides of having killed tragedy, he adds: "you could easily put in its place an imitation that, like Heracles' monkey, would trick itself out in the master's robes" (69). Here, too, ambiguity rules. For Marsyas' face behind his flute was often likened to a player's mask, not so different from the "masked myth" that Nietzsche identified with Heracles' ape. The reference was to Lucian's *Piscator*, whose accuser of false philosophers (but also of "true" ones) remarked to Plato and others that the former were "as if some actor in tragedy . . . should act the part of Achilles or Theseus, or even Heracles himself . . . showing off airs and graces in a mask of such dignity." They "made bold . . . though but apes, to wear heroic masks." He ended by asking: "Have their sort anything to do with you, or have they displayed any similarity or kinship in their mode of life? Aye, 'Heracles and the monkey,' as the proverb has it!" (Lucian of Samosata 1969: 47–9, 55–7).

Later, the ape became for Nietzsche more clearly other than masked imitator, more clearly sign of a passage from a world of wholeness to one of division and abyss. It became the symbol of what was left behind when humans rose to a new stage: "What is the ape to me? A laughing-stock or a painful embarrassment. And just so shall man be to the Super-man: a laughing stock or a painful embarrassment" (1961: 42: "Prologue" §3). This explained why the ape could *only* be a masked imitator of the human. Like tragedy, the ape marked steps in a tragic disjunction of humans from the world. This sense of dissonance, scission, and otherness was already in Plato's *Symposium*, when young Alcibiades arrives at the banquet, heard first as a voice shouting outside. When he does enter the dining area, he is leaning drunkenly on a flute-girl – a Dionysian eruption into reasoned debate. All the others having spoken on love, Alcibiades is asked for a contribution, which, it is finally agreed, will be a praise of Socrates. He starts by likening Socrates to a commonly found small statue of Silenus playing the flute and then to Marsyas, known, we saw, for the ugliness of his face when playing and for having been flayed alive by Apollo for daring to rival him. Adriana Cavarero suggests that this flaying symbolizes rejection of Marsyas' playing as itself figuring pure *phone* (or *voce*) against Apollo's *logos*, body expressive against rational mind. Socrates, speaker and flute-player (Alcibiades recalls), was put to death for maybe analogous reasons. By the end of the written *Symposium*, Platonic *logos* has replaced Socratic *logoi*, his plural voices, the dialogue stressing for its readers that Plato, not vocalic Alcibiades of the suspect Dionysian lifestyle, was Socrates' true heir

(Cavarero 2003: 80–90). Socrates' defense of speech against Thoth's claims and Plato's writing at the end of *Phaedrus* signals the same division. The time of original tragedy, organic representation of the city's cultural, social, political, and religious life has also gone. Femi Osofisan has a like thought in remarking that contemporary African authors have access to a felt reality of corporeal "space," lost to Europeans, because "our continent never produced a Sophocles or an Aeschylus," mediators between voice and *logos* – or not so as to bind the future (2001: 59–60).

Her gloss on the *Symposium* is part of Cavarero's historical study of how *logos* replaced *voice* (vital mark of living body's presence). Socrates as Dionysian flute-player was an image that escaped Nietzsche, for whom, also, Marsyas and apes figured a stage inferior to tragedy, already a falling-off from its voice and music. This figuring especially reveals how tragedy, in its origins and long history, represents the *logos* of a European culture which has seen, and sees, itself essentially in terms of autonomies, disjunctions, and ruptures: human from divine, reason from unreason (or emotion), beauty from ugliness, tame from savage, written from spoken, culture from barbarism, us from others (Reiss 2002). In other cultures, ape figures directly oppose Nietzsche's vision. He, like most Western commentators, saw tragedy as showing Europeans "keenly aware of the terrors and horrors of existence" (1956: 29). Tragedy controlled terror via Aristotelian "pity and fear," casting horror into Form. The ape and flayed Marsyas figured unreason and misrule.

Elsewhere, however, in almost all non-Western cultures, the ape is, or is companion of, trickster gods – Chinese Sun Wu K'ong, Indian Hanuman, sub-Saharan Esu Elegbara, Egyptian Thoth – who mark unions between human and divine, life and death, here and elsewhere, born and unborn, individual and community. They are an imagining of the world as rooted not so much

> in the coincidence of opposites or in the mere passage between structure and antistructure as it is in a perception of life as a rounded wholeness whose faces both mask and disclose each other. These faces are simultaneously present, but this is a simultaneity of process, a turning by which one face not only succeeds but is transformed into the other. (Pelton [1980] 1989: 104)

Even myths of taboo or awful acts have no "aura of tragedy." They are *"overcome"* to ground a "conviction that reality is always moving in a spiral of growth drawing even rebellion, incestuous desire, paternal rage, murderous jealousy,' and death into the service of life" (214). This worldview has no place for a tragic sense of "discrepancy" (270).

Derek Walcott writes that the 1950s–1960s Caribbean stage had to catch "not only nostalgia for innocence, but the enactment of remorse for the genocides of civilization, a search for the wellspring of tragic joy in ritual . . . gropings for the outline of pure tragedy, rituals of washing in the first darkness." For actor and director, says this reader of Nietzsche, the "darkness which yawns before them is terrifying. It is the journey back from man to ape" (Walcott 1970: 5–6). Osofisan echoes the sense of a "space filled with dramatic terror when, according to the Yoruba myth, gods invaded the earth and drama was born" (2001: 55). They also forged ties that only later inflictions broke. Contrariwise, the Caribbean, for Walcott and others, had *always* lived a vast series of dislocations, figured in forms like the "tragic bulk" of Christophe's Haitian citadel, as tragic as the man, who "believed then that the moral of tragedy could only be Christian" and lived in a "tragic anguish" that was the harvest of "divisions" imposed by Europe (Walcott 1970: 12). The return from tragic scission to the ape's prior time would begin delivery "from servitude" by making "a language that went beyond mimicry" (17). The Caliban-like ape would make a new "revelatory" language. If Western culture, in late centuries, has used tragedy to grasp different cultures and control some of their aspects and practices (Reiss 2002: 141–8), Walcott urges uses of tragedy to invert that grasp, Caliban turning, turning on, Prospero and his books.

Tragedy and Wholeness

That is why Soyinka calls his *The Bacchae of Euripides* "a communion rite" and wants it played "as a communal feast, a tumultuous celebration of life" ("Production Note"). It certainly exhibits (among other things) fraught agonies of decolonization, conflicts between "collaborators" and "refusers," marked especially by the now added Slave Leader, enabling a harder probing of specific historical context. But that probing also joyfully reaffirms a culture that unites death and life, divine and secular, social and natural worlds. The disaster and exile that end Euripides' *Bacchae* are upturned. In Soyinka's play a kind of Hegelian *Aufhebung* is performed, whereby dissension and dissonance, conflicts of slavery and rule, belief and disbelief, freedom and force, are overridden, transformed, and conjoined in a "communal feast." The final tearing apart of Pentheus and removal of what Agave saw as his lion "mask" repeat the flaying of Marsyas, enabling the deforming mask to bring new life, as red jets spurt "from every orifice of the impaled head": "What is it, Kadmos, what is it?" asks Tiresias. "Again blood, Tiresias, nothing but blood." "No," says Tiresias, nearing the jets: "It's wine." So Agave, too, steps to the mask to share the liquid, the curtain falling as the "light contracts to a final glow around the heads of Pentheus and Agave" (97): Eucharist aped to meld a deeper union of culture, history, and place, absorbing scraps of another Western tradition to new ends (cannibalizing it, as Maryse Condé has said). For mission Christianity was a potent instrument of European colonial empires. To impose it, they tried to erase local beliefs, to the ruin of culture and language. In Soyinka's *Bacchae*, a chief scrap of that Christianity is taken from its destructive use and transfigured, like tragedy, the play having drawn us to know a dialectic of slavery and racism, religious creed and secular order, metropolitan dominion and colonial underdevelopment – with an optimism (in 1973, three years after the Biafran War) that Soyinka's and others' works would not show for much longer, as political conditions across sub-Saharan Africa fast decayed.

For the theater in Africa, like much artwork in the underdeveloped/"developing" world, is rooted in the sociopolitical – *making*, not allegorizing it. Here – and given this reading of Soyinka's *Bacchae*, what Biodun Jeyifo says of tragedy in Africa is material (despite its contrary take on Soyinka) – Aristotle on tragedy typifies alienated Western *logos*: "a spirit and a vision sublimated from life into an 'organic' form which is eternally 'true' and indifferent to the unfolding of 'life' in history" (1985: 23). Hegel and Marx/Engels disalienated this. For Hegel, tragedy "distilled the *necessary* collisions which the World Historical Spirit, in every age and in its manifestations in racial or national communities, must go through in its self-actualization in history." So opposing forces are "themselves and *more* than themselves..., reflect[ing] the contradictions which must be 'annulled', must be negated for spirit to realize itself in an age or epoch." To *this* abstraction, Marx/Engels added an idea of "tragedy based on historical events – reflect[ing] the socio-historical roots of the tragic issue," tragedy waged between social classes or forces (24–5).

I want to show that African writers, directors, and actors who use tragedy annul such a distinction. Yet it is a useful one, just because Western aesthetics after Aristotle *has* taken tragedy to give a universal view of humans' condition and their action. The context and aesthetic choices of African writers seem to deter this view. But if Jeyifo does not comment here on the *Bacchae*, he sees an Aristotelian spirit as a basic temptation of Soyinka's *Death and the King's Horseman* (1975). Soyinka does say in an "Author's Note" that the "Colonial Factor is . . . a catalytic incident merely" for seeing a "metaphysical" conflict "contained in the human vehicle which is Elesin [the King's horseman] and the universe of the Yoruba mind." This conflict can be "fully realised only through an evocation of music from the abyss of transition" between "the living, the dead and the unborn" (2003: 3). For Jeyifo, the play's deviations from historical fact only ratify the Aristotelian "Author's Note" (1985: 27–8). The play is a straightforward, alienated "European" tragedy.

Based on an event that occurred in colonial Nigeria in 1946, the play opens to Elesin Oba gaily entering the marketplace with his followers. During an exchange with his Praise-Singer we learn that he is to commit suicide, following the custom that the King's Horseman joins his dead king, the Alafin, to travel to the ancestral world. The Alafin had died a month earlier; his funeral is now. Their passage to the other world confirms the jointure between the worlds of the dead, the living, and the unborn. Elesin now insists on taking as bride a lovely young woman who walks by. Their issue, he claims, will further tighten the world's bonds. Although she is betrothed to the son of Iyaloja, "mother" of the marketplace, the latter feels bound to reply to the market-women's objections: "The voice I hear is already touched by the waiting fingers of our departed. I dare not refuse" (2003: 16). These first scenes figure a deeper breach. Benedict Ibitokun writes that life's "market phase (in-between birth and death) is notorious for its transitoriness and contingency for which the Yorùbá man provides the ethic of industry, combativity and heroism as its most efficient panacea" (1995: ix). Elesin has grievously destabilized communal bonds.

Forcing himself on mother and daughter, Elesin already betrays the personal, familial, and racial honor that he sees verified by his willing death, vital aspect of their family's ancestral role:

> Life has an end. A life that will outlive
> Fame and friendship begs another name.
> What elder takes his tongue to his plate,
> Licks it clean of every crumb? He will encounter
> Silence when he calls on children to fulfill
> The smallest errand! Life is honour.
> It ends when honour ends.
>
> (2003: 11)

Later, he admits that forcing himself on his bride was a failing, "a weight of longing on my earth-held limbs" (53), one "tainted with the curses of the world," that Iyaloja angrily confirms (55). Elesin's worldly failing actually showed right after the longer passage above, when he threatened, only partly as a joke, that the market-women had not given him a new set of clothes (11–12).

Soon, the white District Officer Pilkings and his wife learn from the local policeman and their house servant of Elesin's planned suicide. We first see them dancing in the confiscated attire of the Oyo ancestral masquerade of death, *egungun*, which they are to wear to a fancy-dress ball that night. We see their blithe racism – surrounded as they are by "pagans" believing in "barbaric customs" (19, 22, 25) – Pilkings' arrogance, bragging of taking Elesin's son Olunde to send him to England to become a doctor (over his father's fury, since an eldest son has to take his father's place if the Horseman's death precedes the Alafin's: 22–3), and their further arrogance in aiming to stop the suicide willy-nilly. And they do, after the wedding, after the successful start of the death rite, after the ball, and after we find that Olunde has returned in time to tell Pilkings how glad he is that he had not prevented his father's death; for to have done so "would have been a terrible calamity . . . for the entire people" (47). Right away, Elesin is brought in in chains, struggling: "Give me back the name you have taken away from me you ghost from the land of the nameless!" to see and face Olunde: "O son, don't let the sight of your father turn you blind!" Olunde, struck motionless at hearing his father's voice, now turns, picking up on his father's much earlier proud statement to the market-women: "I have no father, eater of left-overs" (49–50).

In jail, Elesin tells Pilkings: "You have shattered the peace of the world forever . . . If I wished you well, I would pray that you do not stay long enough on our land to see the disaster you have brought upon us." Pilkings has prevented Elesin "from fulfilling my destiny": "Did you think it all out before, this plan to push our world from its course and sever the cord that links us to the great origin? . . . The world is set adrift and its inhabitants are lost. Around them there is nothing but emptiness" (50–1). Eventually Iyaloja is let in, along with women bearing the body of Olunde, whose own suicide has saved "the honour of your household and of our race" (61). Prevented by Pilkings from leaving his cell to recite words of passage to his dead son, Elesin strangles himself with his chains. Iyaloja condemns Pilkings and all he represents:

> you who play with strangers' lives, who even usurp the vestments of our dead, yet believe that the stain of death will not cling to you. The gods demanded only the old expired plantain but you cut down the sap-laden shoot to feed your pride. There is your board, filled to overflowing. Feast on it." But even as she says this, she calls on the Bride properly to close Elesin's eyes and to rebuild bonds: "Now forget the dead, forget even the living. Turn your mind only to the unborn. (62–3)

Jeyifo sees the play as showing "the conflict between a traditional African, organic vision of life and an alien system of discrete laws and social polity, with tragic results for the indigenous system. In other words, it is a confrontation at the level of categorical superstructures wrested from their economic and social foundations" (1985: 34). Elesin's honor marks a patriarchal class distinction whose ready acceptance by the women and others signals its repression. Yet he shows how the policeman Amusa – to say nothing of the Pilkings' house servant Joseph and the market-women – introduces enough of "the real, objective differences between conflicting groups and classes" (35) as to be seen to be depicting them. Nor is the "traditional" vision pure. Jeyifo thinks Soyinka was trying to show the colonized world as one of fragmentation and bewilderment (31). Elesin's failings suggest as much. More gravely, Jeyifo ignores the play's end, seeing as final a prior scene where Iyaloja and the Praise-Singer lament Elesin's and his people's lost honor and his having let the world "plunge over the edge of the bitter precipice" (2003: 62; Jeyifo 1985: 30). Agreeing, Osofisan asserts that "the possibility of tragedy crumbles. Deprived of his status as communal scapegoat, Elesin goes to his death all alone, in a private tragedy which no longer involves the larger human community or our collective destiny" (2001: 81). *His* tragedy *is* that privacy and exile, but the play's *actual* end is Iyaloja's scornful fury at Pilkings and her telling the Bride to care now for the unborn. Also, given Elesin's behavior toward Iyaloja and the Bride, it matters that this exchange is between the two women, and that the women bearing Olunde's body back them as chorus. Consciousness of gender – as well as of race – forces in history is clearly a major ground of the play's conflicts.[5]

The play is more complex than a simple Aristotelian versus Marxist analysis allows. Some things could be analyzed through an Aristotelian grille: Elesin as flawed tragic hero overcome by preordained fate – save that that fate was a communal one he welcomed. Not preordained was the intervention of a colonial world. *That* world made his weakness fatal (as the successful start of the death rite shows). *His* fate was one confirming a community across life and death that the play shows in its insistence on a temporality that makes present, past, and future one whole, and on a spatiality figured by the market, with its community of women, its constant process of exchange, its song and dance. There was no supposal of scission between worlds. That supposal came from outside, as Olunde finds, knowing what he "took" with him to England and what the colonizers had "over there" (2003: 44): here and there marking not just lack of understanding but, on the colonizers' part, lack of *wanting* to do so. Also, as the plot progresses, the forces of oppression, the fact of internal weakness, and the play of gender and racial forces *together* forge the possibility not just of rejecting the colonizing interloper whom Iyaloja accuses of inability *ever* to understand, but of letting the Bride turn her "mind only to the unborn." *Death and the King's Horseman* may lack the *Bacchae*'s optimism. It establishes the source of disjunction and offers more than a hope of rejoining produced from the play of social and political forces.[6]

That most African and Caribbean tragedies probe sociopolitical realities is a critical cliché. While clearly not limited to African and Caribbean cases, this probing is key to their experience of tragedy. Looking at some of these tragedies, we start to see how cultural contexts shape those realities and attitudes toward them, leading to a perhaps new idea of tragedy. The probing and its centrality are easily explicable: "my theatre," said Aimé Césaire in 1966, "is above all a political theatre because the major problems of Africa are political problems. I would like to reactualize black culture to ensure its permanence, so that it becomes a culture contributing to the building of a new order, a revolutionary order where the African personality can bloom" (cited by Brichaux-Houyoux 1993: 12). Even to its architectural metaphor, the remark rests on and stresses the originally affirmative end of Césaire's *Une saison au Congo* (A season in the Congo, 1966), implying possible achievement of new community and tying the political sphere to a wider jointure, buttressed by culturally embedded spiritual and aesthetic values and media mostly unfamiliar to – or now merely exotic in – European tragedy.

Narratives of Wholeness and Ambiguity

Political probings tend to be focused via four narratives, always overlapping. One involves colonization and its horrors; a second, conflicts that weakened cultures before colonial onslaught; a third, present struggles of cultural values, often involving failures of combative will or action; a fourth, neocolonialism and crimes and corruptions of its elites. All mean to raise awareness and enable political action. Ola Rotimi's *Ovonramwen Nogbaisi* typifies the first (Rotimi saying it also did the fourth; Alston 1989: 95), exploring the ruin of the Empire of Benin by an English army: death of a culture, end of an era, loss of values.[7] Ama Ata Aidoo's *Anowa* tells this first narrative otherwise, showing how Kofi Ako's collusion with the colonizers in the 1870s makes him wealthy but destroys him, his wife Anowa, and traditions. Rotimi's *Kurunmi* epitomizes the second, telling of a precolonial war to uphold traditional values against new deforming ones. Sofola's *Old Wines Are Tasty* illustrates the third, with strife between traditional and neocolonial values baldly direct – ending in the death of the latter's misguided delegate. Césaire's *Saison* exemplifies the fourth – notably in its final version (1973), which ends not with its sanza player's optimistic banter and opening to a new future (we shall see), but with the tyrant Mokutu publicly "rehabilitating" the Lumumba he has murdered but, fast enraged by the crowd's enthusiasm, calling on his guards to shoot, killing many, including the sanza player (3.8.117). Another such is Rotimi's *If* (1979), bitterly showing the poverty, abusive oppression of the people, "the tragedy of the ruled," and ferociously damning the corrupt wealth and misused power of the neocolonial elites.

A particularly well-known instance of the first narrative is the Swahili playwright Ebrahim Hussein's *Kinjeketile*, which tells the story of the 1906 Maji Maji Uprising against German colonizers in southern Tanganyika. Its first act tells of growing oppression – reaching its peak in the rape of Kitunda's daughter and the whipping of him and his wife. The people fail to rally against the Germans because the tribes continually quarrel. Kitunda advises against war, as this will lead only to myriad deaths, while "the few who will survive will get the same treatment, or worse, as before" (Hussein 1970: 8). Kinjeketile, meanwhile, withdraws into prayer and ritual. As the second act starts we find that "Kitunda is now the leader of the people" and see Kinjeketile come from his house in a trance, do a violent dance around the compound, and finally writhe, possessed (by the spirit Hongo) into the river, where he disappears (12). A day later, he reappears, announcing the tribes' uniting in a new community:

> We will unite and we will be one body
> And as it is in a human body
> when a toe gets hurt,
> the whole body feels the pain.
> When a Mmatumbi gets whipped,
> it is the Mzaramo who will feel the pain.
> When a Mrufiji gets tortured,
> it is the Mngoni who will cry out.
> When we reach this stage, then we will be united,
> We will be one people.
>
> (16)

He says that he has been given water (Swahili *maji*) that will stop bullets from harming its drinker. Together, water and unity will enable them to win. Ritualistically, Kinjeketile blesses messengers who will spread the word and with the water anoints Kitunda as military leader: "Partake of this water and believe. / Believe in the power of the water. / Believe in the water of life" (19).

The next scene shows a different Kinjeketile. When Kitunda asks him worriedly who is the Seyyid Said whose "children" Kinjeketile had said in his post-river trance they would be once they freed themselves (16), the latter replies: "the Sultan of Zanzibar." But he is an Arab, says Kitunda. Kinjeketile is shocked at learning he had said this: "I've been cheated! They have killed me – no, I have killed myself! . . . No, no, no, no! I have been cheated! No! (*He gives a terrible cry and falls down*)" (21): one oppression would be swapped for another. But everyone is gathering, eager for war.

Kinjeketile is unsure whether Hongo is deceiving them and urges "patience." Kitunda insists that all are ready for war and accuses Kinjeketile of crossing the people, who came "because they believe in you" (27). The latter says they will fight, but "must not depend on the water." "You brought the water," Kitunda replies. "You brought these people together. You made them believe in you." Kinjeketile is a liar, and he will tell the people so. "Go tell them," says the other, "And by tomorrow there won't be a single soul out there. And you will be under the white man's rule for ever" (28–9). That's a reason not to wait, says Kitunda, "the people have been made strong by the water, and they want to start the war as soon as possible." Says Kinjeketile: "A man gives birth to a...word. And the word...grows...it grows bigger and bigger. Finally, it becomes bigger than the man who gave it birth" (30). War fervor wins and as all rush off, Kinjeketile is left to say a third time: "The word...man breeds a word...and it knocks down its creator, destroying him" (39).

Carried away by faith in the water, despite many deaths, the armies ignore Kitunda's plans. Thousands are killed, others are prisoners in the fort they had been attacking. There, they find an unconscious Kinjeketile, terribly beaten by the Germans to force him to say "that the water was a lie." "He has refused" (51). Finally, he is told that if he admits it everyone else will be freed. Alone with Kinjeketile, Kitunda tries to get him to save the people. Kinjeketile cannot:

> Do you know what they will say tomorrow? The officer will say that we were wrong in fighting him. He will tell that to our children, Kitunda. That to fight him is wrong! *That to fight for one's country is wrong!* And he wants me to help him by retracting all that I said. He wants me to say that the water was a lie. Do you know what that means? The moment I say that, people in the north, south, east and west will stop fighting. They will fall into hopeless despair – they will give up. I will not say that! A word has been born. Our great-grandchildren will hear of it. One day the word will cease to be a dream, it will be a reality! (53)

He goes to his death. The insuperable contradictions – the people's unity needs belief in the magic water, that very belief ruins them – may be overcome. Kinjeketile now knows that what matters is the people's belief that unity is possible (shown by the war itself) and that, properly mobilized and ordered, it can liberate. He and Kitunda finally know the military and political realities that need ordering. If they do, so will others. To achieve this collective knowledge and action, Kinjeketile's refusal and death are as necessary as the process leading to them. They may create new cultural and political realities (cf. Jeyifo 1985: 35–40; Etherton 1982: 155–65).

One may say the same of Ngugi wa Thiong'o and Micere Mugo's *The Trial of Dedan Kimathi*, where the young finally know why Kimathi also refuses words and thoughts the British and neocolonial Africans seek to impose; or of Maryse Condé's *Mort d'Oluwémi d'Ajumako* (Death of Oluwémi d'Ajumako), where, after trying to evade the fruits of his craven flight from customary death, King Oluwémi realizes that the real act of resistance is to return, appropriating his death and reasserting the force of a threatened culture. These plays join commentary on colonization to one on present conditions. So, too, does Condé's *Dieu nous l'a donné* (God gave him to us), a tragedy epitomizing the third kind of sociopolitical play: that of failed will or action. Dieudonné, having trained in the colonial capital as a doctor, returns to a small Caribbean town resolved to start a revolt against corrupt rule. Like Kinjeketile, he uses ritual and magic to bring people to him. Unlike Kinjeketile, he is undone by friends' failings and enemies' tricks, and finally killed out of mere sexual jealousy: no hopeful apotheosis here. Divisions are incurably forlorn. So, too, in Rotimi's *If*, where, faced with boundless corruption, "community" is class conflict, union of the poor against the elites, the police, the military: "The day our solidarity dissolves is the day our humanity ends, and our worthlessness begins" (1983: 16). But the same speaker finally knows that these are already the divisions of "individual self-preservation," giving power to those with guns and money. His resolute cry: "We must survive: *together*," yields to the groan of the community's old moral leader: "It is finished" (82–3).

Sylvain Bemba's *Noces posthumes de Santigone* (Posthumous wedding of Santigone, 1988) differs. A tragedy of neocolonial corruption, "inspired" by Sophocles' *Antigone*, it "turns" that play against its tradition, damning division and the violence and agony it fosters and depends on. The actress Melissa Yadé, fiancée, then wife, of her nation's slain leader, is famed worldwide for her performances in England of *Antigone*. *Noces'* action resonates with that play: "We must link up. The audience must feel something real's going on on stage. Has Antigone heard my call to come halfway on the path separating her from me?" ([1988] 1995: 44). Melissa's "halfway" denies familiar individualist readings of *Antigone*, offers reworkings, even as it adopts it. She *knows* that her "inexplicable fear" is due "to what will happen" to her beloved Titus Saint-Just Bund (45). Polynices, she says, will die twice on the night of his assassination (56), once as Titus, once on stage, for her to bury both deniers of colonial and neocolonial power, Saint-Just echoing Lumumba (57). After his killing (recalling that of Burkina Faso's Thomas Sankara in 1987 [10]), she is, like Antigone over Polynices, "watchful" guardian over the "wounded memory of her heroic husband" (62–3).[8] Her African nation, Amandla, slides into violent neocolonialism under the rule of the new "strongman"/Creon, who equates and forbids the old colonial power and Saint-Just's once-hopeful new utopia (70–1) – inspired by Thomas More (30), conservative chancellor made revolutionary. Melissa/Antigone returns home, popular symbol of the good lost by the strongman's coup. She will not be silent on his corruption and butchery, she finally tells him, but not now cause more bloodshed. Leaving to fly back to England, she takes with her as a relic More's book soaked with Titus's blood (88): utopia departing for now. Her plane is destroyed. The Griot has the last word: "Melissa–Antigone blazes from the depths of the ocean-necropolis like a supernova that bursts with all its fires into the vexed dreams of our orphan nights. No superman diver to bring to the surface our memories scattered into twisted starfish. But I tell you, the people's memory will one day spring up again" (93). Like *Kinjeketile* and many others, *unlike Antigone*, the tragedy ends on a note of collective hope.

Soyinka writes of the "tragedy" of "man . . . grieved by a consciousness of the loss of the eternal essence of his being" that traditional Yoruba drama shows: a "severance, . . . fragmentation of essence from self." Simultaneously this drama performs "symbolic transactions to recover his totality of being" (1976: 144–5). That totality alters what the West calls "tragedy." The play takes its protagonist "through areas of terror and blind energies into a ritual empathy with the gods, the eternal presence, who once preceded him in parallel awareness of their own incompletion" (146). Performance conjoins – no finally blasted Pentheus or lasting blind Oedipus here:

> Morality for the Yoruba is that which creates harmony in the universe, and reparation for disjunction within the individual psyche cannot be seen as compensation for the individual accident to that psyche. Thus good and evil are not measured in terms of offenses against the individual or even the physical community, for there is knowledge from within the corpus of Ifa oracular wisdoms that a rupture is often simply one aspect of the destructive-creative unity, that offenses even against nature may be part of the exaction by deeper nature from humanity of acts which alone can open up the deeper springs of man and bring about a constant rejuvenation of the human spirit. Nature in turn benefits by such broken taboos, just as the cosmos does by demands made upon its will by man's cosmic affronts. Such acts of hubris compel the cosmos to delve deeper into its essence to meet the human challenge. Penance and retribution are not therefore aspects of punishment for crime but the first acts of a resumed awareness, an invocation of the principle of cosmic adjustment. (1976: 156)

This helps us read Rotimi's redoing of Sophocles' *Oedipus the King. The Gods Are Not to Blame* (1968) opens at Ogun's shrine, where Baba Fakunle, "oldest and most knowing / of all Ifa priests" is to divine "the future that this boy / has brought / with him" (1971a: 2), telling King Adetusa and Queen Ojuola "what it is that the boy has brought / as mission from the gods / to carry out on earth" (3). Told he will kill his father and wed his mother, they choose to avert this "bad future," giving the child as "sacrifice / to the gods who have sent / boy down to this Earth" (3). Next we learn that 32 years have passed and that 11 years before, Adetusa was killed and his kingdom of Kutuje instantly attacked by its neighbors, killing, pillaging, and enslaving. The farmer Odewale, hearing of this calamity "in the course of my countless wanderings / from land to land, town to town, village to village," came to Kutuje and gathered its people to defeat those of Ikolu. The Kutuje people elected him king and he took "for wife, / as custom wishes, / Ojuola, the motherly Queen," with whom he has four children. But now sickness has broken out (4–8).

In light of Soyinka's remarks, this opening gives a different frame from that of Sophocles' play. Odewale has a specific future, not unlike Oedipus, but bears it as a "mission from the gods." This mission will open deeper springs of humanity and renew the spirit. Breaking "taboos," it may "compel the cosmos to delve deeper into its essence," to echo Soyinka's phrase. The unborn has knelt before Olodumare, father of the gods, to choose this mission (Etherton 1982: 124; Rotimi 1984: 3–4). Chosen in a divine place of nothing but the good, the choice to defend his people has to be executed in a world where bad and good mix and matter and emotion are in play (Rotimi 1984: 4–6). Yet equivocal as things are in life, the fact is that the unborn Odewale's choice is still a mission approved by Olodumare. Except for a general sense of dissymmetry between gods and humans (a Gloucester-like sense of "Like flies are we to the gods, they kill us for their sport"), little explains Oedipus' fate. But Odewale is still conjoined to the gods, whose mission he bears – whether or not humans understand it. If Laius and Jocasta cannot hope to stop what Apollo has ordained, they do no wrong in trying to. Adetusa and Ojuola directly counter their son's mission and his divinely ratified free choice. Toward the play's end, the priest of Ogun says: "It is the custom: when the gods command, we men must obey!" (68).[9] They have not. Whatever might have happened (in some unimagined alternative), objectively their acts cause the later calamities.

That his mission binds Odewale to Ogun is marked not just by the Prologue's shrine, but by his "wanderings from land to land, town to town, village to village." Ogun is god of the road, maker of the road over which he led the other gods to earth. "From the earthwomb, Ogún sighted and dug an iron ore which he later forged into a cutlass and, at the head of the other deities, used this artefact to cut a path and throw up a bridge of transition and fraternization between men and deities" (Ibitokun 1995:23). As he led "the procession [that] braved disjunctive chaos and linked man with god, his 'weapon' was not language significantly, but the iron artifact of his forge" (Osofisan 2001: 57). Odewale again echoes Ogun, god of iron and war, always using language to second his use of objects. References throughout the play to his use of iron tools, hoe as farmer, machete and sword as warrior and king (on which he often orders his courtiers to swear), further the association – and hint that by killing Adetusa with a hoe he was effecting part of his mission. Doing so, he indeed called on Ogun; before, for help that the god gives; after, from fear at what he has done: "Ogun . . . Ogun . . . I have used your weapon, and I have killed a man. Ogun . . . !" (49). Adetusa was arrogantly misusing his power and attendants to take the land Odewale had bought, gratuitously insulting and assaulting Odewale (the farmer, too, plowing and reshaping the land, echoes Ogun's primal gesture). The horror that Odewale feels at having killed a man and breached the living community signals the mix of good and bad, matter and emotion that define this world. Rotimi speaks of the "tragic flaw" of Odewale's temper (1984: 5), but this "temper" marks that difference and shows why the *human* agent of renewal suffers even as the community is healed.

Odewale's leadership made him king. Unlike Oedipus' lone defeat of a predatory Sphinx, he attained Kutuje's relief by forging a community for mutual good (1.1 shows the same effort to defeat the epidemic by not just human community but firm bond with land and gods: Odewale is also a healer; 12–13). It is in community, too, that he leaves Kutuje. After Ojuola's death and his self-blinding, their four children run out to greet him, taking his hand, quarreling as if all were normal. As they leave to resume roaming, they pass "through a mass of Kutuje townspeople who kneel or crouch in final deference to the man whose tragedy is also their tragedy" (72). Michael Etherton sees this as a fraud: "what is seen at the end of the play is the tragedy of one man, not of Kutuje or of the Yoruba kingdom" (1982: 127) – a note bred in part by what he sees as Rotimi's failed melding of ancient Greek and Yoruba cosmologies, in part by the playwright's claim that a major aspect of the play was its gloss on the Biafran War (e.g., Rotimi 1984: 1–2). As to the first, I am saying that Rotimi is melding nothing. He is *turning* the Greek story, making it one joining realms of being and experience, not marking their division – Odewale's is fundamentally, as Sofola says more generally of tragedy, "a life-saving action" (1994: 11). As to the second (where the gods not being blamed were superpowers whom many blamed for the outbreak and continuance of war), however such a gloss may be analyzed in detail, it is inescapably an aspect of the play. Grievous as Odewale's departure is, it does achieve an apotheosis – more *Oedipus at Colonus* than *Oedipus the King*. His leaving heals Kutuje, and him. He is returning to the road, following again Ogun's path to "anywhere," as he answers one of his children: "wherever we get tired, there we rest to continue again" – a life-journey in the company of children, offspring of a broken taboo whose breaching has led to a deeper sense of a community of humans, the world, and the gods.[10]

Efua Sutherland's reworking of *Alcestis* in *Edufa* (1967), out of Akan tradition, shows an analogous reshaping, but now one that stresses the irrevocable harm of breaching necessary bonds between levels of being – no demigod can bring back Ampoma as Heracles does Alcestis. But nor is *Edufa*'s emphasis on divine intervention or virtue and its redemptive value, as it is in *Alcestis*. The change of titular protagonist matters. In *Edufa* emphasis falls on the husband Edufa's belief that he can defeat ties of past, present, and future world(s), here and there, gods and humans. It falls on his belief that he can do so by manipulating them as he has his townspeople, buying his way into a postcolonial present whose very existence would mark the passage of a traditional world of beliefs into a dustbin of time hammered from a History supplied by another's narrative. He thinks that if he replaces traditional history with a new present and future, its forces lose their power. Admetos at last knows that he must die his own death, sacrificing another's life strips his of value (198, 895–9, 940, 1082). With the *voluntariness* of Alcestis' sacrifice, this knowledge may justify her recovery. Edufa finds that to play with life and death is to play not with powers whose divinity sets them somehow "elsewhere" but with powers of the human heart and soul. It is they that embody and forge ties with the worlds of the gods, the ancestors, and the unborn. It is they that make the path between them irrevocable.

The plays differ in tone, structure, and plotting. By moderns, *Alcestis* may be set among Greek tragedies. This was less clear in antiquity. A Hellenistic grammarian says that it was fourth in a tetralogy. *Alcestis*, while not a satyr play, held the position of one, and the grammarian adds that, like *Orestes*, it was "rejected from tragic poetry in that they begin with disaster and end in joy and delight, which belong rather to comedy" (Euripides 1988: 63). This was partly to differ with Aristotle, who held that a happy end to a tale of catastrophe was often best, and did not by itself make a play not a tragedy (e.g., *Poetics* 1545a4–9). *Alcestis'* form is that of all tragedy. From the start, catastrophe impends. It does so via *hamartia*, which may be what Pheres,

Admetos' father, calls his cowardice, but which may, as so often, be ignorance: of the reality of death, of his need for Alcestis, of the fact that the greater hurt may be to live – with loss, ignobility, weakness, of people's bonds. It does so, too, by direct divine intervention. Alcestis knowingly agrees to die for Admetos, once Apollo had tricked the Fates into letting another die for him, in return for his generous care of the god, doomed by Zeus to a year's slavery for having killed the Cyclops (*Alcestis* 10–18).[11] We know this at the start, and the play is both a dirge and Admetos' gradual learning of his own character, and that to live without Alcestis is not to live at all.

An equivalent to Apollo's elucidative prologue has no place in *Edufa*. Rather than serving as an explanation, Edufa's sister's opening presence is elegiac. Abena's lament evokes a feeling of being embedded in place, even as it elicits a mysterious sense of other, not quite this-worldly places:

> Dreamlike views of mist rising
> Above too much water everywhere.
> I heard tonight,
> And stretched thin through the mist, calling.
> Heard in that calling, the quiver of Ampoma's voice.
> Thought I saw suddenly in the restless white waters,
> The laterite red of an ant hill jutting
> And rocking.
> A misty figure on its topmost tip,
> Flicking her fingers like one despairing.
> I panicked, and came to this door, listening,
> But all was silence—
>
> (Sutherland [1975] 1987: 97)

The wealthy Edufa, benevolent, generous, and popular throughout the town, has abruptly changed his lifestyle. His doors are no longer open; he is no longer welcoming or laughing. "True that Ampoma, his wife, is unwell; but . . . she is not mortally ill," so better to keep doors open and laughter alive (98–9). Now, the place is shut, people excluded, the communal ideal of hospitality shut down. The audience no more knows the sense of this than does Abena that of her brother's change. Later, we find that Ampona, too (unlike Alcestis), did not know the seriousness of her oath to die for Edufa, since it was elicited during what he passed off as a joke.

As in *The Gods Are Not to Blame* (which is not to elide Akan and Yoruba beliefs), *people* make or break ties. Just as society needs their maintenance and an equitably balanced exchange of obligations, duties, and mutual recognitions, so do relations across times, places, and worlds. Gods are no more responsible than people, people no less so than gods and spirits. That is why, in most African traditions, people "believe that they can plead, question and dialogue with the forces that govern and control their lives" (Chinyowa 2001: 8). People's bonds in time, place, life and death are stressed in *Edufa*'s first scene as a chorus of women go by, singing a dirge for a woman who has died earlier, reminding Edufa and Seguwa ("a matronly member of the household," 95) that "the bridge we are now crossing is between the bands of life and the banks of death" (102). Only little by little do we come to understand that something is off kilter in the matter of Ampoma's illness:

> Yet, how good that I should not be the one to live beyond your days. I could not live where you are not. I could not live without you, my husband. (104)
> Let me talk with you a little longer in the sun before I step into the dark where you cannot see me. Soon, my pledge will be honoured. (104)
> Over me, the sun is getting dark . . . My husband! Watch the death that you should have died . . . Stay over there in the sun. Children! My children! If I could cross this water I would pluck you back from the mountain side. Children! Hold my hand! (105)

By scene 3, through Seguwa, we begin to see more clearly:

> I wish I could break this lock on my lips.
> Let those who would gamble with lives,
> Stake their own.
> None I know of flesh and blood,
> Has right to stake another's life
> For his own.
>
> (106)

The next scene explains fully, doing so via Edufa's father, Kankam, in a major departure from *Alcestis*. There, Pheres' and Admetos' fight is one of acrid mutual accusation that ends with Pheres indicting Admetos for his cowardice and Admetos disowning his father for not dying in his place, old and decrepit as he is. In *Edufa*, we learn that Kankam had disowned his son three years earlier, because, aching "to be emancipated," Edufa sought wealth, power over others, a name for philanthropy (self-centered lie as this was), and capitalistic *possession* – a sense of self and practice drawn from that imperial History named earlier as oppressive of traditional, local histories. This is quite unlike Admetos, whose generosity and hospitality signaled just rule, whether shown to Apollo, Heracles, or veiled Alcestis at the end. Kankam's first words to Edufa accuse him of the opposite: "Don't let us fail, however, on the sacredness of courtesy. Had I entered the house of a total stranger, he would have given me water to drink, seeing I'm a traveller" (108). Even Pheres accused Admetos of nothing such. But Kankam says of Edufa: "He grew greedy and insensitive; insane for gain; frantic for the fluff of flattery" (113), uneasy of his "reputation" (114), and fearful now that Kankam "might have turned tongues against me" (108). Without parallel in *Alcestis* is our learning of Edufa's fears and his savage trick on Ampoma. Kankam wants Edufa to accept the responsibility essential to being a human, in all the bonds that that means: "What do I want, you say? . . . I want the courage that makes responsible men. I want truthfulness. Decency. Feeling for your fellow men. These are the things I've always wanted. Have you got them to give?" (108). Above all, he adds, he wants: "The life of your wife Ampoma, from you" (109).

In Euripides, Heracles plays the savior. Here, Kankam might have done the same, thereby reaffirming natural human ties. He tells his son that he knows Edufa visited a diviner who forecast his death, knows the diviner gave him a charm to enable another to die in his stead if they swore an oath to do so, recalls the evening when Edufa joked about the request to know who would die for him. Kankam adds that he knows that Edufa later told Ampoma of her peril, only to elicit greater resolve, even after showing her the charm (112). Edufa angrily denies all this. How could one "educated . . . to another plane of living" believe such things (109)? He desperately accuses his father of speaking "drivel," lying, and then says: "Father, are you mad?" Silence reigns. Kankam cries: "[*Shocked*] Nyame above! To say father and call me mad! My *ntoro* within you shivers with the shock of it!" (111). Edufa has broken another taboo. In Akan belief, says Kwasi Wiredu, a human being is four joined elements: *ōkra*, a bit like Greek *psuchē*, life force, part of *Onyame*, the supreme being, and whose leaving is death; *sunsum*, character, the specific person you are; *ntoro*, received from your father, site of inherited traits; *mogya*, received from your mother, fixing clan identity (1980: 47). This joining means that "a human creature is not a human person except as a member of a community" – communities (1996: 19). Edufa has broken the joining. He is thus obsessed with false speech, while Kankam stresses the power of oath-swearing and truth of diviners, saying that if needed he can "broadcast my [true] story in the market place" (110) – whose significance we saw. Edufa's sham on the fatal evening is a "treacherous" misuse of language (111). To Edufa's offer to swear that all Kankam's facts are false, he just asks how his son can confuse oath-swearing and lying (112).

Finally, he asserts that the only way to defeat a true oath is with even stronger and truer language. "An oath once sworn will always ride its swearer. But there might still be a chance to save her." Edufa suggests paying for a Western-style doctor. He has the money to "pay their fees." The only way, his father pleads, is to "confess and denounce your wrong," publicly destroy the charm, and then "raise the prayer of our souls together." It is now that Edufa offers to swear that the whole affair is false. "If you must lie," says Kankam, "don't swear about it in a house in which death is skirmishing, and the ancestral spirits stand expectantly by. A man may curse himself from his own lips. Do not curse the house in which your children have to grow" (112–13). Edufa again replies: "I hope you haven't talked like this to anyone. You could do so much harm. Unjustly" (114). Kankam leaves in scorn, while Edufa regrets that his "emancipation" will not let him wholly deny the reality of charm and oath. The scene is crucial. The breach with his father, the breach in himself, the role of true language and balanced ties between humans, spirits, and the world are the play's core. More, it is the breach that takes effort, the "market" exchange is normal, natural, and wholesome: as the chorus soon says: "While we mourn another's death, it's our own death we also mourn" (117), or: "Crying the death day of another / Is crying your own death day" (120).

Breaking taboos in the name of "emancipation," these are the ties Edufa ruptures. Once split, they cannot easily be repaired. That is why Heracles' counterpart, Senchi, may be appealing, in a nomadic beachcomber kind of way, but his strengths are those of raising a smile and a song. It is why Ampoma, not believing Edufa's earlier vow that he will not remarry, enacts an elaborate and "embarrassingly" public ceremony to shame him into keeping it (146–7). It is why her several falls on the sign of the sun drawn on the house's steps take on such sinister meaning. Says Seguwa: "Bad signs. They would pose no menace if no oath had been sworn, and we were free to read in her present condition normal disabilities for which remedy is possible. As it is, the reality of that oath makes Edufa for all time guilty, no matter how or when she meets her end" (149). Once "the oath [is] sworn" on the "evil charm," it cannot be undone: "We cannot reason without it now" (151). That is why Ampoma cannot return from death. If the chorus can hope to begin repairing the breach by calling on tears to "make a river of sorrow," the same river with which the play began, and for someone to "go and tell her mother" (153–4), tying back to the earlier funeral chant, Edufa cannot. In his false emancipation, he is, as Seguwa said, guilty for all time.

So it is little wonder if, in *his* final madness – for where Kankam's continuing beliefs and behavior were *not* mad, Edufa's are – he turns into a crazed version of Euripides' *Heracles*:

> Where is my leopard skin? I'll teach Death to steal my wives. . . . Death, I will lie closely at the grave again, and when you come gloating with your spoil, I'll grab you, unlock her from your grip and bring her safely home to my bed. And until then, no woman's hand shall touch me.

"She is dead," the Chorus says with finality, while Senchi holds Edufa. But he "wrenches free":

> The last laugh will be mine when I bring her home again. I will bring Ampoma back. Forward, to the grave. [*He moves in strength towards the back courtyard, roaring.*] I will do it. I am conqueror! [*His last word, however, comes as a great questioning lament.*] Conqueror . . . ? (153)

This parodies Heracles: "Once I've run out from my place of ambush and seized [Death] and encircled him in these strong arms of mine, there's no one alive who will ever drag him thence, his lungs bursting for breath, till he has yielded the woman up to me" (*Alcestis* 846–9). He does just that (1141–2). Not so Edufa. If his leopard-skin parodies Heracles' traditional lion-skin, it also picks up on Kankam's earlier remark about Edufa's demanding abnormal sacrifices: "Beasts are normal sacrifices, but surely you know they are without speech. Beasts swear no oath to die for others, Edufa" (110). Nor did Edufa, who now misuses language, even more so in his final madness. His is a beast's roaring. Having split, and split from, community, he is no longer human.

There may be no need to point out the play's other dimension, to which Rotimi refers, in writing of *The Gods Are Not to Blame*, as the "secular." At the end of *Alcestis*, Admetos declares that life will now be better. Lessons have been learned and he knows what real happiness can and should be (1157–8) – although over the end of the play hangs the possibility that if Alcestis has not died for him, then Admetos must now die his own death. *Edufa* ends with the madness brought on by the hope and results of a false emancipation. Traditional bonds are shattered. "Blank," says Senchi, Heracles' counterpart:

> I have ended up blank once again. All that is left, the laughter of the flowers in her
> lifeless arms, and the lingering smell of incense. [*He descends*]
> And over me, the taut extension of the sky – to which I raise my song.
> Will someone go and tell her mother? [*He sings*]
> And if I find you
> I'll have to worship you
> I must adore you
> Nne
> Nne nne
> O mother.
>
> (154)

Edufa was written when early hopes of cultural recovery and political sovereignty in Ghana were fading, when hopes for mutual enriching of cultures were being devoured by realities that looked more like a ruin of values. If Sutherland's "comedy," *The Marriage of Anansewa*, seemed to hold that these hopes might be realized, Ananse's daughter's "modern" values joining traditional ones of "Chief-of-chiefs," *Edufa* implies that a ruined culture may be irrecoverable – at least for its Edufas.[12] Yet not all may be lost; a flicker of ongoing cycles stays. The split world that Edufa has made is neither good nor real. It is blank. People may or may not "find" and "worship" this broken world. As its potential loss points to colonial causes, its very blankness points to a still alive wholeness. One recalls again Dionysus' companion Silenus in Nietzsche's *Birth of Tragedy*: "What would be best for you is quite beyond your reach: not to have been born, not to *be*, to be *nothing*" (29). Out of this nothing art is born, out of this blank life can come, and social renewal: "not only does the bond between man and man come to be forged once more..., but nature itself, long alienated [, hostile], or subjugated, rises again to celebrate the reconciliation with her prodigal son, man" (23). "Our joy," echoes the Slave Leader in Soyinka's *The Bacchae of Euripides*, "Is the great joy of union with mother earth / And the end of separation between man and man":

> Said Bromius,
> I am the gentle comb of breezes on the slope of vines
> The autumn flush on clustered joy of grapes
> I am the autumn sacrament, the bond, word, pledge
> The blood rejuvenated from a dying world
> I am the life that's trodden by the dance of joy
> My flesh, my death, my re-birth is the song
> That rises from men's lips, they know not how.
>
> (38)

Spiritual and social, material and political, moral and epistemological intertwine, and the very intertwining signals not just the possibility, but the actuality of cultural wholeness. The ones are not "allegories," "symbols," or "representations" of the others (as some have suggested of art and culture, with respect to the political). Together they provide a mutual *poiesis*, to use another old Greek word, an organic *making*, a *forging* of lived actuality and its understanding. Such tragedies in their context approach something like the original meaning of *mimesis*, which Aristotle held the capacity – necessity – that most made humans *human*: not *re*production but production, a making that was the same as that of the gods. One sees why, speaking of no wholly different context, Nietzsche asserted, in the first foreword to *The Birth of Tragedy*, "that art is the highest human task, the true metaphysical activity" (1956: 17). These reworkings of tragedy give meanings to the intertwinings of social life in the world. They bring people, we shall see Ato Quayson argue, into engagement with their history. Doing so, they are an organic part of the making of that history.

A like figuring of ruptured bonds and potential wholeness, and yet their final bringing-together, is in 'Zulu Sofola's *Wedlock of the Gods*. Two lovers, Ogwoma and Uloko, have been forbidden to marry by Ogwoma's father. Wanting a high bride-price to buy a cure for Ogwoma's sick brother, Ogwoma's father forced her to wed the hated Adigwu, who, three years later, has died. Ignoring the three-month mourning period at the end of which she must marry Adigwu's brother, the widowed Ogwoma has urged Uloko to visit: she is pregnant with their child. Odibei, Ogwoma's spying mother-in-law, catches them together. She thinks that her unfounded and untrue suspicions that Adigwu was murdered are confirmed. From then on Odibei plans to kill Ogwoma. Taboos and bonds have been broken, families shamed, but nothing allows Odibei to judge – especially as she is seeking "vengeance" on Ogwoma from the first, when she has no cause to believe in murder – save only that she knows, as did Ibekwe and Nneka, Ogwoma's parents, that she hated Adigwu. They had forced her to marry him despite this, for which the family later upbraid Ibekwe, causing further breaches. They insist that he had resources other than unjustly forcing Ogwoma into a hostile marriage. He accuses them of hypocrisy, since they had not helped at other times.

What we see, again, are results of familial, social, and spiritual ruptures in the destruction of lives. Odibei finally manages to poison Ogwoma, Uloko kills Odibei and poisons himself with the drug Ogwoma drank, falling next to her, singing over her body a song of hope:

> Your love will now come with you.
> Ours is the wedlock of the gods.
> Together we shall forever be lightning
> and thunder – inseparable . . .
> (1972: 55–6)

Here, too, a breach was initially made by a demand for wealth that blasted the lives of two others. No balance can be set by destroying vital bonds, and a first disequilibrium leads to a rushing spiral of disaster. The final breach of the taboo on mourning and a widow's marrying her dead husband's brother confirms the ruptures of ties between families, between gods, spirits, and humans, present, past, and future. Of the violence ending *Wedlock*, Sofola noted that what matters are not so-called "age-old traditions," not even, in a simple way, immoral behavior, but that "those violent deaths are going to affect the families because of reincarnation." Disrupting life instantly, they more importantly unbalance the long-term course of community and persons (James 1990: 148–9).

Something not dissimilar is found in Sofola's *King Emene I*, where the king of the title is on the throne because his mother, Agrippina-like, has murdered his half-brother. Emene is ignorant of this, but takes from the start a kind of Neronian stance, insisting on hectoring and bullying everyone. Yet his authority is visibly in doubt. He rejects the oracle that repeatedly tells of something rotten in the state and of an evildoer in the heart of the royal family. He takes this, rather, Oedipus- or Odewale-like, as proof that ministers and council are plotting against him. Exiling the oracle's interpreter, he becomes increasingly paranoid, more and more insistent on holding the ceremonial week of peace, even as his people tell him he cannot do so until the oracle says that state and palace have been "cleansed." The result is rebellion, effort to overcome ever-widening gaps and oppositions. In the end, Emene finds that his mother Nneobi is indeed guilty. The fact makes him more guilty: it had been in his power to discover and atone for the murder. At first, his response is to rage and threaten his mother with a dagger, but as he does so, "it thunders violently, lightning barely misses the King; he stops abruptly, turns away and walks steadily and deliberately to the inner palace." As "those on stage stare at him not knowing what to make of the sudden change," it thunders again. Going after him, they discover that he has used the knife on himself (Sofola 1974: 45).

Emene knows the thunder and lightning are divine signs of *his* responsibility. This is not Oedipus saying that while Apollo ordained his actions, he has finally taken responsibility for them on himself. Nothing in Thebes is healed, save briefly. The disasters of the House of Thebes continue down the years: we know what will happen to Antigone, Ismene, Eteocles, and Polynices. The world's divisions continue, ordained by gods, accepted by humans. In *Emene*, the world had been whole. And while Emene may not at first be liable for the growing disjunction (Nneobi is), his behavior affirms it. In the end, the gods let him know that only he can ravel up the world's soul again. He does so, remaking jointure. Here, the *fact* of violence has a contrary role to that in *Wedlock*. There, it ratified the breach, here it hopes to heal it. The final violence is on him who upheld and prevented atonement for the first. Only thus is there hope of healing ruptured bonds; here, by destroying their advocate. That was Soyinka's and Rotimi's point: these experiences involve lived bonds with past, present, and future worlds which are all part of a person, however much they must often be read in "secular," sociopolitical terms – though I think that risky in the case of these two Sofola plays.

Debate on Tragedy and Its Utility

Emene, like *The Gods Are Not to Blame*, *The Bacchae of Euripides*, and *Noces posthumes de Santigone*, is also a commentary on and manifestation of the uses of tragedy; more exactly, perhaps, on how tragedy can be turned to the needs of new contexts, demands, and desperations. Likewise, John Pepper Clark-Bekederemo turns to many of these matters in his dramatic duo, *Song of a Goat* and *The Masquerade*. These interrogate forms, meanings, and uses of tragedy, adapting a very Greek tone of divine implacability to the story of a family suffering under a curse which has made an elder son, Zifa, unable to conceive more children (he who as "a dutiful son" had "brought back home among his people" for proper burial his dead father, outcast by his village for "the white taint," – leprosy: 1961: 9). We are not told why Zifa must suffer personally from impotence or communally from constant fear of personal attack – save perhaps that he has put family honor before village safety. As *Song* opens, the Masseur (a Tiresias-like character) tells Ebiere, Zifa's wife, whom Zifa has sent to consult him, that the "ways of our land" say that she should no longer have just one child, but lie with her husband's younger brother – enabling "a retying / Of knots" (5). As she indignantly runs off, Zifa arrives, uttering vague hints that he has been cast out by the village and will be more so if it learns his impotence. "All this is folly, Zifa," says the Masseur. "No / Man ever built a house or cleared / A piece of ground all by himself" (6). Singular hardships are always solved communally. In the springtime of her life (a constant theme evoking Greek tragedy's performance at the Spring Dionysia), Ebiere, says the Masseur, should not be forced to "Wait still when all the world is astir / With seed and heavy from flow of sap" (7). The Masseur's efforts stir an Oedipal outbreak on Zifa's part: "You lame thing, you crawling piece / Of withered flesh with the soul of a serpent" (10). Along with clear commentary on the genre of tragedy, at stake are the situations of person and family in the community and cycles of time and place.

Finding later that his brother Tonye has indeed had sex with his wife, Zifa first humiliates him in a scene heavy with symbolism by forcing him to break a cooking pot by stuffing into it the head of a ritually slaughtered goat, then chases him with a cutlass, only for Tonye to hang himself first, so, Zifa cries, "again perform[ing his, the elder son's] part" (32). Zifa drowns himself in the ocean. *Masquerade* continues this Oedipal story, with Tufa, son of Tonye and Ebiere (but not knowing his incestuous origins), going to another village and courting Titi. His past is revealed just before they are to marry, but Titi refuses to give Tufa up, saying that he is not responsible for or to this ancestry. Her furious father shoots Titi dead and, during a later fight, Tufa as well.

Besides Greek-like elements of the story itself, both plays' titles refer to that tradition. The word "tragedy" derives from *trágos*, "goat." Tragedians always played in mask. Both plays have choruses. They stress, as do most of these plays, what critics see common to African drama, no matter what its origin: "Song and dirge, drum and dance, color and costuming, poetry and pageantry, all commingle" (Osofisan 2001: 65). "Some of the characteristics of an African Theatre," Rotimi adds, should be those that can be easily identified with African culture itself. Music is one, dance is another. Again, there is the use of crowds. Most African celebrations involve some amount of communal participation, and the use of crowds in a play is one way of establishing some definition of an African Theatre. (Alston 1989: 83)

What Mineke Schipper says of Wale Ogunyemi's "music-drama," *Obalúayé*, applies widely: "Music, dancing, drama, décor and light effects unite towards a multi-faceted performance" (1982: 55). "Rather than rely on the written word *per se*," says Kennedy Chinyowa, "the African's histrionic sensibility... derive[s] its context from ritual celebration and its meaning from symbolic enactment, direct audience participation and stylised artistic forms such as mime, song, dance, movement, music, poetic rhythm, costume, gesture, dialogue and role-playing" (2001: 4). The presence of these media varies; massive in the Rotimi and Soyinka plays mentioned and in Sofola's *King Emene*, more muted in *Wedlock* or in Clark-Bekederemo's two plays, if not in his *Ozidi*, which not only uses all these media but, as so often in these plays, various practices (not least a "Storyteller") to draw in the "so-called" audience, made "an integral part of that arena of conflict; it contributes spiritual strength to the protagonist through its choric reality which must first be conjured up and established" (Soyinka 1976: 39).

Such media, with ancient Greek equivalents but few in later European traditions, extend the staged community to Soyinka's "so-called" audience. This is what makes these plays secular commentary as well as communal rite. Writing of *Ozidi*, Lokangaka Losambe thus remarks:

> As in several other African plays, such as Ngugi wa Thiong'o and Ngugi wa Mirii's *I Will Marry When I Want* (1982) and Sonny Labou Tansi's *Parentheses of Blood* (1986), in *Ozidi* the main tragic "hero" is a community. The main tragic flaw of Ozidi and that of his son cannot be separated from the communal tragic flaw of the whole Orua community, whose eccentric power and material lust has led them to ravage neighbouring communities and enslave many people. (2001: 83–4)

To this end, too, *Ozidi* appropriates

> the English language, making it carry the baggage of the expressive culture of the Ijo people [the author's father was Ijo]. Clark-Bekederemo's use in this play of what he calls "indirection," punctuated by Ijo riddles, songs, ritualistic incantation and invocation, gives a sense of conviction to characters' actions and enhances the tragic effect of the play. (Losambe 2001: 91)

This appropriation is usual. Suzanne Brichaux-Houyoux notes that the Martinican Aimé Césaire used African terms in *Une saison au Congo* "to make the theatre into an authentic cultural instrument," using not just local languages to achieve "an African tonality," but "calling on Bantu symbolism and modes of thought and expression by using in particular many proverbs and animal stories to reinforce" it (1993: 15). That this itself marks collective investment is seen by Ngugi's experience while working on *Ngaahika Ndeenda* (I will marry when I want):

> when it came to song, dance and ceremony, the peasants, who of course knew all about it, were particular about the accuracy of detail..., *they were also particular about language.... They were concerned that the various characters, depending on age and occupation, be given the appropriate language.* 'An old man cannot speak like that', they would say. 'If you want him to have dignity, he has to use this or that kind of proverb'. Levels of language and language-use and the nuances of words and phrases were discussed heatedly. (Ngugi 1986: 54, emphasis in original)

The language used in these plays and performance itself creates *local* space.

This is why a play like *Ozidi*, written in 1966, the year before the Biafran War erupted, as tensions in Nigeria neared breaking pitch, can be read as forceful comment on events. *Song of a Goat* (1961) and *The Masquerade* (1964), it is true, have been seen to "omit...any deep sense of communal engagement across time or place." Gerald Moore adds that if most African traditions "offer means by which contamination can be explained or cleansed," and if these "may involve the death or expulsion of a single person," these two plays expiate nothing, while *Masquerade* ends by predicting more disaster, "full of danger / And portent for all of us" (1991: 69; Moore [1969] 1970: 149). Moore recalls a creation myth of the Ijo that tells how the unborn make an irrescindable choice of attributes to be carried through life, but with no suggestion "that the consequences of choice endure beyond the life-span of the person making it" ([1969] 1970: 150). Written as political conditions were already showing grave signs of falling apart, one could hold that *Masquerade* was saying exactly that: its tragedy, too, was to be a communal one. But Zifa's case is already so, for his values are indeed set against the community's welfare. Ebiere's first reaction to the Masseur is not continued; Zifa's is, and it is his acts that bring disaster. One might also hold that Clark used the very form, tragedy, to show how colonial impositions had broken traditional ties, set individualist against communal values. *Song of a Goat* in particular is a play *about* the genre, tragedy. Tragedy itself, then, guides the spectator to how that history and its deformations are to be seen, Western *ratio* setting its grip on a different culture. Ezenwa-Ohaeto has been concerned to argue that disaster ensues when "the individual refuses to accept the dictates of his society" (1982: 9), when he splits from community. Here, tragedy would show the onset of deep scission in community and its long consequences. In this context, tragedy may end by drawing these out, as in *King Emene* or *Edufa*; by leaving them as a peril hanging over some hopeful reconnection, as in *The Gods Are Not to Blame*, *Wedlock of the Gods*, or *Noces posthumes de Santigone*, or it may offer a healing like the dance ending *Ozidi*, rejoining actors and audience, or the "Eucharistic" ceremony that ends *The Bacchae of Euripides*.

Césaire attains such a transfiguration in his *Tragédie du roi Christophe*, whose protagonist also walks narrowly between using Western history and fighting it. Ex-slaves above all (especially in the diaspora of a Middle Passage whose perpetrators purposely destroyed their victims' cultures) have no choice but to use their oppressors' tools to dismantle their power and their victims' alienation. His Christophe thus exclaims:

> All humans have the same rights. I agree. But among common peoples some have more duties than others. There is the inequality. An inequality of obligations, you understand? Whom will you have believe that all humans, all I say, without exception, without particular reason, have gone through deportation, slave trade, slavery, collective reduction to bestiality, total violation, utter insult, that all have received, spattered on body and face, all-denying sputum! Only us, madame, do you hear? only us niggers! ([1966] 1970: 59)

That is why one has to "succeed in the impossible" in fighting "against History," while using tools from that History (62), just as, I suggested, Clark-Bekederemo was *using* tragedy. Here, the oppressors have disjoined colonized Haiti, remade it in their own disjunctive image:

> Stone, I'm looking for stone!
> Cement! I'm looking for cement!
> Everything is disjoined, oh! to get all that upright!
> Upright and in the world's face, and solid!
> ([1966] 1970. 45)

His citadel becomes the image of this demand and duty. Like Pentheus, Christophe dies in the trap forged by this disjointed history.

In this sense, Christophe is a familiar tragic figure, "walking to death through the solitude that progressively settles around him, and the distance that gradually settles between him and his people" (Césaire, in Auclaire-Tamaroff and Auclaire-Tamaroff 1986: 124). But as his last followers bear his body through the mountains toward the citadel, it is ever more "weighty." They set him down, stand him "upright," "facing south," to make his own journey, his own "stature," remaking Africa in, and bringing Shango to, Haiti; "upright King" standing in newly affirmed liberty (Césaire [1966] 1970: 150–1). For "Christophe is the incarnation of Shango, violent, brutal, tyrannical god, but also beneficent, god of destructive thunder and, at the same time, of fertilizing rain." In the play, he is attended and softened by Hugonin: "As Christophe is Shango," says Césaire, "Hugonin is Esu," the Yoruba trickster god. "Alongside inflexible Shango, Hugonin, Protean character, forming an inseparable pair. Alongside power weighing with all its weight, fluidity and change. That is why the moment of revolution, which is Time's operative moment, is Hugonin's" (in Auclaire-Tamaroff and Auclaire-Tamaroff 1986: 124). When his followers leave Christophe/Shango's body erect, in the open, he (re)joins those mountains and forests of Haiti whose praises he had sung as the symbol of liberty (Césaire [1966] 1970: 23), asserting a history in, specific to, his Caribbean geography. Not unlike Kinjeketile, a word makes bond: for those bearing his ever more "weighty" body to the mountains, "his weight is his word" (Césaire [1966] 1970: 150), word that will bear a new community into its future.

This differs wholly from Walcott's earlier *Henri Christophe* (1949), which tells of Haiti's revolt, whose leaders, Dessalines, Christophe, Pétion, Sylla, Brelle, and Vastey, brawl in a swirl of self-interest, marking not community but venalities of power. At the end, Pétion arrives offstage, killing a shrieking Vastey: the cycle of bloodshed and corruption continues. The curtain falls on Christophe raising a pistol to his head (Walcott 2002: 107). The disparity marks the import of historical context. Walcott wrote not just as Haiti was falling into the further horrors of the Duvalier regime but when the rest of the Caribbean was still colonial. By the 1960s, much of the Caribbean and Africa was, was soon to be – or thought it might be – politically sovereign. This counts, too, in Césaire's next tragedy, *Une saison au Congo*, whose 1973 ending has Mokutu killing the once-hopeful sanza player. In 1966, this play enacted *Tragédie*'s hopes. Lumumba, "victim and hero," was also "conqueror. Breaking himself against the bars of the cage, but also making a breach in them. Through this man . . . the whole history of a continent and of a people is played out in an exemplary and symbolic manner."[13] The sanza player ends the play by reviving a metaphor used earlier by Lumumba. Knowing he is likely soon to die, Lumumba had recalled the architectural terms Descartes used in the *Discours de la méthode* (1637) to name his new edifice of knowledge, history, identity, and the *polis*. Lumumba speaks of creating a new state *from* a postcolonial zero point and he speaks *to* colonial power: "I regret nothing, Mpolo. Doesn't the architect go directly to the goal, projecting the whole house at once? When the sky was black and the horizon blocked, it was my job to set out the sweeping path with one magic stroke" (Césaire 1973: 3.1.87). One thinks of Kinjeketile's word-made future or Christophe's heavy word. The sanza player ends the play by recalling this, speaking of "growing straight," "rising from the ground," "standing on feet of your own," concluding with the droll banter of his own chatter (3.8.103–4). It is not scission and lasting divide that are at issue, but community, jointure, and remaking. These turn tragedy on its head. Sociopolitical critique joins with what Soyinka calls the "sacred," others the spiritual, and yet others the metaphysical. History and cultural traditions alter tragedy's effect and meaning.

In all these regards, the Swahili dramatist Penina Muhando suggestively remarks:

> There is still much more to be done with the African tradition. To give this simple example, I have noticed the way the African audience laughs, even when the play is tragic. The point is that Africans are not callous people, it doesn't mean they enjoy seeing people murdered, it means they have a different perception. Maybe they are laughing at the perfection of the acting, seeing that the actor has managed to imitate the action so well. I don't know, but these are things that need to be researched. (James 1990: 88)

Osofisan reports K. A. B. Jones-Quartey's comments on the same phenomenon:

> The typical African audience giggles, guffaws, eventually roars in laughter at what was meant – or at least hoped – to evoke from them the reactions of horror, pity, tears . . . Medea, towering in the grandeur of her utter prostration before the Fates;

Hamlet battling with the blood splashed terror of eternal night; Orukorere [Zifa's Cassandra-like aunt in *Song of a Goat*], half-crazed in her fate-filled obsession with the fate-loaded song of the goat – the whole gamut, from ancient Greece through Shakespeare's Europe to renascent Africa itself: any representation at all of human tragedy in dramatic form, from anywhere, evokes from a typically African audience, in "the bush" or in the city, laughter, not tears.

Glossing this, Osofisan sees the answer as a matter of technique (2001: 84 n. 4). Everything implies, rather, people laughing at acts that falsify life's ultimate jointure. This nears Clark-Bekederemo's *Song* and *Masquerade*, the second uttering decisive ignorance and breach: "Who / The gods love they visit with calamity" (1991: 69). "History," Walcott's Christophe, echoes Shakespeare's Gloucester: "Kills us like flies, wings torn, held up to light" (106).

Soyinka's communion rite and Sofola's thought that *Wedlock of the Gods* marks not death and scission differ from such an idea of tragedy. They insist on continuities and interlockings which the breach of taboos suspends but which tragedies like *Wedlock* or *The Bacchae of Euripides* depict as always existing. Ato Quayson shows that this sense of tragedy gives another way to set "real-life events ... in the emotionally and philosophically charged discourse of literary tragedy" (2003: 58). He argues that seeing Sani Abacha's murder of Ken Saro-Wiwa (who wrote of his Ogoni people's genocide as a "tragedy") in *this* tragic prism "arouse[s] a silent people into an engagement with their history" (74). It translates the solidarity of Rotimi's *If* into wider mutual (here global) need. A worldview antagonistic to this sense of wholeness and community may well provoke laughter – circling us back to Nietzschean gaiety, yet rejoicing in a renewed idea of tragedy as a celebration of jointure.

Notes

1 Through antiquity into late sixteenth-century Europe, no one *really* had this sense of self. Maybe it uttered Nietzsche's "terrors and horrors" (1956: 29). It needs interpreting with care not to presume modern understandings (Reiss 2003).

2 I thank Stanley Corngold for this passage.

3 It proved incredibly hard to obtain Sofola's 1994 inaugural lecture. I thank Michael J. Hannon and his bombarded staff for their multiple Interlibrary Loan efforts, Ato Quayson for successful pointers, and most of all Nasrin Qader, who exceeded bounds of collegiality in getting me a copy.

4 I do not look at Shakespeare, whose tragedies have much been used against their grain.

Besides a play like South African Murray Carlin's *Not Now, Sweet Desdemona* (written and performed in 1968 when he was teaching at Uganda's Makerere College), Tayib Salih's 1969 novel *Season of Migration to the North* (*Othello*), or Akira Kurosawa's 1957 film, *Throne of Blood* (*Macbeth*) – elements in a transcultural phenomenon of vast proportions – one need but think of Lemuel Johnson's work on *Shakespeare in Africa* (1998), and others' on Shakespeare in India, where adaptations to local contexts and conventions, and rewritings in local languages show divers "turnings" (see Sisson 1926; Shankar 1999a, 1999b).

5 Jeyifo, then grounded in a fairly straight Marx–Engels line, shared their blind spots on

race and gender as *historical* forces. Soyinka answered him and others (not on these grounds) in "Who's Afraid of Elesin Oba?" (1993: 62–81).

6   Unlike Duro Ladipo's telling of the same story as the result of Olori Elesin's belief "in a new time: in a new law" brought by the "white man," which ends with the chorus of women lamenting: "As yet we cannot tell / How much of our world you have destroyed" (Ladipo 1964: *Oba Waja* 71–2).

7   This rejects Michael Etherton's view that Rotimi's Ovonramwen yields to a "fatalistic bias" (1982: 155), taking the war's outcome as foreordained (164). Whatever his doubts on *how* to resist, Ovonramwen does *not* give up. Captured, he escapes so "that the fight with the Whiteman begins afresh" (Rotimi 1974: 64). That those he most trusts betray him as "a wisp of cotton wool, fiercely yanked off its stalk by the wind in harmattan and cast into space . . . at the mercy of airy whims far beyond its control" (71) does not mean he accepts what has happened, especially not when he plans to restart the fight. Nor does his final defiant sarcasm about Queen Victoria addressed to the crudely overbearing English Captain Roupell imply willing yielding (78).

8   Titus is Melissa's "fiancée" alive, her "husband" dead, in a sense Polynices *and* Hemon, both slain by the power "Creon" represents. In *Noces*, the strongman is also directly responsible for the death of her "young brother" (80–2), Eteocles, if Titus is Polynices. Neocolonial power is all-destructive and has no companions among its own people. *Noces* is not a version of *Antigone*; it plays off it.

9   It has been suggested that the priest of Ogun orders Odewale's death. But while he does the rituals, he *orders* nothing. He could never deny the boy's divinely approved mission.

10 Two "taboos" may be in contradiction. None knows that Ojuola is Odewale's mother; all know that "custom" dictates that the new king wed the widowed queen. This Gordian knot again signals the ambiguous ethical condition of the human world.

11 The Cyclops forged the thunderbolts with which Zeus slew Apollo's son Asclepios (whose temple was seen by the audience just to the west of the theatre of Dionysus where *Alcestis* was performed), for having brought a dead man back to life, thus interfering with the prerogative of the Fates. In *Alcestis*, Death accuses Apollo of doing the same, taking Admetos from the Fates by a "wrestler's trick" (30–4: in the myth, he got them drunk). Heracles also wrestles Alcestis from Death (846–50, 1140–2), after being drunk. Does the play mock the Fates and gods? or wonder what they have in immediate store for Admetos, now that Alcestis has *not* died for him?

12 So may *Marriage*, satirizing corrupt consumerism of a false vision of cultural and social fusion: Anansewa sold to the highest bidder, induced into the object of her and his desire, "completing" whatever she thought herself to be. "Chief of Chiefs" is then romanticized negritude, not even the "other" of colonial capitalist values, since their union absorbs "traditional" (financial) competition.

13 These comments are from Césaire's *Postface* to the 1966 edition of *Une saison au Congo* (Brichaux-Houyoux 1993: 14), which I have been unable to get. They were repeated in the program of the November 1967 Théâtre de l'Est Parisien production – for a copy of which I thank A. James Arnold. Césaire cut the matter from the 1973 Seuil edition (although the back cover gives the last sentence). The English is from the back of the Grove translation of the 1966 edition.

References and Further Reading

Agbaw, S. Ekema. (1996). "Africanizing *Macbeth*: 'Down-fall'n Birthdom'." *Research in African Literatures* 27.1 (Spring), 102–9.

Aidoo, Ama Ata. (1970). *Anowa*. Harlow: Longman.

Alston, J. B. (1989). *Yoruba Drama in English: Interpretation and Production*. Lewiston, NY: Edwin Mellen Press.

Aristotle. (1995). *Poetics*, ed. and trans. Stephen Halliwell; Longinus. *On the Sublime*, ed. and trans. W. H. Fyfe and Rev. Donald Russell; Demetrius, *On Style*, ed. and trans. Doreen C. Innes. Based on W. Rhys

Roberts. Cambridge, MA and London: Harvard University Press.

Auclaire-Tamaroff, Élisabeth, and Auclaire-Tamaroff, Barthélémy. (1986). *Jean-Marie Serreau découvreur de théâtres* [Jean-Marie Serreau, discoverer of theaters]. Paris: L'Arbre Verdoyant.

Bemba, Sylvain. [1988] (1995). *Noces posthumes de Santigone*. Solignac: Le Bruit des Autres.

Brichaux-Houyoux, Suzanne, ed. (1993). *Quand Césaire écrit, Lumumba parle*. Édition commentée de *Une Saison au Congo* [When Césaire writes, Lumumba speaks. Edition with commentary of *Une Saison au Congo*]. Paris: L'Harmattan.

Cavarero, Adriana. (2003). *A più voci: Filosofia dell'espressione vocale* [More in voices: philosophy of vocal expression]. Milan: Feltrinelli.

Césaire, Aimé. [1966] (1970). *La tragédie du roi Christophe: Théâtre*. Paris: Présence Africaine. (See also Brichaux-Houyoux 1993 *and* Théâtre de l'Est Parisien 1967.)

Césaire, Aimé. (1968). *A Season in the Congo*, trans. Ralph Manheim. New York: Grove Press.

Césaire, Aimé. (1973). *Une saison au Congo*. "Points." Paris: Seuil.

Clark-Bekederemo, John Pepper. [1961] (1991). *Song of a Goat*. In *Collected Plays 1964–1988*, intro. Abiola Irele. Washington, DC: Howard University Press, 3–39.

Clark-Bekederemo, John Pepper. (1991). *Collected Plays 1964–1988*, intro. Abiola Irele. Washington, DC: Howard University Press.

Chinyowa, Kennedy C. (2001). "The Context, Performance and Meaning of Shona Ritual Drama." In *Pre-colonial and Post-Colonial Drama and Theatre in Africa*, ed. Lokangaka Losambe and Devi Sarinjeive. Trenton, NJ and Asmara: Africa World Press, 3–13.

Condé, Maryse. (1972). *Dieu nous l'a donné*, [God gave him to us] foreword by Guy Tirolien, preface by Lilyan Kesteloot. Paris: Pierre Jean Oswald.

Condé, Maryse. (1973). *Mort d'Oluwémi d'Ajumako* [The death of Oluwémi d'Ajumako]. Paris: Pierre Jean Oswald.

Etherton, Michael. (1982). *The Development of African Drama*. New York: Africana Publishing.

Euripides. (1988). *Alcestis*, ed., trans., and commentary by D. J. Conacher. Warminster: Aris & Phillips.

Ezenwa-Ohaeto. (1982). "The Nature of Tragedy in Modern African Drama." *The Literary Half-Yearly* 23:2 (July), 3–17.

Hussein, Ebrahim N. (1970). *Kinjeketile*. Dar es Salaam: Oxford University Press.

Ibitokun, Benedict M. (1995). *African Drama and the Yorùbá World-View*. Ibadan: Ibadan University Press.

James, Adeola, ed. (1990). *In Their Own Voices: African Women Writers Talk*. London and Portsmouth, NH: James Currey and Heinemann.

Jeyifo, Biodun. (1985). *The Truthful Lie: Essays in a Sociology of African Drama*. London and Port of Spain: New Beacon.

Johnson, Lemuel A. (1998). *Shakespeare in Africa (and Other Venues): Import and the Appropriation of Culture*. Trenton, NJ and Asmara: Africa World Press.

Kafka, Franz. (1954). *Dearest Father*, trans. Ernest Kaiser and Eithne Wilkins. New York: Schocken Books.

Ladipo, Duro. (1964). *Oba waja*. In *Three Yoruba Plays: Oba koso, Oba moro, Oba Waja*, English adaptations by Ulli Beier. Ibadan: Mbari Publications, 53–72; also in Wole Soyinka, *Death and the King's Horseman*, ed. Simon Gikandi. New York: Norton, 2003, 74–89.

Losambe, Lokangaka. (2001). "Dialogic Forces in J. P. Clark-Bekederemo's *Ozidi*." In *Pre-colonial and Post-Colonial Drama and Theatre in Africa*, ed. Lokangaka Losambe and Devi Sarinjeive, Trenton, NJ and Asmara: Africa World Press, 81–94.

Losambe, Lokangaka and Sarinjeive, Devi, eds. (2001). *Pre-colonial and Post-Colonial Drama and Theatre in Africa*. Trenton, NJ and Asmara: Africa World Press, 81–94.

Lucian of Samosata. (1969). "The Dead Come to Life, or the Fisherman [*Piscator*]." *The Works*, ed. and trans. Austin Morris Harmon, 8 vols. Vol. 3, 1921–6; Cambridge, MA and London: Harvard University Press and Heinemann, 1–81.

Moore, Gerald. [1969] (1970). *The Chosen Tongue: English Writing in the Tropical World*. New York and Evanston, IL: Harper & Row.

Ngugi wa Thiong'o. (1986). *Decolonising the Mind: The Politics of Language in African Literature*. London: James Currey.

Ngugi wa Thiong'o. and Mugo, Micere Githae. (1977). *The Trial of Dedan Kimathi*. 1976; rpt. Oxford: Heinemann.

Nietzsche, Friedrich. (1956). *The Birth of Tragedy and the Genealogy of Morals*, trans. Francis Golffing. Garden City, NJ: Doubleday Anchor.

Nietzsche, Friedrich. (1961). *Thus Spoke Zarathustra: A Book for Everyone and No One*, trans. R. J. Hollingdale. Harmondsworth: Penguin.

Osofisan, Femi. (2001). *The Nostalgic Drum: Essays on Literature, Drama and Culture*. Trenton, NJ and Asmara: Africa World Press.

Pelton, Robert D. [1980] (1989). *The Trickster in West Africa: A Study of Mythic Irony and Sacred Delight*. Berkeley, Los Angeles, and London: University of California Press.

Quayson, Ato. (2003). *Calibrations: Reading for the Social*. Minneapolis: University of Minnesota Press.

Reiss, Timothy J. (2002). "The Law, the Tragic, and Cultures of Dissonance." In *Against Autonomy: Global Dialectics of Cultural Exchange*. Stanford, CA: Stanford University Press, 108–49.

Reiss, Timothy J. (2003). *Mirages of the Selfe: Patterns of Personhood in Ancient and Early Modern Europe*. Stanford, CA: Stanford University Press.

Rotimi, Ola. (1971a). *The Gods Are Not to Blame*. London: Oxford University Press.

Rotimi, Ola. (1971b). *Kurunmi: An Historical Tragedy*. Ibadan: Oxford University Press.

Rotimi, Ola. (1974). *Ovonramwen Nogbaisi: An Historical Tragedy in English*. Benin City: Ethiope Publishing; Ibadan: Ibadan University Press.

Rotimi, Ola. (1983). *If: A Tragedy of the Ruled*. Ibadan: Heinemann Educational.

Rotimi, Ola. (1984) *Understanding the Gods Are Not to Blame*, preface by Chidi Maduka. Lagos: Kurunmi Adventures Publication.

Schipper, Mineke. (1982). *Theatre and Society in Africa*, trans. Ampie Coetzee. Johannesburg: Ravan Press.

Shankar, D. A. (1999a). *Appropriating Shakespeare (A Study of Shakespeare's Plays Rendered into Kannada between 1895–1932)*. Shimla: Indian Institute of Advanced Study.

Shankar, D. A., ed. (1999b). *Shakespeare in Indian Languages*. Shimla: Indian Institute of Advanced Study.

Sisson, Charles Jasper. (1926). *Shakespeare in India: Popular Adaptations on the Bombay Stage*. London: Humphrey Milford, Oxford University Press.

Sofola, 'Zulu [Onuekwuke Nwazuluoha]. (1972). *Wedlock of the Gods*. London: Evans.

Sofola, 'Zulu [Onuekwuke Nwazuluoha]. (1974). *King Emene: Tragedy of a Rebellion*. London: Heinemann Educational.

Sofola, 'Zulu [Onuekwuke Nwazuluoha]. [1979] (1981). *Old Wines Are Tasty. A Play*. Ibadan: Ibadan University Press.

Sofola, 'Zulu [Onuekwuke Nwazuluoha]. (1994). *The Artist and the Tragedy of a Nation*. Ibadan: Caltop Publications.

Sophocles. [1982] (1984). *The Three Theban Plays: Antigone, Oedipus the King, Oedipus at Colonus*, trans. Robert Fagles, intro. and notes by Bernard Knox. Harmondsworth: Penguin.

Soyinka, Wole. (1974). *The Bacchae of Euripides: A Communion Rite*. 1973; rpt. New York: Norton.

Soyinka, Wole. [1975] (2003). *Death and the King's Horseman*, ed. Simon Gikandi. New York: Norton.

Soyinka, Wole. (1976). *Myth, Literature and the African World*. Cambridge: Cambridge University Press.

Soyinka, Wole. [1988] (1993). *Art, Dialogue, and Outrage: Essays on Literature and Culture*, ed. and intro. by Biodun Jeyifo. New York: Pantheon.

Sutherland, Efua Theodora. [1975] (1987). *The Marriage of Anansewa* and *Edufa*. Harlow: Longman.

Théâtre de l'Est Parisien. [1967]. *Une saison au Congo* de Aimé Césaire, directed by Jean-Marie Serreau (theater program).

Walcott, Derek. (1970). "What the Twilight Says: An Overture." In *Dream on Monkey Mountain and Other Plays*. New York: Farrar, Straus & Giroux, 3–40.

Walcott, Derek. (2002). *Henri Christophe*. In *The Haitian Trilogy*. New York: Farrar, Straus & Giroux, 1–107.

Wiredu, Kwasi. (1980). *Philosophy and an African Culture*. Cambridge: Cambridge University Press.

Wiredu, Kwasi. (1996). *Cultural Universals and Particulars: An African Perspective*. Bloomington: Indiana University Press.

Index